Knowledge Discovery for Business Information Systems

The Kluwer International Series in Engineering and Computer Science

Knowledge Discovery for Business Information Systems

Edited by

Witold Abramowicz
The Poznań University of Economics, Poland

Jozef Zurada
University of Louisville, U.S.A.

KLUWER ACADEMIC PUBLISHERS
Boston / Dordrecht / London

Distributors for North, Central and South America:
Kluwer Academic Publishers
101 Philip Drive
Assinippi Park
Norwell, Massachusetts 02061 USA
Telephone (781) 871-6600
Fax (781) 681-9045
E-Mail <kluwer@wkap.com>

Distributors for all other countries:
Kluwer Academic Publishers Group
Distribution Centre
Post Office Box 322
3300 AH Dordrecht, THE NETHERLANDS
Telephone 31 78 6392 392
Fax 31 78 6392 254
E-Mail <services@wkap.nl>

Electronic Services <http://www.wkap.nl>

Library of Congress Cataloging-in-Publication Data

Knowledge discovery for business information systems / edited by Witold Abramowicz, Jozef Zurada.
p. cm. - - (The Kluwer international series in engineering and computer science ; SECS 600)
Includes bibliographical references (p) and index.
ISBN 0-7923-7243-3 (alk. paper)
1. Data mining. 2. Knowledge acquisition (Expert systems) 3. Database searching. I. Abramowicz, Witold. II. Zurada, Jozef, 1949- III. Series.

QA76.9.D343 K56 2000
006.3--dc21 00-048482

Printed on acid-free paper.

Printed in the United States of America

Contents

Preface

Current database technology and computer hardware allow us to gather, store, access, and manipulate massive volumes of raw data in an efficient and inexpensive manner. However, the amount of data collected and warehoused in all industries is growing every year at a phenomenal rate. As a result, our ability to discover critical, obscure nuggets of useful information that could influence or help in the decision making process is still limited.

Knowledge discovery in databases (KDD) is a new, multidisciplinary field that focuses on the overall process of information discovery in large volumes of warehoused data. KDD concerns techniques that can semi-automatically or automatically find fundamental properties and principles in data. These properties and principles are supposed to be non-trivial, useful, and understandable, and can be used in business decision making.

The KDD field combines database concepts and theory, machine learning, pattern recognition, statistics, artificial intelligence, uncertainty management, and high-performance computing. The problem of information discovery involves many factors such as data retrieval and manipulation, mathematical and statistical inference, search, and uncertain reasoning. In particular, KDD is a process that includes the following stages: learning the application domain; data acquisition, preparation, selection, and cleaning; model and hypothesis development; data mining (DM); assessing the discovered knowledge (testing and verification); interpretation and using discovered knowledge; and visualization of results.

The field of KDD has become very important not only in business but also in academia. Several prominent US universities, such as Carnegie-Mellon University, now offer an MS degree program exclusively focused on KDD. Also, several top business schools, including the Stern School of Business at New York University, regularly teach a KDD course in a traditional MBA degree program.

In our April 1999 call for chapters we sought contributions to the book that would present new and unconventional trends in the KDD process. We solicited from a diverse body of authors, including the leading scientists and practitioners in the field, to stimulate a new wave of knowledge beyond the main stream in this area. The envisioned readers of the book are scientists and practitioners who perform research in KDD and/or implement the discoveries.

Because the KDD field is so comprehensive but not yet coherent and fully defined, editing a book on KDD for Business Information Systems has been a challenging task. After spending one and a half years on the book's preparation, we are delighted to see it appearing on the market. We believe that the book will inspire academics, practitioners, and graduate students alike to engage in this new field.

We hope that the book may also be useful to a broader audience of readers, who are not necessarily experts in the field of KDD but would like to learn about the current developments in the field and gain some practical experience in the use of the DM tools. Selected chapters from the book, especially those that discuss the DM applications, might also be valuable to senior undergraduate computer science and computer information systems students.

The book contains a collection of seventeen chapters written by a truly international team of thirty eight experts representing academia and business institutions from ten countries: Austria, Canada, Estonia, Denmark, Germany, Hong Kong, Italy, Poland, Singapore, and the United States. Many of the authors who contributed to the book have worked and published extensively in the KDD and DM field or closely related areas.

We want to thank the participants of the KnowBIS workshop organized as part of the 4th International Business Information Systems Conference in Poznań, Poland, April 12-14, 2000, for their useful comments and suggestions which we tried to incorporate to the book. We extend our gratitude to Professors Foster Provost, New York University, Leszek Maciaszek, Macquarie University, Sydney, Australia, and Eberhard Stickel, Germany, for writing excellent comments about the book. We are also thankful to a group of anonymous reviewers whose work greatly enhanced each chapter in the book. We are indebted as well to Krzysztof Węcel and Paweł Jan Kalczyński from the Poznań University of Economics, Poland, for their invaluable help in preparation of camera-ready copy of the manuscripts and conducting most of the correspondence with the authors. Finally, we would also like to express our sincere thanks to Scott Delman and Melissa Fearon, Kluwer Academic Publishers, for their help and enthusiastic encouragement throughout the entire project.

Witold Abramowicz and Jozef Zurada
Editors

Foreword

Our analytical capabilities are overloaded with data from transaction systems, monitoring systems, financial systems, the Web, third-party vendors, and increasingly from electronic commerce systems. That which previously we would have called "information", now has ceased to inform. We are unable to process even a small fraction of it.

As a result of the glut of data, the field of Knowledge Discovery and Data Mining (KDD) is receiving increasing attention. Until very recently, KDD research focused primarily on the data mining algorithm – the engine that searches through a vast space of patterns for interesting ones. However, the process of discovering knowledge from data involves much more than simply the application of a data mining algorithm. Practitioners routinely report that applying the algorithms comprises no more than 20% of the knowledge discovery process. Therefore, it's important to keep in mind that no matter how efficient data mining algorithms become, we still will be faced with 80% of the knowledge discovery task.

This book stands out because it compiles research on all phases of the knowledge discovery process, presenting issues that have received little attention by the KDD research community. The seventeen chapters address data integration and warehousing, diverse data representations, problem formulation, evaluation of discoveries and models, integration with business processes, and maintenance of discovered knowledge, in addition to the data mining algorithm. The book's perspective is refreshing because in many chapters these issues appear in combination, as they do in actual business information systems.

Let me highlight just a few examples. Enterprise-wide business intelligence systems coalesce data from diverse systems, which in traditional organizations usually are isolated. Mining these data can pay huge dividends. However, building an enterprise-spanning system is a tremendous undertaking. If it is not designed well the ultimate goal of gaining insight collectively across many departments will never be realized. We hear often about large-scale data mining successes, but many large-scale projects fail before any significant data mining gets done. From a practical point of view, in Chapter 11, Mrazek discusses data modeling, aggregation/transformation, and warehousing issues that are seldom considered in data mining research, but which are crucial if enterprise-wide knowledge discovery is to succeed on a regular basis.

As I suggested above, the data mining algorithm has received the bulk of research attention. In Chapter 15, Schlösser et al. examine how to make the rest of the process more efficient. Starting with the „visual programming" paradigm of KDD process representation, pioneered by the developers of Clementine and now used by several tools, they ask what technical advances are necessary to facilitate the exploratory and preparatory phases of the KDD process.

As a third example, in Chapter 10, Mani et al. provide an excellent description of the use of multiple techniques to discover knowledge helpful for customer relationship management. They interleave statistical methods and data mining methods to produce personalized customer lifetime value models (an important component of customer relationship management) that are accurate and understandable. Each method addresses a weakness of the other. Specifically, statistical techniques (such as hazard functions) are used to transform the problem so that it is suitable for the application of a powerful neural network. The resultant neural network, albeit quite accurate, is difficult to interpret. However, postprocessing with clustering analysis uncovers several distinct customer groups. Using decision-tree mining on these groups yields concise, comprehensible descriptions, that can be translated by business users into actions.

I'm happy that the book's editors saw fit to compile a book specifically targeted to knowledge discovery for business information systems. Up until now, KDD research has been dominated by computer scientists, and to their tremendous credit we now have an impressive toolkit of data mining algorithms. Going forward we need more research addressing the rest of the knowledge discovery process. This book is filled with thought-provoking ideas. I would be very surprised if you left it without some new ideas of your own.

Foster Provost

Information Systems Department
Stern School of Business
New York University

List of Contributors

Witold Abramowicz
Department of Computer Science, The Poznań University of Economics, al. Niepodległości 10, 60-967 Poznań, Poland

Ken Barker
Advanced Database Systems and Applications Laboratory, Department of Computer Science, University of Calgary, 2500 University Dr. NW, Calgary, Alberta, Canada

Andrew Betz
GTE Laboratories Incorporated, 40 Sylvan Road, Waltham, MA 02451, USA

David Cheung
Department of Computer Science and Information Systems, The University of Hong Kong, H. K.

Manoranjan Dash
School of Computing, National University of Singapore

Piew Datta
GTE Laboratories Incorporated, 40 Sylvan Road, Waltham, MA 02451, USA

James Drew
GTE Laboratories Incorporated, 40 Sylvan Road, Waltham, MA 02451, USA

Sandhya Dwarkadas
Computer Science Department, University of Rochester, Rochester, NY 14627, USA

Benjamin P. Foster
School of Accountancy, University of Louisville, Louisville, KY 40292, USA

Matthias Gimbel
Institut für Programmstrukturen und Datenorganisation, Universität Karlsruhe, Am Fasanengarten 5, 76128 Karlsruhe, Germany

Hele-Mai Haav
Institute of Cybernetics, Tallinn Technical University, Akadeemia tee 21, 12618 Tallinn, Estonia

Zdzisław S. Hippe
Rzeszów University of Technology, Al. Powstańców Warszawy 6, 35-041 Rzeszów, Poland

Janusz Kacprzyk
Systems Research Institute, Polish Academy of Sciences, ul. Newelska 6, 01-447 Warsaw, Poland

Paweł Jan Kalczyński
Department of Computer Science, The Poznań University of Economics, al. Niepodległości 10, 60-967 Poznań, Poland

Ramon Lawrence
Department of Computer Science, University of Manitoba, 545 Machray Hall, Winnipeg, Manitoba, Canada

Sau Dan Lee
Department of Computer Science and Information Systems, The University of Hong Kong, H. K.

Beate List
Vienna University of Technology, Institute of Software Technology, Austria

Huan Liu
Department Computer Science & Engineering, Arizona State University

Peter C. Lockemann
Institut für Programmstrukturen und Datenorganisation, Universität Karlsruhe, Am Fasanengarten 5, 76128 Karlsruhe, Germany

D.R. Mani
GTE Laboratories Incorporated, 40 Sylvan Road, Waltham, MA 02451, USA

Jan Mrazek
Bank of Montreal, Global Information Technology, Business Intelligence Solutions, 4100 Gordon Baker Road, Toronto, Ontario, Canada

Jørgen Fischer Nilsson
Department of Information Technology, Technical University of Denmark, Building 344 DK-2800 Lyngby, Denmark

Mitsunori Ogihara
Computer Science Department, University of Rochester, Rochester, NY 14627, USA

Srinivasan Parthasarathy
Computer Science Department, University of Rochester, Rochester, NY 14627, USA

Witold Pedrycz
Department of Electrical & Computer Engineering, University of Alberta, Edmonton, Canada, and Systems Research Institute, Polish Academy of Sciences, 01-447 Warsaw, Poland

Jaroslav Pokorny
Department of Software Engineering, Charles University of Prague, Malostranské nam. 25, 118 00 Prague, Czech Republic

Giuseppe Psaila
Università degli Studi di Bergamo - Facoltà di Ingegneria, Viale Marconi 5, I-24044 Dalmine, Italy

Gerald Quirchmayr
University of Vienna, Institute for Computer Science and Information Systems, Austria

Josef Schiefer
Vienna University of Technology, Institute of Software Technology, Austria

Jörg A. Schlösser
Heyde AG, Auguste-Viktoria-Strasse 2, 61231 Bad Nauheim, Germany

A Min Tjoa
Vienna University of Technology, Institute of Software Technology, Austria

Terry J. Ward
Department of Accounting, Middle Tennessee State University, Murfreesboro, TN 37132, USA

Krzysztof Węcel
Department of Computer Science, The Poznań University of Economics, al. Niepodległości 10, 60-967 Poznań, Poland

Ronald R. Yager
Machine Intelligence Institute, Iona College, New Rochelle, NY 10801, USA

Jun Yao
School of Computing, National University of Singapore

Sławomir Zadrożny
Systems Research Institute, Polish Academy of Sciences, ul. Newelska 6, 01-447 Warsaw, Poland

Mohammed J. Zaki
Computer Science Department, Rensselaer Polytechnic Institute, Troy, NY 12180, USA

Jozef Zurada
Department of Computer Information Systems, University of Louisville, Louisville, KY 40292, USA

Chapter 1

INFORMATION FILTERS SUPPLYING DATA WAREHOUSES WITH BENCHMARKING INFORMATION

Witold Abramowicz, Paweł Jan Kalczyński, Krzysztof Węcel
Department of Computer Science
The Poznań University of Economics
al. Niepodległości 10
60-967 Poznań, Poland
{W.Abramowicz, P.Kalczynski, K.Wecel}@kie.ae.poznan.pl

Keywords: data warehousing, metadata, information filtering, selective distribution of information, user profiles, unstructured content, hypertext

Abstract: Alphanumeric data contained within a data warehouse represents "structured content". In contrast, the web is mostly composed of static pages of text and images, generally referred to as "unstructured content". As information systems grow to deliver better decision support, adding the unstructured content from the web to the structured content from the data warehouse becomes an important issue. In this chapter we establish the framework for supplying data warehouses with relevant information filtered from the web.

1. INTRODUCTION

Every human activity – particularly business activity – is based on some information resources that ought to be collected beforehand. Business people collect information in order to gain knowledge about the processes taking part within their organizations and beyond them. This knowledge helps the organization to perform better, in accordance to the specified goals.

It is assumed that information stored in electronic format can be divided into structured, unstructured and semi-structured ([Abramowicz1990b]

[Dittrich1999]). Structured information is usually stored as objects in a database. Correspondingly, unstructured and semi-structured information is usually stored as text, hypertext and hypermedia documents in a proper collection. Hence, we can distinguish information systems which help to build knowledge either out of structured information or out of unstructured information (i.e. data warehouses, information retrieval systems).

In this paper we present the idea of combining "textual" and "numerical" knowledge representations. "Numerical" knowledge will be understood as user-organized structured information such as data derivatives (i.e. charts, reports, aggregates or indexes) in a company's data warehouse. Appropriately, "textual knowledge" will be grasped as hypertext-organized collection of unstructured and semi-structured information stored as digital documents. We think that combining these two knowledge representations may positively affect a company's knowledge on the processes, which take part inside and outside the organization.

2. DATA WAREHOUSES

2.1 The Significance of Metadata

Metadata is the most important organizing element in a company's data warehouse structure. Metadata describes properties of data and information stored in the repository. Talking about a data warehouse without metadata does not make sense. Metadata enables users to navigate within the warehouse by supplying them with information about available data. Value of information in the warehouse depends on how detailed descriptions its metadata contains.

Defining data models and setting metadata repository is the distinctive stage of building a company's data warehouse when Information Technology and business experts must intensively work together. Metadata links IT experts with business experts in the organization. It enables end-users to interpret data by means of tools designed specially for them. Such organized collection of structured information may be understood as a company's knowledge repository based on historical data.

2.2 Logical Organization of Data Warehouse

All data warehouse examples mentioned in this paper will be based on a logical organization of a sample data warehouse implemented in

SAS/Warehouse Administrator [SAS/WA]. *Figure 1* shows the logical model of a sample data warehouse environment.

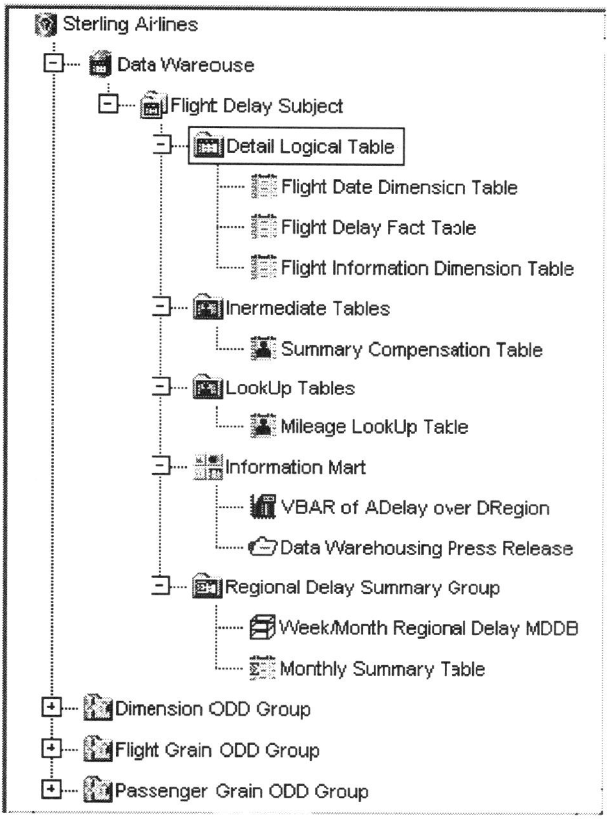

Figure 1. Logical organization of the data warehouse in SAS/Warehouse Administrator

The superior unit of SAS implementation is the data warehouse environment. A number of data warehouses can be defined within a single environment. Thanks to such a solution, all data warehouses inherit suitable pieces of metadata such as owners, supervisors, servers and data libraries. All objects defined within a particular warehouse share its metadata.

According to the data warehousing paradigm, the repository is organized into a number of *subjects*. A warehouse *subject* can be defined as a collection of data and information concerning a particular issue. Each subject must contain a single *detail logical table*. The detail logical table consists of a single multidimensional detail table or a number of detail tables organized into a star-schema. Subjects may also contain *intermediate tables* and *summary groups* of various aggregation levels.

2.3 Data Warehouses and the Web

Technologies that enable users to access a company's warehouse data through the Web are mostly based on Java. A thin client (Web browser) can log on and access warehouse data through a Java applet from anywhere in the world [Flangan1998]. One of the most common methods of making warehouse data available on the Web is generating reports as HTML pages by warehouse applications such as *SAS/IntrNet Software*[1]. Other more interactive approaches enable users to perform SQL queries by sending them to data warehouse via CGI. The queries are then processed by applications such as *Oracle WebDB*[2]or *SAS/IntrNet Software* and the results are sent back to the browser as regular Web pages.

So far the solutions connecting data warehouses with the Web focused on publishing data and structured information on Web pages. In this paper we aim at presenting a new approach to this issue. In our concept, not only does a data warehouse act as a source of information on the Web, but also it uses the Internet to retrieve more information. For instance, a customer relationship manager of an aviation company who accesses the "Flight Delays" subject of a company's data warehouse would also receive documents on flight delays in other airlines. Those documents would be retrieved from various subscribed Web services such as press news or special business information services. Information that increases a company's knowledge on the processes, which take part within and beyond the organization, will be further referred to as *benchmarking information.*

3. THE HYPERSDI SYSTEM

The idea of HyperSDI was developed in 1995 in the Department of Computer Science at the University of Economics in Poznań, Poland [Abramowicz1990b] [Abramowicz1998] and based on our previous projects (e.g. [Abramowicz1985] [Abramowicz1990a]). The concept is based on three principal topics: hypertext, information retrieval and information filtering.

[1] http://www.sas.com/software/components/intrnet.html
[2] http://www.oracle.com/tools/webdb

3.1 HyperSDI Basis

Hypertext was invented by Vannevar Bush in 1945 [Bush1945] and popularized by Ted Nelson in 1965 [Nelson1965]. As T. Nelson puts it, hypertext is *...a body of written or pictorial material interconnected in a complex way that it could not be conveniently represented on paper* [Nelson1965]. Hypertext enables creating hyperlinks between nodes which represent portions of information. This feature makes hypertext information storage similar to human brain perception. Thus, hypertext can be understood as an interconnected set of information pieces.

The concept of information retrieval systems emerged in the late 1950s. *An information retrieval system is an information system; that is, a system used to store items of information that need to be processed, searched, retrieved and disseminated to various user populations* [Salton1983]. Users usually represent their information needs as queries specified in an adequate query language. The idea of connecting the hypertext and information retrieval has a firm theoretical and practical basis e.g. [Clitherow1989] [Croft1989] [Kuhlen1991] [Weyer1982].

The concept of selective distribution of information (SDI) is derived from the concept of selective dissemination of information. The latter was created by H.P.Luhn [Luhn1958] in order to improve scholarly communication among universities. SDI systems should provide users with relevant information while possibly rejecting irrelevant information. Information producers, who offer information stored as digital documents to users, provide sources for SDI systems [Abramowicz1998] [Brzoskowski1997] [Houseman1970] [Latanowicz1996]. As opposed to traditional retrieval systems (described by Salton [Salton1983], van Rijsbergen [Rijsbergen1979]) SDI systems are information filters. In the typical Information Retrieval system, a single query is performed on the set of documents. Whereas in the SDI system, a set of queries is applied to a single document [Abramowicz1984]. The functionality of SDI systems requires a specific representation of user information needs – a user profile. A typical query performed in a traditional information retrieval system would check which documents in the collection meet user needs specified in the query. In the SDI system, a single document is compared to the set of profiles (queries) and distributed to users whose information needs are met. SDI profiles usually contain a list of terms with corresponding parameters (i.e. weights) [Abramowicz1998].

The HyperSDI system is an information filter that retrieves information from information sources on the Web. Information is filtered against user profiles (see 3.3.1 Information Supply) by measuring similarity between documents and user profiles. Similarity is measured in one of commonly applied similarity measures. Documents that are similar to a particular profile are distributed to its owner. The user then estimates the relevance of the document by deciding either to include the document in his private collection or to reject it. In addition to this the HyperSDI system automatically updates user profiles according to relevance evaluation.

3.2 The HyperSDI System Model

The HyperSDI system architecture is based on *the thin client* model. The client in the client-server model is considered thinner when the *fat server* does most of processing. The main parts of the HyperSDI system architecture are users, Internet sources of documents, HyperSDI server, collection of documents, collection of profiles and HyperSDI database. *Figure 2* shows the architecture of the HyperSDI system.

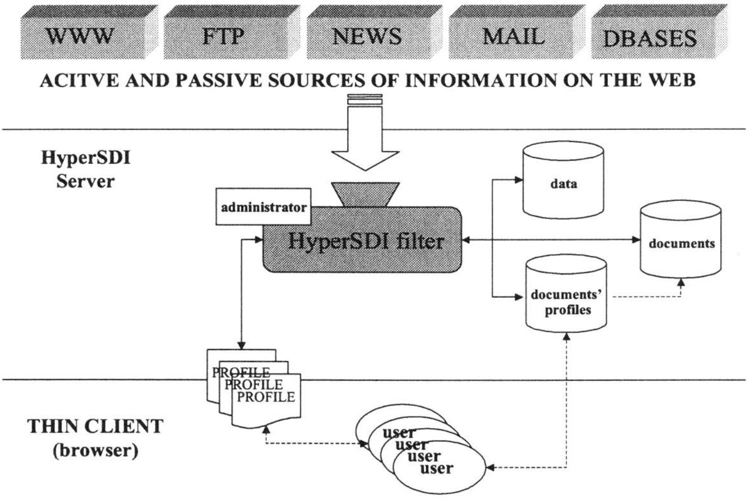

Figure 2. The HyperSDI system architecture

3.2.1 HyperSDI Users

A HyperSDI system's user can be grasped as a unit in the organization structure (i.e. Customer Relationship Manager) or as a superposition of functions in the organization workflow. A warehouse subject (see *Figure 3*) or a role in workflow may also be considered a HyperSDI user. Thus, the definition of a HyperSDI user is broad and enables us to include the process of collecting benchmarking information in the organizational workflow.

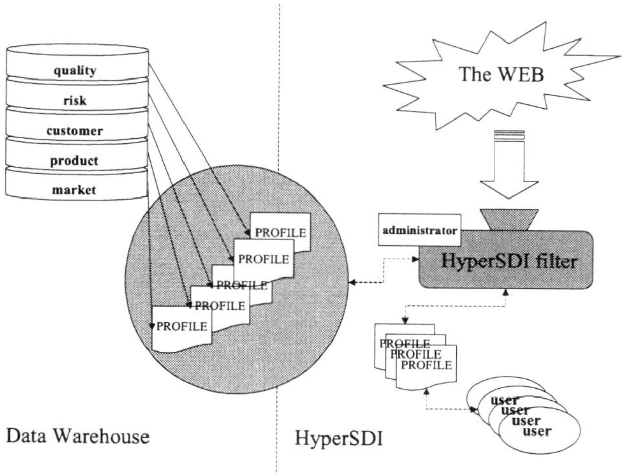

Figure 3. Warehouse subjects as HyperSDI users

3.2.2 Information Sources

We distinguish two sorts of benchmarking information sources on the Web: passive information sources and active information sources. The active information sources deliver documents independently from the system (i.e. e-mail, distribution lists, newsgroups). Consequently, information from passive information sources must be retrieved by the system (i.e. downloading a Web page). Heterogeneous active and passive information sources imply various retrieving techniques (see 3.3.1 Information Supply).

We assume that benchmarking information sources for HyperSDI systems are provided (i.e. subscriptions to benchmarking or financial services on the Web). Under such an assumption only trusted information sources may deliver information to HyperSDI systems.

3.2.3 The HyperSDI Server

The HyperSDI server is the main module of the system. It performs the following functions:

- collecting, storing and managing user data
- collecting, storing and managing user profiles

- storing, managing and extending the set of information sources
- informing users of new documents similar to their profiles
- estimating relevance of documents
- storing, hypertext-way organizing, retrieving and presenting information in the document collection
- building, storing and organizing metainformation on documents in the collection

3.2.4 Document Collection, Document Profile Collection and HyperSDI Database

The HyperSDI *document collection* is a set of documents owned by all HyperSDI system users. Documents in the collection are automatically organized as interconnected groups (see 3.3.2 Organizing Information). Analysis of preexisting hyperlinks plays an important role in automatic reorganization of the document collection.

The HyperSDI *document profile* contains metainformation about a particular document such as author, size, word count, revision date and a hyperlink to this document. Thus, the profile can be understood as a sort of view to the *document collection* that enables users to access a particular document. Also, document profiles enable users to create hyperlinks to other documents in the collection or on the Web. The number of document profiles corresponding to a particular document depends on user information needs. All document profiles that belong to a single profile form the *document profiles collection* (DPC).

A HyperSDI *database* stores data about sources of benchmarking information on the Web, documents in the document collection, users and their information needs (profiles) and – finally – document profiles.

3.3 Building Knowledge out of Information

Transforming information into knowledge requires certain information supply, certain information organization and certain information presentation.

3.3.1 Information Supply

Benchmarking information sources on the Web are mostly dispersed and they store information as heterogeneous documents [Drożdżyński1997]. The HyperSDI system makes use of *software agents* in order to retrieve relevant information from heterogeneous Web sources of benchmarking information.

HyperSDI agents exploit the sources seeking documents that may be included in user collections. In particular agents navigate among and browse Web pages. They decide on navigation strategy based on rules stored in the knowledge base. Facts and rules that concern information sources are defined by experts on information retrieval. As navigating agents compare documents against user profiles, they notify users when they find sufficient similarity level.

According to the classification of software agents described by Franklin [Franklin1996], HyperSDI agents should be considered:

- reactive – they start exploiting active sources of benchmarking information when the system is notified of new documents available
- autonomous – they decide on navigation strategy regardless of other HyperSDI agents that exploit other sources
- temporal – they are deleted from the system after they finish checking the particular source
- communicative – they synchronize information about analyzed documents so as not to analyze documents more than once
- artificially intelligent – they decide on navigation strategy by means of a rule-based expert system and frequently updated user profiles
- learning – their knowledge on user information needs is improved over time

Users are given access to the documents they evaluated as relevant by adequate document profiles. Other documents are ultimately rejected by the system. Thus, users estimate the relevance of pre-filtered documents that contain benchmarking information and decide which of them will supply their private collections.

3.3.2 Organizing Information

Before a particular document is included in the hypertext document collection, it should possibly be converted into hypertext format [Dudziński1997] [Krzyżaniak1998] [Mytych1994] [Płuciennik1997] [Sachanowicz1994]. Conversion should be performed semi-automatically according to the rules described by DeBra [DeBra1996], Schneiderman [Schneiderman1989]. Also, reorganization (understood here as re-linking) of the document collection can be performed by the system. Reorganization can be executed periodically or every time the specified number of new documents is accepted. The main techniques used in organizing document collection are similarity analysis described by van Rijsbergen [Rijsbergen1979] and Salton [Salton1983] and cluster analysis described by Abramowicz [Abramowicz1998], Bijnen [Bijnen1973] and Xu [Xu1999]. Reorganization does not affect hyperlinks and attributes previously defined by users as they are included in document profiles [Łysiak1996]. The desirable result of reorganization is more efficient exploitation of the collected resources by supplying users with more relevant documents.

3.3.3 Presentation of Information

Every user profile should be accompanied by a proper user profile collection (UPC). UPC contains document profiles of documents evaluated as relevant to adequate user profiles. Consequently, every user collection is comprised of a number of user profile collections.

Users may access documents through their private user collections (UC). Document profiles in such collections are linked to documents in a system's document collection. Additionally, users can perform traditional queries on the HyperSDI document collection.

3.4 Hyperlinks Connecting HyperSDI Document Collection and a Company's Data Warehouse

Most data warehouse solutions enable users to store hyperlinks as metadata objects. Hence, these solutions enable the inclusion of documents in the warehouse according to hypertext paradigm. Documents are included in the warehouse by generating hyperlinks to document profiles that represent metadata structure such as the Flight Delays Subject (see 3.2.1 HyperSDI Users). Relevance of incoming documents is estimated by the subject supervisor.

Correspondingly, document profiles in HyperSDI DPC may contain hyperlinks to warehouse data available on the Web (see 2.3 Data Warehouses and the Web). These hyperlinks may vary as they are defined by different users who access the particular document.

Establishing connections between a company's data warehouse and the HyperSDI document collection requires some pieces of information to be semantically similar to each other. Thus, the HyperSDI system should be capable of retrieving information that meets information *needs* of a particular subject (see *Figure 3*). This requires a specific profile that covers both metadata and user information needs.

4. USER PROFILES IN THE HYPERSDI SYSTEM

4.1 Representing User Information Needs

As we mentioned before, HyperSDI users (information consumers) specify their information needs in user profiles. A traditional profile contains a list of terms. Users may define numerous profiles to represent various issues [Abramowicz1990b]. Profiles are transferred to the HyperSDI server via e-mail or via a proper Java applet. HyperSDI profiles are encoded in XML.

4.2 User Profile Elements

A proper HyperSDI user profile should contain the following elements:

- name that distinguishes it from other user profiles
- list of information sources which are most probable to supply user with relevant documents; only documents from registered sources will be compared against the profile
- source weights that represent user interest in a particular source
- similarity threshold that represents the minimum value of similarity between the profile and the analyzed document
- similarity measure used for comparing documents with the profile
- set of records that represent user interests. Each record should contain term, its weight, a case-sensitiveness parameter and term-concentration parameter. The former shows how frequency of term in a particular document influences its weight when evaluating similarity. Additionally, terms may be defined as *whole word*, *prefix*, *suffix* or *infix*.

All postulates listed above were taken into consideration while defining the Extended Markup Language (XML) profile format for the HyperSDI system.

5. BUILDING DATA WAREHOUSE PROFILES

5.1 The Concept of Data Warehouse Profiles

We decided to adapt information retrieval techniques for automatic text indexing to use them in data warehouses.

In our solution we use two types of profiles:

- warehouse subject profile linked to a structure of data warehouse,
- user profile linked to a person.

The warehouse subject profile represents information needs of a virtual user. Each subject profile is managed by a human, referred to as the profile supervisor.

Furthermore, we distinguish three types of warehouse subject profiles:

- metaprofile – built automatically out of metadata, the starting point for further improvement
- current subject profile (referred to as subject profile) – used for documents retrieval, continuously improved during system exploitation
- multiprofile – a compound consisting of repeatedly improved user profiles

Another important issue connected with warehouse profiles is the way they are linked to a company's data warehouse. Particularly when a user profile is meant to be utilized within a data warehouse, it should be assigned to a selected element of the warehouse's structure. Assigning user profiles to the element of the warehouse structure may be initiated by users themselves, it may result from the function they perform within the organization or from the process they belong to.

Assigning profiles to selected warehouse structure elements can result in the following advantages:

- exercising control over access to information retrieved for the warehouse; profiles are assigned by subject profile supervisor
- possibility of improving subject profiles

Hence, warehouse subject users are supplied with documents compared to the profile of the subject. They estimate relevance of the retrieved documents and the HyperSDI system improves the subject profile. However, users do not equally influence changes in the profile. Profile supervisors specify users whose functions, positions or roles affect the particular profile most.

We assume that numerous HyperSDI profiles may represent interests of a single user. Thus, it is likely that each warehouse subject may contain various profiles. These profiles may be brought together as a subject profile that represents knowledge of all subject users. Due to the security demands, warehouse profiles should not be accessed (modified) by users. Instead of representing information needs of a particular user, subject profiles depict the needs of the whole metadata structure (i.e. subject).

In our project, we assume that all changes in metadata must be confirmed by a human supervisor. Thus, warehouse supervisors control information that is included in subjects. If supervisors accept a metaprofile they can assign it as a current subject profile. Such a profile will be then improved by users of this subject. The functionality of the HyperSDI system includes techniques which improve user profiles. When metaprofiles change due to changes in warehouse metadata, profiles should be automatically improved; however, this should be confirmed by users. Users should be informed about improvement suggestions and should be able to adjust their profiles according to the suggestions. New profiles should never be imposed on users.

5.2 Automatic Text Indexing

Every information retrieval system provides its users with information stored in a specific format – mostly as digital documents. Currently IR systems store documents' bodies and provide access to them via views. In the past, memory was expensive, processing capabilities were low and the majority of documents were available only as hard copies. Instead of storing the whole documents, IR systems stored their specific representations: indexes. Indexes are created automatically, semi-automatically or manually. The process of creating an index out of a document will be further referred to as indexing. *The indexing task consists first of assigning to each stored item terms, or concepts, capable of representing document content, and second of assigning to each term a weight, or value, reflecting its presumed importance for purposes of content identification* [Salton1983].

5.3 Traditional Information Retrieval and Metadata Structures

As we mentioned before, a company's data warehouse contains a number of subjects. Apart from "numerical" knowledge subjects may contain one or more *information marts* that consist of documents.

Before a metaprofile is created it should be taken into consideration whether *information mart* documents will be indexed along with metadata. Consequently, we can distinguish narrow and broad warehouse indexing. In both cases, data warehouse is considered as a collection of documents. Depending on the indexing techniques, various algorithms may be applied to creating indexes.

In broad warehouse indexing it is assumed that *information mart* documents affect the analysis. Every subject may contain several *information marts*, which adds one more level in metadata hierarchy.

Cluster analysis is defined as grouping objects by similarity measured in the specified space of object attributes [Bijnen1973]. In information retrieval systems, a document is considered an object and attribute space is grasped as limited number of terms. The idea of cluster analysis is to find terms that clearly distinguish collections of documents (called clusters). Clusters may be then organized into hierarchies by creating broader clusters that group narrower collections [Abramowicz1998].

Similarity between metadata hierarchy and the hierarchy of clusters in traditional cluster analysis made us consider using clustering algorithms for creating metaprofiles. *Table 1* summarizes our reasoning.

Table 1. Similarity between data warehouses and cluster analysis

Data warehouses	Cluster analysis
data warehouse	set of all documents
subject	broader cluster
information mart	narrower cluster
document in an information mart	document in a cluster

We believe that a company's data warehouse can be understood as the broadest cluster. Thus, instead of searching terms in the whole space of attributes, we could seek the ones that caused the existing organization of documents in the warehouse to be created. Consequently, if we consider the problem of clustering documents in the warehouse according to such terms, we expect the solution to resemble metadata hierarchy.

We assume that in narrow metadata indexing only metadata alone is analyzed. When subject metadata stands for a document, we may comb metadata in the search of indexing terms. These terms should meet the same conditions as traditional indexes. They should represent the analyzed subject and distinguish it from the other subjects. The search process is similar to traditional indexing (see *Table 2*).

Later we will prove that the indexing algorithm does not require subjects to be exclusive from the issue point of view. Similar documents may be indexed with the same keywords. Similarly, data warehouse subjects may be indexed with the same terms.

Table 2. Similarity of data warehouse structures and indexing

Data warehouses	Traditional indexing
data warehouse	set of all documents
subject metadata	indexed documents

Thus, another way of creating metaprofiles is to make use of well-known indexing techniques. This method will be discussed further in this paper.

5.4 Justification of Narrow Metadata Indexing

In our opinion, narrow metadata indexing is more functional than broader indexing for the following reasons.

The number of documents included in a company's data warehouse may significantly increase over the years. According to the data warehousing paradigm, documents included in the repository should never be removed. This is opposite to traditional SDI systems where documents are usually stored temporarily and later removed from the collection. Identifying changes in a massive amount of old information is extremely hard. Therefore, organizing documents seems to have a very high priority in implementing the system. These changes should affect quality not quantity of information retrieved by the system. That is why profiles should be improved only by incoming documents alone.

In comparison with broader metadata indexing, the amount of data being analyzed in narrow indexing seems to be more reasonable. Accordingly, the results will be produced faster.

Although it seems that *information mart* documents are not considered in narrow indexing, in fact it affects only the preliminary metaprofile. The metaprofile evolves as data warehouses evolve and users become more and more experienced in information retrieval. Documents included in the warehouse through the working HyperSDI system affect the way profiles are improved. Consequently, only the documents that preceded HyperSDI system deployment do not affect profiles.

Another reason for introducing narrow indexing is the fact that data warehouses are not designed for collecting documents. For years this functionality has belonged to information retrieval systems. Information marts were introduced specially for users who wanted to access information from a single storage. We also assume that documents can be accessed independently from the warehouse via hyperlinks (see 3.4 Hyperlinks Connecting HyperSDI Document Collection and a Company's Data Warehouse). The idea of creating metaprofiles out of metadata will be discussed below.

The first assumption is that metadata properly describes information stored in warehouse subjects. We also assume that any changes made in metadata will be accompanied by appropriate descriptions according to the data warehousing paradigm. Appropriate metadata is the basis of proper warehouse indexing.

5.5 Searching for Indexing Terms in Warehouse Subjects

As we stated before, metaprofiles are constructed of terms found exclusively in metadata (narrow indexing).

Below we present the algorithm searching for terms that clearly distinguish one particular subject from other subjects. Commonly known statistics such as **term concentration index** or **inverse document frequency** can be applied to estimate weights of indexing terms.

Metaprofiles should follow the rules of constructing regular document profiles and should preferably be:

- sufficient – representing as much subject information as possible
- discriminating – enabling to distinguish subjects
- concise – represented in limited number of terms

5.6 Term Concentration Index

The concentration of term **i** can be estimated by the following formula:

$$\rho_i^{(y)} = \frac{\max^{(y)}\left(F^i\right)}{sum\left(F^i\right)}$$

where:

F^i - indicates the vector that represents the frequency of term **i** in every subject,

$\max^{(y)}(v)$ - indicates the function that returns the sum of **y** biggest elements in vector **v**,

sum(v) - indicates the function that returns the sum of all elements in vector **v.**

If the concentration index of term **i** $\rho_i^{(y)}$ is small, the term is dispersed among warehouse subjects. Consequently, it is considered to be inappropriately discriminating and is not taken into account when building a metaprofile. If the index is large, it means that the term is clustered round **y** warehouse subjects and is considered appropriately discriminating. Estimating the **y** parameter is somewhat difficult. In our opinion the **y** parameter should increase as the number of warehouse subjects increase; however, precise evaluation requires further research.

To conclude, metaprofile generation requires finding and including terms with large concentration indexes $\rho_i^{(y)}$.

5.7 Inverse Document Frequency

The concept of inverse document frequency (IDF) is based on the hypothesis that says: terms common in analyzed documents and rare in other documents are particularly good for indexing. This hypothesis is true for the limited set of documents. Under some conditions, a relatively stable data warehouse may be considered such a limited set of documents.

The advantages of the IDF method include satisfactory results and easy implementation. One of the disadvantages is the necessity of modifying weights each time metadata changes. In our opinion it is not an obstacle as repeatedly improved HyperSDI profiles keep up with changes made in metadata.

We adapted formulas applied to automatic document indexing described by Salton [Salton1983]. It is assumed that the meaning of term is inversely proportional to the number of warehouse subjects (S_i) it describes. The (modified) formula looks as follows:

$$IDF_i = \log_2 \frac{N}{S_i} + 1$$

where:

IDF_i - indicates inverse document frequency index of term **i**

N - indicates number of warehouse subjects

S_i - indicates number of subjects that contain term **i**

The next stage of warehouse indexing is the estimation of weights. They may be resolved by means of the following formula:

$$IDFW_i^k = F_i^k \cdot (\log_2 N - \log_2 S_i + 1),$$

where:

$IDFW_i^k$ - indicates inverse document frequency weight of term **i** in subject **k**

F_i^k - indicates frequency count of term **i** in subject **k.**

The above formula makes significant only those terms that occur in few subjects.

5.8 The Algorithm for Generating Metaprofiles

The algorithm for generating metaprofiles appears as follows:

1. Searching for terms in metadata
2. Limiting the number of terms
3. Generating metaprofiles

Because of the limited size of this paper we are not going to describe the algorithm in detail.

6. TECHNIQUES FOR IMPROVING PROFILES

6.1 Introduction to Improving HyperSDI Profiles

The techniques used for improving user profiles in our project are derived from traditional SDI techniques developed once metadata has been taken into consideration [Callan1998].

HyperSDI user profile may be improved by modifying weights of significant terms. Additionally, users may insert terms found in metadata by the system. Users can declare their profiles as members of a particular subject. Superposition of these profiles forms a multiprofile. Every warehouse subject collects documents that were evaluated as relevant by subject users. Such documents may be considered as superposition of subject users' knowledge. Hence, all users of a particular subject can access information retrieved by other users within this subject. However, they can not access information about document owners.

6.2 Improving User Profiles by Modifying Weights

HyperSDI profiles are improved by modifying weights of terms. This is usually performed automatically after considering a particular document as either relevant or irrelevant to user. Generally weights of terms, which appear often in relevant documents, are increased and weights of terms, which appear often in rejected documents, are diminished [Abramowicz1998] [Greiff1998]. Moreover, information on how a particular term is useful for document indexing is applied. Weights in user profile are usually modified when the specified number of new documents is evaluated by a user.

Further reasoning will be conducted under the assumption that users received and analyzed **n** documents, which were estimated similar to their **k** profile. Additionally, it is assumed that users either accepted or rejected each document (evaluated its relevance). The last assumption is that information on the level of term usefulness for document indexing is available for each document. This information is represented by the following parameters.

Let a_i^k be the sum-of-usefulness index of term **i** in the profile **k** for documents accepted by user. Let **A** be the set of documents (**D**$_j$) accepted by the user. The sum-of-usefulness index is estimated as:

$$a_i^k = \sum_{D_j \in A} p_i^k(D_j),$$

where:

$p_i^k(D_j)$ - indicates usefulness index of term **i** in profile **k** in document $\mathbf{D_j}$

A similar index can be counted for rejected documents. Let o_i^k be the sum-of-usefulness index of term **i** in the profile **k** for documents rejected by the user.

$$o_i^k = \sum_{D_j \notin A} p_i^k(D_j)$$

After estimating **a** and **o** parameters the term-acceptance index can be assessed. This index represents the level of term acceptance for term **i** in profile **k** in **n** evaluated documents similar to profile **k** [Ceglarek1997].

$$acc_i^k = \frac{a_i^k}{a_i^k + o_i^k}$$

When a particular term does not frequently appear in relevant documents, a_i^k is relatively small. If $a_i^k > o_i^k$ ($acc_i^k > 0{,}5$), it indicates that term **i** more frequently appears in relevant documents than in irrelevant ones. If a particular term more often appears in relevant documents and its usefulness is on average higher than in irrelevant documents, it positively influences the retrieval of documents that meet user needs. Weights of such terms should be increased. Otherwise, when a particular term frequently appears in rejected (irrelevant) documents and its usefulness is on average higher than in relevant documents, its weight should be diminished.

Having estimated the term-acceptance index, it is feasible to assess the average-term-acceptance index π^k for user profile **k** [Ceglarek1997].

$$\pi^k = \frac{1}{n_k} \sum_{i=1}^{n_k} acc_i^k ,$$

where:

n_k - indicates total number of terms in profile **k**

Let $\Delta_i^k = acc_i^k - \pi^k$.

The weights in the analyzed user profile are modified according to the parameters mentioned above. The weight of term **i** should be increased by $\Delta_i^k \cdot (1 - w_i^k)$ if $\Delta_i^k > 0$. Otherwise, the weight should be diminished by

$\left|\Delta_i^k\right| \cdot w_i^k$ [Ceglarek1997]. Terms, which weights reached the specified minimum, are removed from the profile. The modified profile is presented to users who can either accept or reject changes. Also they may want to manually modify their profiles.

6.3 Improving Subject Profiles by Modifying Weights

We assume that user profile **k** is assigned to subject profile **t**. Thus the subject profile **t** is improved every time user profile **k** is improved.

When subject supervisor binds a user profile to a subject profile he assigns it a weight. The weight denotes the importance of the user in the subject profile improvement process. Let w_k^t be the weight of user profile **k** in subject **t**.

The Δ_i^k parameter is the same as described in the previous section. Let w_i^t be the weight of term **i** in subject profile **t**. If term **i** from the user profile exists in the subject profile then the weights of the subject profile are modified. If $\Delta_i^k > 0$, then the weight of term **i** should be increased by $w_k^t \cdot \Delta_i^k \cdot \left(1 - w_i^t\right)$. Otherwise, the weight should be diminished by $w_k^t \cdot \left|\Delta_i^k\right| \cdot w_i^t$.

When term **i** from user profile does not exist in the subject profile, the system checks whether this term can be added to the subject profile. The new weight is estimated according to the formula below:

$$w_i^t = w_k^t \cdot w_i^k$$

If the computed weight is higher than a specified threshold, then term **i** is added to the subject profile with this weight. The modified profile is presented to the profile supervisor who can either accept changes or reject them. The profile supervisor may also manually modify the profile.

6.4 Indirect Information about Relevance

Indirect information about relevance is sent to users along with the documents retrieved by HyperSDI server. It contains terms that do not occur in the particular user profile but they occur in other profiles that were estimated similar to the analyzed document. This information is also called *inspiring information* [Abramowicz1990b].

In a traditional SDI system, information consumers receive from information producers not only documents but also terms from other profiles. These special terms made the system consider the document interesting to other users. Thus, it is assumed that users properly depict their interests in their profiles. Document acceptance is not as important as user potential interest in this document.

Due to the requirements of data warehousing, the traditional HyperSDI models have been altered. Instead of physical distribution (i.e. via e-mail) documents are stored on the HyperSDI server. Users access documents via *document profiles* (see 3.2.4 Document Collection, Document Profile Collection and HyperSDI Database). In that way it is easy to find user profiles that correspond with accepted documents. Additionally, it is possible to determine whether a user accepted a document or not. The latter was impossible in traditional SDI systems.

In our concept a user should receive *inspiring information* first and foremost from profiles of the same warehouse subject. Then the probability of choosing proper terms is highest.

6.5 Using Metaprofiles

As it was stated before, metaprofiles are built out of metadata for each subject. In traditional SDI systems, metaprofiles are the elements of the information producer's knowledge. Metaprofiles are profiles representing information interests of the whole group of information consumers. In our concept metaprofiles are grasped as automatically created profiles on the basis of warehouse metadata. They are exploited mostly by users who have no idea how to create their initial profile. The metaprofile can be either accepted or modified by users and saved as their own profiles. Hence, the HyperSDI system helps users create their own profiles.

6.6 Using Multiprofiles

Multiprofile was defined as superposition of all user profiles in the subject. Thus, strict restrictions must be imposed on metaprofiles in order not to disclose information on users' interests. Multiprofiles are created by users themselves. Therefore, they represent the interest of the group of users in the same warehouse subject. Users would loose confidence in the system if it enabled other users to view their private profiles. Consequently, multiprofiles should never be revealed. Hence, users may only access documents evaluated similar to the multiprofile. More terms can be added to user profile when *inspiring information* is exploited.

Moreover, multiprofiles are flexible since they change as users' profiles change. These changes affect the information retrieval process.

Comparing metaprofile with multiprofile by means of some similarity measure (i.e. cosine) can produce very interesting results. The less similar the profiles are the less interested in warehouse documents users are. This may be the sign of warehouse's drift toward misinformation.

7. IMPLEMENTATION NOTES

The HyperSDI working model was created on the basis of object oriented methodology. The System's database model is relational and its document collection is based on hypertext systems.

7.1 Base Objects

The base classes of the HyperSDI system model are *document*, *source*, *user*, *profile*, *doc_profile* and *dw_structure*. The links between objects are mostly of *has-a* type. *Figure 4* presents the links among simplified HyperSDI classes.

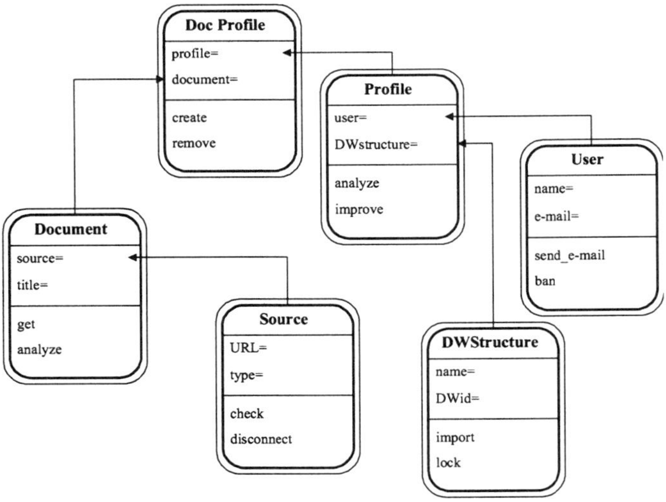

Figure 4. Base objects of the HyperSDI system

7.2 Database and Knowledge Base of the HyperSDI System

The relational database of the HyperSDI system contains basic information on system objects and system knowledge about information sources [Płuciennik1997]. The most important tables in the database are *document*, *profile*, *user*, *source*, *document_profile* and *dw_structure* as shown on *Figure 5*.

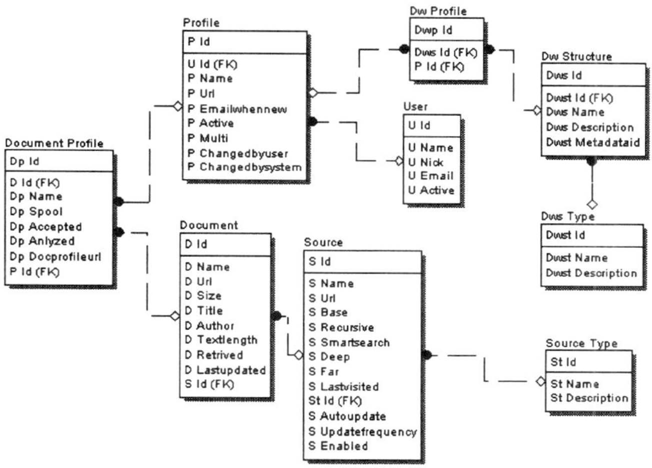

Figure 5. The HyperSDI Database Model

The knowledge base is a part of system database. It contains facts and rules concerning retrieved documents and sources. These rules enable HyperSDI agents to decide which navigation strategy should they use. The decision depends on source type, source structure, document format and document body. The main tables of the HyperSDI knowledge base are *fact*, *value*, *rule* and *condition*. These tables are not linked to those in the database as *knowledge* is applied to temporal (just analyzed) instances of *document* class. *Figure 6* shows the HyperSDI knowledge base relational model.

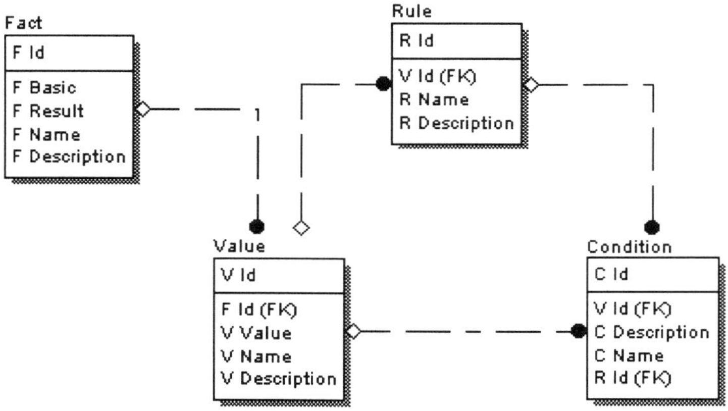

Figure 6. The HyperSDI Knowledge Base Model

The HyperSDI agent knowledge base contains the following objects:

- facts on documents and sources,
- discrete values of facts,
- rules that create values,
- conditions that form rules.

Facts can be divided into base facts, result facts (conclusions) and intermediate facts. The base facts must have their values assigned before the knowledge is applied. When concluding is complete at least one conclusion must have its value assigned. The knowledge base is independent from the system. Hence, advanced users may modify intermediate facts and rules that lead agents to conclusions.

7.3 HyperSDI Server

The HyperSDI server can be defined as the set of applications and data placed on some operating system. In our model The HyperSDI server works on the *Microsoft Windows NT Server* with a working WWW server (i.e. *Microsoft WWW Server*, *HyperWave*) and working *Java Virtual Machine* (JVM). The HyperSDI server builds its own files and folders under *Windows NT* file system. These files are available on the Web via WWW server. HyperSDI server application manipulates documents within main HyperSDI folder and manipulates data through Java Database Connectivity –

Open Database Connectivity (JDBC-ODBC). HyperSDI database is available via standard *Windows NT* ODBC.

7.4 Document Collection and Document Profile Collection

In the physical model of the system, the document collection is a set of hypertext documents stored as files under *Windows NT* file system. These files are named according to their id number in HyperSDI database and their format extension such as "html", "txt" or "xml". Document profiles are placed in user private folders (password-protected). They may be modified either by users (user-defined hyperlinks and comments) or by the system (document updates information). Users may change their document profiles via Java applets.

7.5 HyperSDI Profile Format

HyperSDI profile format was frequently reviewed during our research. The reason for this review was continuous extending HyperSDI functionality, which required changes in profile format. Also some of the functionality was abandoned due to implementation difficulties.

Encoding HyperSDI profiles in XML seems to be the most beneficial idea as popularity of this language has increased recently. While experimenting with the system, new XML tools emerged on the market. Microsoft introduced XML in the latest version of Internet Explorer (5.0). Netscape declared to implement XML in its future Navigator 5.0. We anticipate that XML may prove to be the base Web document format in the future.

Using XML to encode HyperSDI profiles makes them accessible from numerous operating systems. Consequently, creating information filters would be easier if user interests were described in the standard format.

8. CONCLUSIONS

The concept of connecting "numerical" knowledge, based on structured information processing, with "textual" knowledge, based on unstructured information processing, will hopefully extend the meaning of term "knowledge" in information systems.

The users of data warehouse profiles form interest groups, which appear to have similar interests. Documents collected by one user may appear relevant to other users within the same warehouse subject [Herlocker1999].

Hence, it is essential to make all relevant documents in the subject accessible to users. Creating proper structures that would make organizing documents in the warehouse possible could help users to make use of the retrieved information.

Occasionally, user profiles should be compared to the *typical* profile of a particular subject. The results of such comparison might be useful as far as improvement of profiles is concerned. Thus, user profiles should be compared against both metaprofiles and multiprofiles within the subject.

It is also possible to exchange users' knowledge among subjects. It may appear that some subjects are similar to other subjects and they may contain the same documents. The similarity between subjects can be measured by cluster analysis. A warehouse attribute (term) space must be created beforehand. Similar warehouse subjects would form clusters. A special structure should be introduced to navigate among such clusters.

Applying the HyperSDI system to supply a company's data warehouse with benchmarking information may significantly increase a company's knowledge. However, this must be proved in practice. *Figure 7* summarizes our paper.

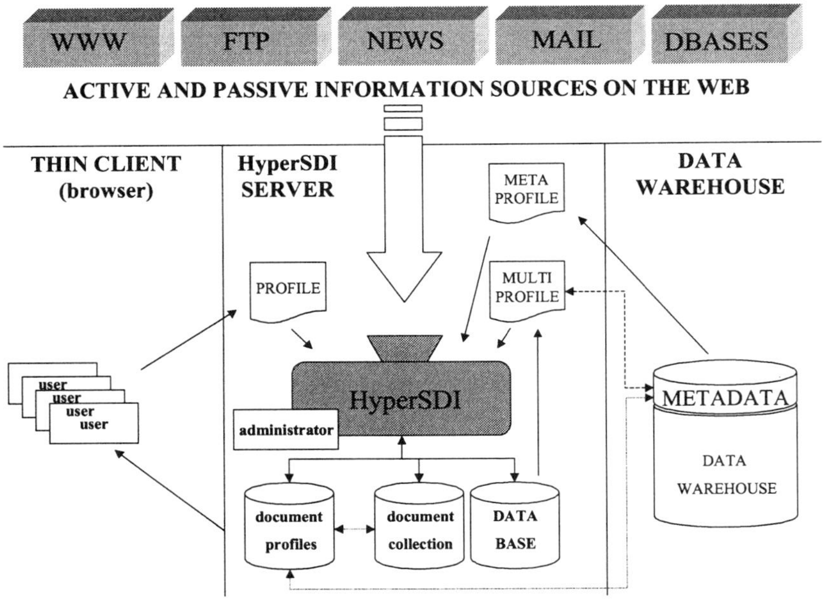

Figure 7. HyperSDI supplying data warehouse with benchmarking information from the Web

REFERENCES

[Abramowicz1984] Abramowicz, W. *Ein mathematisches Modell eines IR-Systems zur Verbreitung von Informationen in einem Netz*, Institut für Informatik, Eidgenössische Technische Hochschule, Zürich, 1984, 44pp.

[Abramowicz1985] Abramowicz W. *Computer Added Dissemination of Information on Software in Networks*, Proceedings of Compas '85 - The European Software Congress, December 10-13, Berlin West, 1985, 491-505.

[Abramowicz1990a] Abramowicz W. *Hypertexte und ihre IR- basierte Verbreitung*, Humboldt Universität Berlin 1990, 292 +VII

[Abramowicz1990b] Abramowicz W. *Information Dissemination to Users with Heterogenous Interests*. Grabowski J. (ed.), Computers in Science and Higher Education, Mathematical Research, Vol. 57, Akademie-Verlag, Berlin 1990, pp. 62-71

[Abramowicz1998] Abramowicz, W. Ceglarek, D. *Applying Cluster-Based Connection Structure in the Document Base of the SDI System*. WebNet'98 World Conference of the WWW, Internet & Intranet, Nov. 7-12, 1998, Orlando, Florida, USA

[Bijnen1973] Bijnen E.J. *Cluster analysis*. Tilburg University Press, 1973

[Brzoskowski1997] Brzoskowski, P. *Possibilities and Means of Distributing Legal Information on the Web*, The Poznan University of Economics, Faculty of Economics, Poznań 1997

[Bush1945] Bush, W. *As We May Think*, Atlantic Monthly, July 1945, 101-108.

[Callan1998] Callan, J. *Learning while Filtering Documents*, 22nd International Conference on Research and Development in Information Retrieval

[Ceglarek1997] Ceglarek, D. *Applying Taxonomous Methods in Selective Distribution of Information (SDI) Systems Supplying Users with Business Information*, Ph.D. Thesis, The Poznan University of Economics, Faculty of Economics, Poznań1997

[Clitherow1989] Clitherow, P.; Riecken, D.; Muller M., *VISAR: A System for Interference and Navigation in Hypertext*, Hypertext'89, Proceedings, November 5-8, 1989, Pittsburgh, Pennsylvania, 293-304.

[Croft1989] Croft, W. B.; Tutle H. *A Retrieval Model for Incorporating Hypertext Links*, Hypertext'89, Proceedings, November 5-8, 1989, Pittsburgh, Pennsylvania, 213-224.

[DeBra1996] De Bra, P.M.E. *Hypermedia Structures and Systems*. TUE course http://win-www.uia.ac.be/u/debra/INF706

[Dittrich1999] Dittrich, K. R. *Towards Exploitation of the Data Universe – Database Technology for Comprehensive Query Services*. Proceedings of the 3rd International Conference on Business Information Systems in Poznań; Springer Verlag London Ltd. 1999

[Drożdżyński1997] Drożdżyński, W. *Identifying Sources of Information and Specifying Revisiting Periods on the Basis of User Profiles*, Master Thesis, The Poznan University of Economics, Faculty of Economics, Poznań 1997

[Dudziński1997] Dudziński, P. *Delinearization of Legal Documents Based on Their Structure*, Master Thesis, The Poznan University of Economics, Faculty of Economics, Poznań 1997

[Flangan1998] Flangan, Thomas; Safdie, Elias. *Java Gives Data Marts a Whole New Look*, Copyright © 1998 The Applied Technology Group

[Franklin1996] Franklin, Stan; Graesser, Art. *Is it an Agent, or Just a Program ? A taxonomy for Autonomous Agents*; Proceedings of the Third International Workshop on Agent Theories, Architectures, and Languages, Springer-Verlag, 1996

[Greiff1998] Greiff, W.R., A Theory of Term Weighting Based on Exploratory Data Analysis, 21st International Conference on Research and Development in Information Retrieval.

[Herlocker1999] Herlocker, J.L. et al. *An Algorithmic Framework for Performing Collaborative Filtering,* 22nd International Conference on Research and Development in Information Retrieval.
[Housman1970] Housman, E.M. Kaskela, E.D. *State of the art in Selective dissemination of information.* IEEE Transactions on Engeeneering Writing and Speech, Vol. 13, pp. 78-83
[Inmon1996] Inmon, William H., Hackathorn, Richard D. *Using the Data Warehouse*, John Wiley & Sons, New York, 1994
[Kimball1996] Kimball, R. *The Data Warehouse Toolkit - Practical Techniques for Building Dimensional Data Warehouses*, John Wiley & Sons, Inc., New York, 1996
[Kuhlen1991] Kuhlen, R., Hypertext, Ein nicht-lineares Medium zwischen Buch und Wissensbank, Springer-Verlag, 1991, pp.353.
[Krzyżaniak1998] Krzyżaniak M., *Multiplatform Legal Documents and Their Processing Based on Markup Languages Consistent With SGML*, Master Thesis, The Poznan University of Economics, Faculty of Economics, Poznań 1998
[Latanowicz1996] Latanowicz, W. S. *Applying SDI for Mail Filtering Based on Sample Mail Processor Application*, Master Thesis, The Poznan University of Economics, Faculty of Economics, Poznań 1996
[Luhn1958] Luhn H.P., *A Business Intelligence System*, IBM Journal of Research and Development, Vol. 2, No. 2, pp. 159-165
[Łysiak1996] Łysiak, B. M. *Interactive Linking Legal Documents in the „Hyper Themis" System*, Master Thesis, The Poznan University of Economics, Faculty of Economics, Poznań 1996
[Mytych1994] Mytych, R. *Storing Polish Legal Documents in SGML Format*, Master Thesis, The Poznan University of Economics, Faculty of Economics, Poznań 1994
[Nelson1965] Nelson, T.; *A file structure for The Complex, The Changing and The Indeterminate*, ACM 20th National Conference, 1965
[Płuciennik1997] Płuciennik, P. *A Relational Data Model for the Hypertext Legal Information System*, Master Thesis, The Poznan University of Economics, Faculty of Economics, Poznań 1997
[Rijsbergen1979] Rijsbergen van, C.J.; *Information Retrieval;* Butterworths, London, 1979. http://www.dcs.gla.ac.uk/Keith/Preface.html
[Sachanowicz1994] Sachanowicz, M. *Automatic Building of Hypertext Intratext anf Intertext Structure of Legal Documents*, Master Thesis, The Poznan University of Economics, Faculty of Economics, Poznań 1994
[Sager1976] Sager, Wolfgang K.; Lockemann Peter C. *Classification of Ranking Algorithms.* International Forum on Information and Documentation, vol 1, No. 4., 1976
[Salton1983] Salton, Gerard; McGill, Michael. *Introduction to Modern Information Retrieval*, McGraw-Hill Book Company 1983;
[SAS/WA] SAS Institute Inc., *SAS/Warehouse Administrator˜ User's Guide, Release 1.1, First Edition*, Cary, NC, SAS Institute Inc., 1997. 142 pp. ; http://www.sas.com/software/components/wadmin.html
[Schneiderman1989] Schneiderman, B. Kearlsley, G. *Hypertext Hands-On: An Introduction to a New Way of Organizing and Acessing Information.* Addison Wesley, 1989
[Sprague1978] Sprague, Robert J. Freudenreich, L. Ben, *Building Better SDI Profiles for Users of Large, Multidisciplinary Data Bases*, Journal of the American Society for Information Science, John Wiley & Sons, November 1978, Vol. 29, No. 6, pp. 278-282
[Weyer1982] Weyer, Stephen A. "The Design of a Dynamic Book for Information Search." International Journal of Man-Machine Studies, 17 (1982): 87-107.
[Xu1999] Xu, J., Croft, B., Cluster-based Language Models for Distributed Retrieval. 22nd International Conference on Research and Development in Information Retrieval.

Chapter 2

PARALLEL MINING OF ASSOCIATION RULES

David Cheung
Department of Computer Science and Information Systems, The University of Hong Kong, H. K.
dcheung@csis.hku.hk

Sau Dan Lee
Department of Computer Science and Information Systems, The University of Hong Kong, H. K.
sdlee@csis.hku.hk

Keywords: association rules, data mining, data skewness, workload balance, parallel mining, partitioning.

Abstract: Data mining requires lots of computation—a suitable candidate for exploiting parallel computer systems. We have developed a new parallel mining algorithm FPM on a distributed share-nothing parallel system. The new algorithm outperforms several previous parallel mining algorithms. It's efficiency is found to be sensitive to two data distribution characteristics, data skewness and workload balance. We have developed methods to preprocess a database to attain good skewness and balance, so as to accelerate FPM.

1 INTRODUCTION

Mining *association rules* in large databases is an important problem in data mining research [1, 10]. It can be reduced to finding *large itemsets* with respect to a given *support threshold* [1]. The problem demands a lot of CPU resources and disk I/O to solve. It needs to scan all the transactions in a database which introduces much I/O, and at the same time search through a large set of candidates for large itemsets. Thus, employing multiple processors to do data mining in parallel may deliver an effective solution to this problem. In this chapter, we study the behavior of parallel association rule mining algorithms in parallel systems with a share-nothing memory. Under this model, the database is partitioned and distributed across the local disks of the processors. We investigate how the partitioning method affects the performance of the algorithms, and then propose new partitioning methods to exploit this finding to speed up the parallel mining algorithms.

The cost of finding large itemsets is dominated by the computation of *support counts* of candidate itemsets. Two different paradigms have been proposed for parallel system with distributed memory for this purpose. The first one is *count distribution* and the second one is *data distribution* [2]. In this chapter, we investigate parallel mining employing the count distribution approach.

In the count distribution paradigm, each processor is responsible for computing the *local support counts* of *all* the candidates, which are the support counts in its partition. By exchanging the local support counts, all processors then compute the *global support counts* of the candidates, which are the total support counts of the candidates from all the partitions. Subsequently, large itemsets are computed by each processor independently. The merit of this approach is the simple communication scheme: the processors need only one round of communication to exchange their support counts in every iteration. This makes it very suitable for parallel system when considering response time. However, since every processor is required to keep the local support counts of *all* the candidates at each iteration, count distribution requires much memory space to maintain the local support counts of a large number of candidate sets. This is a drawback of this approach. Algorithms that use the count distribution paradigm include CD (Count Distribution) [2] and PDM (Parallel Data Mining) [11]. CD [2] is a representative algorithm in count distribution. It was implemented on an IBM SP2. PDM [11] is a modification of CD with the inclusion of the direct hashing technique proposed in [10].

To tackle the problem of large number of candidate sets in count distribution, we adopt two effective techniques, *distributed pruning* and *global pruning*, to prune and reduce the number of candidates in each iteration. These two techniques make use of the local support counts of large itemsets found in an iteration to prune candidates for the next iteration. These two pruning techniques have been adopted in a mining algorithm FDM (Fast Distributed Mining) previously proposed by us for distributed databases [4, 5]. However, FDM is not suitable for parallel environment, it requires at least two rounds of message exchanges in each iteration that increases the response time significantly. We have adopted the two pruning techniques to develop a new parallel mining algorithm FPM (Fast Parallel Mining), which requires only one round of message exchange in each iteration. Its communication scheme is as simple as that in CD, and it has a much smaller number of candidate sets due to the pruning.

We will focus on studying the performance behavior of FPM against CD. It depends heavily on the distribution of data among the partitions of the database. To study this issue, we first introduce two metrics, *skewness* and *balance* to describe the distribution of data in the databases. Then, we analytically study their effects on the performance of the two mining algorithms, and verify the results empirically. Next, we propose algorithms to produce database partitions that give "good" skewness and balance values. In other words, we propose algorithms to partition the database so that good skewness and balance values are obtained. Finally, we do experiments to find out how effective these partitioning algorithms are. We would like to note that the two pruning techniques and the partitioning algorithms not only can be used in the count distribution algorithm such as FPM, but it can also be integrated into data distribution algorithms.

We have captured the distribution characteristics in two factors: *data skewness* and *workload balance*. Intuitively, a partitioned database has high data skewness if most globally large itemsets[1] are locally large[2] only at a very few partitions. Loosely speaking, a partitioned database has a high workload balance if all the processors have similar number of locally large itemsets.[3] We have defined quantitative metrics to measure data skewness and workload balance. We found out that both distributed and global prunings have super performance in the best case of high data skewness and high workload balance. The combination of high balance with moderate skewness is the second best case. On the other hand, the high skewness, moderate balance combination only provides moderate improvement over CD, while the combination of low skewness and low balance is the worst case in which only marginal improvement can be obtained. Inspired by this finding, we investigate the feasibility of planning the partitioning of the database. We want to divide the data into different partitions so as to maximize the workload balance and yield high skewness. Mining a database by partitioning it appropriately and then employing FPM thus gives us excellent mining performance. We have implemented FPM on an IBM SP2 parallel machine with 32 processors. Extensive performance studies have been carried out. The results confirm our observation on the relationship between pruning effectiveness and data distribution.

For the purpose of partitioning, we have proposed four algorithms. We have implemented these algorithms to study their effectiveness. K-means clustering, like most clustering algorithm, provides good skewness. However, it in general would destroy the balance. Random partitioning in general can deliver high balance, but very low skewness. We introduce an optimization constraint to control the balance factor in the k-means clustering algorithm. This modification, called $Bk\mu$ (balanced k-means clustering), produces results which exhibit as good a balance as the random partitioning and also high skewness. In conclusion, we found that $Bk\mu$ is the most favorable partitioning algorithms among those we have studied.

2 PARALLEL MINING OF ASSOCIATION RULES

2.1 ASSOCIATION RULES

Let $I = \{i_1, i_2, \cdots, i_m\}$ be a set of items and D be a database of transactions, where each transaction T consists of a set of items such that $T \subseteq I$. An *association rule* is an implication of the form $X \Rightarrow Y$, where $X \subseteq I$, $Y \subseteq I$ and $X \cap Y = \phi$. An association rule $X \Rightarrow Y$ has support s in D if the probability of a transaction in D contains both X and Y is s. The association rule $X \Rightarrow Y$ holds in D with confidence c if the probability of a transaction in D which contains X also contains Y is c. The task of mining association rules is to find all the association rules whose support is larger than a given minimum support threshold and whose confidence is larger than a given minimum confidence threshold. For an itemset X, we use $X_{.sup}$ to denote its *support count* in database D, which is the number of transactions in D containing X. An itemset $X \subseteq I$ is *large* if $X_{.sup} \geq minsup \times |D|$, where $minsup$ is the given minimum support threshold and $|D|$ denotes the number of transactions in database D. For the purpose of presentation, we sometimes just use *support* to stand for support count of an itemset.

It has been shown that the problem of mining association rules can be decomposed into two subproblems [1]: (1) find all large itemsets for a given minimum support threshold, and (2) generate the association rules from the large itemsets found. Since (1) dominates the overall cost, research has been focused on how to efficiently solve the first subproblem.

In the parallel environment, it is useful to distinguish between the two different notions of *locally large* and *global large* itemsets. Suppose the entire database D is partitioned into $D_1, D_2, \cdots, D_n$ and distributed over n processors. Let X be an itemset, the *global support* of X is the support $X_{.sup}$ of X in D. When referring to a partition D_i, the *local support* of X at processor i, denoted by $X_{.sup(i)}$, is the support of X in D_i. X is *globally large* if $X_{.sup} \geq minsup \times |D|$. Similarly X is *locally large* at processor i if $X_{.sup(i)} \geq minsup \times |D_i|$. *Note that in general, an itemset X which is locally large at some processor i may not necessary be globally large. On the contrary, every globally large itemset X must be locally large at some processor i.* This result and its application have been discussed in details in [4].

For convenience, we use the short form k-itemset to stand for size-k itemset, which consist of exactly k items. And use L_k to denote the set of globally large k-itemsets. We have pointed out above that there is distinction between locally and globally large itemsets. For discussion purpose, we will call a globally large itemset which is also locally large at processor i, *gl-large* at processor i. We will use $GL_{k(i)}$ to denote the set of gl-large k-itemsets at processor i. Note that $GL_{k(i)} \subseteq L_k, \forall i, 1 \leq i \leq n$.

2.2 COUNT DISTRIBUTION ALGORITHM FOR PARALLEL MINING

Apriori is the most well known serial algorithm for mining association rules [1]. It relies on the apriori_gen function to generate the candidate sets at each iteration. CD (Count Distribution) is a parallelized version of Apriori for parallel mining [2]. The database D is partitioned into $D_1, D_2, \cdots, D_n$ and distributed across n processors. In the first iteration of CD, every processor i scans its partition D_i to compute the local supports of all the size-1 itemsets. All processors are then engage in one round of support counts exchange. After that, they independently find out global support counts of all the items and then the large size-1 itemsets. The program fragment of CD at processor i, $1 \leq i \leq n$, for the k-th iteration is outlined in Algorithm 1. In step 1, it computes the candidate set C_k by applying the apriori_gen function on L_{k-1}, the set of large itemsets found in the previous iteration. The apriori_gen function takes as input a set of itemsets of size $k-1$ and generates as output a set of itemsets of size k, such that for each such size k itemset, all its size $k-1$ subsets are in the input set. This property of apriori_gen guarantees that the generated set is a superset of the set of large k-itemsets of the same database. So, to look for all large k-itemsets, it suffices to check the output set of apriori_gen in the k-th iteration. In step 2, local support counts of candidates in C_k are computed by a scanning of D_i. In step 3, local support counts are exchanged with all other processors to get global support counts. In step 4, the globally large itemsets L_k are computed independently by each processor. In the next iteration, CD increases k by one and repeats steps 1–4 until no more candidate is found.

Algorithm 1 The Count Distribution Algorithm

1. $C_k = \text{apriori\_gen}(L_{k-1})$;
2. scan partition D_i to find the local support counts $X_{.sup(i)}$ for all $X \in C_k$;
3. exchange $\{X_{.sup(i)} \mid X \in C_k\}$ with all other processors to find out the global support counts $X_{.sup}$, for all $X \in C_k$;
4. $L_k = \{X \in C_k \mid X_{.sup} \geq minsup \times |D|\}$

3 PRUNING TECHNIQUES AND THE FPM ALGORITHM

CD does not exploit information hidden in the data partitioning in the parallel setting to prune its candidate sets. Thus, it has relatively large candidate sets, impeding its performance significantly. We propose a new parallel mining algorithm FPM which has adopted the distributed and global prunings proposed first in [4].

3.1 CANDIDATE PRUNING TECHNIQUES

3.1.1 Distributed Pruning. CD applies apriori_gen on the set L_{k-1} to generate the candidate sets C_k in the k-th iteration. Indeed, in step 4 (Algorithm 1), after the support count exchange in the k-th iteration, each processor can find out not only the large itemsets L_k, *but also the processors at which an itemset X is locally large, for all itemsets $X \in L_k$*. In other words, the subsets $GL_{k(i)}$, $1 \leq i \leq n$, of L_k can be identified at every processor. This information, ignored by CD, of locally large itemsets turns out to be very valuable in developing a pruning technique to reduce the number of candidates. Utilizing this information, many candidates in C_k can be shown to be small (details in the following paragraphs) and hence pruned away before the next scan of the database.

Suppose the database is partitioned into D_1 and D_2 on processors 1 and 2. Further assume that both A and B are two size-1 globally large itemsets. In addition, A is gl-large at processor 1 but not processor 2, and B is gl-large at processor 2 but not processor 1. Then AB can never be globally large, and hence does not need to be considered as a candidate. A simple proof of this result is as follows. If AB is globally large, it must be locally large (i.e. gl-large) at some processor. Assume that it is gl-large at processor 1, then its subset B must also be gl-large at processor 1, which is contradictory to the assumption. Similarly, we can prove that AB cannot be gl-large at processor 2. Hence AB cannot be globally large at all.

Following the above result, no two 1-itemsets which are not gl-large together at the same processor can be combined to form a size-2 globally large itemset. This observation can be generalized to size-k candidates. The subsets $GL_{k-1(i)}$, $(1 \leq i \leq n)$, together form a partition of L_{k-1}, (some of them may overlap). For $i \neq j$, no candidate need to be generated by joining sets from $GL_{k-1(i)}$ and $GL_{k-1(j)}$. In other words, candidates can be generated by applying apriori_gen on each $GL_{k-1(i)}$, $(1 \leq i \leq n)$, separately, and then take their union. The set of size-k candidates generated with this technique is equal to $CG_k = \cup_{i=1}^{n} CG_{k(i)} = \cup_{i=1}^{n}\text{apriori\_gen}(GL_{k-1(i)})$. Since $GL_{k-1(i)} \subseteq L_{k-1}$, $\forall i, 1 \leq i \leq n$, the number of candidates in CG_k could be much less than that in $C_k = \text{apriori\_gen}(L_{k-1})$, the candidates in the Apriori and CD algorithms.

Theorem 1 *For $k > 1$, the set of all globally large k-itemsets L_k is a subset of $CG_k = \cup_{i=1}^{n} CG_{k(i)}$, where $CG_{k(i)} = \text{apriori\_gen}(GL_{k-1(i)})$.*

Based on the above result, we can prune away a size-k candidate if there is no processor at which *all* its size-$(k-1)$ subsets are gl-large. This pruning technique is called *distributed pruning* [4]. The following example taken from [4] shows that the distributed pruning is more effective in reducing the candidate sets than the pruning in CD.

Example 1 Assuming there are 3 processors which partitions the database D into D_1, D_2 and D_3. Suppose the set of large 1-itemsets (computed at the first iteration) $L_1 = \{A, B, C, D, E, F, G, H\}$, in which A, B, and C are locally large at processor 1, B, C, and D are locally large at processor 2, and E, F, G, and H are locally large at processor 3. Therefore, $GL_{1(1)} = \{A, B, C\}$, $GL_{1(2)} = \{B, C, D\}$, and $GL_{1(3)} = \{E, F, G, H\}$.

Based on the above discussion, the set of size-2 candidate sets from processor 1 is $CG_{2(1)}$ = apriori_gen$(GL_{1(1)}) = \{AB, BC, AC\}$. Similarly, $CG_{2(2)} = \{BC, CD, BD\}$, and $CG_{2(3)} = \{EF, EG, EH, FG, FH, GH\}$. Hence, the set of size-2 candidate sets is $CG_{(2)} = CG_{2(1)} \cup CG_{2(2)} \cup CG_{2(3)}$, total 11 candidates.

However, if apriori_gen is applied to L_1, the set of size-2 candidate sets C_2 = apriori_gen(L_1) would have 28 candidates. This shows that it is very effective to use the distributed pruning to reduce the candidate sets.

It is straightforward to see that any itemset which is pruned away by apriori_gen will be pruned away by distributed pruning. The reverse is not necessarily true, though.

3.1.2 Global Pruning. As a result of count exchange at iteration $k-1$, (step 3 of CD in Algorithm 1), the local support counts $X_{.sup(i)}$, for all large $(k-1)$-itemsets, for all processor i, $(1 \leq i \leq n)$, are available at every processor. Another powerful pruning technique called *global pruning* is developed with this information.

Let X be a candidate k-itemset. At each processor i, $X_{.sup(i)} \leq Y_{.sup(i)}$, if $Y \subset X$. Thus, $X_{.sup(i)}$ will always be smaller than $\min\{Y_{.sup(i)} \mid Y \subset X \text{ and } |Y| = k-1\}$. Hence

$$X_{.maxsup} = \sum_{i=1}^{n} \min\{Y_{.sup(i)} \mid Y \subset X \text{ and } |Y| = k-1\}$$

is an upper bound of $X_{.sup}$. X can then be pruned away if $X_{.maxsup} <$ minsup $\times\ |D|$. This technique is called *global pruning*. Note that the upper bound is computed from the local support counts resulting from the previous count exchange.

Table 2.1 is an example that global pruning could be more effective than distributed pruning. In this example, the global support count threshold is 15 and the local support count threshold at each processor is 5. Distributed pruning cannot prune away CD, as C and D are both gl-large at processor 2. Whereas global pruning can prune away CD, as $CD_{.maxsup} = 1 + 12 + 1 < 15$.

In fact, global pruning subsumes distributed pruning, and it is shown in the following theorem.

Items	A	B	C	D	E	F
local support at processor 1	13	33	1	2	2	1
local support at processor 2	1	3	12	34	1	4
local support at processor 3	2	1	2	1	12	33
global support	16	37	15	37	15	38
gl-large at processor 1	√	√	×	×	×	×
gl-large at processor 2	×	×	√	√	×	×
gl-large at processor 3	×	×	×	×	√	√

Table 2.1 High data skewness and high workload balance case

Theorem 2 *If X is a k-itemset ($k > 1$) which is pruned away in the k-th iteration by distributed pruning, then X is also pruned away by global pruning in the same iteration.*
Proof. If X can be pruned away by distributed pruning, then there does not exist a processor at which all the size $(k-1)$ subsets of X are gl-large. Thus, at each processor i, there exists a size $(k-1)$ subset Y of X such that $Y_{.sup(i)} < minsup \times |D_i|$. Hence $X_{.maxsup} < \sum_{i=1}^{n}(minsup \times |D_i|) = minsup \times |D|$. Therefore, X is pruned away by global pruning.

The converse of Theorem 2 is not necessarily true, however. From the above discussions, it can be seen that the three pruning techniques, the one in apriori_gen, the distributed and global prunings, have increasing pruning power, and the latter ones subsume the previous ones.

3.2 FAST PARALLEL MINING ALGORITHM (FPM)

We present the FPM algorithm in this section. It improves CD by adopting the two pruning techniques. The first iteration of FPM is the same as CD. Each processor scans its partition to find out local support counts of all size-1 itemsets and use one round of count exchange to compute the global support counts. At the end, in addition to L_1, each processor also finds out the gl-large itemsets $GL_{1(i)}$, for $1 \leq i \leq n$. Starting from the second iteration, prunings are used to reduce the number of the candidate sets. Algorithm 2 is the program fragment of FPM at processor i for the k-th ($k > 1$) iteration. In step 1, distributed pruning is used and apriori_gen is applied to the sets $GL_{k-1(i)}$, $\forall i = 1, \cdots, n$, instead of to the set L_{k-1}.[4] In step 2, global pruning is applied to the candidates that survive the distributed pruning. The remaining steps are the same as those in CD. As has been discussed, FPM in general enjoys a smaller candidate sets than CD. Furthermore, it uses a simple one-round message exchange scheme same as CD. If we compare FPM with the FDM algorithm proposed in [4], we will see that this simple communication scheme makes FPM more suitable than FDM in terms of response time in a parallel system.

Algorithm 2 The FPM Algorithm

1. compute the candidate sets $CG_k = \cup_{i=1}^{n}\text{apriori\_gen}(GL_{k-1(i)})$; (distributed pruning)
2. apply global pruning to prune the candidates in CG_k;
3. scan partition D_i to find out the local support counts $X_{.sup(i)}$ for all remaining candidates $X \in CG_k$;
4. exchange $\{X_{.sup(i)} \mid X \in CG_k\}$ with all other processors to find out the global support counts $X_{.sup}$, for all $X \in CG_k$;
5. compute $GL_{k(i)} = \{X \in CG_k \mid X_{.sup} \geq minsup \times |D|$ and $X_{.sup(i)} \geq minsup \times |D_i|\}$ and exchange the result with all other processors;
6. return $L_k = \cup_{i=1}^{n} GL_{k(i)}$.

Note that since the number of processors n would not be very large, the cost of generating the candidates with the distributed pruning in step 1 (Algorithm 2) should be on the same order as that in CD. As for global pruning, since all local support counts are available at each processor, no additional count exchange is required to perform the pruning. Furthermore, the pruning in step 2 (Algorithm 2) is performed only on the remaining candidates after the distributed pruning. Therefore, cost for global pruning is small comparing with database scanning and count updates.

3.3 DATA SKEWNESS AND WORKLOAD BALANCE

In a partitioned database, two data distribution characteristics, *data skewness* and *workload balance*, affect the effectiveness of the pruning and hence performance of FPM. Intuitively, the data skewness of a partitioned database is high if most large itemsets are locally large only at a few processors. It is low if a high percentage of the large itemsets are locally large at most of the processors. For a partitioning with high skewness, even though it is highly likely that each large itemset will be locally large at only a small number of partitions, the set of large itemsets together can still be distributed either evenly or extremely skewed among the partitions. In one extreme case, most partitions can have similar number of locally large itemsets, and the workload balance is high. In the other extreme case, the large itemsets are concentrated at a few partitions and hence there are large differences in the number of locally large itemsets among different partitions. In this case, the workload is unbalance. These two characteristics have important bearing on the performance of FPM.

Items	A	B	C	D	E	F
local support at processor 1	6	12	4	13	5	12
local support at processor 2	6	12	5	12	4	13
local support at processor 3	4	13	6	12	6	13
global support	16	37	15	37	15	38
gl-large at processor 1	√	√	×	√	√	√
gl-large at processor 2	√	√	√	√	×	√
gl-large at processor 3	×	√	√	√	√	√

Table 2.2 High workload balance and low data skewness case

Example 2 Table 2.1 is a case of high data skewness and high workload balance. The supports of the itemsets are clustered mostly in one partition, and the skewness is high. On the other hand, every partition has the same number (two) of locally large itemsets.[5] Hence, the workload balance is also high. CD will generate $\binom{6}{2} = 15$ candidates in the second iteration, while distributed pruning will generate only three candidates AB, CD and EF, which shows that the pruning has good effect.

Table 2.2 is an example of high workload balance and low data skewness. The support counts of the items A, B, C, D, E and F are almost equally distributed over the 3 processors. Hence, the data skewness is low. However, the workload balance is high, because every partition has the same number (five) of locally large itemsets. Both CD and distributed pruning generate the same 15 candidate sets in the second iteration. However, global pruning can prune away the candidates AC, AE and CE. FPM still exhibits a 20% of improvement over CD in this pathological case of high balance and low skewness.

We will define formal metrics for measuring data skewness and workload balance for partitions in Section 4. We will also see how high values of balance and skewness can be obtained by suitably and carefully partitioning the database in Section 5. In the following, we will show the effects of distributed pruning analytically for some special cases. Firstly, we give a theorem on the effectiveness of distributed pruning for the case in which the database partition has high database skewness and workload balance.

Theorem 3 *Let L_1 be the set of size-1 large itemsets, $C_{2(c)}$ and $C_{2(d)}$ be the size-2 candidates generated by CD and distributed pruning, respectively. Suppose that each size-1 large itemset is gl-large at one and only one processor, and the size-1 large itemsets are distributed evenly among the processors, i.e., the number of size-1 gl-large itemsets at each processor is $|L_1|/n$, where n is the number of processors. Then $\frac{|C_{2(d)}|}{|C_{2(c)}|} = \frac{(|L_1|/n)-1}{|L_1|-1} \approx \frac{1}{n}$.*

Proof. Since CD will generate all the combinations in L_1 as size-2 candidates, $|C_{2(c)}| = \binom{|L1|}{2} = \frac{|L_1|}{2}(|L_1| - 1)$. As for distributed pruning, each processor will generate candidates independently from the gl-large size-1 itemsets at the processor. The total number of candidates it will generate is $|C_{2(d)}| = \binom{|L_1|/n}{2} \times n = \frac{|L_1|}{2}(|L_1|/n - 1)$. Since n is the number of processor, which is much smaller than $|L_1|$, we have $|L_1| \gg n \geq 1$. Hence, we can take the approximations $|L_1| - 1 \approx |L_1|$ and $|L_1|/n - 1 \approx |L_1|/n$. So, $\frac{|C_{2(d)}|}{|C_{2(c)}|} = \frac{(|L_1|/n)-1}{|L_1|-1} \approx \frac{1}{n}$.

Theorem 3 shows that distributed pruning can dramatically prune away almost $\frac{n-1}{n}$ size-2 candidates generated by CD in the high balance and good skewness case.

We now consider a special case for the k-th iteration ($k > 2$) of FPM. In general, if A_{k-1} is the set of size-$(k-1)$ large itemsets, then the maximum number of size-k candidates that can be generated by applying apriori_gen on A_{k-1} is equal to $\binom{m}{k}$, where m is the smallest integer such that $\binom{m}{k-1} = |A_{k-1}|$. In the following, we use this maximal case to estimate the number of candidates that can be generated in the k-th iteration. Let $C_{k(c)}$ and $C_{k(d)}$ be the set of size-k candidates generated by CD and distributed pruning, respectively. Similar to Theorem 3, we investigate the case in which all gl-large $(k-1)$-itemsets are locally large at only one processor, and the number of gl-large itemsets at each processor is the same. Let m be the smallest integer such that $\binom{m}{k-1} = |L_{k-1}|$. Then, we have $|C_{k(c)}| = \binom{m}{k}$. Hence $|C_{k(c)}| = \frac{m-k+1}{k} \times |L_{k-1}|$. Similarly, let m' be the smallest integer such that $\binom{m'}{k-1} = \frac{|L_{k-1}|}{n}$. Then $|C_{k(d)}| = \binom{m'}{k} \times n$. Hence $|C_{k(d)}| = \frac{m'-k+1}{k} \times \frac{|L_{k-1}|}{n} \times n$. Therefore, $\frac{|C_{k(d)}|}{|C_{k(c)}|} = \frac{m'-k+1}{m-k+1}$. When $k = 2$, this result becomes Theorem 3. In general, $m' \ll m$, which shows that distributed pruning has significant effect in almost all iterations. However, the effect will decrease when m' converges to m as k increases.

Thus, it can be concluded that distributed pruning is very effective when a database is partitioned with high skewness and high balance. On the other hand, in the cases of high skewness with low balance or low skewness with high balance, the effects of distributed pruning degrades to the level of CD. However, we also have observed that global pruning may perform better than CD even in the two worst cases. In order to strengthen our studies, we define metrics to measure the two distribution characteristics.

4 METRICS FOR DATA SKEWNESS AND WORKLOAD BALANCE

We have mentioned above that the data skewness and workload balance (or "skewness" and "balance" for short, respectively) of a database partitioning affect the effectiveness of global and local pruning. This will in turn affect the performance of FPM. To do a study on this, we need to define skewness and balance quantitatively.

Intuitively, we can define balance to be the evenness of distributing transactions among the partitions. However, this definition is not suitable for our studies. The performance of the prunings is linked to the distribution of the large itemsets, not that of the transactions. Furthermore, the metrics on skewness and balance should be consistent between themselves. In the following, we explain our entropy-based metrics defined for these two notions.

4.1 DATA SKEWNESS

We develop a skewness metric based on the well established notion of entropy [3]. Given a random variable X, it's entropy is a measurement on how even or uneven its probability distribution is over its values. If a database is partitioned over n processors, the value $p_X(i) = \frac{X_{.sup(i)}}{X_{.sup}}$ can be regarded as the probability that a transaction containing itemset X comes from partition D_i, $(1 \leq i \leq n)$. The *entropy* $H(X) = -\sum_{i=1}^{n}(p_X(i) \times \log(p_X(i)))$ is an indication of how even the supports of X are distributed over the partitions.[6] For example, if X is skewed completely into a single partition D_k, $(1 \leq k \leq n)$, i.e., it only occurs in D_k, then $p_X(k) = 1$ and $p_X(i) = 0$, $\forall i \neq k$. The value of $H(X) = 0$ is the minimal in this case. On the other hand, if X is evenly distributed among all the partitions, then $p_X(i) = \frac{1}{n}$, $1 \leq i \leq n$, and the value of $H(X) = \log(n)$ is the maximal in this case. Therefore, the following metric can be used to measure the skewness of a database partitioning.

Definition 1 *Given a database with n partitions, the skewness $S(X)$ of an itemset X is defined by*
$S(X) = \frac{H_{max} - H(X)}{H_{max}}$, *where* $H(X) = -\sum_{i=1}^{n}(p_X(i) \times \log(p_X(i)))$ *and* $H_{max} = \log(n)$.

The skewness $S(X)$ has the following properties:

- $S(X) = 0$ when all $p_X(i)$ $(1 \leq i \leq n)$, are equal. So the skewness is at its lowest value when X is distributed evenly in all partitions.
- $S(X) = 1$, when a $p_X(i)$ equals 1 and all the others are 0. So the skewness is at its highest value when X occurs only in one partition.
- $0 < S(X) < 1$, in all the other cases.

Following the property of entropy, higher values of $S(X)$ corresponds to higher skewness for X. The above definition gives a metric on the skewness of an itemset. In the following, we define the skewness of a partitioned database as a weighted sum of the skewness of all its itemsets.

Definition 2 *Given a database D with n partitions, the skewness $TS(D)$ is defined by*

$$TS(D) = \sum_{X \in IS} S(X) \times w(X)$$

where IS is the set of all the itemsets, $w(X) = \frac{X_{.sup}}{\sum_{Y \in IS} Y_{.sup}}$ is the weight *of the support of X over all the itemsets, and $S(X)$ is the skewness of itemset X.*

$TS(D)$ has some properties similar to those of $S(X)$.

- $TS(D) = 0$, when the skewness of all the itemsets are at its minimal value.
- $TS(D) = 1$, when the skewness of all the itemsets are at its maximal value.
- $0 < TS(D) < 1$, in all the other cases.

We can compute the skewness of a partitioned database according to Definition 2. However, the number of itemsets may be very large in general. One approximation is to compute the skewness over the set of globally large itemsets only, and take the approximation $p_X(i) \approx 0$ if X is not gl-large in D_i. In the generation of candidate itemsets, only globally large itemsets will be joined together to form new candidates. Hence, only their skewness would impact the effectiveness of pruning. Secondly, the number of large itemsets is usually much smaller than all the itemsets. So, it is more practical to computing the approximate value instead. In our experimental measurements below, we will use this approximation for the skewness values.

4.2 WORKLOAD BALANCE

Workload balance is a measurement on the distribution of the total weights of the locally large itemsets among the processors. Based on the definition of $w(X)$ in Definition 2, we define $W_i = \sum_{X \in IS} w(X) \times p_X(i)$ to be the *itemset workload* of partition D_i, where IS is the set of all the itemsets. Note that $\sum_{i=1}^{n} W_i = 1$. A database has high workload balance if the W_i's are the same for all partitions D_i, $1 \leq i \leq n$. On the other hand, if the values of W_i exhibit large differences among themselves, the workload balance is low. Thus, our definition of the *workload balance* metric is also based on the entropy measure.

Definition 3 *For a database D with n partitions, the workload balance factor $TB(D)$ is defined as $TB(D) = \frac{-\sum_{i=1}^{n} W_i \log(W_i)}{\log(n)}$.*

The metric $TB(D)$ has the following properties:

- $TB(D) = 1$, when the workload across all processors are the same;
- $TB(D) = 0$, when the workload is concentrated at one processor;
- $0 < TB(D) < 1$, in all the other cases.

Similar to the skewness metric, we can approximate the value of $TB(D)$ by only considering globally large itemsets.

The data skewness and workload balance are not independent of each other. Theoretically, each one of them may attain values between 0 and 1, inclusively. However, some combinations of their values are not admissible. For instance, we cannot have a database partitioning with very low balance and very low skewness. This is because a very low skewness would accompany with a high balance while a very low balance would accompany with a high skewness.

Theorem 4 *Let $D_1, D_2, \cdots, D_n$ be the partitions of a database D.*

1. *If $TS(D) = 1$, then the admissible values of $TB(D)$ ranges from 0 to 1. Moreover, if $TS(D) = 0$, then $TB(D) = 1$.*
2. *If $TB(D) = 1$, then the admissible values of $TS(D)$ ranges from 0 to 1. Moreover, if $TB(D) = 0$, then $TS(D) = 1$.*

Proof.

1. By definition $0 \leq TB(D) \leq 1$. What we need to prove is that the boundary cases are admissible when $TS(D) = 1$. $TS(D) = 1$ implies that $S(X) = 1$, for all large itemsets X. Therefore, each large itemset is large at one and only one partition. If all the large itemsets are large at the same partition D_i, then $W_i = 1$ and $W_k = 0, (1 \leq k \leq n, k \neq i)$. Thus $TB(D) = 0$ is admissible. On the other hand, if every partition has the same number of large itemsets, then $W_i = \frac{1}{n}, (1 \leq i \leq n)$, and hence $TB(D) = 1$. Furthermore, if $TS(D) = 0$, then $S(X) = 0$ for all large itemsets X. This implies that W_i are the same for all $1 \leq i \leq n$. Hence $TB(D) = 1$.
2. It follows from the first result of this theorem that both $TS(D) = 0$ and $TS(D) = 1$ are admissible when $TB(D) = 1$. Therefore the first part is proved. Furthermore, if $TB(D) = 0$, there exists a partition D_i such that $W_i = 1$ and $W_k = 0, (1 \leq k \leq n, k \neq i)$. This implies that all large itemsets are locally large at only D_i. Hence $TS(D) = 1$.

Even though, $0 \leq TS(D) \leq 1$ and $0 \leq TB(D) \leq 1$, we have shown in Theorem 4 that not all possible combinations are admissible. In general, the

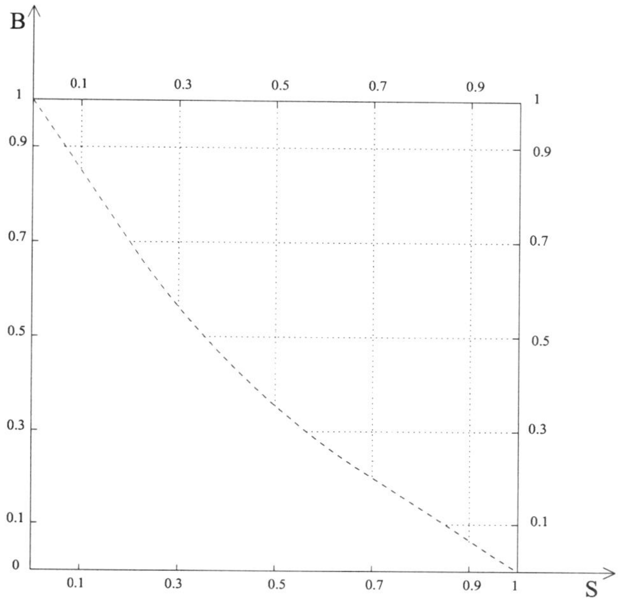

Figure 2.1 Admissible Combinations of Skewness(S) and Balance(B) Values

admissible combinations is a subset of the unit square, represented by the shaded region in Figure 2.1. It always contains the two line segments $TS(D) = 1$ (S = 1 in Figure 2.1) and $TB(D) = 1$ (B = 1 in Figure 2.1), but not the origin, (S = 0, B = 0). After defining the metrics and studying their characteristics, we can experimentally validate our analysis (see Section 3.3) on the relationship between data skewness, workload balance and performance of FPM and CD.

We would like to note that the two metrics are based on total entropy which is a good model to measure evenness (or unevenness) of data distribution. Also, they are consistent with each other.

4.3 PERFORMANCE BEHAVIORS OF FPM AND CD

We study the performance behaviors of FPM and CD in response to various skewness and balance values The performance studies of FPM were carried out on an IBM SP2 parallel processing machine with 32 nodes. Each node consists of a POWER2 processor with a CPU clock rate of 66.7 MHz and 64 MB of main memory. The system runs the AIX operating system. Communication between processors are done through a high performance switch with an aggregated peak bandwidth of 40 MBps and a latency about 40 microseconds. The appropriate database partition is downloaded to the local disk of each processor before

Speedup	FPM/CD					
	B100	B90	B70	B50	B30	B10
D3278K.T5.I2.S90	2.10	1.69	1.36	1.23	1.14	1.06
D3278K.T5.I2.S70	2.07	1.41	1.23	1.13	1.06	—
D3278K.T5.I2.S50	1.88	1.22	1.11	1.06	—	—
D3278K.T5.I2.S30	1.55	1.17	1.08	—	—	—
D3278K.T5.I2.S10	1.36	1.09	—	—	—	—

Table 2.3 Performance Improvement of FPM over CD

mining starts. The database partition on each node is about 100MB in size. The databases used for the experiments are all synthesized according the model described in Section 6, which is an enhancement of the model adopted in [1].

4.3.1 Improvement of FPM over CD. In order to compare the performance of FPM and CD, we have generated a number of databases. The size of every partition of these databases is about 100MB, and the number of partitions is 16, i.e., $n = 16$.[7] We also set $N = 1000$, $L = 2000$, correlation level to 0.5 (refer to [1]). The name of each database is in the form Dx.Ty.Iz.Sr.Bl, where x is the average number of transactions per partition, y is the average size of the transactions, z is the average size of the itemsets. These three values are the control values for the database generation. On the other hand, the two values r and l are the control values (in percentage) of the skewness and balance, respectively. They are added to the name, in the sense that they are intrinsic properties of the database.

We ran FPM and CD on various databases. The minimum support threshold is 0.5%. The improvement of FPM over CD in response time on these databases are recorded in Table 2.3. In the table, each entry corresponds to the results of one database, and the value of the entry is the speedup ratio of FPM to CD, i.e. the response time of CD over that of FPM. Entries corresponding to the same skewness value are put onto the same row, while entries under the same column correspond to databases with the same balance value. The result is very encouraging. FPM is consistently faster than CD in all cases. Obviously, the local pruning and global pruning adopted in FPM are very effective. The sizes of the candidate sets are significantly reduced, and hence FPM outperforms CD significantly.

4.3.2 Performance of FPM with High Workload Balance. Figure 2.2 shows the response time of the FPM and CD algorithms for databases with various skewness values and a high balance value of B = 100 [8]. FPM outperforms CD significantly even when the skewness is in the moderate range,

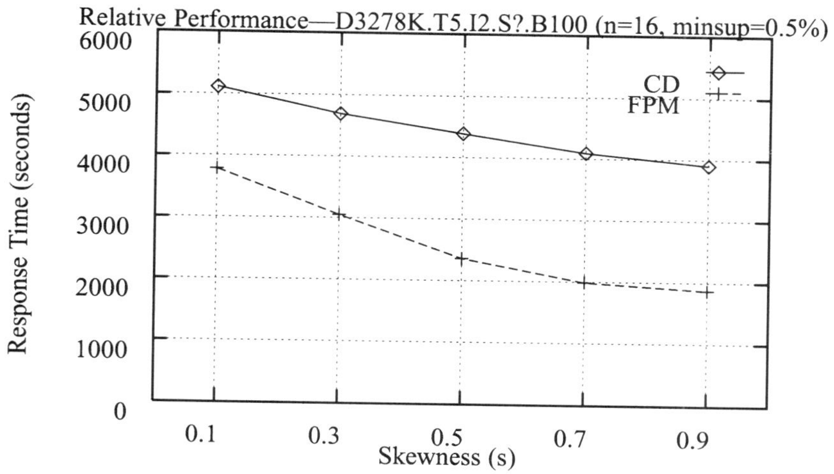

Figure 2.2 Relative Performance on Databases with High Balance and Different Skewness

$(0.1 \leq s \leq 0.5)$. This trend can be read out from Table 2.3, too. When B = 100, FPM is 36% to 110% faster than CD. In the more skewed cases, i.e., $70 \leq S \leq 90$, FPM is at least 107% faster than CD. When skewness is moderate $(S = 30)$, FPM is still 55% faster than CD. When B = 90, FPM maintains the performance lead over CD. The results clearly demonstrate that given a high workload balance, FPM outperforms CD significantly when the skewness is in the range of high to moderate.

These results clearly demonstrate that given a high workload balance, FPM outperforms CD significantly if the skewness is high. More importantly, in this case of high workload balance, FPM can have a substantial improvement even if the skewness is at a moderate value.

4.3.3 Performance of FPM with High Skewness. Figure 2.3 plots the response time of FPM and CD for databases with various balance values. The skewness is maintained at S = 90. In this case, FPM behaves slightly differently from the high workload balance case presented in the previous section. FPM performs much better than CD when the workload balance is relatively high $(b > 0.5)$. However, its performance improvement over CD in the moderate balance range, $(0.1 \leq b \leq 0.5)$, is marginal. This implies that FPM is more sensitive to workload balance than skewness. In other words, if the workload balance has dropped to a moderate value, even a high skewness cannot stop the degradation in performance improvement.

This trend can also be inferred from Table 2.3. When S = 90, FPM is 6% to 110% faster than CD depending on the workload balance. In the more balanced

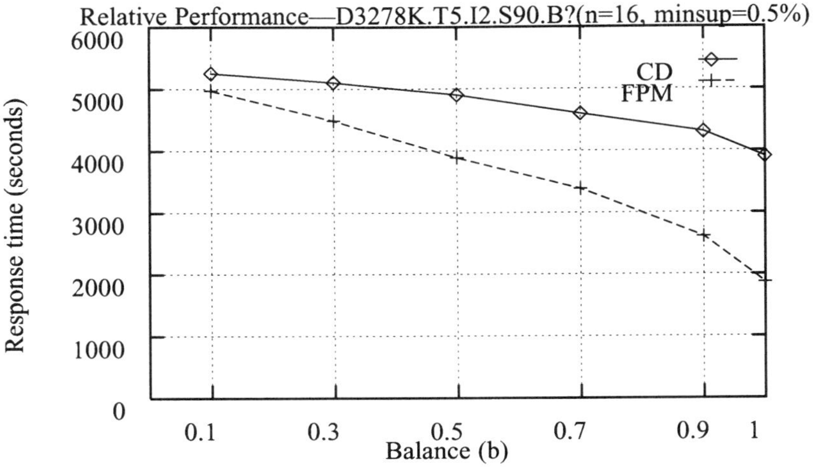

Figure 2.3 Relative Performance on Databases with High Skewness and Different Workload Balance

databases, i.e., $90 \leq B \leq 100$, FPM is at least 69% faster than CD. In the moderate balance case ($50 \leq B \leq 70$), the performance gain drops to the 23% to 36% range. This result shows that a high skewness has to be accompanied by a high workload balance in order for FPM to deliver a good improvement. The effect of a high skewness with a moderate balance is not as good as that of a high balance with a moderate skewness.

4.3.4 Performance of FPM with Moderate Skewness and Balance. In Figure 2.4, we vary both the skewness and balance together from a low values combination to a high values combination. The trend shows that the improvement of FPM over CD increases from a low percentage at $s = 0.5$, $b = 0.5$ to a high percentage at $s = 0.9$, $b = 0.9$. Reading Table 2.3, we find that the performance gain of FPM increases from around 6% (S = 50, B = 50) to 69% (S = 90, B = 90) as skewness and balance increase simultaneously. The combination of S = 50, B = 50 in fact is a point of low performance gain of FPM in the set of all admissible combinations in our experiments.

4.3.5 Summary of the Performance Behaviors of FPM and CD. We have done some other experiments to study the effects of skewness and balance on the performance of FPM and CD. Combining these results with our observations in the above three cases, we can divide the admissible area of Figure 2.1 into several regions, as shown in Figure 2.5. Region A is the region in which FPM outperforms CD the most. In this region, the balance is high and the

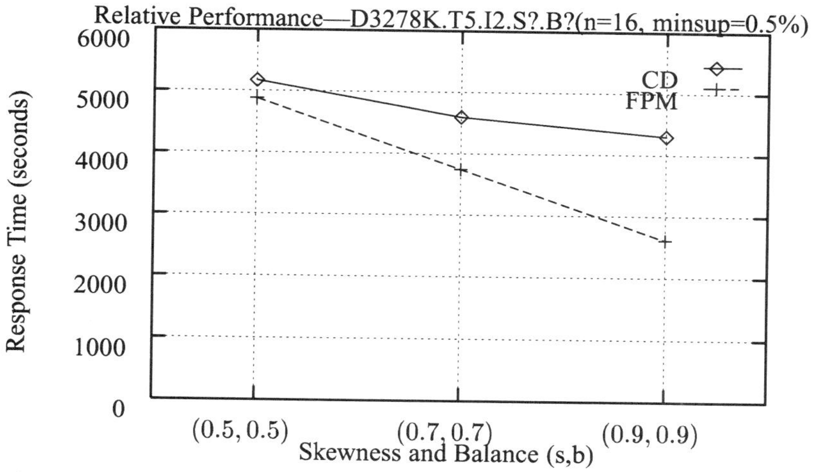

Figure 2.4 Relative Performance on Databases when both Skewness and Balance are varied

skewness varies from high to moderate, and FPM performs 45% to 221% faster than CD. In region B, the workload balance value has degraded moderately and the skewness remains high. The change in workload balance has brought the performance gain in FPM down to a lower range of 35% to 45%. Region C covers combinations that have undesirable workload balance. Even though the skewness could be rather high in this region, because of the low balance value, the performance gain in FPM drops to a moderate range of 15% to 30%. Region D contains those combinations on the bottom of the performance ladder in which FPM only has marginal performance gain.

Thus, our empirical study clearly shows that high values of skewness and balance favors FPM. This is consistent with our analysis in Section 3.3. Furthermore, between skewness and balance, workload balance is more important than skewness. we have discovered that balance has more effects on the improvement of FPM than skewness. FPM outperforms CD significantly when skewness and balance are both high. When balance is extremely high and skewness is moderately high, FPM still shows substantial improvements over CD.

The study here has shown that the effectiveness of the pruning techniques is very sensitive to the data distribution. Moreover, the two metrics that we defined are useful in distinguishing "favorable" distributions from "unfavorable" distributions. In Figure 2.5, regions C and D may cover more than half of the whole admissible area. For database partitions fall in these regions, FPM may not be much better than CD. Because of this, it is important to partition a database in such a way that the resulted partitions would be in a more favorable

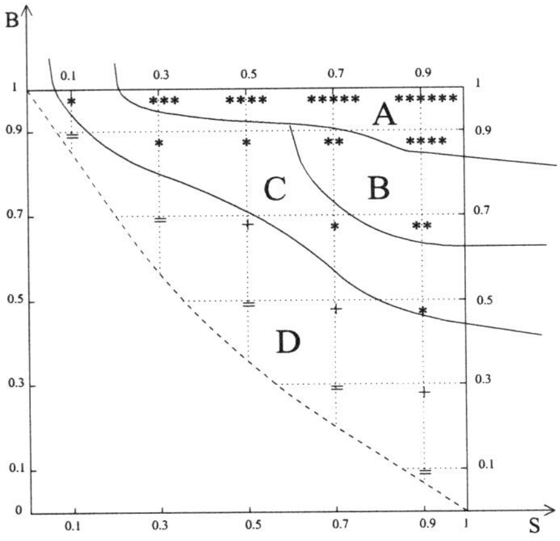

legend	FPM/CD
**** … *****	(1.60, 3.21]
***	(1.45, 1.60]
**	(1.30, 1.45]
*	(1.15, 1.30]
+	(1.10, 1.15]
=	(1.00, 1.10]

Figure 2.5 Division of the admissible regions according to the performance improvement of FPM over CD (FPM/CD)

region. In Sections 5 and 6, we will show that this is in fact possible by using partitioning algorithms we will proposed.

5 PARTITIONING OF THE DATABASE

Suppose now that we have a centralized database and want to mine it for association rules. If we have a parallel system, how can we take advantage of FPM? We have to divide the database into partitions and then run FPM on the partitions. However, if we divide it arbitrarily, the resulting partitions may not have high skewness or workload balance. In that case, FPM is only marginally better than CD. If we can divide the database in a way to yield high balance and skewness across the partitions, we can have much more savings on resources by using FPM. Even for an already partitioned database, redistributing the data among the partitions may also increase the skewness and balance, thus benefiting FPM. So, how to divide the database into partitions to achieve high balance and skewness becomes an interesting and important problem.

Note that not all databases can be divided into a given number of partitions to yield high skewness and balance. If the data in the database is already highly uniform and homogeneous, with not much variations, then any method of dividing it into the given number of partitions would produce similar skewness and balance. However, most real-life database are not uniform, and there are many variations within them. It is possible to find a wise way of dividing the data tuples into different partitions to give a very high balance and skewness than an arbitrary partition. Therefore, if a database intrinsically has non-uniformness, we may dig out such non-uniformness and exploit it to partition the database. to get very high balance and skewness.

So, it would be beneficial to partition the database carefully. A good partitioning can boost the performance of FPM significantly. Ideally, the partitioning method should maximize the skewness and balance metrics for any given database. However, doing such an optimization would be no easier than finding out the association rules. The overhead of this would be too high to worth doing. So, instead of optimizing the skewness and balance values, we would use low-cost algorithms that produce reasonably high balance and skewness values. These algorithms should be simple enough so that not much overhead is incurred. Such small overhead would be far compensated by the subsequent savings in running FPM.

5.1 FRAMEWORK OF THE PARTITIONING ALGORITHMS

To make the partitioning algorithms simple, we will base on the following framework. The core part of the framework is a clustering algorithm, for which we will plug in different clustering algorithms to give different partitioning algorithms. The framework can be divided into three steps.

Conceptually the first step of the framework divides the transactions in the database into equal-sized chunks C_i. Each chunk contains the same number y of transactions. So, there will be a total of $z = \left\lceil \frac{|D|}{y} \right\rceil$ chunks. For each chunk, we define a signature γ_i, which is an $|I|$-dimensional vector. The j-th ($j = 1, 2, \ldots, |I|$) element of the signature, $\gamma_{i,j}$, is the support count of the 1-itemset containing item number j in chunk C_i. Note that each signature γ_i is a vector. This allows us to use functions and operations on vectors to describe our algorithms. The signatures γ_i are then used as representatives of their corresponding chunks C_i. All the γ_i's can be computed by scanning the database once. Moreover, we can immediately deduce the support counts of all 1-itemsets as $\sum \gamma_i$. This can indeed be exploited by FPM to avoid the first iteration, thus saving one scan in FPM (see Section 7.1 for details). So, overall, we can obtain the signatures without any extra database scans.

The second step is to divide the signatures γ_i into n groups G_k, where n is the number of partitions to be produced. Each group corresponds to a partition in the resulting partitioning. The number of partitions n should be equal to the number of processors to be used for running FPM. A good partitioning algorithm should assign the signatures to the groups according to the following criteria. To increase the resulting skewness, we should put the signatures into groups so that the distance[9] between signatures in the same group is small, but the distance between signatures in different groups is high. This would tend to make the resulting partitions more different from one another, and make the transactions within each partition more similar to themselves. Hence, it would have higher skewness. To increase the workload balance, each group should have similar signature sum. One way to achieve this is to assign more or less the same number of signatures to each group such that the total signatures in each group are very close.

The third step of the framework distributes the transactions to different partitions. For each chunk C_i, we check which group its signature γ_i was assigned to in step 2. If it was assigned to group G_k, then we send all transactions in that chunk to partition k. After sending out all the chunks, the whole database is partitioned.

It can be easily noticed that step 2 is the core part of the partitioning algorithm framework. Steps 1 and 3 are simply the pre-processing and post-processing parts. By using a suitable chunk size, we can reduce the total number of chunks, and hence signatures, to a suitable value, so that they can all be processed in RAM by the clustering algorithm in step 2. This effectively reduces the amount of information that our clustering algorithm have to handle, and hence the partitioning algorithms are very efficient.

We like to note that in our approach, we have only made use of the signatures from size-1 itemsets. We could have used those of larger size itemsets. However, that would cost more and eventually it becomes the problem of finding the large itemsets. Using size-1 itemsets is a good trade-off, and the resources used in finding them as we have noted is not wasted. Furthermore, our empirical results (in Section 6) have shown that by just using the size-1 itemsets, we can already achieve reasonable skewness and high balance.

5.2 THE CLUSTERING PROBLEM

With this framework, we have reduced the partitioning problem to a clustering algorithm. Our original problem is to partition a given database so that the resulting partitions give high skewness and balance values, with balance receiving more attention. Now, we have turned it into a clustering problem, which is stated as follows.

Problem. Given z I-dimensional vectors γ_i $(i = 1, 2, \ldots, z)$, called "*signatures*", assign them to n groups G_j $(j = 1, 2, \ldots, n)$ so as to achieve the following to criteria:

1. (Skewness)

$$\sum_{i=1}^{z} \sum_{j=1}^{n} ||\gamma_i - \theta_j||^2 \cdot \delta(i, j)$$

is minimized, where $\theta_j = \frac{1}{\sigma_j}\sum_{i=1}^{z} \gamma_i \cdot \delta(i,j)$

and $\delta(i,j) = \begin{cases} 1 & \text{if } \gamma_i \text{ is assigned to } G_j \\ 0 & \text{otherwise} \end{cases}$ and $\sigma_j = \sum_{i=1}^{z} \delta(i,j)$

2. (Balance)

$$\sigma_{j_1} = \sigma_{j_2}$$

for all $j_1, j_2 = 1, 2, \ldots, n$

Note that here, the vector θ_j is the geometric centroid of the signatures assigned to group G_j, while σ_j is the number of signatures assigned to that group.[10] The notation $||x||$ denotes the distance of vector x from the origin, measured with the chosen distance function.

The first criterion above says that we want to minimize the distance between the signatures assigned to the same group. This is to achieve high skewness. The second criterion reads that each group shall be assigned the same number of signatures, so as to achieve high balance.

Note that it is non-trivial to meet both criteria at the same time. So, we develop algorithms that attempt to find approximate solutions. Below, we will give several clustering algorithms, that are to be plugged into step 2 of the framework to give various partitioning algorithms.

5.3 SOME STRAIGHTFORWARD APPROACHES

The simplest idea to solve the clustering problem is to assign the signatures γ_i to the groups G_j randomly.[11] For each signature, we choose a uniformly random integer r between 1 and n (the number of partitions) and assign the signature to group G_r. As a result, each group would eventually receive roughly the same amount of signatures, and hence chunks and transactions. This satisfies the balance criterion (see Section 5.2), but leaves the skewness criterion unattacked. So, this clustering method should yield high balance, which is close to unity. However, skewness is close to zero, because of the completely random assignment of signatures to groups. With this clustering algorithm, we get a partitioning algorithm, which we will refer to "random partitioning".

To achieve good skewness, we shall assign signatures to groups such that signatures near to one another should go to the same group. Many clustering algorithms with such a goal have been developed. Here, we shall use one of the most famous ones: the k-means algorithm [8]. (We refer the readers to relevant publications for a detailed description of the algorithm.) Since the k-means algorithm minimizes the sum of the distances of the signatures to the geometric centroids of their corresponding groups, it meets the skewness criterion (see Section 5.2). However, the balance criterion is completely ignored, since we impose no restrictions on the size of each group G_j. Consequently some groups may get more signatures then the others and hence the corresponding partitions will receive more chunks of transactions. Thus, this algorithm should yield high skewness, but does not guarantee good workload balance. In the subsequent discussions, we shall use the symbol "$k\mu$" to denote the partitioning algorithm employing the k-means clustering algorithm.

Note that the random partitioning algorithm yields high balance but poor skewness, while $k\mu$ yields high skewness but low balance. They do not achieve our goal of getting high skewness *as well as* balance. Nonetheless, these algorithms does give us an idea of how high a balance or skewness value can be achieved by suitably partitioning a given database. The result of the random algorithm suggests the highest achievable balance of a database, while the $k\mu$ algorithm gives the highest achievable skewness value. Thus, they give us reference values to evaluate the effectiveness of the following two algorithms.

5.4 SORTING BY THE HIGHEST-ENTROPY ITEM (SHEI)

To achieve high skewness, we may use sorting. This idea comes from the fact that sorting decreases the degree of disorder and hence entropy. So, the skewness measure should, according to Definitions 1 and 2, increase. If we sort the signatures γ_i ($i = 1, 2, \ldots, z$) in ascending order of the k_1-th coordinate value (i.e. γ_{i,k_1}), which is the support count of item number k_1, and then divide the sorted list evenly into n equal-length consecutive sublists, and then assign each sublist to a group G_j, we can obtain a partitioning with good skewness. Since each sublist has the same length, the resulting groups have the same number of signatures. Consequently, the partitions generated will have equal amount of transactions. This should give a balance better then $k\mu$.

This idea is illustrated with the example database in Table 2.4. This database has only 6 signatures and we divide it into 2 groups ($z = 6$, $n = 2$). The table shows the coordinate values of the items k_1 and k_2 of each signature. Using the idea mentioned above, we sort the signatures according to the k_1-th coordinate values. This gives the resulting ordering as shown in the table. Next, we divide the signatures into two groups (since $n = 2$), each of size 3, with the order of the signature being preserved. So, the first 3 signatures are assigned to group G_1, while the last 3 signatures are assigned to G_2. This assignment is also shown in the table. The database is subsequently partitioned by delivering the corresponding chunks C_i to the corresponding partitions. Observe how the sorting has brought the transactions that contribute to the support count of item k_1 to the partition 2. Since the coordinate values are indeed support counts of the corresponding 1-itemsets, we know that partition 1 has a support count of $0+3+3 = 6$ for item k_1, while partition 2 has a support count of $3+5+7 = 15$. Thus, the item k_1 has been made to be skewed towards partition 2.

group	signature	coordinate values				
		$\cdots$	k_1	$\cdots$	k_2	$\cdots$
G_1	γ_1	$\cdots$	0	$\cdots$	1	$\cdots$
	γ_6	$\cdots$	3	$\cdots$	1	$\cdots$
	γ_3	$\cdots$	3	$\cdots$	1	$\cdots$
G_2	γ_2	$\cdots$	3	$\cdots$	0	$\cdots$
	γ_5	$\cdots$	5	$\cdots$	0	$\cdots$
	γ_4	$\cdots$	7	$\cdots$	2	$\cdots$

Table 2.4 An example demonstrating the idea of SHEI

Now, why did we choose item k_1 for the sort key, but not item k_2? Indeed, we should not choose an arbitrary item for the sort key, because not all items can give good skewness after the sorting. For example, if the item k_1 occurs equally frequently in each chunk C_i, then all signatures γ_i will have the same value in the coordinate corresponding to the support count of item k_1. Sorting the signatures using this key will not help increasing the skewness. On the other hand, if item k_1 has very uneven distribution among the chunks C_i, sorting would tend to deliver chunks with higher occurrence of k_1 to the same or near-by groups. In this case, skewness can be increased significantly by sorting. So, we shall choose the items with uneven distribution among the chunks C_i for the sort key. To measure the unevenness, we use the statistical entropy measure again. For every item X, we evaluate its statistical entropy value among the signature coordinate values $\gamma_{i,X}$ over all chunks C_i. The item with the highest entropy value is the most unevenly distributed. Besides considering the unevenness, we have to consider the support count of item X, too. If the support count of X is very small, then we gain little by sorting on X. So, we should consider both the unevenness and the support count of each item X in order to determine the sort key. We multiply the entropy value with the total support count of the item in the whole database (which can be computed by summing up all signature vectors). The product gives us a measure of how frequent and how uneven an item is in the database. The item which gets the highest value for this product is chosen for the sort key, because it is both frequent and unevenly distributed in the database. In other words, we choose as the sort key the item X which has the largest value of

$$\pi_X = \left(\operatorname*{entropy}_{i=1}^{z} \gamma_{i,X}\right) \cdot \left(\sum_{i=1}^{z} \gamma_{i,X}\right)$$

The item with the second highest value for this product is used for the secondary sort key. We can similarly determine tertiary and quaternary sort keys, etc.

Sorting the signatures according to keys so selected will yield reasonably high skewness. However, the balance factor is not good. The balance factor is primarily guaranteed by the equal size of the groups G_j. However, this is not sufficient. This is because the sorting will tend to move the signatures with large coordinate values and hence the large itemsets to the same group. The "heavier" signatures will be concentrated in a few groups, while the "lighter" signatures are concentrated in a few other groups. Since the coordinate values are indeed support counts, the sorting would thus distribute the workloads unevenly. To partly overcome this problem, we sort on the primary key in ascending order of coordinate values (which is the support count of the item), the secondary key in descending order of the coordinate values, etc. By alternating the direction of sorting in successive keys, our algorithm can distribute the workload quite evenly, while maintaining a reasonably high skewness.

This idea of using auxiliary sort keys and alternating sort orders is illustrated in Table 2.4. Here, the primary sort key is k_1, while k_2 is the secondary sort key. The primary sort key is processed in ascending order, while the secondary key is processed in descending order. Note how the secondary sort key has helped assigning γ_6 and γ_3 to one group and γ_2 to another, when they have the same value in the primary sort key. This has helped in increasing the skewness by gathering the support counts of k_2 for those signatures sharing the same value in the primary sort key. Note also how the alternating sort order has slightly improved the balance, by assigning one less unit of support count, carried by C_2 (corresponding to γ_2), to G_2.

So, this resulting partitioning algorithm, which we shall call "Sorting by Highest Entropy Item", abbreviated as "SHEI", should thus give high balance and reasonably good skewness.

5.5 BALANCED K-MEANS CLUSTERING ($BK\mu$)

The balanced k-means clustering algorithm, which we will abbreviate as "$Bk\mu$", is a modification of the k-means algorithm. As described in Section 5.3. The major difference is that $Bk\mu$ assigns and reassigns the signatures γ_i to groups G_j in a quite different way. Instead of simply (re)assigning the signatures to the group with the nearest centroid, we add one more constraint to the (re)assignment: each group must be assigned the same amount[12] of signatures. This constraint guarantees good workload balance while sacrificing a certain amount of skewness. The $k\mu$ algorithm achieves the skewness criterion. However, it does not pay any effort to achieve to the balance criterion. In $Bk\mu$, we remedy this by assigning the signatures γ_i to the groups G_j while minimizing the value of the following expression. We also add the *constraint* that each group receives the same number of signatures. The problem is stated as follows.

$$\begin{array}{ll} \text{Minimize} & F = \frac{1}{\lambda+\mu}\left(\lambda \sum_{i=1}^{z} \sum_{j=1}^{n} ||\gamma_i - \alpha_j||^2 \cdot \delta(i,j) \right. \\ & \qquad \left. + \mu \sum_{j=1}^{n} \sigma_j \cdot ||\alpha_j - E||^2 \right) \\ \text{subject to} & \begin{cases} \sigma_{j_1} = \sigma_{j_2} & (j_1, j_2 = 1, 2, \ldots, n) \\ \delta(i,j) = 0 \text{ or } 1 & (i = 1, 2, \ldots, z; \quad j = 1, 2, \ldots, n) \end{cases} \end{array}$$

where $E = \frac{1}{z} \sum_{j=1}^{n} \sigma_j \theta_j$ is constant (which depends on the whole database) and λ, μ are constant control parameters. Actually, E is the arithmetic mean of all the signatures. (Note that σ_j and θ_j, $j = 1, \ldots, n$, have been defined in Section 5.2.) All α_j's and $\delta(i,j)$'s are variables in the above problem. Each α_j represents the geometric centroid of each group G_j, while each $\delta(i,j)$ takes the value of 1 or 0 accordingly as whether the signature γ_i is currently assigned to group G_j or not.

Note that the first term inside parenthesis is exactly the skewness criterion when we set $\alpha_j = \theta_j$. Thus, minimizing this term brings about high skewness. The second term inside parenthesis is introduced so as to achieve balance. Since the vector E is the average of all signatures, it gives the *ideal* value of θ_j (the position of the geometric centroids of each group of signatures) for high balance. The second term measures how far away the actual values of α_j are from this ideal value. Minimizing this term would bring us balance. Therefore, minimizing the above expression would achieve both high balance and skewness. The values of λ and μ let us control the weight of each criterion. A higher value of λ gives more emphasis on the skewness criterion, while a higher value of μ would make the algorithm focus on achieving high balance. In our experiments (see Section 6), we set $\lambda = \mu = 1.0$. In addition, we use the Euclidean distance function in the calculations.

This minimization problem is not trivial. Therefore, we take an iterative approach, based on the framework of the $k\mu$ algorithm. We first make an arbitrary initial assignment of the signatures to the groups, thus giving an initial value for each $\delta(i,j)$. Then, we iteratively improve this assignment to lower the value of the objective function.

Each iteration is divided into two steps. In the first step, we treat the values of $\delta(i,j)$ as constants and try to minimize F by assigning suitable values to each α_j. In the next step, we treat all α_j as constants and adjust the values of $\delta(i,j)$ to minimize F. Thus, the values of α_j and $\delta(i,j)$ are adjusted alternatively to reduce minimize value of F. The details are as follows. In each iteration we first use the same approach as $k\mu$ to calculate the geometric centroids θ_j for each group. To reduce the value of the second term (balance consideration) in the objective function F, we treat temporarily the values of $\delta(i,j)$ as constants and find out the partial derivatives of the object function w.r.t. each α_j. Solving

$\frac{\partial F}{\partial \alpha_j} = 0$ $(j = 1, 2, \ldots, n)$, we find that we shall make the assignments

$$\alpha_j = \frac{\lambda\theta_j + \mu E}{\lambda + \mu} \qquad j = 1, 2, \ldots, n$$

in order to minimize the objective function F. After determining α_j, we next adjust the values of $\delta(i, j)$, treating the values of α_j as constants. Since the second term inside parenthesis now does not involve any variable $\delta(i, j)$, we may reduce the minimization problem to the following problem:

$$\begin{array}{ll} \text{Minimize} & \sum_{i=1}^{z} \sum_{j=1}^{n} ||\gamma_i - \alpha_j||^2 \cdot \delta(i, j) \\ \text{subject to} & \begin{cases} \sigma_{j_1} = \sigma_{j_2} & (j_1, j_2 = 1, 2, \ldots, n) \\ \delta(i, j) = 0 \text{ or } 1 & (i = 1, 2, \ldots, z; \quad j = 1, 2, \ldots, n) \end{cases} \end{array}$$

where $\delta(i, j)$ are the variables. Note that this is a linear programming problem. We shall call it the "generalized assignment problem". It is indeed a generalization of the Assignment Problem and a specialization of the Transportation Problem in the literature of linear programming. There are many efficient algorithms for solving such problems. The Hungarian algorithm [6], which is designed for solving the Assignment Problem, has been extended to solve the generalized assignment problem. This extended Hungarian algorithm is incorporated as a part of the $Bk\mu$ clustering algorithm. Like $k\mu$, $Bk\mu$ iteratively improves its solution. The iterations are stopped when the assignment becomes stable.

Since the $Bk\mu$ algorithm imposes the constraint that each group gets assigned the same number[13] of signatures, workload balanced is guaranteed in the final partitioning. Under this constraint, it strives to maximize the skewness (by minimizing signature-centroid distance) like the $k\mu$ algorithm does. So, skewness is not very high, but is still reasonable high. So, the skewness is in a reasonably high level. The $Bk\mu$ algorithm actually produces very high balance, and while maintaining such high balance workload, it attempts to maximize skewness. So, essentially the balance factor is given primary consideration. This should suit FPM well.

6 EXPERIMENTAL EVALUATION OF THE PARTITIONING ALGORITHMS

To find out whether the partitioning algorithms introduced in Section 5 are effective, we have done two sets of experiments. In these experiments, we first generate synthetic databases. That generated databases are already partitioned, with the desired skewness and workload balance. So, the databases are intrinsically non-uniform. This is, however, not suitable for the experiments for evaluating whether our partitioning algorithms can dig out the skewness and workload balance from a database. So, we "destroy" the apparent skewness and workload balance that already exist among the partitions, by concatenating the partitions to form a centralized database and then shuffling the transactions in the concatenated database. The shuffling would destroy the orderness of the transaction, so that arbitrary partitioning of the resulting database would give a partitioning with low balance and skewness. We can then test whether our partitioning algorithms can produce partitions that give higher workload balance and skewness than an arbitrary partitioning.

The databases used here are synthesized. Because of space limits, we are not describing the details here. The number of partitions in the databases is 16. Each partition has 100,000 transactions. Chunk size is set to 1000 transactions; hence each partition has 100 chunks, and the total number of chunks is 1600. In order to evaluate the effectiveness of the partitioning algorithms, we have to compare the skewness and workload balance of the resulting partitions against the skewness and balance intrinsic in the database. For this purpose, we take the skewness and workload balance *before* concatenation as the *intrinsic* values. All the skewness and balance values reported below are obtained by measurement on the partitions before the concatenation as well as after the partitioning, not the corresponding control values for the data generation. So, they reflect the actual values for those metrics.

For each generated database, we run all the four partitioning algorithms given in Section 5. The skewness and workload balance of the resulting partitions are noted and compared with one another together with the intrinsic values. As discussed in Section 5.3, the result of the random algorithm suggests the highest achievable balance value, while the result of $k\mu$ gives the highest achievable skewness value.

We did two series of experiments: (1) the first series varied the intrinsic skewness while keeping the intrinsic balance at a high level; (2) the second series varied the intrinsic balance value while keeping the intrinsic skewness almost constant.

6.1 EFFECTS OF HIGH INTRINSIC BALANCE AND VARIED INTRINSIC SKEWNESS

The first series of experiments we did was to find out how the intrinsic balance and skewness values would affect the effectiveness of SHEI and $Bk\mu$ given that the intrinsic balance is in a high value and the skewness changes from high to low. Figure 2.6 shows the results for the skewness of the resulting partitionings. The vertical axis gives the skewness values of the resulting databases. Every four points on the same vertical line represent the results of partitioning the same initial database. The intrinsic skewness of the database is given on the horizontal axis. For your reference, the intrinsic balance values are given in

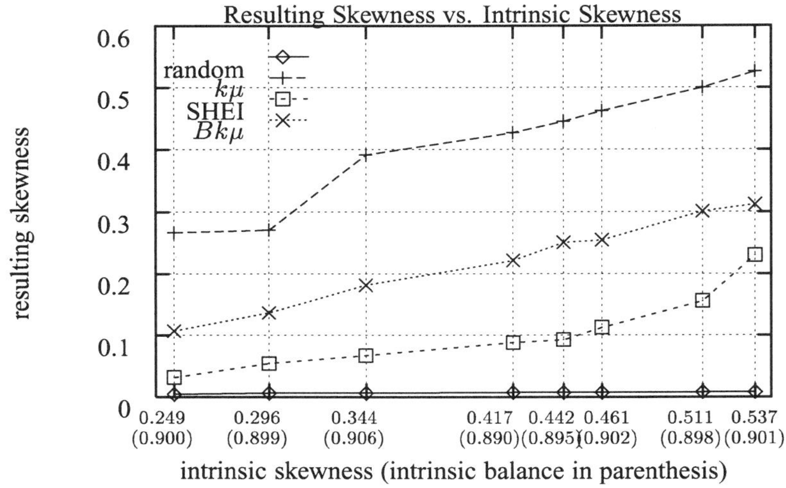

Figure 2.6 High intrinsic balance and varied intrinsic skewness—resulting skewness

parenthesis directly under the skewness value of the database. Different curves in the figure show the results of different partitioning algorithms.

The $k\mu$ algorithm, as explained before gives the highest skewness achievable by a suitable partitioning. Indeed, the resulting skewness values of $k\mu$ are very close to the intrinsic values. Both SHEI and $Bk\mu$ do not achieve this skewness value. This is primarily because they put more emphasis on balance than skewness. Yet, the results show that some of the intrinsic skewness can be recovered. According to the figure, the resulting skewness of $Bk\mu$ is almost always twice of that of SHEI. So, the $Bk\mu$ algorithm performs better than SHEI in terms of resulting skewness. This is due to the fact that $Bk\mu$ uses a more sophisticated method of achieving high skewness. SHEI is much simpler and hence is expected to perform not as well as $Bk\mu$. Most importantly, the skewness achieved by $Bk\mu$ is between 50% to 60% of that of the benchmark algorithm $k\mu$, which indicates that $Bk\mu$ can maintain a significant degree of the intrinsic skewness. This shows that $Bk\mu$ can deliver a good level of skewness.

Figure 2.7 shows the workload balance values for the same partitioned databases. This time, the vertical axis shows the resulting balance. Again, every four points on the same vertical line represent the partitioning of the same original database. The horizontal axis gives the intrinsic balance values of the databases, with the intrinsic skewness values of the corresponding databases given in parenthesis. Again, different curves show the results of different algorithms. The workload balance was controlled at a constant value of 90%. So, the generated databases all have an intrinsic balance very close to 0.90. Random partitioning of course yields a high balance value very close to

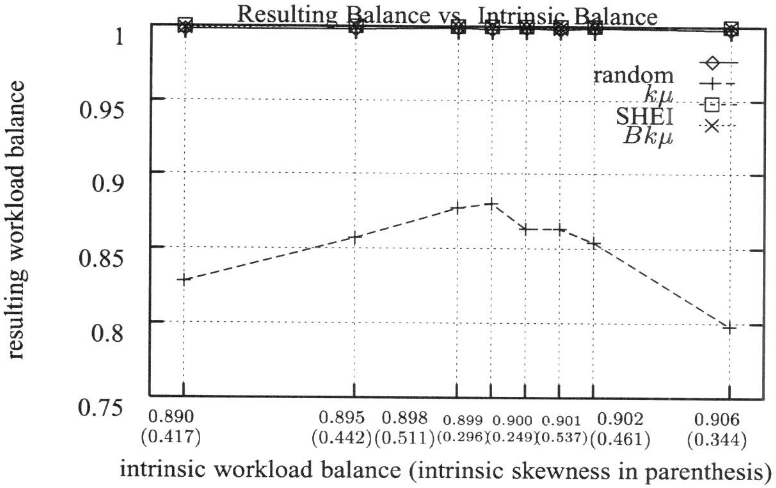

Figure 2.7 High intrinsic balance and varied intrinsic skewness—resulting balance

1.0, which can be taken as the highest achievable balance value. It is encouraging to discover that SHEI and $Bk\mu$ also give good balance values which are very close to that of the random partitioning. This results from the design that high balance is the primary goal of these two algorithms. Both algorithm give good resulting workload balance.

From this series of experiments, we can conclude that: given a database with good intrinsic balance, even if the intrinsic skewness is not high, both $Bk\mu$ and SHEI can increase the balance to a level as good as that in a random partitioning; in addition, $Bk\mu$ can at the same time deliver a good level of skewness, much better than that from the random partitioning, the skewness achieved by $Bk\mu$ is also better than SHEI and is in an order comparable to what can be achieved by the benchmark algorithm $k\mu$.

Another way to look at the result of these experiments is to fit the intrinsic skewness and balance value pairs (those on the horizontal axis of Figure 2.6) into the regions in Figure 2.5. These pairs, which represent the intrinsic skewness and balance of the initial partitions, all fall into region C. Combining the results from Figures 2.6 and 2.7, among the resulting partitions from $Bk\mu$, five of them have moved to region A, the most favorable region. For the other three, even though their workload balance have been increased, their skewness have not been increased enough to move them out of region C. In summary, a high percentage of the resulting partitions have been benefited substantially from using $Bk\mu$This shows the effectiveness of $Bk\mu$.

6.2 EFFECTS OF REDUCING INTRINSIC BALANCE

Our second series of experiments attempted to find out how SHEI and $Bk\mu$ would be affected when the intrinsic balance is reduced to a lower level. while the skewness is maintained in a moderate level.

Figure 2.8 presents the resulting skewness values against the intrinsic skewness. The numbers in parenthesis show the intrinsic balance values for the corresponding databases. Figure 2.9 shows the resulting balance values of the four algorithms on the same partitioning results.

Again, the random algorithm suggests the highest achievable balance value, which is close to 1.0 in all cases. Both SHEI and $Bk\mu$ are able to achieve the same high balance value which is the most important requirement (Figure 2.9). Thus, they are very good at yielding a good balance even if the intrinsic balance is low. As for the resulting skewness, the results of the $k\mu$ algorithm gives the highest achievable skewness values, which are very close to the intrinsic values (Figure 2.8). Both SHEI and $Bk\mu$ can recover parts of the intrinsic skewness. However, the skewness is reduced more when the intrinsic balance is in the less favorable range (< 0.7). These results are consistent with our understanding. When the intrinsic balance is low, spending effort in re-arranging the transactions in the partitions to achieve high balance would tend to reduce the skewness.

Both $Bk\mu$ and SHEI are low-cost algorithms, they spend more effort in achieving a better balance while at the same time trying to maintain certain level of skewness. Between $Bk\mu$ and SHEI, the resulting skewness of $Bk\mu$ is at least twice of that of SHEI in all cases. This shows that $Bk\mu$ is better than SHEI in both cases of high and low intrinsic balance. It is also important to note that the skewness achieved by $Bk\mu$ is always better than that of the random partitioning.

Again, we can fit the skewness and balance values of the initial databases and their resulting partitions (Figures 2.8 and 2.9) into the regions in Figure 2.5. What we have found out is that: after the partitioning performed by $Bk\mu$, four partitionings have moved from region C to A, two from region D to C, two others remain unchanged. This again is very encouraging and shows the effectiveness of $Bk\mu$ — more than 70% of the databases would have their performance improved substantially by using $Bk\mu$ and FPM together.

6.3 SUMMARY OF THE EXPERIMENTAL RESULTS

The above experiments confirms our analysis of the properties of the four partitioning algorithms: Random partitioning gives excellent balance, but very poor skewness. The $k\mu$ algorithm yields very high skewness, but the resulting balance may not be high. Both SHEI and $Bk\mu$ give high balance, and while doing so, they still try to achieve reasonably high skewness values. $Bk\mu$ in

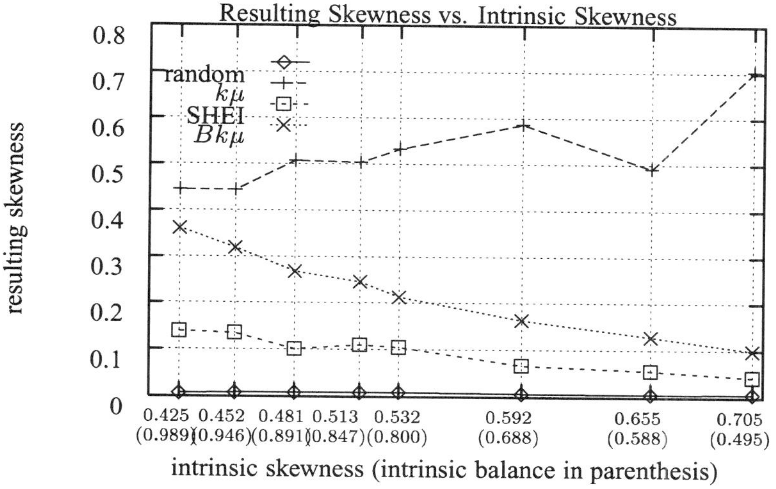

Figure 2.8 Reducing intrinsic balance—resulting skewness

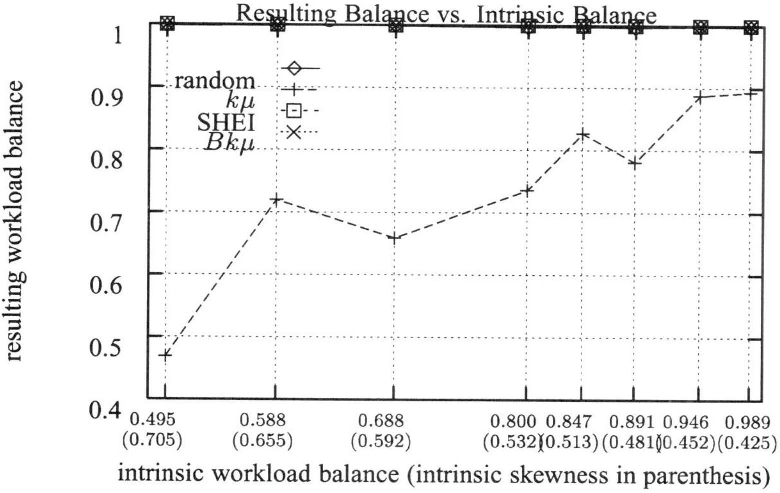

Figure 2.9 Reducing intrinsic balance—resulting balance

general gives much better skewness values than SHEI, because it uses a more sophisticated method to achieve high skewness. These results are true for a wide range of intrinsic skewness and balance values. Given that FPM benefits the most from a database partitioning with very high workload balance and sufficiently high skewness, we would recommend using SHEI or $Bk\mu$ for the partitioning (or repartitioning) of the database before running FPM. Also, the results are true for a wide range of intrinsic balance and skewness values.

Note that we did no study on the time performance of the partitioning algorithms. This is primarily because the algorithms are so simple that they consume negligible amounts of CPU time. In our experiments, the amount of CPU time is no more than 5% of the time spent by the subsequent running of FPM. As for I/O overhead, the general framework of the partitioning algorithms (see Section 5.1) require only one extra scan of the database, whose purpose is to calculate the signatures γ_i. This cost can be compensated by the saving of the first database scan of FPM (see Section 7.1). After that, no more extra I/O is required. We assume that the chunk size y, specified by the user, is large enough so that the total number of chunks z is small enough to allow all the signatures γ_i be handled in main memory. In this case, the total overhead of the partitioning algorithms is far compensated by the subsequent resource savings. For a more detailed discussion on the overhead of these partitioning algorithms, please refer to Section 7.1.

7 DISCUSSIONS

To restrict the search of large itemset in a small set of candidates is very essential to the performance of mining association rules. After a database is partitioned over a number of processors, we have information on the support counts of the itemsets at a finer granularity. This enables us to use distributed and global prunings discussed in Section 3. However, the effectiveness of these pruning techniques are very dependent on the distribution of transactions among the partitions. We discuss two issues here related to the database partitioning and performance of FPM.

7.1 OVERHEAD OF USING THE PARTITIONING ALGORITHMS

We have already shown that FPM benefits over CD the most when the database is partitioned in a way such that the skewness and workload balance measures are high. Consequently, we suggest that partitioning algorithms such as $Bk\mu$ and SHEI be used before FPM, so as to increase the skewness and workload balance for FPM to work faster. But this suggestion is good only if the overhead of the partitioning (or repartitioning in the case of already partitioned databases) is not high. We will make this claim by dividing the overhead of the partitioning algorithms into two parts for analysis.

The first part is CPU cost. First, the partitioning algorithms calculate the signatures of the data chunks. This involves only simple arithmetic operations. Next, the algorithms call a clustering algorithm to divide the signatures into groups. Since the amount of signatures is much smaller than the number of transactions in the whole database, the algorithms process much less information than a mining algorithm. Moreover, the clustering algorithms are designed to be simple, so that they are computationally not costly. Finally, the program delivers transaction in the database to different partitions. This involves little CPU cost. So, overall, the CPU overhead of the partitioning algorithms is very low. Experimental results show that it is no more than 5% of the CPU cost of the subsequent run of FPM.

The second part is the I/O cost. The partitioning algorithms in Section 5 all read the original database twice and write the partitioned database to disk once. In order to enjoy the power of parallel machines for mining, we have to partition the database anyway. Comparing with the simplest partitioning algorithm, which must inevitably read the original database once and write the partitioned database to disk once, our partitioning algorithms only does one extra database scan. But it shall be remarked that in our clustering algorithm, this extra scan is for computing the signatures of the chunks. Once the signatures are found, the support counts of *all* 1-itemsets can be deduced by summation, which involves no extra I/O overhead. So, we can indeed find out the support counts of all 1-itemsets essentially for free. This can be exploited to eliminate the first iteration of FPM, so that FPM can start straight into the second iteration to find large 2-itemsets. This saves one database scan from FPM, and hence as a whole, the 1-scan overhead of the partitioning algorithm is compensated.

Thus, the partitioning algorithms essentially introduce negligible CPU and I/O overhead to the whole mining activity. It is therefore worthwhile to employ our partitioning algorithms to partition the database before running FPM. The great savings by running FPM on a carefully partitioned database far compensates the overhead of our partitioning algorithms.

7.2 SCALABILITY IN FPM

Our performance studies of FPM were carried out on a 32-processor SP2 (section 4.3). If the number of processors n is very large, global pruning may need a large memory to store the local support counts from all the partitions for all the large itemsets found in an iteration. Also, there could be cases that candidates generated after pruning is still too large to fit into the memory. We suggest to use a cluster approach to solve this problem. The n processors can be grouped into p clusters, ($p \ll n$), so that each cluster would have $\frac{n}{p}$ processors.

In the top level, support counts will be exchanged between the p clusters instead of the n processors. The counts exchanged in this level will be the sum of the supports from the processors within each cluster. Both distributed and global prunings can be applied by treating the data in a cluster together as a partition. Within a cluster, the candidates are distributed across the processors, and the support counts in this second level can be computed by count exchange among the processors inside the cluster. In this approach, we only need to ensure that the total distributed memory of the processors in each cluster is large enough to hold the candidates. From the setting, this approach is highly scalable.

8 CONCLUSIONS

We have investigated the parallel mining of association rules on a shared-nothing distributed machine architecture. A parallel algorithm FPM for mining association rules has been proposed. Performance studies carried out on an IBM SP2 system show that FPM consistently outperforms CD. The gain in performance in FPM is due mainly to the pruning techniques incorporated.

We have found that the effectiveness of the pruning techniques depend highly on two data distribution characteristics: data skewness and workload balance. An entropy-based metric has been proposed to measure these two characteristics. Our analysis and experiment results show that the pruning techniques are very sensitive to workload balance, though good skewness will also have important positive effects. The techniques are very effective in the best case of high balance and high skewness. The combination of high balance and moderate skewness is the second best case.

This motivates us to develop algorithms to partition database in a wise way, so as to get higher balance and skewness values. We have proposed four partitioning algorithms. With the balanced k-means ($Bk\mu$) clustering algorithm, we can achieve a very high workload balance, while at the same time a reasonably good skewness. Our experiments have demonstrated that many unfavorable partitions can be repartitioned by $Bk\mu$ into partitions that allow FPM to perform more efficiently.

Moreover, the overhead of the partitioning algorithms is negligible, and can be compensated by saving one database scan in the mining process. Therefore, we can obtain very high association rule mining efficiency by partitioning a database with $Bk\mu$, and then mining it with FPM. We have also discussed a cluster approach which can bring scalability to FPM.

Notes

1. A itemset is *globally large* if it is large with respect to the whole database [4, 5].
2. An itemset is *locally large* at a processor if it is large within the partition at the processor.
3. More precise definitions of skewness and workload balance will be given in Section 4.

4. Compare this step with step 1 of Algorithm 1 would be useful in order to see the difference between FPM and CD.

5. As has been mentioned above, the support threshold in Table 2.1 for globally large itemsets is 15, while that for locally large itemset is 5 for all the partitions.

6. In the computation of $H(X)$, some of the probability values $p_X(i)$ may be zero. In that case, we take $0 \log 0 = 0$, in the sense that $\lim_{h \to 0} h \log h = 0$.

7. Even though the SP2 we use has 32 nodes, because of administration policy, we can only use 16 nodes in our experiments.

8. We use B and S to represent the control value of the balance and skewness in the databases in Table 2.3. Here their unit is in percentage and their value is in the range of [0, 100]. On the other hand, in Figures 2.2 to 2.5, we use s and b to represent the skewness and balance of the databases, which are values in the range of $[0, 1]$. In real term, both B and b, S and s have the same value except different units.

9. Any valid distance function in the $|I|$-dimensional space may be used.

10. In the subsequent sections, the index j will be used for the domain of groups. So, it will *implicitly* take values from 1 to n.

11. In the subsequent sections, the index i will be used for the domain of signatures. So, it will *implicitly* take values $1, 2, \ldots, z$.

12. up to a difference of 1, due to the remainder when the number of signatures is divided by the number of groups

13. Practically, the constraint is relaxed to allow up to a difference of 1 between the σ_j's, due to the remainder when the number of signatures is divided by the number of groups

References

[1] R. Agrawal and R. Srikant. Fast algorithms for mining association rules. In *Proc. of the 20th VLDB Conference*, Santiago, Chile, 1994.

[2] R. Agrawal and J.C. Shafer. Parallel mining of association rules: Design, implementation and experience. Technical Report TJ10004, IBM Research Division, Almaden Research Center, 1996.

[3] T. M. Cover, T. A. Thomas. Elements of information theory. John Wiley & Sons, Inc., 1991.

[4] D. W. Cheung, J. Han, V. T. Ng, A. W. Fu, Y. Fu. A fast distributed algorithm for mining association rules. In *Proc. of 4th Int. Conf. on Parallel and Distributed Information Systems*, 1996.

[5] D. W. Cheung, V. T. Ng, A. W. Fu, and Y. Fu. Efficient Mining of Association Rules in Distributed Databases. Special Issue in Data Mining, *IEEE Trans. on Knowledge and Data Engineering*, IEEE Computer Society, V8, N6, December 1996, pp. 911–922.

[6] S.K. Gupta, "*Linear Programming and Network Models*", Affiliated East-West Press Private Limited, New Delhi, Madras HyderBrabad Bangalore. (ISBN: 81-85095-08-6)

[7] E. Han, G. Karypis and V. Kumar. Scalable parallel data mining for association rules. In *Proc. of 1997 ACM-SIGMOD Int. Conf. On Management of Data*, 1997.

[8] L. Kaufman, and P.J. Rousseeuw. *Finding Groups in Data : An Introduction to Cluster Analysis.*, John Wiley & Sons, 1990.

[9] Message Passing Interface Forum. MPI: A Message-Passing Interface Standard, May 1994.

[10] J. S. Park, M . S. Chen, and P. S. Yu, An effective hash-based algorithm for mining association rules. In *Proc. of 1995 ACM-SIGMOD Int. Conf. on Management of Data*, San Jose, CA, May 1995.

[11] J. S. Park, M. S. Chen, and P. S. Yu, Efficient parallel mining for association rules. In *Proc. of the 4th Int. Conf. on Information and Knowledge Management*, Baltimore, Maryland, 1995.

[12] T. Shintani, M. Kitsuregawa. Hash based parallel algorithms for mining association rules. In *Proc. of 4th Int. Conf. on Parallel and Distributed Information Systems*, 1996.

Chapter 3

UNSUPERVISED FEATURE RANKING AND SELECTION

Manoranjan Dash
School of Computing, National University of Singapore, manoranj@comp.nus. edu.sg

Huan Liu
Department Computer Science & Engineering, Arizona State University,hliu @asu.edu

Jun Yao
School of Computing, National University of Singapore, yaojun@yahoo.com

Keywords: unsupervised data, feature selection, clustering, entropy

Abstract: Dimensionality reduction is an important issue for efficient handling of large data sets. Feature selection is effective in dimensionality reduction. Many supervised feature selection methods exist. Little work has been done for unsupervised feature ranking and selection where class information is not available. In this chapter, we are concerned with the problem of determining and choosing the important original features for *unsupervised data* . Our method is based on the observation that removing an irrelevant feature may not change the underlying concept of the data, but not so otherwise. We propose an entropy measure for ranking features, and conduct experiments to verify that the proposed method is able to find important features. For verification purpose, we compare it with a feature ranking method (Relief) that requires class information, and test the reduced data for tasks of clustering and model construction. This work can also be extended to dimensionality reduction for data with continuous class.

1. INTRODUCTION

In real-world applications the size of a database is usually large. The largeness can be due to the excessive number of features (variables, dimensions), the huge number of instances (records, data points), or both. For data mining algorithms to work efficiently one can try to reduce the data size [Wyse et al., 1980]. In this chapter we focus on reducing the size by decreasing the number of features. One approach is to determine the relative importance of the features and then select a subset of important features. This can be achieved in various ways, for example, by feature selection [Kira and Rendell, 1992] or feature extraction [Jolliffe, 1986].

There are a number of feature selection methods [Dash and Liu, 1997] that determine the relative importance of the features before selecting a subset of important ones. Examples are Relief [Kira and Rendell, 1992, Kononenko, 1994], ABB [Liu et al., 1998]. A typical feature selection method tries to choose a subset of features from the original set that is ideally necessary and sufficient to describe the target concept [Kira and Rendell, 1992]. Target concepts are denoted by class labels. Data with class labels are called supervised data; data without class labels unsupervised. Although original features are selected based on some evaluation function, *these methods require class labels*. Hence, feature selection methods largely fail for unsupervised data.

Feature extraction methods create new features which are uncorrelated and retain as much variation as possible in the database ([Wyse et al., 1980], [Jolliffe, 1986]). One commonly known method is principal component analysis (PCA). Although PCA does not need class labels for extracting the features or Principal Components (PCs), *usually original features are still needed in order to calculate PCs since each PC is a function of original features*. Also, it is difficult to get an intuitive understanding of data *using the extracted features only*.

In practice, we often encounter databases that have large dimensionality and no class information. Data is normally collected for organizational or book-keeping purposes, and not particularly for data mining. For example, transactional data does not contain any class information, and it could have a huge number of features. It is often desirable to pre-process the data before applying a knowledge discovery tool [Uthurusamy, 1996]. Dimensionality reduction without creating any new feature offers an effective solution to reducing data size while keeping original features intact. This helps in obtaining intuitive understanding of the data as one can know the important features for describing underlying concept. PCA or feature selection methods cannot help much for this type of dimensionality reduction due to the reasons given above. This problem surfaces as the need for data mining arises. It is also an interesting research problem, and solutions for this will be welcome by both research and industry community handling data with large dimensionality.

In this chapter we address the problem of determining and choosing important original features for unsupervised data. Our contributions are:

1. an entropy based method to do feature ranking and selection,

2. an application of our method to an important unsupervised task, i.e. clustering.

The chapter is organized as follows. We discuss the advantages and disadvantages of the existing methods that conduct feature ranking and selection for unsupervised data in Section 2. An entropy measure that determines importance of original features with respect to underlying clusters is described in Section 3. This measure works for both nominal and continuous data types. In Section 4 a sequential backward selection algorithm is given that ranks features in order of their importance, and the problem of determining a threshold for a selected number of features is discussed. The experimental study in Section 5 shows that proposed algorithm is able to find the important features for data sets with known important features. It also shows that performance of the proposed algorithm without using class labels is very close to and sometimes better than that of Relief-F [Kononenko, 1994] (a generalized version of Relief [Kira and Rendell, 1992] for multiple class labels) which ranks original features using class labels. Experiments with two classifiers show the advantages of feature elimination in unsupervised data. In Section 6 we report results of our experiments that shows the usefulness of our method for clustering and prediction using model construction. The chapter concludes in Section 7 with discussions on future work.

2. BASIC CONCEPTS AND POSSIBLE APPROACHES

2.1 NOTATIONS AND PROBLEM

In the chapter N is number of instances and M is number of features. The problem we are concerned with is how to rank M features according to their importance and then select d number of features. For supervised data which has class information this problem can be stated as: selecting d features from the given M features from a data set of N instances where each instance x_i is represented by a vector of M values followed by a class label (i.e., $\{x_{i1}x_{i2}...x_{iM}, c\}$). But unsupervised data does not have class (c) information which makes the feature selction methods (see [Dash and Liu, 1997] for a survey) unsuitable for dimensionality reduction. As discussed in introduction PCA is unsuitable to choose important original features. Another method that may be applied is clustering. In the following we discuss an intuitive way of applying clustering to do feature ranking and selection, and some associated difficulties.

2.2 FEATURE RANKING AND SELECTION VIA CLUSTERING

Clustering is a task of grouping similar data together [Bradley et al., 1999]. The most general approach is to view clustering as a density estimation problem [Silverman, 1986, Scott, 1992]. Clustering has been formulated in various ways in the literature of machine learning [Fisher, 1987], pattern recognition [Duda and Hart, 1973, Fukunaga, 1990], optimization [Bradley et al., 1997], and statistics [Kaufman and Rousseeuw, 1989, Bishop, 1995]. All existing clustering algoirthms can be classified into hierarchical and non-hierarchical. K-means [Lloyd, 1982, Bishop, 1995] and EM [Dempster et al., 1977, Bishop, 1995] are commonly used ones for non-hierarchical clustering, numerical taxonomy [Duda and Hart, 1973] and conceptual clustering [Michalski and Stepp, 1983, Fisher, 1987, Lebowitz, 1987] are examples of hierarchical clustering. We briefly describe K-means and Cobweb [Fisher, 1987] below and then examine how to use them for unsupervised ranking or selecting features.

Suppose there are N data points $\mathbf{x}^n$ in total, and we know there are K disjoint clusters containing N_j data points with representative vectors μ_j where $j = 1, ..., K$. The K-means algorithm attempts to minimize the sum-of-squares clustering function given by

$$J = \sum_{j=1}^{K} \sum_{n \in S_j} ||\mathbf{x}^n - \mu_j||^2$$

where μ_j is the mean of the data points in cluster S_j and is given by

$$\mu_j = \frac{1}{N_j} \sum_{n \in S_j} \mathbf{x}^n.$$

The training is carried out by assigning the points at random to K clusters and then computing the mean vectors μ_j of the N_j points in each cluster. Each point is re-assigned to a new cluster according to which is the nearest mean vector. Many distance measures are available for dealing with different types attributes. The mean vectors are then recomputed. This procedure is repeated until there is no further change in clustering.

Cobweb [Fisher, 1987] uses a heursitic measure called category utility (CU) suggested in [Gluck and Corter, 1985]. CU attempts to maximize both the probability that two objects in the same ctegory have values in common and the probability that objects in different categories will have different property values. High CU meansures indicate a high likelihood that objects in the same category will share proerties, while decreasing the likelihood that objects in the different categories having properties in common. The clustering is done in a top-down fashion: (1) start with the root (in the beginning, it contains only one instance (object)), for each subsequent instance, do (2) find the best choice for it among (a) creating a new child cluster (under the current cluster) to accommodate the instance, (b) hosting the instance in an existing cluster, (c) merging the best two child clusters to accommodate the instance, and (d) splitting the best cluster (upgrading its child nodes) to find a cluster that can accommodate the instance. The result of clustering is a concept hierarchy in which the root is the most general concept and the leaves are the more specific concepts (objects themselves).

Now let us examine whether we can make use of existing clustering algorithms to rank and select features. To recall, our task is to remove redundant and/or irrelevant attributes. Intuitively, the general procedure of using clustering algorithms is (1) applying a clustering algorithm to form clusters; (2) collecting attributes used by all clusters; and (3) identifying those not being used in any cluster as irrelevant attributes, and ranking the used attributes according to their frequencies of useage in the clusters. If the clustering algorithm is K-means, we deduce that the result of feature selection is sensitive to the value of K. If K is too large, there could exist unnatrual clusters so that irrelevant attributes are used and therefore considered as relevant; if K is too small, there could be a danger to remove relevant features. When outliers exist, the situation gets worse as they can also make irrelevant attributes relevant. However, removing outliers can help. In short, unless we know exactly what K should be, too large or too small a K can sway from one extreme to the other. If the clustering algorithm is Cobweb like, clustering results in a hierachy of clusters. Now we face a problem in choosing which layer of clusters for feature ranking and clustering as it is obvious that all attributes will be chosen if we take the whole hierarchy of clusters. The idea is to use those base-leval concepts [Rosch, 1978], then attributes used in these clusters are selected and the feature ranking can be determined according to features' occurrence in the selected clusters. However, to determine the base-level clusters itself is a difficult problem. It is usually hard for us to make a good guess. This will result in either too general or too specific concepts to be chosen. The dire consequences are wrong selection of features. In a nut shell, it is not trivial to apply existing clustering algorithms to solve the problem of unsupervised feature ranking and selection.

2.3 SOME RECENT APPROACHES

Some recent works on clustering try to handle high-dimensionality by selecting important features. In [Agrawal et al., 1998] and later in [Cheng et al., 1999] it is observed that dense regions may be found in subspaces of high dimensional data. An algorithm called CLIQUE in [Agrawal et al., 1998] divides each dimension into a user given divisions. It starts with finding dense regions in 1-dimensional data and works upward to find k-dimensional dense regions using candidate generation algorithm Apriori [Agrawal and Srikant, 1994]. This approach is different from the conventional clustering that partitions the whole data. In [Aggarwal et al., 1999] a new concept is presented called "projected clustering" to discover interesting patterns in subspaces of high-dimensional data. It first finds clusters and then selects a subset of features for each cluster.

It searches for the subset of features by putting a restriction on the minimum and the maximum number of features.

We address the problem of selecting a subset of important features for the *whole data and not just for clusters*. This helps in knowing the important features before applying any unsupervised learning task such as clustering. A clustering task becomes more efficient and focused as only the important features can be used. Finding important original features for the whole data helps in understanding the data better unlike principal components. Data storage, collection and processing tasks become more efficient and noise is reduced as the data is pruned.

3. AN ENTROPY MEASURE FOR CONTINUOUS AND NOMINAL DATA TYPES

In this section we introduce an entropy measure for determining relative importance of variables. This measure is applicable to both nominal and continuous data types, and does not need class information to evaluate the variables unlike some other entropy measures, for example, information gain measure in ID3 [Quinlan, 1986].

3.1 PHYSICAL SIGNIFICANCE

Consider an instance in a data set, which is described by a set of variables. If the data has distinct clusters, this instance should belong to some cluster, and the instance must be well separated from some instances in other clusters and very close to others in the same cluster. Irrelevant variables have no influence, but relevant ones do, on forming distinct clusters. Our method is based on the observation that removing an irrelevant variable from the variable set should not change the underlying concept of the data, but not so otherwise. Consider a set of N instances in an M dimensional hyper-space. Removing a variable from original set of variables (i.e., decreasing dimensionality of the hyper-space by one) is to project data onto an $M - 1$ dimensional hyper-space. Distinctness among clusters after removal varies for different variables according to their importance, and is shown below.

An Example: Iris data (summarized in Table 3.1) has four variables in total. Figure 3.1 (a) and (b) show instances in a 3-dimensional space of subset (v_1, v_3, v_4). Removing variable v_4 is equivalent to projecting data onto a 2-dimensional plane of subset (v_1, v_3) (Figure 3.1 (c)), and removing variable v_1 is equivalent to projecting data onto a 2-dimensional plane of subset (v_3, v_4) (Figure 3.1 (d)). By examining the figures, we notice that data in Figure 3.1 (d) for subset (v_3, v_4) displays more distinct clusters than data in Figure 3.1 (c) for subset (v_1, v_3). This implies that variable v_4 is more important than variable v_1. Also, as the clusters in Figure 3.1 (d) for subset (v_3, v_4) are roughly as

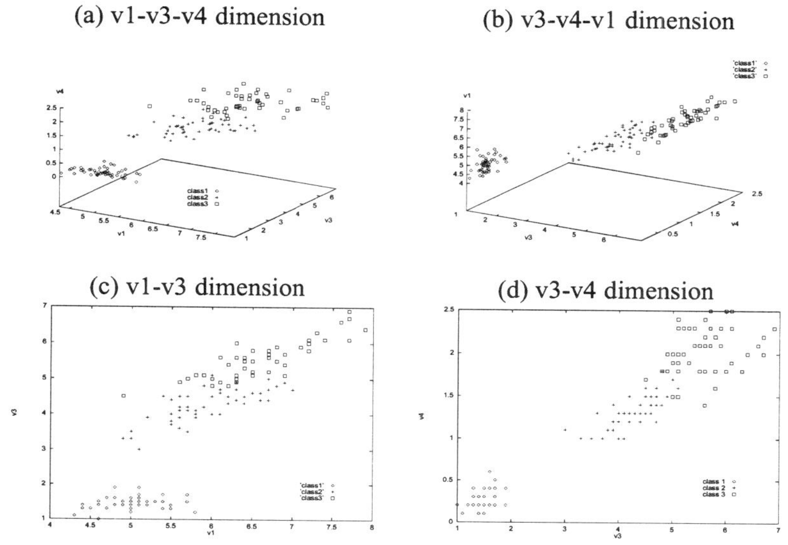

Figure 3.1 Importance of different dimensions for Iris data set

distinct as the clusters in Figure 3.1 (b) for subset (v_3, v_4, v_1), variable v_1 may be removed if only two variables are allowed.

3.2 THE MEASURE

We wish to find a measure that can rank features according to their importance in defining underlying clusters. If we start with the complete set of features, a feature, whose removal retains the distinctness most among the clusters, should be removed first. Notice that when we remove a feature we project original data of M dimensions to $M-1$ dimensions, and for M features we create M different projections. Hence our task is to compare all these projections and find out the one that retains the distinctness most. We say data has orderly configurations if it has distinct clusters, and has disorderly or chaotic configurations otherwise. From entropy theory [Fast, 1962], we know that entropy (or probability) is low for orderly configurations, and more for disorderly configurations for the simple reason that there are few orderly configurations compared to disorderly configurations. Thus, if we can measure the entropy content in a data set after each projection, then we can determine which feature to remove. Notice that in a data set entropy should be very low between two instances if they are very close or very far, and very high if they are separated by the mean of all distances. We use a similarity measure (S) that is based on distance, and assumes a very small value (close to 0.0) for very close pairs of instances, and a very large value (close to 1.0) for very distant pairs. For two instances, the entropy measure is $E = -S\log_2 S - (1-S)\log_2(1-S)$ that assumes the maximum value of 1.0 for $S = 0.5$, and the minimum value of 0.0 for $S = 0.0$ and $S = 1.0$ [Klir and Folger, 1988].

For a data set of N instances entropy measure is given as:

$$\mathbf{E} = -\sum_{i=1}^{N}\sum_{j=1}^{N}(S_{ij} \times \log S_{ij} + (1 - S_{ij}) \times \log(1 - S_{ij})) \quad (3.1)$$

where S_{ij} is similarity between the instances x_i and x_j normalized to [0,1].

When all variables are *numeric* or *ordinal*, similarity value of two instances is:

$$S_{ij} = e^{-\alpha \times D_{ij}} \quad (3.2)$$

where D_{ij} is distance between x_i and x_j, and α is a parameter. If we plot similarity against distance, the curve will have a bigger curvature for a larger α. In this work, α is calculated automatically by assigning 0.5 in Eqn. 3.2 at which entropy is maximum. This, in fact, produces good results for the tested data sets. Mathematically, it is given as: $\alpha = \frac{-\ln 0.5}{\overline{D}}$ where $\overline{D}$ is the average distance among instances. Euclidean distance is used to calculate D_{ij}. In a multi-dimensional space, it is defined as: $D_{ij} = [\sum_{k=1}^{M}(\frac{x_{ik}-x_{jk}}{max_k - min_k})^2]^{1/2}$ where max_k and min_k are maximum and minimum values of kth dimension. The range of kth dimension is normalized by dividing it by the maximum interval $max_k - min_k$.

Similarity for *nominal* variables is measured using the Hamming distance. Similarity value of two instances is given as:

$$S_{ij} = \frac{\sum_{k=1}^{M} |x_{ik} = x_{jk}|}{M} \quad (3.3)$$

where $|x_{ik} = x_{jk}|$ is 1 if x_{ik} equals x_{jk} and 0 otherwise.

For mixed data (i.e., both numeric and nominal variables), one may discretize numeric values first before applying our measure [Liu and Setiono, 1995].

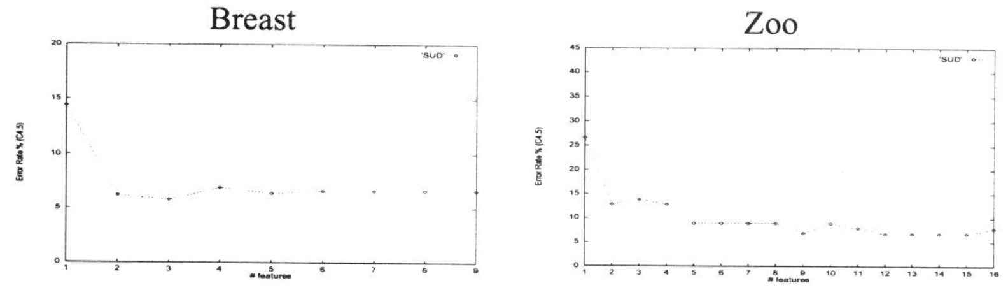

Figure 3.2 Typical trends of performance vs. number of features

4. ALGORITHM TO FIND IMPORTANT VARIABLES

We use a **S**equential Backward Selection algorithm [Devijver and Kittler, 1982] to determine the relative importance of variables for **U**nsupervised **D**ata (SUD). In the algorithm D is the given data set.

SUD(D)

  T = Original Variable Set

  For $k = 1$ to $M - 1$ /* Iteratively remove variables one at a time */

    For every variable v in T /* Choose a variable to removed */

      $T_v = T - v$

      Calculate E_{T_v} using Eqn. 3.1

    Let v_k be the variable that minimizes E_{T_v}

    $T = T - v_k$ /* Remove v_k as the least important variable */

    Output v_k

In each iteration, entropy **E** is calculated using Eqn. 3.1 after removing one variable from the set of remaining variables. A variable is removed as the least important if its removal gives the least entropy. This continues until all features are ranked.

As we are interested in dimensionality reduction, naturally we want to know how many variables we should keep for a task. If we know that an application only needs d variables, we can simply choose the first d variables. The automated selection of d is more complicated. We investigate this issue through experiments on a number of data sets with class labels. We ran SUD after removing class labels. Then we performed 10-fold cross-validation of C4.5 [Quinlan, 1993] using subsets consisting of d most important variables, where d varies from 1 to M, to obtain average error rates. Two results are shown in Figure 3.2 and more in Figure 3.3. They clearly show that increasing d may not improve the performance of the chosen classifier (C4.5) much. But in most cases the performance ceases to improve after a certain point which varies from one data set to another (in case of the Parity3+3 data, in Figure 3.3, the performance falls sharply as more variables are added). In order to determine d for any data having class information, one may perform such experiments, and choose d to be the number of variables beyond which the error rate does not fall. If this is not possible, one may use a windowing technique to find d. That is, stop including more variables if the performance does not improve for a few more extra variables. This issue is being investigated in more detail.

5. EXPERIMENTAL STUDIES

Experiments are conducted to test whether: (1) SUD can find important variables for continuous and nominal data; (2) its performance is comparable to a popular feature ranking method that requires class information unlike SUD; and (3) it does well for an important unsupervised task, i.e. clustering.

Datasets: a summary of 17 data sets is given in Table 3.1. Parity3+3 data set is a modified version of the original Parity3 data set with extra three redundant and six irrelevant variables. In the last column of the Table 3.1 the important variables are shown for Iris, Chemical Plant, Non-linear, CorrAL, Monk3, and Parity3+3. For CorrAL, Monk3, and Parity3+3 data sets the target concepts are also known. The important variables for Iris and Chemical Plant are based on the results of other researchers. For Iris data, Chiu [Chiu, 1996] and Liu and Setiono [Liu and Setiono, 1995] conclude that v_3 (petal-length) and v_4 (petal-width) are the most important variables. Both Chemical Plant and Non-linear data sets are taken from Yasukawa and Sugeno's paper [Sugeno and Yasukawa, 1993]. For Chemical Plant data, they conclude that the first three variables are important. Non-linear data set has an output or class variable y and two input variables v_1 and v_2, and is defined as: $y = (1 + v_1^2 + v_2^{-1.5})^2, 1.0 \leq v_1, v_2 \leq 5.0$. The other two variables in this data set are irrelevant. Most data sets can be found in the machine learning repository in University of California at Irvine [Blake and Merz, 1998].

Experimental Set-up: for part (1) we test SUD over 6 data sets having continuous or nominal variables whose important variables are known. For part (2) we select Relief-F [Kononenko, 1994] as it is a generalized version of Relief, and also it is quite efficient in ranking the features given the class labels. We run SUD and Relief-F over 15 data sets (Chemical Plant and Non-linear data have continuous class variables, hence, are not considered), and obtain ranking of features. Then performance (error rate %) is compared by performing 10-fold cross-validation of C4.5 and OC1 [Murthy et al., 1994] using subsets consisting of d most important variables, d varies from 1 to M. For part (3) see Section 6..

Results: we produce experimental results in Tables 3.2 and 3.3, and Figures 3.3 and 3.4. In all the experiments with SUD class variables are removed first.

Data Set	Data Type	M	N	# Classes	I.V.
Parity3+3	Nominal	12	128	2	{1,7},{2,8},{3,9}
CorrAL	Nominal	6	64	2	1,2,3,4
Monk3	Nominal	6	122	2	2,4,5
Vote	Nominal	16	135	2	NK
Zoo	Nominal	16	74	7	NK
Mushroom	Nominal	22	7125	2	NK
Breast Cancer	Nominal	9	699	2	NK
Lymphography	Nominal	18	148	4	NK
Iris	Continuous	4	150	3	3,4
Bupa	Continuous	6	345	2	NK
New-Thyroid	Continuous	5	215	3	NK
Pima-Diabetes	Continuous	8	768	2	NK
Glass	Continuous	10	214	7	NK
Wine	Continuous	13	178	3	NK
Ionosphere	Continuous	34	351	2	NK
Chemical Plant	Continuous	5	70	∞	1,2,3
Non-linear	Continuous	4	50	∞	1,2

Table 3.1 Summary of data sets. I.V. – Important Variables, ∞ – Class variable is continuous, NK – Not Known, N and M are defined earlier.

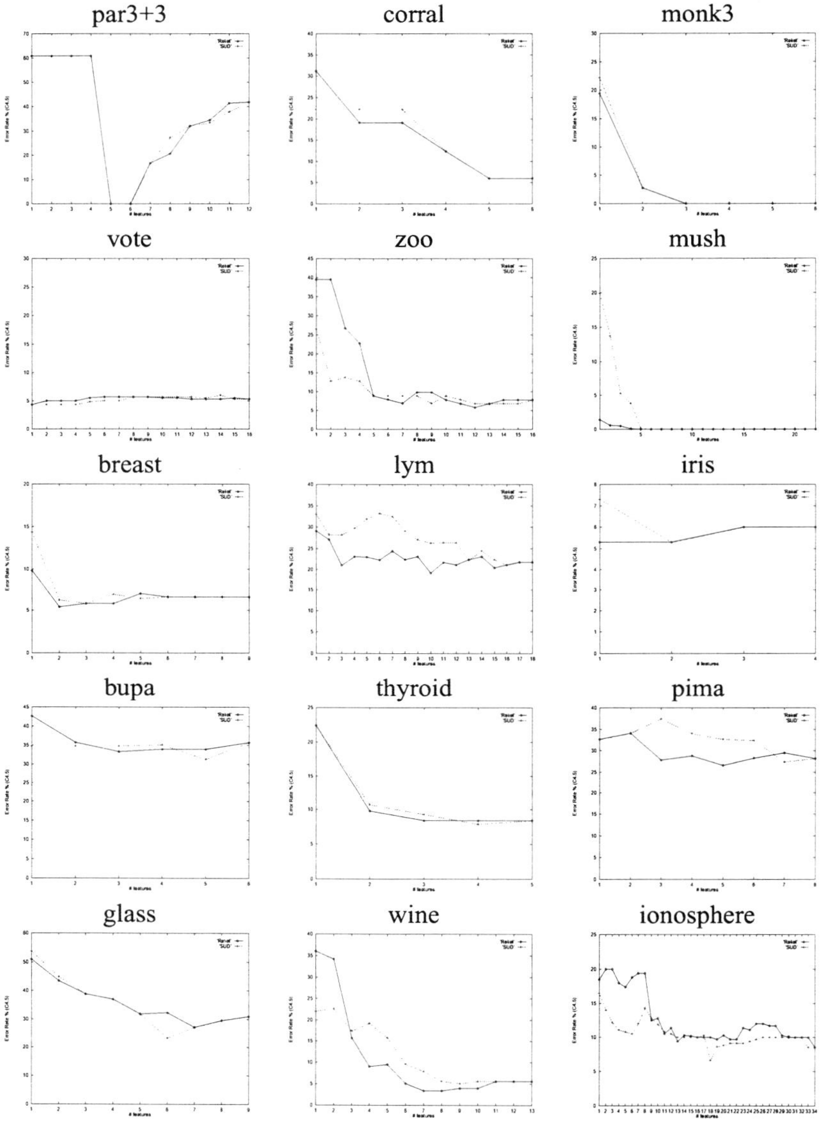

Figure 3.3 Comparison of error rates (%) of 10-fold cross validation of C4.5 using subsets of features ranked by SUD (without using class variable) and Relief-F (using class variable)

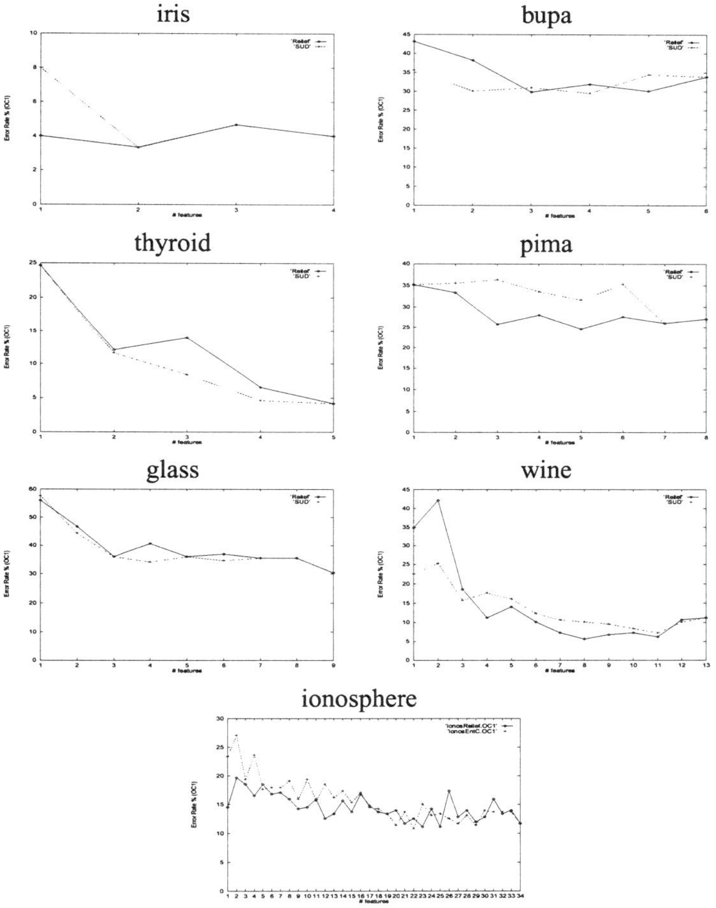

Figure 3.4 Comparison of error rates (%) of 10-fold cross validation of OC1 using subsets of features ranked by SUD (without using class variable) and Relief-F (using class variable)

Data set	Important variables	Decreasing order of importance
Iris	3,4	**3,4**,1,2
Plant	1,2,3	**3,1,2**,4,5
Non-linear	1,2	**2,1**,3,4
Monk3	2,4,5	**5,2,4**,1,6,3
CorrAL	1,2,3,4	**3**,6,**1,2,4**,5
Parity3+3	{1,7},{2,8},{3,9}	**9,3,8,2,7,1**,4,10,6,5,11,12

Table 3.2 Ranking of features by SUD for data sets with known important variables.

Table 3.2 shows that SUD is able to find the important variables although it assigns high importance to the redundant variables in Parity3+3 and CorrAL. Table 3.3 shows the order of importance by SUD and Relief-F for 15 data sets with discrete class variables. Figure 3.3 and 3.4 compares SUD and Relief-F by performing 10-fold cross-validation of C4.5 (inducing axis-parallel decision trees) and OC1 (producing oblique decision trees) using subsets consisting of d most important variables, $d = 1...M$. We run OC1 only on continuous data as is suggested in [Murthy et al., 1994]. In each of these graphs average error rates are plotted in Y-axis and the number of variables in X-axis. It shows that performance of SUD (without using class variable) is close to and sometimes even better than that of Relief-F (using class variable).

6. CLUSTERING USING SUD

In this section, we will apply our dimensionality reduction method for clustering. Before we go into the details of test, we briefly describe a fuzzy clustering algorithm using SUD. We call it *E*ntropy-based *F*uzzy *C*lustering (EFC) [Yao et al., 2000].

We consider the same notations as before: N is number of data points and M number of dimensions. EFC evaluates entropy at each data point x_i as follows:

$$E_i = - \sum_{j=1...N}^{j \neq i} (S_{ij} \times \log S_{ij} + (1 - S_{ij}) \times \log(1 - S_{ij})) \quad (3.4)$$

It selects the data point with the least entropy value as the first cluster center. Then it removes this cluster center and all the data points that have similarity with this center greater than a threshold β from being considered for cluster

Data	Decreasing order of importance	
	SUD	Relief-F
Par3+3	9,3,8,2,7,1,4,10,6,5,11,12	3,9,7,1,8,2,6,11,12,10,4,5
CorrAL	3,6,1,2,4,5	1,2,6,3,4,5
Monk3	5,2,4,1,6,3	2,5,4,3,6,1
Vote	14,6,5,13,4,12,16,8,7,3,9, 15,2,1,10,11	4,3,5,14,11,12,13,8,15,9, 10,2,1,6,16,7
Zoo	13,3,4,1,8,16,6,5,2,14,9, 10,12,11,15,7	4,3,8,1,13,2,9,10,14,16,12, 5,6,7,11,15
Mush	9,3,20,22,5,11,21,2,19,15,14, 1,13,12,4,10,8,7,18,6,17,16	5,20,11,8,19,4,10,22,9,12,13, 21,7,3,2,15,14,18,6,17,16,1
Breast	1,7,3,2,5,6,4,8,9	6,2,3,7,5,1,4,8,9
Lym	18,12,10,13,1,15,11,6,2,16, 8,5,17,3,7,4,9,14	2,13,15,10,17,18,5,7,14,11, 9,1,3,16,12,6,8,4
Iris	3,4,1,2	4,3,1,2
Bupa	5,3,4,6,1,2	6,5,3,2,4,1
Thyroid	4,5,3,2,1	4,3,1,2,5
Pima	8,1,3,6,5,7,2,4	8,1,2,5,6,4,7,3
Glass	9,7,4,8,3,2,5,6,10,1	7,4,9,3,8,5,2,6,10,1
Wine	7,6,12,9,11,10,5,13,1,4,3,8,2	6,9,1,11,5,7,10,4,12,2,13,3,8
Iono-sphere	13,15,11,9,7,17,19,21,5, 3,23,25,27,29,31,33,10,4, 6,12,14,8,16,20,18,22,28, 26,24,30,32,34,2,1	34,22,33,6,4,8,16,14,21, 9,27,15,30,20,29,24,32,7, 12,18,10,11,3,5,28,25,26, 19,23,1,31,13,17,2

Table 3.3 Ranking of features by SUD and Relief-F.

centers in the rest of the iterations. Then the second cluster center is selected that has the least entropy value among the remaining data points, and again this cluster center and the data points having similarity greater than β are removed. This process is repeated until no data point is left. At the end, we get a number of cluster centers. To obtain crisp clusters, it assigns each data point to the cluster center to which it has the highest similarity among all cluster centers.

6.1 TEST ON CLUSTERING

We choose four data sets with class labels for the experiment. The reason to choose these data sets are they have continuous values and they are appropriate for clustering analysis. We apply EFC to these data sets after removing class labels, and then compare clustering results of EFC with the given classes.

To apply our dimensionality reduction method to clustering, we conduct tests as follows: first, for each data set features are ranked according to their importance. Second, the clustering method is applied on each data which consists of d most important variables, d varies from 1 to M. Discrepancies arising from mismatch between the given classes and the achieved clusters for each data set are obtained from each stage in which different number of variables are included. Figure 3.5 shows experimental results for the four data sets. We get the minimum discrepancies when $\{8, 8 \text{ and } 4\}$ most important variables are chosen for BC, Wine and Thyroid data sets respectively. For Iris data, the discrepancies do not decrease significantly when more than two variables are included. In other words, only two variables (variable 4 and 3) are sufficient to get distinct clusters in which there are few discrepancies.

7. DISCUSSION AND CONCLUSION

In this chapter we focus on reducing the number of original features for unsupervised data – a problem that concerns data with large dimensionality. Neither feature selection methods for supervised data nor PCA solves this problem directly. We discuss the difficulties involved if we use clustering for this task. An entropy measure is proposed to measure the importance of a variable. The measure is applicable to both numeric and nominal data types. A sequential backward selection algorithm, SUD, is implemented to determine the relative importance among the features. The issue of choosing d important features is discussed. We carried out experiments to show that (a) SUD is able to find important features, (b) it compares well with a feature ranking algorithm that requires class variables unlike SUD, and (c) it does well for an important unsupervised task, i.e. clustering.

This chapter deals with an interesting problem from both research and industry point of view, and a number of issues that are associated with it. Selecting d important features is one and the time complexity of the algorithm is another.

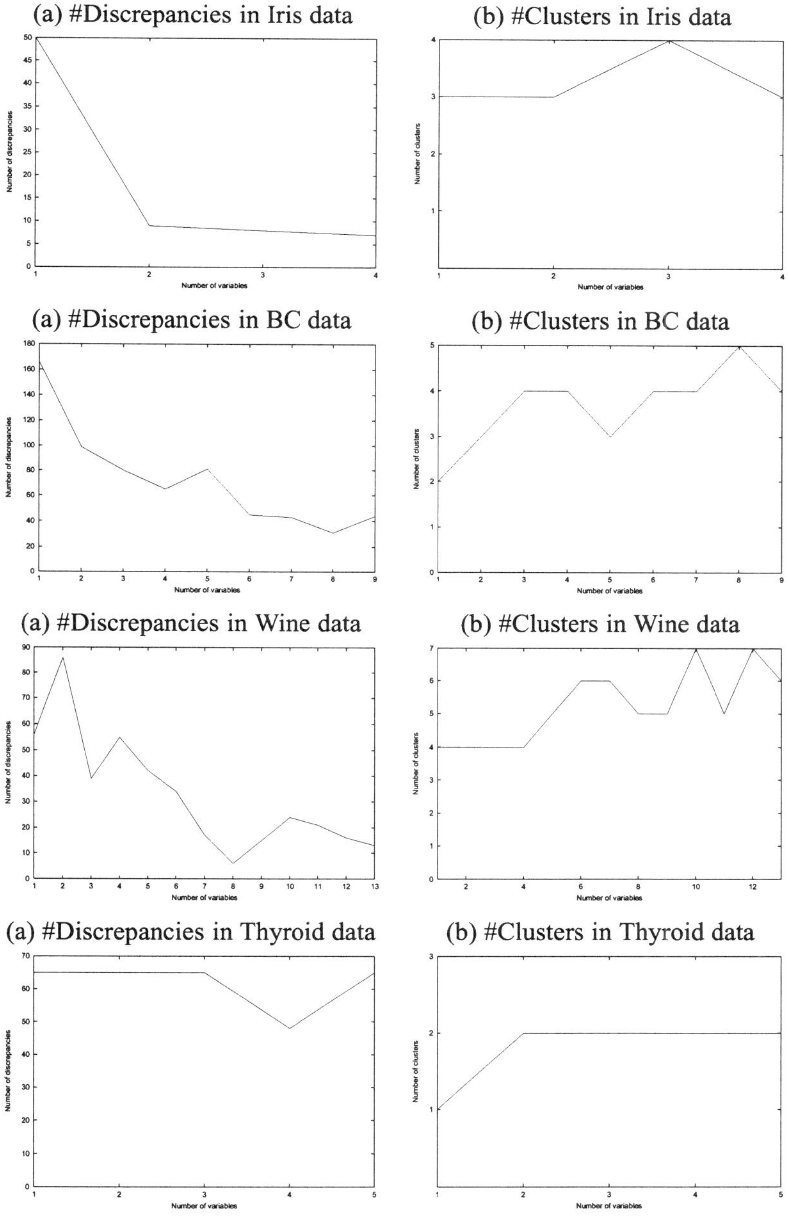

Figure 3.5 Clustering results on four data sets

To find a threshold (number of features) to stop selecting features is a difficult task as shown by our results in Figures 3.3 and 3.4. Although the performances of the classifiers rapidly improve with addition of features, the points (d values), beyond which it no longer improves substantially, vary from one data to another. The graphs also give an insight about how the irrelevant features affect the underlying clustering. Addition of irrelevant features generally do not reduce the distinctness, rather the distinctness becomes stagnant (flat curve). Because of this, determining a robust threshold is difficult. Our experiments on clustering and model construction did show that our method for ranking works well for these important unsupervised tasks. An open question is "how many top ranking features to select for optimal performance?".

In conclusion, our method is useful for unsupervised classification and clustering as it helps in removing the irrelevant features. It helps in getting insight into the data as the important original features are known. Overall, this chapter shows convincingly the advantages of feature elimination in unsupervised clustering.

References

[Aggarwal et al., 1999] Aggarwal, C. C., Procopiuc, C., Wolf, J. L., Yu, P. S., and Park, J. S. (1999). Fast algorithms for projected clustering. In *Proceedings of ACM SIGMOD Conference on Management of Data*, pages 61–72.

[Agrawal et al., 1998] Agrawal, R., Gehrke, J., Gunopulos, D., and Raghavan, P. (1998). Automatic subspace clustering of high dimensional data for data mining applications. In *Proceedings of ACM SIGMOD Conference on Management of Data*.

[Agrawal and Srikant, 1994] Agrawal, R. and Srikant, R. (1994). Fast algorithm for mining association rules. In *Proceedings of the 20th VLDB Conference*, Santiago, Chile.

[Bishop, 1995] Bishop, C. (1995). *Neural Networks for Pattern Recognition*. Oxford University Press.

[Blake and Merz, 1998] Blake, C. L. and Merz, C. Z. (1998). UCI repository of machine learning databases. http://www.ics.uci.edu/~mlearn/MLRepository.html.

[Bradley et al., 1999] Bradley, P., Fayyad, U., and Reina, C. (1999). Scaling clustering algorithms to large databases. In *Proceedings of the Fourth International Conference on Knowledge Discovery & Data Mining*, pages 9 –15. AAAI PRESS, California.

[Bradley et al., 1997] Bradley, P., Mangasarian, O., and Street, W. (1997). Clustering via concave minimization. In Mozer, M., Jordan, M., and Petsche,

T., editors, *Advances in Neural Information Processing Systems*, pages 368 – 374. MIT Press.

[Cheng et al., 1999] Cheng, C., Fu, A. W., and Zhang, Y. (1999). Entropy-based subspace clustering for mining numerical data. In *Proceedings of Internationl Conference on Knowledge Discovery and Data Mining (KDD'99)*.

[Chiu, 1996] Chiu, S. L. (1996). Method and software for extracting fuzzy classification rules by subtractive clustering. In *Proceedings of North American Fuzzy Information Processing Society Conf. (NAFIPS'96)*.

[Dash and Liu, 1997] Dash, M. and Liu, H. (1997). Feature selection methods for classifications. *Intelligent Data Analysis: An International Journal*, 1(3). `http://www-east.elsevier.com/ida/free.htm`.

[Dempster et al., 1977] Dempster, A., Laird, N., and Rubin, D. (1977). Maximum likelihood from incomplete data via the em algorithm. *Journal of the Royal Statistical Society, Series B*, 39(1):1 – 38.

[Devijver and Kittler, 1982] Devijver, P. A. and Kittler, J. (1982). *Pattern Recognition : A Statistical Approach*. Prentice Hall.

[Duda and Hart, 1973] Duda, R. and Hart, P. (1973). *Pattern Classification and Scene Analysis*. John Wiley & Sons, New York.

[Fast, 1962] Fast, J. (1962). *Entropy : the significance of the concept of entropy and its applications in science and technology*, chapter 2: The Statistical Significance of the Entropy Concept. Eindhoven : Philips Technical Library.

[Fisher, 1987] Fisher, D. (1987). Knowledge acquisition via incremental conceptual clustering. *Machine Learning*, 2:139–172.

[Fukunaga, 1990] Fukunaga, K. (1990). *Introduction to Statistical Pattern Recognition*. San Diego: Academic Press.

[Gluck and Corter, 1985] Gluck, M. and Corter, J. (1985). Information, uncertainty, and the utility of categories. In *Proceedings of the Seventh Annual Conference of the Cognitive Science Society*, pages 283–87. Lawrence Erlbaum, Irvine, CA.

[Jolliffe, 1986] Jolliffe, I. T. (1986). *Principal Component Analysis*. Springer-Verlag.

[Kaufman and Rousseeuw, 1989] Kaufman, L. and Rousseeuw, P. (1989). *Finding Groups in Data*. New York: John Wiley and Songs.

[Kira and Rendell, 1992] Kira, K. and Rendell, L. A. (1992). The feature selection problem: Traditional methods and a new algorithm. In *Proceedings of Ninth National Conference on AI*.

[Klir and Folger, 1988] Klir, G. and Folger, T. (1988). *Fuzzy Sets, Uncertainty, and Information*, chapter 5: Uncertainty and Information. Prentice-Hall International Editions.

[Kononenko, 1994] Kononenko, I. (1994). Estimating attributes : Analysis and extension of RELIEF. In Bergadano, F. and De Raedt, L., editors, *Proceedings of the European Conference on Machine Learning, April 6-8*, pages 171–182, Catania, Italy. Berlin: Springer-Verlag.

[Lebowitz, 1987] Lebowitz, M. (1987). Experiments with incremental concept formation. *Machine Learning*, 1:103–138.

[Liu et al., 1998] Liu, H., Motoda, H., and Dash, M. (1998). A monotonic measure for optmial feature selection. In Nedellec, C. and Rouveirol, C., editors, *Machine Learning: ECML-98, April 21 - 23, 1998*, pages 101–106, Chemnitz, Germany. Berlin Heidelberg: Springer-Verlag.

[Liu and Setiono, 1995] Liu, H. and Setiono, R. (1995). Chi2: Feature selection and discretization of numeric attributes. In *Proceedings of the 7th IEEE International Conference on Tools with Artificial Intelligence(TAT'95)*, pages 388–391.

[Lloyd, 1982] Lloyd, S. (1982). Least squares quantization in PCM. *IEEE Transactions on Information Theory*, 28(2):129 – 137.

[Michalski and Stepp, 1983] Michalski, R. and Stepp, R. (1983). Learning from observation: conceptual clustering. In Michalski, R., Carbonell, J., and Mitchell, T., editors, *Machine Learning I*, pages 331–363. Tioga, Palo Alto, CA.

[Murthy et al., 1994] Murthy, S. K., Kasif, S., and Salzberg, S. (1994). A system for induction of oblique decision trees. *Journal of Artificial Intelligence Research*, 2:1–32.

[Quinlan, 1986] Quinlan, J. (1986). Induction of decision trees. *Machine Learning*, 1(1):81–106.

[Quinlan, 1993] Quinlan, J. (1993). *C4.5: Programs for Machine Learning.* Morgan Kaufmann.

[Rosch, 1978] Rosch, E. (1978). Principles of categorization. In Rosch, E. and Lloyd, B., editors, *Cognition and Categorization*. Erlbaum, N.J.

[Scott, 1992] Scott, D. (1992). *Multivariate Density Estimation: Theory, Practice, and Visualization*. Newy York: John Wiley.

[Silverman, 1986] Silverman, B. (1986). *Density Estimation for Statistics and Data Analysis*. London: Chapman & Hall.

[Sugeno and Yasukawa, 1993] Sugeno, M. and Yasukawa, T. (1993). A fuzzy-logic-based approach to qualitative modeling. In *IEEE Transactions on Fuzzy system Vol.1, No.1*.

[Uthurusamy, 1996] Uthurusamy, R. (1996). From data mining to knoweldge discovery: Current challenges and future directions. In Fayyad, U., Piatetsky-Shapiro, G., Smyth, P., and Uthurusamy, R., editors, *Advances in Knowledge Discovery and Data Mining*, pages 561–569. AAAI Press / The MIT Press.

[Wyse et al., 1980] Wyse, N., Dubes, R., and Jain, A. (1980). A critical evaluation of intrinsic dimensionality algorithms. In Gelsema, E. and Kanal, L., editors, *Pattern Recognition in Practice*, pages 415–425. Morgan Kaufmann Publishers, Inc.

[Yao et al., 2000] Yao, J., Dash, M., Tan, S., and Liu, H. (2000). Entropy-based fuzzy clustering and fuzzy modeling. *Fuzzy Sets and Systems - International Journal of Soft Computing and Intelligence*, 113(3):381–388.

Chapter 4

APPROACHES TO CONCEPT BASED EXPLORATION OF INFORMATION RESOURCES

Hele-Mai Haav
Institute of Cybernetics at Tallinn Technical University, Estonia

Jørgen Fischer Nilsson
Department of Information Technology, Technical University of Denmark

Keywords: concept based retrieval, conceptual modeling, ontology, formal concept analysis, and algebraic lattices

Abstract: This paper discusses methods for improving the usual keyword based retrieval from information resources. Common to these methods is the use of lattices to structure the conceptual content of the information resources. The first method discussed relies on construction of ontology by a human being acquainted with a considered knowledge domain. The second approach constructs a formal concept lattice by algorithmic analysis of keyword patterns in the text.

1. INTRODUCTION

This paper discusses methods aiming at facilitating access to relevant parts of text sources, which are supported traditionally by simple keyword search facilities. At focus are methods enabling content-based retrieval of pertinent units of information by establishment of an appropriate conceptual model formalized as a concept access structure.

In conventional data base methodology versatile accessing of information is offered by structuring the available information into given data structures and putting at disposal a query language geared to the applied data forms.

In the prevailing relational data base model data is cast into n-ary relations supported by query languages applying set operations and constructs from predicate logic. However, such mathematical query languages are intended for IT professionals, they being in concept based access general to be difficult to master for IT users. In addition conventional data base models and supporting technology is of little use for loosely structured knowledge sources such the Web, and for unstructured sources such as conventional text sources.

Ideally, a supporting conceptual model identifies the conceptual content of the user's access demand and then retrieves those information units which conceptually match the demand.

We discuss methods for approaching such concept based retrieval functionality in software systems by

1. formalizing essentials of the user's conceptual model of the domain; and/or
2. extracting a conceptual structure inherent in the available information sources.

We address concept-based retrieval of unformatted text sources. These sources are to be conceptually well structured such as textbooks, handbooks, manuals, and encyclopedias.

Of particular interest are here on-line information sources such as dictionaries and encyclopedias where a selected major knowledge domain or subject is usually fragmented into a large number of alphabetically ordered articles.

The system is to serve a user posing a specific question with no obvious or simple connection to the alphabetical list of articles. Such a problem may typically involve relationships between concepts for which indices are of little use. Moreover, the system is to assist a user in a general attempt to come to grips the key concepts as well as their mutual relationships within a knowledge domain.

In focus of the conceptualization process is the use of lattices as formal basis for conceptual modeling and ontology construction. Lattices support hierarchical classifications, which are lacking in the classical relational data model. Lattices, however, transcend hierarchical classification by opening for cross-categorization by partially overlapping categories.

The rest of the paper is structured as follows. In section 2 we introduce conceptual taxonomies used for conceptual modeling and ontology construction. In section 3 we discuss ontology driven concept-based retrieval. Search based on formal concept lattices is described in section 4. We conclude our discussion in section 5.

2. CONCEPTUAL TAXONOMIES

In this section we describe the background and the mathematical foundations of our modeling approach to be applied in the following sections.

2.1 Words and concepts

We consider conceptual structures consisting of concepts and binary relationships between concepts. In the tradition of semantic nets and entity-relationship (E-R) modeling, and conceptual graphs [Sowa 2000] such structures are visualized as directed graphs with concepts associated with nodes. In natural language, there is no simple one-to-one relationship between words and concepts: synonymous words represent the same concept and one word may represent two or more distinct and unrelated concepts (homonyms).

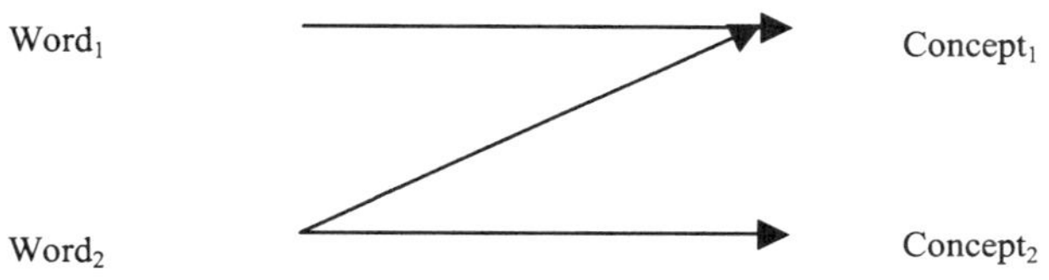

Figure 1. Words and concepts

The many-to-many relationship indicated in Fig.1 is further complicated by metonymic usage of words and use of compound words and phrases. The left part of Fig. 1 constitutes what we call a lexicon comprising morphological and other linguistic descriptions of words. The right part of the figure belongs to the conceptual structure, which is to be independent on natural language peculiarities. It is important to realize that conceptual relationships are conceived of as relationships between abstract concepts rather than relationships between words, although concepts are named by words.

2.2 Relationships between concepts

There is a general consensus that the most important relationship between concepts is the conceptual inclusion relationship (is-a relationship). The conceptual inclusion relationship

c_1 is-a c_2

is here to signify that instances of c_1 comprise all the properties possessed by instances of c_2. For instance, "tomato is-a vegetable" informs that tomatoes possess the attributes of vegetables and in addition possibly tomato-specific attributes not possessed by vegetables in general (e.g. such as being red and round).

It follows from this intensional definition that instances falling under c_1 form a subset of the instances falling under c_2 by virtue of c_1 instances comprising properties in addition to those of c_2 instances. Thus, in the so-called extensional set oriented view the set of c_1 instances is a subset of c_2 instances. However it should be observed that although intensional inclusion implies extensional inclusion, the reverse does not hold in general.

Many other conceptual relationships can be identified and introduced, e.g. locational, structural, causal, and temporal relationships. The most important one among these additional relationships is perhaps the part-of relationship, which is a structural relationship.

However, in the rest of this section we focus on the conceptual inclusion relationship, which is crucial for establishing conceptual taxonomies, returning to the remainder relationships in section 3.

The conceptual inclusion relationship possesses the following properties for any concept c_1, c_2, and c_3:

- Reflexivity — c_1 is-a c_1
- Antisymmetry — c_1 is-a c_2 and c_2 is-a c_1 implies that c_1 and c_2 are identical
- Transitivity — c_1 is-a c_2 and c_2 is-a c_3 implies that c_1 is-a c_3

This means that the inclusion relationship is a weak partial order relationship with the implication that the conceptual graph has no cycles between distinct concepts. In our conceptual graphs, relationships implied by the transitivity are omitted as in the following Fig. 2.

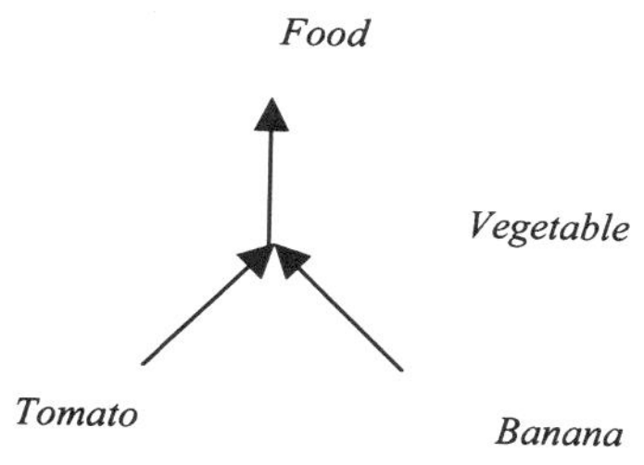

Figure 2. Sample conceptual structure

In Fig. 2, the is-a labels on the upward pointing inclusion arcs are left implicit. Moreover, the inclusion arc from Tomato to Food is given by transitivity. The conceptual structure in the Fig. 2 is a simple example of a concept hierarchy. However, partial orders go beyond hierarchies as exemplified in the below Fig. 3 by telling that vitamin-C is classified as a vitamin as well as an antioxidant. We take the domain of nutrition as a running example domain. Upward pointing arrowheads are left implicit.

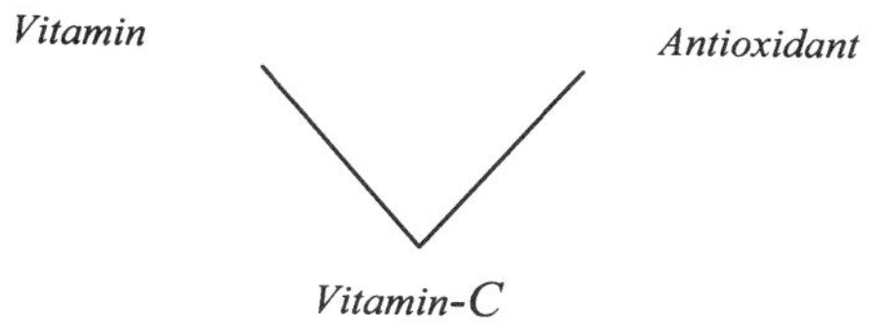

Figure 3. Multiple inclusion

This multiple inclusion situation implies multiple inheritance as well, since the reverse inclusion arc propagates properties downwards. Imagine now in the course of analyzing our target domain it is realized that other vitamins are antioxidants as well as indicated in the following Fig. 4.

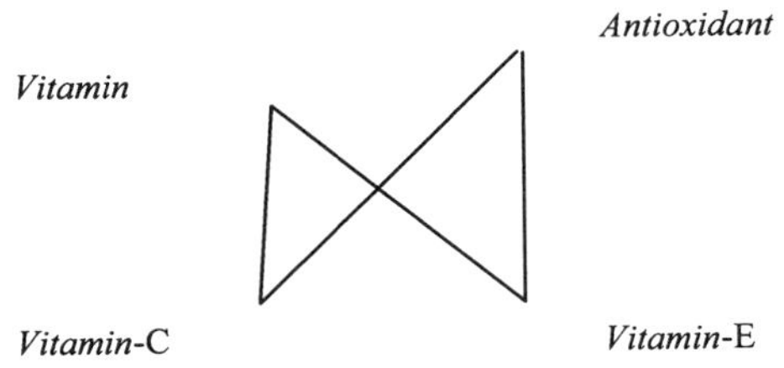

Figure 4. Conceptual structure

This conceptual structure comprising 4 nodes is still a partial order. However, it is feasible for a logical account of conceptual structures to impose certain restrictions on the partial order, which leads us to lattice structures.

2.3 Lattice structures

A lattice is a partial order visualized as above diagrams in Fig. 2 and 3, subjected in addition to the following restrictions, cf. Fig. 5 below:

Existence of Supremum. For any two concepts c_1 and c_2 there exists a concept c_{sup} superior to c_1 and c_2 and being a specialization of any other concept c' superior to both c_1 and c_2.

Existence of Infimum. For any two concepts c_1 and c_2 there exists a concept c_{inf} inferior to c_1 and c_2 and being a generalization of any other concept c'' inferior to both c_1 and c_2.

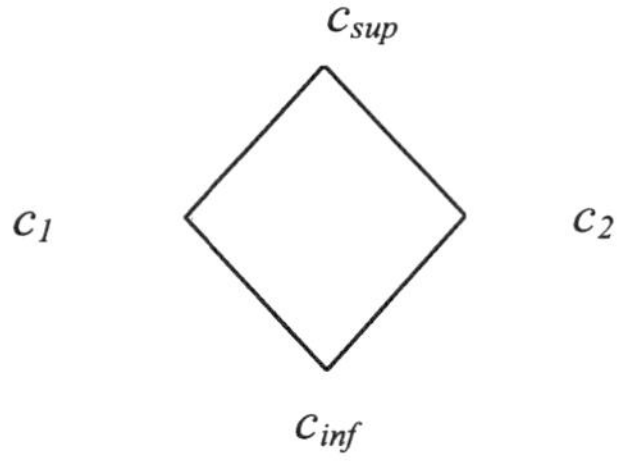

Figure 5. Supremum and infimum of concepts

The structure in Fig. 4 violates the existence of supremum condition since the concept Vitamin is superior to Vitamin-C and Vitamin-E, but so is the concept Antioxidant without there being any inclusion relationship between Vitamin and Antioxidant. Similarly, this structure violates existence of the infimum condition. However, the conceptual structure can be turned into a lattice simply by introduction of an anonymous node expressing the concept of being Vitamin as well as Antioxidant as shown in the following Fig. 6.

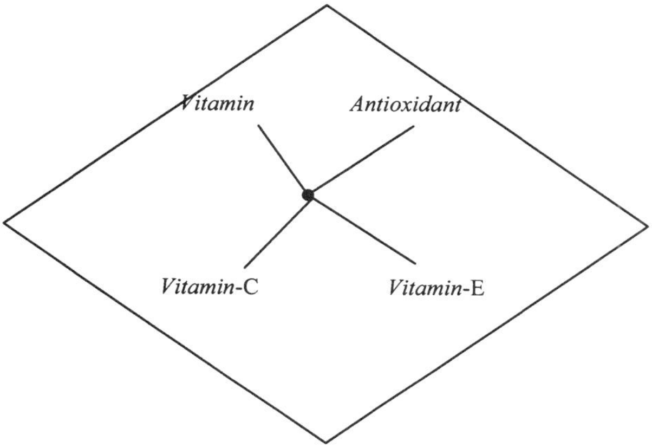

Figure 6. An anonymous connecting concept

Recall that in Fig. 6 arcs from Vitamin-C to Vitamin and Vitamin-E to Antioxidant are given implicitly by transitivity via the unlabelled node. In this figure the infimum of concepts Vitamin and Antioxidant is an anonymous node, which is at the same time supremum of concepts Vitamin-C and Vitamin-E. In order to ensure existence of supremum and infimum of all concepts is formally introduced a top and a bottom element into the lattice as shown in Fig. 7.

The top element represents the universal concept, which includes any other concept. Dually the bottom element represents the absurd null concept, which is included in any concept. The situation that the infimum of a pair of concepts is bottom, $\perp$, expresses non-overlap (disjointness) of the concepts.

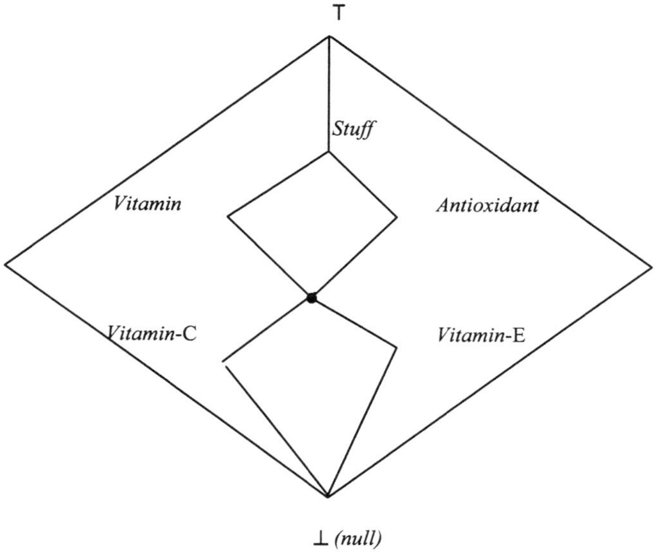

Figure 7. A lattice conceptual structure

2.4 Lattice algebra

The previous subsection introduced lattices as partial orders imposed existence conditions. The conceptual structure diagrams (known as Hasse diagrams in lattice theory) facilitate elaboration of conceptual models. In addition to diagrams lattice theory provides an algebraic language in the form of an equational logic for concepts. This algebraic logic comes about by introducing a binary operator, say +, for supremum and a dual operator, say ×, for infimum. Thus, c_1+c_2 is the supremum of the concept nodes c_1 and c_2, and similarly $c_1 \times c_2$ gives the infimum. As an example, the conceptual structure in Fig. 7 can be specified as the following equations:

$$Stuff = Vitamin + Antioxidant$$

$$Vitamin\text{-}C + Vitamin\text{-}E = Vitamin \times Antioxidant$$

In lattice theory the two operators and lattice bounds, top and bottom, are characterized by appropriate axioms, see e.g. [Davey & Priestley 1990].

For instance, there are laws of commutativity as follows:

$$X + Y = Y + X$$

$$X \times Y = Y \times X$$

The laws in effect for + and × are similar to those for logical operators *or* and *and* known from Boolean algebra. They are also similar to those for the set operators for union and intersection in the set theory in the assumed case of so-called distributive lattices.

As yet a fragment of a conceptual model for nutrition let us consider the below Fig. 8 corresponding to the following equations:

$$\textit{Vitamin} = \textit{Vitamin-A} + \textit{Vitamin-B} + \textit{Vitamin-C}$$

$$\textit{Vitamin-A} \times \textit{Vitamin-B} = \textit{null}$$

$$\textit{Vitamin-B} \times \textit{Vitamin-C} = \textit{null}$$

$$\textit{Vitamin-A} \times \textit{Vitamin-C} = \textit{null}$$

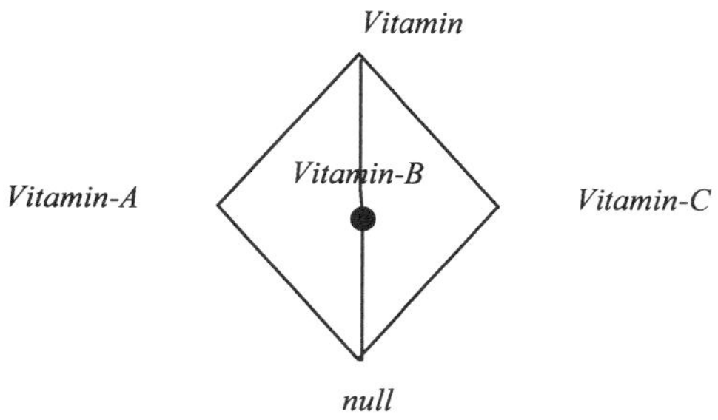

Figure 8. A fragment of a conceptual model

Actually, the shown diagram is *simplified* since it does not show the nodes corresponding to the concepts *Vitamin-A+Vitamin-B, Vitamin-A+Vitamin-C,* and *Vitamin-B+Vitamin-C* situated below the concept Vitamin. For simplicity's sake we often refrain from showing such non-lexicalized sum nodes in diagrams.

The three last equations expressing disjointness are assumed implicitly according to the default principle that concepts c_1 and c_2 are disjoint unless an overlapping concept distinct from *null* is introduced explicitly as *Vitamin×Antioxidant* in Fig. 6.

The diagrams and the equations support and complement each other in the course of elaborating concept taxonomies.

The equations constitute a logico-algebraic counterpart of a fragment of predicate calculus dealing with monadic predicates. For instance, the first equation of Fig. 8 conforms with the logical sentence

$$\forall x\ (Vitamin(x) \leftrightarrow Vitamin\text{-}A(x) \vee Vitamin\text{-}B(x) \vee Vitamin\text{-}C(x))$$

Here it is assumed that *Vitamin-A*, etc are predicates. If *Vitamin-A* is conceived to be an individual the sentence has to be reformulated using *Vitamin(Vitamin-A)*. This logical complication arises often in conceptual modeling since an individual concept such as *Vitamin-B* becomes in a refined model a compound term with specialization $Vitamin\text{-}B_1$, $Vitamin\text{-}B_2$, etc. with corresponding equation:

$$Vitamin\text{-}B = Vitamin\text{-}B_1 + Vitamin\text{-}B_2 + \ldots$$

Such an open-ended specification can be stated in the algebra as

$$Vitamin\text{-}B = Vitamin\text{-}B_1 + Vitamin\text{-}B_2 + Vitamin\text{-}B$$

This equation states that $Vitamin\text{-}B_1$ and $Vitamin\text{-}B_2$ are sub-concepts of *Vitamin-B*, leaving open presence of additional immediate sub-concepts. Thus this equation expresses the inclusion relationships

$Vitamin\text{-}B_1$ is-a *Vitamin*

$Vitamin\text{-}B_2$ is-a *Vitamin*

2.5 Conceptual modeling and ontology

In the above subsections we have presented an equational language supported by diagrams for establishing concept taxonomies. If the conceptual model at the top level comprises metaphysical categories such as stuff, events, states, and time, it is often referred to as ontology. In the ontological approach, domain specific concept structures are to be appropriately situated below the relevant general categories as sketched below for our target domain of nutrition.

Fig. 9 shows three major disjoint categories of the nutrition domain. The diagrams in Fig. 7 and 8 are to reside below the Nutrient node. According to the introduced default principle the edges to the bottom element are left implicit.

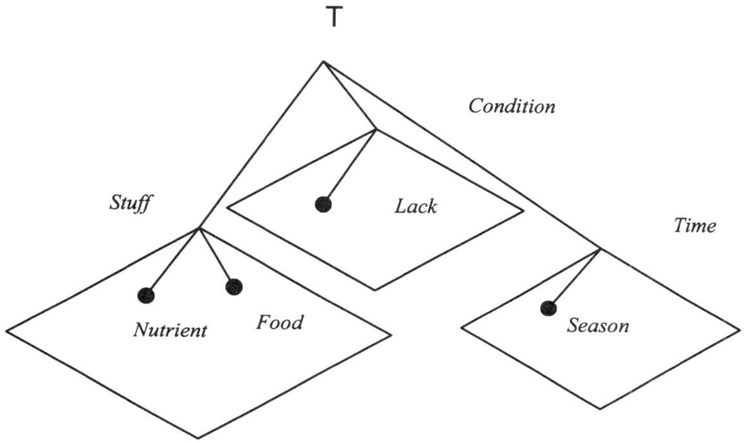

Figure 9. Top of ontology for the domain of nutrition.

The above concept classification taxonomies are called skeleton ontologies, since they are made more expressive in the below section 3.

3. ONTOLOGY DRIVEN CONCEPT RETRIEVAL

In this section, we are going to discuss how the above notions and models can be used for easing retrieval of information pertaining to a concept or to a combination of concepts. However, before involving the above methods we briefly discuss conventional keyword based search.

Let us stress that focus here is on the desirable search and retrieval principles and functionality rather than the implementation techniques in the form of appropriate indices and algorithms to be used for speeding up retrieval.

3.1 Basic search methods for text sources

There are two basic access methods for text sources: keyword search and navigation (browsing) in a given classification. Often searches combine the two methods.

Keyword based search applies a very simple logical search language basically comprising expressions of the form w_1 *AND* w_2 *AND*.... This search expression is to retrieve those units of the text source, which contain all the keywords w_1, w_2... Here it is assumed that the text source is pre-structured into units, say in the form of pages on the Web or articles in a dictionary. This search facility, which is well known from Web search engines can be generalized by logical *OR* and other operators. However, logical OR can be reduced to a series of conjunctive *AND* queries.

Suppose, for instance, in context of our nutrition domain that a user wants to inquire about lack of vitamin. He/she could then state the query

Vitamin AND *Lack*

This query is supposed to retrieve the set of articles addressing lack of vitamins. However, this keyword query may retrieve articles, which just happen to contain the two keywords without addressing the subject of lack of vitamin.[1] Even worse, the query may fail to retrieve entries dealing with lack of vitamin either because the concept of lack is represented by the synonym, say, deficiency - or because the article discusses a specific vitamin, say vitamin-C.

3.2 Concept based search

We now consider the same representative query example in the context of conceptual models discussed in section 2. The mentioned shortcomings of the keyword-based search can now be overcome by letting synonyms be identified by the system, and furthermore by letting sub- and super-concepts be recognized by the system.

Let us introduce the notion of conceptual distance between concept c_1 and concept c_2 defined as the number of edges of the shortest path between c_1 and c_2 in the conceptual structure. Then synonyms have the distance of 0 and immediate super and sub-concepts have the distance of 1. Thus, an article describing lack of vitamin-D can be retrieved within a distance horizon of 1 with respect to lack of vitamin. However, this scheme still and

[1] Search machines offer a more restrictive operator NEAR, which requires that the two keywords be close to each other in the text.

even more than before tends to produce spurious retrieval results since the constituent concepts are not combined into a compound concept.

3.3 Combining concepts

At this point it is important to realize the difference between the operators in keyword expressions and the conceptual operators in the skeleton ontologies. Although the search expression *Vitamin AND Lack* conforms *prima facie* with the concept term

$$Vitamin \times Lack$$

the latter term is identified with null in the ontology (cf. Fig. 9) since there is nothing, which is a vitamin (chemical substance) as well as lack (state). The two concepts do not combine directly ontologically. Thus, the representation of lack of vitamin calls for more operators in the algebraic language used for the ontology. It is tempting at the informal level to represent lack of vitamin formally by attribution of vitamin to lack in a feature structure with attribute say *wrt* (i.e. with respect to) as in

Lack [wrt: Vitamin].

Similarly the compound concept "lack of vitamin-D in winter" might be represented as the extended feature structure of type Lack with two qualifying features

$$Lack \begin{bmatrix} wrt\text{: } Vitamin\text{-}D \\ tmp\text{: } Winter \end{bmatrix}$$

where *tmp* is a common attribute for temporal periods. These examples illustrate the following two important principles:

1. Addition of features specializes concepts.
2. Specialization of a concept within an attribute specializes the entire concept. For instance, *Lack [wrt: Vitamin-D]* is a subordinate concept of *Lack [wrt: Vitamin]* since vitamin-D is a sub-concept of vitamin.

The introduction of attributes overcomes the problem of disjoint concepts since *Lack* × *[wrt: Vitamin]* may well be non-null in the ontology even though *Lack* and *Vitamin* are kept as disjoint concepts, that is

Lack $\times$ *Vitamin = null.*

Observe further that according to the stated principles

Lack $\times$ *[wrt: Vitamin]*

must be situated below the node Lack.

3.4 Accommodating feature structures in lattices

It is possible formally to extend the lattice algebra described above with feature structures in the following way (cf. [Nilsson 1994], [Larsen & Nilsson, 1997], [Nilsson 1999], [Nilsson & Haav 1999]):

1. Every attribute *a* is turned into one argument operator (function) *a(...)*. Hence the feature *[wrt: Vitamin]* is re-expressed as the term *wrt(Vitamin)*. The attribute function turns the stuff vitamin into the property of being something with respect to vitamin. Similarly, in *tmp(Winter)* the time period winter is turned into the property of taking place during winter.
2. Feature terms are attached to a concept as restricting properties by means of the $\times$ operator. Thus the feature structure expressing lack of vitamin-D in winter from last subsection becomes *Lack* $\times$ *wrt(Vitamin-D)* $\times$ *tmp(Winter).*

The attributes jointly possess a number of formal algebraic properties as discussed in [Nilsson 1994]. Let us mention the monotonicity of attribution (cf. the second principle of sect. 3.3), which claims that

If X is-a Y, then $a(X)$ is-a $a(Y)$

This property is visualized in the below partial ontology comprising compound concepts.

Condition

|

Lack

|

Lack×wrt(Vitamin)

|

Lack×wrt(Vitamin-D)

|

Lack×wrt(Vitamin-D) × tmp(Winter)

Figure 10. Specialization of concepts by attribution

This attribute-enriched lattice language may be understood as a fragment of relation-algebraic logic presented in [Brink et al. 1994]. Since the attributes can be viewed as binary relationships between concepts there are strong affinities to the entity-relationship model known from the database field as well as to conceptual graphs as discussed in [Bräuner et al. 1999]. In an informal comparison this means that the compound concept

Lack × wrt(Vitamin-D) × tmp(Winter)

corresponds to the conceptual graph in Fig. 11.

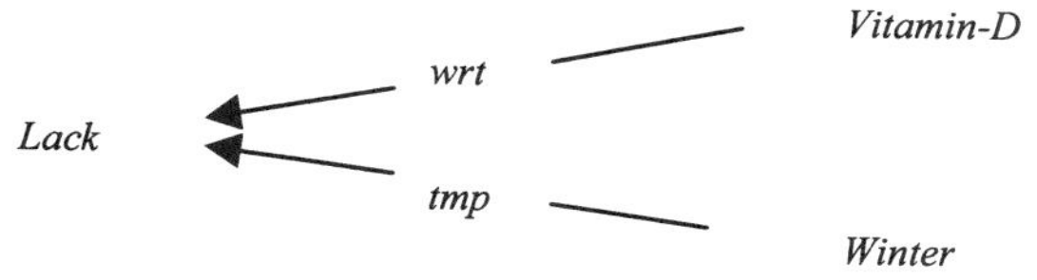

Figure 11. Conceptual graph of a compound concept

Thus in this resulting enriched ontology specification language the skeleton lattice diagrams are extended with attribute-relations in addition to the is-a relationships spanning the lattice.

3.5 Exploiting ontology for search

We now consider ways of exploiting the above-extended ontological language comprising relationships between concepts in the form of attached attributes.

In section 3.1 we considered the keyword query *Vitamin AND Lack.* This query failed within the basic skeleton ontology framework since *Vitamin×Lack=null.* Using the attribute extended ontology this sample query can be handled as follows.

1. The keyword query can be translated into ontologically acceptable terms by means of the established ontology. Thus the ontological analysis is to identify the term *Lack×wrt(Vitamin)* as connecting term (node) between lack and vitamin. An appropriate previous indexing of the text would then provide pointers from this ontological node to relevant text parts.
2. In addition to or as replacement of stating keywords a user may prefer to browse in ontology along the various relationships connecting nodes. For instance, the user finds a lack of specific vitamins situated immediately below the nodes reached with the keyword expression *vitamin* AND *lack.* From these nodes by traversing the relationships one reaches the nodes for lack of vitamins. Again appropriate indexing is to provide pointers from nodes to text sources.
3. In a more sophisticated version of this framework as addressed in the Ontoquery project [OntoQuery] the user may enter noun-phrases as queries instead of keyword expressions. Through a combined linguistic and ontological analysis the noun-phrase may be mapped into a node in the ontology. For instance, the phrase lack of vitamin may be mapped into the node *Lack×wrt(Vitamin).* The admissible attribute(s) (relations) between - in this case - lack and vitamin are to be singled out by *ontological combinability restrictions* imposed by the ontology. The text indices may be also be constructed by combined linguistic and ontological analysis of noun-phrases in the text.

4. SEARCH BASED ON FORMAL CONCEPT ANALYSIS

We now turn to an alternative principle for text search based on the so-called formal concept analysis [Ganter & Wille 1999a]. This technique also applies lattices so there is an unfortunate potential risk of confusing terminology.

The above ontologies are to be constructed manually from common sense and domain knowledge, such as the information that tomatoes are vegetables and that vitamin-C is a vitamin. This process is time-consuming and tedious for an application domain as also reported in [Embley & Campbell 1999]. By contrast the formal concept analysis establishes concept lattices automatically.

Generally speaking this technique takes as basis two sets (called object set and attribute set) and a binary relationship between the two, and constructs a so-called formal concept lattice with a concept inclusion ordering. Formal concept analysis is also based on lattice theory and an understanding of a concept as constituted by its extent (a subset of the objects) and its intent (a subset of available attributes).

Formal concept analysis has several applications in the field of conceptual information systems, data analysis, in Business IS [Ganter & Wille 1999b], document retrieval systems [Godin 1993], and in OODB field [Godin & Mili 1993], [Haav 1997].

In formal concept analysis the notions of concept, conceptual structure, and context are mathematized to become mathematical notions of formal context, formal concept, and formal concept lattice. This formal conceptualization may support human understanding of conceptual structures and may assist in the establishing of ontologies created by humans.

We now rather informally consider and explain the main notions of formal concept analysis using the previously explored nutrition application domain.

4.1 Formal concept analysis of text sources

Let us consider a set of text sources T (e.g. articles) described by a set of keywords W. The largest set of keywords W is the set of all words present in the text sources. We are interested in constructing automatically a formal concept lattice, which is to facilitate information access, and which may also assist in establishing and understanding ontologies. As objects of the analysis we choose the sentences of the text source. The attributes of an object are the keywords present in the sentence. The rationale for this choice is that the keywords used to describe a concept often appear together in sentences. For instance, the keywords vitamin and lack can be found in different text sources or in the same source but without relation to the concept of "lack of vitamin". However, if vitamin and lack are mentioned in one sentence, then probably the concept of lack is used with respect to vitamin. Recall that in the above ontology for the nutrition domain the following holds:

$$Vitamin \times Lack = null$$

By contrast in the formal concept analysis, the concepts vitamin and lack can have a common sub-concept in the lattice. Thus the lattice to be constructed in formal concept analysis from the text sources and without use of human background knowledge of the domain differs from the above-considered ontological lattices.

Now let us consider a set of sentences S from T; each sentence from S is then described by a subset of words from W used in the sentence. This is described as a binary relationship between sentences and keywords denoted by R; i.e. a relationship between the sets S and W so that $R \subseteq S \times W$.

For example, consider the following sample subset of sentences from a set of different text sources taken from nutrition domain and the binary relationship between the sentences and keywords describing the sentences. In Table 1, a reference to the text source is embedded into the sentence identifier (e.g. A*i* denotes *i*'th sentence from text source A, B*i* denotes the *i*'th sentence from B etc.). We do not show all the keywords contained in the sentences but rather we feel free to display only keywords relevant to the nutrition domain. This is in order to obtain a small sample lattice in the example.

Table 1 Description of sentence-keyword relationship

Sentence	**Keywords**
A1	{Vitamin, Vitamin-C, Vitamin-D}
A2	{Vitamin, Vitamin-C}
B1	{Vitamin, Vitamin-B, Vitamin-D}
B2	{Vitamin, Vitamin-D, Lack }
N1	{Vitamin, Lack}

Following [Ganter & Wille 1999a] a formal concept is a pair of sets *(X, Y)*, where $X \subseteq S$ and $Y \subseteq W$ with respect to sentence-keyword relationship R satisfying the following two conditions:

1. *X* is a set of sentences containing all the keywords in *Y*
2. *Y* is the set of keywords common to all the sentences in *X*

This pair of sets represents a formal concept with *extent X* and *intent Y*. Extent and intent of a formal concept determine each other and the formal concept. For example, one of the formal concepts of the context described in Table 1 is as follows:

$$\{A1, A2, B1, B2, N1\} \times \{Vitamin\},$$

where the set *{A1, A2, B1, B2, N1}* is the extent of a concept and the set *{Vitamin}* is its intent.

It is shown in [Ganter & Wille 1999a], that the two conditions given above establish a so-called Galois connection between powersets of sentences (2^S) and keywords (2^W). If we consider the set of all formal concepts *(X, Y)* derived from the relationship R (sentence-keyword relationship) and define the partial order relation on this set so that

$$X \times Y \leq X' \times Y' \text{ iff } X' \subseteq X \text{ and } Y \subseteq Y',$$

then we get the Galois lattice induced by the relationship R on $S \times W$.

Each node in this lattice is a formal concept, so the lattice is also called a formal concept lattice in [Ganter & Wille 1999a]. Construction of concept lattices is presented in [Ganter & Wille 1999a]. One of the best algorithms for computing formal concepts is found in [Ganter 1984]. The formal concept lattice corresponding to the relationships shown in table 1 is displayed in the following Fig. 12

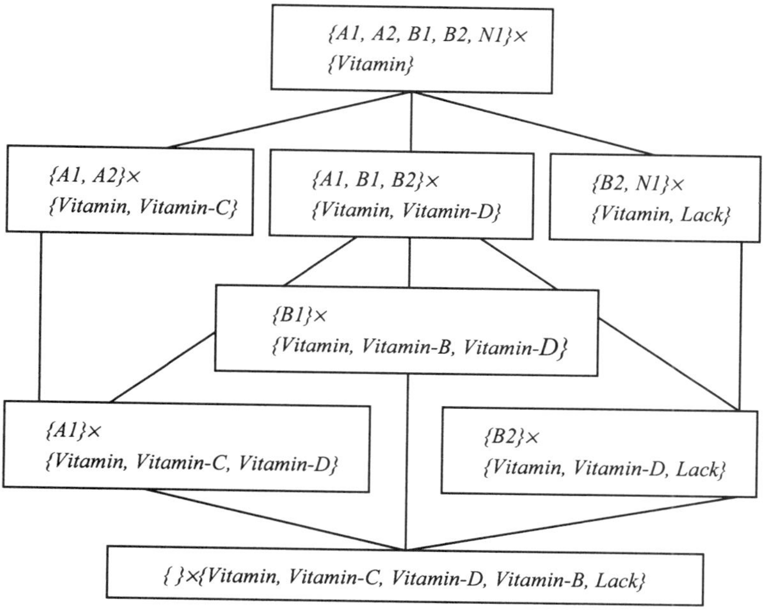

Figure 12. The formal concept lattice of the sentence-keyword relationship

Sub and super-concept relationships between the formal concepts are represented by edges in the Hasse diagram in Fig 12.

If we have two formal concepts (X_1, Y_1) and (X_2, Y_2), then (X_1, Y_1) is called a sub-concept *of* (X_2, Y_2) provided that $X_1 \subseteq X_2$, which is equivalent to $Y_2 \subseteq Y_1$. Thus, X and Y are contravariant, smaller X sets correspond to large Y sets.

In this case (X_2, Y_2) conversely is a super-concept of (X_1, Y_1) written as

$$(X_1, Y_1) \leq (X_2, Y_2),$$

where the relation $\leq$ is called hierarchical order of concepts in [Ganter&Wille 1999a].

For example,

$$\{B2, N1\} \times \{Vitamin, Lack\}$$

is a super-concept of

$$\{B2\} \times \{Vitamin, Vitamin\text{-}D, Lack\}.$$

The sub and super-concept relationship also represents inheritance of properties by concepts.

In practical applications, where the number of features per instance (number of keywords for each sentence in our case) is usually bounded, the worst case complexity of the structure (lattice) is linearly bounded with respect to the number of instances [Godin 1991]. There exists also an incremental algorithm for updating the structure by adding (removing) instances or features to existing instances [Godin 1991].

4.2 Retrieval in formal concept lattice

For a given formal concept (X, Y), the set of keywords Y appearing in a conjunctive query retrieves the set of sentences X (with accompanying context). It can be considered as the maximally specific set of sentences for sentences in X (i.e. the most general concept described by the keywords Y).

Let us reconsider the keyword query *Vitamin AND Lack*. Referring to Fig. 12 this query retrieves a set of sentences *{B2, N1}* as a maximally specific set of sentences matching the query. These sentences in turn identify the two text sources B and N containing these sentences.

An alternative to keyword-based search retrieval is browsing in the formal concept lattice. Following an edge downward corresponds to minimal refinement (specialization) of the relevant query. Conversely, following an edge upward corresponds to a minimal generalization. The structure of the formal concept lattice makes it possible to combine these two retrieval approaches.

For instance, having retrieved a concept *{B2, N1}×{Vitamin, Lack}* one can refine the search by moving down in the lattice to the node representing formal concept *{B2}×{Vitamin, Vitamin-D, Lack}*. The set of retrieved text sources is smaller - now containing only one source, *B*.

5. CONCLUSION

We have considered two methods for obtaining concept-based access to text sources. The notion of lattice is fundamental to both of these methods. In the conceptual model based method of section 3 ontology is to be specified as a lattice by a human possessing understanding of the target domain. By contrast in the formal concept analysis of section 4 a concept lattice is constructed algorithmically by analysis of the text sources.

The resulting lattices differ in that the ontological approach encodes commonsense relationships between concepts, which cannot be captured in general in the formal concept analysis. On the other hand, the ontological approach requires that the target domain is small and well structured, whereas formal concept analysis is applicable for large loosely structured domains. An interesting idea is to use the formal concept analysis as auxiliary tool for the ontologist in the construction of domain ontology.

We plan to carry out experimental comparison of these approaches in the OntoQuery project.

ACKNOWLEDGEMENTS

The first author of this paper is grateful to Estonian Research Foundation for supporting this work by the Grant no 2772. The Ontoquery project is supported by a grant from the Danish Research Councils.

REFERENCES

[Bräuner et al., 1999] T. Bräuner, J. Fischer Nilsson, and A. Rasmussen: Conceptual Graphs as Algebras -- with an Application to Analogical Reasoning, in Proceedings of the 7th Int. Conf. on Conceptual Structures, Blacksburg, Virginia, July 1999, W. Tepfenhart and W. Cyre (eds.), *Lecture Notes in Artificial Intelligence LNAI 1640*, Springer, 1999.

[Brink et al. 1994] C. Brink, K. Britz, and R.A. Schmidt: Peirce Algebras, *Formal Aspects of Computing*, Vol. 6, 1994, pp. 339-358.

[Cook 1992] W. R. Cook, Interfaces and Specifications for the Smalltalk-80 Collection Classes, *Proc. of OOPSLA'92*, ACM Press, 1992, pp. 1-15.

[Davey & Priestley 1990] Davey, and B. A., Priestley, H. A., *Introduction to Lattices and Order*, Cambridge University Press, 1990.

[Embley & Campbell 1999] D.W. Embley, D.M. Campbell, Y.S. Jiang, S.W. Liddle, D.W. Lonsdale, Y.-K. Ng, R.D. Smith: Conceptual-model-based data extraction from multiple-record Web pages, *Data & Knowledge Engineering*, 31 (1999), pp. 227-251.

[Ganter 1984] B. Ganter, Two Basic Algorithms in Concept Analysis (Preprint 831), Darmstadt: Technische Hochschule, 1984

[Ganter & Wille 1999a] B. Ganter and R. Wille, *Formal Concept Analysis, Mathematical Foundations*, Springer, 1999.

[Ganter & Wille 1999b] B. Ganter and R. Wille, Contextual Attribute Logic, in Proceedings of the 7th Int. Conf. on Conceptual Structures, Blacksburg, Virginia, July 1999, W. Tepfenhart and W. Cyre (eds.), *Lecture Notes in Artificial Intelligence LNAI 1640*, Springer, 1999.

[Godin 1993] R. Godin, R. Missaoui and A. April, Experimental comparison of navigation in a Galois lattice with conventional information retrieval methods, *Int. J. Man-Machine Studies*, 1993, (38) pp. 747-767.

[Godin 1991] R. Godin, R. Missaoui and H. Alaoui, Learning Algorithms Using a Galois Lattice Structure, *Proc. of the Third Int. Conference on Tools for Artificial Intelligence*, IEEE Computer Society Press, CA, 1991, pp. 22-29.

[Godin & Mili 1993] R. Godin and H. Mili, Building and Maintaining Analysis-Level Class Hierarchies Using Galois Lattices, *Proc. of OOPSLA'93*, ACM Press, 1993, pp. 395-410.

[Haav 1997] H-M. Haav, An Object Classifier Based on Galois Approach: H. Kangassalo, J. F. Nilsson, H. Jaakkola, S. Ohsuga, *Information Modelling and Knowledge Bases VIII*, IOS Press, 1997, pp. 309-321.

[Larsen & Nilsson, 1997] H. L. Larsen and J. F. Nilsson, Fuzzy Querying in a Concept Object Algebraic Datamodel, in:T. Andreasen, H. Christiansen, H. L. Larsen (Eds), *Flexible Query Answering Systems*, Kluwer Academic Publishers, 1997, pp. 123-140.

[Nilsson 1994] J. F. Nilsson, An Algebraic Logic for Concept Structures, *Information Modelling and Knowledge Bases V*, IOS Press, Amsterdam, 1994, pp. 75-84.

[Nilsson 1999] J. Fischer Nilsson, A Conceptual Space Logic, 1999, in E. Kawaguchi et al. (eds.): *Information Modeling and Knowledge Bases XI*, IOS Press, Amsterdam, 2000.

[Nilsson & Haav 1999] J. F. Nilsson and H-M. Haav, Inducing Queries from Examples as Concept Formation, *Information Modelling and Knowledge Bases X*, H. Jaakkola et al. (eds), IOS Press, 1999.

[OntoQuery] OntoQuery Project, www.ontoquery.dk

[Sowa 2000] J.F. Sowa, *Knowledge Representation, Logical, Philosophical, and Computational Foundations*, Brooks/Cole Thomson Learning, 2000.

Chapter 5

HYBRID METHODOLOGY OF KNOWLEDGE DISCOVERY FOR BUSINESS INFORMATION

Zdzisław S. Hippe
Rzeszow University of Technology
E-mail: zshippe@prz.rzeszow.pl

Keywords: data mining, knowledge discovery, hybrid methodology, virtual visualisation

Abstract: Recently, some machine learning methods are applied to find regularities and chunks of knowledge hidden in data. It is proven that combined (hybrid) application of various machine learning algorithms may supply more profound understanding of the investigated processes or phenomena. This is particularly true for various branches of business, like banking and finance, retail and marketing, management and logistics. In this chapter different ways of knowledge discovery (aimed at finding the quasi-optimal learning model) and its basic steps are dealt with. Then, a short background for three fundamental approaches of data mining (classification studies, clustering studies and visualization studies) is given, assigning particular attention to problem of visualization of multidimensional data (further called *virtual visualization).* In the last part of the text, using a set of business data extracted from a large anonymous database, various machine learning algorithms are used to exemplify hybrid (combined) extraction of useful knowledge.

1. INTRODUCTION

Under increasing competitive pressure many corporations and enterprises are forced to rethink about the ongoing decision-making procedures, or management method used. Thus, we are unavoidably interested in rationalisation of the decisive processes. There are now some information technologies available that can help all these things and can support, through innovative use, various areas of business, and can improve effectiveness of management, logistics, or enhancing the flow of information. One of these technologies, having currently enormous impact on various types of business activities, is data mining and knowledge discovery. Data mining is the process of automating information discovery, allowing elucidation of knowledge structures hidden in data. According to some sources [Wong, 1998] the discovery process is much more profound, and may flow from data to wisdom (see Figure 1).

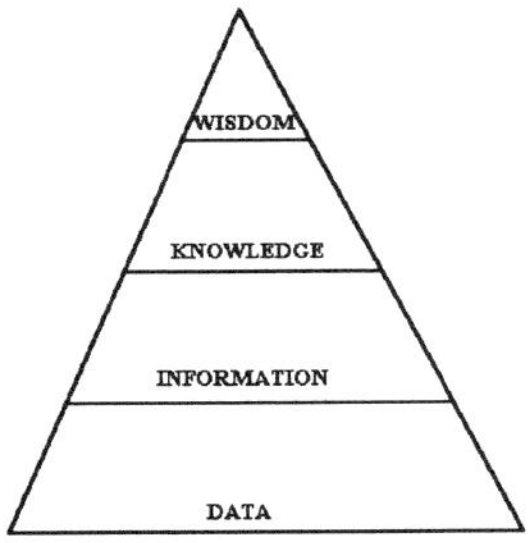

Figure 1. The data ⇒ wisdom triangle

Central to data mining is the process of model building using existing data, or - in other words - the process of advancing from data to knowledge. Yet this knowledge is implicit in data, therefore it must be mined and expressed in a concise, useful form of decision trees, rules, simulated neural networks, statistical patterns, equations, conceptual hierarchies, or other forms of knowledge representation. The final result of the passage from data to knowledge should display distinct features of a common sense. Learning model created in this way may enable to get deeper insight into trends, patterns and/or correlation, usually not recognizable by simple statistical methods.

The process of extracting knowledge from data, treated usually in the literature as discovery of regularities in data, stepwise became an essential goal of machine learning. Despite the diversity of scientific domains that machine learning and discovery systems treat, there are many distinct similarities in representations of models, in problem-solving methods and heuristics used in model construction (for a profound discussion of these similarities, see [Valdez-Perez et all, 1993]. Basing on actual trends of information science, it may be assumed that discovery systems for mining large databases would play an important role also in business and economy. These mutually and tightly connected disciplines, in foreseeable future, will be faced with necessity to search large databases that encompass gigabytes or even terabytes of information. This is particularly valid for extraction of knowledge from such sources, as: records of financial operations in banks, collected on daily basis; real-time repository protocols in chains of big stores and shopping centers; social and urban data, etc.

The purpose of this paper is to show how selected approaches of machine learning used for extracting regularities from data, can be applied *together* in a hybrid form. This idea uses the observation flowing from the basic paradigm of data mining and machine learning: we should use various data mining and/or knowledge discovery methods (computer program tools) to develop different learning models, and then make collective (hybrid) interpretation of their suitability for solving of the investigated problem. From among various data mining methods touched in the paper, particular attention will be paid to advanced visualization (further called *virtual visualization*) of the database content. As a working example, a case of application for credit loan[1] has been selected. Simplicity of the example allows for easy tracing of possibilities and inherent limitations of the approach.

2. PRESENT STATUS OF DATA MINING

Advances in data mining, gained within last decade, are based on development and implementation of some innovative techniques, in the first line of a new approach to decision trees technology [Quinlan, 1993], Bayesian belief networks [Charniak, 1991; Druzdzel et all, 1998], influence diagrams [Ramoni and Sebastiani, 1998], simulated neural networks [Zurada et all, 1996], genetic algorithms and evolutionary programming [Michalewicz, 1996], or the networked agent-based methodology [Groth, 1998]. Detailed treatment of these techniques is given elsewhere [Fayyad et all, 1996; Michalski et all, 1998]; here it should be emphasized that in close relation to mining knowledge from data are some tasks of machine learning, particularly **(i)** concept learning from examples, and **(ii)** conceptual clustering.

Learning from examples is directly related to searching for regularities in data. The database contains in that case a collection of examples (records) described by means of arbitrary number of attributes (or features). These attributes display values indicating for each example whether it belongs to a given class or not, that is, whether it is an example or counterexample (binary classification is here regarded, however, there are no distinct difficulties with treatment of multi-category data). Usually, examples used for learning create vectors, labeled with the class-membership. The target class itself may readily be an action, a decision, an object, a phenomenon, or a process, etc. The learning model developed conveys the best definition of the target class. This definition may be viewed here as a special case of regularity; it may then be applied to predict the

[1] A set of business data extracted from a large anonymous database

class-membership of an unseen object. However, all other regularities that may be present in the data, are not considered and exploited.

Conceptual clustering is an another field of machine learning related to discovering knowledge from data. The task here is somewhat more open: for a given database conceptual clustering seeks to divide all examples into classes, which display the highest intraclass similarity, and simultaneously the highest interclass dissimilarity, with defining general description of each class. Therefore, the task is clearly different from regularity detection. A regularity does not separate existing examples (records) in a base into classes, but it specifies a model obeyed by all (or roughly all) examples, applied later in classification of unseen cases. We may say that this learning (and data mining) method is similar to traditional cluster analysis [Michalski et all, 1998], but is defined in a different way. Let us given a set of attributional descriptions of some entities (say, a vector in the typical decision table), a description language for characterizing classes of such entities, and a classification quality criterion. The problem is to partition entities into classes of business problems (in a way that maximizes the classification quality criterion) and simultaneously to determine extensional description of these classes in the given description language. Thus, a conceptual clustering method seeks not only a classification structure of entities (a dendrogram), but also a symbolic description of the proposed clusters (classes). It should be noted that a conventional clustering method typically determines clusters on the basis of a similarity measure, defined as a multidimensional distance between the entities being compared. In contrast, a conceptual clustering algorithm clusters entities on the basis of a *conceptual cohesiveness*. It is a function of not only properties of the clustered entities, but also of two other factors: the *description language,* L, used to describe the classes of entities, and the *environment*, E, which is the set of neighboring examples. Hence, two objects may be similar, i.e. close according to some distance (or similarity) measure, while having a low conceptual esiveness, or vice versa (see Figure 2).

Figure 2. Difference between closeness and conceptual cohesiveness. The points **1** and **2** are "close" to each other therefore they would be placed into the same cluster by any technique based solely upon the distances between them. However, these points have small conceptual cohesiveness due to the fact that they belong to two different concepts: the letter **R** and the letter **S**.

Let us now focus the attention on inductive learning from examples, as one of basic methods of knowledge acquisition from databases. The key concern of this intricate process is to discover knowledge structures hidden in the data, and to present them in a proper form, say decision trees, or production rules.

There are many inductive learning methods proposed to automatize the knowledge acquisition process. These methods may be tentatively assigned to **(i)** divide-and-conquer methods, and **(ii)** covering methods.

Divide-and-conquer methods received considerable attention due to pioneering work by J. Ross Quinlan, summarized recently [Quinlan, 1993]. His first algorithm, commonly known as **ID3**, constructs a decision tree for classification of objects (abstractions, notions, patterns, etc.) in a given set of examples, called frequently a training set. Nodes of the construed tree are selected according to entropy of information, associated with a given attribute of objects. The use of entropy of information measure provides a convenient and effective way to construct decision trees, although in some instances the decision trees might not be very general, and/or may contain irrelevant conditions. Additionally, the inherent feature of the **ID3** algorithm forces to break up a large collection of data into subsets (divide-and-conquer!). In consequence, the algorithm not always yields the same decision tree as would be obtained for the complete training set. **ID3** is also sensitive to sequence of attributes used for the description of cases in the training set. The original algorithm has been improved several times by a number of researchers, leading to **ID4** and **ID5** [Piatetsky-Shapiro and Frawley, 1992], and finally has been converted by Quinlan himself to **C4.5** – a package of utility programs for machine learning. The **C4.5** is able to generate optimum decision tree for a given set of cases, and to convert it into a set of production rules.

Searching databases with algorithms based on *covering methods* yields the classification model(s) representing disjunctive logical expressions, describing each class. Hence, covering algorithm searches for a set of possible generalizations attempting to find correct hypotheses that satisfy selected boundary conditions. The search proceeds from partially ordered (according to class membership) training set; it tries to find all possible criteria describing selected class of objects. If the working hypotheses satisfy certain criteria, the search is terminated. Otherwise, the current hypotheses are slightly modified (generalization, or specialization of rules), and tested, if they satisfy the termination criteria. Covering algorithm developed initially by R.S. Michalski in 1969, was from that time distinctly improved.

Before we head off into the next paragraph, it seems reasonable to give at least a touch of some other approaches to find regularities within the same kind of data. One way to carry out this task is to recall a similar case whose class is known, and to assume that the new (unseen) case will have the same class membership. This philosophy supports instance-based reasoning, which classifies unknown cases by referring to similar remembered cases. Central issues in instance-based systems are: Which training cases should be remembered? (If all cases will be retained, the classifier can become ineffective and slow); How can the similarity of cases be measured? (For continuous attributes we can compute the distance between two cases, however, when attributes are mixed (numeric with symbolic) the interpretation of such distance becomes more problematic.

Also, learning using neural networks and genetic algorithms may be used for searching regularities in data, but even the shortest explanation of these approaches is far beyond the scope of this chapter.

Before we proceed to discuss basic steps of the data mining process, let us explain the difference between query tools (which allow end users to ask questions oriented towards database management system), and data mining tools. Query tools allow finding out new and interesting facts from the data stored in a database. However, creating a query for the database management system (like, for example a question "*What is the number of cars sold in the South-East versus the North-West?*"), we are making an assumption that the sales volumes of cars are affected by regional market dynamics. On the other side, a data mining study tackles much broader goal – instead assuming the link between regional location and sales volumes – it is trying to determine the most significant factors involved, doing it without any assumption. Following the example discussed data mining tries additionally to discover relationships and hidden patterns that may not always be obvious.

2.1 Data mining process and its basic steps

Regardless of the methodology used, the data mining process consists generally of five distinct steps:

(i) ***Data manipulation,***
(ii) ***Defining a study,***
(iii) ***Building a model,***
(iv) ***Understanding a model,*** and
(v) ***Prediction***

The first step, **(i)**, may be considered as a process of data preparation for mining. We may employ here such operations as data cleaning, e.g. making various names of an object consistent (for example, *Pepsi Cola* vs. *Pepsi*), removing typographical errors, filling of missing values, making data derivation, and data merging. The second **(ii)** step, always under control of the decision-maker, is devoted to specification of a goal of the data mining process. This goal may be different depending whether the data mining relies on supervised or unsupervised learning. Building a model (step **(iii)**) is the main task of data mining process; the learning model developed should not only embody relations among particular variables, it additionally explains the meaning of weights, conjunctions, and differentiation of important variables, and their combinations. Step **(iv)** (understanding a model) is connected with verification and validation of the developed learning model, whereas the last step **(v)** serves for classification of unseen cases and for prediction the behavior of the investigated object in a new, unknown situation(s).

2.2 Common features of data mining algorithms

There are three fundamental approaches applied in data mining algorithms:

- ***Classification studies (supervised learning),***
- ***Clustering studies (unsupervised learning),*** and
- ***Visualization studies.***

Notions *supervised learning* and *unsupervised learning* do not need special explanation; they are widely addressed in many books, for example in [Winston, 1992]. Additionally, both approaches have been briefly discussed in the introductory part of this paragraph. However, the idea of application of advanced visualization tools in profound application of data mining, although intuitive, needs some substantiation. For this reason, this approach will be briefly discussed in the next section.

2.3 Visualization studies in data mining

Current status of research in the field stated strongly supports the idea that visualization would play more and more important role in professional data mining. The essence of data mining yet is the process of creating a model that makes complex data more understandable. But some pictures often represent data better than reports or numbers; therefore data visualization – especially in business – is clearly a powerful way of data mining. But then starting the discussion it seems necessary to emphasize that the term ***visualization*** is understood here in a profound sense, well *beyond* the simple graphical representation of data mining results in such forms as curves, diagrams, pie-charts, schemes, etc. In many domains data can be best perceived by showing boundaries, outliers, exemptions, decision trees, and/or by presenting some specific features of mined structures in the form of **3D**-view, well understandable for a human being. Therefore, in the research devoted to this problem, a **V**irtual **V**isualization **T**ools (**VVT***1* for supervised learning and **VVT***2* for unsupervised learning), elaborated recently in our group [Mazur, 1999], were used to *disclose the spatial distribution* of raw experimental data. As visualization engine, the **SAHN**-procedures (**SAHN** – **S**equential, **A**gglomerative, **H**ierarchical, and **N**on-overlapping) were used with the aim to get better insight into data being mined, and then to apply the developed model in classification of unseen cases.

Fundamentals of the **SAHN** methods have been described elsewhere [Hippe, 1998]; the **VVT*n*** modules extensively use the generalized Lance-Williams recursive formula [Lance and Williams, 1966] with some improvements done recently, allowing for controlled transformation of data – usually located within a multidimensional solution space – into **3D**-data. Generally, the following **SAHN**-procedures were applied: *Single Linkage Method* (**SLM**), *Group Average Method* (**GAM**), *Weighted Average Method* (**WAM**), *Complete Linkage Method* (**CLM**), *Unweighted Centroid Method* (**UCM**), *Weighted Centroid Method* (**WCM**), *Minimum Variance Method* (**MVM**), and *Flexible SAHN Strategy* (**FSS**), with various metrics to calculate distances in the similarity matrix (Euclidean, City Block and Tshebyshev's). Basic equation and respective coefficients, used by internal **SAHN**-algorithms in **VVT*n*** modules, are presented in Table 1.

3. Experiments with mining regularities from data

In this section a set of business data, extracted from a large anonymous database, is exploited to disclose some hidden regularities. The following tools were used: **(i)** an algorithm constructing decision trees (**ID3**), **(ii)** two algorithms that directly induce production rules (**LERS** [Grzymala-Busse et all, 1993], and **GTS** [Hippe, 1997]), **(iii)** simulated neural nets, and **(iv)** two visualization modules (**VVT*1*** **&** **VVT*2***). It may be stated that results presented here, derived from own research, illustrate development of learning models by supervised and unsupervised machine learning, augmented by visualization studies.

The following training set was used as a benchmark for evaluation of the mentioned types of knowledge discovery algorithms:

	Credit_rating	Experience_at_job	Salary	Real_estate_owner	I	LOAN
1	excellent	low	medium	yes	I	accepted
2	excellent	low	medium	no	I	accepted
3	excellent	low	low	yes	I	denied
4	good	high	high	yes	I	accepted
5	good	very_high	low	no	I	denied
6	good	moderate	medium	no	I	denied
7	poor	low	medium	no	I	denied

Figure 3. Fragment of the database used in the research.

Table 1. Basic SAHN-formula and coefficients used in various specific algorithms of clustering

$$d(s_a,s_k) = \alpha_i d(s_i,s_k) + \alpha_j d(s_k,s_k) + \beta d(s_i,s_j) + \gamma \left| d(s_i,s_k) - d(s_j,s_k) \right|$$

Here:

$d(.,.)$	denotes distance (similarity) between two clusters,
s_i, s_j, s_k	denote clusters i, j, k,
s_a	denotes a new agglomerated cluster obtained by combining clusters s_i and s_j,
$\alpha_i, \alpha_j, \beta, \gamma$	denote parameters describing clustering methods

No	**Way of clustering**	α_i	α_j	β	γ
1	Single **L**inkage **M**ethod	0.5	0.5	0.0	- 0.5
2	Group **A**verage **M**ethod	0.5	0.5	0.0	0.0
3	Weighted **A**verage **M**ethod	$n_i/(n_i + n_j)$	$n_j/(n_i + n_j)$	0.0	0.0
4	Complete **L**inkage **M**ethod	0.5	0.5	0.0	0.5
5	Unweighted **C**entroid **M**ethod	0.5	0.5	-0.25	0.0
6	Weighted **C**entroid **M**ethod	$n_i/(n_i + n_j)$	$n_j/(n_i + n_j)$	$-n_i n_j/(n_i + n_j)^2$	0.0
7	**M**inimum **V**ariance **M**ethod	$(n_i + n_k)/(n_i + n_j + n_k)$	$(n_j + n_k)/ /(n_i + n_j + n_k)$	$-n_k/(n_i + nj + n_k)$	0.0
8	Flexible **SAHN** Strategy	(1 -ß)/2	(1 - ß)/2	< 1	0.0

This problem is based on four descriptive attributes that are the outcomes of an interview (managed by a bank representative) with a candidate for a credit loan. Each attribute has own domain of values; all of them (for simplicity) are symbolic. The decision of the bank representative is binary: the loan application is either accepted or denied. Actually, data contained in this training set are a very small part of an extended database, collecting records from credit line operations in an anonymous bank, gathered over a larger period of time.

The following questions are associated with the attributes that cover cases in the training set (allowed values of respective attributes are given in parentheses):

* What is your current credit history?
  [*excellent, good, poor*]

* What is your experience in fulfilling current position?
  [*low, moderate, high, very_high*]

* How do you estimate your monthly salary?
  [*low, medium, high*]

* Are you the owner of real estate, like private house or apartment?
  [*yes, no*]

3.1 Decision tree model

The decision tree developed by **ID3** for the working example is shown in Figure 4. Efficiency of a decision tree developed for the identifications of a set of alternatives **X** = {x1, x2, x3, ... , xN}, may be evaluated by calculation of the mean number of questions, **E(S)**, required to classify all elements of

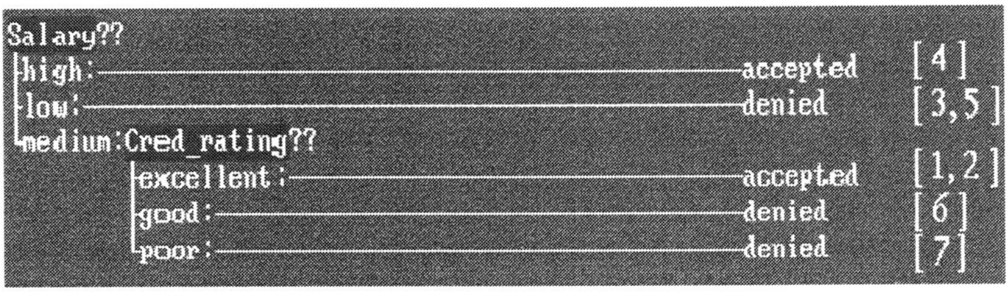

Figure 4. Decision tree (apparently optimal) developed by **ID3** for the mined data (identifiers of examples from the data set are given in brackets).

the set **X** [Hippe, 1991]. The mean number of questions, S_k, in the tree constituting the learning model, may be defined as:

(1) $$E(S_K) = \sum S_K(X_i) \cdot P_i$$

Here: $S_K(X_i)$ - is the number of questions that must be issued to identify the alternative X_i, and
P_i - denotes the probability of occurrence of the alternative X_i.

Evaluation the quality (goodness?) of a decision tree may be based on a lemma that for any learning model **S** holds the inequality:

(2) $$E(S_k) \geq H(X)$$

where **H(X)** is the entropy of information, calculated from the equation:

(3) $$H(X) = -\sum P_i \cdot \log_2 P_i$$

At this very moment, an important question should be issued: for which sets **X**, and for which learning models S_k, inequality (2) is valid? Putting it in a different way, we are interested in the problem whether for a given set of alternatives there exists such a learning model (here a decision tree) which satisfies the general equality $E(S) = H(X)$. Helpful here is a theorem stating that if the learning model S_k identifying elements of the set **X**, meeting the mentioned equality is to exist, it is necessary and sufficient that for every i = 1, 2, ... , N, $\log_2 p_i$ be an integer. This implies that only some sets of alternatives have absolutely the best (i.e. that $E(S) = H(X)$ learning model. All remaining sets of alternatives obey a rule that there always exists a learning model in which the average number of questions differs from **H(X)** by not more than one, i.e.

(4) $$H(X) \leq E(S_k) \leq H(X) + 1$$

Simple calculation, not included here, has proven the learning model (decision tree) developed for the investigated data is optimal, or – at least – *quasi*-optimal; additionally it i very compact.

3.2 Decision rules models

Learning models developed by **GTS** and **LERS**, working directly on mined data, contain in both cases sets with five rules (see Figure 5a,b). It was found, that generated sets of decision rules classify errorless all working examples. However, neither **GTS**-rules nor **LERS**-rules come out clearly from pathways (nodes and branches) of the very concise decision tree (Figure 4) based on two attributes only. It should be emphasized, that **GTS** develops decision rules using one additional attribute (<Exp_at_job>), whereas **LERS** uses also the same three attributes (<Salary>, <Cred_rating>, <Exp_at_job>), and one additional – the <Real_estate>).

(a)

RULE 1
IF Cred_rating **IS** excellent
AND Salary **IS** medium
THEN LOAN **IS** accepted

RULE 2
IF Salary **IS** low)
THEN LOAN **IS** denied

RULE 3
IF Exp_at_job **IS** high
THEN LOAN **IS** accepted

RULE 4
IF Exp_at_job **IS** moderate
THEN LOAN **IS** denied

RULE 5
IF Cred_rating **IS** poor
THEN LOAN **IS** denied

(b)

1. (cred_rating,excellent) & (salary,medium) → (loan,accepted

2. (exp_at_job,high) → (loan,accepted)

3. (real_estate,no) & (cred_rating,good) → (loan,denied)

4. (cred_rating,poor → (loan,denied

5. (salary,low) → (loan,denied)

Figure 5. Sets of decision rules developed by **GTS** (*a*) and **LERS** (*b*). Rules (*a*) are developed using keywords (in bold) from the **KKL** (**K**nowledgebase **K**ernel **L**anguage), rules (*b*) are typical production rules written in specific **LERS**-format.

3.3 Neural networks model

In a series of separate experiments, a network was found that directly supports the observation made *via* the decision tree model. Namely, among various networks designed, that one shown in Fig. 6a,b, trained using *Conjugate Gradient Descent algorithm* [Bishop, 1995], is based on the same two input attributes employed in the decision tree model (<Cred_rating>, and

<Salary>). This network displayed very high performance in identification of unseen examples.

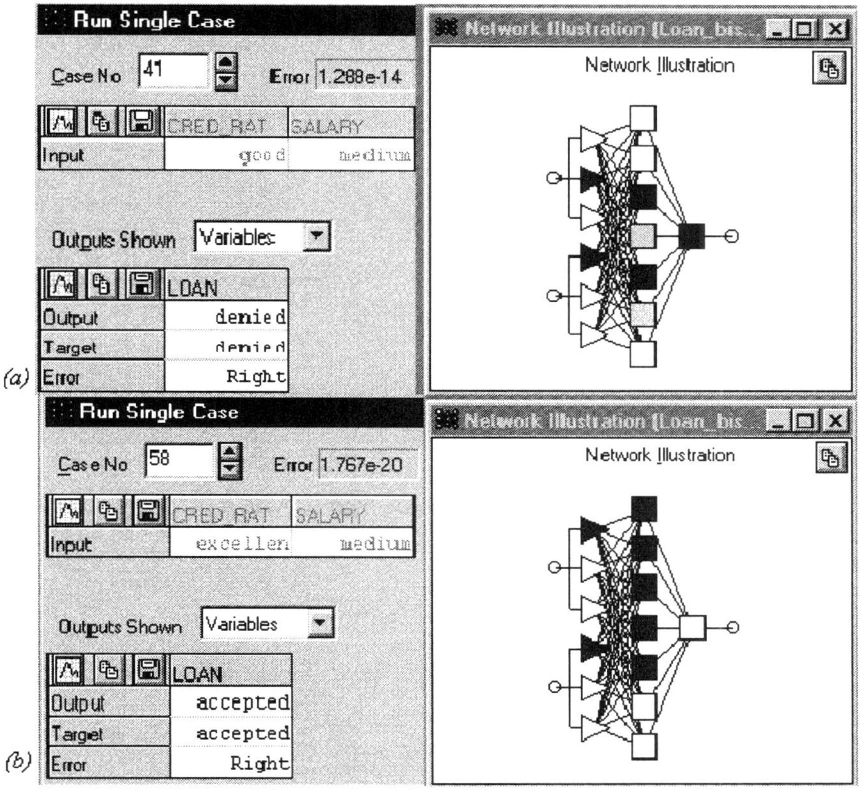

Figure 6. Neural network developed explains well knowledge structures hidden in mined data. Here, two unseen cases were run successfully: **(a)** negative case (LOAN denied), and **(b)** positive case (LOAN accepted). Input, hidden, and output neurons are shown together with states of their activation.

3.4 Visualization model

In order to visualize the spatial distribution of data mined, the initial training set was modified by controlled conversion of symbolic values of the decisive variable ("LOAN") into numeric values (i.e. "*Accepted*" was converted to '**1**', and "*Denied*" to '**-1**'). The cases from the data set, converted automatically, were correctly split into two clusters (#**1** and #**2**, Fig. 7), what is in consistence with the binary status of the decisive attribute. Spatial location of clusters, showing very fine separation, may be achieved by proper selection of eigenvectors along **X,Y,Z** axes, and rotation of displayed objects. It seems necessary to stress, that separation of clusters was based on supervised learning, however, using in further research the**VVT2** module, unsupervised data mining was executed.

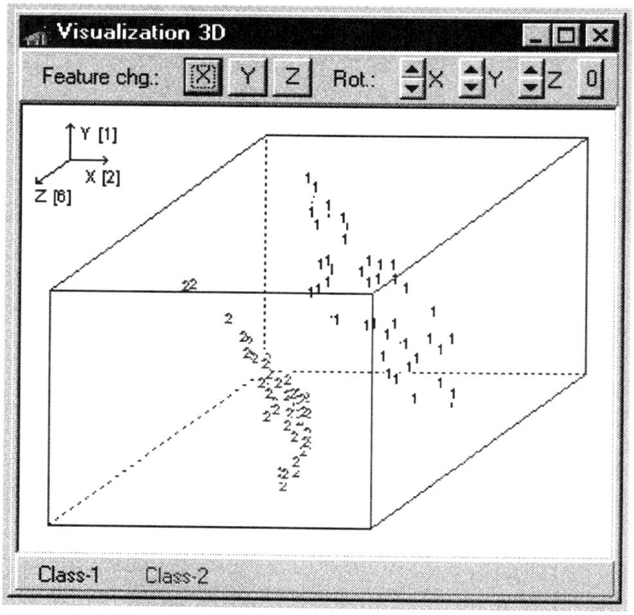

Figure 7. Spatial separation of data (supervised Learning): cluster #1 represents "LOAN *accepted*", cluster #2 – "LOAN *denied*"

Numerous tests along these lines, with carefully selected "unseen" cases, have proven that this new visualization technique may be used with high reliability (especially in the *prediction step*) in mining data for business information. One of selected examples of unseen cases (being well outside of the training set) is referred to in Fig. 8. As in other cases tested, unanimous decision may be arrived whether or not a given unseen case, representing unknown applicant, may be identified as good or bad credit risk.

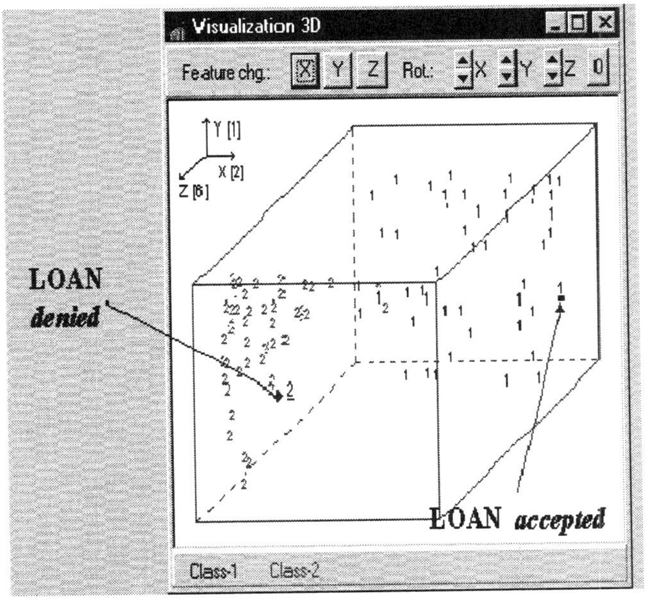

Figure 8. Location of two unseen cases (initially represented by five-dimensional vectors) in **3D**-space. This representation allows to assign correctly class-membership of an investigated example.

4. DISCUSSION

The research performed provide the conclusion, that classification of unseen cases (with values well outside the bounds settled in the data set) may be executed with confidence using the elaborated **SAHN**-visualization methodology. The following approach for mining a visual model from data may be suggested: any of **SAHN**-procedures may be used for ***supervised learning***, whereas for ***unsupervised learning*** - the best results are obtained with **CLM**, **WCM**, and **FSS** procedures. The visual model generated from data may readily be applied to overcome basic restrictions met while working with other mining strategies, especially when learning model was developed using the decision rules format. These restrictions clearly come out from the inherent properties of decision rules themselves. In one respect, decision rules contain chunks of explicit knowledge mined from data: this knowledge usually is obvious, easy to perceive and to understand. On the other hand, however, decision rules cast serious "rigidity" over the reasoning process. This phenomenon relies on hindering or even complete blocking the data mining process, especially if attributes describing unseen objects are discrete. The main cause of the discussed finding is that reasoning, using data mining model relied on decision rules is directly dependent on what is known as the "exact match". It means that a new, unseen case with properties selected at random can be correctly classified if, and only if, exactly the same case is contained in the data set. But this situation is of very low probability, especially when objects are described by many attributes representing such fuzzy properties as those met in business data.

Advanced visualization techniques (beyond the trivial graphical presentation of data) are of paramount importance for knowledge discovery process. Additionally, these techniques supported by hybrid methodology (i.e. critical comparison and evaluation of various learning models developed for the investigated data), allow to get in many cases better insight into the data mined. This conclusion may be treated as an additional argument for the well known paradigm of machine learning and artificial intelligence: *we should use different learning methods for development various learning models, and then use **all** of them in the interpretation of knowledge discovery results.*.

ACKNOWLEDGMENTS

Preparation of this paper was possible owing to excellent job done by my co-workers: Dr. hab. B. Dębska, and MSc. M. Mazur

REFERENCES

[Bishop, 1995] Bishop C.: ***Neural Networks for Pattern Recognition***. Oxford University Press, Oxford 1995.

[Charniak, 1991] Charniak E.: ***Bayesian networks without tears.*** AI Magazine **1991(12,** No. 4) **50-63.**

[Druzdzel et all, 1998] Druzdzel M.J., Onisko A., Wasyluk H.: ***A probabilistic model for diagnosis of liver disorders.*** In: Klopotek M.A., Michalewicz M., Raś Z.W. (Eds.) *Intelligent Information Systems*, IPIPAN Edit. Office, Warsaw 1998, pp. 379-387.

[Fayyad et all, 1996] Fayyad U.M., Piatesky-Shapiro G., Smyth D., Uthurusamy R.: ***Advances in Knowledge Discovery and Data Mining.*** AAAI Press/MIT Press, Cambridge 1996.

[Groth, 1998] Groth R.: ***Data Mining. A Hands-On Approach for Business Profesionals.*** Prentice Hall PTR, Upper Saddle River 1998.

[Grzymala-Busse et all., 1993] Grzymala-Busse J.W., Chmielewski M.R., Peterson N.W., Than S.: ***The Rule Induction System LERS – A Version for Personal Computers.*** Foundations Comp. and Decision Sci. **1993(18,** No. 3-4) **181-211.**

[Hippe, 1991] Hippe Z.S.: ***Artificial Intelligence in Chemistry: Structure Elucidation and Simulation of Organic Reactions.*** Elsevier, Amsterdam 1991.

[Hippe, 1997] Hippe Z.S.: ***Machine Learning - A Promising Strategy for Business Information Processing?.*** In: Abramowicz W. (Ed.) *Business Information Systems*, Academy of Economy Edit. Office, Poznań 1997, pp. 603-622.

[Hippe, 1998] Hippe Z.S.: ***New Data Mining Strategy Combining SAHN Visualization and Case-Based Reasoning.*** Proc. Joint Conference on Information Sciences (JCIS'98), Research Triangle Park (NC), 23-29 October 1998, Vol. II, pp. 320-322.

[Lance and Willians, 1966] Lance G.N., Williams N.T.: ***A Generalized Sorting Strategy for Computer Applications.*** Nature **1966(1)212-218.**

[Mazur, 1999] Mazur M.: ***Virtual Visualization Tool.*** In: Res. Report 8T11C 004 09, Department of Computer Chemistry, Rzeszów University of Technology, Rzeszów 1999.

[Michalewicz, 1996] Michalewicz Z.: ***Genetic Algorithms + Data Sructures = Evolution Programs.*** Springer Verlag, Heidelberg 1996.

[Michalski et all., 1998] Michalski R.S., Bratko I., Kubat M.: ***Machine Learning and Data Mining: Methods and Applications.*** J. Wiley & Sons Ltd., Chichester 1998.

[Piatetsky-Shapiro and Frawley, 1992] Piatetski-Shapiro G. and Frawley W. (Eds.): ***Knowledge Discovery in Databases.*** AAAI-Press, Menlo Park 1992.

[Quinlan, 1993] Quinlan J.R.: *C4.5:* ***Programs for Machine Learning.*** Morgan Kaufmann Publishers, San Mateo 1993.

[Ramoni and Sebastiani, 1998] Ramoni M., Sebastiani P.: ***Bayesian Knowledge Discoverer, Ver. 1.0 for MSWindows95/NT.*** KMi, The Open University, Milton Keynes, UK.

[Valdez-Perez et all., 1993] Valdez-Perez R.E., Zytkow J.M., Simon H.A.: ***Scientific model building as a search in matrix spaces.*** Proc. 11th Nat. Conference on Artificial Intelligence. AAAI-Press, Meblo Park (CA) 1993, pp. 472-478.

[Winston, 1992] Winston P.H.: ***Artificial Intelligence.*** Addison-Wesley Publishing Company, Reading 1992.

[Wong, 1998] Wong A.K.C.: *private information.*

[Zurada at all, 1996] Żurada J., Barski M., Jędruch W.: ***Artificial Neural Networks.*** Polish Scientific Publishers, Warsaw 1996 (in Polish).

Chapter 6

FUZZY LINGUISTIC SUMMARIES OF DATABASES FOR AN EFFICIENT BUSINESS DATA ANALYSIS AND DECISION SUPPORT

Janusz Kacprzyk[*], Ronald R. Yager[**] and Sławomir Zadrożny[*]
[*]*Systems Research Institute, Polish Academy of Sciences*
ul. Newelska 6, 01-447 Warsaw, Poland
Email: {kacprzyk, zadrozny}@ibspan.waw.pl

[**]*Machine Intelligence Institute, Iona College*
New Rochelle, NY 10801, USA
Email: yager@panix.com

Keywords: linguistic data summaries, fuzzy logic, fuzzy linguistic quantifier, fuzzy queryting

Abstract: We present the use of fuzzy logic for the derivation of linguistic summaries of data (databases) for providing efficient and human consistent means for the analysis of large amounts of data to be used for a more realistic business decision support. We concentrate on the issue of how to measure the goodness of a linguistic summary, and on how to embed data summarization within the fuzzy querying environment, for an effective and efficient computer implementation. Finally, we present an implementation for deriving linguistic summaries of a sales database at a small-to-medium size computer retailer. By analyzing the linguistic summaries obtained we indicate how they can help make decisions by the business owner.

1. INTRODUCTION

The recent growth of Information Technology (IT) has implied, on the one hand, the availability of a huge amount of data (from diverse, often remote databases). What is important is that the cost of having those data available has become low, even for small businesses and organizations due to falling prices of hardware and a rising efficiency of software products. Unfortunately, the raw data alone are often not useful and do not provide "knowledge", hence are not useful per se for supporting any rational human activity, notably those related to business where requirements for speed and efficiency are particularly pronounced.

More important than data themselves are relevant, nontrivial dependencies that are encoded in those data. Unfortunately, they are usually hidden, and their discovery is not a trivial act that requires some intelligence.

One of interesting and promising approaches to discover such dependencies in an effective, efficient and human consistent way is to derive linguistic summaries of a set of data (database). Here we discuss linguistic summarization of data sets in the sense of Yager (1982, 1989 - 1996) [for some extensions and other related issues, see, e.g., Kacprzyk and Yager (2000), Rasmussen and Yager (1996 – 1999), Yager and Rubinson (1981), etc.].

In this approach linguistic summaries are derived as linguistically quantified propositions, exemplified – when the data in question concern employees – by "most of the employees are young and well paid", with which a degree of validity is associated.

Basically, in the source Yager's (1982, 1989 – 1996) works that degree of validity was meant to be the degree of truth of a linguistically quantified proposition that constitutes a summary. This was shown to be not enough, and other validity (quality) indicators were proposed, also in the above Yager's works. As a relevant further attempt, we can mention George and Srikanth's (1996) solution in which a compromise between the specificity and generality of a summary is sought, and then some extension given in Kacprzyk and Strykowski's (1999a, b) works in which a weighted sum of 5 quality indicators is employed. Kacprzyk and Yager's (2000) recent proposal is the most comprehensive account of that direction as it includes proposals of new validity (performance) degrees.

In this paper we also follow Kacprzyk and Zadrożny's (1998, 1999, 2000a, b, c), Kacprzyk's (1999a), and Zadrożny and Kacprzyk's (1999) idea of an interactive approach to linguistic summaries. Basically, since a fully automatic generation of linguistic summaries is not feasible at present, an interaction with the user is assumed for the determination of a class of summaries of interest. This is done via Kacprzyk and Zadrożny's (1994 - 1996) fuzzy querying add-on to Microsoft Access.

We show that the approach proposed is implementable, and we present an implementation for a sales database of a computer retailer. We show that the linguistic summaries obtained may be very useful for supporting decision making by the management.

2. IDEA OF LINGUISTIC SUMMARIES USING FUZZY LOGIC WITH LINGUISTIC QUANTIFIERS

First, we will briefly present the basic Yager's (1982) approach to the linguistic summarization of sets of data. This will provide a point of departure for our further analysis of more complicated and realistic linguistic summaries.

In Yager's (1982) approach, we have:

- V is a quality (attribute) of interest, e.g. salary in a database of workers,
- $Y = \{y_1, \ldots, y_n\}$ is a set of objects (records) that manifest quality V, e.g. the set of workers; hence $V(y_i)$ are values of quality V for object y_i,
- $D = \{V(y_1), \ldots, V(y_n)\}$ is a set of data ("database").

A *summary* of a data set consists of:

- a summarizer S (e.g. young),
- a quantity in agreement Q (e.g. most),
- truth (validity) T - e.g. 0.7,

as, e.g., T(*most* of employees are *young*)=0.7.

Given a set of data D, we can hypothetize any appropriate summarizer S and any quantity in agreement Q, and the assumed measure of truth (validity) will indicate the truth (validity) of the statement that Q data items satisfy the statement (summarizer) S.

First, we should comment on the form of the basic elements of the summary, i.e. the summarizer, quantity in agreement, and how to calculate the degree of truth (validity).

Since the only fully natural and human consistent means of communication for the humans is natural language, then we assume that the summarizer S is a linguistic expression semantically represented by a fuzzy set. For instance, in our example a summarizer like "young" would be represented as a fuzzy set in the universe of discourse, say, {1, 2, ..., 90}, i.e. containing possible values of the human age, and "young" could be given as, say, a fuzzy set with a nonincreasing membership function in that universe such that, in a simple case of a piecewise linear membership function, the age up to 35 years is for sure "young", i.e. the grade of membership is equal to 1, the age over 50 years is for sure "not young", i.e. the grade of membership is equal to 0, and for the ages between 35 and 50 years the grades of membership are between 1 and 0, the higher the age the lower its corresponding grade of membership. Clearly, the meaning of the summarizer, i.e. its corresponding fuzzy set is in practice subjective, and may be either predefined or elicited from the user when needed.

Such a simple one-attribute-related summarizer exemplified by "young" does well serve the purpose of introducing the concept of a linguistic summary, hence it was assumed by Yager (1982). However, it is of a lesser practical relevance. It can be extended, for some confluence of attribute values as, e.g, "*young* and *well paid*", and then to more complicated combinations.

Clearly, when we try to linguistically summarize data, the most interesting are non-trivial, *human-consistent* summarizers (concepts) as, e.g.:

- *productive* workers,
- *stimulating* work environment,
- *difficult* orders, etc.

involving complicated *combinations of attributes* like, e.g.: a hierarchy (not all attributes are of the same importance), the attribute values are ANDed and/or ORed, k out of n, *most*, ... of them should be accounted for, etc.

The generation and processing of such non-trivial summarizers needs some specific tools and techniques that will be discussed later.

The quantity in agreement, Q, is a proposed indication of the extent to which the data satisfy the summary. Once again, a precise indication is not human consistent, and a linguistic term represented by a fuzzy set is employed.

Basically, two types of such a linguistic quantity in agreement can be used:

- absolute as, e.g., "about 5", "more or less 100", "several", and
- relative as, e.g., "a few", "more or less a half", "most", almost all", etc.

Notice that the above linguistic expressions are the so-called fuzzy linguistic quantifiers (cf. Zadeh, 1983, 1985) that can be handled by fuzzy logic.

As for the fuzzy summarizer, also in case of a fuzzy quantity in agreement, its form is subjective, and can be either predefined or elicited from the user when needed.

The calculation of the truth (validity) of the basic type of a linguistic summary considered in this section is equivalent to the calculation of the truth value (from the unit interval) of a linguistically quantified statement (e.g., "*most* of the employees are *young*"). This may be done by two most relevant techniques using either Zadeh's (1983) calculus of linguistically quantified statements [cf. Zadeh and Kacprzyk (1992)] or Yager's (1988) OWA operators [cf. Yager and Kacprzyk (1997)]; for a survey, see Liu and Kerre (1998).

A linguistically quantified proposition, exemplified by "most experts are convinced", is written as "Qy's are F" where Q is a linguistic quantifier (e.g., most), $Y = \{y\}$ is a set of objects (e.g., experts), and F is a property (e.g., convinced). Importance B may be added yielding "QBy's are F", e.g., "most (Q) of the important (B) experts (y's) are convinced (F)". The problem is to find truth(Qy's are F) or truth(QBy's are F), respectively, provided we know truth(y is F), $\forall y \in Y$, which is done here using Zadeh's (1983) fuzzy-logic-based calculus of linguistically quantified propositions.

First, property F and importance B are fuzzy sets in Y, and a (proportional, nondecreasing) linguistic quantifier Q is assumed to be a fuzzy set in [0,1] as, e.g., for Q = "most"

$$\mu_Q(x) = \begin{cases} 1 & \text{for } x \geq 0.8 \\ 2x - 0.6 & \text{for } 0.3 < x < 0.8 \\ 0 & \text{for } x \leq 0.3 \end{cases} \tag{1}$$

Then, due to Zadeh (1983), we have:

$$\text{truth}(Qy\text{'s are } F) = \mu_Q[\tfrac{1}{n}\textstyle\sum_{i=1}^{n} \mu_F(y_i)] \tag{2}$$

$$\text{truth}(QBy\text{'s are } F) = \mu_Q[\textstyle\sum_{i=1}^{n} (\mu_B(y_i) \wedge \mu_F(y_i)) / \sum_{i=1}^{n} \mu_B(y_i)] \tag{3}$$

An OWA operator [Yager (1988); Yager and Kacprzyk (1997)] of dimension p is a mapping $F : [0,1]^p \rightarrow [0,1]$ if associated with F is a weighting vector $W = [w_1, \ldots, w_p]^T$, $w_i \in [0,1], w_1 + \cdots + w_p = 1$, and

$$F(x_1, \ldots, x_p) = w_1 b_1 + \cdots w_p b_p = W^T B \tag{4}$$

where b_i is the i-th largest element among $x_1, \ldots, x_p$, $B = [b_1, \ldots, b_p]$.

The OWA weights may be found from the membership function of Q due to [cf. Yager (1988)]:

$$w_i = \begin{cases} \mu_Q(i) - \mu_Q(i-1) & \text{for i} = 1, \ldots, p \\ \mu_Q(0) & \text{for i} = 0 \end{cases} \tag{5}$$

The OWA operators can model a wide array of aggregation operators (including linguistic quantifiers), from $w_1 = \cdots = w_{p-1} = 0$ and $w_p = 1$ which corresponds to "all", to $w_1 = 1$ and $w_2 = \cdots = w_p = 0$ which corresponds to "at least one", through all intermediate situations.

An important issue is related with the OWA operators for importance qualified data. Suppose that we have $A = [a_1, \ldots, a_p]$, and a vector of importances $V = [v_1, \ldots, v_p]$ such that $v_i \in [0,1]$ is the importance of $a_i, i = 1, \ldots, p$, and $v_1 + \cdots v_p = 1$.

The case of an *OWA operator with importance qualification*, denoted OWA_Q is not trivial. In Yager's (1988) approach to be used here, which seems to be highly plausible (though is sometimes critisized), some redefinition of the OWA's weights w_i's into $\overline{w}_i$'s is performed, and (4) becomes

$$F_I(x_1, \ldots, x_p) = \overline{w}_1 b_1 + \cdots \overline{w}_p b_p = \overline{W}^T B \tag{6}$$

where

$$w_j = \mu_Q\left(\frac{\sum_{k=1}^{j} u_k}{\sum_{k=1}^{p} u_k}\right) - \mu_Q\left(\frac{\sum_{k=1}^{j-1} u_k}{\sum_{k=1}^{p} u_k}\right) \tag{7}$$

and u_k is the importance of b_k, that is the k-largest element of A (i.e. the corresponding v_k).

3. ON OTHER VALIDITY CRITERIA

The basic validity criterion introduced in the source Yager's (1982) work and employed by many authors later on, i.e. the truth of a linguistically quantified statement given by (2) and (3), is certainly the most important in the general framework. However, it does not grasp all aspects of a linguistic summary. Some attempts at devising other quality (validity) criteria will be briefly surveyed following Kacprzyk and Yager (2000).

As one of first attempts, Yager (1982, 1991) proposed a measure of informativeness that may be summarized as follows. Suppose that we have a data set, whose elements are from a measurement space X. One can say that the data set itself is its own most informative description, and any other summary implies a loss of information. So, a natural question is whether a particular summary is informative, and to what extent.

However, it turns out that the degree of truth used so far is not a good measure of informativeness [cf. Yager (1982, 1991)]. Let the summary be characterized by the triple (*S*, *Q*, *T*), and let a related summary be characterized by the triple (S^c, Q^c, *T*), such that S^c is the negation of *S*, i.e. $\mu_S^c(.) = 1 - \mu_S(.)$, and $\mu_Q^c(.) = 1 - \mu_Q(.)$.

Then, Yager (1982, 1991) proposes the following measure of informativeness of a (linguistic) summary

$$I = [T \cdot SP(Q) \cdot SP(S)] \vee [(1-T) \cdot SP(Q^c) SP(S^c)] \qquad (8)$$

where *SP*(*Q*) is the specificity of *Q* given as

$$SP(Q) = \int_0^1 \frac{1}{\mathrm{card} Q_\alpha} d_\alpha \qquad (9)$$

where Q_α is the α-cut of *Q* and card(.) is the cardinality of the respective set; and similarly for Q^c, *S* and S^c.

This measure of informativeness results from a very plausible reasoning which can be found, e.g., in Yager (1982, 1991).

Unfortunately, though the above measure of informativeness has much sense and is a considerable step forward, it is by no means a definite solution. First, let us briefly mention George and Srikanth's (1996) proposal.

Suppose that a linguistic summary of interest involves more than 1 attribute (e.g., "age", "salary" and "seniority" in the case of employees). Basically, for the same set of data, two summaries are generated:

- a *constraint descriptor* which is the most specific description (summary) that fits the largest number of tuples in the relation (database) involving the attributes in question,
- a *constituent descriptor* which is the description (summary) that fits the largest subset of tuples with the condition that each tuple attribute value takes on at least a threshold value of membership.

George and Srikanth (1996) use these two summaries to derive a fitness function (goodness of a summary) that is later used for deriving a solution (a best summary) via a genetic algorithm. This fitness function represent a compromise between the most specific summary (corresponding to the constraint descriptor) and the most general summary (corresponding to the constituent descriptor).

Then, Kacprzyk (1999a, b), and Kacprzyk and Strykowski (1999a, b) propose some additional measures that have been further developed by Kacprzyk and Yager (2000).

First, let us briefly repeat some basic notation. We have a data set (database) D that concerns some objects (e.g. employees) $Y = \{y_1, ..., y_n\}$ described by some attribute V (e.g. age) taking on values in a set $X = \{x_1, x_2, ...\}$ exemplified by {20, 21, ..., 100} or {very young, young, ..., old, very old}. Let $d_i = V(y_i)$ denote the value of attribute V for object y_i. Therefore, the data set to be summarized is given as a table

$$D = [d_1,...,d_n]=[V(y_1), V(y_2), ..., V(y_n)] \tag{10}$$

In a more realistic case the data set is described by more than one attribute, and let $V=\{V_1, V_2,..., V_m\}$ be a set of such attributes taking values in X_i, i=1, ..., m; $V_j(y_i)$ denotes the value of attribute V_j for object y_i, and attribute V_j takes on its values from a set X_j.

The data set to be summarized is therefore:

$$D = \{[V_1(y_1), V_2(y_1),..., V_m(y_1)], [V_1(y_2), V_2(y_2),..., V_m(y_2)], ..., [V_1(y_n), V_2(y_n),..., V_m(y_n)]\} \tag{11}$$

In this case of multiple attributes the description (summarizer) S is a family of fuzzy sets $S=\{S_1, S_2,... S_m\}$ where S_i is a fuzzy set in X_i, $i=1,...,m$. Then, $\mu_S(y_i)$ may be defined as:

$$\mu_S(y_i) = \min_{j\in\{1,2,...,n\}}[\ \mu_{Sj}\ (V_j(y_i))] \tag{12}$$

So, having S, we can calculate the truth value T of a summary for any quantity in agreement. However, to find a best summary, we should calculate T for each possible summarizer, and for each record in the database in question. This is computationally prohibitive for virtually all non-trivial databases and numbers of attributes.

A natural line of reasoning would be to either limit the number of attributes of interest or to limit the class of possible summaries by setting a more specific description by predefining a "narrower" description as, e.g. very young, young and well paid, etc. employees. This will limit the search space.

We will deal here with the second option. The user can limit the scope of a linguistic summary to, say, those for which the attribute "age" takes on the value "young (employees)" only, i.e. to fix the summarizer related to that attribute. That is, this will correspond to the searching of the database using the query w_g equated with the fuzzy set in X_g corresponding to "young" related to attribute V_g (i.e. age), i.e. characterized by $\mu_{w_g}(.)$. In such a case, $\mu_S(y_i)$ given by (12) becomes

$$\mu_S(y_i) = \min_{j\in\{1,2,\ldots,m\}}[\mu_{Sj}(V_j(y_i)) \wedge \mu_{w_g}(V_g(y_i)], \quad i=1,\ldots,n \tag{13}$$

where "$\wedge$" is the minimum (or, more generally, a t-norm), and then we have

$$r = \frac{\sum_{i=1}^{n}\mu_S(y_i)}{\sum_{i=1}^{n}\mu_{w_g}(V_g(y_i))} \tag{14}$$

and $T=\mu_Q(r)$.

Now, we will present the 5 new quality measures of quality of linguistic database summaries introduced in Kacprzyk (1999a, b), Kacprzyk and Strykowski (1999a, b), and then further developed in a more profound way in Kacprzyk and Yager (2000):

- truth value [which basically corresponds to the degree of truth of a lingustically quantified proposition representing the summary given by, say, (2) or (3)],
- degree of imprecision (fuzziness),
- degree of covering,
- degree of appropriateness, and
- length of a summary,

and these degrees will now be formally defined.

For further notational simplicity, let us rewrite (13) and (14) as:

$$\mu_S(d_i) = \min_{j\in\{1,2,\ldots,m\}}[(\mu_{Sj}(V_j(y_i))], \quad i=1,\ldots,n \tag{15}$$

and

$$r = \frac{\sum_{i=1}^{n}[\mu_S(y_i)\wedge\mu_{w_g}(V_g(y_i))]}{\sum_{i=1}^{n}\mu_{w_g}(V_g(y_i))} \tag{16}$$

The **degree of truth**, T_1, is the basic validity criterion introduced in the source Yager's (1982, 1991) works and commonly employed. It is equal to

$$T_1 = \mu_Q(r) \tag{17}$$

that results from the use of Zadeh's (1983) calculus of linguistically quantified propositions.

The **degree of imprecision (fuzziness, specificity)** is an obvious and important validity criterion. Basically, a very imprecise (fuzzy) linguistic summary (e.g. "on almost all winter days the temperature is rather cold") has a very high degree of truth yet it is not useful.

Suppose that description (summarizer) S is given as a family of fuzzy sets $S=\{s_1, s_2,, \dots s_m,\}$. For a fuzzy set s_j, $j=1, \dots, m$, we can define its degree of fuzziness as, e.g.:

$$\text{in}(s_j) = \frac{\text{card}\,\{x \in X_j : \mu_{s_j}(x) > 0\}}{\text{card}\, X_j} \tag{18}$$

where card{.} denotes the cardinality of the corresponding (nonfuzzy) set. That is, the "flatter" the fuzzy set s_j the higher the value of in(s_j). The degree of imprecision (fuzziness), T_2, of the summary – or, in fact, of S – is then defined as:

$$T_2 = 1 - \sqrt[m]{\prod_{j=1,\dots,m} \text{in}(s_j)} \tag{19}$$

Notice that the degree of imprecision T_2 depends on the form of the summary only and not on the database, that is its calculation does not require the searching of the database (all its records) which is very important.

The **degree of covering**, T_3, is defined as

$$T_3 = \frac{\sum_{i=1}^{n} t_i}{\sum_{i=1}^{n} h_i} \tag{20}$$

where:

$$t_i = \begin{cases} 1 & \text{if } \mu_S(y_i) > 0 \quad \text{and} \quad \mu_{w_g}(V_g(y_i)) > 0 \\ 0 & \text{otherwise} \end{cases}$$

$$h_i = \begin{cases} 1 & \text{if } \mu_{w_g}(V_g(y_i)) > 0 \\ 0 & \text{otherwise} \end{cases}$$

The degree of covering says how many objects in the data set (database) corresponding to the query w_g are "covered" by the summary corresponding to the particular description S. Its interpretation is simple as, e.g., if it is equal to 0.15, then this means that 15% of the objects are consistent with the summary in question. The value of this degree depends on the contents of the database.

The **degree of appropriateness** is the most relevant degree of validity. To present its idea, suppose that the summary containing the description (fuzzy sets) $S = (S_1, S_2, \ldots, S_m)$ is partitioned into m partial summaries each of which encompasses the particular attributes $S_1, S_2, \ldots, S_m$, such that each partial summary corresponds to one fuzzy value only. So, if we denote:

$$S_j(y_i) = \mu_{Sj}(V_j(y_i)) \tag{21}$$

then

$$r_j = \frac{\sum_{i=1}^{n} h_i}{n}, \quad j=1, \ldots, n \tag{22}$$

where:

$$h_i = \begin{cases} 1 & \text{if } S_j(y_i) > 0 \\ 0 & \text{otherwise} \end{cases}$$

and the degree of appropriateness, T_4, is defined as:

$$T_4 = \text{abs}\Big(\prod_{j=1,\ldots,m} r_j - T_3\Big) \tag{23}$$

The degree of appropriateness means that if we have a database concerning the employees, then if 50% of them are less than 25 year old and 50% are highly qualified, then we may expect that 25% of the employees would be less than 25 year old and highly qualified; this would correspond to a typical, fully expected situation. However, if the degree of appropriateness is, say, 0.39 (i.e. 39% are less than 25 years old and highly qualified), then the summary found reflects an interesting, not fully expected relation in our data. This degree describes therefore how characteristic for the particular database the summary found is. T_4 is very important because, for instance, a trivial summary like "100 % of sale is of any articles" has full validity (truth) if we use the traditional degree of truth but its degree of appropriateness is equal 0 which is clearly what it should be.

The **length** of a summary is relevant because a long summary is not easily comprehensible by the human user. This length, T_5, may be defined in various ways, and the below form has proven to be useful:

$$T_5 = 2\,(0.5^{\text{card}\,S}) \tag{24}$$

where card S is the number of elements in S.

Now, the (total) degree of validity, T, of a particulat linguistic summary is defined as the weighted average of the above 5 degrees of validity, i.e.:

$$T = T(T_1, T_2, T_3, T_4, T_5; w_1, w_2, w_3, w_4, w_5) = \sum_{i=1,2,\ldots,5} w_i T_i \quad (25)$$

And the problem is to find an optimal summary, $S^* \in \{S\}$, such that

$$S^* = \arg\max_S \sum_{i=1,2,\ldots,5} w_i T_i \quad (26)$$

where $w_1,\ldots,w_5$ are weights assigned to the particular degrees of validity, with values from the unit interval, the higher the more important, such that $\sum_{i=1,2,\ldots,5} w_i = 1$.

The definition of weights, $w_1,\ldots,w_5$, is a problem in itself, and will not be dealt with here in more detail. The weights can be predefined or elicited from the user. In the case study presented later the weights are determined by using the well-known Saaty's (1980) AHP (analytical hierarchy process) approach that works well in the problem considered.

4. DERIVATION OF LINGUISTIC SUMMARIES VIA A FUZZY LOGIC BASED DATABASE QUERYING INTERFACE

The roots of the approach are our previous papers on the use of fuzzy logic in database querying [cf. Kacprzyk and Zadrożny (1994 - 1997c), Kacprzyk, Zadrożny and Ziółkowski (1989), Zadrożny and Kacprzyk (1995)] in which we argued that the formulation of a precise query is often difficult for the end user [see also Zemankova and Kacprzyk (1993)]. For example, a customer of a real-estate agency looking for a house would rather express his or her criteria using imprecise descriptions as *cheap*, *large* garden, etc. Also, to specify which combination of the criteria fulfillment would be satisfactory, he or she would often use, say, *most* of them or *almost all*. All such vague terms may be relatively easily interpreted using fuzzy logic. This has motivated the development of the whole family of fuzzy querying interfaces, notably our FQUERY for Access package [cf. Kacprzyk and Zadrożny (1994 - 1997c), Zadrożny and Kacprzyk (1995)].

The same arguments apply, to an even higher degree, when one tries to summarize the content of a database in a short (linguistic) statement. For example, a summary like "*most* our customers are *reliable*" may very often be more useful than, say "65% of our customers have paid at least 70% of their duties in less than 10 days".

In the previous section we studied the summarization independently, and here we will restate it in the fuzzy querying context. We start with the reinterpretation of (2) and (3). Thus, (2) formally expresses a statement:

"Most records match query S" (27)

where S replaces F in (2) since we refer here directly to the concept of a summarizer.

We assume a standard meaning of the query as a set of conditions on the values of fields from the database tables, connected with AND and OR. We allow for fuzzy terms in a query that implies a degree of matching from [0,1] rather than a yes/no matching. So, a query S defines a fuzzy subset on the set of the records, and the membership of them is determined by their matching degree with the query.

Similarly, (3) may be interpreted as expressing a statement of the following type:

"Most records meeting conditions F match query S" (28)

Thus, (28) says something only about a subset of records taken into account by (27). That is, in database terminology, F corresponds to a *filter* and (28) claims that *most* records passing through F match query S. Moreover, since the filter may be fuzzy, a record may pass through it to a degree from [0,1].

We seek, for a given database, propositions of the type (3), interpreted as (28) that are highly true, and they contain three elements: a fuzzy filter F (optional), a query S, and a linguistic quantifier Q. There are two limit cases where we:

- do not assume anything about the form of any of these elements,
- assume fixed forms of a fuzzy filter and query, and look only for a linguistic quantifier Q.

In the first case data summarization will be extremely time-consuming but may produce interesting results. In the second case the user has to guess a good candidate formula for summarization but the evaluation is fairly simple being equivalent to the answering of a (fuzzy) query. Thus, the second case refers to the summarization known as *ad hoc queries*, extended with an automatic determination of a linguistic quantifier.

In between these two extreme cases there are different types of summaries with various assumptions on what is given and what is sought. In case of a linguistic quantifier the situation is simple: it may be given or sought. In case of a fuzzy filter *F* and a fuzzy query *S*, more possibilities exist as both *F* and *S* consist of simple conditions, each stating what *value* a *field* should take on, and connected using logical connectives. Here we assume that the table(s) of interest for the summarization are fixed.

We will use the following notation to describe what is given or what is sought with respect to the fuzzy filter *F* and query *S* (*A* will stand below for either *F* or *S*):

- A - all is given (or sought), i.e. attributes, values and the structure,
- A^{fc} - attributes and structure are given but values are left out,
- A^{v} - denotes sought left out values referred to above, and
- A^{f} - only a set of attributes is given and the other elements are sought.

Using such a notation we may propose a classification of linguistic summaries as shown in Table 1.

Table 1. Classification of linguistic summaries

Type	Given	Sought	Remarks
1	S	Q - sought	Simple summaries through ad-hoc queries
2	S F	Q - sought	Conditional summaries through ad-hoc queries
3	Q S^{fc}	S^{v}	Simple value oriented summaries
4	Q S^{fc} F	S^{v}	Conditional value oriented summaries
5	Nothing	S F Q	General fuzzy rules

Thus, we distinguish 5 main types of data summarization. Type 1 may be easily produced by a simple extension of fuzzy querying as proposed and implemented in our FQUERY for Access package. Basically, the user has to construct a query – a candidate summary. Then, it has to be determined what is the fraction of rows matching this query and what linguistic quantifier best denotes this fraction. The primary target of this type of summarization is certainly to propose such a query that a large proportion (e.g., *most*) of the rows satisfies it. On the other hand, it may be interesting to learn that only *few* rows satisfy some meaningful query. A Type 2 summary is a straightforward extension of a Type 1 summary by adding a fuzzy filter. As soon as a fuzzy querying engine deals with fuzzy filters, the computational complexity of this type of summaries is the same as for Type 1. For more on these types of summaries, see for instance Anwar, Beck and Navathe (1992), or Kacprzyk and Zadrożny (1998).

The summaries of Type 3 require much more effort. A primary goal of this type of summary is to determine typical (exceptional) values of an attribute. In such a special case, query *S* consists of only one simple condition built of the attribute whose typical (exceptional) value is sought, the '=' relational operator and a placeholder for the value sought. For example, using the following summary in a context of personal data:

Q = "*most*" and S = "age=?" ("?" denotes a placeholder mentioned above) (29)

we look for a typical value of the age of the employees. Then, we try to find such a (possibly fuzzy) value that the query matches to a high degree in Q of the rows. Depending on the category of the Q used as, e.g., *most* versus *few*, typical or exceptional values are sought, respectively. Some more considerations are required as in some cases all values may turn out to be exceptional and none to be typical. This type of summaries may be used with more complicated, regular queries but it may quickly become computationally infeasible (due to the combinatorial explosion) and the interpretation of results becomes vague. A Type 4 summary may produce typical (exceptional) values for some, possibly fuzzy, subset of rows. From the computational point of view, the same remarks apply as for Type 1 versus Type 2 summaries.

A Type 5 summary represents the most general form considered here. In its full version this type of summaries produce fuzzy rules describing dependencies between specific values of particular attributes. Here the use of a filter is essential, in contrast to the previous types where it was optional. The very meaning of a fuzzy rule obtained is that if a row meets a filter's condition, then it meets also the query's conditions – this corresponds to a classical IF-THEN rule. For a general form of such a rule it is difficult to devise an effective and efficient generation algorithm. Full search may be acceptable only in case of restrictively limited sets of rule building blocks, i.e. attributes and their possible values. Here, some genetic algorithm based approaches may be employed [cf. George and Srikanth (1996)] to alleviate the computational complexity, and additional assumptions may also be made. For example, some sets of relevant (interesting, promising, etc.) attributes for the query (S^f) and the filter (F^f) may be selected in advance. Some constraints may also be put on the structure of the query S and filter F (in terms of the number of logical connectives allowed). Another important special case of Type 5 summaries refers to the situation where the query (S) is fixed and only the filter (F) and quantifier (Q) are sought, i.e. we look for causes of given data features. For example, we may set in a query that profitability of a venture is *high* and look for the characterization of ventures (rows) securing such a high profitability.

The summaries of Type 1 and 3 have been implemented as an extension to our FQUERY for Access.

FQUERY for Access is an add-in that makes it possible to use fuzzy terms in queries [cf. Kacprzyk and Zadrożny (1994 - 1997c), Zadrożny and

Kacprzyk (1995)]. Briefly speaking, the following types of fuzzy terms are available:

- fuzzy values, exemplified by *low* in "profitability is *low*",
- fuzzy relations, exemplified by *much greater than* in "income is *much greater than* spending", and
- linguistic quantifiers, exemplified by *most* in "*most* conditions have to be met".

The elements of the first two types are elementary building blocks of fuzzy queries in FQUERY for Access. They are meaningful in the context of numerical fields only. There are also other fuzzy constructs allowed which may be used with scalar fields.

If a field is to be used in a query in connection with a fuzzy value, it has to be defined as an *attribute*. The definition of an attribute consists of two numbers: the attribute's values lower (LL) and upper (UL) limit. They set the interval that the field's values are assumed to belong to. This interval depends on the meaning of the given field. For example, for the *age* (of a person), a reasonable interval would be, e.g., [18,65], in a particular context, i.e. for a specific group. Such a concept of an attribute makes it possible to universally define fuzzy values.

Fuzzy values are defined, for technical reasons, as fuzzy sets on [-10, +10]. Then, *the matching degree* $md(\cdot,\cdot)$ of a simple condition referring to attribute AT and fuzzy value FV against a record R is calculated by:

$$md(\mathrm{AT} = \mathrm{FV}, \mathrm{R}) = \mu_{\mathrm{FV}}(\tau(\mathrm{R}(\mathrm{AT})) \tag{30}$$

where: R(AT) is the value of attribute AT in record R, μ_{FV} is the membership function of fuzzy value FV, τ: $[\mathrm{LL}_{\mathrm{AT}},\mathrm{UL}_{\mathrm{AT}}] \rightarrow [-10,10]$ is the mapping from the interval defining AT onto [-10,10] so that we may use the same fuzzy values for different fields. A meaningful interpretation is secured by τ which makes it possible to treat all fields domains as ranging over the unified interval [-10,10].

For simplicity, it is assumed that the membership functions of fuzzy values are trapezoidal as in Figure 1 and τ is assumed linear.

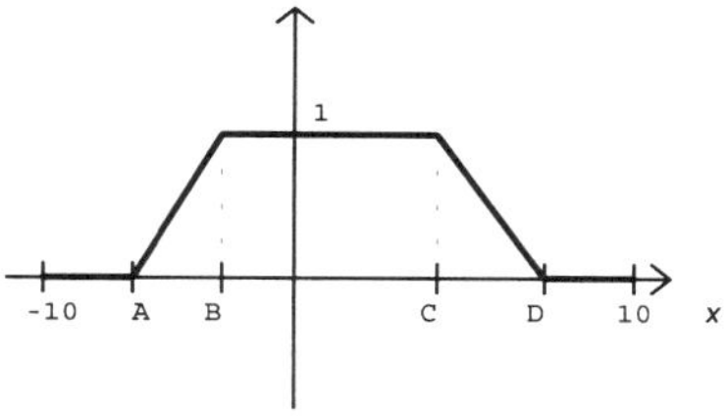

Figure 1. An example of the membership function of a fuzzy value

Linguistic quantifiers provide for a flexible aggregation of simple conditions. In FQUERY for Access the fuzzy linguistic quantifiers are defined in Zadeh's (1983) sense (see Section 2) as fuzzy set on the [0, 10] interval instead of the original [0, 1]. They may be interpreted either using original Zadeh's approach or via the OWA operators (cf. Yager, 1988, Yager and Kacprzyk, 1997); Zadeh's interpretation will be used here. The membership functions of fuzzy linguistic quantifiers are assumed piece-wise linear, hence two numbers from [0,10] are needed. Again, a mapping from [0,N], where N is the number of conditions aggregated, to [0,10] is employed to calculate the matching degree of a query. More precisely, the matching degree, $md(\cdot,\cdot)$, for the *query* "*Q* of *N* conditions are satisfied" for record R is equal to

$$md(Q, \text{condition}_i, \text{R}) = \mu_{\text{Q}}[\tau(\sum_i md(\text{condition}_i, \text{R}))] \tag{31}$$

We can also assign different importance degrees for particular conditions. Then, the aggregation formula is equivalent to (3). The importance is identified with a fuzzy set on [0,1], and then treated as property *B* in (3).

FQUERY for Access has been designed so that queries containing fuzzy terms still be syntactically correct queries in Access. It has been attained through the use of parameters. Basically, Access represents the queries using SQL. Parameters, expressed as strings limited with brackets, make it possible to embed references to fuzzy terms in a query. We have assumed a special naming convention for parameters corresponding to particular fuzzy terms. For example, a parameter like:

[FfA_FV *fuzzy value name*] will be interpreted as a fuzzy value

[FfA_FQ *fuzzy quantifier name*] will be interpreted as a fuzzy quantifier

To be able to use a fuzzy term in a query, it has to be defined using the toolbar provided by FQUERY for Access and stored internally. This feature, i.e. the maintenance of dictionaries of fuzzy terms defined by users, strongly supports our approach to data summarization to be discussed next. In fact, the package comes with a set of predefined fuzzy terms but the user may enrich the dictionary too.

When the user initiates the execution of a query it is automatically transformed by appropriate FQUERY for Access's routines and then run as a native query of Access. The transformation consists primarily in the replacement of parameters referring to fuzzy terms by calls to functions implemented in the package that secure a proper interpretation of these fuzzy terms. Then, the query is run by Access as usually.

FQUERY for Access provides its own toolbar. There is one button for each fuzzy element, and the buttons for declaring attributes, starting the querying, closing the toolbar and for help (cf. Figure 2). Unfortunately, these are shown for a Polish version of Access but an interested reader can easily figure out their equivalents in English or any other versions.

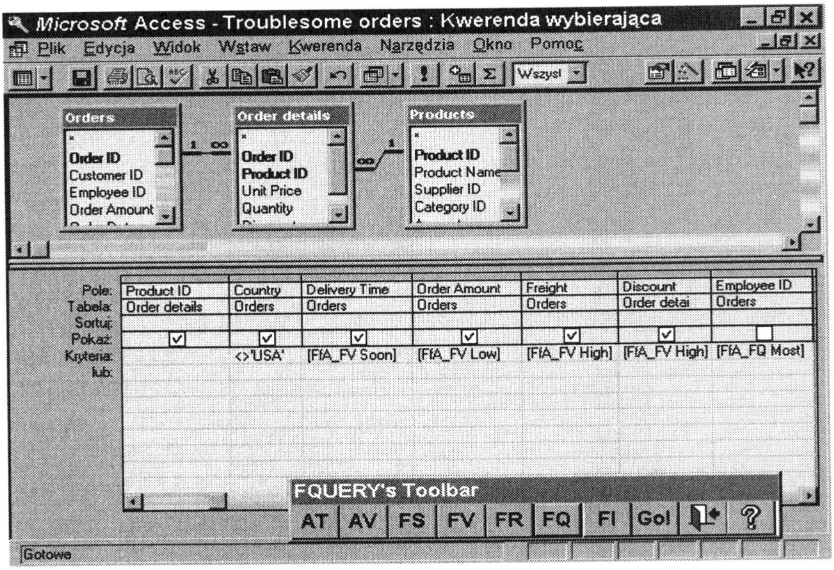

Figure 2. Composition of a fuzzy query

Details can be found in Kacprzyk and Zadrożny (1994 - 1997c) and Zadrożny and Kacprzyk (1995).

5. IMPLEMENTATION FOR A SALES DATABASE AT A COMPUTER RETAILER

The proposed data summarization procedure was implemented on a sales database of a computer retailer in Southern Poland [cf. Kacprzyk (1999a, b), Kacprzyk and Strykowski (1999a, b)].

The basic structure of the database is as shown in Table 2.

Table 2. Structure of the database

Attribute name	Attribute type	Description
Date	Date	Date of sale
Time	Time	Time of sale transaction
Name	Text	Name of the product
Amount (number)	Numeric	Number of products sold in the transaction
Price	Numeric	Unit price
Commission	Numeric	Commission (in %) on sale
Value	Numeric	Value = amount (number) x price; of the product
Discount	Numeric	Discount (in %) for transaction
Group	Text	Product group to which the product belongs
Transaction value	Numeric	Value of the whole transaction
Total sale to customer	Numeric	Total value of sales to the customer in fiscal year
Purchasing frequency	Numeric	Number of purchases by customer in fiscal year
Town	Text	Town where the customer lives

In the beginning, after some initialization, we provide some parameters concerning mainly: definition of attributes and the subject, definition of how the results should be presented, definition of parameters of the method (i.e. a genetic algorithm or, seldom, full search). Then, we initialize the search and obtain results shown in the tables to follow. Their consecutive columns contain: a lingustic summary, values of the 4 indicators, i.e. the degrees of appropriateness, covering, truth, and fuzziness (the length is not accounted for in our simple case), and finally the weighted average. The weights have been determined by employing Saaty's AHP procedure using pairwise comparisons importance of the particular indicators evaluated by experts. Some simple learning and finetuning has also been employed taking into account experience gained in previous sessions with the users.

We will now give a couple of examples. First, if we are interested in the relation between the commission and the type of goods sold, then we obtain the linguistic summaries shown in Table 3.

As we can see, the results can be very helpful in, e.g., negotiating commissions for various products sold.

Table 3. Linguistic summaries expressing relations between the group of products and commission

Summary	Degree of appropriateness	Degree of covering	Degree of validity
	Degree of imprecision	Weighted average	
About ½ of sales of network elements is with a high commission	0.2329 0.1872	0.4202 0.3165	0.3630
About ½ of sales of computers is with a medium commission	0.2045 0.3453	0.5498 0.3699	0.4753
Much sales of accessories is with a high commission.	0.1684 0.4095	0.5779 0.3919	0.5713
Much sales of components is with a low commission	0.1376 0.5837	0.7212 0.4449	0.6707
About ½ of sales of software is with a low commission	0.1028 0.5837	0.4808 0.3162	0.4309
About ½ of sales of computers is with a low commission	0.0225 0.5837	0.5594 0.3202	0.4473
A few sales of components is without commission	0.0237 0.2745	0.0355 0.2346	0.0355
A few sales of computers is with a high commission	0.1418 0.1872	0.0455 0.1881	0.0314
Very few sales of printers is with a high commission	0.1288 0.1872	0.0585 0.1820	0.0509

Table 4. Linguistic summaries expressing relations between the groups of products and times of sale

Summary	Degree of appropriateness	Degree of covering	Degree of validity
	Degree of imprecision	Weighted average	
About 1/3 of sales of computers is by the end of year	0,0999 0,2010	0,3009 0,1274	0,2801
About ½ of sales in autumn is of accessories	0,0642 0,4095	0,4737 0,1143	0,4790
About 1/3 of sales of network elements is in the beginning of year	0,0733 0,2124	0,2857 0,0982	0,1957
Very few sales of network elements is by the end of year	0,0833 0,2010	0,1176 0,0980	0,0929
Very few sales of software is in the beginning of year	0,0768 0,2124	0,1355 0,0929	0,0958
About ½ of sales in the beginning of year is of accessories	0,0348 0,4095	0,4443 0,0860	0,4343

About 1/3 of sales in the summer is of accessories	0,0464 0,2745	0,3209 0,0853	0,3092
About 1/3 of sales of peripherals is in the spring period	0,0507 0,2525	0,3032 0,0809	0,2140
About 1/3 of sales of software is by the end of year	0,0446 0,2010	0,2455 0,0768	0,2258
About 1/3 of sales of network elements is in the spring period	0,0458 0,2525	0,2983 0,0763	0,2081
About 1/3 of sales in the summer period is of components	0,0336 0,2745	0,3081 0,0745	0,3081
Very few sales of network elements is in the autumn period	0,0485 0,1956	0,1471 0,0692	0,0955
A few sales of software is in the summer period	0,0402 0,1362	0,1765 0,0691	0,1765

Next, suppose that we are interested in relations between the groups of products and times of sale. We obtain the results as in Table 4. Notice that in this case the summaries are much less obvious than in the former case.

Finally, let us show in Table 5 some of the obtained linguistic summaries expressing relations between the attributes: size of customer, regularity of customer (purchasing frequency), date of sale, time of sale, commission, group of product and day of sale. This is an example of the most sophisticated form of linguistic summaries allowed in the system. These sets of most valid summaries (normally, not just one summary) will give much inside into relations between the attributes chosen.

Table 5. Linguistic summaries expressing relations between the attributes: size of customer, regularity of customer (purchasing frequency), date of sale, time of sale, commission, group of product and day of sale

Summary	Degree of appropriateness	Degree of covering	Degree of validity
	Degree of imprecision	Weighted average	
Much sales on Saturday is about noon with a low commission	0,3843 0,2748	0,6591 0,3863	0,3951
Much sales on Saturday is about noon for bigger customers	0,3425 0,4075	0,7500 0,3648	0,4430
Much sales on Saturday is about noon	0,3133 0,4708	0,7841 0,3564	0,4654
Much sales on Saturday is about noon for regular customers	0,3391 0,3540	0,6932 0,3558	0,4153
A few sales for regular customers is with a low commission	0,3882 0,5837	0,1954 0,3451	0,1578

A few sales for small customers is with a low commission	0,3574 0,5837	0,2263 0,3263	0,1915
A few sales for one-time customers is with a low commission	0,3497 0,5837	0,2339 0,3195	0,1726
Much sales for small customers is for nonregular customers	0,6250 0,1458	0,7709 0,5986	0,5105

6. CONCLUDING REMARKS

In this paper we presented an idea of how fuzzy logic can be employed to derive linguistic summaries of a set of data (database). We proposed the use of two extensions of the basic Yager's (1982, 1989 - 1996) general approach to the linguistic summarization of a set of data (database) were given. The first extension is through the use of additional degrees of validity (quality), namely those of: truth, imprecision (fuzziness), covering, appropriateness, and length. Their weighted average is the quality (performance) measure of a linguistic summary (cf. Kacprzyk and Yager, 2000). The second extension is related to the structure of a linguistic summary and consists of embedding the summarization procedure within a flexible (fuzzy) querying environment, here within Kacprzyk and Zadrożny's (1994 – 1997c) FQYERY for Access, an add in to Microsoft Access.

We advocated the use of such linguistic database summaries for supporting business decision making by presenting application for the derivation of linguistic summaries of a sales database at a computer retailer, and show that the summaries obtained may of a considerable practical value for the management.

We strongly believe that linguistic summarization of (large) sets of data is a crucial step in an attempt to devise efficient and human consistent means for handling the glut of data that exists today in virtually all environments, notably in business.

REFERENCES

Anwar T.M., Beck H.W. and Navathe S.B. (1992) Knowledge mining by imprecise querying: A classification based system, in: Proceedings of the International Conference on Data Engineering, Tampa, USA, 622-630.

George R. and R. Srikanth (1996) Data summarization using genetic algorithms and fuzzy logic. In F. Herrera and J.L. Verdegay (Eds.): Genetic Algorithms and Soft Computing. Physica-Verlag, Heidelberg, pp. 599-611.

Kacprzyk J. (1999a) An Interactive Fuzzy Logic Approach to Lingustic Data Summaries, Proceedings of NAFIPS'99 - 18th International Conference of the North American Fuzzy Information Processing Society - NAFIPS, IEEE, pp. 595-599.

Kacprzyk J. (1999b) A New Paradigm Shift from Computation on Numbers to Computation on Words on an Example of Linguistic Database Summarization, In: N. Kasabov (ed.): Emerging Knowledge Engineering and Connectionist-Based Information Systems – Proceedings of ICONIP/ANZIIS/ANNES'99, University of Otago, pp. 179-179.

Kacprzyk J. and Strykowski P. (1999a) Linguistic data summaries for intelligent decision support, In: R. Felix (ed.): Fuzzy Decision Analysis and Recognition Technology for Management, Planning and Optimization – Proceedings of EFDAN'99, pp. 3-12.

Kacprzyk J. and Strykowski P. (1999b) Linguitic Summaries of Sales Data at a Computer Retailer: A Case Study. Proceedings of IFSA'99 (Taipei, Taiwan R.O.C), vol. 1 pp. 29-33.

Kacprzyk J. and Yager R.R. (2000) Linguistic Summaries of Data Using Fuzzy Logic. International Journal of General Systems (in press)

Kacprzyk J., Zadrożny S. and Ziółkowski A. (1989) FQUERY III+: a 'human consistent` database querying system based on fuzzy logic with linguistic quantifiers. Information Systems 6, 443 - 453.

Kacprzyk J. and Zadrożny S. (1994) Fuzzy querying for Microsoft Access, Proceedings of FUZZ-IEEE'94 (Orlando, USA), vol. 1, pp. 167-171.

Kacprzyk J. and Zadrożny S. (1995a) Fuzzy queries in Microsoft Access v. 2 , Proceedings of FUZZ-IEEE/IFES '95 (Yokohama, Japan), Workshop on Fuzzy Database Systems and Information Retrieval, pp. 61-66.

Kacprzyk J. and Zadrożny S. (1995b) FQUERY for Access: fuzzy querying for a Windows-based DBMS, in P. Bosc and J. Kacprzyk (eds.): Fuzziness in Database Management Systems. Physica-Verlag: Heidelberg, pp. 415-433.

Kacprzyk J. and Zadrożny S. (1996) A fuzzy querying interface for a WWW-server-based relational DBMS. Proc. of IPMU'96 (Granada, Spain), vol. 1, pp. 19-24.

Kacprzyk J. and Zadrożny S. (1998) Data Mining via Linguistic Summaries of Data: An Interactive Approach, in T. Yamakawa and G. Matsumoto (eds.): Methodologies for the Conception, Design and Application of Soft Computing (Proceedings of IIZUKA'98, Iizuka, Japan), pp. 668-671.

Kacprzyk J., Zadrożny S. (1999) On Interactive Linguistic Summarization of Databases via a Fuzzy-Logic-Based Querying Add-On to Microsoft Access. W: Bernd Reusch (Ed.)(Red.): Computational Intelligence: Theory and Applications, Springer-Verlag, Heidelberg, pp. 462-472.

Kacprzyk J. and Zadrożny S. (2000a) On combining intelligent querying and data mining using fuzzy logic concepts. In: G. Bordogna and G. Pasi (ed.): Recent Research Issues on the Management of Fuzziness in Databases, Physica - Verlag, Heidelberg and New York (in press).

Kacprzyk J. and Zadrożny S. (2000b) Data Mining via Fuzzy Querying over the Internet. In: Pons O., Vila M.A. and Kacprzyk J. (ed.): Knowledge Management in Fuzzy Databases, Physica - Verlag, Heidelberg and New York, pp. 211-233.

Kacprzyk J. and Zadrożny S. (2000c): Using Fuzzy Querying over the Internet to Browse Through Information Resources. In: P.P. Wang(Red.): Computing with Words, Wiley, New York (in press).

Kacprzyk J. and Ziółkowski A. (1986b) Database queries with fuzzy linguistic quantifiers. IEEE Transactions on Systems, Man and Cybernetics SMC - 16, 474 - 479.

Liu Y. and E.E. Kerre (1998) An overview of fuzzy quantifiers. (I) Interpretations. Fuzzy Sets and Systems 95, 1 – 21.

Pons O., M.A. V., Kacprzyk J. (Eds.): Knowledge Management in Fuzzy Databases, Physica-Verlag, Heidelberg, New York, Seria: Studies in Fuzziness and Soft Computing.

Rasmussen, D. and Yager, R.R. (1996) Using summarySQL as a tool for finding fuzzy and gradual functional dependencies, Proceedings of IPMU'96 (Granada, Spain), pp. 275-280.

Rasmussen, D. and Yager, R.R. (1997a) A fuzzy SQL summary language for data discovery, In: Dubois, D., Prade, H. and Yager, R.R. (eds.): Fuzzy Information Engineering: A Guided Tour of Applications, Wiley, New York, pp. 253-264, 1997.

Rasmussen, D. and Yager, R.R. (1997b) SummarySQL-A fuzzy tool for data mining, Intelligent Data Analysis - An International Journal 1 (Electonic Publication), URL-http//:www-east.elsevier.com/ida/browse/96-6/ida96-6.htm.

Rasmussen, D. and Yager, R.R. (1999) Finding fuzzy and gradual functional dependencies with summarySQL, Fuzzy Sets and Systems 106, 131-142.

Saaty, T.L. (1980) The Analitic Hierarchy Process: Planning, Priority Setting, Resource Allocation.. McGraw-Hill, New York.

Yager R.R.(1982) A new approach to the summarization of data. Information Sciences, 28, 69 – 86.

Yager R.R. (1988) On ordered weighted avaraging operators in multicriteria decision making. IEEE Trans. on Systems, Man and Cybern. SMC-18, 183-190.

Yager, R.R. (1989) On linguistic summaries of data, Proceedings of IJCAI Workshop on Knowledge Discovery in Databases, Detroit, 378-389.

Yager, R.R. (1991) On linguistic summaries of data, In: Piatetsky-Shapiro, G. and Frawley, B. (eds.): Knowledge Discovery in Databases, MIT Press, Cambridge, MA, pp. 347-363.

Yager, R.R. (1994) Linguistic summaries as a tool for database discovery, Proceedings of Workshop on Flexible Query-Answering Systems, Roskilde University, Denmark, pp. 17-22.

Yager, R.R. (1995a) Linguistic summaries as a tool for database discovery, Proceedings of Workshop on Fuzzy Database Systems and Information Retrieval at FUZZ-IEEE/IFES, Yokohama, pp. 79-82.

Yager, R.R. (1995b) Fuzzy summaries in database mining, Proceedings of the 11th Conference on Artificial Intelligence for Applications (Los Angeles, USA), pp. 265-269.

Yager, R.R. (1996) Database discovery using fuzzy sets, International Journal of Intelligent Systems 11, 691-712.

Yager R.R. and Kacprzyk J. (1997) The Ordered Weighted Averaging Operators: Theory and Applications. Kluwer, Boston.

Yager R.R. and Kacprzyk J. (1999) Linguistic Data Summaries: A Perspective. Proceedings of IFSA'99 Congress (Taipei), vol. 1, 44-48

Yager, R. R. and Rubinson, T. C. (1981) Linguistic summaries of data bases, Proceedings of IEEE Conf. on Decision and Control (San Diego, USA), pp. 1094-1097.

Zadeh L.A. (1983) A computational approach to fuzzy quantifiers in natural languages. Computers and Maths with Appls. 9, 149-184.

Zadeh L.A. (1985) Syllogistic reasoning in fuzzy logic and its application to usuality and reasoning with dispositions. IEEE Transaction on Systems, Man and Cybernetics, SMC-15, 754--763.

Zadeh L.A. and Kacprzyk, J. (eds.) (1992) Fuzzy Logic for the Management of Uncertainty, Wiley, New York.

Zadeh L. and Kacprzyk J. (eds.) (1999a) Computing with Words in Information/Intelligent Systems 1. Foundations. Physica-Verlag, Heidelberg and New York, 1999.

Zadeh L. and Kacprzyk J. (eds.) (1999b) Computing with Words in Information/Intelligent Systems 2. Applications. Physica-Verlag, Heidelberg and New York, 1999.

Zadrożny S. and Kacprzyk J.: On database summarization using a fuzzy querying interface, Proceedings of IFSA'99 World Congress (Taipei, Taiwan R.O.C.), vol. 1, pp. 39-43.

Chapter 7

INTEGRATING DATA SOURCES USING A STANDARDIZED GLOBAL DICTIONARY

Ramon Lawrence and Ken Barker*
Department of Computer Science, University of Manitoba, Canada

**Department of Computer Science, University of Calgary, Canada*

Keywords: database, standard, dictionary, integration, schema, relational, wrapper, mediator, web

Abstract: With the constantly increasing reliance on database systems to store, process, and display data comes the additional problem of using these systems properly. Most organizations have several data systems that must work together. As data warehouses, data marts, and other OLAP systems are added to the mix, the complexity of ensuring interoperability between these systems increases dramatically. Interoperability of database systems can be achieved by capturing the semantics of each system and providing a standardized framework for querying and exchanging semantic specifications.

Our work focuses on capturing the semantics of data stored in databases with the goal of integrating data sources within a company, across a network, and even on the World-Wide Web. Our approach to capturing data semantics revolves around the definition of a global dictionary that provides standardized terms for referencing and categorizing data. These standardized terms are then stored in record-based semantic specifications that store metadata and semantic descriptions of the data. Using these semantic specifications, it is possible to integrate diverse data sources even though they were not originally designed to work together.

A prototype of this integration system called the Relational Integration Model (RIM) has been built. This paper describes the architecture and benefits of the system, and its possible applications. The RIM application is currently being tested on production database systems and integration problems.

1. INTRODUCTION

Interoperability of database systems is becoming increasingly important as organizations increase their number of operational systems and add new decision-support systems. The construction, operation, and maintenance of these systems are complicated and time-consuming and grow quickly as the number of systems increases. Thus, a system that simplifies the construction and integration of data sources is of great importance.

Our work attempts to standardize the description of information. Behind most web sites and applications is a database storing the actual data. Our goal is to capture the semantics of the data stored in each database so that they may operate together. Capturing data semantics and integrating data sources is applicable to companies and organizations with multiple databases that must interoperate. More importantly, by presenting a framework for capturing data semantics, it is more likely that databases that were never intended to work together can be made to interoperate. This is especially important on the World-Wide Web, where users want to access data from multiple, apparently unrelated sources.

This work outlines a model for capturing data semantics to simplify the schema integration problem. The major contribution of the work is a systemized method for capturing data semantics using a standardized global dictionary and a model that uses this information to simplify schema integration in relational databases. This chapter describes the structure of the global dictionary and the benefits of the Relational Integration Model (RIM). Section 2 discusses the integration problem, and how capturing data semantics is fundamental to its solution. Previous work in the area is detailed in Section 3. Section 4 overviews our integration architecture which utilizes a global dictionary (Section 5) for identifying similar concepts, and a record-based integration language, the Relational Integration Model (Section 6), used to exchange metadata on systems. Details on integration related problems are given in Section 7, and applications of our integration technique are presented in Section 8. The chapter closes with future work and conclusions.

2. DATA SEMANTICS AND THE INTEGRATION PROBLEM

Integrating data sources involves combining the concepts and knowledge in the individual data sources into an integrated view of the data. The integrated view is a uniform view of all the knowledge in the data sources so that the user is isolated from the individual system details. By isolating the user from the data sources and the complexity of combining their knowledge, systems become "interoperable", at least from the user's perspective, as they can access the data in all data sources without worrying about how to accomplish this task.

Constructing an integrated view of many data sources is difficult because they will store different types of data, in varying formats, with different meanings, and will be referenced using different names. Subsequently, the construction of the integrated view must, at some level, handle the different mechanisms for storing data (structural conflicts), for referencing data (naming conflicts), and for attributing meaning to the data (semantic conflicts).

Although considerable effort has been placed on integrating databases, the problem remains largely unsolved due to its complexity. Data in individual data sources must be integrated at both the schema level (the description of the data) and the data level (individual data instances). This chapter will focus on schema-level integration. Schema integration is difficult because at some level both the operational and data semantics of a database need to be known for integration to be successful.

The schema integration problem is the problem associated with combining diverse schemas of different databases into a coherent integrated view by reconciling any structural or semantic conflicts between the component databases. Automating the extraction and integration of this data is difficult because the semantics of the data are not fully captured by its organization and syntactic schema.

Integrating data sources using schema integration is involved in constructing both a multidatabase system and a data warehouse. Both of these architectures are finding applications in industry because they allow users transparent access to data across multiple sites and provide a uniform, encompassing view of the data in an organization. On an even wider-scale, a standardized mechanism for performing schema integration would allow a user's browser to automatically combine data from multiple web sites and present it appropriately to the user. Thus, a mechanism for performing schema integration would be of great theoretical and practical importance.

The literature has proposed various methods for integrating data sources. However, the fundamental problem in these systems is the inability to capture data semantics. Automated integration procedures cannot be applied without a systematic way of capturing the meaning of the stored data. In this work, we propose a method for capturing data semantics which bridges the theoretical work and the pragmatic approach used in industry. A standardized global dictionary is defines words to reference identical concepts across systems. We then demonstrate a systematic method of storing data semantics using these dictionary words for integrating relational schemas.

3. PREVIOUS WORK

The integration problem involves combining data from two or more data sources and is often required between databases with widely differing views on the data and its organization. Thus, integration is hard because conflicts at both the structural and semantic level must be addressed. Further complicating the problem is that most systems do not explicitly capture semantic information. This forces designers performing the integration to impose assumptions on the data and manually integrate various data sources based on those assumptions. To perform integration, some specification of data semantics is required to identify related data. Since names and structure in a schema do not always provide a good indication of data meaning, it often falls on the designer to determine when data sources store related or equivalent data. The integration problem is related to the database view integration problem[1]. Batini[2] surveys early manual integration algorithms.

Previous work in this area has focused on capturing metadata about the data sources to aid integration. This metadata can be in the form of rules such as the work done by Sheth[3], or using some form of global dictionary such as work done by Castano[4]. We believe that the best approach involves defining a global dictionary rather than using rules to relate systems because rules are more subject to schema changes than a global dictionary implementation and grow exponentially as the number of systems increase.

Other research efforts include the definition of wrapper and mediator systems such as Information Manifold[5] and TSIMMIS[6]. These systems provide interoperability of structured and unstructured data sources by "wrapping" data sources using translation software. Once a data source has been integrated into the overall system, distributed querying is possible. However, the construction of the global view is mostly a manual process. Our approach is complimentary to these systems by studying how standardized dictionaries can be used to simplify and automate the construction of the integrated or global view.

Work on capturing metadata information in industry has resulted in the formation of a metadata consortium involving many companies in the database and software communities. The goal of the consortium is to standardize ways of capturing metadata so that it may be exchanged between systems. The consortium has defined the Metadata Interchange Specification (MDIS) version 1.1[7] as an emerging standard for specifying and exchanging metadata. The structured format is very good at specifying the data structure, names, and other schema information in record-form. However, the only method for capturing data semantics, besides the schema names used, are by using text description fields or storing semantic names in long name fields. The problem with this method is that systems cannot automatically process these optional description fields to determine equivalent data using the metadata information. Basically, this system lacks a global dictionary to relate terms.

Another emerging metadata standard is Extensible Markup Language (XML) [8]. The power of XML as a description language is its ability to associate markup terms with data elements. These markup terms serve as metadata allowing formalized description of the content and structure of the accompanying data. Unfortunately, the use of XML for integration is limited because XML does not define a standardized dictionary of terms. Thus, our approach extends industrial methodologies by systematically defining and applying a dictionary of terms that can be used across domains, industries, and organizations.

Global dictionaries have been used before to perform integration. Typically, the dictionary chosen consists of most (or all) of the English language terms. For example, the Carnot Project[9] used the Cyc Knowledge base as a global dictionary. The problem with such large dictionaries is that they lead to ambiguity that further complicates integration.

4. THE INTEGRATION ARCHITECTURE

Our integration architecture consists of two separate and distinct phases: the *capture process* and the *integration process*.

In the capture process (see Figure 1), the semantics and the metadata of a given data source are represented in record form using terms extracted from a global dictionary. This capture process is performed independently of the capture processes that may be occurring on other data sources. The only "binding" between individual capture processes at different data sources is the use of the global dictionary to provide standardized terms for referencing data.

The inputs of the capture process are a relational database and the global dictionary. Using a customized tool called a specification editor, the database administrator (DBA) attempts to capture the data semantics in a record-based form. The records storing the data description are called RIM specifications (explained in Section 6).

From the relational database schema, the specification editor extracts typical metadata information such as table names, field sizes and types, keys, indices, and constraints. All this information is readily available in the database schema and does not require any input by the DBA. This schema information is then stored in the appropriate fields in the RIM specification.

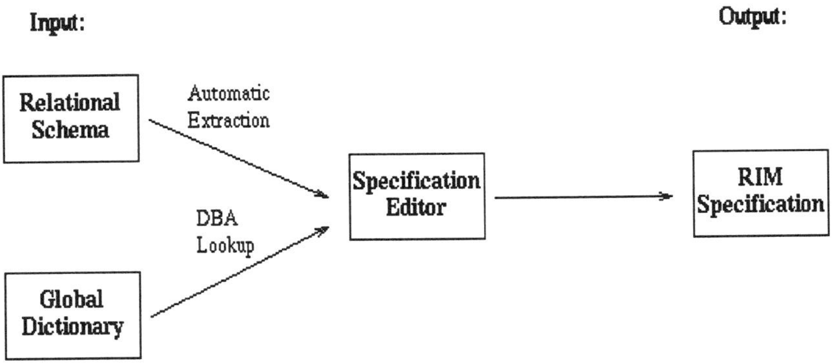

Figure 1. The Capture Process on a Relational Database

The second step in the capture process is less automatic. While the specification editor is parsing the database schema, it attempts to match attribute and table names to entries in the global dictionary. Since field names in schemas are not always descriptive, this matching process works by comparing the field names on a best effort basis to existing global dictionary terms. In addition, as system field names are matched to their global counterparts, this information is stored in the global dictionary for future use. Basically, the system remembers mappings between system names and global concepts, so if a system name is encountered again, the mapping is performed automatically.

The system's initial attempt at mapping system names to global concepts will almost always miss the semantic intent of some fields. It then falls on the DBA to determine the correct global dictionary terms for all concepts in the database. Depending on the size of the database, this may be a time consuming task, but it only needs to be performed once.

After all system names are mapped to terms in the global dictionary, these global terms are stored in the RIM specifications along with the schema information. The output of the capture process is a complete RIM specification which contains the necessary information to describe the data stored in the data source and to integrate it with other data sources. These RIM specifications are similar to export schemas in federated systems[10] with one difference; they also contain sufficient metadata to automate the integration process.

The integration phase of the architecture (see Figure 2) actually performs the integration of various data sources. The integration process begins when a client accesses two or more data sources. To access the data sources, a client connects and is authenticated by each data source required. The data source provides the client with its RIM specification describing its data. These RIM specifications are then combined at the client site by an integration algorithm which detects and resolve structural and semantic conflicts between the data sources. The output of the integration algorithm is an integrated view on which the client poses queries.

The integration algorithm is responsible for combining the RIM specifications for each data source and for partitioning a query posed on the integrated view into subtransactions on the individual data sources (de-integration). A brief description of the integration algorithm is provided in Section 6.

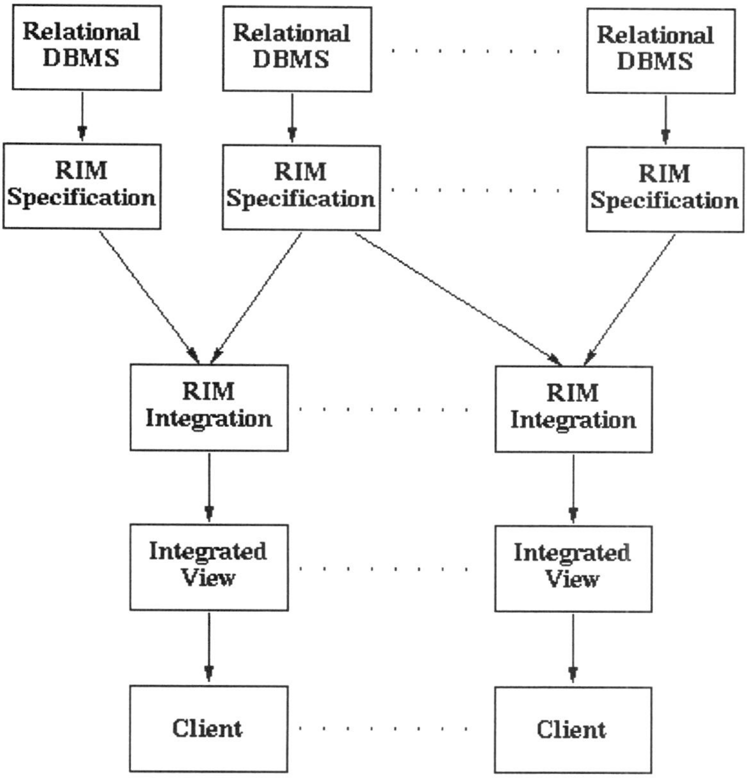

Figure 2. The Integration Process for Relational Databases

The two-phase architecture has several desirable properties:

1. Performs dynamic integration - schemas are combined one at a time into the integrated view
2. Captures both operational and structural metadata to resolve conflicts
3. Performs automatic conflict resolution
4. Metadata is captured only at the local level and semi-automatically which removes the designer from most integration-related problems
5. Local schemas are merged into an integrated view using a global dictionary to resolve naming conflicts

The key benefit to the two phase process is that the capture process is isolated from the integration process. This allows multiple capture processes to be performed concurrently and without knowledge of each other. Thus, the capture process at one data source does not affect the capture process at any other data source. This allows the capture process to be performed only once, regardless of how many data sources are integrated. This is a significant advantage as it allows application vendors and database designers to capture the semantics of their systems at design-time, and the clients of their products are able to integrate them with other systems with minimum effort.

The underlying framework which ties these capture processes together is the RIM specification. The RIM specification contains the schema information and semantic terms from the global dictionary. Using these terms, the integration algorithm is able to identify similar concepts even though their structural representations may be very different. As the global dictionary and its structure are central to the integration architecture, it is discussed in detail in the following sections.

5. THE GLOBAL DICTIONARY

To provide a framework for exchanging knowledge, there must be a common language in which to describe the knowledge. During ordinary conversation, people use words and their definitions to exchange knowledge. Knowledge transfer in conversation arises from the definitions of the words used and the structure in which they are presented. Since a computer has no built-in mechanism for associating semantics to words and symbols, an on-line dictionary is required to allow the computer to determine semantically equivalent expressions.

The problem in defining a global dictionary is the complexity of determining semantically equivalent words and phrases. The English language is very large with many equivalent words for specifying equivalent concepts. Thus, using an on-line English dictionary for the computer to consult is not practical. Not only is the size of the database a problem, but it is complicated for the computer to determine when two words represent semantically equivalent data. Bright used an English language dictionary in defining the Summary Schemas Model (SSM)[11] to query multidatabases using imprecise words, but it is difficult to base an integration methodology on such a model.

The other alternative is to construct a global dictionary using words as they appear in database schema. This has the advantage that the global dictionary is only storing the required terms. However, it still may be difficult to integrate global dictionaries across systems that are derived in this manner depending on the exact words chosen to represent the data. Castano[4] studied creating a global dictionary during integration.

Our approach is a hybrid of the two methodologies. The basis of the shared dictionary is a standardized concept hierarchy containing hypernym links relating concepts. This dictionary contains the most common concepts stored in databases. Each node in the hierarchy consists of a default term and definition. Synonyms for the default term in the node are also provided. The vast majority of the concepts in a database including dates, addresses, names, id/key fields, and description fields are captured using this simplified hierarchy.

The second component of the global dictionary is component relationships. Component relationships relate terms using a 'Part of' or 'HAS A' relationship. For example, an address has (or may have) city, state, postal code, and country components. Similarly, a person's name may have a first, last, and full name components. These component relationships are intended to standardize how common concepts with subcomponents are represented.

Ideally, a global dictionary consisting of a concept hierarchy and a set of component relationships would be enough to represent all data in databases. However, this is not possible as new types of data and very specialized data would not appear in the dictionary. Although a standards organization could continually evolve the global dictionary, this would not occur rapidly enough. Thus, we allow an organization to add nodes to the global dictionary to both the concept hierarchy and component relationships to capture and standardize names used in their organization which are not in the standardized global dictionary. These additional links are stored in a record format and are transmitted along with the metadata information during integration.

5.1 Using the Global Dictionary

The global dictionary serves as a mechanism for agreeing on the vocabulary describing the data. Without a standardized dictionary, it would be next to impossible to determine the meaning of data. The dictionary provides the computer with a framework for comparing individual words across database systems to determine if they are semantically equivalent. Obviously, when hypernym links are involved, there must be some mechanism for defining partial equivalence; terms that are related but not exactly similar. For this paper, we will use an approach proposed by Castano[4]. The semantic similarity between two words in the dictionary is based on the number of hypernym links between them. Each hypernym link has a value of 0.8, so traversing two hypernym links would result in a semantic similarity of 0.64.

Using a single word to describe the semantics of a database field or relation is insufficient. It is highly unlikely that a given dictionary word is able to capture all the semantics of a database element. We are proposing capturing data semantics using a semantic name with the following structure:

Semantic Name = [CT_1;CT_2; ... ;CT_N] Concept name
where CT_i is a context term

A context term is used to define the general context to which the semantic term applies, and typically corresponds to an entity or a relationship in the database. It is possible to have a hierarchy of context terms. For example, the city field of an address of a person has two contexts: the person and the person's address (i.e. [Person;Address] City). The concept name is a dictionary term which represents the semantics of the attribute describing the context. A semantic name does not have to include a concept name. Typically, a semantic name will contain a concept name only if it is describing an attribute of a table. A semantic name will not have a concept name if it is defining a context. Context terms and concept names are either extracted directly from the global dictionary or added to the global dictionary as needed.

The semantic names defined using this procedure can then be included in a metadata specification such as MDIS version 1.1 (in the description field), a RIM specification, as a XML tag, or another model capturing semantic metadata using records. The system will be able to use this information more readily to integrate metadata automatically than a plain-text description field.

5.2 Comparing semantic names

The first step in integrating RIM specifications is identifying equivalent or semantically similar names. The semantic similarity of two terms can be measured by the semantic distance between the two terms in the dictionary. The definition of semantic distance can vary by application. In some cases, two semantic names may be only deemed equivalent if they are exactly identical. For the purpose of this paper, we will define a simple formula for semantic distance based on the number of hypernym links separating the terms in the dictionary. However, other definitions of semantic distance are equally valid and may be more effective in certain applications.

Given a global dictionary *D*, a set of added global terms *A*, and two metadata specifications M_1 and M_2, an automated integration system must take the two specifications and use the dictionary to construct an integrated schema. Ideally, this process would be performed with minimal user input, although some user tuning may have to be performed at the end of the process. The first step is identifying semantically similar terms in the two specifications.

Let $F_{SD}(T_1,T_2)$ be a function that computes the semantic distance between two terms T_1 and T_2 in the dictionary. $F_{SD}(T_1,T_2) = 0.8^N$, where N = Number of hypernym links separating T_1 and T_2. For any semantic names S_1 from M_1 and S_2 from M_2, the system determines their semantic equivalence by first matching context terms then comparing concept names (if present).

The first step in comparing two semantic names S_1 and S_2 is to separate each semantic name S_i into a set of N context terms, $CT_{i(1..N)}$, and a concept name CN_i. Then, given the two sets of context terms $CT_{1(1..N)}$ and $CT_{2(1..M)}$, the individual global dictionary terms are compared in the order they appear.

Assume that S_1 is a semantic name already in the Integrated View (IV), and S_2 is the semantic name to be integrated into the IV. The distance between the two contexts is given by:

$$\mathrm{CT_{SD}} = \prod_{i=1..\min(N,M)} \mathrm{F_{SD}}(\mathrm{CT}_{1(i)},\mathrm{CT}_{2(i)})$$

That is, the semantic distance between the two contexts is the product of the semantic distances between the individual context terms taken pairwise in the order that they appear. If the contexts are sufficiently similar, then the concept names are compared. The semantic distance between two concept names is given by: $CN_{SD} = F_{SD}(CN_1,CN_2)$.

Thus, the unmodified semantic distance between S_1 and S_2 is $U_{SD} = CT_{SD} * CN_{SD}$. The unmodified semantic distance is not the final semantic distance calculated. Since the integration algorithm will be comparing the new semantic term S_2 to all semantic terms in the integrated view, modification constants are used to indicate more desirable matches in addition to semantic similarity in the global dictionary.

For example, assume S_2 = [A;B] C. If S_1 = [A;B;C], U_{SD} = 1 as the first two contexts (A,B) are identical and S_1 and S_2 do not both have concept names to compare. However, modification constants are applied to "penalize" S_1 for having an extra context (C) and no concept name. These constants insure that if S_3 = [A;B] C, then the semantic similarity of S_2 and S_3 is 1, while the similarity of S_1 and S_3 would be slightly less than 1.

6. THE RELATIONAL INTEGRATION MODEL

Using semantic names and the global dictionary, the system can more readily determine identical concepts in a metadata specification than by using only plain-text description fields or logical names. These semantic names can be inserted into a metadata specification model such as MDIS version 1.1[7], but we have also defined our own model for capturing and specifying metadata.

The Relational Integration Model (RIM) is designed to capture metadata and semantic names to allow automatic integration of relational database systems. The core idea behind the model is that semantic names are used to determine equivalent concepts across metadata specifications, and the model has been designed to represent schema in a way that makes it easy to convert the structure of the data as needed during integration.

The system is based on the ER model and models data as an entity, relationship, or attribute. A semantic name is associated with all entities and attributes (and optionally relationships), so that they may be identified during integration. Once identical (or semantically similar) concepts are found, it is easy to transform the concept's structural representation. For example, if an identical concept is represented as an entity in one schema and a relationship in another, the concept can be represented as either an entity or a relationship in the integrated schema, and the other representation can be mapped or converted into the chosen one.

RIM is similar to MDIS as it captures semantic information in record-form. However, we are planning on expanding RIM to capture behavioral characteristics in the future, hence the departure from MDIS. Using RIM and capturing semantic names, we can identify related global concepts across systems and transform their structures into an integrated schema.

6.1 The Integration Algorithm

To produce an integrated view of data sources, RIM specifications are first constructed containing metadata on each data source and semantic names describing their data. These RIM specifications then must be combined using the global dictionary and an integration algorithm into an integrated view. The integration algorithm combining RIM specifications consists of two distinct phases:

1. **Matching phase:** combines the semantic terms in the specification using the global dictionary into an integrated view
2. **Metadata phase:** uses additional metadata from the individual data sources (including relationships, constraints, and comments) to refine the integrated view

The matching phase proceeds by taking a RIM specification M_I and combining it with the integrated view. The algorithm can be abstracted as follows:

```
Procedure RIM_integration(M as RIM spec., IV as Int_View)
   For each RIM header (context) Hi in M
      sn = semantic name of Hi
      match_sname(sn,Hi,IV)
   Next i

   For each RIM schema (concept) Ti in M
      sn = semantic name of Ti
      match_sname(sn,Ti,IV)
   Next i
End Procedure

Procedure match_sname(sn as semantic_name, V as
     Context/Concept, IV as Int_View)

   max = 0
   For all root-level contexts Ci in the IV
      Recursive_match(sn,Ci,best_match,sem_dist)
      If sem_dist > max Then Keep Best Match (max)
   Next
   // Add sn to IV: If there is a best_match use it
   //   otherwise add new name
   Integrate_semantic_name(sn, best_match, IV)
End Procedure

Procedure Recursive_match(sn as Semantic name, CT as Context,
     best_match as Variant, max as double)

   max = 0
   sd = Compute_SD(sn,CT)
   cutoff_value = 0.5
   If sd > cutoff_value Then
```

```
      If sn has more context terms than CT Then
         For each subcontext SCj of CT
            Recursive_match(sn,SCj,best_match,sem_dist,status)
            If sem_dist > max Then Keep best match (max)
         Next
      End If

      For each concept CNj in CT
         sd = Compute_SD(sn, CNj)
         If sd > max Then Keep best match (max)
      Next
   End If
End Procedure
```

It is important to note that each semantic name in the RIM specification is separately integrated into the integrated view. Thus, once a term from the specification is added to the view, the next term from the specification will also be integrated with the newly added term. This is desirable because the integration algorithm is consistent regardless of the number of RIM specifications combined into the integrated view, even if there are none. Another desirable feature is that integration occurs "within" a specification itself which combines contexts and concepts into a better form than they originally appear. Thus, RIM headers (contexts) are added first, in order to provide a framework for the RIM schemas (concepts) to be integrated into.

The majority of the integration work is performed by the semantic name matching algorithm. This algorithm takes a semantic name to be integrated, and finds and combines the term appropriately into the integrated view. The matching algorithm recursively matches a given semantic name S_i to all contexts and concepts in the integrated view.

The *recursive_match* function takes the semantic name of S_i (**sn** in code), and the root-level context C_i, and recursively matches S_i with C_i and all of its subcontexts. The *recursive_match* function then returns the best matching context or concept, and its semantic distance from S_i. If a match is found, the type of match is important because it indicates if schema changes may be necessary. The type of match depends on if the integrated view term and S_i are contexts or concepts. For example, a context-concept type match occurs if the integrated view term is a context and S_i is a concept. Similarly, 3 other types of matches are possible: context-context, concept-concept, and concept-context.

At this point, the semantic name S_i has been compared to the integrated view, and its proper integration point has been determined. The *integrate_semantic_name* procedure takes this information and updates the view. The exact result will depend on if a match was made and its type. The procedure may add contexts, subcontexts, and concepts to the integrated view, especially when S_i did not perfectly match anything in the view. Regardless, this procedure records S_i in the integrated view and the database source information for use in querying. Replication of this procedure for all terms S_i in the RIM specification completes the integration.

Once all semantic terms of the RIM specification are initially integrated into the view, a second integration phase is performed. The second step uses metadata in the individual data sources to refine the integration. Semantic names are not used in this procedure. The metadata phase of the integration algorithm performs the following actions:

1. Uses relationship information such as cardinalities in the specification to promote/demote hierarchical contexts created in the initial phase.
2. Uses field sizes and types to validate initial matchings.
3. Creates views to calculate totals for data sources that are integrated with data sources containing totals on semantically similar data.

6.2 Integration Example using RIM

To illustrate the application of RIM specifications and a global dictionary, this section presents a very simple example of its use. For this example, a reduced RIM specification format will be used which consists only of the system names and their associated semantic names for each table and field in the databases. Normally, field sizes, types, indices, foreign keys, and other syntactic metadata is also present in a RIM specification.

Consider XYZ shipping company which has a relational database storing damage claim information, and ABC hauling company which uses a similar database. XYZ shipping company just bought out ABC hauling company and would like to use both databases together instead of building a new one. The structure of the XYZ database is: *Claims_tb(claim_id, claimant, net_amount, paid_amount)*. The structure of the ABC database is: *T_claims(id, customer, claim_amount)* and *T_payments(cid, pid, amount)*. Notice that the ABC database may store multiple payments per claim, whereas the XYZ database only stores one payment amount.

A capture process is performed on each database to produce a RIM specification describing their data. The RIM specifications for the XYZ database and the ABC database are given in Tables 1 and 2 respectively.

Table 1. RIM Specification for XYZ Database

Type	System Name	Semantic Name
Table	Claims_tb	[Claim]
Field	Claim_id	[Claim] Id
Field	Claimant	[Claim] Claimant
Field	Net_amount	[Claim] Net amount
Field	Paid_amount	[Claim;Payment] Amount

Table 2. RIM Specification for ABC Database

Type	System Name	Semantic Name
Table	T_claims	[Claim]
Field	Id	[Claim] Id
Field	Customer	[Claim] Customer
Field	Claim_amount	[Claim] Amount
Table	T_payments	[Claim;Payment]
Field	Cid	[Claim] Id
Field	Pid	[Claim;Payment] Id
Field	Amount	[Claim;Payment] Amount

Each table has a semantic name associated with the entity (record instance) it contains. (i.e. "Claim" and "Payment") A field of a table modifies or describes the entity which is the context of the attribute. Thus, the *claim_id* field in *Claims_tb* has a context of "Claim" because it describes the claim entity, and a concept (or attribute) name of "id". In the case of the field *pid* in table *T_payments*, the id attribute actually describes two contexts: a payment and a claim, as a payment itself describes a claim.

It is obvious from examining the two tables that the integration algorithm would detect equivalent concepts for many fields using strict equivalence on the semantic names. However, in some cases a measure of semantic distance is required. For example, the semantic names [Claim] Claimant and [Claim] Customer are not equivalent, but would have a very low semantic distance as the two terms would be very close together in the dictionary.

The integrated view produced is: *Claim(id, claimant, amount, Payment(id, amount))*. Note that in the case of the XYZ company database the payment id is NULL as there is only one payment. Using the global dictionary the integrated view is produced automatically using the RIM specifications. The integrated view is a hierarchy of concepts rather than a physical structure. Thus, a mapping is performed during querying from semantic names representing concepts to the system names of physical fields and tables in the underlying data sources.

A major benefit of this procedure is that no explicit mappings or rules are produced relating the two systems. This means that the schemas of the systems can be changed without requiring the integration to be totally re-done. Only the RIM specification of the affected database would need to be changed, and the integration procedure should be able to automatically reconstruct an updated view which reflects the changes. Finally, integrating new data sources is significantly easier as only one new RIM specification would have to be created. Suppose CDE company bought out ABC and XYZ companies. To integrate all three databases, a RIM specification is only constructed for the CDE database, which is then combined with the two other databases without any knowledge of their structure. Thus, this architecture scales well as the number of databases to be integrated increases.

7. SPECIAL CASES OF INTEGRATION

With properly selected semantic terms, most integrations produce expected results. However, there are some special cases to consider. This section explains how to resolve some of these issues.

The most serious integration problem is false matchings between semantic terms. Consider the previous example. One database stores a claimant and the other stores a customer. In the global dictionary, the term claimant is one link (subtype) below customer, so the semantic distance between the two terms is 0.8. The system then combines these terms together which is a desirable result.

However, consider how phone numbers will be integrated. In the global dictionary, the term phone number has subtypes home phone number, fax number, and cell number among others. If phone number is already in the integrated view, and fax number is added, the two concepts will be combined as they have a semantic distance of 0.8. Unfortunately, unlike the customer-claimant combination, phone and fax numbers are separate concepts which should not be combined even though they are semantically similar.

This false integration problem is called **hierarchical mis-integration**. The reason for these faulty integrations is that two semantically similar, hierarchical concepts are combined together based on their high semantic similarity even though they are distinct, real-world concepts and should not be combined.

One possible solution to this problem is to add weighted links between terms in the dictionary instead of using a uniform link value. Thus, the link between phone and fax number may only be 0.4, whereas the link between phone number and home phone number may be 0.8. The problem with this approach is the loss of uniformity in the global dictionary, and the difficulty in assigning link values to insure correct integrations.

Our approach involves the detection and promotion of related, hierarchical terms. The general idea is if term A currently exists in the integrated view and term B which is a subtype of A is added, then term A is promoted to a context ([A]), and the concept [A] A is added. Finally, the concept B is inserted as [A] B.

For example, consider the previous case of phone and fax numbers. Let the integrated view contain the semantic name [Customer] Phone Number (a customer's phone number), and we wish to add the fax number of the customer. The concept [Customer] Phone Number gets promoted to a context, i.e. [Customer;Phone Number], then, a concept phone number is inserted [Customer;Phone Number] Phone Number. Finally, the new concept [Customer;Phone Number] Fax Number is added. The final view is: [Customer], [Customer;Phone Number], [Customer;Phone Number] Phone Number, [Customer;Phone Number] Fax Number.

Thus, the phone and fax number concepts are kept separate, and a higher-level notion (that of all phone numbers regardless of usage) is also defined. In most cases, this hierarchical promotion feature is desirable for integration. However, in some cases it may be inappropriate. In the claims database example, the merger of customer and claimant in the two databases would produce an integrated view of: [Claim], [Claim;Customer], [Claim;Customer;Claimant]. Ideally, the integrated view should be:[Claim], [Claim;Claimant]. That is, the user is generally not interested in the distinction between a customer and a claimant, as the distinction is more terminology than semantics. Thus, although the user is still allowed to query only on the customer and claimant "levels", for most queries the users wants to see only the claimant "level" with all customer and claimant information merged into it. This demotion or merger activity is performed in the metadata phase of integration and is based on the relationships between the concepts/contexts.

Another integration challenge is the handling of totals and aggregates. In the claims database example, it may be possible that the payment amount in the XYZ database is actually the total amount of all payments, and not the value of one payment. In this case, it makes more sense to name the field [Claims;Total;Payment] Amount, so that it is not integrated with the individual payment amounts in the ABC database. This implies the system should calculate the payment totals for the ABC database as required.

Finally, in some cases a default concept name should be assumed for a semantic name, even if it already has a concept name. For example, the semantic name for a city in a database may be given as [Address] City, however this should really be represented as [Address;City] Name. Depending on the dictionary term, a default concept name of "name" or "description" may be appropriate.

8. APPLICATIONS TO THE WWW

Integrating data sources automatically would have a major impact on how the World-Wide Web is used. The major limitation in the use of the Net, besides the limited bandwidth, is in the inability to find and integrate the extensive databases of knowledge that exist. When a user accesses the Web for information, they are often required to access many different web sites and systems, and manually pull together the information presented to them. The task of finding, filtering, and integrating data consumes the majority of the time, when all the user really requires is the information. For example, when the user wishes to purchase a product on-line and wants the best price, it is up to the user to visit the appropriate web sites and "comparison shop". It would be useful if the user's web browser could do the comparison shopping.

In our architecture, these types of queries are now possible. To achieve this, each web site would specify their database using a RIM specification. The client's browser would contain the global dictionary and a list of web sites to access to gather information. When the user wishes to purchase an item, the browser downloads the RIM specifications from the on-line stores, integrates them using the global dictionary, and then allows the user to query all databases at once through the "integrated view of web sites" that was constructed. Obviously, the integration itself is complex, but a system which achieves automatic integration of data sources would have a major impact on how the Web is used and delivered.

9. FUTURE WORK AND CONCLUSIONS

In this chapter, we have detailed how a standardized global dictionary, a formalized method for capturing data semantics, and a systematic approach for calculating semantic distance between phrases can be used to identify similar concepts across data sources. These semantic names can then be inserted into a metadata descriptive model such as MDIS or RIM, and can be automatically processed during integration. This reduces the amount of user input required to integrate diverse data sources and serves as a mechanism for capturing and displaying semantics of the data.

Future work includes refining the standardized dictionary and modifying the integration software. We have already completed construction of RIM software including a specification editor tool and integration module. We plan to test its performance on existing systems and integration problems in the near future.

REFERENCES:

1. R. Hull and G. Zhou. A framework for supporting data integration using the materialized and virtual approaches. In *Proceedings of ACM SIGMOD Conference on Management of Data*, Montreal, Canada, 1996, pages 481-492.
2. C. Batini, M. Lenzerini and S. B. Navathe. A Comparative Analysis of Methodologies for Database Schema Integration. *ACM Computing Surveys*, 18(4) Dec. 1986, pages 323-364.
3. A. P. Sheth and G. Karabatis. Multidatabase interdependencies in industry. In *Proceedings of ACM SIGMOD Conference on Management of Data*, Washington, DC, USA, 1993, pages 481-492.
4. S. Castano and V. Antonellis. Semantic dictionary design for database interoperability. In *Proceedings of the 13th International Conference on Data Engineering (ICDE'97)*, 1997, pages 43-54.
5. T. Kirk, A. Levy, Y. Sagiv and D. Srivastava. The Information Manifold. In *AAAI Spring Symposium on Information Gathering*, 1995.
6. C. Li, R. Yerneni, V. Vassalos, H. Garcia-Molina, Y. Papakonstantinou, J. Ullman and M. Valiveti. Capability Based Mediation in TSIMMIS. . In *Proceedings of ACM SIGMOD Conference on Management of Data*, Seattle, WA, USA, 1998, pages 564-566.
7. The Metadata coalition. Metadata interchange specification. Technical Report version 1.1, August 1997.
8. W3C. Extensible Markup Langauge (XML) specification. Technical Report version 1.0, February 1998.
9. C. Collet, M. Huhns, and W-M. Shen. Resource integration using a large knowledge base in Carnot. *IEEE Computer*. 24(12), December 1991, pages 55-62.
10. A. Sheth and J. Larson. Federated database systems for managing distributed, heterogenous and autonomous databases. *ACM Computing Surveys*, 22(3) Sept. 1990, pages 183-236.
11. M. Bright, A.Hurson, and S. Pakzad. Automated resolution of semantic heterogeneity in multidatabases. In *ACM Transactions on Database Systems*, 19(2) June 1994, pages 212-253.

Chapter 8

MAINTENANCE OF DISCOVERED ASSOCIATION RULES

Sau Dan Lee
Department of Computer Science and Information Systems, The University of Hong Kong, H. K.
sdlee@csis.hku.hk

David Cheung
Department of Computer Science and Information Systems, The University of Hong Kong, H. K.
dcheung@csis.hku.hk

Keywords: data mining, knowledge discovery, association rules, rule maintenance

Abstract: While data mining large databases has become a very hot topic these years, few researches look into the maintenance of the information mined. We argue that incremental updating of discovered knowledge is no less important than data mining itself. In this chapter we define the problem of incrementally updating mined association rules. We present efficient technique that we have developed to solve this non-trivial problem. The proposed techniques are implemented and both theoretically and empirically verified.

1 INTRODUCTION

With the rapid development of technology, it has now become much easier to collect data. Many new data collection devices have been invented or improved to make the data collection process more efficient and more accurate. For example, bar-code readers in point-of-sales systems can identify the type and model of the purchased items, enabling the collection of data about the sales of items in a department store. Many data collection processes which used to be performed manually have become either semi-automated or fully-automated. As a result, the amount of data that can be collected per man-hour has increased.

Meanwhile, new and improved technologies have caused storage devices to drop in price and increase in variety and performance. RAID implementations, both software-based or hardware-based, have become affordable and practical options for robust storage. New storage media such as rewritable compact disks make it possible to store very large volumes of data conveniently. The decrease in price to capacity ratio has lowered the cost of storing large amounts of data. It is now possible to store large amounts of data on computers at very affordable costs.

As a result many organizations and corporations can now collect and store gigabytes of data with ease. Such data is also considered by these corporations as important assets, as many useful information can potentially be discovered from these data. Researchers and practitioners are looking for tools to extract useful information from these on-line or archived treasures. Many interesting studies and important techniques have been performed and proposed [1, 2, 6]. Data mining has the following special characteristics.

1. The size of the database is generally very large.
2. The rules or knowledge discovered from the database only reflect a particular state of the database.

Because of the second characteristic, maintenance of discovered rules or knowledge is an important issue in data mining. Without efficient incremental updating techniques, it will be difficult to adopt data mining in practical applications.

Mining *association rules* is an important problem in data mining [2]. A representative class of users of this technique is the retail industry. A sales record in a retail database typically consists of all the items bought by a customer in a transaction, together with other pieces of information such as date, card identification number, etc. Mining association rules in such a database is to discover from a huge number of transaction records the strong associations among the items sold such that the presence of one item in a transaction may imply the presence of another. It has been shown that the problem of mining association rules can be decomposed into two subproblems [1]. The first is to find out all *large itemsets* which are *contained* by a significant number of transactions with respect to a threshold *minimum support*. The second is to generate all the association rules from the large itemsets found, with respect to another threshold, the *minimum confidence*. Since it is straight forward to generate association rules if the large itemsets are available, the challenge is in computing the large itemsets. The cost of computing the large itemsets consists of two main components.

1. The I/O cost in scanning the database.
2. For each transaction read, the cost of identifying all candidate itemsets which are contained in the transaction.

For the second component, the dominant factor is the size of the search domain, i.e., the number of candidate itemsets.

One of the earliest proposed algorithm for association rules mining is Apriori [1, 2]. It has adopted a level-wise pruning technique which prunes candidate sets by levels. The pruning makes use of the large itemsets found in one level (size k) to generate the candidates of the next level (size $k+1$). This in general could reduce significantly the amount of candidate sets after the first level. The DHP (Direct Hashing and Pruning) [6] algorithm is a variant of Apriori. It uses a hash table to perform some look ahead counting on the candidates of the next level to enhance the pruning power of Apriori. The essence these two algorithms is the technique of using the search result in one level to prune the candidates of the next level, and hence reduce the searching cost. The smaller the number of candidate sets is, the faster the algorithm would be.

In this chapter, we give a solution to the incremental update problem of association rules after a nontrivial number of updates have been performed on a database. The updates in general would include insertions, deletions and modifications of transaction records in the database. There are several important characteristics in the update problem.

1. The update problem can be reduced to finding the new set of large itemsets. After that, the new association rules can be computed from the new large itemsets.

2. Generally speaking, an old large itemset has the potential to become small in the new database.

3. Similarly, an old small itemset could become large in the new database.

One possible approach to the update problem is to re-run the association rule mining algorithm on the whole updated database. This approach, though simple, has some obvious disadvantages. All the computations done previously in finding out the old large itemsets are wasted and all large itemsets have to be computed again from scratch. Although it is relatively straight forward to find out the new large itemsets among the old large itemsets (by simply using their old support counts in the previous mining exercise plus a single scan of the inserted and deleted transactions), finding out the new large itemsets among the previously small ones presents a great challenge. The reason is that the support counts of the previously small itemsets are far too numerous to be kept across mining exercises. The key to performance here is to develop very effective pruning techniques that can vastly reduce the number of old small itemsets that have to be checked, resulting in a much smaller number of candidate sets in the update process.

We will see in this chapter how an algorithm, called "FUP2 ", is developed for the incremental update problem. We will first briefly go through the problem definition, and then study the cases for the insertion-only and deletion-only cases The algorithm FUP2 for the general case is then given. Performance study and further discussions are then presented.

We have previously proposed the FUP algorithm for the special case in which the updates consist of insertions but no deletion nor modification [3]. FUP2 is a generalization of FUP, which handles the general case in which insertions, deletions, and modifications could all be applied on the database. Another major difference of FUP2 from FUP is the development of pruning techniques on the set of candidates.

Extensive experiments have been conducted to study the performance of our new algorithm FUP2 and compare it against the cases in which either Apriori or DHP is applied to the updated database to find the new large itemsets. FUP2 is found to be 4 to 6 times faster than re-running Apriori or DHP. More importantly, the number of candidate sets generated by FUP2 is found to be only about 40% of that in Apriori. This shows that FUP2 is very effective in reducing the number of candidate sets.

2 PROBLEM DESCRIPTION

First, we give an informal description of the mathematical concepts employed in this chapter. More precise definitions of the notations are given in later subsections.

The problem of mining association rules is modeled after a supermarket *transaction database.* When a supermarket customer checks out his *items* at the cashier, the machine can keep a record of what items he has purchased in that *transaction.* In this problem, we are concerned only with *whether or not* certain items are purchased in a transaction. The amounts of such items bought in the transaction are irrelevant. Neither is the customer ID (in case he pays with credit card or by any other means such that he can be identified) within the interest of this problem.

The customer can choose any items $i_1, i_2, \ldots, i_m$ from the set I of all the m available items in the supermarket. This m is typically of the order of thousands. Since the amounts purchased is unimportant, a transaction T is just a subset of the available items I. Throughout a day (or any long span of time), there will be many checkout instances at all the opened cashier counters of the supermarkets. So, a large number of transactions can be collected over such a period of time. Such a collection is called a transaction database (or simply "database") D. As time passes, new transactions are added to the database and obsolete transactions are removed. The set of new transactions are denoted "Δ^+" while the obsolete transactions are denoted "Δ^-". The database so updated is named "D'".

Association rules are rules of the form "In a transaction, if the p items $i_{k_1}, i_{k_2}, \ldots, i_{k_p}$ are all purchased, then the q items $i_{l_1}, i_{l_2}, \ldots, i_{l_q}$ are also *likely* to be purchased, too." For convenience, we call any set of available items an *itemset*. So, the set of items $i_{k_1}, i_{k_2}, \ldots, i_{k_p}$ can be denoted as an itemset X. Similarly, we can write $Y = \{i_{l_1}, i_{l_2}, \ldots, i_{l_q}\}$. Thus, the above verbal rule can be abbreviated as "$X \Rightarrow Y$". Of course, such a rule does not always hold in a real transaction database. Exceptions are often. We emphasize the word *likely* in the above rule. The measure of how likely the rule will hold is called the *confidence* of the rule.

Not all association rules in the database are interesting or useful. In particular, rules that are applicable to only a few transactions are not very useful. A rule "$X \Rightarrow Y$" is *applicable* to transaction T if T contains all the items in X, i.e. $T \supseteq X$. The percentage of transactions in a database for which an association rule is applicable is called the *support* of the rule. So, we are only interested in rules with high *support*. Moreover, among such rules, only those with high *confidence* are useful. Therefore, the association rule mining problem is to discover all association rules in the database with *support* and *confidence* higher than some specified thresholds. Naturally, the maintenance problem is to find out new association rules satisfying these threshold in the updated database, and to remove stale rules that no longer satisfy these thresholds.

2.1 MINING OF ASSOCIATION RULES

Let $I = \{i_1, i_2, \ldots, i_m\}$ be a set of literals, called *items*. Let D be a database of transactions, where each transaction T is a set of items such that $T \subseteq I$. For a given *itemset* $X \subseteq I$ and a given transaction T, we say that T *contains* X if and only if $X \subseteq T$. The *support count* σ_X of an itemset X is defined to be the number of transactions in D that contain X. We say that an itemset X is *large*, with respect to a given *support threshold* of s, if $\sigma_X \geq s \times |D|$, where $|D|$ is the number of transactions in the database D. An *association rule* is an implication of the form "$X \Rightarrow Y$", where $X \subseteq I$, $Y \subseteq I$ and $X \cap Y = \emptyset$. The association rule $X \Rightarrow Y$ is said to hold in the database D with *confidence* c if the ratio of $\sigma_{X \cup Y}$ over σ_X equals c. The rule $X \Rightarrow Y$ has *support* t in D if $\sigma_{X \cup Y} = t \times |D|$. For a given pair of confidence and support thresholds, the problem of mining association rules is to find out all the association rules that have confidence and support greater than the corresponding thresholds. This problem can be reduced to the problem of finding all large itemsets for the same support threshold [1].

Thus, if s is the given support threshold, the mining problem is reduced to the problem of finding the set $L = \{X | X \subseteq I \ \wedge \ \sigma_X \geq s \times |D|\}$. For the convenience of subsequent discussions, we call an itemset that contains exactly k items a *k-itemset*. We use the symbol L_k to denote the set of all k-itemsets in L.

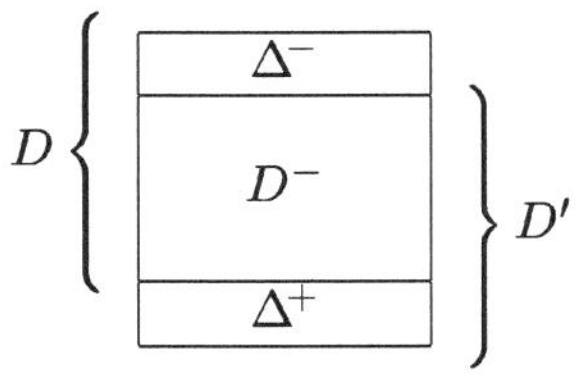

Figure 8.1 Definitions of D, D', Δ^-, D^- and Δ^+

database	**support count of itemset X**	**Large k-itemsets**
Δ^+	δ_X^+	—
D^-	—	—
Δ^-	δ_X^-	—
$D = \Delta^- \cup D^-$	σ_X	L_k
$D' = D^- \cup \Delta^+$	σ'_X	L'_k

Table 8.1 Definitions of several symbols

2.2 UPDATE OF ASSOCIATION RULES

After some update activities, old transactions are deleted from the database D and new transactions are added. We can treat the modification of existing transactions as deletion followed by insertion. Let Δ^- be the set of deleted transactions and Δ^+ be the set of newly added transactions. We assume, without loss of generality, that $\Delta^- \subseteq D$. Denote the updated database by D'. Note that $D' = (D - \Delta^-) \cup \Delta^+$. We denote the set of unchanged transactions by $D^- = D - \Delta^- = D' - \Delta^+$. Since the relative order of the transactions within the database does not affect the mining results, we may assume that all of the deleted transactions are located at the beginning of the database and all of the new transactions are appended at the end, as illustrated in Figure 8.1.

As defined in the previous section, σ_X is the support count of itemset X in the original database D. The set of large itemsets in D is L. Define σ'_X to be the new support count of an itemset X in the updated database D', and L' and L'_k to be the set of large itemsets and large k-itemsets in D' respectively. We further define δ_X^+ to be the support count of itemset X in the database Δ^+ and δ_X^- to be that of Δ^-. These definitions are summarized in Table 8.1. We define $\delta_X = \delta_X^+ - \delta_X^-$ which is the change of support count of itemset X as a result of the update activities. Thus, we have:

Lemma 1 $\sigma'_X = \sigma_X + \delta_X^+ - \delta_X^- = \sigma_X + \delta_X$
Proof. By definition.

As the result of a previous mining on the old database D, we have already found L and σ_X $\forall X \in L$. Thus, the update problem is to find L' and σ'_X $\forall X \in L'$ efficiently, given the knowledge of D, D', Δ^-, Δ^+, L and σ_X $\forall X \in L$. In other words, we need to find out the new large itemsets and their supports given the old large itemsets and their supports.

3 THE FUP ALGORITHM FOR THE INSERTION ONLY CASE

Since modification can be treated as a deletion followed by an insertion, an update algorithm only has to handle the insertion and deletion cases. Although the same approach will be used to solve the problem for both cases, there are asymmetrical characteristics in the techniques required for the two cases. Therefore, we first restrict the updates to insertions only and discuss the techniques used for this special case in this section. In the next section, the technique will be extended to solve the general case.

Now, we consider the case of insertions of new transaction records only. In this case, $\Delta^- = \emptyset$. Hence $D' = D \cup \Delta^+$, and $D = D^-$. The algorithm for this case is called the FUP algorithm (FUP stands for Fast UPdate). Similar to Apriori, FUP computes large itemsets of different sizes by levels iteratively, beginning at the size-one itemsets at level one. Moreover, the candidate sets (size k) at each iteration are generated based on the large itemsets (size $k-1$) found at the previous iteration. The features of FUP which distinguish it from Apriori are listed as follows.

1. At each iteration, the supports of the old large k-itemsets in L are updated against the increment Δ^+ to filter out the *losers*, i.e., those that are no longer large in D'. The increment Δ^+ is scanned only once to perform this update.

2. While scanning the increment Δ^+, a set of candidate itemsets, C_k, is extracted from Δ^+, together with their supports in Δ^+ counted. The supports of these candidates are then updated against the database D to find the "new" large itemsets.

3. More importantly, many sets in C_k can be pruned away by a simple check on their support counts in Δ^+ before their support is updated against D. (This check will be discussed in the following.)

The pruning of the candidates in C_k provides FUP with a strong edge over a re-running of Apriori or DHP on the updated database. The following is a detailed description of the algorithm FUP. The first iteration of FUP is discussed followed by the discussion of the remaining iterations.

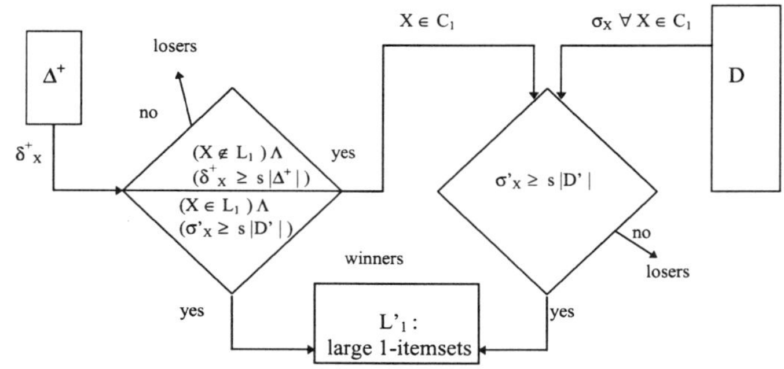

Figure 8.2 Processes in the first iteration of FUP.

3.1 FIRST ITERATION OF FUP

The following properties are useful in the derivation of the large 1-itemsets for the updated database.

Lemma 2 *If $\Delta^- = \emptyset$, a 1-itemset X not in the original large 1-itemsets L_1, (i.e. $X \notin L_1$), can become large in D', (i.e., $X \in L'$), only if $\delta_X^+ > s \times |\Delta^+|$.*
Proof. Since X is not in the original large 1-itemsets L_1, $\sigma_X < s \times |D|$. If $\delta_X^+ \leq s \times |\Delta^+|$, then $\sigma'_X = \sigma_X + \delta_X^+ < s \times (|D| + |\Delta^+|) = s \times |D'|$. That is, X cannot become a large itemset in D'. Thus we have the lemma.

Lemma 2 implies a powerful pruning technique to select the candidates for new size-1 large itemsets. We can restrict the search domain on the subset of all size-1 itemsets which are large in Δ^+. This subset is much smaller than the set of all size-1 old small itemsets. Following this result, the following procedure can be used to compute the large 1-itemset L'_1 in D'. (The steps are described graphically in Figure 8.2 for easy understanding.)

1. Scan the increment Δ^+ to compute the support count δ_X^+ for all itemsets $X \in L_1$. Remove the losers from L_1 by checking the condition $\sigma'_X = \sigma_X + \delta_X^+ < s \times |D'|$ on all $X \in L_1$. The remaining itemsets in L_1 are the old large itemsets that remain large in D', i.e., they become members of L'_1.

2. In the same scan on Δ^+, store in C_1 all size-one itemsets found in Δ^+ which do not belong to L_1. The support counts δ_X^+ $\forall X \in C_1$ are also computed in the scan. According to Lemma 2, if $X \in C_1$ and $\delta_X^+ \leq s \times |\Delta^+|$, X can never be large in D'. Therefore, we can prune off all the itemsets in C_1 whose support counts in Δ^+ are less than $s \times |\Delta^+|$. This gives us a small candidate set for finding the new size-one large itemsets.

3. Scan D to compute σ_X and hence σ'_X $\forall X \in C_1$. New large itemsets in C_1 can then be found by checking their support counts against the threshold. All size-one large itemsets in L'_1 can then be obtained by combining the large itemsets found in steps 1 and 3.

Example 1 A database D is updated with an increment Δ^+ such that $|D| = 1000$, $|\Delta^+| = 100$ and $s = 3\%$. $\mathcal{A}$, $\mathcal{B}$, $\mathcal{C}$, and $\mathcal{D}$ are four items, and $\mathcal{A}$ and $\mathcal{B}$ are the large itemsets in L_1 with $\sigma_{\mathcal{A}} = 32$, and $\sigma_{\mathcal{B}} = 31$.

After a scan on Δ^+, assume that we find $\delta^+_{\mathcal{A}} = 4$ and $\delta^+_{\mathcal{B}} = 1$. Hence $\sigma'_{\mathcal{A}} = 36 \geq 3\% \times 1100$ and $\sigma'_{\mathcal{B}} = 32 < 3\% \times 1100$. Therefore $\mathcal{B}$ is a loser, and only $\mathcal{A}$ is included in L'_1 (i.e., remains to be large in D'.)

Assume that $\mathcal{C}$ and $\mathcal{D}$ are two itemsets which are not in L_1 but occur in the increment Δ^+. Both $\mathcal{C}$ and $\mathcal{D}$ are potential candidate sets. In the scan of Δ^+, it is found that $\delta^+_{\mathcal{C}} = 6$ and $\delta^+_{\mathcal{D}} = 2$. Since $\delta^+_{\mathcal{D}} < s \times |\Delta^+| = 3\% \times 100$, it is removed from the candidate set C_1, (i.e., it is unnecessary to check $\mathcal{D}$ against D). Only $\mathcal{C}$ is included in C_1. Suppose that $\sigma_{\mathcal{C}} = 28$ is obtained in the scan of D. Thus, $\sigma'_{\mathcal{C}} = \sigma_{\mathcal{C}} + \delta^+_{\mathcal{C}} = 34 \geq 3\% \times 1100$, and $\mathcal{C}$ is included in L'_1.

Compared to Apriori and DHP, FUP first filters out the losers from L_1 and obtains the first set of winners by examining only the incremental database Δ^+. It also filters out from the remaining candidate sets in Δ^+ those items whose occurrence frequencies are too small to be considered as potential winners. Both functions are performed together in a single scan of Δ^+. It then scans the original database D once to check the remaining potential winners. In contrast, Apriori and DHP must take all the data items as size-one candidate sets and check them against the whole updated database D'.

3.2 REMAINING ITERATIONS OF FUP

The major issue in the remaining iterations of FUP is the generation of candidate sets. Following the technique in the Apriori algorithm, in iteration k ($k > 1$), the candidate sets is generated by applying the Apriori-gen function on the new itemsets L'_{k-1} found in the database D' in the previous iteration [2]. However, because of the existence of L_k and the pruning done during the update of L_{k-1}, not all itemsets generated by the Apriori-gen are necessary. The following properties are useful in the discussion of the generation of candidate sets.

Lemma 3 *Suppose $\Delta^- = \emptyset$. If an itemset X is a* loser *at the $(k-1)$-th iteration (i.e., the itemset is in L_{k-1} but not in L'_{k-1}), a large k-itemset in L_k (for any k) containing the itemset X cannot be a winner in the k-th iteration (i.e., being included in the large k-itemset L'_k).*

Proof. This is based on the property that *all the subsets of a large itemset must* *also be large*, proved in [2].

Lemma 4 *A k-itemset X not in the original large k-itemsets L_k can become a* winner *(i.e., being included in the large k-itemset L'_k) in D' only if $\delta^+_X > s \times |\Delta^+|$.*
Proof. Based on the similar reasoning as for Lemma 2.

Lemma 4 has an effect similar to Lemma 2 in pruning size-k candidate sets. Following the results, we can use the following procedure to compute the large k-itemsets in D' in iteration k ($k > 1$).

1. Filter winners from L_k. Firstly, following Lemma 3, insert into a candidate set P_k all $X \in L_k$ such that no subset of X belongs to $L_{k-1} - L'_{k-1}$. (This is equivalent to set $P_k = L_k \cap$ Apriori-gen(L'_{k-1}).) Secondly, compute δ^+_X and σ'_X for all $X \in P_k$ by performing a scan on Δ^+. Subsequently, find out the new large itemsets X from P_k by comparing σ'_X against the threshold.

2. Find the winners which were small. Let $Q_k =$ Apriori-gen$(L'_{k-1}) - L_k$. The sets in L_k has been handled in step 1 and hence are removed from the candidate set Apriori-gen(L'_{k-1}). In the same scan performed on Δ^+ in step 1, the support counts δ^+_X $\forall X \in Q_k$ are found. Following Lemma 4, all candidates $X \in Q_k$ such that $\delta^+_X \leq s \times |\Delta^+|$ are pruned from Q_k

3. The last step is to scan D to compute σ_X for all the reminding X in Q_k and hence their support counts σ'_X in D'. At the end of the scan, all the sets $X \in Q_k$ such that $\sigma'_X \geq s \times |D'|$ are identified as the new large itemsets. The set L'_k, which contains all the large itemsets identified from P_k and Q_k above, is the set of all the new large k-itemsets.

Example 2 A database D is updated with an increment Δ^+ such that $|D| = 1000$, $|\Delta^+| = 100$ and $s = 3\%$. $\mathcal{A}, \mathcal{B}, \mathcal{C}$, and $\mathcal{D}$ are four items and the size-1 and size-2 large itemsets in D are $L_1 = \{\mathcal{A}, \mathcal{B}, \mathcal{C}\}$ and $L_2 = \{\mathcal{AB}, \mathcal{BC}\}$, respectively. (For convenience, we write XYZ for the itemset $\{X, Y, Z\}$ when no ambiguity arises.) Also $\sigma_{\mathcal{AB}} = 50$ and $\sigma_{\mathcal{BC}} = 31$. Suppose FUP has completed the first iteration and found the "new" size-1 itemsets $L'_1 = \{\mathcal{A}, \mathcal{B}, \mathcal{D}\}$. This example illustrates how FUP will find out L'_2 in the second iteration.

FUP first filters out losers from L_2. Note that $\mathcal{C} \in L_1 - L'_1$, therefore, the set $\mathcal{BC} \in L_2$ is a loser and is filtered out. For the remaining set $\mathcal{AB} \in L_2$, FUP scans Δ^+ to update its support count. Assume that $\delta^+_{\mathcal{AB}} = 3$. Since $\sigma'_{\mathcal{AB}} = (3 + 50) > 3\% \times 1100$, therefore, $\mathcal{AB}$ is large in D' and is stored in L'_2.

Next, FUP will try to find out the "new" large itemsets from Δ^+. Note that Apriori-gen applied on L_1' generates the candidate set $C_2 = \{\mathcal{AB}, \mathcal{AD}, \mathcal{BD}\}$. Since $\mathcal{AB} \in L_2$ has already been handled, it is not included in Q_2. For the candidates in $Q_2 = \{\mathcal{AD}, \mathcal{BD}\}$, FUP scans Δ^+ to update their support counts. Suppose $\delta^+_{\mathcal{AD}} = 5$ and $\delta^+_{\mathcal{BD}} = 2$. Since $\delta^+_{\mathcal{BD}} = 2 < 3\% \times 100$, it cannot be a large itemsets in D'. Therefore, $\mathcal{BD}$ is removed from the candidate set Q_2.

For the remaining set $\mathcal{AD} \in Q_2$, FUP scans D to update its support count. Suppose $\sigma_{\mathcal{AD}} = 29$. Since $\sigma'_{\mathcal{AD}} = 29 + 5 > 3\% \times 1100$, it is a large itemset in the updated database. Therefore $\mathcal{AD}$ is added into L_2'. At the end of the second iteration, $L_2' = \{\mathcal{AB}, \mathcal{AD}\}$ is returned.

At the k-th iteration of FUP, the whole updated database D' is scanned once. However, for the large k-th itemsets in L_k, they only have to be checked against a much smaller increment Δ^+. For the new large itemsets, their candidate sets are extracted from the much smaller Δ^+ and are pruned further with their support count in Δ^+. This pool of candidate sets is much smaller than those found by using either Apriori or DHP on the updated database. The smaller number of candidates has ensured the efficiency of FUP.

3.3 THE FUP ALGORITHM (INSERTIONS ONLY)

After the new candidate sets L_{k-1}' has been found, in the k-th iteration of the FUP algorithm, the set of candidates is given by C_k = Apriori-gen(L_{k-1}'). It can be seen from our previous discussion that C_k should be partitioned into two sets to be handled differently, and hence more efficiently. The first partition is $P_k = C_k \cap L_k$. For any candidate $X \in C_k \cap L_k$, its support count σ'_X can be found with a scan on Δ^+, and it can be determined efficiently if X remains large. The second partition is $Q_k = C_k - L_k$. For any itemset $X \in C_k - L_k$, δ^+_X can be found in the same scan performed on Δ^+ and if $\delta^+_X \leq s \times |\Delta^+|$, then it is pruned away. The support count σ'_X for the remaining candidates $X \in C_k - L_k$ can be found by performing a scan on D. Following that, large itemsets from $C_k - L_k$ can also be identified. The FUP algorithm is given as Algorithm 1 below.

4 THE FUP ALGORITHM FOR THE DELETIONS ONLY CASE

Before the introduction of the general case, let us discuss the algorithm for the deletion only case. Even though the frame work of the algorithm for the deletion only case is similar to that of the insertion only case, the techniques used are asymmetrical to those in the FUP for insertions only. In the deletion only case, $\Delta^+ = \emptyset$ and hence $D' = D - \Delta^-$. Note also that $\delta^+_X = 0$ for all itemsets X.

Algorithm 1 FUP (insertions only case)

The 1st iteration:

1. Let $C_1 = I$ and scan Δ^+ to find δ_X^+ for all $X \in C_1$.
2. Let $P_1 = L_1$. For all $X \in P_1$, compute $\sigma'_X = \sigma_X + \delta_X^+$ and insert X into L'_1 if $\sigma'_X \geq s \times |D'|$.
3. Let $Q_1 = C_1 - L_1$. Remove X from Q_1 if $\delta_X^+ \leq s \times |\Delta^+|$.
4. Scan D to find σ_X and σ'_X for all the remaining $X \in Q_1$.
5. Insert $X \in Q_1$ into L'_1 if $\sigma'_X \geq s \times |D'|$.
6. Return L'_1.

The k-th iteration ($k > 1$):

1. Let $C_k = \text{Apriori-gen}(L'_{k-1})$. Halt if $C_k = \emptyset$.
2. Scan Δ^+ to find δ_X^+ for all $X \in C_k$.
3. Let $P_k = C_k \cap L_k$. For all $X \in P_k$, compute $\sigma'_X = \sigma_X + \delta_X^+$ and insert X into L'_k if $\sigma'_X \geq s \times |D'|$.
4. Let $Q_k = C_k - L_k$. Remove X from Q_k if $\delta_X^+ \leq s \times |\Delta^+|$.
5. Scan D to find σ_X and σ'_X for all the remaining $X \in Q_k$.
6. Insert $X \in Q_k$ into L'_k if $\sigma'_X \geq s \times |D'|$.
7. Return L'_k.
8. Halt if $|L'_k| < k + 1$; else goto the $(k + 1)$-th iteration.

Rationale: The rationale of the algorithm follows from our previous discussion in this section. The halting condition in step 1 of the k-th iteration is straight forward. The one in step 8 follows from the candidate set generation in the Apriori-gen function, because every candidate set $X \in C_{k+1}$ must have $k + 1$ subsets in L'_k.

To discover the large itemsets in the updated database D', the algorithm again executes iteratively. In the k-th iteration, the large itemsets L'_k is a subset of the candidate set Apriori-gen(L'_{k-1}). Similar to the insertion only case, the set $P_k = L_k \cap$ Apriori-gen(L'_{k-1}) is the set of candidates which were large in D. The support counts $\sigma'_X = \sigma_X - \delta^-_X$ for all $X \in P_k$ can be found efficiently by a scan on Δ^-. Thus, a candidate $X \in P_k$ becomes a winner and is inserted into L'_k if $\sigma'_X \geq s \times |D'|$.

For those candidates in $Q_k =$ Apriori-gen$(L'_{k-1}) - L_k$, they were small in D, and the goal is to prune away as many candidates from them as possible to create a smaller candidate set by using the information in the small decrement Δ^-. For the candidates in Q_k, we only know that they were small in the original database D; their old support counts in D are not known. However, since they were small, $\sigma_X < s \times |D| \; \forall X \in Q_k$. By using this information and the result of the following lemma, we can distinguish which candidates from Q_k *may* be large and which *will not.*

Lemma 5 *If* $\Delta^+ = \emptyset$, *a k-itemset X not in the original large k-itemsets L_k can become a* winner *(i.e., being included in the large k-itemset L'_k) in D' only if* $\delta^-_X < s \times |\Delta^-|$, *(i.e., only if it is small in Δ^-).*
Proof. Since $X \notin L_k$, we have $\sigma_X < s \times |D|$. Suppose $\delta^-_X \geq s \times |\Delta^-|$, then

$\sigma'_X = \sigma_X - \delta^-_X + \delta^+_X < s \times |D| - s \times |\Delta^-| + 0 = s \times (|D| - |\Delta^-|) = s \times |D'|$.
Hence X cannot be a winner. Thus we have the lemma proved.

That is to say, for each candidate in Q_k, if it is large in Δ^-, then it cannot be large in L'_k. This is the major difference from the insertion-only case. Here, we are not inspecting Q_k for large itemsets, but small itemsets. An intuitive explanation is that an itemset can remain large after the deletion only if a small amount of it is deleted from the main database D. Thus, the algorithm FUP first scans Δ^- and obtains δ^-_X for each $X \in Q_k$. Those candidates for which $\delta^-_X \geq s \times |\Delta^-|$ are removed from Q_k and those left behind in Q_k are the true candidates. Note that not all small itemsets in Δ^- are taken as candidate sets which would be quite large. We only need to consider those small itemsets of Δ^- that are in Q_k. The number of such itemsets is not large because $Q_k \subseteq$ Apriori-gen(L'_{k-1}), (recall that $Q_k = C_k - L_k$). For the candidates X remaining in Q_k, we scan D^- to obtain their new support counts σ'_X. Finally, we insert into L'_k those itemsets X from Q_k for which $\sigma'_X \geq s \times |D'|$. Thus, we have discovered which candidates from P_k and Q_k are large and put them into L'_k. Algorithm 2 shown below gives the update algorithm FUP for the deletion only case.

Algorithm 2 FUP (deletions only case)

The 1st iteration:

1. Let $C_1 = I$ and scan Δ^- to find δ_X^- for all $X \in C_1$.
2. Let $P_1 = L_1$. For all $X \in P_1$, compute $\sigma'_X = \sigma_X - \delta_X^-$ and insert X into L'_1 if $\sigma'_X \geq s \times |D'|$.
3. Let $Q_1 = C_1 - L_1$. Remove X from Q_1 if $\delta_X^- \geq s \times |\Delta^-|$.
4. Scan D^- to find σ'_X for all the remaining $X \in Q_1$.
5. Insert $X \in Q_1$ into L'_1 if $\sigma'_X \geq s \times |D'|$.
6. Return L'_1.

The k-th iteration ($k > 1$):

1. Let $C_k = \text{Apriori-gen}(L'_{k-1})$. Halt if $C_k = \emptyset$.
2. Scan Δ^- to find δ_X^- for all $X \in C_k$.
3. Let $P_k = C_k \cap L_k$. For all $X \in P_k$, compute $\sigma'_X = \sigma_X - \delta_X^-$ and insert X into L'_k if $\sigma'_X \geq s \times |D'|$.
4. Let $Q_k = C_k - L_k$. Remove X from Q_k if $\delta_X^- \geq s \times |\Delta^-|$.
5. Scan D^- to find σ'_X for all the remaining $X \in Q_k$.
6. Insert $X \in Q_k$ into L'_k if $\sigma'_X \geq s \times |D'|$.
7. Return L'_k.
8. Halt if $|L'_k| < k + 1$; else goto the $(k + 1)$-th iteration.

Rationale: The pruning in step 3 of the 1st iteration and step 4 of the k-th iteration follows from Lemma 5. The rationale of the algorithm follows from our discussion in this section.

4.1 AN OPTIMIZATION IN THE DELETION ONLY CASE

One straightforward optimization of Algorithm 2 (k-th iteration) is to reduce the number of itemsets for which we need to compute their supports in Δ^- in step 2. Observe that the supports in Δ^- is required only for the condition checking in step 4 for those in Q_k. For some itemsets in Q_k, we can determine very early after step 1 that they are small in Δ^- and hence don't need to compute their supports in Δ^-. It should be noted that any superset of a small itemset in Δ^- is also small. Hence, if we remember which 1-itemsets are small in Δ^- during the first iteration, then in the subsequent iterations, once step 1 is finished, we can quickly determine if a candidate from Q_k is small in Δ^- without knowing its support in Δ^-. Accordingly, we can remove all candidates from C_k which was not large and contains a small 1-itemset in Δ^- and store them in a set R. Thus these sets won't involve in the computation in step 2. Subsequently, we need to insert them back into Q_k after step 4. In summary, we can optimize Algorithm 2 by adding the following two steps after steps 1 and 4, respectively:

1.5 Remove all candidates X from C_k such that $X \notin L_k$ and X contains any small 1-itemset in Δ^-, and insert the removed sets into R.

4.5 Move all candidates sets from R back into Q_k.

This modification significantly reduces the number of candidates that has to be handled during the scan of Δ^-. The only additional cost is to maintain the set of small 1-itemset in the first iteration. This requires extra memory space of size linear to $|I|$. The CPU overhead involved is negligible, since we have to find δ_X^- for all 1-itemsets X anyway. The number of candidates for scanning D' is not affected by this optimization, but the number of candidates for scanning Δ^- is significantly reduced.

Example 3 Let us illustrate the FUP algorithm for the deletion only case with the example shown in Table 8.2. The original database D contains 5 transactions and the support threshold s is 25%. So, itemsets with a support count σ_X greater than $5 \times 25\% = 1.25$ are large. The large itemsets in L are shown in the same table. One transaction is deleted, leaving 4 transactions in the final database D'. Now, let us apply FUP to see how L' is generated.

In the first iteration, $C_1 = I = \{\mathcal{A}, \mathcal{B}, \mathcal{C}, \mathcal{D}, \mathcal{E}\}$. Of these candidates, only $\mathcal{E}$ was not large in D. So, after partitioning, $P_1 = \{\mathcal{A}, \mathcal{B}, \mathcal{C}, \mathcal{D}\}$ and $Q_1 = \{\mathcal{E}\}$. Next, we scan Δ^- and update the support counts of the candidates in P_1. Only $\mathcal{A}$ and $\mathcal{B}$ occur in Δ^-. So, the counts are updated as $\sigma'_\mathcal{A} = \sigma'_\mathcal{B} = \sigma'_\mathcal{C} = 2$, $\sigma'_\mathcal{D} = 3$. In the same scan of Δ^-, we find out that $\delta_\mathcal{E}^- = 1 \geq 0.25 = 25\% \times |\Delta^-|$. Hence, $\mathcal{E}$ is large in Δ^-, and it was small in D. It cannot be large in D'. So,

Transactions: ($I = \{\mathcal{A}, \mathcal{B}, \mathcal{C}, \mathcal{D}, \mathcal{E}\}$)

		Transaction	
D	Δ^-	$\mathcal{A}$ $\mathcal{B}$ $\mathcal{E}$	
D	D^-	$\mathcal{A}$ $\mathcal{B}$ $\mathcal{C}$	D'
D	D^-	$\mathcal{A}$ $\mathcal{D}$	D'
D	D^-	$\mathcal{B}$ $\mathcal{D}$	D'
D	D^-	$\mathcal{C}$ $\mathcal{D}$	D'

Large itemsets (support threshold $s = 25\%$) in $D = \Delta^- \cup D^-$:

Itemsets(X)	$\mathcal{A}$	$\mathcal{B}$	$\mathcal{C}$	$\mathcal{D}$	$\mathcal{AB}$
σ_X	3	3	2	3	2

Table 8.2 An example for the deletion-only case

it is removed from Q_1. This leaves Q_1 empty; therefore, we need not scan D^- at all in this iteration. Since all the remaining candidates in $P_1 \cup Q_1$ have a support count in D' no less than $25\% \times |D'| = 1$, they all fall into L'_1. Hence $L'_1 = \{\mathcal{A}, \mathcal{B}, \mathcal{C}, \mathcal{D}\}$. We remember that $\mathcal{C}$ and $\mathcal{D}$ are small in Δ^- for optimization.

In the second iteration, we first obtain C_2 by applying the Apriori-gen function on L'_1. This gives $C_2 = \{\mathcal{AB}, \mathcal{AC}, \mathcal{AD}, \mathcal{BC}, \mathcal{BD}, \mathcal{CD}\}$, of which only $\mathcal{AB}$ was large in D. So, the partitioning results in $P_2 = \{\mathcal{AB}\}$ and $Q_2 = \{\mathcal{AC}, \mathcal{AD}, \mathcal{BC}, \mathcal{BD}, \mathcal{CD}\}$. Next, we scan Δ^- and update the count $\sigma'_{\mathcal{AB}} = \sigma_{\mathcal{AB}} - \delta^-_{\mathcal{AB}} = 2 - 1 = 1$. All the candidates in Q_2 contain either item $\mathcal{C}$ or $\mathcal{D}$, which are small in Δ^-. So, we know that all the candidates in Q_2 are definitely small in Δ^- and hence potentially large in D' (Lemma 5). There is no need to find out δ^-_X for these candidates $X \in P_2$. So, the next job is to scan $D^- = D'$ to obtain σ'_X for the candidates in Q_2. This gives $\sigma'_{\mathcal{AC}} = \sigma'_{\mathcal{AD}} = \sigma'_{\mathcal{BC}} = \sigma'_{\mathcal{BD}} = \sigma'_{\mathcal{CD}} = 1$. Consequently, $\mathcal{AB}$, $\mathcal{AC}$, $\mathcal{AD}$, $\mathcal{BC}$, $\mathcal{BD}$, $\mathcal{CD}$ are large in D' and hence are included in L'_2.

In the third iteration, Apriori-gen gives a candidate set $C_3 = \{\mathcal{ABC}, \mathcal{ABD}, \mathcal{ACD}, \mathcal{BCD}\}$. None of these candidates were large. So, $P_3 = \emptyset$ and $Q_3 = C_3$. Since all the candidates contain item $\mathcal{C}$ or item $\mathcal{D}$, we know that they are all small in Δ^- without having to find out their support counts in Δ^-. So, there is no need to scan Δ^- in this iteration! We only have to scan D^- to obtain the support counts in D' for the candidates. The results are $\sigma'_{\mathcal{ABC}} = 1$, $\sigma'_{\mathcal{ABD}} = \sigma'_{\mathcal{ACD}} = \sigma'_{\mathcal{BCD}} = 0$. So, only $\mathcal{ABC}$ goes to L'_3. There is only 1 large itemset found in this iteration. This is insufficient to generate any candidates in the next iteration. So, the algorithm stops after 3 iterations.

Iteration	Apriori	FUP	
	scan D^-	scan D^-	scan Δ^-
1	5	0	5
2	6	5	1
3	4	4	0
Total	15	9	6

Table 8.3 Size of candidates for the example

The above example illustrates how the algorithm makes use of the previous mining results to reduce the size of the candidate sets (Q_k) used to scan the database D^- as compared to that (C_k) of applying Apriori directly on $D' = D^-$. Note also how FUP wisely uses available information to avoid the scan of D^- in the first iteration, and the scan of Δ^- in the third. Table 8.3 compares the size of candidates when Apriori is applied on D' and when FUP is employed. While Apriori scans D' three times, with a total of 15 candidate itemsets, FUP scans D^- only twice, with a total of 9 candidates only. Although FUP has to scan Δ^- with 6 candidate sets, the time spent on this is insignificant, as $|D^-| \gg |\Delta^-|$ in real applications. Thus, FUP has reduced the size of candidates for scanning D^- by $\frac{15-9}{15} = 40\%$. This gives much improvement on the performance.

5 THE FUP2 ALGORITHM FOR THE GENERAL CASE

Now, it is time to generalize the algorithm FUP introduced in the previous sections to the general case which admits transaction insertions as well as deletions. The extended algorithm is called FUP2 . In this case, both Δ^+ and Δ^- are non-empty, and δ_X^+ and δ_X^- may be non-zero for any itemset X. Consequently, none of Lemmas 4 and 5 can be applied.

As in the special cases, we find out L'_k and $\sigma'_X \; \forall \; X \in L'_k$ in the kth-iteration. In each iteration, the candidate set C_k is partitioned into two parts P_k and Q_k as before. For each candidate $X \in P_k$, σ_X is known from the previous mining result. So, only Δ^- and Δ^+ have to be scanned to find out δ_X^- and δ_X^+ to compute the support count σ'_X for every candidate $X \in P_k$. In the FUP2 algorithm, Δ^- is scanned first to find δ_X^- for each candidate X. As we scan Δ^-, we can decrease the support count at the same time, and remove a candidate from P_k as soon as its support count drops below $s \times |D'| - |\Delta^+|$. This is because such a candidate has no hope to have $\sigma'_X \geq s \times |D'|$, as $\delta_X^+ \leq |\Delta^+|$. Next, Δ^+ is scanned to find δ_X^+ for each candidate X that remains in P_k. Finally, σ'_X is calculated for each candidate in P_k using Lemma 1, and those with $\sigma'_X \geq s \times |D'|$ are inserted into L'_k.

For the candidates $X \in Q_k$, again we do not know σ_X, but we know that $\sigma_X < s \times |D|$. By a generalization of Lemmas 4 and 5, some candidates in Q_k can be pruned away without knowing their support counts in D.

Lemma 6 *A k-itemset X not in the original large k-itemsets L_k can become a winner (i.e., being included in the large k-itemset L'_k) in D' only if* $\delta_X = \delta_X^+ - \delta_X^- > s \times (|\Delta^+| - |\Delta^-|)$.

Proof. If $X \notin L_k$, then $\sigma_X < s \times |D|$. Suppose $\delta_X = \delta_X^+ - \delta_X^- \leq s \times (|\Delta^+| - |\Delta^-|)$. Hence, $\sigma'_X = \sigma_X + (\delta_X^+ - \delta_X^-) < s \times |D| + s \times (|\Delta^+| - |\Delta^-|) = s \times (|D| + |\Delta^+| - |\Delta^-|) = s \times |D'|$. Thus $X \notin L'_k$. Thus we have the lemma proved.

So, for each candidate X in Q_k, FUP2 obtains the values of δ_X^+ and δ_X^- during the scans of Δ^+ and Δ^-. Then, δ_X is calculated and those with $\delta_X \leq s \times (|\Delta^+| - |\Delta^-|)$ are removed, because Lemma 6 shows that they will not fall into L'_k. For the remaining candidates $X \in Q_k$, FUP2 scans D^- to obtain their support counts in D^-. Adding this count to δ_X^+ gives σ'_X. Those candidates with $\sigma'_X \geq s \times |D'|$ are inserted into L'_k. This finishes the iteration.

The FUP2 algorithm scans Δ^- and Δ^+ with a candidate set of size $|P_k \cup Q_k| = |C_k|$, the same as Apriori does. However, it scans D^- with a candidate set which is a subset of $Q_k \subseteq C_k$, and is thus much smaller than C_k. Whereas Apriori scans D^- with all the candidates in C_k, thereby FUP2 is more efficient than Apriori. In real applications, we have $|D^-| \gg |\Delta^-|$ and $|D^-| \gg |\Delta^+|$. So, the algorithm saves a lot of time when compared to Apriori. The algorithm FUP2 is given below as Algorithm 3.

5.1 OPTIMIZATIONS ON FUP2

In the FUP2 algorithm, the databases Δ^+ and Δ^- have to be scanned with a candidate set of size $|C_k|$. As an improvement, we can reduce this size by finding bounds on the value of δ_X^+ for each candidate X prior to the scans of Δ^- and Δ^+.

Note that for any itemsets X, $\delta_X^+ \leq \delta_Y^+$, if $Y \subseteq X$. At the k-th iteration ($k > 1$), we can obtain an upper bound b_X^+ for δ_X^+ of candidate X before scanning Δ^+. The bound $b_X^+ = \min\{ \delta_Y^+ \mid Y \subset X \wedge |Y| = |X| - 1\}$. Since X is a candidate generated by the Apriori-gen function, all its size-($k-1$) subsets Y must be in L'_{k-1} and hence C_{k-1}; thus δ_Y^+ has been found in the previous iteration. It is important to note that it may be more convenient to calculate b_X^+ during the generation of the candidate X by slightly modifying the Apriori-gen function.

Before the scan of Δ^- at step 2 (k-th iteration), the values of δ_X^- and δ_X^+ for each candidate X are not known. Lemma 6 cannot be applied directly.

Algorithm 3 FUP2 (general case)

The 1st iteration:

1. Let $C_1 = I$ and scan Δ^- to find δ_X^- for all $X \in C_1$.
2. Let $P_1 = L_1$. Remove X from P_1 if $\sigma_X - \delta_X^- < s \times |D'| - |\Delta^+|$. /* It implies that $\sigma'_X = \sigma_X + \delta_X^+ - \delta_X^- < s \times |D'|$ */
3. Let $Q_1 = C_1 - L_1$. Scan Δ^+ to find δ_X^+ for all 1-itemsets in $P_1 \cup Q_1$.
4. For all $X \in P_1$, compute $\sigma'_X = \sigma_X + \delta_X^+ - \delta_X^-$ and insert X into L'_1 if $\sigma'_X \geq s \times |D'|$.
5. Remove X from Q_1 if $\delta_X = \delta_X^+ - \delta_X^- \leq s \times (|\Delta^+| - |\Delta^-|)$. /* follows Lemma 6 */
6. Scan D^- to obtain the support counts and σ'_X for all remaining $X \in Q_1$.
7. Insert $X \in Q_1$ into L'_1 if $\sigma'_X \geq s \times |D'|$.
8. Return L'_1.

The k-th iteration ($k > 1$):

1. Let C_k = Apriori-gen(L'_{k-1}). Halt if $C_k = \emptyset$.
2. Scan Δ^- to find δ_X^- for all $X \in C_k$.
3. Let $P_k = C_k \cap L_k$. Remove X from P_k if $\sigma_X - \delta_X^- < s \times |D'| - |\Delta^+|$.
4. Let $Q_k = C_k - L_k$. Scan Δ^+ to find δ_X^+ for all remaining itemsets X in $P_k \cup Q_k$.
5. For all $X \in P_k$, compute $\sigma'_X = \sigma_X + \delta_X^+ - \delta_X^-$ and insert X into L'_k if $\sigma'_X \geq s \times |D'|$.
6. Remove X from Q_k if $\delta_X = \delta_X^+ - \delta_X^- \leq s \times (|\Delta^+| - |\Delta^-|)$.
7. Scan D^- to obtain the support counts and σ'_X for all remaining $X \in Q_k$.
8. Insert $X \in Q_k$ into L'_k if $\sigma'_X \geq s \times |D'|$.
9. Return L'_k.
10. Halt if $|L'_k| < k + 1$; else goto the $(k + 1)$-th iteration.

Rationale: The pruning in step 5 of the 1st iteration and step 6 of the k-th iteration follows from Lemma 6. The rationale of the algorithm follows from our discussion in this section.

However, some pruning can be done at this stage. Firstly, for each candidate X in Q_k, if $b_X^+ \leq s \times (|\Delta^+| - |\Delta^-|)$, then $\delta_X \leq \delta_X^+ \leq b_X^+ \leq s \times (|\Delta^+| - |\Delta^-|)$, and X cannot be in L'_k. So, such X can be removed from Q_k. Secondly, the bound b_X^+ can be used to remove the candidates X in P_k which satisfy $\sigma_X + b_X^+ < s \times |D'|$, because $\sigma'_X \leq \sigma_X + b_X^+ < s \times |D'|$. This reduces the number of candidates before scanning Δ^- at a negligible cost.

After scanning Δ^- and before scanning Δ^+ at step 4, the value of δ_X^-, but not δ_X^+ is known for a candidate X. Again, Lemma 6 cannot be applied directly. However, we can delete from Q_k those candidate for which $b_X^+ - \delta_X^- \leq s \times (|\Delta^+| - |\Delta^-|)$, because $\delta_X = \delta_X^+ - \delta_X^- \leq b_X^+ - \delta_X^- \leq s \times (|\Delta^+| - |\Delta^-|)$. Furthermore, for the candidates X in P_k, those satisfying $\sigma_X + b_X^+ - \delta_X^- < s \times |D'|$ can be removed from P_k, because $\sigma'_X = \sigma_X + \delta_X^+ - \delta_X^- \leq \sigma_X + b_X^+ - \delta_X^- < s \times |D'|$. Thus, the number of candidates is reduced at a negligible cost before scanning Δ^+.

To summarize our discussion on the optimization, we give the optimized algorithm as Algorithm 4. (We only present the algorithm for the k-th iteration. The first iteration can be derived straightforwardly.)

It is of theoretical interest to note that the FUP2 algorithm (Algorithm 3) reduces to Apriori [2] if $\Delta^- = D^- = \emptyset$, to FUP (Algorithm 1) if $\Delta^- = \emptyset$, and to FUP (Algorithm 2) if $\Delta^+ = \emptyset$. So, it is a generalization of these three algorithms.

A further improvement can be made by applying the DHP technique [6]. The technique can be introduced into the FUP2 algorithm to hash the counts of itemsets in D'. This brings the benefits of the DHP algorithm into the FUP2 algorithm immediately. We call this DHP-enhanced update algorithm FUP2H, to distinguish it from FUP2 .

Let us illustrate this final Algorithm 4 with an example from Table 8.2 again.

Example 4 This example is a modification of Example 3. This time, Δ^+ has one transaction $\{\mathcal{C}, \mathcal{D}\}$. The new situation is depicted in Table 8.4. Again, the support threshold s is set to 25%. In the first iteration, $C_1 = I = \{\mathcal{A}, \mathcal{B}, \mathcal{C}, \mathcal{D}, \mathcal{E}\}$, $P_1 = \{\mathcal{A}, \mathcal{B}, \mathcal{C}, \mathcal{D}\}$, $Q_1 = \{\mathcal{E}\}$. Note that for this iteration, $b_X^+ = |\Delta^+|$ for all $X \subseteq I$, and steps 3 and 4 do not have any effects. Next, Δ^- is scanned and we find $\delta_\mathcal{A}^- = \delta_\mathcal{B}^- = \delta_\mathcal{E}^- = 1$ and $\delta_\mathcal{C}^- = \delta_\mathcal{D}^- = 0$. After pruning (step 7 of Algorithm 4), $Q_1 = \emptyset$. Then, Δ^+ is scanned and we have $\delta_\mathcal{A}^+ = \delta_\mathcal{B}^+ = 0$; $\delta_\mathcal{C}^+ = \delta_\mathcal{D}^+ = 1$. Since Q_k is empty, steps 11 and 12 can be skipped. D^- need not be scanned in this iteration. Finally, $\sigma'_\mathcal{A} = \sigma'_\mathcal{B} = 2$; $\sigma'_\mathcal{C} = 3$ and $\sigma'_\mathcal{D} = 4$. All of them are large in D'. So, $L'_1 = \{\mathcal{A}, \mathcal{B}, \mathcal{C}, \mathcal{D}\}$.

In the second iteration, $C_2 = \{\mathcal{AB}, \mathcal{AC}, \mathcal{AD}, \mathcal{BC}, \mathcal{BD}, \mathcal{CD}\}$, $Q_2 = \{\mathcal{AC}, \mathcal{AD}, \mathcal{BC}, \mathcal{BD}, \mathcal{CD}\}$ and $P_2 = \{\mathcal{AB}\}$. Since $b_{\mathcal{AC}}^+ = b_{\mathcal{AD}}^+ = b_{\mathcal{BC}}^+ = b_{\mathcal{BD}}^+ = 0$ (because $\delta_\mathcal{A}^+ = \delta_\mathcal{B}^+ = 0$), the corresponding candidates are removed from Q_2 in step 4, leaving $Q_2 = \{\mathcal{CD}\}$. Next, we scan Δ^- and obtain $\delta_{\mathcal{AB}}^- = 1$,

Algorithm 4 FUP2 (general case with optimization)

The k-th iteration ($k > 1$):

1. Let C_k = Apriori-gen(L'_{k-1}). Halt if $C_k = \emptyset$.
2. Calculate b^+_X for each $X \in C_k$.
3. Let $P_k = C_k \cap L_k$. Remove X from P_k if $\sigma_X + b^+_X < s \times |D'|$.
4. Let $Q_k = C_k - L_k$. Remove X from Q_k if $b^+_X \leq s \times (|\Delta^+| - |\Delta^-|)$.

5. Scan Δ^- to find δ^-_X for all $X \in C_k = P_k \cup Q_k$.
6. Remove X from P_k if $\sigma_X + b^+_X - \delta^-_X < s \times |D'|$.
7. Remove X from Q_k if $b^+_X - \delta^-_X \leq s \times (|\Delta^+| - |\Delta^-|)$.
8. Scan Δ^+ to find δ^+_X for all itemsets in $P_k \cup Q_k$.
9. For all $X \in P_k$, compute $\sigma'_X = \sigma_X + \delta^+_X - \delta^-_X$ and insert X into L'_k if $\sigma'_X \geq s \times |D'|$.
10. Remove X from Q_k if $\delta_X = \delta^+_X - \delta^-_X \leq s \times (|\Delta^+| - |\Delta^-|)$.
11. Scan D^- to obtain the support counts and σ'_X for all remaining $X \in Q_k$.
12. Insert $X \in Q_k$ into L'_k if $\sigma'_X \geq s \times |D'|$.
13. Return L'_k.
14. Halt if $|L'_k| < k + 1$; else goto the $(k+1)$-th iteration.

Transactions: $(I = \{\mathcal{A}, \mathcal{B}, \mathcal{C}, \mathcal{D}, \mathcal{E}\})$

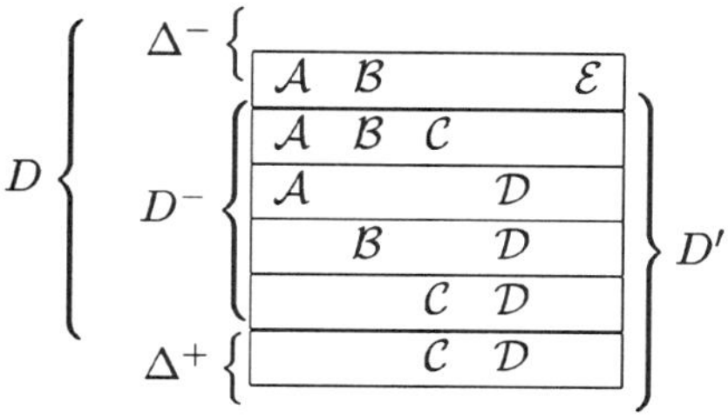

Large itemsets (support threshold $s = 25\%$) in $D' = D^- \cup \Delta^+$:

Itemsets(X)	$\mathcal{A}$	$\mathcal{B}$	$\mathcal{C}$	$\mathcal{D}$	$\mathcal{CD}$
σ'_X	2	2	3	4	2

Table 8.4 An example for the general case

$\delta^-_{\mathcal{CD}} = 0$. Since $b^+_{\mathcal{AB}} = 0$, $\mathcal{AB}$ is removed from P_2 in step 6, leaving $P_2 = \emptyset$. Then, Δ^+ is scanned to get $\delta^+_{\mathcal{CD}} = 1$, followed by the scan of D^-. Finally $\sigma'_{\mathcal{CD}}$ is found to be 2, enough for $\mathcal{CD}$ to be large. Thus $L'_2 = \{\mathcal{CD}\}$. This is the last iteration, since $|L'_2| < 3$ is insufficient to generate a C_3 in the third iteration.

Hence, we find that in the updated database D', $L' = \{\mathcal{A}, \mathcal{B}, \mathcal{C}, \mathcal{D}, \mathcal{CD}\}$. The large itemset $\mathcal{AB} \in L$ is obsoleted and the new large itemset $\mathcal{CD}$ is added to L'. Note that FUP2 scans D^- only once, to obtain the count of $\mathcal{CD}$ in the second iteration. If we apply the Apriori algorithm on D' instead, we will have to scan D^- twice, with 11 candidates from C_1 and C_2. So, FUP2 reduces the candidate size by $\frac{11-1}{11} = 91\%$. This significantly increases the performance of FUP2 .

6 PERFORMANCE STUDIES

We have implemented the algorithms, Apriori [1, 2], DHP [6], FUP2 and FUP2$\mathcal{H}$ on an RS/6000 workstation (model 410) running AIX. Several experiments are conducted to compare their performance. Synthetic data are usd in the experiments. The data are generated using the techniques as introduced in [2] and modified in [6], with a further modification. The purpose of our modifications are to create *skewness* in the data, so as to model the change of association rules as a result of inserting and deleting transactions. The details of the data generation method is described below, and results of the experiments follow.

6.1 GENERATION OF SYNTHETIC DATA

The data generation process is governed by various parameters, which are listed Table 8.5. We will explain Their meanings as we go through the data generation procedure. The data generation procedure consists of 2 major steps. In the first step, a set $\mathcal{L}$ of potentially large itemsets is generated. In the second step, the itemsets in $\mathcal{L}$ are used to generate the database transactions.

To model the existence of association rules in the "real" world, we first generate a set $\mathcal{L}$ of itemsets. Each of these itemsets is *potentially* a large itemset in the generated database. For example, such an itemset might be { bread, butter, cheese, milk, orange juice } and this indicates that people usually buy these items together. However, they may not buy *all* of them at the same time. The size of each potentially large itemset is determined from a Poisson distribution with mean $|\mathcal{I}|$. A total of $|\mathcal{L}|$ such itemsets are generated. In the first itemset, items are picked randomly from a total of N items. In order to have common items in the subsequent S_q itemsets, in each of these S_q itemsets, some fraction of items are picked from the first itemset, and the remaining items are chosen randomly. This fraction is called the correlation level and is chosen from an exponential distribution with mean 0.5. After the first $(S_q + 1)$ itemsets are

Parameter	Value	Description
$\|\Delta^-\|$	j	number of deleted transactions
$\|D^-\|$	$i-j$	number of unchanged transactions
$\|\Delta^+\|$	k	number of added transactions
$\|T\|$	x	mean size of transactions
$\|\mathcal{I}\|$	y	mean size of potentially large itemsets
$\|\mathcal{L}\|$	2100	number of potentially large itemsets
N	1000	number of items
S_q	5	length of clusters in $\mathcal{L}$
P_s	50	pool size
M_f	200	multiplying factor for the pool
p	2000	number of p.l. itemsets that generate Δ^-
q	2000	number of p.l. itemsets that generate Δ^+

Table 8.5 Parameters for data generation for the case Tx.Iy.D$i-j+k$

generated, the process resumes a new cycle and the next $(S_q + 1)$ itemsets are generated. This repeats until a total of $|\mathcal{L}|$ itemsets are generated. Thus, we have $\frac{|L|}{S_q+1}$ clusters of itemsets such that similarity within each cluster is high. By adjusting S_q, we can vary the length of these clusters and hence the degree of similarity among the itemsets in $\mathcal{L}$. In addition, each potentially large itemset is given a weight taken from an exponential distribution with unit mean. This weight determines the probability that the itemset will be chosen to generate transactions as described below. The weights of the itemsets in $\mathcal{L}$ are normalized so that the total is one.

Next, transactions are generated from the potentially large itemsets in $\mathcal{L}$. The transactions are generated one after another. To generate a transaction, its size is first determined from a Poisson distribution with mean $|T|$. Then, we start with an empty transaction. We choose a potentially large itemset from a *pool*, and assign it to the transaction. The items from the assigned itemset are then added to the transaction. This is repeated until the transaction reaches the desired size. If the last assigned itemset would cause the transaction to become larger than the desired size, items in that itemset will be added to the transaction with a probability of 0.5. The *pool* of itemsets mentioned above has a size of P_s. It is initialized by choosing and inserting P_s itemsets from $\mathcal{L}$ into it. The probability that an itemset from $\mathcal{L}$ is chosen is equal to its weight. When an itemset from $\mathcal{L}$ is inserted into the pool, this itemset is assigned a *count*, initialized to the product of its weight and a factor M_f. When an itemset in the pool is chosen and assigned to a transaction, its counter is decremented. If the counter reaches 0, the itemset is replaced by choosing and inserting an itemset from $\mathcal{L}$ into the pool. With this arrangement, the number of large k-itemsets can be controlled by M_f and S_q.

In fact, when an itemset is assigned to a transaction, not all items in the itemset are added to the transaction. Each itemset is given a *corruption level* c which is normally distributed with mean 0.5 and variance 0.1. If the size of the itemset is l, then all the l items are added to the transaction with probability $1-c$, or $l-1$ items are added to the transaction with probability $c(1-c)$, or $l-2$ items are added with probability $c^2(1-c)$, etc. This is to model the customer behaviour that not all the items in a potentially large itemset are always bought together.

To model a change of association rules as D is updated to D', transactions in them are not generated from the same set of potentially large itemsets. We choose two integers p and q in the range from zero to $|\mathcal{L}|$. The first p potentially large itemsets from $\mathcal{L}$ are used to generate Δ^- and the last q potentially large itemsets from $\mathcal{L}$ to generate Δ^+. D^- is generated from the whole $\mathcal{L}$. As a result, the first p potentially large itemsets in $\mathcal{L}$ have a higher tendency to be large in $D = \Delta^- \cup D^-$ than in $D' = D^- \cup \Delta^+$. They correspond to large itemsets that turn *obsolete* due to the updates. Similarly, the last q potentially large itemsets have a higher tendency to be large in D' than in D. They correspond to *new* large itemsets in the updated database. When $p+q \geq |\mathcal{L}|$, the middle $p+q-|\mathcal{L}|$ potentially large itemsets take part in the generation of all of Δ^-, D^-as well as Δ^+. So, they would be large in both D and D'. They represent the association rules that remain unchanged despite the update. By varying the values of p and q, we can control the *skewness*, i.e. the degree of similarity, between D and D'.

In the following sections we use the notation Tx.Iy.D$i-j+k$, modified from the one used in [2], to represent an experiment with databases of following sizes: $|D| = |\Delta^-| + |D^-| = i$ thousand, $|\Delta^-| = j$ thousand, $|\Delta^+| = k$ thousand, $|T| = x$ and $|\mathcal{I}| = y$. In the experiments, we set the other parameters as shown under the "values" column in Table 8.5. For DHP and FUP2$\mathcal{H}$, we use a hash table of 4096 entries, which is of the same order of magnitude as $N = 1000$. The hash table is used to prune size-2 candidates *only*.

In each experiment, we first use DHP to find out the large itemsets in D. Then, we run FUP2 and FUP2$\mathcal{H}$, supplying to them the databases Δ^-, D^- and Δ^+ and the large itemsets and their support counts in D. The time taken is noted. To compare with the performance of Apriori and DHP, we run these two algorithms on the updated database D', and note the amounts the time they have spent. The time taken by the algorithms are then compared.

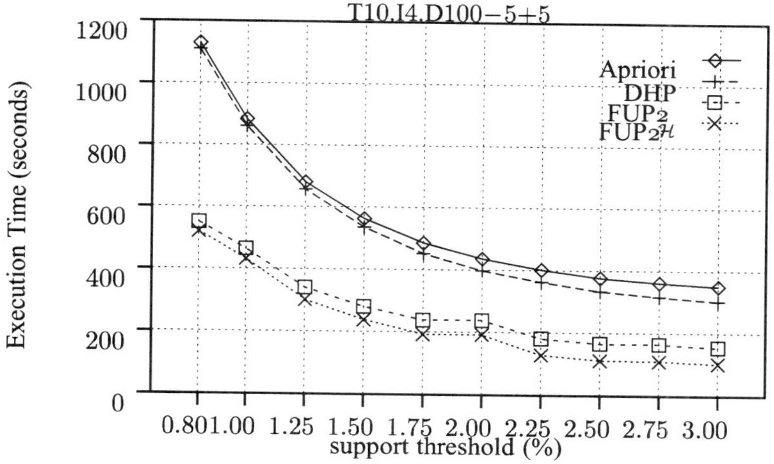

Figure 8.3 Comparison of the four algorithms

6.2 COMPARING THE ALGORITHMS FUP2 AND FUP2H WITH APRIORI AND DHP

We first present an experiment comparing the performances of Apriori and DHP against the general update algorithms FUP2 and FUP2$\mathcal{H}$. The database sizes are T10.I4.D100−5+5. and the support threshold s is varied between 1.0 and 3.0. The results are plotted in Figure 8.3.

It is found that FUP2 is 1.83 to 2.27 times faster than Apriori, while FUP2$\mathcal{H}$ is 1.99 to 2.96 times faster than DHP and is 2.05 to 3.40 times faster than Apriori. To see why we get so much performance gain with FUP2 and FUP2$\mathcal{H}$, let us have a look at the number of candidate itemsets generated by each algorithm in the scan of D^- for the particular instance with support threshold 2.0 (see Table 8.6). Since the sizes of $\Delta^+$and $\Delta^-$are relatively small when compared to D^-, the number of candidates in the scan of D^- is a dominating factor in the speed of the algorithms. The total number of candidates generated by FUP2 is 38% of that of Apriori. The candidate size of FUP2$\mathcal{H}$ is 28% of that of DHP and is 21% of that of Apriori. The numbers of candidates for other support thresholds are plotted in Figure 8.4. It can be observed that FUP2 and FUP2$\mathcal{H}$ are very effective in reducing the number of candidates. This brings about significant performance gain for the overall algorithms.

Clearly, FUP2$\mathcal{H}$ is very efficient because it combines two different techniques, namely that of FUP2 and that of DHP, to reduce the number of candidates. The combination of different pruning techniques results in high pruning ratio, therefore effectively reducing the number of candidates. In FUP2$\mathcal{H}$, only

Itera-tion	Apriori	DHP	FUP2	FUP2$\mathcal{H}$
1	99	99	2	2
2	4095	1615	1794	75
3	3814	3814	2018	2018
4	805	805	34	34
5	697	697	29	29
6	495	495	20	20
7	258	258	7	7
8	92	92	1	1
9	20	20	0	0
10	2	2	0	0
Total	10377	7897	3905	2186
$\frac{\text{Total}}{\text{Apriori}}$	100%	76.1%	37.6%	21.1%
$\frac{\text{Total}}{\text{DHP}}$	131%	100%	49.4%	27.7%

Table 8.6 Number of candidate itemsets

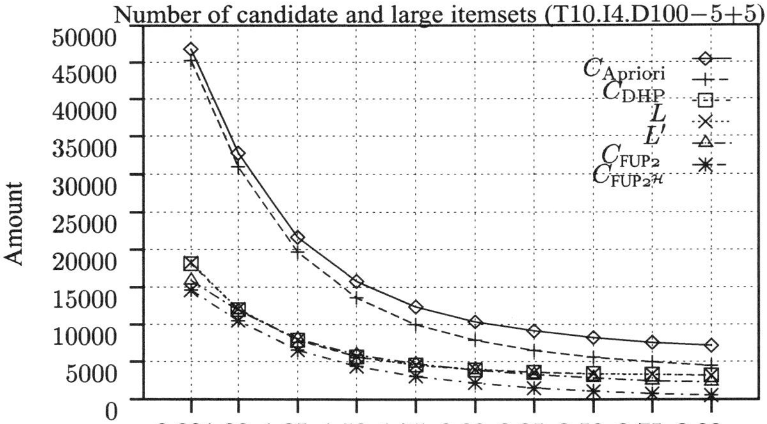

Figure 8.4 Comparison of the number of candidates (general case)

the itemsets in the intersection of the candidate sets of FUP2 and DHP have to be considered. So, the number of candidates is much smaller and hence the performance improvement.

6.3 EFFECTS OF THE SIZE OF UPDATES

To find out how the size of Δ^- and Δ^+ affects the performance of the algorithms, we use the setting T10.I4.D100$-x+x$ for the experiment, with a support threshold of 2%. In other words, we use an initial database of 100 thousand transactions. From this database, x thousand transactions are deleted and another x thousand are added to it. So, the size of the database remains unchanged after the update, i.e. $|D| = |D'|$. This is to simulate the practical situation where the size of a dynamic database remains steady in the long run. Figure 8.5 shows the results of this experiment. As expected, both FUP2 and FUP2$\mathcal{H}$ have to spend more and more time as the size of updates increases. On the other hand, since the size of the final database is constant, the amounts of time spent by Apriori and DHP are insensitive to x. Note that FUP2 is faster than Apriori as long as $x \leq 30$ and FUP2$\mathcal{H}$ is faster than DHP for $x < 40$. As Apriori and DHP do not have to scan through Δ^-, their performances are better when $|\Delta^-|$ is very large. The experimental results indicate that the incremental update algorithms are very efficient for a small to moderate size of updates. When the size of the updates exceeds 40% of the original database, Apriori and DHP perform better. This is because as the amount of changes to the original database becomes large, the updated database becomes very different from the original one. The difference is so great that the previous mining results are not helpful. So, when the amount of updates is too large, mining the updated database from scratch using Apriori or DHP would save more time.

6.4 EFFECTS OF THE NUMBER OF DELETED AND ADDED TRANSACTIONS, VARIED SEPARATELY

Another experiment is conducted to find out how the size of Δ^- affects the performance of the algorithms. We use the setting T10.I4.D100$-x+10$ for the experiment. The support threshold is 2%. In other words, we use an initial database of 100 thousand transactions. Ten thousand transactions are added to the database and x thousand are deleted. The results are shown in Figure 8.6. It is observed that as the number of deleted transactions increases, the amounts of time taken by Apriori and DHP decrease. This is because the size of the final database decreases. For example, at $x = 1.0$, FUP2 is 4.5 times faster than Apriori. As x increases, the number of transactions that FUP2 and FUP2$\mathcal{H}$ have to handle increases; therefore, these algorithms take more and more time as x grows. However, FUP2 and FUP2$\mathcal{H}$ still outperform Apriori and DHP in the range $x < 30$. Beyond that, Apriori and DHP take less time to finish. This

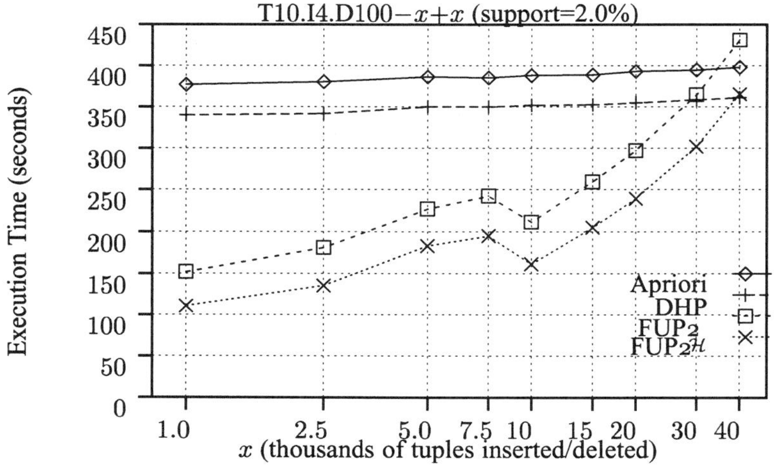

Figure 8.5 Effects of $|\Delta^-|$ and $|\Delta^+|$

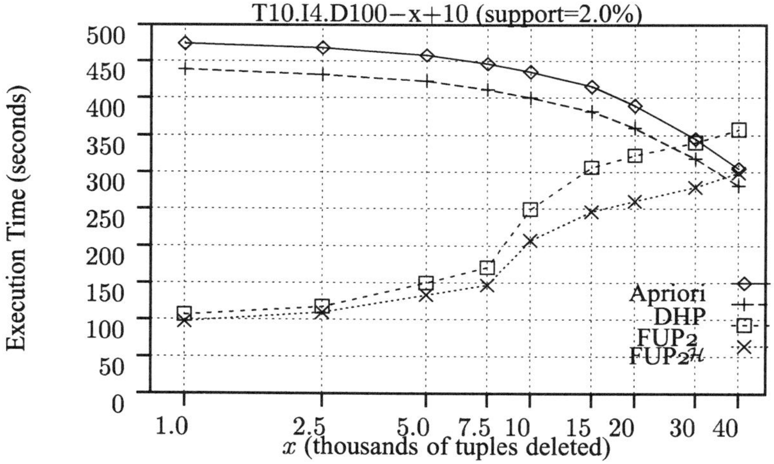

Figure 8.6 Effects of $|\Delta^-|$

means that as long as the number of deleted transactions is less than 30% of the original database, the incremental algorithms win. Practically, the original database D in a data mining problem is very large. The amount of updates should be much less than 30% of D.

A similar experiment is performed using the setting T10.I4.D100−10+x and the same support threshold of 2%. This time, we keep the size of Δ^- constant

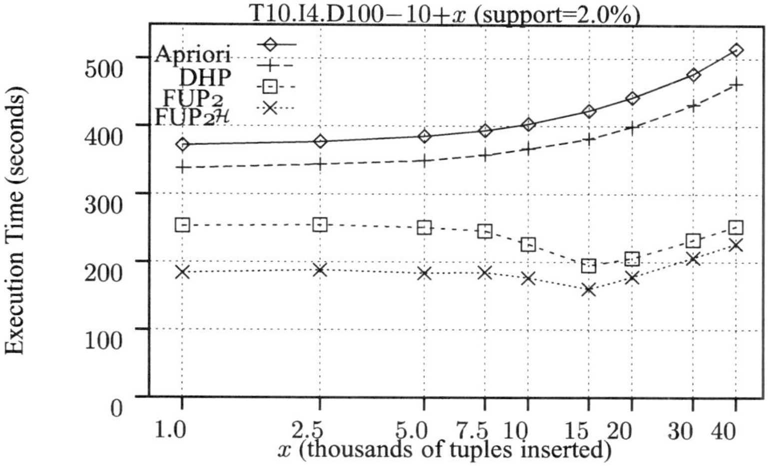

Figure 8.7 Effects of $|\Delta^+|$

and vary the size of Δ^+. The results are plotted in Figure 8.7. As x increases, $|D'|$ increases. So, the execution time of Apriori and DHP increases with x. They do not run faster than FUP2 and FUP2$\mathcal{H}$ even when x is as large as 40.

Examining Figure 8.7 more closely, we notice that the execution times of FUP2 and FUP2$\mathcal{H}$ are quite steady in the range $1.0 \leq x \leq 7.5$. For $x > 15$, the execution times increase with x. This is because the greater the value of x, the more the number of transactions the algorithms have to handle. However, in the range $7.5 \leq x \leq 15$, the execution time drops as x increases! Indeed, if we examine Figure 8.6 more carefully, we can also notice sharper rises in the execution times of FUP2 and FUP2$\mathcal{H}$ in the same range of x.

To explain this phenomenon, let us recall that in the k-th iteration, if an itemset V was not large in D but is in C_k, it is put in Q_k. Suppose that V is also small in D'. Then, since V is small in both D and D', it does not occur frequently in D and D'. Statistically, δ_V^+ and δ_V^- are small in magnitude and they are close to each other. So, $\delta_V = \delta_V^+ - \delta_V^-$ has a very small magnitude. It may be positive or negative. When Lemma 6 is applied to prune Q_k in step (10) of Algorithm 4, a candidate X in Q_k is pruned if $\delta_X \leq (|\Delta^+| - |\Delta^-|) \times s\%$. Now, if $|\Delta^+| \gg |\Delta^-|$, then the right hand side of the pruning condition is positive and it has a great magnitude. So, V has a very high change of being deleted from Q_k. If, however, $|\Delta^+| \geq |\Delta^-|$ but they are close to each other, then the right hand side is slightly positive. V may escape the pruning if δ_V is large enough, although there is still a high chance that V is pruned away. However, if $|\Delta^+| < |\Delta^-|$, then the right hand side of the pruning condition is

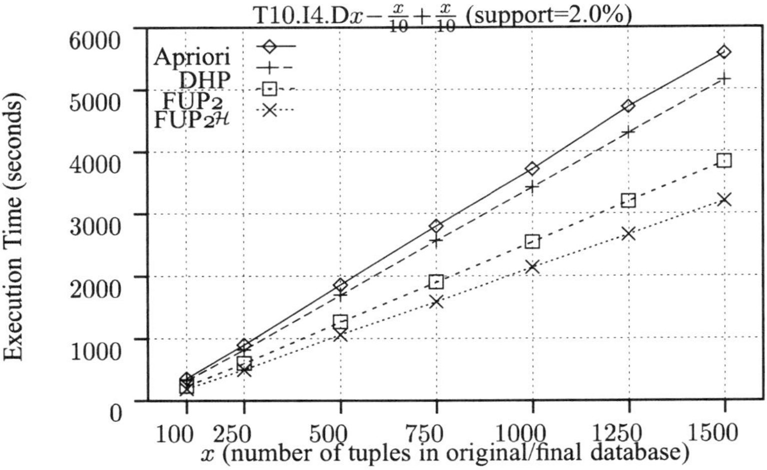

Figure 8.8 Scale-up experiment

negative. In this case, V will only be pruned away if δ_V is negative enough, but the chance of this is low. Hence, as $|\Delta^+| - |\Delta^-|$ increases from a negative value to a small positive value (e.g., as x in Figure 8.7 varies from 10 to 15 thousands), the chance that V gets pruned increases sharply.

There are many itemsets that behave like V; therefore, the drop in execution time of FUP2 and FUP2$\mathcal{H}$ is very dramatic when $|\Delta^+|$ increases from slightly below $|\Delta^-|$ to slightly above $|\Delta^-|$. A similar effect is observed as $|\Delta^-|$ decreases from slightly above $|\Delta^+|$ to slightly below it.

6.5 SCALING UP

To find out if FUP2 and FUP2$\mathcal{H}$ work well also for very large databases, experiments with scale-up databases are conducted. We use the setting of T10.I4.D$x - \frac{x}{10} + \frac{x}{10}$. So, we delete 10% of the transactions from the original database and then insert the same amount of new transaction to it. The size of the original database is varied from 100 thousand transactions to 1.5 million transactions. Again, the support threshold is set to 2%. The results of the experiment are shown in Figure 8.8. The graph illustrates that the execution times of all the four algorithms are found to increase *linearly* as x increases. This shows that FUP2 and FUP2$\mathcal{H}$ are scalable and can work with very large databases.

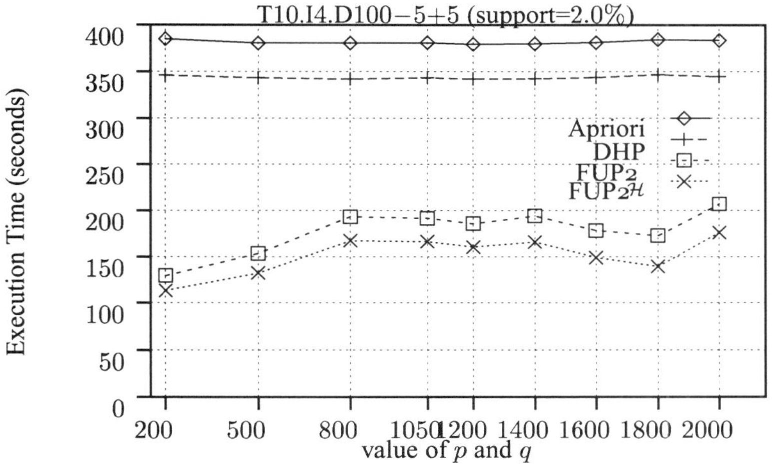

Figure 8.9 Effects of p and q

6.6 EFFECTS OF THE SKEWNESS OF DATA

As mentioned in Section 6.1, the parameters p and q can be used to control the *skewness* of the synthetic databases. Smaller values of p and q generate more skewed data, because the transactions in Δ^+ and Δ^- are generated from very different potentially large itemsets. To find out how the skewness affects the performance of the incremental algorithms, an experiment is performed. While keeping $p = q$ and $|\mathrm{L}| = 2100$, the value of $p(= q)$ is varied between 200 and 2000 and the effects are observed. The database sizes are T10.I4.D100−5+5 and the support threshold used is 2.0%. The results are shown in Figure 8.9. The skewness has little effect on Apriori and DHP. The general trend is that for more skewed data (smaller values of p and q), the incremental algorithms FUP2 and FUP2$\mathcal{H}$ are faster. To see why this is so, the amounts of candidates generated by the algorithms are plotted in Figure 8.10, together with the numbers of the large itemsets in L and L'. In this figure, the curve labeled $L \ominus L'$ shows the number of itemsets in the *symmetric difference*[1] of the sets L and L'. The size of the symmetric difference indicates the degree of dissimilarity between L and L'. It also, to a certain extent, reflects the amount of additional (as compared with Apriori and DHP) work that the incremental algorithms have to do in order to discard old large itemsets and discover new ones. The size of the symmetric difference is small for very small values of p and q. Hence, we can observe from the graph that FUP2 and FUP2$\mathcal{H}$ generate less candidates when the data is more skewed. So, they are more efficient when faced with skewed databases.

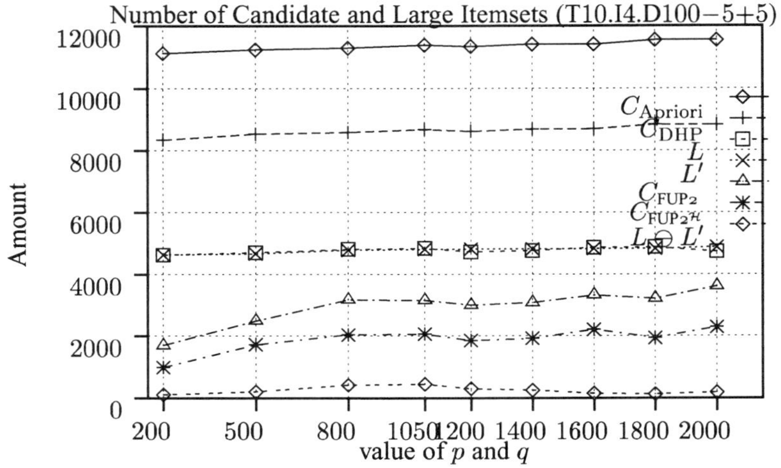

Figure 8.10 Number of candidates for different values of p and q

7 DISCUSSIONS

We have just seen how we designed FUP2 algorithm, which incorporates several effective pruning techniques to solve the incremental update problem efficiently. We discuss several issues in this section which relate to the performance of FUP2 .

7.1 REDUCING THE NUMBER OF DATABASE SCANS

As has been discussed in Section 1, the efficiency of mining large itemsets depends mainly on two factors:

1. the number of candidate itemsets;
2. the number of scannings of the database.

Since checking transactions read from the database against the candidate sets is very computation-intensive, it is critical to have a small number of candidate sets. In the level-wise pruning introduced in Apriori, the candidate sets reduction is achieved by scanning the database once in each level. However, this would inevitably incur some I/O costs. An orthogonal approach would be to reduce the I/O costs by performing less scannings but enduring a larger set of candidate sets. These two opposite effects also have bearing on the maintenance.

In the k-th iteration of FUP2 , after C_k is generated, we divide C_k into P_k and Q_k and perform pruning on them based on the information in Δ^+ and Δ^-. In the end, we scan D^- to find the support counts of the reminding candidates in Q_k. This will return the large itemsets in L'_k, and it will be used to generate the candidates for the $(k+1)$-th iteration. In order to optimize the scannings on D^-, we can skip the scanning of D^- and use $C'_k = P_k \cup Q_k$ instead of L'_k to generate the candidate sets $C_{k+1} = \text{Apriori-gen}(C'_k)$. The prunings in FUP2 can be applied on C_{k+1} with some modifications. The set of candidate sets can be accumulated in this way for several iterations until its size is larger than a threshold, and a scan can be used subsequently to find out the new large itemsets among them. With this optimization, the I/O costs would be reduced with the increase in the cost of tolerating a larger set of candidate sets. The key in applying this technique is in the selection of an appropriate threshold on the maximum number of candidate sets that can be accumulated over several iterations before a scanning is performed.

7.2 TRADING STORAGE SPACE FOR EFFICIENCY

Besides the trade-off between the number of candidate sets and the amount of scannings, there is one additional dimension in the maintenance cost, which is the amount of support counts kept in each update.

This study of incremental update is based on the availability of the following pieces of information:

1. the original database D,
2. the inserted portion of the database Δ^+,
3. the deleted portion of the database Δ^-,
4. the large itemsets and the associated support counts in D, and
5. the support threshold s is given and does not change from time to time.

In the FUP2 algorithm, we assume that no additional support counts are stored for the database D. It is reasonable to assume that all the large k-itemsets and their associated support counts for D are stored and available. However, is it reasonable to assume that some additional support informations are also available? It would be tempting to store the support of all itemsets, whether or not they are large or small. Then, the incremental update would have been much simpler: we would have never had to search through the original D again to find their support counts. Unfortunately, such an approach is unrealistic, because there are exponentially too many such itemsets. However, it is beneficial to store the supports of all the 1-itemsets in D because they have been computed in the initial computation of association rules already. This becomes an issue of trade-off between storage space and computation time: it saves the search on the large D^- in the computation of large 1-itemsets L_1' with the cost of some space to store the 1-itemsets.

This approach has been extended further into a proposal of storing support counts of all the *border sets* [4]. The set of border sets is the minimal itemsets which were not large in D. In addition to all small size-1 itemsets, it also contains all the candidate sets in Apriori, which were found to be small in D. The set of border sets has an interesting property: if X is a new large itemset found in D', (X is small in D), then either X is a border set, or it contains a border set, which is also large in D'. By storing also the support counts of all the border sets in the original mining, the information can be utilized in two ways.

1. It is straight forward to check if any border set has become large in D'. If there exists no such border set, then there is no need to compute the new large itemset.

2. The new large itemsets among the old large itemsets and the border sets can be computed without scanning D^-, and their closure under Apriori-gen contains all new large itemsets and hence could be used as a set of candidate sets. The trade-off in adopting (1) is the possibly large storage required to maintain the support counts of the border sets. The set of all the border sets contains all size-2 candidate sets which were small.

Thus, its size is at least in the order of $|I|^2$, where I is the set of all the items. In general, $|I|$ is quite large in basket databases. In fact, the set of border sets could be on the order of $2^{|I|}$ in the worst case. As for (2), the set of candidate sets could be quite large as well, because it is the result of applying Apriori-gen iteratively without pruning. For example, if the new size-1 large itemsets found among the old large itemsets and border sets cover a large number of the size-1 itemsets, then the size of the candidate sets will be at least in the order of $|I|^2$, and could be much larger in general. We can improve this by applying the prunings developed in FUP2 . During the course of generating the closure from the new large itemsets found among the old large itemsets and the border sets, the prunings in FUP2 , in particular, those resulted from Lemma 6, can be used to remove candidates in the closure. In addition, if the number of candidate sets become too large, a database scanning can be performed to find out some large itemsets, and the candidate set closure computation can be restarted on this newly found smaller set of large itemsets.

7.3 LOOK AHEAD COMPUTATION OF SUPPORT COUNTS

The technique of storing all the size-1 itemsets and their support counts can be generalized to store more support counts by doing some controlled look ahead computation. For a given support threshold s, let s' be a *reduced threshold* such that $s > s' > 0$. In the initial computation of large itemsets in D, assume that not only the large itemsets in L are found, but also the *medium-large* itemsets whose support counts are larger than s' but smaller than s. The same algorithm such as Apriori can be used to compute the set of medium-large itemsets M by adjusting the threshold to s'. If support counts of the medium-large itemsets in M are stored together with those in L, then we can improve the result in Lemma 6 to the one in the following.

Lemma 7 *An itemset $X \notin L \cup M$ (i.e., it is neither large nor medium-large) can become a* winner *in D' only if $\delta_X = \delta_X^+ - \delta_X^- > s \times (|\Delta^+| - |\Delta^-|) + (s - s') \times |D|$.*

We omit the proof of Lemma 7. Both Lemmas 4 and 5 can also be modified similarly.

Following these lemmas, both FUP and FUP2 can be improved. For example, for the insertion only case, in the k-th iteration of Algorithm 1, the set P_k would be equal to $C_k \cap (L_k \cup M_k)$, where M_k are the size-k medium-large itemsets. More importantly, Q_k would be reduced to $C_k - (L_k \cup M_k)$, and an itemset $X \in Q_k$ would be pruned away if $\delta_X^+ \leq s \times |\Delta^+| + (s - s') \times |D|$. It is clear that, with the look ahead computation, the resulted Q_k would be much smaller than that in Algorithm 1, because those in M_k would not be included in Q_k. Also, the pruning performed for itemsets in Q_k is more powerful in this case. Essentially, with the look ahead computation, support counts of more itemsets were found in the initial computation of the large itemsets in D. Hence less candidate sets would be required to be checked against the original database during the update. In the extreme case, if $|\Delta^+| < (s - s') \times |D|$, then all itemsets in Q_k would be pruned away. In other words, if s' is small enough such that $(s - s') \times |D|$ is greater than the size of the increment Δ^+, then there is no need to scan the original database D in the update process.

The above observation applies also to both the deletion only and general cases. The look ahead computation of medium-large itemsets is an appealing technique. However, it suffers from at least two problems.

1. Substantial time and space costs are required to compute and store the support counts of the medium-large itemsets.

2. The technique becomes very difficult to implement when updates are being done repetitively. In particular, after an update of the large itemsets in D with the help of the support counts of the medium-large itemsets, it

may not be possible to identify another threshold and a set of medium-large itemsets useful in the next updated database.

In short, the look ahead technique has a limited applicability, and can only be used as a supporting techniques for FUP or FUP2 .

7.4 UPDATE FREQUENCY

The last issue that we want to discuss is the update frequency. If the updates are done with a high frequency, many updates could find very few new large itemsets and hence consume wasteful efforts. The other extreme of updating too seldom could render the rules being obsoleted for a long time. The most ideal strategy is to do the update at the time when the changes in large itemsets is larger than a predefined threshold. However, this would be feasible only if a measurement on the changes could be done with low cost. In particular, it must be much cheaper than computing the exact amount of new large itemsets in the maintenance. We have proposed to use sampling technique to solve this problem. In FUP2 , after we have pruned the candidate sets, instead of scanning D^-, we use a sample from it to estimate the supports in D^- [5], which is much cheaper. Following that, we can estimate the total changes in large itemsets. We also compute a bound on the estimation error. If the estimated changes is not too large, we suggest no update; otherwise, FUP2 will be triggered to perform a complete update.

8 CONCLUSIONS

In this chapter, we identified the need for incremental updating knowledge mined from large databases. Then, we concentrated on the problem of mining association rules. We gave a mathematical definition for the incremental updating of mined association rules. Efficient incremental updating techniques for the maintenance of the association rules are described. The method strives to determine the promising itemsets and hopeless itemsets in the inserted and deleted portions and optimize the efficiency by reducing the number of the candidate sets to be searched against the original large database. Efficient algorithms have been suggested.

The algorithms have been implemented and their performance have been studied. The study shows that the proposed incremental updating technique has superior performance on database updates in comparison with direct mining from an updated database in all the three cases. Moreover, it also confirms that the speed up is more significant when the size of the inserted or deleted portions is a small percentage of that of the original database, which is the most usual case. The performance study also reveals that the number of candidate sets generated in the proposed algorithms is substantially smaller than that in the direct mining. Moreover, scale up experiments have been carried out which show that the efficiency of the technique are consistent over databases with different sizes.

We also have studied several issues relating to the maintenance cost. The trade-offs among prunings, database scannings and storing of support counts, have been discussed in details. Recently, there have been some interesting studies at finding generalized, quantitative, and numeric association rules in large transaction databases. Future research directions include the extension of our incremental updating technique for maintenance of generalized, quantitative, and numeric association rules in transaction databases.

Notes

1. The symmetric difference of two sets A and B is defined as: $A \ominus B = (A - B) \cup (B - A)$

References

[1] R. Agrawal, T. Imielinski, and A. Swami. Mining Association Rules between Sets of Items in Large Databases. In *Proc. 1993 ACM-SIGMOD Int. Conf. Management of Data*, 207–216, May 1993.

[2] R. Agrawal and R. Srikant. Fast algorithms for mining association rules. In *Proc. 1994 Int. Conf. Very Large Data Bases*, pages 487–499, Santiago, Chile, September 1994.

[3] D.W. Cheung, J. Han, V. Ng, and C.Y. Wong. Maintenance of discovered association rules in large databases: An incremental updating technique. In *Proc. 1996 Int'l Conf. on Data Engineering*, New Orleans, Louisiana, Feb. 1996.

[4] R. Feldman, Y. Aumann, A. Amir, and H. Mannila. Efficient Algorithms for Discovering Frequent Sets in Incremental Databases. In *Proc. 1997 ACM-SIGMOD Workshop on Data Mining and Knowledge Discovery*, Tucson, Arizona, USA, May 1997.

[5] S.D. Lee and D.W. Cheung. Maintenance of Discovered Association Rules: When to Update? In *Proc. 1997 ACM-SIGMOD Workshop on Data Mining and Knowledge Discovery*, Tucson, Arizona, USA, May 1997.

[6] J.S. Park, M.S. Chen, and P.S. Yu. An effective hash-based algorithm for mining association rules. In *Proc. 1995 ACM-SIGMOD Int. Conf. Management of Data*, San Jose, CA, May 1995.

[7] A. Savasere, E. Omiecinski, and S. Navathe. An efficient algorithm for mining association rules in large databases. In *Proc. 1995 Int. Conf. Very Large Data Bases*, pages 432–443, Zurich, Switzerland, Sept. 1995.

[8] H. Toivonen. Sampling large databases for finding association rules. In *Proc. 1996 Int. Conf. Very Large Data Bases*, pages 134–145, Bombay, India, Sept. 1996.

Chapter 9

MULTIDIMENSIONAL BUSINESS PROCESS ANALYSIS WITH THE PROCESS WAREHOUSE

Beate List[1], Josef Schiefer[1], A Min Tjoa[1] and Gerald Quirchmayr[2]
1) Vienna University of Technology, Institute of Software Technology, Austria
2) University of Vienna, Institute for Computer Science and Information Systems, Austria

Keywords: workflow management systems, data warehousing, business process analysis and improvement

Abstract: A data warehouse is a global information repository, which stores facts originating from multiple, heterogeneous data sources in materialised views. Up to now, a data warehouse has always been used for application data and never for control data. As efficiency, accuracy, transparency and flexibility of enterprise's business processes have become fundamental for process reengineering programmes, paying attention to monitoring and controlling of workflow execution at an formal and strategic level will become a focus of information management in the near future.

We present the concept of the process warehouse that is a separate read-only analytical database, which provides the foundation of a process oriented decision support system with the aim to analyse and improve business processes continuously. This huge historic database, prepared for analysis purposes, enables process analysts to receive comprehensive information on business processes very quickly, at various granularity levels, from various, multidimensional points of view, over a long period of time.

1. INTRODUCTION

Efficient business processes are an important success factor in today's competitive markets. In the past few years enterprises have put the focus of business reengineering projects on reducing cost and measuring service efficiency and quality [20]. This has significantly contributed to the recent popularity of workflow management systems (WFMS). They have been developed to support and automate the execution of business processes according to the workflow specification. Workflow monitoring, controlling and reporting are playing a key role as an enabling technology for achieving and improving the efficiency of workflows, which is crucial for the success of continuous business process reengineering. Current state-of-the-art workflow management systems [1] are mainly concerned with the routing and assignment of tasks, providing little support for administration and management tasks such as workflow monitoring and reporting, management of resources, tracking the status of ongoing processes and exception handling. Supporting these tasks [18] is essential for establishing a robust and manageable work environment and providing quality guarantees. Overall business planning and operations control require comprehensive mechanisms, such as workflow history management, for performance monitoring.

Workflow history management provides the mechanisms for storing and querying the history of both ongoing and past processes for monitoring, business process reengineering, recovery and authorisation purposes [11]. In this paper we focus on business process reengineering and improvement purposes, as defined in [24]: Aggregating and mining the histories of all workflows over a longer time period form the basis for analysing and assessing the efficiency, accuracy and the timeliness of the enterprise's business processes. Therefore, this information provides feedback for continuous business process reengineering. For pointing out the distinction between business process reengineering and monitoring purposes of workflow history management, we agree with [20] and define workflow monitoring as follows: During the execution of a workflow, the need may arise for looking up some piece of information in the process history, for example, to figure out who else has already been concerned with the workflow at what time and in which role, or to monitor the current states of the tasks of an executing process instance when the administrator should make an interruption to the normal execution of the process instance. The ability of the workflow system to reveal such kind of information contributes to more transparency, flexibility and overall work quality.

Over the years, various definitions of WFMSs have been proposed, but one of the chief goals of WFMSs is to separate process logic from task logic, which is embedded in individual user applications [20]. This separation allows the two to be independently modified as well as analysed.

Most WFMSs' [20] servers use a relational DBMS as the repository for keeping track of workflow process definitions, organisation structure, runtime information on process and activity instances, workflow data, etc.

Addressing the fact, that the workflow repository is mostly a relational DBMS, performs mostly update transactions, has highly concurrent accesses and a crucial availability constraint [19], we have chosen a data warehouse approach for analysing and assessing business processes, because querying, aggregating and mining the operational workflow repository will cause a bottleneck or even a collapse of the entire workflow system. Due to the increasing competition and pace in today's industry, continuous analysis and assessment of business processes based on intelligent information technology is a major aspect of keeping up with competitors.

2. RELATED WORK

Workflow history management for business process reengineering purposes has not been extensively studied in the literature. Weikum has already out pointed in [25], that advanced workflow monitoring facilities are completely lacking in the current generation of commercial and research workflow management systems, and claimed also that the monitoring aspect bears a huge potential for improving the transparency, efficiency and accuracy of workflows and is crucial for the success of business process reengineering. He proposed and compared an audit trail approach and a special kind of temporal database management system.

LabFlow-1 is a benchmark that concisely captures the DBMS requirements of high throughput WFMSs [2]. The system is especially designed for controlling, tracking and managing high-volume, mission-critical workflows. Unlike our approach, LabFlow1 uses only one DBMS for monitoring and analysing the event history. The DBMS requirement is to quickly retrieve information about any activity for day-to-day operations. The history is also used to explore the cause of unexpected workflow results, to generate reports on workflow activity, and to discover workflow bottlenecks during process reengineering. As they are expecting even more throughput, DBMS bottlenecks will occur. Our process warehouse could reduce the workload of the DBMS and prevent these bottlenecks.

A light-weight system architecture, consisting of a small system kernel on top of which extensions like history management and work list management are implemented as workflows themselves is described in [21]. The history management consists of two components: A database system for storing the history data and a library of sub-workflows handling the access to the history database. History management sub-workflows are specified as state and activity charts. History data is aggregated during workflow execution and queries are implemented on these data. The workflow history serves simple monitoring as well as business process improvement purposes. Unlike our approach, which uses data warehouse techniques for improving business process quality, [21] selects and aggregates history data at runtime and is only intended for a very small amount of data.

The Process Performance Measurement System (PPMS) is focused on improving performance of business processes in general and evaluates financial as well as non-financial measures. While traditional controlling covers the firm in its entirety, workflow-based controlling and PPMS are focusing on business processes. Kueng argues in [12] that workflow-based controlling is mainly technology-driven, the selection of process performance indicators is primarily influenced by data, which can be gathered through the automated or semi-automated execution of activities by a WFMS and is therefore lacking the qualitative performance data and performance data about activities that are carried out manually. Our process warehouse approach addresses the fact and considers also external data sources, e.g. data from the human resource department, opinion surveys, employee surveys or advertising means. Although the PPMS can be seen as primarily business driven approach, and the database side is not considered at all, an enterprise prototype stores data in an additional database and uses SAP[1]-EIS for presentation.

PISA (Process Information System with Access) [23], [29] is a prototype that provides process monitoring and analysing functionality, using the IBM MQSeries[2] Workflow event history and the corresponding data from the process modelling tool ARIS[3] Toolset. Data is stored in an additional relational database at process instance level. Retrieving information on these workflows requires a lot of complex database operations and causes a negative performance impact.

Workflow history management for improving business processes and monitoring purposes is an important link between computer science and business science. We have seen that both research groups are working on this topic, using different approaches. Business science is more concerned with improving efficiency, presenting a comprehensive view of process performance and goal-orientation through target values, while computer science focuses mainly on the database side. In this work, we try to bridge the gap by embedding technology in a way that ensures not only the orientation towards business goals, but also the integration in environments traditionally supporting business decision-making.

[1] SAP is a registered trademark of SAP AG

[2] MQSeries Workflow is a registered trademark of IBM

[3] ARIS is a registered trademark of IDS Prof. Scheer AG

3. GOALS OF THE DATA WAREHOUSE APPROACH

Current commercial and research WFMSs are lacking extended workflow analysis capabilities [25]. We address these needs by applying a data warehouse approach, called process warehouse, which is an enabling technology for accurate and comprehensive business process analysis and is defined as follows:

The process warehouse (PWH) is a separate read-only analytical database that is used as the foundation of a process oriented decision support system with the aim to analyse and improve business processes continuously [15].

We have chosen the data warehouse approach and already extensively discussed in [15], because

a) Operational workflow repositories store workflow histories only for a few months, but analysing data patterns and trends over time requires large volumes of historical data over a wide range of time. Several years of data would be useful for such analysis [22]. Though, workflow repositories are not capable for analysis purposes, but comprehensive business process analysis requires an analytical database storing a high volume of workflow histories.
b) Most existing WFMSs are built on top of a centralised database that acts as a single point of failure: When the database fails no user can continue executing processes [1]. As WFMS perform mostly update transactions[19], querying, aggregating and mining the operational workflow repository will cause a bottleneck or even lead to a collapse of the entire workflow system. An analytical database, designed as a separate read-only database, will avoid a negative performance impact on the operational workflow repository.
c) Performing comprehensive data analysis using very large normalised databases causes costly joins and provides slow query response times. To avoid this, we use an OLAP approach, which is dedicated to analytical processing and well suited for fast performance in mining applications towards bottleneck diagnosis and other important decision supporting analysis.
d) Adding data from various source systems, e.g. Workflow Management Systems, Business Process Management Systems, Enterprise Resource Planning Systems, etc. leads to a very balanced and enterprise wide business process analysis.

The data warehouse approach provides information at various granularity levels with navigation capabilities, addressing users at strategic, tactical and operational levels. It enables process analysts to receive comprehensive information on business processes very quickly, at different aggregation levels, from different and multidimensional points of view, over a long period of time, using a huge historic data basis prepared for analysing purposes to effectively support the management of business processes.

4. DATA SOURCE

WFMSs carry out business processes by interpreting the process definition. A workflow participant or the workflow engine creates a new process instance and at the same time the workflow engine assigns an instance state. Basically, workflow participants can explicitly request a certain process instance state. When the process is running, the workflow engine creates sub-process, activity or work item instances according to the process definition and assigns work items to the process participant's work list. The work item is withdrawn from the work list after completion.

WFMSs store audit trails of all instances in log files, recording all state changes that occur during a workflow enactment in response to external events or control decisions taken by the workflow engine. Audit data, the historical record of the progress of a process instance from start to completion or termination [28], is the main data source of the PWH. In [27] a detailed specification of audit data can be found, which we have applied in this work as the foundation for the data model. In our current concept we focus primarily on audit data, but basically we plan to integrate also other data sources, e.g. Business Process Management Systems, Enterprise Resource Planning Systems, Balanced Scorecard [9], Knowledge Maps [4] etc. in order to receive a balanced business process analysis. As audit data is to be used in conjunction with meta data [27], we enhance the audit trail with the corresponding process definition, which is defined in the build time component of the WFMS.

5. BASIC PROCESS WAREHOUSE COMPONENTS REPRESENTING BUSINESS PROCESS ANALYSIS REQUIREMENTS

The analysis of business processes requires the integration of theoretical aspects. We capture business process theory in four views, which we present in this paper. Two of these views, the Business Process Improvement Support View and the Business Process Information Detail View are already discussed in [15] and extended in this section.

5.1 Business Process Information Detail View

This view is targeting process, activity and work item information on instance level or slightly aggregated level. It enables the analysis of instance development over time and supports to determine the cause of performance gaps and deviations.

In organisations knowledge becomes embedded in routines, processes, practices and norms [4]. Knowledge can be evaluated by decisions or actions to which it leads, for example measurable efficiencies, speed or quality gains [4], therefore the PWH can measure knowledge. Davenport and Prusak discern in [4] between knowledge that is fully embedded in the process design and human knowledge that keeps the process going. The latter correlates directly with the business process information detail view.

Knowledge develops over time, through experience that includes what we absorb from courses, books, and mentors as well as informal learning [4]. For example a process performer, who has just joined a company or started a new job will need a considerable amount of time to perform a work item, but after some days the person should become faster due to gained experience. A poor or unskilled process performer, who has finished an education program, should increase his/her performance because of improved skills. Knowledge generation can be measured through the business process information detail view, which enables the analysis of experience and skill development over time.

A continuous reduction of process, activity or work item duration represents the development of a learning participant. A very high process duration represents either an indicator for further education in order to improve the skill level or that the employee is not suitable or motivated for the job at all and a job rotation initiative has to be considered. Constant process durations and low deviations represent a well-qualified process participant and a well-designed process.

Knowledge is not bound to a high level occupation, even assembly line work, often considered merely mechanical, benefits from the experience, skill, and adaptability of human expertise [4]. Therefore, even simple production workflows are suitable for knowledge measurement.

5.2 Business Process Improvement Support View

This view is based on the histories of several instances together. The aggregation of instances is aiming at identifying major performance gaps and deviations, which give evidence of improvement needs. As single instances do not have an impact on aggregated performance, gaps reflect a fundamental performance problem. Drilling-down to the business process information detail view, to get information on the development processes, activities and work items over time, is one way to determine the cause of these gaps and deviations.

The expert's knowledge is embedded in the process design [4]. This knowledge can be measured firstly by the identification of highly aggregated performance deviations indicating that the designer could not deal with complexity and secondly by comparison with competitors.

5.3 Business Process View

A process is defined as a group of tasks that together create a result of value to the customer [6] or a structured, measured set of activities designed to produce a specified output for a particular customer or market [3]. The analysis of this view focuses on the process as a complete entity from a process owner's point of view, who is an individual concerned with the successful realisation of a complete end-to-end process, the linking of tasks into one body of work and making sure that the complete process works together [6].

Modern companies' problems do not lie in the performance of individual tasks and activities, the units of work, but in the processes, how the units fit together into a whole [6]. This view completely disregards the functional structure, but fully represents the approach of process-centered organisations and looks horizontally across the whole organisation. Both views, the Business Process Improvement Support View as well as the Business Process Information Detail View can be applied to the Business Process View.

5.4 Organisational View

The Industrial Revolution had turned its back on processes, deconstructing them into specialised tasks and then focusing on improving the performance of these tasks [6]. Tasks-orientation formed the basic building blocks – the functional, mostly hierarchical structure - of twentieth century corporations. In the 1990s the application of process-oriented business improvement programs has begun, but the functional structure has remained unchanged. Therefore, we face two organisational concepts, existing side by side: A functional structure and business process orientation.

As business processes typically flow through several organisational units and cross a lot of responsibilities, it is obvious that the process reflects the hierarchical structures of the organisation [14]. The analysis of this view addresses the organisational structure of a business process and the fact that business processes, which cross organisational boundaries very often tend to be inefficient because of changing responsibilities, long delay times and so on [14]. Therefore, the analysis of the organisational structure is an important aspect of process improvement, as it supports the detection of delay causing organisational units. The Business Process Improvement Support View as well as the Business Process Information Detail View can be applied to this view.

6. DATA MODEL AND ANALYSIS CAPABILITIES

We have adopted Jacobson's forward business engineering approach, which is part of an object oriented business process reengineering method [8], as the basic development strategy for the data model. Jacobson proposes to build two models in parallel: An ideal and a real model. The ideal model is seen as the desired objective, showing the direction and the vision, whereby the real model is intended to capture restrictions found in the business [8].

Our ideal model is based on standards of the Workflow Management Coalition [26], [27], [28] and is not restricted to a commercial product or meta model. The real model is integrated in a research prototype based on a commercial WFMS. In this work we focus on the ideal model that gives us the opportunity to develop an unrestricted, unbiased and visionary data model. We present three examples, which capture basic concepts of the PWH and discuss their analysis capabilities.

6.1 Business Process Duration Analysis

Most enterprises, even very large and complex ones, can be broken down into fewer than 20 - typically between 5 and 15 - key processes, which include product development, customer order fulfilment, order acquisition, after sales support or financial asset management [3], [6]. Workflows are not as complex as key processes, but indeed they consist of a lot of activities, sub-processes and work items. In order to enable the detection of the deviation causing part in the process, a detailed analysis of activities and work items is required.

A process is a set of one or more linked process activities, which may result in several work items [28]. Processes, activities and work items have hierarchical dependencies and therefore a lot of attributes in common such as workflow participants, but differ in other aspects like instance states. Therefore, we have decided to separate process, activity and work item fact tables. Those dimensions, which are needed by all fact tables, enable a drill-across from one fact table to the other.

6.1.1 Granularity

In the build time component of a WFMS or BPMS the target duration of processes is defined, during execution a deviation between the actual duration and the target value is generated. We store the deviation, because on one hand using the target value creates a highly redundant fact table, which should be normalised [10], and on the other hand when the target duration changes the model of the PWH is not affected. The Process Duration Fact Table (*Figure 1* - semantic model proposed by Kurz in [13]) is targeting business processes as a complete entity.

Process instances can turn into seven basic states: Active, running, archived, initiated, suspended, completed and terminated [28]. Any state change is logged in an audit trail. We calculate the duration of all states, which result accumulated in the process duration. As the final process states - completed or terminated – must not turn into a new state, we integrate these states into the category dimension.

6.1.2 Process Dimension

At process ID level, multiple instances are aggregated by process definition. This level enables the analysis of a certain process and represents the Business Process Improvement Support View. Drilling-down to the instance level represents the Business Process Information Detail View.

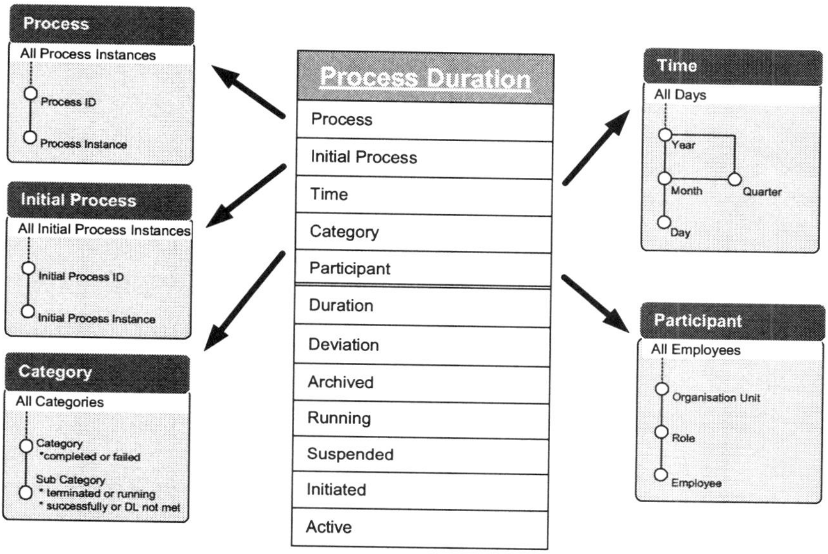

Figure 1: Process Duration Fact Table

6.1.3 Initial Process Dimension

A process may consist of various sub-processes, which can be also called by other initiating processes or sub-processes. A sub-process has its own process definition and is therefore a process without any restrictions. To access a sub-process with our PWH process dimension, it is necessary to choose the initiating process dimension, because sub-processes are reusable components within other processes and can be identified through the initiating process. With the initiating process dimension, we can choose a special instance or ID and refer to certain sub-process instance or ID.

6.1.4 Time Dimension

Time is a very complex data warehouse dimension and has been extensively discussed by [10]. As this dimension requires a comprehensive analysis of business needs, we use a generic time dimension for demonstration purposes only.

6.1.5 Participant Dimension

Workflow participants act as the performers of various activities in the process [26]. The workflow participant declaration does not necessarily refer to a single person (employee or user id), but may also identify a set of appropriate skill (role) or responsibility (organisation unit), or machine automated resources rather than human [26]. In the process definition a workflow participant is assigned to perform a particular work item. During execution, work items are assigned to an employee or a group of employees, but performed only by one person, who is in a particular role and belongs to an organisation unit. The participant dimension represents the Organisational View and is dedicated to analyse the duration that organisation units require accomplishing a process. It enables the detection of deviation-causing departments.

6.1.6 Category Dimension

We have introduced two levels for the category dimension: Categories and sub-categories. Categories distinguish between 'completed' processes and 'failed' processes. When a process has 'completed', it has either the sub-category 'successfully completed' or 'deadline not met'. The category 'completed' is equal to the process instance state completed. The process has 'completed successfully' when it has completed within the proposed target. When the process has completed, but not within the target time limit and an escalation procedure has been started, the process sub-category is 'deadline not met'.

When a process has 'failed', the sub-category is either 'terminated' or 'running'. The 'terminated' process is equal to the terminated workflow process state, so the process instance has been stopped before its normal completion. A process is 'running' means that the process has not completed within the deadline multiplied by a certain factor. In our opinion this process has failed, because the first principle is that process design must be customer-driven [6]. When a customer orders a book and requests the delivery within 24 hours and the book turns up after a week, than the company has probably lost a customer. The process has completed, but in terms of customer relationship management the process has totally failed. If the process had completed within the deadline multiplied by a certain factor and the cycle time is greater than the deadline, than the sub-category is 'deadline not met'. The category dimension enables the analysis of processes that finished similarly.

6.2 Work Item Performance Analysis

6.2.1 Granularity

A work item performer requires for the execution of a work item a certain amount of time, what we call working time. The time span between the actual duration and the target duration is the deviation, which can be seen as a performance assessment. The work item performance fact table (*Figure 2*) is targeting the analysis of work items performed by certain participants or qualification groups, without considering involved processes or activities. We do not discuss the work item dimension, because the functionality is similar to the process dimension.

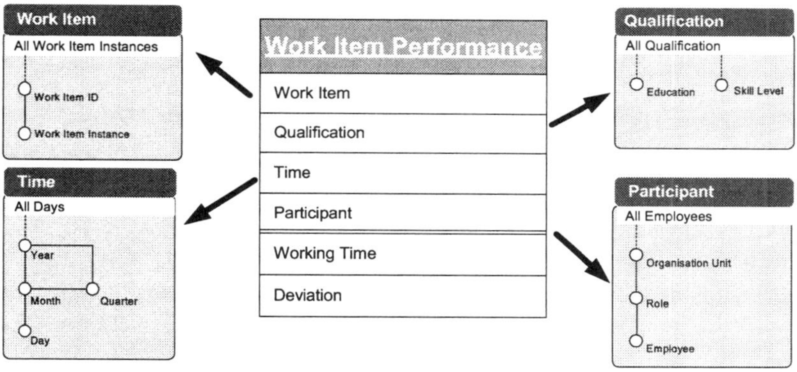

Figure 2: Work Item Performance Fact Table

6.2.2 Participant Dimension

The participant dimension enables the performance analysis of work item participants. On work item instances level the performance development over time is provided, which represents the gathered knowledge of the performer.

6.2.3 Qualification Dimension

The qualification dimension filters by education (A-level, bachelor, etc.) or skill level (beginner, professional, etc.) and enables a performance analysis of certain qualification types. For example, when a company is going to hire a new employee, we recommend finding out the best performing education level for the required work items, in order to support the preparation of an adequate job announcement.

6.3 Workload Analysis

6.3.1 Granularity

A user's work list can consist of several work item instances, categorised by priorities, and a work item instance can be assigned to several participants. When a user selects a work item, it is withdrawn from all work lists. If the work item is not completed, it will be reassigned to all work lists.

Employees face various working periods, e.g. at peak times the workload is higher and during vacation periods a stand-in concept is required. The workload fact table (*Figure 3*) focuses on achieving a balanced workload and represents the Organisational View.

6.3.2 Participant Dimension

In organisations groups of people work together and workload has to be balanced between group members. The participant dimension enables the detection of unbalanced stand-in concepts or staff schedules. When all group members face an extremely high workload, a new schedule or even an additional employee is required. When group members face different workloads, a balanced stand-in or work schedule concept is required.

6.3.3 Qualification Dimension

At the beginning of training the overall performance is very low. The qualification dimension enables the workload analysis of beginners and professionals, in order to detect an overload. When beginners have a very high amount of assigned work items and a high average time of work items assigned to their work list, it represents a familiarisation process with work and has nothing to do with work overload. But when professional face this high amount of work, evidence of work overload is given.

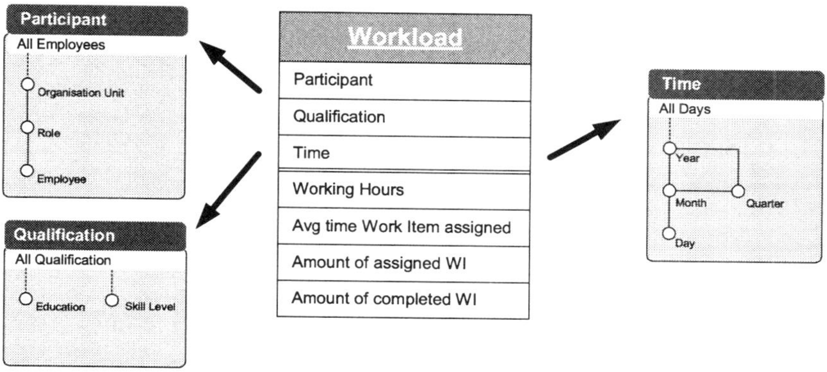

Figure 3: Workload Fact Table

7. CONCLUSION AND FURTHER RESEARCH

As competition is growing in all sectors, well-designed business processes and their continuous improvement is a prerequisite for survival in the global economy. We think the Process Warehouse is a very promising approach to a comprehensive business process analysis, because of the multiple data sources, fast database, multidimensional analysis, navigation capabilities and the opportunity to use data mining and OLAP tools.

Due to very powerful labour unions in western countries, especially in Europe, we think that the implementation of the Process Warehouse within organisations is rather difficult. In [16], [17] we have extended the Process Warehouse for inter-organisational e-business processes, because highly competitive and fast developing environments face aggressive competition and provide an opportunity for realisation.

REFERENCES

[1] ALONSO, G., AGRAWAL, D., ABBADI, A. El, and MOHAN, C., Functionality and Limitations of Current Workflow Management Systems; IEEE Expert, 1(9), 1997, Special Issue on Cooperative Information Systems.

[2] BONNER, A., SHRUFI, A., ROZEN, S., LabFlow-1: A Database Benchmark for High-Throughput Workflow Management, In Proceedings of the International Conference on Extending Database Technology (EDBT), 1996

[3] DAVENPORT, T. H., Process Innovation – Reengineering Work through Information Technology, Harvard Business School Press, Boston 1993

[4] DAVENPORT, T. H., PRUSAK, L. Working Knowledge: How Organizations Manage What They Know. Harvard Business School Press, 1998.

[5] GEORGAKOPOULOS, D., HORNIK, M., SHETH, A. (1995). An overview of workflow management: From process modelling to infrastructure for automation. Journal on Distributed and Parallel Database Systems, 3(2): 119 – 153.

[6] HAMMER, M., Beyond Reengineering, Harper Collins Publishers 1996.

[7] INMON, W. H., Building the Data Warehouse, Wiley & Sons, 1996.

[8] JACOBSON, I., ERICSON, M., JACOBSON, A., The Object Advantage – Business Process Reengineering with Object Technology, ACM Press, Addison-Wesely Publishing 1995

[9] KAPLAN, R., NORTON, D., The Balanced Scorecard: Translating Strategy into Action. Harvard Business School Press, Boston, 1996.

[10] KIMBALL, R., The Data Warehouse Toolkit: Practical Techniques For Building Dimensional Data Warehouse, John Wiley & Sons 1996.

[11] KOKSAL, P.; ARPINAR, S. N.; DOGAC; A.; Workflow History Management; SIGMOD Record, Vol. 27 No.1, 1998.

[12] KUENG, P., Supporting BPR through a Process Performance Measurement System, Business Information Technology Management, Conference Proceedings of BITWorld'98. Har-Anand Publications, New Delhi, 1998.

[13] KURZ, A., Data Warehousing – Enabling Technology, MITP-Verlag, 1999.

[14] LEYMANN, F., ROLLER, D., Production Workflow – Concepts and Techniques, Prentice Hall PTR, 2000.

[15] LIST, B., SCHIEFER, J., TJOA, A. M., QUIRCHMAYR, G., The Process Warehouse - A Data Warehouse Approach for Business Process Management, To appear in: e-Business and Intelligent Management - Proceedings of the International Conference on Management of Information and Communication Technology (MiCT1999), Copenhagen, Denmark, September 15 – 16 1999, Austrian Computer Society Bookseries, books @ocg.at, 2000.

[16] LIST, B., SCHIEFER, J., TJOA, A. M., QUIRCHMAYR, G., The Process Warehouse Approach for Inter-Organisational e-Business Process Improvement, In: Proceedings of the 6th International Conference on Re-Technologies for Information Systems (ReTIS2000) Preparing to E-Business, Zurich, Switzerland, February 29 – March 3 2000, Austrian Computer Society Bookseries, books @ocg.at, vol. 132, 2000.

[17] LIST, B., SCHIEFER, J., TJOA, A. M., Customer driven e-Business Process Improvement with the Process Warehouse, To appear in: Proceedings of the 16th International Federation for Information Processing (IFIP) World Computer Congress, International Conference on Information Technology for Business Management (ITBM), Beijing, China, August 21 – 25 2000, Kluwer Academic Publishers, 2000.

[18] MARAZAKIS, M., PAPADAKIS, D., NIKOLAOU, C., Management of Work Sessions in Dynamic Open Environments, Proceedings of the 9th International Conference on Database and Expert Systems Applications (DEXA 1998), Vienna, IEEE Press, 1998.

[19] MOHAN, C., Tutorial: State of the Art in Workflow Management System Research and Products, Presented at: NATO Advanced Study Institute (ASI) on Workflow Management Systems and Interoperability Istanbul, August 1997; 5th International Conference on Database Systems for Advanced Applications (DASFAA'97), Melbourne, April 1997; ACM SIGMOD International Conference on Management of Data, Montreal, June 1996; 5th International Conference on Extending Database Technology, Avignon, March 1996.

[20] MOHAN, C., Recent Trends in Workflow Management Products, Standards and Research, Proc. NATO Advanced Study Institute (ASI) on Workflow Management Systems and Interoperability, Istanbul, August 1997, Springer Verlag, 1998.
[21] MUTH, P., WEISSENFELS, J., GILLMANN, M., WEIKUM, G., Workflow History Management in Virtual Enterprises using a Light-Weight Workflow Management System, Workshop on Research Issues in Data Engineering, Sydney, March 1999.
[22] POE, V., Building a Data Warehouse for Decision Support. Prentice Hall, 1995.
[23] ROSEMANN, M., DENECKE, TH., PÜTTMANN, M., PISA – Process Information System with Access, Design and realisation of an information system for process monitoring and controlling (German), Working paper no. 49, 1996.
[24] WEIKUM, G., Personal Communication with P. Koksal, S. N. Arpinar, A. Dogac in Workflow History Management [11].
[25] WEIKUM, G., Workflow Monitoring: Queries On Logs or Temporal Databases, HPTS'95, Position Paper.
[26] Workflow Management Coalition, http://www.aiim.org/wfmc/, Interface 1 – Process Definition Interchange 1998.
[27] Workflow Management Coalition, Interface 5 – Audit Data Specification, 1998.
[28] Workflow Management Coalition, Workflow Handbook, John Wiley & Sons, 1997.
[29] zur Muehlen, M.; Rosemann, M., Workflow-based Process Monitoring and Controlling – Technical and Organizational Issues, *Proceedings of 33rd Hawaii International Conference on System Sciences (HICSS),* January 4 – 7 2000, Wailea Maui.

Chapter 10

AMALGAMATION OF STATISTICS AND DATA MINING TECHNIQUES: EXPLORATIONS IN CUSTOMER LIFETIME VALUE MODELING

D. R. Mani, James Drew, Andrew Betz and Piew Datta
GTE Laboratories Incorporated, 40 Sylvan Road, Waltham, MA 02451 USA

Keywords: survival analysis, neural networks, lifetime value, tenure prediction, proportional hazards regression

Abstract: We illustrate how one can exploit the complementary strengths of Statistics and Data Mining techniques to build accurate, intuitively understandable and ultimately actionable models for business problems. We show how accurate, but not-so-transparent, models built by data mining algorithms (like neural networks) can be understood—and the interesting patterns captured in these models appropriately used in a business context—by bringing to bear statistical formalisms and business domain knowledge. The work will be presented in the context of lifetime value modeling for GTE cellular telephone subscribers.

1. INTRODUCTION

One of the primary goals of business data analysis is to model and analyze data, using a variety of techniques, in order to gain *actionable insights* that can be used to ultimately promote the profitability of the business. Furthermore, business data analysis must provide enough accurate quantitative information, usually in the form of data models, so that the insights of analysis can be effectively implemented.

Traditionally, business data analysis has been the responsibility of statisticians. Over the span of almost a century, statistics as a discipline has developed a gamut of sound, simple-yet-powerful, and intuitively understandable techniques for data modeling and analysis. Of late, knowledge discovery and data mining (KDD) is becoming increasingly popular as an approach to business data analysis. Data Mining uses a variety of scalable machine learning techniques—including neural networks, decision trees, association rules and *k*-nearest neighbor models—to develop automated, highly non-linear and accurate models by sifting through large amounts of data.

Data analysts with a statistical background have generally stayed away from using data mining techniques. These analysts do not trust data mining algorithms for a range of reasons, some of which include ad-hoc and unsystematic approaches, inscrutable black-box like models, etc. Data miners, on the other hand, have cavalierly gone on to invent more ad-hoc methods for dealing with situations for which the statisticians already have elegant answers.

In this chapter, we argue that business data analysis can be transformed to a new level by appropriately adapting techniques from *both* the statistics and data mining disciplines. Using the problem of customer lifetime value (LTV) modeling to set the business context, we demonstrate how data mining tools can be apt complements of classical statistical methods, and show that their combined usage overcomes many of the shortcomings of each separate set of tools.

This amalgam of data mining and classical statistics is motivated by the observation that many real-world business problems have requirements for both accuracy and understanding. The former is often superbly addressed by data mining techniques, while the latter is generally suited to the data model building which is the hallmark of classical statistics. The illustration we present below revolves around the need to both estimate and understand customer lifetimes and churn patterns. We will show that the data mining technique of an artificial neural net, built on the statistical concept of hazard functions, gives a highly accurate estimate of customer lifetimes. Subsequent data mining (clustering) and statistical modeling then produces models of churn patterns to be used by the business analyst as he or she develops customer relationship strategies.

The data analyst whose tool kit includes a repertoire of statistical and data mining techniques can harness the systematic, elegant and eminently understandable framework of statistics along with the accuracy, power and scalability of data mining methods to tame business problems like never before—leading to good business insight, accurate and targeted implementation and ultimately to competitive advantage!

1.1 Overview

Section 2 briefly compares the salient features of statistics and data mining for data analysis. The next section, Section 3, defines the business problem of evaluating customer lifetime value (LTV) and summarizes the key challenges in tenure modeling for LTV. The data used in exploring and comparing various techniques for tenure modeling is described in Section 4. Classical survival analysis for LTV tenure modeling is discussed in Section 5, while the neural network model is the subject of Section 6. Comparison of experimental results in Sections 5 and 6 show that neural network models are significantly more accurate. In Section 7, we discuss methods to explicate and interpret the neural network, and demonstrate techniques that go beyond data modeling to provide actionable business insight. The final section summarizes the chapter, and revisits the amalgamation of statistics and data mining techniques for business data analysis.

2. STATISTICS AND DATA MINING TECHNIQUES: A CHARACTERIZATION

Statistics encompasses a large, well-defined body of knowledge including statistical inference and modeling, exploratory data analysis, experimental design and sampling (Glymour et. al., 1997). Data mining is more nebulously defined, since the term takes on different meanings with different audiences. For our purposes, we use data mining to represent the application of machine learning techniques (Mitchell, 1997) to data analysis. From a business data analysis standpoint, both statistics and data mining techniques would be used in understanding data—i.e., transforming raw data into useful information.

Figure 2.1 is a graphic representation of the complementary strengths of statistics and data mining. Statistics excels at providing a structured and formal mathematical framework for data modeling and analysis. Though this enables rigorous analysis of correlations, uncertainties and errors, this same structure forces models to be mostly linear and parametric (or semi-parametric). When modeling complex systems represented by large amounts of data, these model restrictions result in less than maximal accuracy. Data mining algorithms, on the other hand, are highly non-linear and generally free from underlying restrictive assumptions about model structure. While this is an asset in producing accurate models, it makes the models complex and difficult to comprehend. Furthermore, data mining algorithms result in disaggregated models which capture nuances in the data at the level of individual records (or cases), making these models extremely accurate. This is unlike statistical models, which generally capture more aggregate and average characteristics. The disaggregated nature of data mining models adds to the opaqueness and makes them more difficult to interpret.

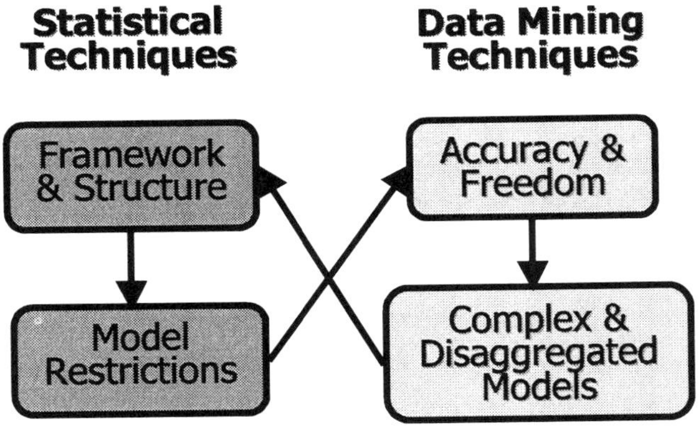

Figure 2.1. Strengths and weaknesses of statistics and data mining techniques.

In this chapter, we demonstrate that the framework and structure introduced by statistical techniques can provide the context for the data mining algorithms. In this context, data mining produces highly accurate and disaggregated models. These models are then explained and understood by going back to statistical formalisms. The result of this amalgamation of statistics and data mining techniques are models that are not only highly accurate, but can also be probed and understood by business analysts. We further show how models built by data mining techniques can, when analyzed in the appropriate statistical framework, lead to direct and actionable business insight and knowledge.

3. LIFETIME VALUE (LTV) MODELING

Customer *lifetime value* (LTV)—which measures the revenue and profit generating potential of a customer—is increasingly being considered a touchstone for administering one-on-one *customer relationship management* (CRM) processes in order to provide attractive benefits to, and retain, high-value customers, while maximizing profits from a business standpoint. LTV is usually considered to be composed of two independent components—

tenure and value. Though modeling the value component of LTV is a challenge in itself, our experience has been that finance departments, to a large degree, dictate this aspect. We therefore focus exclusively on modeling tenure.

In the realm of CRM, modeling customer LTV has a wide range of applications including: special services (e.g., premium call centers and elite service) and offers (concessions, upgrades, etc.) based on customer LTV; targeting and managing unprofitable customers; segmenting customers, marketing, pricing and promotional analysis based on LTV.

LTV is a composite of tenure and value: LTV = tenure × value. Tenure and value could be computed as an aggregate over customer segments or time periods. The central challenge of the prediction of LTV is the production of estimated, *differentiated* (disaggregated) tenures for *every* customer with a given service supplier, based on the usage, revenue, and sales profiles contained in company databases. Tenure prediction models we develop generate, for a given customer *i*, a *hazard curve* or *hazard function* that indicates the probability $h_i(t)$ of cancellation at a given time *t* in the future. Figure 5.1 shows an example of a hazard function. A hazard curve can be converted to a *survival curve* or *survival function*, which plots the probability $S_i(t)$ of "survival" (non-cancellation) at any time *t*, given that customer *i* was "alive" (active) at time $(t-1)$, i.e., $S_i(t) = S_i(t-1) \times [1 - h_i(t)]$ with $S_i(1)=1$. Section 5 formally defines hazard and survival functions. Armed with a survival curve for a customer, LTV for that specific customer *i* is computed as: $\text{LTV} = \sum_{t=1}^{T} S_i(t) \times v_i(t)$ where $v_i(t)$ is the expected value of customer *i* at time *t*, and *T* is the maximum time period under consideration. This approach to LTV computation provides customer specific estimates (as opposed to average estimates) of total expected future (as opposed to past) revenue based on customer behavior and usage patterns.

There are a variety of standard statistical techniques arising from *survival analysis* (e.g. Cox and Oakes, 1984) which can be applied to tenure modeling. We look at tenure prediction using classical survival analysis and compare it with "hybrid" data mining techniques that use neural networks in conjunction with statistical techniques. We demonstrate, as highlighted in Section 2, how data mining tools can be apt complements of the classical statistical models, and show that their combined usage overcomes many of the shortcomings of each separate tool set—resulting in LTV models that are both accurate and understandable.[1]

[1] When modeling LTV using tenure and value, we are implicitly assuming that for a given customer, revenue and behavior do not change significantly. This may not always be true,

3.1 Challenges

Given that LTV is defined in terms of a survival function, a distinguishing and challenging feature of tenure prediction is computing the disaggregated or differentiated hazard function for every customer. Classical statistical techniques (Section 5) like proportional hazards regression provide estimates of hazard functions that are dependent on often questionable assumptions and can yield implausible tenure estimates.

If each customer can be observed from subscription to cancellation, predictive modeling techniques can be directly applied. In reality, where a large majority of customers are still currently subscribers, the data are *right censored.* While classical survival analysis can handle right censoring, data mining techniques like neural nets are ill adapted to directly dealing with censored data. The situation is further complicated by the fact that company databases often do not retain information on customers who have cancelled in the past. Thus, observed (and censored) lifetimes are biased by the exclusion of (relatively short-lived) customers canceling before the database's observation start period. This is *left truncation*, recognized by Bolton (1998) and Helson and Schmittlein (1993), which needs to be systematically addressed in order to build reliable and unbiased tenure models.

Evaluating tenure models by comparing against actual cancellations is another challenge due to the prevalence of right censoring. Furthermore, the small fraction of cancellations that are observed could be a biased sample.

Lastly, real world customer databases have large amounts of data (Section 4), and relatively frequent recomputation of LTV is needed to accommodate for changes in customer behavior and market dynamics. We therefore need a reasonably automated technique that can handle large amount of data.

4. CUSTOMER DATA FOR LTV TENURE PREDICTION

We have applied statistics and data mining techniques to model LTV for GTE Wireless' cellular telephone customers. GTE Wireless has a customer data warehouse containing billing, usage and demographic information. The warehouse is updated at monthly intervals with summary information by

either due to customer life changes, or due to targeted marketing efforts by the service provider. Such change is extremely difficult to model directly. We assume that the LTV models will be periodically recalibrated to capture such change.

adding a new record for every active customer, and noting customers who have cancelled service. GTE Wireless offers cellular services in a large number of areas—divided into *markets*—scattered throughout the United States. Because of differences arising from variations in the geography, composition and market dynamics of the customer base, we build individual LTV tenure models for each market.

For LTV tenure modeling, we obtain a data extract from the warehouse where each customer record has about 30–40 fields including: identification (cellular phone number, account number); billing (previous balance, charges for access/minutes/toll); usage (total calls, minutes of use); subscription (number of months in service, rate plan); churn (a flag indicating if the customer has cancelled service); and other fields (age, optional features). We use data from a single, relatively small, market containing approximately 21,500 subscribers. The data represents customer behavior summary for the month of April 1998. The *churn* flag in this data would indicate those customers who cancelled service during the month of April 1998. Approximately 2.5% of customers churned in that period, resulting in 97.5% of censored observations. This dataset is used in both the statistical and data mining approaches, and facilitates comparison of the various techniques.

5. CLASSICAL STATISTICAL APPROACHES TO SURVIVAL ANALYSIS

There are three classic statistical approaches for the analysis of survival data, largely distinguished by the assumptions they make about the parameters of the distribution(s) generating the observed survival times. All deal with censored observations by estimating hazard functions $\{h_i(t)\}$ where

$h_i(t)$ = Probability of subject *i*'s death at time *t* given subject *i*'s lifetime is *t* or greater

or the survival function $\{S_i(t)\}$ where

$S_i(t)$ = Probability that subject *i*'s lifetime is no less than *t*

Parametric survival models (see, e.g., Lawless, 1982) estimate the effects of covariates (subject variables whose values influence lifetimes) by presuming a lifetime distribution of a known form, such as an exponential or Weibull. While popular for some applications (especially accelerated failure models), the smoothness of these postulated distributions makes them inappropriate for our data with its contract expiration date and consequent built-in hazard "spikes" (for example, see Figure 5.1.)

In contrast, Kaplan-Meier methods (Kaplan and Meier, 1958) are non-parametric, providing hazard and survival functions with no assumption of a parametric lifetime distribution function. Suppose deaths occur at times $t_1 < t_2 < ... < t_K$, with d_k deaths at time t_k. Let r_k be the number of subjects at risk at time t_k. (In our data situation, where we observe all subscribers active within a one-month time period, r_k is the number of subjects of age k at the start of the month, and d_k is the number of customers dying during that month. Different data sampling methods—including all customers active within a larger range of time, for instance—require more complicated accounting for those at risk.) Then the hazard estimate for time t_k is

$$h(t) = \frac{d_k}{r_k}, t_k < t < t_{k+1} \qquad \text{Equation 5.1}$$

and the survival function is estimated by

$$S(t) = \prod_{k:_k t<t} (1 - h(t)) \qquad \text{Equation 5.2}$$

Note that this estimator cannot easily estimate the effects of covariates on the hazard and survival functions. Subsets of customers can generate separate Kaplan-Meier estimates, but sample size considerations generally require substantial aggregation in the data, so that many customers are assigned the same hazard and survival functions, regardless of their variation on many potential covariates.

This latter problem has a classic solution in proportional hazards (PH) regression (Cox, 1972). This model is semi-parametric in the sense that all subjects have a common, arbitrary baseline hazard function $\lambda_0(t)$ which is related to an individual's hazard function by a multiple which is a parametric function of covariates $\{x_{ic}\}, i = 1,2,...,n; c = 1,2,...,C$:

$$h_i(t) = \lambda_0(t) exp\left\{\sum_{c=1}^{C} \beta_c x_{ic}\right\} \qquad \text{Equation 5.3}$$

where i=1,2,. . .,n indexes the n subjects, c=1,2,. . .,C indexes the C covariates, and $\{\beta_c\}$ represent parameters estimated during the PH regression. In our situation covariates include data such as various charges per month, as well as dummy variables to indicate presence of a discrete attribute:

$$A_i = \begin{cases} 1, & \text{if attribute } A \text{ is present in the } i^{th} \text{ subject} \\ 0, & \text{otherwise} \end{cases}$$

This model has two conceptual and one operational sets of shortcomings. First, the form of the multiplier $exp\left\{\sum_{c=1}^{C} \beta_c x_{ic}\right\}$ is usually chosen for convenience, except in the rare instance where substantive knowledge is available. The form is, of course, reasonable as a first step, to uncover influential covariates, but its essentially linear form tends to assign extreme values to subjects with extreme covariate values. There is no mechanism to stop any component of the estimated hazard function from exceeding 1.0. Second, the presumption of proportional hazards is restrictive in that there may not be a single baseline hazard for each subject, and the form of that baseline's variation may not be well modeled by the time-dependent covariates or stratification that are the traditional statistical extensions of the original PH model.

An operational difficulty of PH regression lies in its de-emphasis of explicit calculation of baseline hazards. This problem is particularly acute in our situation of observing subjects over one month only of their lifetimes instead of following a cohort from birth until death/censoring. The standard statistical packages (e.g. Allison, 1995) do not allow the direct estimation of a baseline hazard function when time-dependent covariates are used, and our data situation described above (in which subjects are taken to be available only during the one month observation period) is construed as introducing a time-dependence.

Fortunately, deaths are only recorded as occurring during a particular month, so there are typically many deaths that effectively occur simultaneously. Prentice and Goeckler (1978) showed that the PH coefficients can be estimated via a form of logistic regression. The complementary-log-log (CLL) model

$$log[-log\{1 - h_i(t)\}] = \alpha_t + \sum_{c=1}^{C} \beta_c x_{ic} \qquad \text{Equation 5.4}$$

yields theoretically the same coefficients $\{\beta_c\}$ as the PH model, and furthermore gives baseline age effects $\{\alpha_t\}$ which can be translated into baseline hazard components via

$$\lambda_o(t) = 1 - exp(-exp(\alpha_t)) \qquad \text{Equation 5.5}$$

Direct estimation of the baseline hazard function values is very useful, both in itself, and facilitates the hazard function estimations for each individual subject. Once the hazard function $h_i(t)$ is estimated for each subject i, the individual survival function is estimated as

$$S_i(t_k) = \prod_{t=0}^{t_k} \left(1 - h_i(t)\right) \qquad \text{Equation 5.6}$$

and the median lifetime is estimated as the interpolated value of t for which $S_i(t) = 0.5$. It is important to note that the later estimate is very sensitive to the choice of the baseline hazard function.

5.1 Results

The CLL model was fit to the data described above. The covariates were chosen by a combination of classical variable selection techniques, subject matter expert opinion and intuitive examination of coefficients. The resulting baseline hazard function is shown in Figure 5.1.

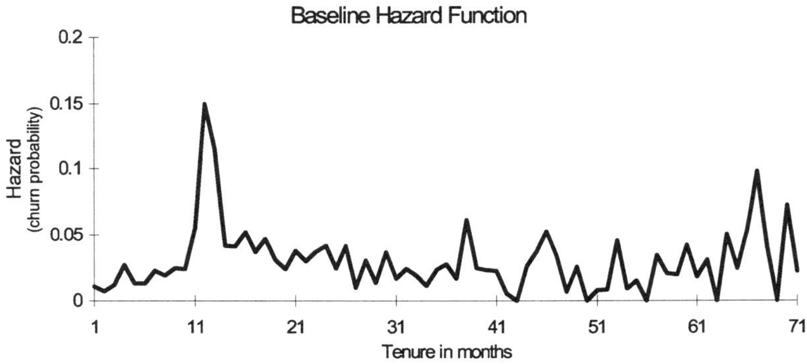

Figure 5.1: The baseline hazard function.

By many statistical standards, the CLL model producing this hazard function fits the data well. The covariates, including the baseline hazard coefficients, are highly significant (X^2=10059.75 with 71 df, p<0.0001), and Somer's D=0.502.

However, the graph in Figure 6.1b shows the "relation" of tenure predicted by this model, and actual tenures observed from those who died during the observation period. For these data, the predicted lifetimes are quite poor.

These classical statistical techniques are subject to three major problems in estimating lifetimes. First, the functional forms for the effect of the covariates must be assumed, and are typically chosen to be linear or some mild extension thereof. More sophisticated choices tend to be cumbersome and major exploration of better-fitting forms is generally manual, ad-hoc, and destructive of the significance tests which motivate the statistical approaches. Second, many of these forms work poorly with outlying values of the covariates, so it is possible that some customers with extreme covariate values may be assigned an unlikely or impossible hazard function, e.g. one in which some of its components exceed 1.0. Both of these situations are possible in the usual proportional hazards model, where for covariates $\{x_c\}, c = 1,2,\ldots,C$ the traditional functional form for the multiple of the baseline hazard is $\exp(\sum_{c=1}^{C} \beta_c x_{ci})$ for the ith customer. Third, the baseline hazard function is not easily made to vary across subsets of the customer population. This is a particularly serious defect when the object is to estimate individual customer lifetimes, rather than covariate effects as in traditional in PH analysis. Incorrect specification of a customer's hazard function can seriously misestimate tenure, frequently through the misestimate of any isolated "spikes."

6. NEURAL NETWORKS FOR SURVIVAL ANALYSIS

When applied to survival analysis, multilayer feed-forward neural networks (NN) (Haykin, 1994)—being non-linear, universal function approximators (Hornick, et. al., 1989)—can overcome the proportionality and linearity constraints imposed by classical survival analysis techniques (Section 5), with the potential for more accurate tenure models. But the large fraction of censored observations in real world data (Section 4) for LTV modeling precludes using the neural network to directly predict tenure. The actual tenure to cancellation is unknown for censored customers since they are currently active—all we know is their tenure to date, and using this instead of tenure to cancellation would be inaccurate and unsatisfactory. Ignoring censored customers, on the other hand, not only results in discarding a lot of data, but also results in a small and biased training dataset. To address this problem, we draw from the statistical concept of hazard functions, and use the neural network to model hazards rather than tenure.

6.1 Neural Network Architecture for Hazard Curve Prediction

Our approach to harnessing multilayer feedforward neural networks for survival analysis (for LTV tenure prediction) involves predicting the hazard function for every customer. We begin with data from the data warehouse and run it through a preprocessing step where the data is readied for neural network training. The second step involves setting up and training one or more neural networks for hazard prediction. The final data post-processing is used to evaluate the performance of the neural network and compare it with classical statistical approaches. We describe this process in detail in the following sections.

6.1.1 Data Preprocessing

Customer data for LTV modeling should have, in addition to a variety of independent input attributes (Section 4), two important attributes: (i) tenure, and (ii) a censoring flag. In our data, the TENMON attribute has the customer tenure in months, and a CHURN flag indicates if the customer is still active or has cancelled. If CHURN=0, the customer is still active and TENMON indicates the number of months the customer has had service; if CHURN=1, the customer has cancelled and TENMON is his age in months at the time of cancellation. In order to model customer hazard for the period $[1,T]$, for every record or observation i, we add a vector of T new attributes, $h_i(1), \ldots, h_i(T)$ with the following values (for $1 \leq t \leq T$):

$$h_i(t) = \begin{cases} 0 & 1 \leq t \leq \text{TENMON} \\ 1 & \text{CHURN} = 1 \;\&\; \text{TENMON} < t \leq T \\ \frac{d_t}{n_t} & \text{CHURN} = 0 \;\&\; \text{TENMON} < t \leq T \end{cases}$$

Here, d_t is the number of cancellations (churners) in time interval t; n_t is the number of customers at risk, i.e., total number of customers with TENMON $= t$. The ratio d_t/n_t is the Kaplan-Meier hazard estimate for time interval t (Kaplan and Meier, 1958). Intuitively, we set hazard $h_i(t)$ to 0 when a customer is active, 1 when a customer has cancelled, and to the Kaplan-Meier hazard if censored.

Table 1 shows an example. This approach is similar to Street (1998), except that we use the hazard function instead of the survival function. Hazard functions do not have any monotonicity constraints, and support customer segmentation (Section 7) which has important ramifications from a marketing perspective.

i	*Phone #*	...	*TENMON*	*CHURN*	*h(1)*	*h(2)*	*h(3)*	*h(4)*	*h(5)*	*h(6)*
1	456-1234	...	3	1	0	0	0	1	1	1
2	123-4567	...	4	0	0	0	0	0	0.03	0.1
...	...	...	...	...	...	...	...	...	...	...
N	987-6543		2	0	0	0	0.06	0.04	0.03	0.1

Table 1: Showing the computation of $h_i(t)$ with T=6. Kaplan-Meier hazard for t=3, 4, 5 and 6 are assumed to be 0.06, 0.04, 0.03 and 0.1 respectively.

6.1.2 Training the Neural Network

The hazard vector $h_i(1)$, …, $h_i(T)$ serves as the output target or training vector for the respective neural network input case i. The remainder of the attributes, *except* TENMON and CHURN, serve as inputs to the neural network[2].

Most modern neural network packages or data mining tool sets with neural networks provide the following automated processing:

- Ignore identification attributes like cellular phone number and account number;
- Standardize (or normalize) continuous attributes;
- Prune and group categorical attribute values and create the of binary dummy attributes to represent each categorical attribute.

These operations must be manually executed if the neural network software does not provide automated support.

Finally, the dataset is split into train, test and holdout (or validation) datasets. The train and test datasets are used to train the neural network and avoid overfitting. The holdout data is used to evaluate performance of the neural network and compare it with classical statistical techniques.

We use a standard feedforward neural network with one or two hidden layers and experiment with the number of hidden units to obtain the best network (see Section 6.2). The number of input units is dictated by the number of independent input attributes. The network is set up with T output units, where each output unit o_t learns to estimate hazard rate $h(t)$. The parameters of the neural network are set up to learn probability distributions (Baum and Wilczek, 1988; Haykin, 1994):

[2] We have experimented with including TENMON. The resulting neural networks perform similarly with or without TENMON. Including *both* CHURN and TENMON is tantamount to indirectly providing the output targets as inputs, and the neural network trivially detects this correlation. Furthermore, when predicting hazards for existing customers, CHURN will always be 0. Hence CHURN should always be excluded.

- The standard linear input combination function is used for the hidden and output units. The internal activation of these units is therefore the weighted sum of its inputs.
- The logistic activation function $\varphi(v) = \dfrac{1}{1+e^{-v}}$ is used (in both the hidden and output layers) to transform the internal activation of a unit to its output activation. The logistic activation function for output units also ensures that the predicted hazard rates are between 0 and 1.
- The *relative entropy* or *cross entropy* error function is used. The total error function is given by:

$$E = \sum_i f_i \sum_k 2\left\{ y_{ik} \ln\left(\frac{y_{ik}}{\mu_{ik}}\right) + (1 - y_{ik}) \ln \frac{1 - y_{ik}}{1 - \mu_{ik}} \right\}$$

where μ_{ik} is the predicted output value (or posterior probability) for the k-th unit of the i-th input case, y_{ik} is the target value for the k-th unit of the i-th case, and f_i is the frequency of the i-th case. With this error function, the objective function (SAS Institute, 1998) which the neural network minizes is $O = E \Big/ \sum_i \sum_k f_i$.

6.1.3 Post-Processing

Once the neural network has been trained, we use the network to score the holdout dataset. For every observation i in the holdout dataset, the neural network outputs a predicted hazard function $\{ h_i(t) \}$, $1 \le t \le T$. In the post-processing step, we convert this hazard function into a survival function $s_i(t) = s_i(t-1) \times [1 - h_i(t)]$ for $1 \le t \le T$ and $s_i(1)=1$. We compute *predicted median tenure* for the neural network (NNPRED) as that value of t for which $s(t) \le 0.5$. We score the same holdout dataset with a complementary log-log model (Section 5) built using the same training set as the neural network. We also compute predicated median tenure for the complementary log-log predictions (CLOGPRED) in an identical manner.

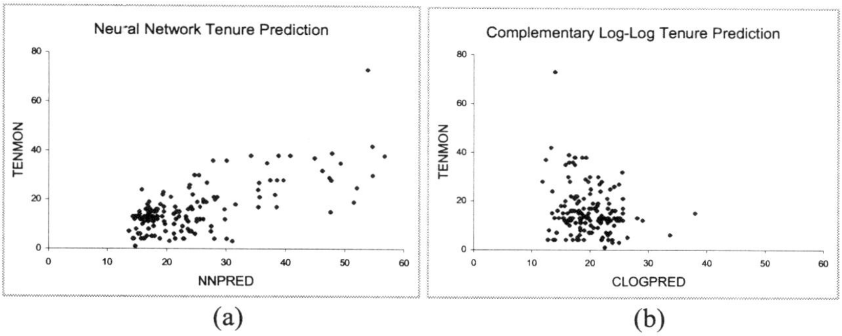

Figure 6.1: Comparison of (a) neural network and (b) complementary log-log model for LTV tenure prediction.

6.2 Experimental Results

The data described in Section 4 was used in our experiments with the neural network and classical statistical techniques. For the neural network, 40% of the data (8,600 records) was used for training, and 30% (6,450 records) each for the test and holdout datasets. We use a time period of T = 60 months[3].

We built several neural networks: single hidden layer networks with 25, 50 and 100 hidden units, and a two hidden layer network with 25 units in the first hidden layer and 10 units in the second hidden layer. After training, all four networks had very similar mean square error rates on the holdout data. We report results from the two hidden layer neural network.

Figure 6.1 shows predicted median tenure (based on the survival curve) for the neural network (NNPRED) and complementary log-log model (CLOGPRED) plotted against actual tenure (TENMON) for customers in the holdout dataset who have already cancelled. Of the 6,450 customers included in the holdout dataset, 161 have already cancelled service (i.e., churned). Figure 6.1 plots predicted vs. actual tenure for these 161 customers. It is clear from the graphs that the neural network is much better at predicting tenure than the complementary log-log model. The complementary log-log tenure predictions are clustered around 20 months, and rarely exceed 30 months, resulting in grossly underestimating LTV for long-lived customers. The neural network predictions, on the other hand, have a more reasonable distribution, even for long-lived customers.

[3] We have also experimented with T=36 months (3 years). The neural network performs somewhat better with the shorter time period, since this is an inherently easier problem.

Figure 6.1 is a comparison of the residuals—i.e., differences between actual tenure and the NN/CLL prediction for those subjects dying during the observation period—from predictions on the holdout set. We observe how close these residuals—NNRES and CLLRES—are to zero, respectively, and how that distance varies for different ages of subjectsBoth residuals show a systematic bias with respect to age. The CLL residuals have an average value near 0.0, but the extreme ages are either overestimated (for low ages) or underestimated (for high ages). The NN residuals show much less variation than do the CLL residuals, and are substantially closer to zero for the high age groups.

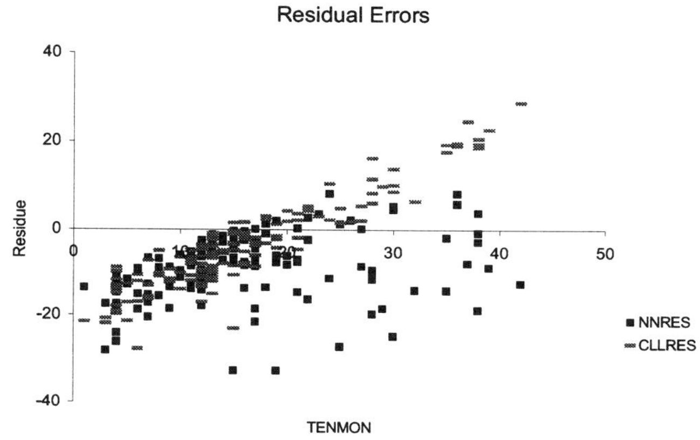

Figure 6.1: Residual errors for the neural network and complementary log-log model.

Given that neural networks do not enforce proportionality and linearity constraints, one would expect these models to be better than proportional hazards-like models. In comparisons reported in the literature (Ravdin et. al., 1992; Ohno-Machado, 1997), neural networks have performed comparably to proportional hazards models for medical prognosis. Tenure modeling for LTV is one of those challenging applications where the power of the neural network manifests itself in significantly better models in comparison with proportional hazards-like methods.

7. FROM DATA MODELS TO BUSINESS INSIGHT

Having built neural network models for LTV tenure prediction, we have shown that these models are much more accurate than traditional statistical models. But we are still left with the task of deriving business insight from the neural network. A statistical model, like proportional hazards regression, gives a clear indication of the importance of the various covariates and their contribution to the final tenure (or hazard) prediction. A neural network, on the other hand, is essentially a black box, and provides very little intuitive information on how it comes up with its (accurate!) predictions. We now switch back to statistical framework to interpret the neural network models.

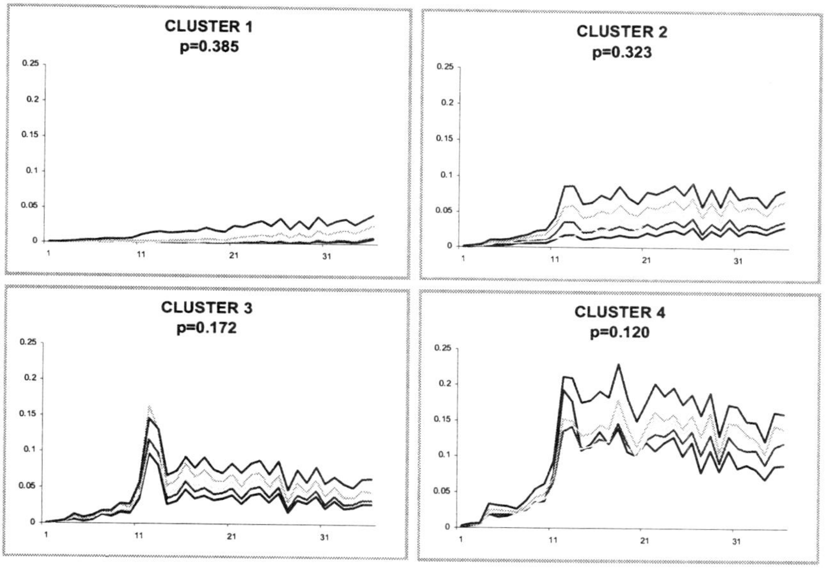

Figure 7.1: Hazard clusters.

7.1 Patterns of Hazards: Clustering Hazard Functions

The neural network produces a *T*-month hazard function, i.e., a *T*-component vector $h_i(1), \ldots, h_i(T)$, for each customer *i*. To group the disaggregated hazard functions into segments that we can hopefully explain and understand, we begin by clustering the individual hazard functions. We parameterize the shape of the hazard curve by defining a set of derived attributes that collectively capture the geometric aspects of the curves, and were judged as likely to yield behavioral information. These include: average hazard rate, average hazard rate for the pre-contract expiration period (with 12-month contracts); overall slope of the hazard curve; initial and terminal slope of the hazard curve; and relative size of the contract expiration (12-month) "spike". These attributes were computed for each customer, and then standardized to have a mean of 0 and a standard deviation of 1.

Augmented by these additional attributes, the hazard functions were then segmented into clusters using *k*-means clustering, in combination with manual inspection and assimilation of small-size clusters. The resulting four clusters are illustrated in Figure 7.1. In order to display the thousands of hazard functions in each cluster, a principal components analysis (see, e.g., Morrison, 1967) was performed. The figure shows the hazard functions on the 10th, 25th, 50th, 75th and 90th percentiles along the first principal component. We observe also that within each of these four clusters, the constituent hazard functions are all very nearly multiples of each other. This conclusion derives from the results of the principal components analysis, where the first component—the average hazard rate—accounts for nearly all (88–99%) of the functions' variation. Thus, the neural network hazard functions are, to a first approximation, four groups of proportional hazard models.

Cluster	Cluster Description	Characterization of Cluster	Implications for Retention Effort
1	No effect of contract expiration.	Detailed Bill. Few calls/month.	No pre-expiration contact required. Contact may trigger churn.
2	Small increase in churn propensity at expiration. Post-expiration churn remains elevated.	The average, prototypical customers.	Moderate pre-expiration effort needed. New contract or continued contacts needed.
3	Large spike in churn at expiration. Low churn thereafter.	Two types: ▪ No charge for MOU, many calls/month. ▪ No detailed bill, low total charge.	Concentrate effort on pre-expiration. Contract renewal may not be required.
4	Large increase in churn at expiration. Post-expiration churn high and increasing.	High total charge.	High intensity effort pre-expiration. Continued competitive offers to designated customers.

Table 2: Characterizing hazard clusters for targeted marketing and retention.

7.2 Business Insights and Implications of Hazard Clusters

The business implications of the clusters shown in Figure 7.1 are indicated in

Table 2. It is evident that this segmentation has important interpretations of a customer's state of mind in using cellular service, and important intuitive implications for the company's retention efforts for these different segments. In order to characterize customers in each segment, we build a decision tree with the explanatory covariates as independent attributes and the cluster number as target. The "Characterization of Cluster" column in

Table 2 summarizes splitting rules to the most discriminatory leaf in the tree for each cluster. The table also indicates potential implications for marketing and retention efforts.

Intuitively, it seems that Cluster 1 is composed of "safety and security" customers, who possess their cellular telephone as an emergency and convenience device. Cluster 3 comprises users who have a moderate flat-rate access charge which accommodates all their calling needs. Cluster 4, in contrast, comprises customers with rate plans whose flat rates do not fit their high calling volumes. These may well be customers who would be better served by a different rate plan; their high post-contract churn probabilities indicate that such improved plans are often obtained through alternative suppliers. It may be that Cluster 2, which is a scaled-down version of Cluster 4, may also comprise customers with inappropriate contracts.

8. CONCLUSION: THE AMALGAMATION OF STATISTICAL AND DATA MINING TECHNIQUES

It is of interest to summarize the preceding analysis in terms of the overview provided in Section 2, specifically the hybrid statistics and data mining approach outlined in Figure 2.1. In the process of LTV tenure modeling and analysis, we have used techniques that have been viewed as the province of classical statistics, or of data mining. The techniques of classical statistics and those of data mining have followed separate development streams, and the tools each school has generated are frequently viewed with skepticism by the other school (Hand, 1998). For the problem of customer tenure estimation, however, we have seen that there is a natural amalgamation between the two, leading to an analysis process where the weaknesses of one are addressed by the strengths of the other.

Initially, at the conceptual level, the statistics literature (Cox, 1972) has suggested the proportional hazards model as described in Section 5 as a framework for understanding sets of hazards, and it is natural to search for subsets of such functions which have the proportionality property. This model thus imposes a framework on an arbitrary set of hazard functions in the sense that a vocabulary, such as baseline hazards and covariate multipliers, exists to describe a clustering of the functions.

The classical statistical models used to originally fit the models corresponding to the proportional hazards concept require certain assumptions and have certain conventions. The most stringent assumption is that the subsets of the customer population can be identified which have unique baseline hazards, by prior knowledge. In fact, most such models will assume a certain unspecified baseline hazard for the entire population. The second assumption is that the covariates affect the hazard via a multiplier which is the exponent of a linear combination of covariates. It is not unusual, however, for the modeler, or the modeler's client, to know that a single baseline is inappropriate, but to be unable to identify the segments that might have distinct baselines. Similarly, the linearity restriction may be felt to be too restrictive based on anecdotal information, but an alternative may not be known.

To address these problems, it is appropriate to use the neural net model described in Section 6 to construct the final tenure model and estimate individual hazard functions and predicted tenures. However, the neural net does not produce a functional model of the relation between covariates and hazards, as the classical statistical models do, nor is any simple structure necessarily imposed on the set of individual hazard functions. These two types of structure, assuming they exist, must be identified by traditional tools. The hazard functions can be described by vectors of shape parameters (such as pre- and post-contract slope and size of the contract expiration "spike") and partitioned into segments by traditional clustering methods. To the extent possible, counterparts to the covariate multipliers can be calculated and fitted to linear and other statistical models to uncover the form of the non-linearities imposed by the neural net.

In a last transition away from classical techniques, our hazard segments are explicated by the classification technique of decision trees. This relates the segments to patterns of underlying covariates without the functional restrictions of statistical classification models, and allows their description in a way that is useful to marketers.

Thus, in our approach, data mining interacts with classical statistics at both conceptual and computational levels. The structure of data for the LTV problem is handled by using the classical concept of a hazard function.

Classical estimation techniques allow the development of individual hazard function targets which can be processed by an artificial neural net. The neural net's output can be clustered into meaningful geometric shapes, which are finally modeled by a form of the classical hazard function model on which our customer lifetimes were based. In this way, by comparing and understanding these techniques, our analysis leads to tenure models based on hybrid statistical and data mining approaches that are richer in meaning and more predictive than either approach by itself.

REFERENCES

Allison, P.D. *Survival Analysis Using the SAS® System*, Cary, NC: SAS Institute, 1995.

Baum, E. B. and Wilczek, F. "Supervised Learning of Probability Distributions by Neural Networks." In *Neural Information Processing Systems*, D. Z. Anderson, editor, pp 52-61, New York, NY: American Institute of Physics, 1988.

Bolton, R. A Dynamic Model of the Duration of the Customer's Relationship with a Continuous Service Provider: The Role of Satisfaction. *Marketing Science*, 1998; 17:1:45-65.

Cox, D. R. Regression Models and Life Tables. *Journal of the Royal Statistical Society*, 1972; B34:187-220.

Cox, D.R. and Oakes, D. *Analysis of Survival Data*, London, UK: Chapman and Hall, 1984.

De Laurentiis, M. and Ravdin, P. M. A Technique for Using Neural Network Analysis to Perform Survival Analysis of Censored Data. *Cancer Letters*, 1994; 77:127-138.

Glymour, C., Madigan, D., Pergibon, D. and Smyth, P. Statistical Themes and Lessons for Data Mining. *Data Mining and Knowledge Discovery*, 1997; 1:11-28.

Hand, D.J. Data Mining: Statistics and More? *The American Statistician*, 1998; 52:2:112-118.

Haykin, S. *Neural Networks: A Comprehensive Foundation*, Upper Saddle River, NJ: Prentice Hall, 1994.

Helson, K. and Schmittlein, D. C. Analyzing Duration Times in Marketing: Evidence for the Effectiveness of Hazard Rate Models. *Marketing Science*, 1993; 11:4:395-414.

Hornick, K., Stinchcombe, M. and White, H. Multilayer Feedforward Networks are Universal Approximators. *Neural Networks*, 1989; 2:359-366.

Kaplan, E.L. and Meier, R. Nonparametric Estimation from Incomplete Observations. *Journal of the American Statistical Association*, 1958; 53:457-81.

Lawless, J.E. *Statistical Models and Methods for Lifetime Data*, New York, NY: John Wiley and Sons, 1982.

Mitchell. T. *Machine Learning*, Boston, MA: WCB/McGraw-Hill, 1997.

Ohno-Machado, L. A Comparison of Cox Propostional Hazards and Artificial Neural Network Models for Medical Prognosis. *Comput. Biol. Med.* 1997; 27:1:55-65.

Prentice, R.L. and L.A. Gloeckler. Regression Analysis of Grouped Survival Data with Application to Breast Cancer Data. *Biometrics* 1978; 34:57-67.

Ravdin, P. M., Clark, G. M., Hilsenbeck, S. G., Owens, M. A., Vendely, P., Pandian, M. R. and McGuire, W. L. A Demonstation that Breast Cancer Recurrence can be Predicted by Neural Network Analysis. *Breast Cancer Research and Treatment* 1992; 21:47-53.

SAS Institute. Neural Network Node: Reference. SAS Enterprise Miner Documentation. Cary, NC: SAS Institute, 1998.

Chapter 11

ROBUST BUSINESS INTELLIGENCE SOLUTIONS

Jan Mrazek
Chief Specialist, Business Intelligence Solutions, Global Information Technology, Bank of Montreal, 4100 Gordon Baker Rd., Toronto, Ontario, M1W 3E8, Canada,
jmrazek@sympatico.ca, jan.mrazek@bmo.com

Keywords: data warehouse, data mart, business intelligence, data mining, On-Line Analytical Processing, star schema, snowflake schema, denormalization, massively parallel processing

Abstract: We discuss implementation of very large multi-purpose Business Intelligence systems. We focus on system architecture and integration, data modelling and productionalisation of data mining. The ideas presented come mostly from the author's experience with implementations of large Business Intelligence projects at the Bank of Montreal. Some of these projects have won major international awards and recognition for unique, integrated, well performing and highly scalable solutions.

1. INTRODUCTION

Business Intelligence (BI) is a new and powerful area of informational expansion in organisations and "getting it right" often makes the difference between a flourishing life and a slow business decay. Business Intelligence is heavy artillery for an organisation and under the assumption of steady supply of quality data, proper maintenance, organisation, integration, focus, mobility/flexibility and readiness to be used, it is arguably the most critical force of today's enterprise. It is supposed to provide easy access to actionable information and knowledge to all decision-makers on all levels in the organisation.

In this practically oriented paper we will essentially describe technical aspects of Business Intelligence systems as they were implemented in the past 3 years at the Bank of Montreal in Toronto.

We will discuss BI architecture, issues of system integration, challenges of information flow design, data transformation, some challenging aspects of data modelling and an integration of data mining. In order to provide a vendor unbiased view on these topics, we will restrain from discussing any technology or product in particular and leave this part fully to the further interest of the reader.

2. BUSINESS INTELLIGENCE ARCHITECTURE

From the business perspective there are two main areas of Business Intelligence Systems: Customer Relationship Management (CRM) and Business Performance Management (BPM). One is outward oriented (on the customer) the other inward oriented (on the business). Often we hear related terms like Customer Value Management (CVM) and Management Information Systems (MIS). From the departmental point of view yet other Decision Support Systems (DSS) are known as Financial Information Systems, Credit Risk Systems, Enterprise Resource Planning Systems, Inventory Management Systems, Product Development Systems, Channel Optimisation Systems, Target Marketing Systems, and others.

Years ago, the recognised need for consistent quality and data content was responsible for the dawn of data warehousing. Conceptually, transactional legacy data is cleansed and transformed only once, when it comes into the data warehouse and where ever it is then presented (data marts), it appears consistent to other presentations. Yet, the problem of data consistency is more complex than that, and the implementation of a data warehouse is not sufficient to resolve it. The major hurdle is the time in which facts and dimensions are constantly changing. Whatever the technical solution, the handling of data consistency and time are the two most crucial challenges of every Business Intelligence System. For a healthy management of any enterprise, it is indispensable that all decision-makers have access essentially to the same information source at the same time. Therefore, from the perspective of a BI architect, there should only be one integrated BI complex satisfying all CRM, BPM and other corporate information needs.

Later in this article we will introduce multi-tier architecture of such a system.

2.1 Iterative approach to building data warehouse integrated with data marts

Let us assume high-level system architecture as in Figure 1.

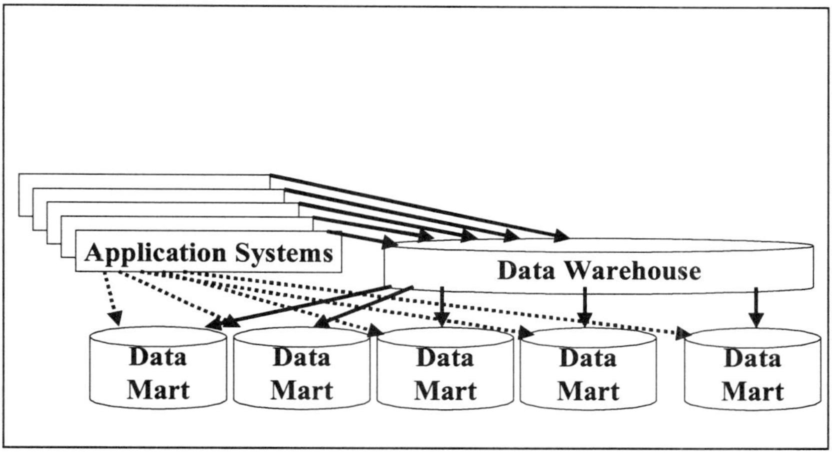

Figure 1. Iterative stage of a high-level system architecture

Data is moved from the application systems through transformation processes to the data warehouse and data marts.

In the ideal world, no direct connection would exist between the applications (core systems) and the data marts and all data flow would be routed through the data warehouse. It is however well known that the data marts are better funded than the data warehouse. Unlike the data warehouse, data marts are usually linked to well-funded projects with a clear business mission and a predictable return on investment (ROI). While the data warehouse represents higher consistency of data and long term savings in the reduction of the transformation processes needed, it is more difficult to secure sufficient funding from just one client or project.

Large organisations that first engaged in building a data warehouse, frequently missed on the business opportunities a data mart would answer. Rapidly changing business needs, organisational structure, distribution channels and product lines not accounted for with necessary detail in the data warehouse design often require significant system changes before a first data mart could be populated solely from the data warehouse.

The other extreme, also very common in large organisations is a collection of departmental data marts existing independently of each other, run on incompatible technologies and failing to follow any consistent corporate BI information designs.

We believe it to be a viable approach to design and develop data marts first, as long as a consistent strategy and design is followed allowing for the growth of the data warehouse incrementally. Even though the final design of most data marts is anything but normalised, it is helpful for future transition to the centralised data warehouse to add and design a data mart's staging area close to a normal form. Normal form is the most stable data structure withstanding most of the business structure changes. While other forms offer better performance or fit to analytical tools, the normal form is the most durable and serves as a data consistency guarantor. The normal staging area of every data mart is the first approximation of a centralised data warehouse, which is indisputably a logical cornerstone of the BI Architecture. In our opinion, experience gained from delivering data marts is crucial to build a functional data warehouse. Our proven and recommended approach is a step by step integration of data marts' normal staging areas and replacement of data marts' direct feeds with processes running through and being shared within the data warehouse. Not surprisingly, the highest value lies on the consistency of dimensional data: customer, business organisation structure, products, time, etc. These dimensions should be the first to be conformed and routed through the data warehouse.

This approach which we strongly advocate, is sometimes called "The third way", considering the first to be a data warehouse feeding data marts exclusively and the second being a collection of data marts only.

2.2 Profitability as the most important derived business measure

For almost any business, the most important questions are about generating a profit. Actually, most BI queries directly or indirectly relate to profitability. Traditionally, every business is able to answer what was the profit delivered in the past fiscal year. That information comes from the Financial Systems/General Ledger and the corporate accounting. But for managing a profitable organisation, this would be too little too late. Detailed, accurate and frequently run calculation of profit on account or transaction level is the most essential derived measure of every Business Intelligence system. As some other organisations have done, the Bank of Montreal has built a very large data mart just to support and analyse profitability calculations on the account level.[1]

This system has only about 50 direct users, mostly analysts responsible for different aspects of profitability. Yet the profitability figures are broadcasted to other data marts and shared by more than 1,000 users.[2]

2.3 Value-adding process; sharing derived measures among data marts

As it is with our profitability system, many data marts present a base for complex value-adding processes whose results are eventually also needed in other data marts. At the same time, a migration of these derived values to the data warehouse level might not be possible or practical.

To illustrate the above point, let us take a look at the historical inheritance of Decision Support Systems. DSS have existed for a long time. For years, each of these isolated systems was able to satisfy all information needs of its departmental users. With the rapid information revolution and often-dramatic changes in the organisational structure, mission and management, the isolated DSS has become more of a limiting factor.

Let us consider a Database Marketing System (DMS) used for the execution of promotional campaigns. In another department of the organisation there exists a new system with detailed profitability information for every customer. So far, marketing has focussed on the execution of campaigns with the maximal response. Yet the maximal response may not be necessarily in line with corporate mission, i.e. the maximisation of return on investment over some time horizon. It is obvious that having the customer profitability figure in the Database Marketing System, better results could be achieved. Unfortunately the DMS and the Profitability System are proprietary, residing on different platforms and non-compatible proprietary databases. Any change is cumbersome and costly and the hardware does not allow for easy communication and fast data transfer between the two systems.

A solution to the presented problem is the integration of both systems to the same hardware platform with high-speed links and the same Database Management System (DBMS). Admitting this, we may see our BI architecture as depicted in Figure 2.

[1] With 13 months of detail history of 18 million accounts the data mart's size is over 2 terabytes.

[2] In the real life, data marts feed frequently other data marts and this fact is largely independent on the level of existence of a corporate data warehouse.

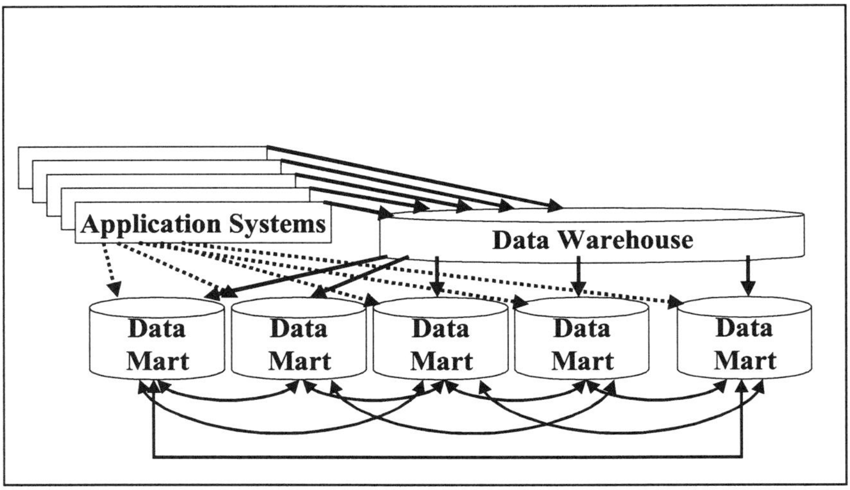

Figure 2. Sharing derived values among data marts

2.4 Hierarchy of data marts and the super mart

Supporting heavy data exchange among data marts going in all directions (as in Figure 2) would be hardly desirable. Fortunately, we found out that a growing number of our data marts could be seen in a certain hierarchy, which limits the number of interconnections and data flow. On the end of the hierarchy we placed a data mart with a special mission – the deployment of CRM and BPM information to massive number of end users. We call this data mart a *super mart.*

The mission of all other data marts is to serve relatively small number of power users who are responsible for additional value-adding processes (profitability figures, identification of households, prediction of credit risk, etc.). The mission of the super mart is to deploy all of this and other derived information to a large number of end users whose interest is "just" to explore and apply the information presented. The new architecture is in the Figure 3.

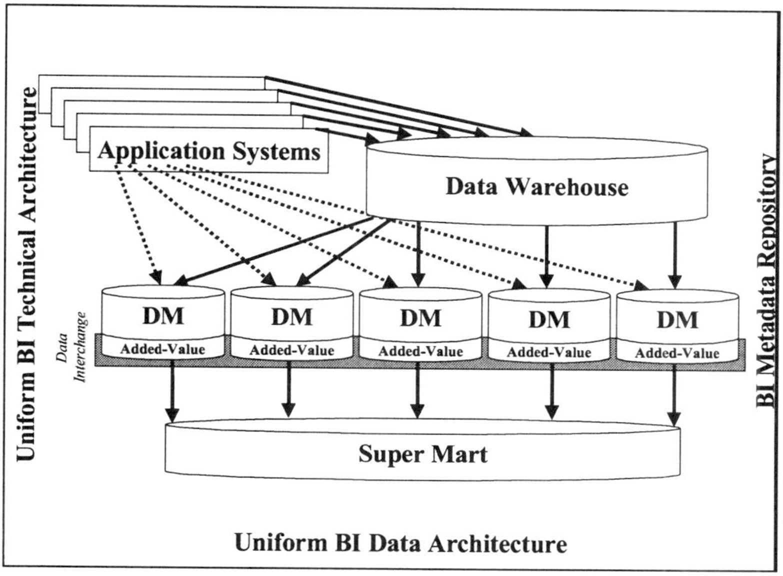

Figure 3. Architecture of a robust integrated BI system

The high level of system integration presented in Figure 3 could be achieved only if aided by consistently applied Uniform Technical Architecture, Uniform Data Architecture and supported by a dynamically managed Metadata Repository.

In summary, we came to the conclusion that

- All BI systems, if possible, should reside on one HW/DBMS platform with high-speed links between them.
- There are three principal BI layers: data warehouse, data marts and the super mart. They are all part of one and only one corporate BI architecture.
- The data warehouse should be responsible in the very minimal for all major corporate dimensions. In ideal world, all transformation of transactional and legacy data should also be routed through the DW. This process could continue gradually while new data marts are being put into place.
- On the data mart level, value-adding processes are run, which result in the creation of new data elements and variables. Examples of those are customer or household identification, profitability figures, performance measures, propensity scores, attrition scores, risk factors, campaigns, any kind of predicted or trending elements: future profits, customer

lifetime value, etc. All these elements could be theoretically redistributed to other data marts via the data warehouse. However, since all our data marts are part of the same architecture and reside on tightly linked platforms with conformed dimensions being used everywhere, the redistribution is easy to implement among the data marts directly on the data mart layer.
There is one data mart with the mission of providing mass access to thousands of end users. This super mart is tuned to handle performance, the challenges presented by data access tools, satisfies CRM, BPM, CVM, MIS and other needs.

3. DATA TRANSFORMATION

The most important part of a BI system design is the transformational data flow. There are 4 different places where data can get derived or be changed. The first place is the transformation process that takes data from the source and moves it to the new destination in the data warehouse or data mart. The second place is in the DW's or DM's database utilising database views. The value-adding processes executed on the database directly or by exporting the data outside and repopulating the final results back to the database represent the third place. The forth place, where the data can be changed, is in the presentation layer. See Figure 4.

There are many good reasons for processing and deriving information in these four principal stages.

In the first stage we cleanse, validate and retransform data to fit the database structure. Also, new complex data might be derived following transformation rules. Most of this processing requires expensive sorts and merges and inter-row[3] processing.

The second stage is reserved for softer intra-row processing and non-expensive aggregations. Let us consider a base level fact table holding 24 months history of 20 million accounts. That is 480 million rows. Now, most of the system users need the information at the customer level. In average, one customer has 1.3 accounts and that would be the compression ratio. Clearly this compression does not justify the creation of a new aggregate table. The aggregation has to happen on the fly using a database view. Another example would be intra-row type processing. Let us assume that in one table there are two columns for "Net Income before Tax" and "Tax".

[3] Inter-row - among many rows, intra-row - within a row

Obviously it is almost a no cost operation to derive the "Net Income after Tax" on the fly through a (non-materialised) database view.

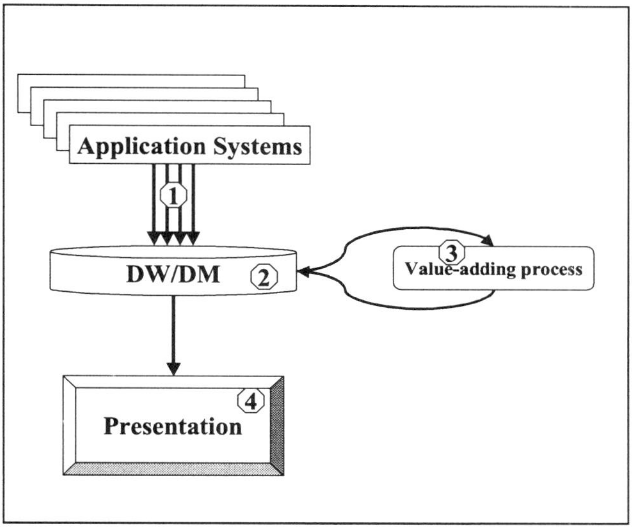

Figure 4. Four stages of data transformation

The value-adding processes are usually complex processing models requiring additional software applications such as automated code generators, data mining kernels and expert knowledge. An example would be the already mentioned Profitability System. Calculating account level profitability in the financial industry is a complex issue. The formulae decompose into many hierarchical levels of sub formulae. Just consider all the revenue and cost factors, fees and all types of transactions, the different rules for every product (and there are thousands of financial products available). As the cost structure changes, so do the rules and the calculations. If these calculations were "hard coded" in the first level of the transformation process, it would be impossible to change these without a complex change management process. Instead, as it is indeed in our case, we have built a Profitability Code Generator with an intuitive graphical user interface and the ability to generate, compile and bind C code, which then executes in parallel streams against the Profitability Database. The group of analysts responsible for profitability calculations uses this code generator whenever there is a need to change these calculations.

The fourth stage of transformation processing is the presentation layer. This usually includes ad-hoc reports and OLAP[4] type of slicing and dicing through data. Because there is usually a vast number of filters applied against the data, it is not practical to calculate report aggregates, rankings and other similar measures elsewhere.

4. DATA MODELLING

In the preceding paragraphs we have touched some of the data modelling issues: dimensions and facts, inter vs. intra row calculations and database views. It is common belief that the data warehouse should be designed in a near to normalised form. The normalised data model is relatively stable and flexible to organisational changes. The mission of a data warehouse is to ensure consistency in data, use of conformed dimensions, allow for control of referential integrity and simplify transformation processes. Very few queries should run directly against the data warehouse. This is the role of data marts, which are designed for the fast response of possibly many concurrent queries.

To allow for a fast query response, data marts are usually designed in some kind of denormalization. The usual forms are either *star* or *snowflake schemas*. Both represent "relational cubes". The tables are divided into two groups: *dimensions and facts*. The dimensional tables contain descriptive non-additive attributes, the facts tables contain additive elements, i.e. measures. The fact tables carry the foreign keys of the dimensions. The facts can then be viewed by their dimensions, i.e. Profitability by Account by Month, etc.

In the star schema, the dimensional table contains all levels of the hierarchy. Thus a row in the Account dimension would contain Account Number, Account Description, Customer (who owns that account), Customer Address, Household (where the Customer belongs to), etc. We say, that all levels of hierarchy are collapsed into one table. Information is fast to retrieve because it is repeated many times - the model is denormalized.

In the snowflake schema, each hierarchy level in a dimension has its own table. The descriptions of individual hierarchies are not denormalized. Denormalized however, are the foreign keys. This allows for "drilling" up and down and skipping the immediate next hierarchical levels. For illustration refer to the Figure 5.

[4] On-Line Analytical Processing viewing data as dimensions and measures.

The star schema has been developed to allow the database optimiser to take special query plans.

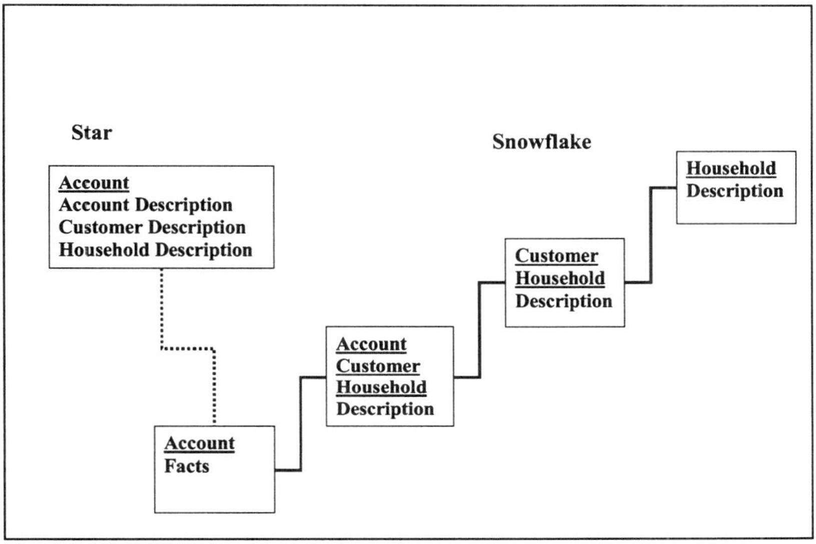

Figure 5. Star vs. snowflake database schema

The major denormalization occurs on the side of the fact tables. The facts are pre-aggregated and stored in aggregate tables. Smart query engines can determine which aggregated fact table the particular query should run against. A two dimensional example with some aggregate tables is shown in Figure 6.

The dimensions are Time and Account, each with three levels of hierarchy. Thanks to the propagated foreign keys, a relation also exists between Household and Account and Year and Date. The base fact table is on the Date and Account level. The two other aggregate tables exist on the Date-Customer and Year-Household levels. Theoretically, 16 different aggregate tables could have been created, if we count tables with one or both collapsed dimensions. In large projects with hundreds of hierarchically expanded dimensional tables, the number of aggregate tables could grow into the thousands. That would not be maintainable and fortunately it is not necessary. Only tables expected to be accessed frequently with high compression ratios over lower granularity tables (1:40+) and with the number of rows reasonably high (20,000+) have to be created.[5] All queries requesting aggregations on levels not directly supported by an aggregate table are satisfied from the next available table with lower granularity and roll up to the sought aggregation in the runtime.

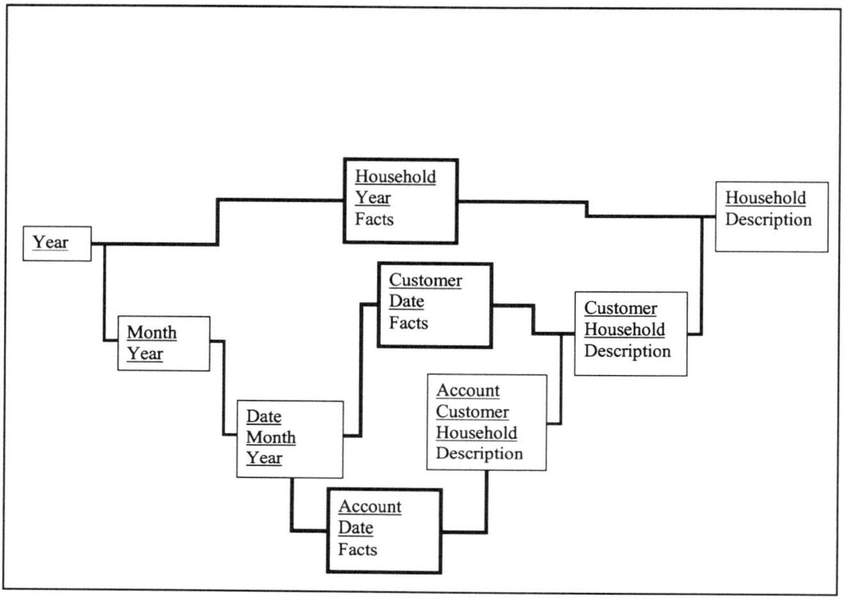

Figure 6. Aggregate tables in the snowflake schema

Understanding these modelling techniques is essential for the design of a well performing super mart[6].

Even though the two major challenges of design of BI databases will always be performance and flexibility to slice and dice through data, there are other major challenges, which are concerns to a data modeller. We will discuss five of these concerns: *slow moving dimensions, historical and current views, restatement of history by current dimensions, decomposition of metrics and finally support for data mining.*

[5] The exact guidelines for determining when to create an aggregate table differ from project to project and depend on the type of hardware and software, average response time requirements and other factors.

[6] See introduction of the super mart in 2.4.

4.1 Slow moving dimensions

Obviously everything is moving in time and base facts always contain the time dimension. Equally obvious should be that dimensions themselves are undergoing changes within time. The nature of the business dictates, when it is necessary to capture and preserve these changes and when we can just update or replace with the latest information.

As an example, let us consider that it has been agreed that the information in our BI system will always be presented with respect to the latest organisational structure. In such a case, there is no need to keep record of historical changes. On the other hand, let us assume that the change in Household - Account Manager relationship ought to be recorded. The Household dimensional table contains among others, Household Number and Account Manager Number.

There are two different approaches to this problem.

One is the generation of an additional surrogate key for the Household table. With a change, a new record is generated and a new higher surrogate key is assigned. New Account Manager Number is recorded and all other columns are copied over from the previous record. Since the additional Household surrogate key represents the relationship between the fact tables and the Household dimension, the old relationships will point to a different record in the Household dimension than the new ones. This solution well reflects the historical change but is causing other problems. One of them is the aggregation by Household dimension. This is because the Household has entries under many different keys in the fact table.

The second approach is time stamping records with changes. We add two columns to the Household table: From-Date and To-Date. The primary key of the Household table will be the Household Number (surrogate or not) and the To-Date. To-Date has the default value of some very distant future. Each new change generates a new record in the Household table with the new Account Manager Number recorded, the From- and To-Dates changed and other columns copied over. This solution has no problem with aggregations. However it does not handle different historical inquires that well. Since ROLAP tools[7] do not efficiently handle joins to dimensional tables based on "Date between From-Date and To-Date", database views have to be created to support that. If the business requirements indicate that the predominant interest is in the latest dimensional status quo, a view can be placed over the Household dimension with the time filter on "To-Date > today".

A hybrid solution could be also created.

[7] Relational OLAP (ROLAP) tools generate SQL queries against a relational database usually designed in star or snowflake schema.

4.2 Historical and current views

The slow moving dimensions are linked to the issue of historical vs. current views. Suppose we have to report on the profit generated by Account Managers and also on profit generated from different Account Manager portfolios. These could be two different things. An Account Manager is actually responsible for the business with a number of Households. Account Managers could be moved and Households may get assigned to different Account Managers. A solution is shown in Figure 7.

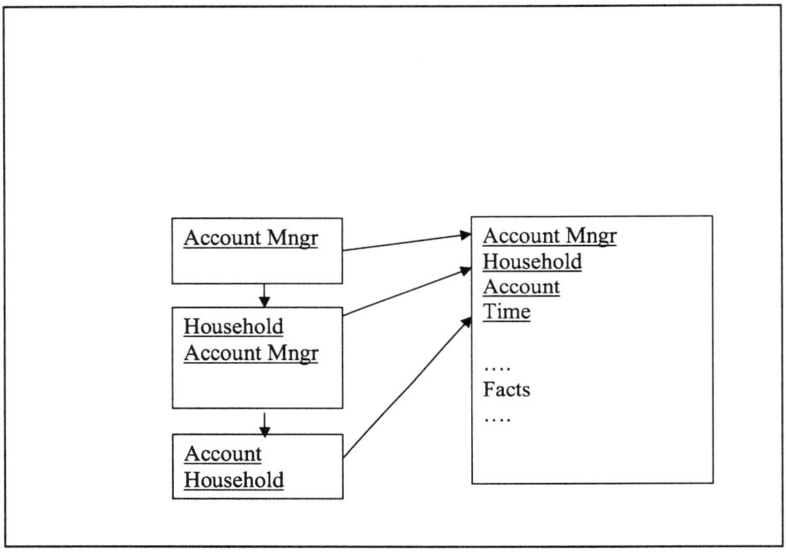

Figure 7. Modelling historical and current relationships

The Household dimension represents the current state only. The question about the profit generated by the Account Manager can be answered through the join of the fact table and Account Manager dimension using the Account Manager key as a link. The question about profit generated by an assigned portfolio of Households can be answered through the join of the fact table to the Household dimension (using Household key) and from here, the join to the Account Dimension table (using Account Manager key). Remember that the Household table holds the current relationship to the Account Manager.

4.3 Restatement of history by current dimensions

Often, there is the requirement to restate history to the current state of dimensions. Fortunately the dimensions don't change on the lowest level of granularity. What changes, are the various hierarchical relationships, which in turn disqualifies the content of the aggregate tables. If we aggregate on the Account Manager level and a Household has been moved from one Account Manager to another and we were asked to restate the history, i.e. to present the history from the perspective of the Account Managers' latest portfolios, the easiest solution would be to abandon aggregate tables containing the Account Manager key and aggregate in real time. From here, we alter our strategy for creating aggregate tables a little and conclude that not only performance and data compression ratios dictate aggregate tables, but also the dimension by which we are requested to restate history. We do not create aggregate tables by these dimensions. If we did, we would have to recreate these tables entirely by every system update. For comparison, note that other aggregate tables grow incrementally by each load and except from occasional purging, their historical entries do not have to be reviewed.

4.4 Decomposition of metrics

Earlier on, we mentioned the complexity of the profitability calculations. Often for the end-user not only is the profitability information of importance but so is the understanding of its full decomposition. Two accounts can generate the same profit but the volume, revenue and cost factors may be completely different. Imagine a simple formulae: Profit = Revenue - Expense. Now in turn, Revenue and Expense break down further and yet again and again.[8]

The decomposition could happen in two different ways. In one, all of the break down elements could be stored in one row of a fact table. Thus, each time the profitability figure is presented, the other elements could be presented as well from the same row. The only disadvantage is the missing structure of decomposition. With other words if the end user does not understand the formulae already, he/she will make little sense from the row of displayed numbers.

The more elegant solution is to allow for actual decomposition layer by layer through the drill down functionality. This can be done by *dimensionalization of metrics (facts)*. That's nothing else but turning a

[8] In our case at the Bank of Montreal up to 12 breakdown levels.

wide/horizontal table into a deep/vertical table. For illustration see the example in Figure 8.

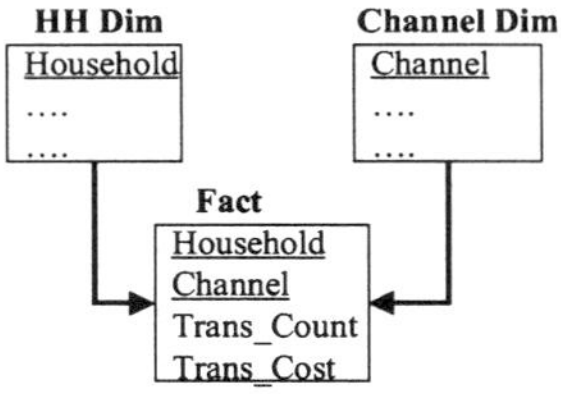

Household	Channel	Count	Cost
998876	ABM	15	6.75
998876	Cheque	5	3.75
998876	Teller	10	12.50
998876	Debit Card	30	15.00
765002	ABM	8	3.60
765002	Cheque	2	1.50
765002	Teller	1	1.25

Household	ABM Count	ABM Cost	Cheque Count	Cheque Cost	Teller Cost	Teller Cost	Debit Card Count	Debit Card Cost
998876	15	6.75	5	3.75	10	12.50	30	15.00
765002	8	3.60	2	1.50	1	1.25	0	0.00

Figure 8. Horizontal vs. vertical table

In this example, a table with one dimension, i.e. Household was turned into a deep table with two dimensions, namely Household and Channel. Only two facts/metrics were left: Count and Cost. In the wide table there is just one row per Household, in the deep table there are many.

In the case of the profitability decomposition, we have to create a new highly hierarchical dimension for the break down of financial terms. The decomposition will happen through the drill down process, level by level. Since the different elements of profitability should be monitored on all levels of aggregation, the aggregate tables have to be changed/turn deep as well.

The dimensionalization of metrics has one important advantage. It allows for new metrics to enter the system without requiring a redesign of the database. Consistently applied dimensionalization of metrics leads to creation of close to "fact-free" fact tables. Performance penalties and inability to create more complex reports with packaged tools often outweigh the convenience of metric decomposition.

4.5 Support for data mining

Earlier we made the statement, that the mission of data marts is primarily to answer large number of analytical queries and therefore the often most appropriate design is a star or snowflake schema. So far, we were not concerned with support for using more advanced exploratory techniques commonly referred to as data mining. Actually, in the data mining world, very little attention has been so far given to the data modelling issues. This is partially because building dedicated data marts just for data mining is still considered an unaffordable luxury, and partially because the data mining community in general has not historically developed as close to relational databases as their OLAP cousins.

From the three principal data modelling techniques, namely normalised models, star and snowflake schemas, it is the latter two, which most closely respond to the needs of data mining. This is because data mining algorithms run best against tables resembling flat files and this is just the nature of fact tables and their aggregates in star and snowflake models. The facts usually represent numerical variables (continuous or integer) and the table's dimensions (foreign keys pointing to dimensional tables) represent the categorical variables. Additional categorical variables could be obtained from star-type joins with the surrounding dimensional tables. Many transformation, reformatting and normalisation requirements could be satisfied through creation of database views, which get materialised in time of processing.

Most data mining techniques require one row per studied subject. I.e. for customer segmentation, one and only one row per customer is needed. This somehow resembles aggregate tables. The only difference is that with aggregate tables, a dimension collapses or is eliminated all together. With data mining, the deep table turns into a wide one with all details of the eliminated dimension preserved in newly created columns. An example of this is shown in Figure 8.

The star fact table of two dimensions, household and channel, collapses into a table with one dimension only – household. The facts are not aggregate but are preserved in newly created columns. This kind of processing could be done inexpensively using a simple generator of database views.

Unlike aggregate tables which are created only for performance reasons to satisfy multiple and frequently concurrent queries, views created for data mining get used less frequently but more systematically and in sequential processing. There is not a real need of having these views existing as permanent tables all the time with indexes created on them.

5. INTEGRATION OF DATA MINING

As we pointed out earlier in this article, most of the large organisations are either in or have already gone through the stadium of disperse decision support systems and non-integrated departmental data marts. In most cases, these systems were/are used by groups of power users, some of which are statisticians and predictive modellers. These specialists usually extract data from their decision support database and process it in adjacent systems. See Figure 9.

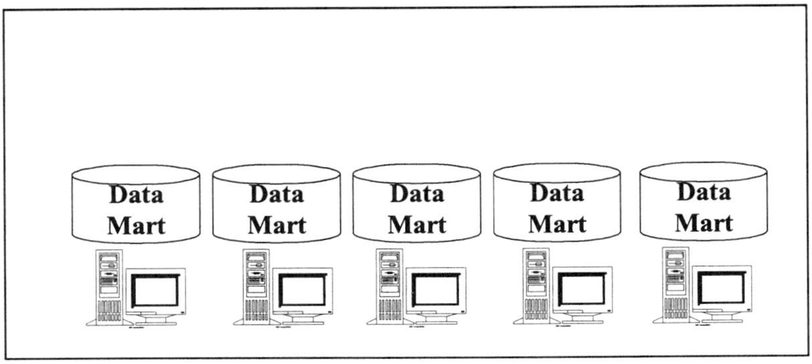

Figure 9. Disperse decision support systems

Solutions similar to the above has outgrown for many principal reasons.

First, it is the data access issue. Advances in data mining software allow for the inclusion of growing number of variables. These and the growing business needs initiate everlasting hunger for additional data. The data in one system is not fully sufficient any more, e.g. our example of optimising marketing campaigns and utilising the profitability figures derived in the neighbouring data mart. Also all analysed data has to be consistent. We have resolved both of these problems with having all data marts on the same BI data architecture and the same platform.

The other problem is the often-inadequate technical equipment for advanced analysis. Most of the analytical processing is occurring on systems, whose mission is to run the database, i.e. systems optimised for I/O. Yet most of the analytical processing is computationally intensive and requires multiple passes through data. Ideally the analytical hardware should be optimised for flow point processing with the emphasis on CPU and memory. Also, the exploratory data mining work requires large dedicated temporary storage. When hosting on a system with different principal mission (i.e. data mart tuned for OLAP) this storage is not usually available. Possible solution might be investments into large dedicated data mining environments adjacent to data marts. However the system maintenance overhead and the unbalanced utilisation makes such investments unattractive.

Another area of concern is the ability to communicate between various teams of analysts. Similarly, as the database systems differ, so do the analytical packages used. Ranging from logistic regression and single-algorithm tools to packages offering dozens of techniques, visualisation and parallel processing. Each tool and vendor are using different terminology and metadata approach, which makes any sensible communication between analysts difficult.

If we remember our conclusion of resolving data access and data consistency problems by migrating all data marts to a single BI data architecture and database and hardware platform, it is intuitive to derive a solution for the above data mining problems, too. We call the solution a Centralised Data Mining Environment. It is depicted in Figure 10.

Centralised Data Mining Environment is a hardware platform supporting massively parallel processing with an installed dedicated parallel database and a set of data mining, statistical and transformation tools. It is fully integrated within the BI complex and has high-speed links to all the major sources of data.

It is shared by all groups of statistical analysts and data miners. A dedicated group of data transformation experts provides acquisition and transformation of consistent data, which is brought into a dedicated database on the mining complex. The exclusive purpose of this database is to provide support for exploratory work only. After models are built and a project ends, most of the used data is removed and space is made available for new projects.

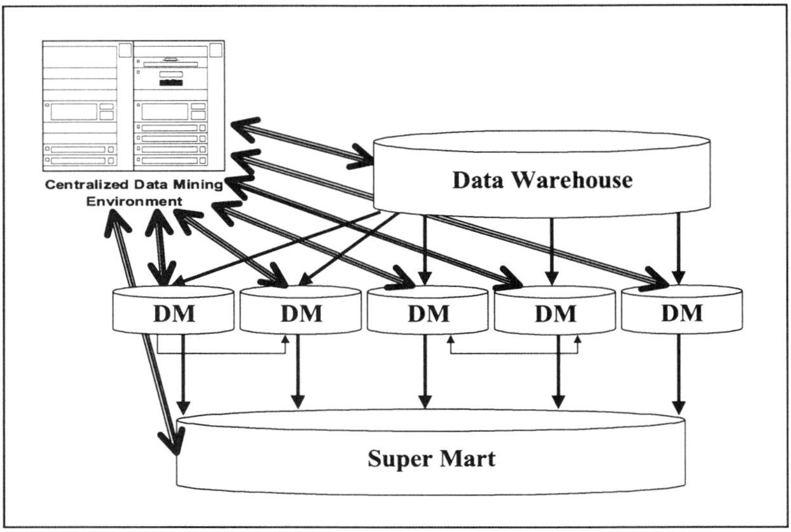

Figure 10. Centralised Data Mining Environment

Data mining projects differ in the number of variables used, in the complexity of data pre-processing and preparation, the complexity of algorithms and in the volumes of processed data. Some projects can suffice working with reasonably sized samples, others, like fraud detection, have to work with all the data available. To train a model, some algorithms require passing through the same data hundreds of times. The shared environment provides robust processing power and data capacity to projects on a when-needed basis and allows multiple projects to execute in parallel. Thus, the investment in the complex is maximally utilised.

The Centralised Data Mining Environment supports communication and exchange of experience among its users. Data mining metadata resides on the same complex and thus supports information sharing, reuse of blocks of work and help in quality assurance and reconciliation.

Similarly, as the need for data in various analytical models is growing beyond a single data source, so is growing the need for sharing the models' results. The original requestor of an analytical project is not the only user. If the project was an assignment of propensity scores to customers likely to buy a new product and this was requested by the marketing department responsible for promoting a new product line, other departments might also be interested in accessing these results. Viewing the propensity scores by customer behaviour segments, channels of communication, customer product mix, time sequence between acquiring two different products, inclination to product cannibalisation, etc. might be of interest to the product lines of business, distribution networks and many other departments. A mechanism should be in place, which allows for publishing the final model results out and beyond the exploratory data mining environment. In other words, data mining is a value-adding process and the results should return to a data mart for further multidimensional presentation, as shown in the Figure 4.

Theoretically we have two ways how to publish data mining results. One is to transmit data, which resulted from models run in the Centralised Data Mining Environment. That would however require change in the mission of the Data Mining Environment itself. The exploratory environment would become a subject of scheduled production runs, which would in turn become limiting factor for new exploratory work and training of new models.

The best solution is to extend the ability to execute data mining models directly on the systems that run the data marts. Unlike the previous solution where we considered transmission of final results, here we talk about transmitting models, i.e. generated code, which then executes as a value-adding transformation process on the dedicated data mart system. Essentially this is the same approach we introduced earlier for the code-generation of profitability calculations and subsequent execution on the Profitability Database system.

The level of difficulty to promote new models to production on the data mart systems depends on the nature of algorithms used and the complexity of the necessary pre-processing. Classification models, for example, result in a set of rules, which could be easily run as stored procedures on the database management system. Other algorithms, like Radial Based Functions, require access to functions of a mining engine kernel. The cost of the deployment of mining engine kernels is dependent on data mining vendors' pricing models. The deployment might range from being free to US $30,000 per processor.

Data pre-processing often represents the most time consuming and tedious work. It includes reformatting of data, data normalisation, derivation of variables and creation of new flat file-like data structures suitable for fast data mining runs. Not surprisingly, the pre-processing is usually the most challenging part of promoting data mining models to production. Usually, during the exploratory work and model building stage, different transformation tools are used than those used for the production environment. The reason being that, during the exploration, emphasis is placed on the convenience of transformation programming. In the production execution, it is the performance, often the ability to execute on massively parallel systems, what matters most. As part of the model promotion, the data pre-processing is often re-programmed and tuned for performance.

Lots of work effort could be saved if data mining experts are invited early in the process of designing a new data mart system. Numerous data pre-processing could be included in the initial data mart transformation process and artificial variables created solely for the purpose of being used in future models, i.e. not in OLAP presentations, could be generated with other facts and dimension keys in the data mart's fact tables.

Production-run models have to be retrained periodically. The retraining happens on the Centralised Data Mining Environment. Retrained models are returned back to production in the form of generated code. This process is smooth as long as no change is required to the data pre-processing.

6. CONCLUSION

In summary, we have discussed some of the most important practical aspects of implementing very large Business Intelligence systems. These include BI system architecture, informational architecture, layers of segmented transformation processing, robust data mining, promotion of data mining models and some key data modelling issues. There are other important topics related to building Robust Business Intelligence systems we did not elaborate on in this article. These include optimisation of databases, parallel transformation processing, backup strategies, dealing with data quality, building behavioural models from transactional data, inclusion of searchable qualitative information in form of binary large objects, support for spatial analysis, design of corporate information portals, creation of automated agents, information broadcasting, metadata repository and much more.

At the Bank of Montreal we have a team of 50 Business Intelligence professionals responsible for mastering the above mentioned areas. This alone is quite an investment for the Bank, but an investment delivering unprecedented returns. Our Business Intelligence complex has more than one thousand daily users spanning from executive management, over different product and channel lines of business to financial service managers in the branches and the call centres. These users turned from passive information recipients to proactive information workers.

The usage of our system clearly demonstrates a process of changing our company from product driven to information driven. This success is a reward for working closely with the scientific as well as the broad vendor communities in a persistent search for new ways of detecting and leveraging actionable information.

REFERENCES

1. Adamson C, Venerable M. *Data Warehouse Design Solutions*. John Wiley & Sons, 1998.
2. Edelstein HA(Editor), et al. *Building, Using, and Managing the Data Warehouse*. Prentice Hall: Data Warehousing Institute Series, 1997.
3. Gleason D. *Creating The No Compromise Data Warehouse*. DM Review, January 1999.
4. Inmon, WH. *Building the Data Warehouse*. John Wiley & Sons, 1996.
5. Kimball R, Merz R. *The Data Webhouse Toolkit: Building the Web-Enabled Data Warehouse*. John Wiley & Sons, 2000.
6. Kimball R, et al. *The Data Warehouse Lifecycle Toolkit: Expert Methods for Designing, Developing, and Deploying Data Warehouses*. John Wiley & Sons, 1998.
7. Kimball R. *The Data Warehouse Toolkit: Practical Techniques for Building Dimensional Data Warehouses*. John Wiley & Sons, 1996.
8. Marquez J, et al. *Building a Data Warehouse With DB2 Universal Database: Time-Saving Methods and Tools for Developers*. John Wiley & Sons, 2000.
9. Morse S, et al. *Parallel Systems in the Data Warehouse*. Prentice Hall: Data Warehousing Institute Series, 1997.

10. www.adtmag.com/Pub/apr2000/bom.cfm
11. www.dmreview.com/master_sponsor.cfm?NavID=193&EdID=1562
12. www.dw-institute.com/whatworks7/montreal.html
13. www2.software.ibm.com/casestudies/swcsdm.nsf/customername/67A6FC99EE97E1360 02568B700161E93
14. www.software.ibm.com/data/solutions/customer/montreal/montreal.htm
15. www.cio.com/archive/051598_mining_content.html
16. www2.computerworld.com/home/print9497.nsf/All/SL42mont16896
17. www.bmo.com
18. www.dmreview.com
19. www.datawarehousingonline.com
20. www.techweb.com
21. www.dw-institute.com

Chapter 12

THE ROLE OF GRANULAR INFORMATION IN KNOWLEDGE DISCOVERY IN DATABASES

Witold Pedrycz

Department of Electrical & Computer Engineering

University of Alberta, Edmonton, Canada (pedrycz@ee.ualberta.ca)

and

Systems Research Institute, Polish Academy of Sciences

01-447 Warsaw, Poland

Keywords: data mining, information granularity, granulation, associations, rules, fuzzy sets, associations versus rules, directionality, attributes

Abstract: In this study, we are concerned with the role of information granulation in processes of data mining in databases. By its nature, data mining pursuits are very much oriented towards end-users and imply that any results need to be easily interpretable. Granulation of information promotes this interpretability and channels all pursuits of data mining (that are otherwise computationally intensive and thus highly prohibitive) towards more efficient processing and feasible processing of information granules. First, we discuss the essence of information granulation and afterwards elaborate on the main approaches to the design of information granules. We distinguish between user-driven, data-driven and hybrid methods of information granulation. Several main classes of membership function of information granules-fuzzy sets are investigated and contrasted in terms of some selection criteria such as parametric flexibility and sensitivity of the ensuing information granules. We revisit two fundamental concepts in data mining such as associations and rules in the setting of information granules. Associations are direction-free constructs that capture the most essential components of the overall structure in database. The relevance of associations is expressed by counting the amount of data standing behind the Cartesian products of the information granules contributing to the construction of the associations. The proposed methodology of data mining comprises two phases. First, associations are constructed and the most essential (relevant) ones are collected in the form of a data mining agenda. Second, some of them are converted into direction-driven constructs, that is rules. The idea of consistency of the rules is discussed in detail.

1. INTRODUCTION

In a very succinct way, data mining in databases aims at making sense of data by revealing meaningful and easily interpretable relationships, see [1][3][4][8][18][21][24]. In spite of many existing variations, this research goal permeates the entire area. The domain of data mining is highly heterogeneous embracing a number of well-established information technologies including statistical pattern recognition, neural networks, machine learning, knowledge-based systems, neural networks, etc [2][6][9][10][11][14][22][23][25][28]. The synergistic character of data mining is definitely one of its dominant and visible features that make this pursuit to emerge as a new area of research and applications. The ultimate goal of data mining is in revealing patterns that are easy to perceive, interpret, and manipulate. One may ask, in turn, what becomes necessary to develop such patterns. To address this essential quest, we should revisit what makes humans so superb at perceiving, understanding, acting in complex worlds and so limited in basic arithmetic operations, manipulating numbers, etc. The cornerstone is the concept of information granules and information granulation. Information granules help us cope with abundance of detailed numeric data. Numbers are important yet humans tend to produce abstractions that are more tangible and easy to deal with. Abstractions manifest in the form of information granules -- entities that encapsulate a collection of fine grain entities (in particular, numbers) into a single construct thus making them indistinguishable. The level of details retained depends on the size of the information granules and is directly implied by the problem at hand. Information granulation makes all data mining pursuits more user-oriented and allows him to become more proactive in the overall data mining process.

Granulation and information granules are carried out in many different frameworks such as set-based environments and their generalizations (fuzzy sets, rough sets, shadowed sets, random sets, etc.) [15][13][19][20][29][30][31][17][16] as well as probabilistic frameworks (subsequently leading to probabilistic information granules such as probability density functions). In this study, we concentrate on the use of the technology of fuzzy sets regarded as a fundamental conceptual environment of information granulation. Nevertheless the developed environment of data mining along with the ensuing methodology is valid for some other environments of information granulation.

The study is organized into a number of sections. First, in Section 2, we concentrate on the very idea of information granulation, formal models of information granules and various algorithms leading to information granulation. Section 3 concentrates on the development side by proposing the design of data-legitimate information granules (fuzzy sets). Such fuzzy sets are then used as building construction modules to design associations (Section 4). The paper makes a strong distinction between associations and rules: rules are regarded as directional constructs resulting from associations. The discussion on this matter is presented in several ensuing sections (Section 5, 6, and 7). The notion of consistency of rules is introduced and studied in detail along with some computational details (Section 8). Conclusions are covered in Section 9.

2. GRANULATION OF INFORMATION

In this section, we concentrate on the essence of information granulation and the role of information granules in a spectrum of perception processes carried out by humans. Then our focus moves into the construction of information granules in the setting of fuzzy sets. In particular, we distinguish between main design avenues pursued in information granulation and contrast their performance.

2.1 Prerequisties: the Role of Information Granulation in Data Mining Processes

The essence of information granulation lies in a conceptual transformation in which a vast amount of numbers is condensed into small number of and meaningful entities - information granules [16][29][31]. Information granules are user-oriented. They are easily comprehended, memorized and used as building blocks helpful when perceiving more complex concepts. Information granules are manifestations of *abstraction*. The level of such abstraction depends upon the objective of perception process carried out by humans. This, in turn, is implied by the goal of data mining and a level of the related decision - making processes. Strategic, long-term decision processes invoke the use of coarse and more stable information granules. Short-term decision-making processes involving immediate actions require another look at the same database that requires fine grain information granules. In this way, the size of information granule becomes crucial to the successful process of data mining. So far, we have not defined information granules and their "size" (granularity) in any formal fashion. As a matter of fact, such definition has to be linked with the formal framework in which such information granules are constructed. For instance, when using fuzzy sets the size of the granules needs to be expressed in terms of the language of fuzzy set theory. Another way of expressing granularity should hold for probabilistic granules. In this case, a plausible option would be to use a standard deviation of the underlying probability density function or probability function. Nevertheless, on the intuitive side, we can envision the general relationship: the larger the number of elements embraced by the information granule, the lower the granularity of such construct. And conversely: the lower the number in the information granule, the higher its granularity. We can also use the term specificity as being opposite in functioning to the notion of granularity.

2.2 Information granulation with the aid of fuzzy sets

In this study, we concentrate on the use of fuzzy sets as a vehicle of information granulation. There are three main ways in which information granules - fuzzy sets or fuzzy relations can be constructed

- User-oriented. It is a user or designer of the system who completely identifies the form of the information granules. For instance, they could be a priori defined as a series of triangular fuzzy numbers. Moreover, the number of these terms as well as their parameters are totally specified in advance.
- Algorithmic approach to information granulation. In this case, information granules come as a result of optimization of a certain performance index (objective function). Clustering algorithms are representative examples of such algorithms of unsupervised learning leading to the formation of the information granules. Quite commonly, the granules are fuzzy sets (or fuzzy relations) when using FCM and alike or sets (or relations) when dealing with the methods such as ISODATA [5][12]
- A combination of these two. The methods that fall under this category come as a hybrid of user-based and algorithmic driven methods. For instance, some parameters of the information granulation process can be set up by the user while the detailed parameters of the information granules can be determined (or refined) through some optimization

mechanism being utilized during the second phase. A level of influence coming from the user and data varies from case to case

One should become aware of the advantages and potential drawbacks of the two first methods (the third one is a compromise between the user and data-driven methods and as such may reduce the disadvantages associated with its components). The user-based approach, even quite appealing and commonly used, may not reflect the specificity of the problem (and, more importantly, the data to be granulated). There could be a serious danger of forming fuzzy sets not conveying any experimental evidence. In other words, we may end up with a fuzzy set whose existence could be barely legitimized in light of the currently investigated data. The issue of the experimental legitimization of fuzzy sets along with some algorithmic investigations has been studied in detail in [15]. On the other hand, the algorithmic-based approach could not be able to reflect the semantics of the problem. Essentially, the membership functions are built as constructs minimizing a given performance index. This index itself may not capture the semantics of the information granules derived in this fashion. Moreover, the data-driven information granulation may be computationally intensive especially when dealing with large sets of multidimensional data (that are common to many tasks of data mining). This may eventually hamper the usage of clustering as a highly viable and strongly recommended option in data mining.

Bearing in mind the computational facet of data mining, we consider a process of granulation that takes place for each variable (attribute) separately. There are several advantages to follow this path. First, the already mentioned computational aspect being essential in data mining pursuits is taken care of. Second, there is no need for any prior normalization of the data that could eventually result in an extra distortion of relationships within the database; this phenomenon has been well known in statistical pattern recognition [10]. The drawback of not capturing the relationships between the variables can be considered minor in comparison to the advantages coming with this approach. In building a series of information granules we follow the hybrid approach, namely we rely on data but provide the number of the linguistic terms in advance along with their general form (type of membership function).

Before proceeding with the complete algorithm, it is instructive to elaborate on different classes of membership functions and analyze their role in information granulation as it applies to data mining.

2.3 Classes of Membership Functions and Their Characterisation

There is an abundance of classes of membership functions encountered in the theory and applications of fuzzy sets. In general, their intent is to model linguistic concepts.

When it comes to data mining, several useful guidelines as to a suitable selection may be sought

Information granules need to be flexible enough to "accommodate" (reflect) the numeric data. In other words, they should capture the data quite easily so that the granules become legitimate (viz. justifiable in the setting of experimental data). This implies membership functions equipped with some parameters (so that these could be adjusted when required). The experimental justification of the linguistic terms can be quantified with the aid of probabilities, say the probability of the fuzzy event [29][30]. Given a fuzzy set A, its probability computed in light of experimental data $\mathbf{X} = \{x_1, x_2, .., x_N\}$ originates as a sum of the membership values

$$\mathrm{Prob}(A) = \sum_{k=1}^{N} A(x_k)$$

We say A is *experimentally justifiable* if the above sum achieves or exceeds a certain threshold value γ.

Information granules need to be "stable" meaning that they have to retain their identity in spite of some small fluctuations occurring within the experimental data. This also raises a question of sensitivity of the membership functions and an issue of its distribution vis-à-vis specific values of the membership grades. We claim that the sensitivity of the membership values should be more evident for higher membership grades and decay for lower membership grades. This is intuitively appealing: we are not concerned that much about the lower membership values while the values close to 1 are of greater importance as those are the values that imply the semantics of the information granule. The quantification of this property can be done by the absolute value of the derivative of the membership function A regarded as a function of membership grade (u), that is

$$s(A)(u) = \left|\frac{dA(x)}{dx}\right| = \varphi(u)$$

In what follows, we analyze three classes of membership functions such as triangular, parabolic, and Gaussian fuzzy sets by studying the two criteria established above.

The triangular fuzzy sets are composed of two segments of linear membership functions, see Figure 1(a). The membership function reads as

$$T(x; a, m, b) = \begin{cases} \dfrac{x-a}{m-a} & x \in [a, m] \\ 1 - \dfrac{x-m}{b-m} & x \in [m, b] \end{cases}$$

(for the rest of the arguments, the membership values are equal to zero).

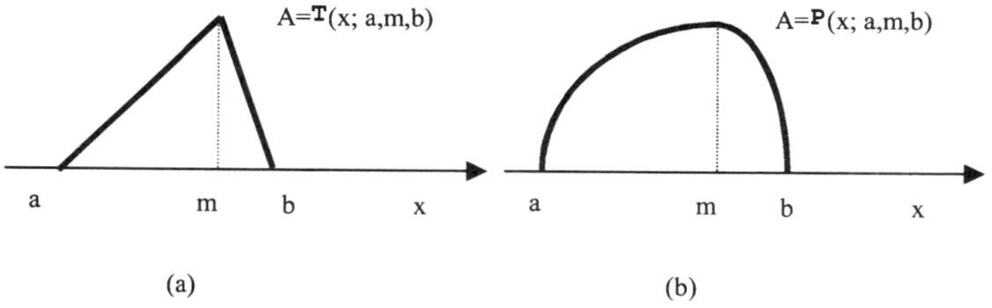

Figure 1. Two general classes of triangular (a) and parabolic membership functions (b)

It is defined by three parameters that is a modal value (m) and two bounds (a and b). The left-hand and right-hand of the fuzzy set are determined separately. Then the parametric flexibility is available in the design of the information granule. The sensitivity of A is constant and equal to the increasing or decreasing slope of the membership function. The sensitivity does not depend on the membership value and does not contribute to the stability of the fuzzy set.

The parabolic membership functions are defined by three parameters (say a, m, and b), Fig 1(b)

$$P(x;a, m, b) = \begin{cases} 1-\left(\dfrac{x-m}{m-a}\right)^2, x \in [a, m] \\ 1-\left(\dfrac{x-m}{b-m}\right)^2, x \in [m, b] \\ 0, \text{otherwise} \end{cases}$$

These parameters can make the fuzzy set asymmetrical and help adjust the two parts of the information granule separately. The sensitivity exhibits an interesting pattern; it achieves the highest values around the membership value equal to 1 and tempers down to zero when the membership values approach zero. In this sense, the range of high membership values of the granule becomes emphasized, Figure 2.

The Gaussian membership function is governed by the expression

$A(x) = \exp(-(x-m)^2/\sigma^2)$

and includes two parameters (m and σ). The first one (m) determines the position of the fuzzy set. The second parameter (σ) controls the spread of the information granule. Gaussian fuzzy sets are symmetrical. This may form a certain problem when the data exhibit a significant asymmetry that cannot be easily copied with. The sensitivity pattern exhibits its maximum around the membership value equal to 0.5, see Figure 3.

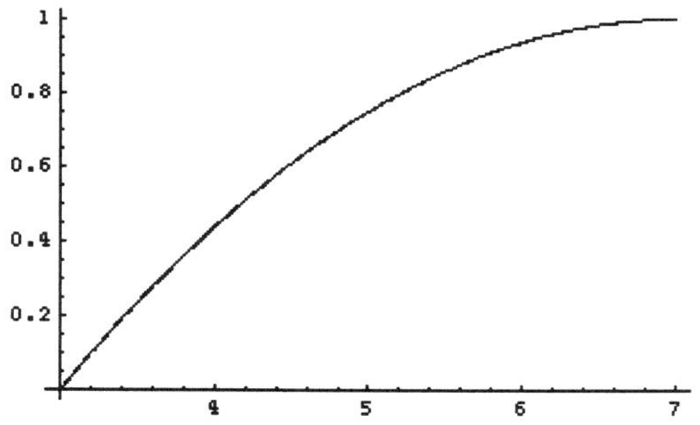

(a)

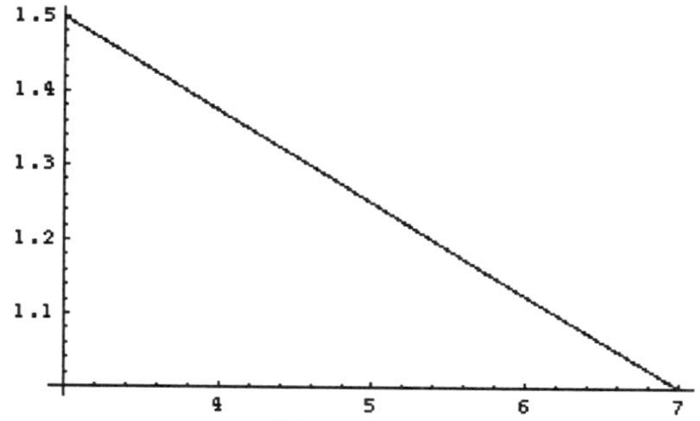

(b)

Figure 2. Sensitivity pattern of the parabolic membership function with m equal to 7 and a = 3; shown is an increasing portion of the membership function (a) and its derivative (b)

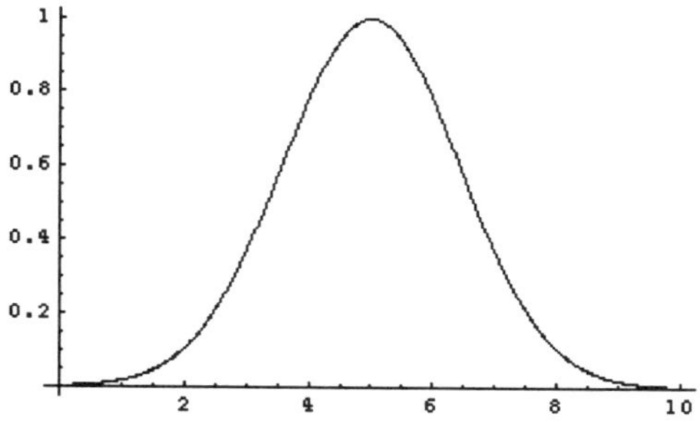

(a)

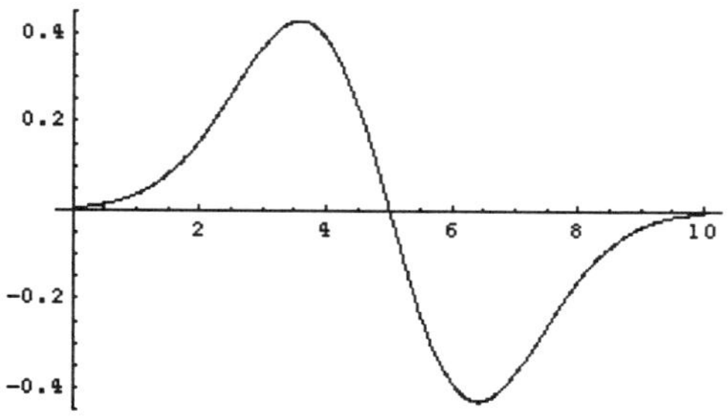

(b)

Figure 3. Sensitivity pattern of the Gaussian membership function with m=5; s =2; membership function (a) and its derivative (b)

3. THE DEVELOPMENT OF DATA-JUSTIFIABLE INFORMATION GRANULES

Our objective is to construct fuzzy sets that are legitimized by data. The problem is posed in the following way:
-given is a collection of numeric one-dimensional data $\mathbf{X} = \{x_1, x_2, \ldots, x_N\}$ where x_k is a real number. Form a collection of fuzzy sets $A_1, A_2, .., A_c$ coming from a certain family of fuzzy sets A (say, triangular, parabolic, etc.) so that each of them carries the same level of experimental evidence. In other words, its probability (as a fuzzy event) is the same and equal to 1/c. Moreover assume that any two adjacent fuzzy sets in A satisfy the condition of zeroing at the modal value of the individual fuzzy set as illustrated in Figure 4 (this requirement prevents us from dealing with fuzzy sets with excessively "long" tails that overlap some other fuzzy sets).

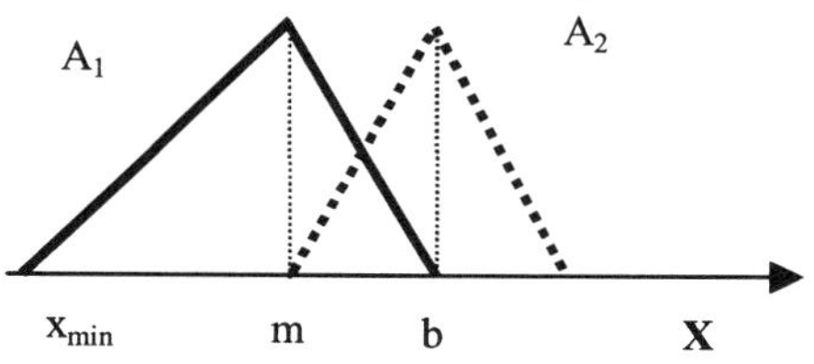

Figure 4. A collection of fuzzy sets with the parameters to be determined

The above formulation of the problem has a strong intuitive underpinning: by making each element of A to be supported by the same amount of data, we construct information granules that will exhibit the same level of experimental evidence, no matter what the details of the ensuing data mining method could be. Similarly, these information granules become detail-neutral, that is data mining architecture independent.

The algorithm of building fuzzy sets of A could be quite straightforward: we scan the universe of discourse **X** from left to right and allocate the characteristic points of the fuzzy sets in such a way so that we reach the required level of experimental evidence. Getting into details, let us illustrate how the algorithm works by constructing a family of parabolic fuzzy sets. The increasing and decreasing parts of the membership functions are determined independently from each other. Regarding the first fuzzy set, its lower bound is equal to the lowest value in **X**, that is a = arg min **X**. The modal value of A is determined by moving towards higher values of **X**, computing the accumulated values of the sum

$$\sum_{i:x_i \le m} A_1(x_i)$$

and terminating the search for such running value of "x" for which the above sum attains the value equal to N/2c (or meets it at some given tolerance level), see Figure 5.

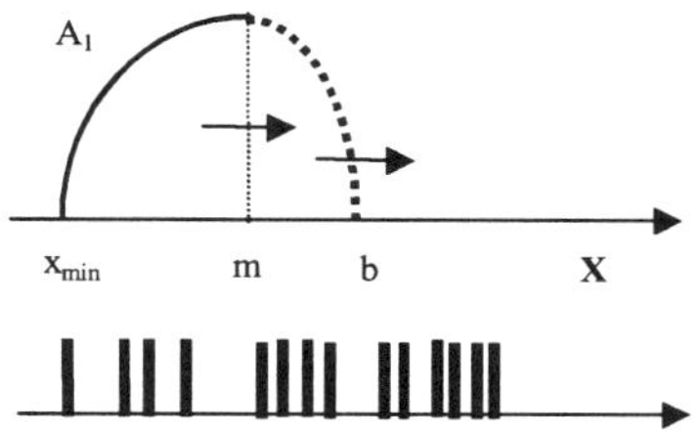

Figure 5. Determination of the membership function of A_1; see description in text

This particular value of x forms then a modal value of A_1, say, equal to m. Then the sweeping towards higher values continues and the overall process is monitored by the value of the sum

$$\sum_{i:m \le x_i \le b} A_1(x_i)$$

As before, this expression should reach the value approximately equal to N/2c (this, as pointed out by the above sum, is achieved for x = b). Summing (1) and (2), the total evidence behind A_1 is equal to N/c. Proceeding with the construction of A_2, we note that the determination of the increasing portion of the membership function has been already done, see Figure 5. We have to compute the experimental evidence behind the increasing part of A_2; this, in general, may not necessarily be equal to N/2c. Denote this value by q. The difference N/2c -q is then used to determine the decreasing part of the membership function of A_2. In this case the mechanism is the same already described. The remaining elements of this family of information granules **A** are computed in an analogous manner.

There are several parameters of the algorithm one may refine in order to carry out the entire construction. In particular, this concerns the sweeping steps across the universe of discourse and the tolerance level at which the thresholds of the evidence have to be determined. One should be vigilant as to the difference

N/2c-q

that is used to construct the decreasing portion of the membership functions. It could well be that this expression could be zero or even negative. This prevents us from building the remaining portion of the fuzzy set. The reason behind this deficiency is linked with the distribution of the experimental data that may exhibit quite substantial "jumps". To avoid this problem, one has to reduce the number of the information granules. This would increase the value of the experimental evidence (N/2c) thus maintaining the final value of (3) positive.

It is worth considering another important scenario of information granulation through fuzzy sets. Here we are provided with a family of numeric data that arise within a fixed granulation window W, refer to Figure 6(a). The granulation is realized in two steps
determination the modal value of the fuzzy set that serves as a representative of all numeric data in W. To assure robustness, we consider a median (m) to be a plausible choice here. The determination of the median is straightforward.The median splits the data into two subsets and each of them is used separately to compute the membership function. Once we agree upon the form of the membership function, say linear, parabolic or alike, we adjust the parameters. In particular this concerns its spread. The optimization of the spread is guided by the following intuitively appealing criterion: the fuzzy set should "embrace" as many data points as possible while being as "specific" as possible. The criterion involves two components. The first one can be captured by the sum of the membership values. The second component can be quantified by the length of the support of the fuzzy set. Adopting the notation as included in Figure 6(b), the performance index Q (criterion) reads as

$$Q = \sum_{k=1}^{n} \frac{A(x_k)}{m-a} = \frac{1}{m-a} \sum_{k=1}^{n} A(x_k)$$

Note that by the two components of the criterion are in competition: by increasing the coverage of the data, we reduce the specificity of the fuzzy set. The optimization of Q is carried out with respect to the value of "a", that is $\min_a Q$. The optimal value of the spread comes from the equality

$$\frac{dQ}{da} = 0$$

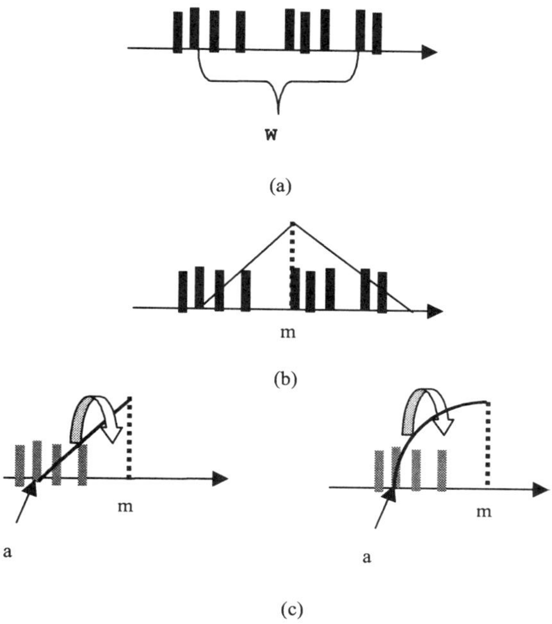

Figure 6. Construction of information granules from numeric data included in some granulation window W

4. BUILDING ASSOCIATIONS IN DATABASES

Once the information granules have been constructed for each variable in the database separately, they need to be combined. The aggregated (composite) granule

granule A_i and granule B_j

is a fuzzy relation defined as a Cartesian product of the corresponding coordinates

$A_{ij} = A_i \times B_j$

The membership function is defined by taking the and-combination (aggregation) of the contributing membership functions, namely

$$(A_i(x) t B_j(y))$$

with "t" denoting the triangular norm. The definition easily extends to any number of the information granules defined in the corresponding universes of discourse, say

$$A_{ij...l} = A_i \times B_j \times ... \times ... Z_l$$

that is

$$A_{ij...l}(\mathbf{x}) = A_{ij...l}(x_1, x_2, ..., x_n) = A_I(x_1) \, t \, B_j(x_2) ... t ... Z_l(x_n)$$

with "n" being the number of the contributing information granules. Assume that for each coordinate (variable, attribute), we have constructed "c" granules. With the fixed number of attributes equal to "n", we come up with c^n different Cartesian products. Only a certain fraction of these combinations would be legitimate in light of the experimental data available in the database. Each Cartesian combination of the information granules as outlined above is quantified by computing its σ-count of (4). The information granules are then ranked according to the values of their σ-counts. We can form an agenda **D** of the most significant Cartesian products that is those ones characterized by the highest values of the σ-counts. The construction of the agenda of a certain size, say "p" can be characterized as follows

cycle through all Cartesian products and retain those with the highest values of σ-counts

With the significant number of the attributes existing in databases, there is an explosion in the number of combinations. Say, for c = 7 (which could be a fairly typical value of the number of the information granules) and n = 40, we end up with possible combinations of 7^{40} composite granules (Cartesian products). Subsequently, if an exhaustive search is out of question, one may consider some alternative and quite often suboptimal approaches. Various evolutionary techniques could be a viable alternative. With the increasing number of the information granules defined for each attribute, the likelihood of having strongly supported Cartesian products may be lower. Larger information granules promote Cartesian products described by higher values of the experimental evidence that is higher values of the corresponding σ-counts.

4.1 Determining links between multidimensional information granules

Once we have derived a collection of associations, one may be interested in revealing whether these associations are linked together and if a certain association is strongly tied with some other. As associations are manifestations of some patterns in data, the relationships between them could be regarded as a certain type of high level data analysis. More descriptively, we start with a collection of the associations (elements of the already developed agenda, **A**) and build a web of links between them. Two approaches can be envisioned. The first one embarks on the notion of Hebbian learning while the second exploits an idea of fuzzy correlation.

The use of Hebbian learning

This is graphically depicted in Figure 7 where the strength of an individual link is reflected by some numeric value (usually the values of which are confined to the interval from -1 to 1). What has been shown in Figure 7 is an undirected graph whose nodes are the associations and the edges represent the level of bonding (influence) occurring between the nodes.

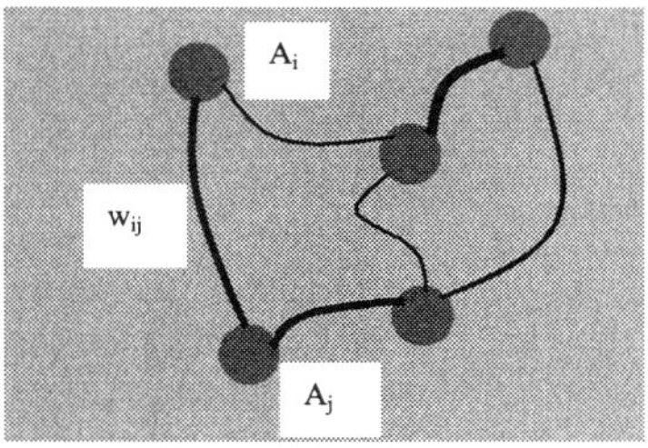

Figure 7. A web of associations; the strength of the bonding is reflected by the width of the link between the corresponding associations

The values associated with the edges can be determined in many different ways. The Hebbian learning comes as a plausible option. Denote by w_{ij} a level of bonding between association A_i and A_j, i, j=1,2, …, p. The Hebbian learning [7] is an example of unsupervised correlation-driven learning where the values of w_{ij} are updated as follows

$$w_{ij}(\text{new}) = w_{ij} + \alpha A_i(\mathbf{x}_k)A_j(\mathbf{x}_k)$$

Where α is a learning rate, $\alpha > 0$. The updates are affected by individual elements of the database (more specifically, their manifestations through the information granules formed at the very beginning of the data mining process). The initial values of the links are set to small random numbers. Noticeably, if both manifestations $A_i(\mathbf{x}_k)$ and $A_j(\mathbf{x}_k)$ are substantial, then the value of w_{ij} increases. For the previous values close to zero, the changes in the value of the corresponding bonding are negligible.

Fuzzy correlation

In addition to the standard Hebbian-like learning discussed in the previous section, we may proceed with a correlation analysis developed for fuzzy sets and fuzzy relations. The crux of this approach is to correlate (determine a strength of correlation) between numeric data that fall under the "umbrella" of the corresponding membership function. Moreover, the correlation coefficient is treated as a fuzzy number defined in the unit interval rather than a single numeric value.

Let us briefly present a way in which the correlation coefficient is formed. For clarity of presentation, we start with two variables only (x and y) and consider that there is a collection of pertinent data coming in the form $\mathbf{D} = (x(k), y(k))$, k=1, 2, ..., K. Given two fuzzy sets A and B defined in $\mathbf{X}$ and $\mathbf{Y}$, respectively we fix the level of the α-cut of A and B. This gives rise to the original subset of the data, namely

$$\mathbf{D}_a = \{(x(k) \mid A(x(k)) \geq \alpha \text{ and } B(y(k)) \geq \alpha\}$$

By definition, $\mathbf{D}_a$ is included in $\mathbf{D}$. The higher the values of α, the less elements involved in the resulting subset of data. Once this data set has been formed, we compute the correlation coefficient in a standard way encountered in statistics. To emphasize the dependency of this coefficient on the level of α, we use the notation $r(\alpha)$ to describe this phenomenon. Several characteristic patterns can be discussed, see below

In general, the data in Figure 8(a) exhibit a very low level of correlation. By decreasing the size of the information granules (A and B), our analysis is confined to a subset of the data in which the linear relationships could become more profound. The curve portrayed in this figure underlines this effect: the less data invoked in the analysis, the higher the value of the correlation coefficient.

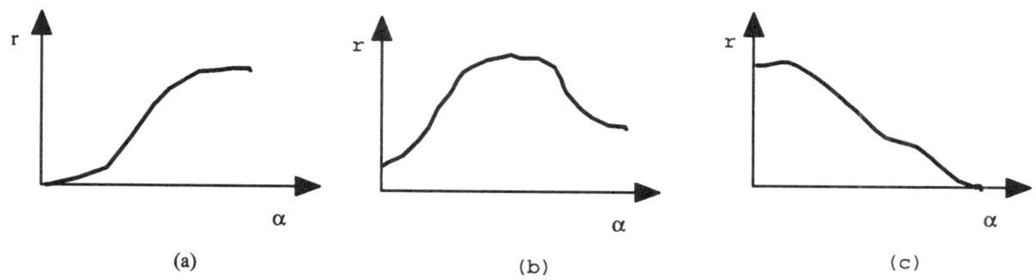

Figure 8. Examples of fuzzy sets of correlation; see detailed description in text.

In Figure 8(b), more specific linguistic granules give rise to the higher values of the correlation coefficient meaning that the linear relationships become more profound in the subset of data "highlighted" by the fuzzy sets under consideration. There is an optimal value of α leading to the highest values of "r". With the increase of the threshold, a decrease in the strength of correlation is observed. This effect can be explained as follows: as a small region of the data set is being concentrated on, some noise being inevitably associated there may be amplified. Noticeably, the maximum corresponds to a point where by selecting a proper level of granularity of linguistic terms, a sound balance is achieved between a global nonlinear pattern in data and the noise factor present there. In Figure 8(c), the correlation is high even for quite large information granules (low values of α) and any further increase of the values of α leads to the lower values of the correlation coefficient. This is due to the high level of noise associated with the data. Too specific information granules generate a "magnification" effect of noise associated with the data. In this sense, the second scenario, Figure 8(b), comes as an intermediate situation between the case of high nonlinearity and high level of noise.

Traditionally, the correlation coefficient captures the relationship between two variables. In case of many variables, say many input variables and a single output variable, we end up with a collection of fuzzy sets of correlation (each for the respective input variable and the output variable). These membership functions are then aggregated (in particular, averaging them).

5. FROM ASSOCIATIONS TO RULES IN DATABASES

The Cartesian products constructed in the previous section, are associations - basic entities that are the tangible results of data mining. The agenda **D** retains the most significant (that is data legitimate) findings in the database. It captures the most essential dependencies. It is important to stress that associations are *direction free*. They do not commit to any causal link between the variables, or more specifically, between the information granules. In this sense, associations are general constructs. One may even emphasize that these are the most generic entities to be used in mining static relationships in data mining. It is needless to say that the form of the associations, their number as well as underlying experimental evidence hinges on the information granules being used across all activities of data mining.

Rules, on the other hand, are *direction-oriented* constructs. They are conditional statements of the form

- if condition(s) then action(s)

The form of the rule clearly stipulates the direction of the construct: the values of the conditions stipulate certain actions. The direction makes the construct more detailed and fundamentally distinct from associations. All rules are associations but not all associations are rules. This observation is merely a translation of associations and rules in the language of mathematics: all relations (Cartesian products) are functions (rules) but not other way around.

In data mining, the issue of distinction between associations and rules plays a primordial role. We may not be certain as to direction between attributes (what implies what). Therefore it is prudent to proceed with a two-phase design: first, reveal associations and then analyze if some of them could become rules. Note that when dealing with rules, they could be articulated once we decide upon the split of attributes (variables) into inputs and outputs. The task looks quite obvious for modeling physical systems (very few variables with an obvious direction between them). In data mining, though, this could be a part of the data mining pursuit. The two-phase process of data mining associations - rules is illustrated in Figure 9.

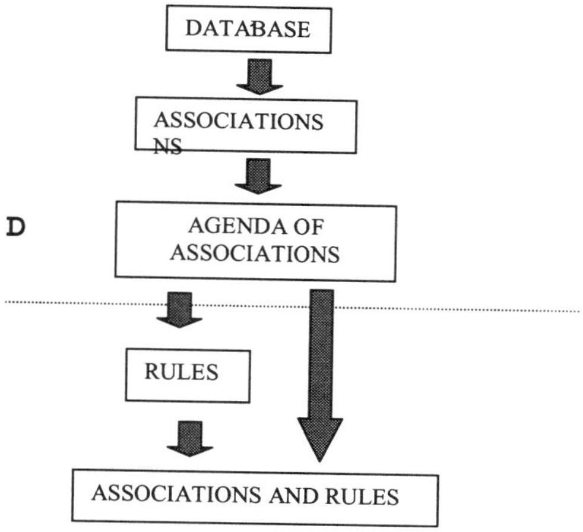

Figure 9. A two-phase process of data mining: from associations to rules

In the next section, we discuss how to realize the second phase producing rules. Hopefully, the objective of this pursuit becomes clear: the data mining of rules realized from the very beginning of the process is false and unnecessary restrictive. This common practice praised and followed by many could be dangerous from the conceptual point of view: seeing functions where there are only relations is not appropriate.

6. THE CONSTRUCTION OF RULES IN DATA MINING

The starting point of this design is a collection of *associations*. Some of them could be recognized as *potential* rules. For the clarity of presentation, we consider only three variables and the associations therein coming in the form of the following Cartesian products

$$A_i \times B_i \times C_i \tag{5}$$

i=1,2, .., r. The first step is to split the variables (attributes) into inputs and outputs. For instance, the first two are regarded as inputs, the third one is an output. The potential rules read as follows

- if A_i and B_i then C_i (6)

By taking C_i as input and retaining the two others as outputs, we get the rules

if C_i then (A_i and B_i) (7)

Obviously, there are far more different arrangements of the variables with respect to their directionality.

In general, when dealing with multivariable associations, they can give rise to numerous rules depending on the allocation of the variables. Figure 10 illustrates this by showing the agenda **D** with its entries being identified as inputs or outputs.

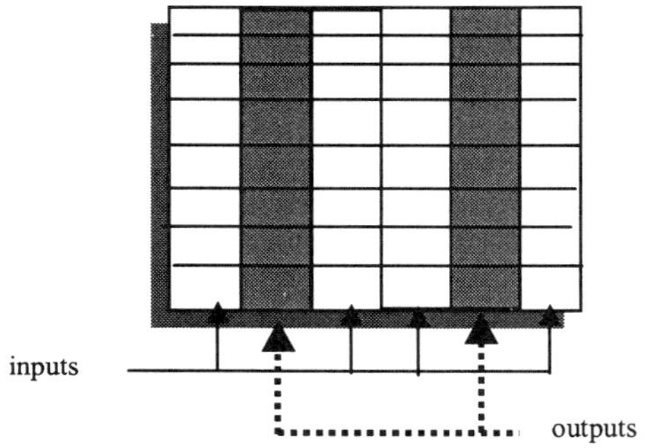

Figure 10. The agenda of associations in database with the attributes identified as inputs (shadowed entries) and outputs

The detailed implementation of the rules (involving various models of the implication operator and a way of their summarization were studied in numerous volumes under the banner of fuzzy inference and is not of particular interest here; the reader may refer to [5][10] as two selected points of reference). The crucial point here is how to identify that some associations are rules. This identification occurs with regard to pairs of associations. The underlying principle is straightforward: the rules obtained from the associations are free of conflict. We say that two rules are conflicting if they have quite *similar* conditions yet they lead to very *different* (distinct) conclusions. The effect of conflict is illustrated succinctly in Figure 11.

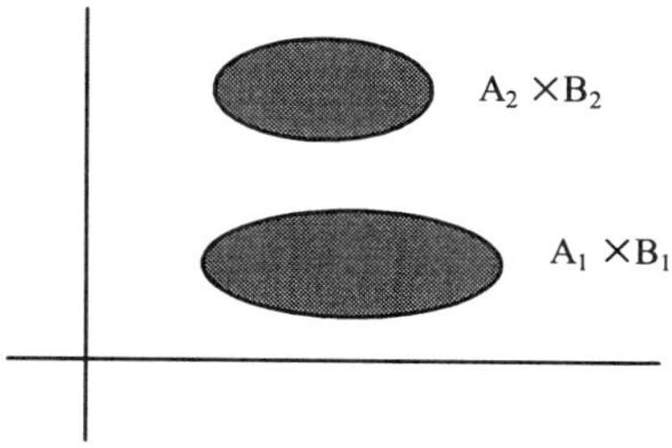

Figure 11. Two associations and rule induction

Here we have two associations: $A_1 \times B_1$ and $A_2 \times B_2$. When converted into rules of the form "if A_i then B_i " then these rules are in conflict. Noticeably, the same associations when converted into rules "if B_i then A_i " do not exhibit a conflict. To measure the level of conflict, we first have to express similarity (or difference) between two fuzzy relations. There are numerous ways of completing this task. By referring to the literature on fuzzy sets, the reader may encounter a long list of methods. The basic selection criteria would involve efficiency of the method as well as its computational overhead. In what follows, we endorse the possibility measure as a vehicle quantifying the similarity between two fuzzy sets or relations. In essence, the possibility describes a degree of overlap between two fuzzy sets. The computations are direct. For example, while discussing two parabolic fuzzy sets A = P(x; a,m,b) and B= P(x; c,n,d) where m < n, the level of matching is expressed in the form, see also Figure 12.

$$\mathrm{Poss}(A, B) = \begin{cases} 0, \text{ if } c > b \\ 1, \text{ if } m = n \\ 3/4 \text{ if } m = b \\ 1 - \left(\dfrac{x_0 - b}{m - b}\right)^2 \text{ if } m < c < b; \text{ here } x_0 = \dfrac{n(b-m) + b(n-c)}{n - m + b - c} \end{cases}$$

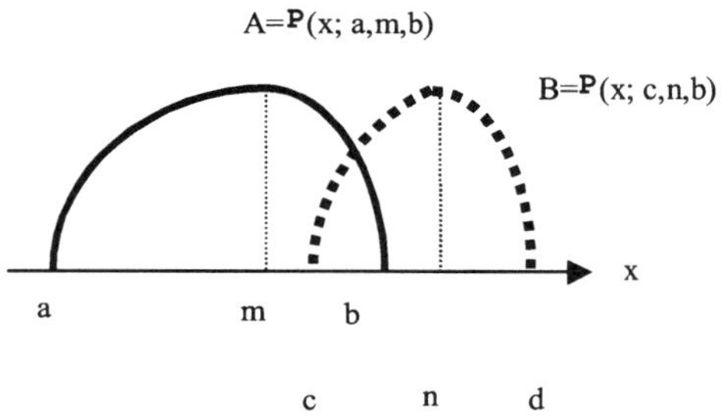

Figure 12. Computing values of the possibility measure Poss(A, B) for two parabolic fuzzy sets A and B

Subsequently, the possibility of the two fuzzy relations $A_1 \times B_1$ and $A_2 \times B_2$ read as

$$\text{Poss}(A_1 \times B_1, A_1 \times B_1) = (\text{Poss}(A_1, A_2)t\text{Poss}(B_1, B_2))$$

so the computations are straightforward as we take a t-norm over the coordinates of the fuzzy relation. Now moving to the consistency of the rules, we can distinguish the following general situations as to the similarity of the conditions and the conclusions of some potential rules, see Table 1.

Table 1. Four general cases of similarity levels between conditions and conclusions of two rules along with their consistency

Conditions	Conclusions	Consistency of rules
similar	different	**inconsistent**
similar	similar	consistent
different	similar	consistent
different	different	consistent

The above scenarios suggest that a plausible consistency index of the two rules can be based on the fuzzy implication

$$\text{Cons(rule-1, rule-2)} = \text{Poss}(A_1 \times B_1, A_1 \times B_1) \Rightarrow \text{Poss}(C_1, C_2) \quad (8)$$

Where " $\Rightarrow$ " denotes a fuzzy implication (residuation operation) defined in the following way

$$a \Rightarrow b = \sup\{c \in [0,1] \mid atc \le b\} \quad (9)$$

where "t" stands for some continuous t-norm. Linking the general formula (9) with the qualitative analysis shown before, it becomes apparent that the values of the consistency index, Cons(., .) attains higher values for lower values of the possibility observed for the condition part and higher values for the matching realized at the conclusion part.

The multidimensional form of the consistency reads as

Cons (rule-1, rule-2) =
= Poss(condition part of -1, condition part of -2) $\Rightarrow$ Poss(conclusion part -1, conclusion part -2) (10)

where the condition part and conclusion part involve the Cartesian products of the information granules of the attributes placed in the condition and conclusion parts of the rules.

So far, we have investigated the two rules. Obviously, when dealing with a collection of associations (and rules afterwards), we would like to gather a global view as to the consistency of the given rule with regard to the rest of the rules. A systematic way of dealing with the problem is to arrange consistency values into a form of a consistency matrix **C** having N rows and N columns (as we are concerned with "N" associations). The (i,j) th entry of this matrix denotes a level of consistency of these two rules. The matrix is symmetrical with all diagonal entries being equal to to 1. As a matter of fact, it is enough to compute the lower half of the matrix. The overall consistency of the ith rule is captured by the average of the entries of the ith column (or row) of **C**,

$$\mathrm{Cons}(i, \mathbf{D}) = \frac{1}{N}\sum_{j=1}^{N} c_{ij} \tag{11}$$

This gives rise to the linear order of the consistency of the rules. This arrangement helps us convert only a portion of the associations into rules while retaining the rest of them as direction-free constructs. What we end up, is a mixture of heterogeneous constructs as illustrated in Figure 13.

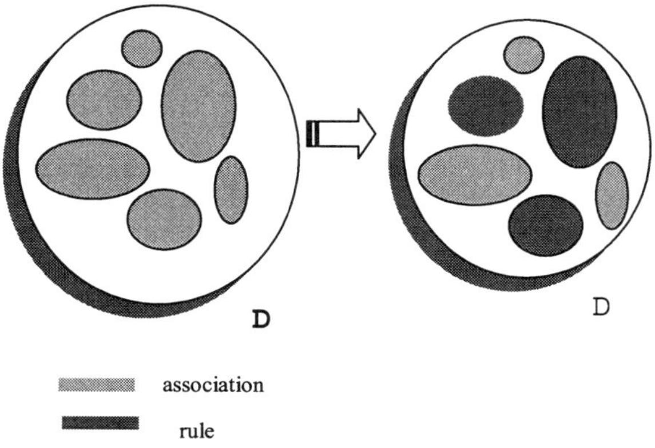

Figure 13. By selecting highly consistent rules, the result of data mining is a mixture of associations and rules

Obviously, by lowering the threshold level (viz. accepting less consistent rules), more associations can be elevated to the position of rules.

An interesting question arises to the quality of rules and an ability of converting associations into rules.

7. PROPERTIES OF RULES INDUCED BY ASSOCIATIONS

How to produce more rules out of associations and make these rules more consistent? There is a lot of flexibility in answering this question. The rules may have a different number of conditions and conclusions. Some attributes can be dropped and not showing up in the rules. To illustrate the point, consider the associations involving four attributes, namely

$$A_i \times B_i \times C_i \times D_i \tag{12}$$

The following are general observations (they come from the interpretation of the consistency index (11) we adhere to)

the increasing number of attributes in the condition part promotes higher consistency of the rules. That is, the rules

- if A_i and B_i and C_i then D_i

are more consistent than the rules in which the first attribute has been dropped, say

- if B_i and C_i then D_i

This is easy to see in light of the main properties of the implication operation that is

$$atb \Rightarrow c \geq a \Rightarrow c \qquad a, b, c \in [0,1].$$

The drop in the number of attributes in the condition part contributes to the rules that tend to be more *general*, i.e., they apply to a broad spectrum of situations. Adding more conditions, we make rules more *specific* (viz. they are appropriate for a smaller number of cases).The increased generality of the rules comes hand in hand with their elevated level of inconsistency.

Interestingly, the analysis of the consistency of the overall set of rules (say, by determining the sum of all entries of **C**, say $\Delta = \sum_{i,j} c_{ij}$) brings us to the examination of the relevance of the attributes: if dropping a certain attribute from the condition part does not reduce the values of Δ then the attribute may be regarded as irrelevant. The more evident reduction in Δ linked with the elimination of the given attribute, the more essential this attribute is. This corresponds to the well-known problem of feature selection in pattern recognition [10]. The difference here lies in the fact that the discriminatory properties of a given attribute are quantified not for the attribute itself but a manifestation of this property is determined for the assumed level of granularity (that is the number of fuzzy sets defined there). In other words, if the granularity of the attribute has been changed (say, by increasing the number of information granules therein), it may happen that its discriminatory properties could be affected as well.

By removing attributes from the conclusion part (for the fixed number of attributes in the condition part), the rules become more consistent. Again, by following the definition of inconsistency, this tendency becomes evident as we have

$$atb \Rightarrow ctd \leq a \Rightarrow c$$

The finding concurs with our intuition: by removing more attributes, the conclusions tend to become less "disjoint" thus reducing the level of potential inconsistency. In principle, the rule becomes less specific (viz. it supports more general conclusions).

One should stress that the above analysis is carried out for the fixed associations. In particular, we have not affected the granularity of the original information granules. The size of information granules may substantially affect the consistency of the resulting rules.

8. DETAILED COMPUTATIONS OF THE CONSISTENCY OF RULES AND ITS ANALYSIS

The way in which information granules have been constructed (that is a method in which they are organized along each attribute) reduce vastly the amount of computing. First, the possibility measure is computed almost instantaneously for triangular (T) and parabolic (P) membership functions.

Consider two triangular fuzzy sets A and B; the following three cases hold

A and B are the same; the possibility is equal to 1

The supports of A and B are disjoint; the possibility is equal to 0

The supports of A and B overlap. Then the overlap is equal to 1/2 and the possibility measure equals (1/2) t (1/2). The result depends on the t-norm being used. For the minimum, Poss(A, B)=1/2. The product operator yields the possibility value equal to 0.25, Poss(A,B)=0.25

Similarly, when dealing with parabolic membership functions, the two first cases are identical as before. For the overlapping supports, one can compute that the overlap is equal to 3/4. Subsequently, the possibility is equal to (3/4) t (3/4).

Now, proceeding with "r" dimensional fuzzy relations A and B rather than fuzzy sets, the values of the possibility measure assumes discrete values. The lowest one is equal to zero, the highest is equal to 1. The intermediate values of the possibility measure Poss(A,B) are equal to a, ata, atata,..., atat...ta (r-times). In these cases, for the product t-norm, Poss(A,B) = a^r (a=1/2 for the triangular fuzzy sets and a=3/4 for the parabolic fuzzy sets). Taking these findings into account, the consistency of the rule with "p" condition parts and "r" conclusion parts assumes the following values (here we consider the implication induced by the product t-norm, that is $a \Rightarrow b = \min(1, b/a), a, b \in [0,1]$)

$\{0, a^{II}, 1, II=1, 2, \ldots, p\} \Rightarrow \{0, a^{JJ}, JJ=1,2,\ldots,r\} = \{0, a^{JJ-II}, 1\}$

The use of the above form of the implication operation, we derive the set of consistency values

$0, \ldots a^{JJ-II}, \ldots 1$

It is noticeable that the consistency of the two rules reveals a direct relationship between the level of consistency regarded as the function of the number of condition and conclusion parts. For II=p and JJ=r, the consistency becomes a power function of the difference r-p.

The level of conflict between two rules can be quantified in more detail. Consider that the overlap level between two fuzzy sets is equal to "a". For two one-dimensional granules, we may have three options as to the values of their overlap

- no overlap (0)
- overlap (a)
- coincidence (two fuzzy sets are identical) (1)

If we consider the number of conditions equal to "p" then the have the following values of the overlap between two fuzzy relations (we assume that all fuzzy sets are the same)

$0, a^p, a^{p-1}, \ldots, a^2, a, 1$

If the conclusion part of this rule has "r" coordinates (fuzzy sets) the overlap is expressed as

$0, a^r, a^{r-1}, \ldots, a^2, a, 1$

In the sequel, the level of conflict expressed in the form of the residuation operation reads as

$$P \Rightarrow Q = \{0, a^p, a^{p-1}, \ldots, a^2, a, 1\} \Rightarrow \{0, a^r, a^{r-1}, \ldots, a^2, a, 1\}$$

Furthermore if we confine ourselves to the specific form of the residuation, more detailed calculations can be carried out. For instance, let us use the following form of the above operation $\alpha \Rightarrow \beta = \min(1, \beta/\alpha)$. Then

$$P \Rightarrow Q = \begin{cases} a^{r-p} \text{if} \quad r \geq p \\ 0, \text{otherwise} \end{cases}$$

And the consistency level becomes a power function of the difference r-p. Noticeably, when "r" increases, the level of consistency gets lower. And conversely, if "r" gets closer to "p" then the consistency level increases.

So far, we have not looked into a relationship between the number of information granules and the consistency of the rules (or the level of overlap between fuzzy sets). To get a better insight into the quantitative aspect of this effect, one should emphasize that the consistency is directly linked with the overlap between the fuzzy sets. Referring to the distribution of the information granules, three cases are distinguished
two granules are the same (coincide)
two granules are adjacent (overlap)
two granules are disjoint (zero overlap)
Considering "n" fuzzy sets, each case comes with its probability. A simple analysis reveals that these probabilities equal to (recall that the total number of different arrangements of two information granules out of "n" is equal to n' =n(n+1)/2)

Prob(two granules are the same) = n/n' = 2/(n+1)
Prob(two granules are adjacent) = 2(n-1)/[n(n+1)]
Prob(two granules are disjoint) = [n(n-3)+2]/[n(n+1)]

Hence it becomes intuitively obvious that when the number of granules goes up, the first two probabilities decrease and the third one increases.

In general, we encounter two modes of evaluation of rule consistency
Data implicit This is the one discussed above. The evaluation of the consistency (the consistency index) does not take the experimental data into consideration directly but rather implicitly as they have already been used in the construction of the information granules.
Data explicit Here we use the data, say a point (x,y) explicitly in the calculations of the expression

$\text{Poss}(A_1(x), A_2(x))$ $\text{Poss}(B_1(y), B_2(y))$

This formula is afterwards averaged over all data. Depending on the data distribution, the consistency of the rule can vary. In other words, we may refer to this definition as data-driven consistency of rules. Following this way, it provides us with some insight into the relationship between data, refer to Figure 14. To maintain the consistency equal to 1, the following relationship should hold

$$\text{Min}(\alpha, 1-\alpha) \quad \text{Min}(\beta, 1-\beta)$$

meaning that "x" should be closer to the crossing (overlap) point of A_1 and A_2 than "y" in the case of B_1 and B_2.

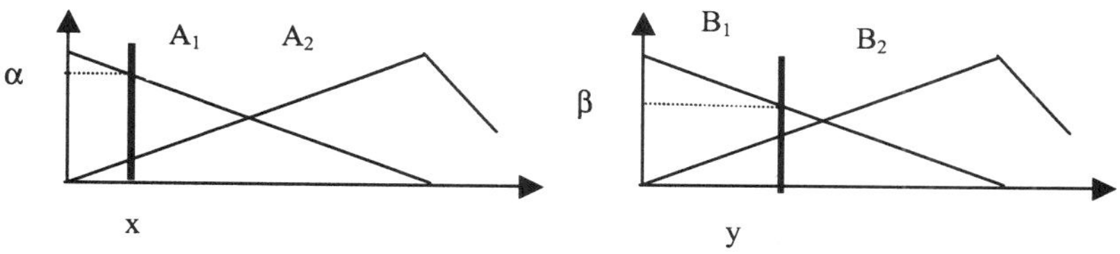

Figure 14. Data explicit computing the consistency of two rules for data point (x, y)

9. CONCLUSIONS

We have discussed the idea of information granulation realized with the aid of fuzzy sets and developed a complete algorithmic framework that helps reveal patterns in databases. The study makes a clear distinction between associations and rules by showing that rules are simply directional constructs that originate from associations. More importantly, as any prior commitment to directionality between variables in databases could be too restrictive, the search for associations does make sense while jumping into the formation of rules could be dangerously premature. By the same token, one should become aware that exploiting standard techniques of model identification and rule-based systems in data mining and endorsing them without any hesitation, as the algorithmic skeleton there is too limited and somewhat biased. In simple systems, the direction between variables is in general quite straightforward and could be done just up front the entire design process. When databases include data about phenomena for which the input - output specification is not obvious at all, one should proceed with associations first and then try to refine them in the form of the rules. It is also likely that we may end up with the heterogeneous topology of a mixture of associations and rules.

ACKNOWLEDGMENT

The support from the Natural Sciences and Engineering Research Council of Canada (NSERC) and ASERC (Alberta Software Engineering Research Consortium) is gratefully acknowledged.

REFERENCES

1. R. Agrawal, T. Imielinski, A. Swami, Database mining: a performance perspective, IEEE Transactions on Knowledge and Data Engineering, 5, 1993, 914-925.
2. J. Buckley, Y. Hayashi, Fuzzy neural networks: a survey, *Fuzzy Sets and Systems*, 66, 1994, 1-14.
3. K. Cios, W.Pedrycz, R. Swiniarski, *Data Mining Techniques*, Kluwer Academic Publishers, Boston, 1998.
4. J. Chattratichat, Large scale data mining: challenges and responses, In: *Proc. 3rd Int. Conf. on Knowledge Discovery and Data Mining*, Newport Beach, CA, August, 14-17, 1997, pp.143-146.
5. B.S. Everitt, Cluster Analysis, Heinemann, Berlin, 1974.
6. C.J. Harris, C.G. Moore, M. Brown, *Intelligent Control - Aspects of Fuzzy Logic and Neural Nets,* World Scientific, Singapore, 1993.
7. D.O. Hebb, *The Organization of Behavior: A Neuropsychological Theory*, J. Wiley, N. York, 1949.
8. P.J. Huber, From large to huge: a statistician's reaction to KDD and DM, In: *Proc. 3rd Int. Conf. on Knowledge Discovery and Data Mining*, Newport Beach, CA, August 14-17, 1997, pp.304-308.
9. J. S. R Jang, C.T. Sun, E. Mizutani, *Neuro-Fuzzy and Soft Computing*, Prentice Hall, Upper Saddle River, NJ, 1997.
10. A. Kandel, *Fuzzy Mathematical Techniques with Applications*, Addison-Wesley, Reading, MA, 1986.
11. N. Kasabov, *Foundations of Neural Networks, Fuzzy Systems, and Knowledge Engineering*, MIT Press, Cambridge, MA, 1996.
12. L. Kaufman and P.J. Rousseeuw, Finding Groups in Data, J. Wiley, New York, 1990.
13. Z. Pawlak, Rough Sets: Theoretical Aspects of Reasoning about Data, Kluwer Academic, Dordrecht, 1991.
14. W. Pedrycz, *Computational Intelligence: An Introduction*, CRC Press, Boca Raton, FL, 1997.
15. W. Pedrycz, F. Gomide, *An Introduction to Fuzzy Sets*, Cambridge, MIT Press, Cambridge, MA, 1998.
16. W. Pedrycz, M.H. Smith, Granular correlation analysis in data mining, *Proc. 18th Int Conf of the North American Fuzzy Information Processing Society (NAFIPS),* New York, June 1-12, 1999, pp. 715-719.
17. W. Pedrycz, E. Roventa, From fuzzy information processing to fuzzy communication channels, *Kybernetes*, vol. 28, no.5, 1999, 515-527.
18. W. Pedrycz, Fuzzy set technology in knowledge discovery, *Fuzzy Sets and Systems*, 3, 1998, 279-290.

19. W. Pedrycz, Shadowed sets: representing and processing fuzzy sets, *IEEE Trans. on Systems, Man, and Cybernetics, part B*, 28, 1998, 103-109.
20. Pedrycz, W. Vukovich, G. (1999) Quantification of fuzzy mappings: a relevance of rule-based architectures, *Proc. 18th Int Conf of the North American Fuzzy Information Processing Society (NAFIPS)*, New York, June 1-12, pp. 105-109.
21. G. Piatetsky-Shapiro and W. J. Frawley, editors. "Knowledge Discovery in Databases", AAAI Press, Menlo Park, California, 1991.
22. J. R. Quinlan, "Induction of Decision Trees", Machine Learning 1, 1, 81-106, 1986.
23. J. R. Quinlan, "C4.5: Programs for Machine Learning", Morgan Kaufmann Publishers, San Mateo, California, 1993.

24 R. Sutton, A. Barto, Toward a modern theory of adaptive networks: expectations and predictions, *Psychological Review*, 88, 1981, 2, 135-170.

24. H. Toivonen, Sampling large databases for association rules. In: Proc. 22nd Int. Conf. on Very Large Databases, 1996, 134-145.
25. L.H. Tsoukalas, R.E. Uhrig, *Fuzzy and Neural Approaches in Engineering*, J. Wiley, New York, 1997.
26. R. R. Yager, Entropy and specificity in a mathematical theory of evidence. Int. J. Gen. Syst., 9, 1983, 249-260.
27. K. Yoda, T. Fukuda, Y. Morimoto, Computing optimized rectilinear regions for association rules, In: Proc. 3rd Int. Conf. on Knowledge Discovery and Data Mining, Newport Beach, CA, August 14-17, 1997, pp.96-103.
28. J. Wnek and R. S. Michalski, "Conceptual Transition from Logic to Arithmetic in Concept Learning", Reports of Machine Learning and Inference Laboratory, MLI 94-7, Center for MLI, George Mason University, December 1994.
29. L. A Zadeh, Fuzzy sets and information granularity, In: M.M. Gupta, R.K. Ragade, R.R. Yager, eds., *Advances in Fuzzy Set Theory and Applications*, North Holland, Amsterdam, 1979, 3-18.
30. L. A. Zadeh, Fuzzy logic = Computing with words, *IEEE Trans. on Fuzzy Systems*, vol. 4, 2, 1996, 103-111.
31. L. A. Zadeh, Toward a theory of fuzzy information granulation and its centrality in human reasoning and fuzzy logic, *Fuzzy Sets and Systems*, 90, 1997, 111-117.

Chapter 13

DEALING WITH DIMENSIONS IN DATA WAREHOUSING

Jaroslav Pokorny
Department of Software Engineering
Faculty of Mathematics and Physics
Malostranské nam. 25
118 00 Prague - Czech Republic
Phone: 00420/2/21914256
Fax: 00420/2/21914323
e-mail: pokorny@ksi.ms.mff.cuni.cz

Keywords: data warehouse, multidimensional modelling, star schema, constellation schema, dimension table, fact table, ISA-hierarchy, dimension hierarchy, join tree

Abstract: In this paper we present a new approach to the notion of dimension in data warehouses modelling. Based on a four-level architecture, a model of dimension and fact tables is considered. A variant of the constellation schema with explicit dimension hierarchies is studied in detail. A dimension hierarchy *H* is extended to contain ISA-hierarchies built as specializations of *H* members. Derived tables can be created by restrictions on attributes of *H* members. Some graph-theoretic properties of *H* are formulated and the correctness of derived table definitions is discussed. As a consequence, the relationship of a correct derivation of tables to so-called join trees known from relational theory is shown. The same principles of correctness testing are applicable on specifications of views over dimensions as well as on queries over DWs designed as constellations with explicit dimension hierarchies.

1. INTRODUCTION

As with other databases, a design of any data warehouse (DW) requires certain modelling stages. Since DW prepares the data for analytical processing, which requires multidimensionality, it seems to be suitable to use a multidimensional model. On the other hand, data sources that serve as input into DW are usually described by E-R schemes on the conceptual level. We will follow the approach given by McGuff (McGuff, 1996) in which the multidimensional modelling for DW makes a separate design stage. It is placed between the business (or conceptual) modelling and the representation (or database) modelling. Then we distinguish

- conceptual modelling,
- multidimensional modelling,
- representation modelling,
- physical modelling.

The conceptual view will cover the aspects of data, which express its associations to real world objects, while the multidimensional view reflects multidimensional requirements on data. We prefer multidimensional or shortly dimensional modelling (DM) based on dimension and fact tables[1]. The representation of facts and dimensions will involve their database description. Finally, in the physical modelling we are interested in indexing, and other implementation aspects, of the database representation of DW. In (Pokorny, 1998) we discussed these stages in detail including a number of necessary algorithms. It is important to remember that the first two stages are often not distinguished and E-R modelling is mixed with DM in one stage (see, e.g., Golfarelli, Maio, and Rizzi, 1998).

With dimension and fact tables it is possible to build more complex data structures like star schemes, constellations etc (e.g. Raden, 1995; Raden, 1996; Kimball, 1996; Kimball, 1997)[2]. The simple star scheme structure, as is popular in the DW community, does not seem to be very flexible and user-friendly in more complicated situations. Structurally complex dimensions are not expressible in these approaches. Moreover, most of the approaches use only intuitive notions with no connection to any powerful query language.

On the other hand, a number of formal dimensional models are at our disposal. We can name the tabular model (Gyssens, Lakshmanan, and

[1] An alternative approach is based on multidimensional cubes (Agrawal, Gupta, and Sarawagi, 1995; Buytendijk, 1996).

[2] A nice survey of various approaches can be found in (Pedersen and Jensen, 1999).

Subramanian, 1996), dimensional model (Li and Wang, 1996) based on cubes and relations, nested dimensional model (Lehner, 1998), the model using attribute trees (Golfarelli, Maio, and Rizzi, 1998), MD model (Cabibbo and Torlone, 1998) etc. None of the mentioned models allows us to model more complex dimensions. We will show examples in which ISA hierarchies of dimension members are useful.

From the conceptual level point of view, dimensions are not only classifications but also regular entity types organized in hierarchies. Based on the formal model developed in (Pokorny, 1998), we present a data structure, called a constellation schema, with explicit dimension hierarchies. This notion generalizes a well-known snowflakes (Raden, 1996). We argue that it is an appropriate framework that offers users a sufficient amount of semantics. These semantics can be used e.g. for clear and correct querying DW.

The paper continues to develop a sound mechanism for deriving tables and their organization in ISA-hierarchies. A motivation for this design decision is determined by the requirement to distinguish two entity types by different attributes. Each of these attributes is applicable only for a specialized entity type. We use a language of easy Boolean expressions for deriving new tables. Although simple, the language is sensitive to the dimension hierarchy structure. This requires appropriate formal conditions for testing the correctness of these table definitions. The same principles of correctness testing are applicable for specifications of views over dimensions as well as for queries over DWs designed as constellations with explicit dimension hierarchies.

In Section 2 we present DM based on the notions of facts, dimensions, and attributes. The notion of a star schema is informally introduced there. In Section 3 various approaches to dimensions are discussed and a simple taxonomy of dimension hierarchies is given. The popular notions of rolling up and drilling down are formulated via functions. Section 4 is devoted to the definition of constellation schemes. First we extend the notion of the star schema to the star schema with explicit dimension hierarchies. Then we define a constellation schema with explicit dimension hierarchies. The core of the paper is presented in Section 5. Hierarchies of tables are defined and possibilities of deriving new tables are discussed. Some conditions about how to ensure their correctness are shown. In Section 6 we discuss some conclusions concerning other generalization of dimensions and a relationship of our approach to querying DW.

2. DW MODELLING WITH TABLES

Informally, a *DM-schema* is a description of *dimension* and *fact tables*. An associated diagram is called *DM-diagram*. A variant of this approach is called *star schema*, i.e. the case with one fact table surrounded by dimension tables (see Figure 1). Each dimension table has a single-part primary key that corresponds exactly to one of the components of the multi-part key in the fact table. Dimension attributes are used as a source of constraints usable in DW queries. A *fact* is a focus of interest for the enterprise. It is modelled by values of non-key attributes in the fact table that functionally depend on the set of key attributes. Each fact is "measured" by values of a tuple of dimension values.

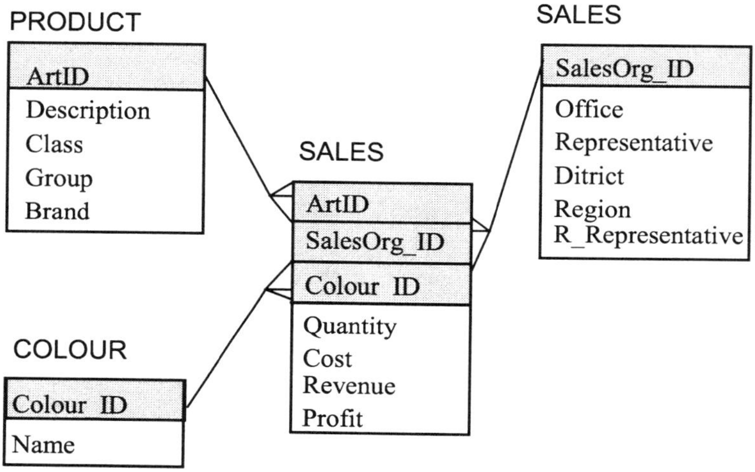

Figure 1: Star schema as a result of the dimensional modelling

Following (Pokorny, 1998) a *star schema* is given by a triple $<\boldsymbol{D}, F, \boldsymbol{CC}>$, where $\boldsymbol{D}$ is a set of *dimension table schemes* D_i with attributes Ω_i, $i=1,\ldots,n$, F is a *fact table schema*, and $\boldsymbol{CC}$ is a set of cardinality constraints. One attribute from Ω_i is called the *key of D_i table* and is denoted as KD_i. The *key of F table* is $\cup_{i=1..n} KD_i$[3]. Other (non-key) attributes of F are usually called *facts*[4].

We use upper letters D, F, ... for table schemes and D^*, F^*, ... for tables. Then the *cardinality constraint* CC_i for F and D_i, $i=1\ldots,n$, is defined as

[3] No functional dependencies are supposed among dimensions.

[4] This often-used terminology is not precise. Facts must be always logically connected with a determinant on which they depend. Here, the key of F table plays its role.

follows. Let F^* and D_i^* be a fact and a dimension table, respectively. The cardinality constraint CC_i is *satisfied* by these tables, when for each row u from F^* there is only one row v in D_i^*, such that

$$u.KD_i = v.KD_i$$

Informally, rows of the fact table and of its any dimension table are in many-to-one relationship. In Figure 1 the well-known crow's feet notation is used for a graphical expressing this statement. In more precise notation, we could express it with the min-max pairs as

$$<F:(1,1), D_i:(0,n)>$$

i.e., some rows from D_i^* need not be associated with any row from F^*. Thus, dimensions are independent on facts, facts can not exist without dimensions. Cardinality constraints also imply an expected observation that each *KD* is a foreign key in *F*.

A *multidimensional database, S^*, over a star schema S* is a set of tables D_i^*, $i=1,\ldots,n$, and F^* that satisfy all cardinality constraints from ***CC***.

This simple environment is not always sufficient for any situation. Sometimes it is necessary to rename key attributes in *F*, i.e. *role names* are needed. A more general approach considers more star schemes at the multidimensional level. Then we obtain so-called *multi-star* or, better said a *constellation schema*. Thus, dimensions are shared, i.e. one dimension table schema can be common for more fact table schemes.

3. DIMENSIONS

In most cases, a dimension consists of multiple hierarchically structured classifications based on a set of basic values. In a DW, a dimension represents the granularity adopted for representing facts (Golfarelli, Maio, and Rizzi, 1998). An element of a dimension could be conceived as a set of tuples, whose components describe an object, on which facts depend. For example, a sale organization is described as (MIC1, Idaho, North) with meaning "the office MIC1 in the district Lublin in the region North".

However, the semantics of a dimension may be deeper. We would like to store, e.g. the information, that the representative of the region North is Smith. Thus, dimensions are described by attributes, some of which are descriptive, e.g. Description, Name, within the others, business-oriented, enterprise-specific *dimension hierarchies* may be included, e.g. PRODUCT: Item → Class → Group → Area. An important dimension is TIME structured, e.g., as date → month → quarter → year. Other attribute hierarchy is SALES_ORGANIZATION: office → district → region → state. Attributes in a dimension hierarchy are called *members* of the hierarchy. It seems that for purposes of DW modelling this approach is not appropriate. For example, in (Lehner, 1998) the lowest member of the hierarchy has to be a primary attribute and the remaining hierarchy members are so-called *classification attributes*. The problem is to which objects to assign other attributes such as a representative of a region (R_representative) etc. These attributes are called *dimension attributes* usually.

On the conceptual level, particular members of each dimension hierarchy are sets of entities. They make it possible to define chains of entity types, where the cardinality of the relationship for each two neighbours is 1:N in top-down direction (see Figure 2).

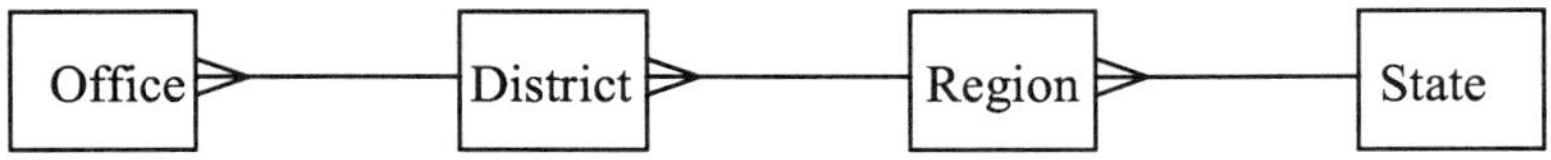

Figure 2. A dimension hierarchy as a chain of entities

3.1 Taxonomy of dimension hierarchies

Similarly to the general object or entity modelling, some hierarchies can be multiple in one dimension. The TIME dimension provides a good example. In fact, the hierarchy date → week is a separate branch of the TIME hierarchy mentioned above. As it is shown in (McGuff, 1996), more structural possibilities are usable in practice. In figure 3, three hierarchy types are shown. In a *simple hierarchy*, the members compose a path in a directed graph. An *alternated hierarchy* contains at least one member with two (ore more) ancestors, but each hierarchy member has at most one predecessor. The third possibility allows the alternate hierarchy to release the restriction. We call such hierarchies *converging*.[5]

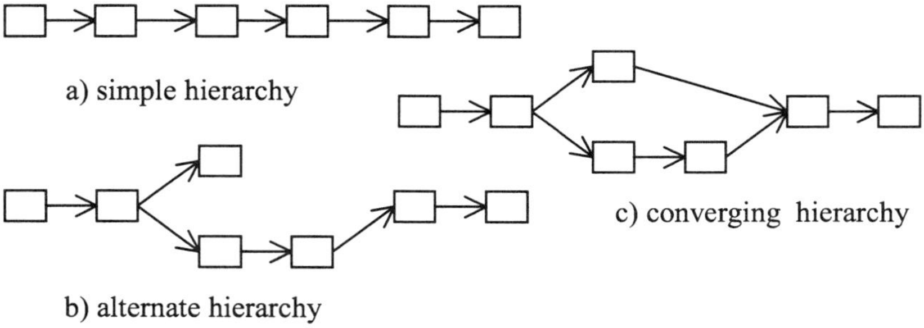

Figure 3. Types of dimension hierarchies

[5] In [McG96] the notion of cyclic hierarchy is used. We do not prefer it because it is confusing in the context of hierarchies.

Remark: In (McGuff, 1996) a resolution of converging hierarchies into simple or alternate ones is recommended and proposed. We do not follow this way.

The notion of a dimension hierarchy can be now formalized as follows.

Definition 1 (Dimension Hierarchy): Consider a set $\boldsymbol{D}$ of dimension table schemes D_i with attributes Ω_i, i=1,...,n. Then a *dimension hierarchy H* is a subset of $\boldsymbol{D} \times \boldsymbol{D}$ or $\{D\}$, $D \in \boldsymbol{D}$, with the following properties:

(a) H is a rooted DAG[6]. *(directed acyclic graph)*

(b) If $(D_j, D_k) \in H$, KD_k is the key of D_k, then KD_k is also an attribute of D_j. *(referential integrity)*

We can observe from the condition (b) that KD_j in D_i is again a foreign key in the same sense as in the connection of a dimension table to a fact table. The condition (a) implies acyclicity of each hierarchy and the existence of its unique root. The root of H plays a significant role. Actually, facts in a fact table are usually dependent on data stored in root tables. By $\boldsymbol{D}_H$ we denote the set of dimension tables occurring in H. Contrary to e.g. (Jagadish, Lakshmanan, and Srivastava, 1999) we do not introduce a special identification attribute for members of the hierarchy.

In practice it is useful to name dimension hierarchies (see e.g. PRODUCT, TIME etc). Then we write N:H, where N is the name of H. If H is a simple hierarchy, we can write N: $D_1 \rightarrow \ldots \rightarrow D_k$.

3.2 Rolling up and drilling down

The hierarchical structure of dimension tables allows easy specification of the well-known notion of rolling up and drilling down. We use some graph-oriented notions for this purpose.

Definition 2 (Path): A *path* in a dimension hierarchy H is a sequence $<D_{i1},...,D_{ik}>$, $k > 1$, where

- $(D_{ij}, D_{i(j+1)}) \in H$, j=$1$,...,$k$-1,

If D_{i1} is the root of H then we will refer to the path as a *rooted path*. The nodes D_1 and D_k of a path are called *start* node and *end* node, respectively. For the path $<D_1,D_2,...,D_k>$, we denote it P, any path $<D_1,D_2,...,D_t>$, where $t \le k$, is called a *prefix* of P. Similarly, $<D_{t+1},D_2,...,D_k>$, where $0 \le t$, is called *suffix* of P. Two paths are *meeting* if they have the same end node.

The condition (b) in Definition 1 allows us to state the following definitions. Consider a path $<D_1,...,D_k>$ in H and the couple (D_j, D_{j+1}), where $1 \le j < k$. Then we say that D_j *rolls up* to D_{j+1} and D_{j+1} *drills down* to D_j. The functional dependency $KD_j \rightarrow KD_{j+1}$ in the table D_j induces a *roll-up*

[6] In (Golfarelli and Rizzi, 1998) this structure is called a *quasi-tree*.

function. This function is total and injective. Its domain is D^*_j and range D^*_{j+1}. In fact, to each row in D^*_j there exists a row in D^*_{j+1} with the same value of KD_{j+1}. Roll-up functions provide a useful tool for querying multidimensional databases. We will use a generalization of roll-up functions defined in the following way.

Let $<D_1,...,D_k>$ be a path in a dimension hierarchy H and f_j be the roll-up function induced by the couple (D_j, D_{j+1}), for each $j \in <1, k\text{-}1>$. We call such roll-up function *simple*. The *composed roll-up functions* are obtainable by the conventional composition operation. Therefore, each roll-up function is either simple or composed. It is easy to see, that for each couple (D_s, D_t), $1 \leq s < t \leq k$, there is the unique induced roll-up function. We denote it f_{st}. Due to their transitivity, it is natural to extend relations roll up and drill down to their transitive closures. Drilling down possibilities are not discussed here. Their semantics could be expressed using roll-up functions.

4. CONSTELLATIONS

We will use explicit hierarchies in constellation schemes. This approach has several of advantages. First, dimensions are structurally visible in the schema. Second, different fact tables are explicitly assigned to those dimensions, which are for given facts relevant.

Definition 3 (Star Schema with Explicit Dimension Hierarchies): Let $\boldsymbol{H}$ be a non-empty set of dimension hierarchies and $\boldsymbol{D}_F$ be the set of its hierarchy roots. A *star schema with explicit dimension hierarchies* is a triple $<\boldsymbol{H}, F, \boldsymbol{CC}>$, such that $<\boldsymbol{D}_F, F, \boldsymbol{CC}>$ is a star schema.

If we consider simple hierarchies we obtain well-known *snowflaking* (Raden, 1996). Our strategy is to extend the star schema with explicit hierarchies in two steps. A natural extension of Definition 3 tends to a constellation schema with explicit dimension hierarchies (Pokorny, 1998; Pokorny, 1999a). There, fact tables model facts on the lowest level of aggregation. Further extension introduces ISA-hierarchies into the explicit dimension hierarchies (Pokorny, 1999b).

Definition 4 (Constellation Schema with Explicit Dimension Hierarchies): Let $\boldsymbol{F}$ be a non-empty set of *fact table schemes*, $\boldsymbol{H}$ a non-empty set of dimension hierarchies, and $\boldsymbol{CC}$ a non-empty set of cardinality constraints. A *constellation schema with explicit dimension hierarchies* is a triple $<\boldsymbol{F}, \boldsymbol{H}, \boldsymbol{CC}>$, such that

- for each fact table F from $\boldsymbol{F}$, there are subsets $\boldsymbol{H}_F \subseteq \boldsymbol{H}$ and $\boldsymbol{CC}_F \subseteq \boldsymbol{CC}$, such that $<\boldsymbol{H}_F, F, \boldsymbol{CC}_F>$ is a star schema with explicit dimension hierarchies; (*star structure*)

- $\boldsymbol{CC} = \cup_{F \in \mathbf{F}} \boldsymbol{CC}_F$ (*constraint completeness*)

An example of a star schema with explicit dimension hierarchies is depicted in Figure 4. Two dimension hierarchies are visible there: SALES_ORGANIZATION: OFFICE → DISTRICT → REGION and PRODUCT: PRODUCT→ CLASS → GROUP.

A *multidimensional database S^* over a constellation schema with explicit hierarchies S* is a set of dimension and fact tables that satisfy all cardinality constraints from ***CC***.

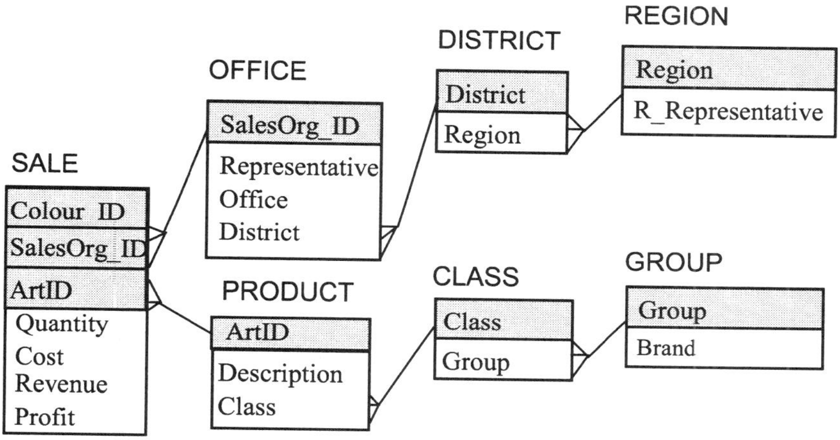

Figure 4: A part of star schema with explicit dimension hierarchies

In summary, the DM includes the principle to express dimension hierarchies both implicitly (Figure 1) and explicitly (Figure 4). Our definition of the constellation schema with explicit dimension hierarchies makes it possible to model fact tables over various members of dimension hierarchies. An extension of this approach by so-called *query constraints* is described in (Pokorny, 1999b).

5. DIMENSION HIERARCHIES WITH ISA-HIERARCHIES

A natural extension of the notion of dimension hierarchy is the introduction of ISA-hierarchies (in Pokorny, 1999b). In a convenient entity framework we can distinguish two possibilities how to do it.

First, an entity type can be specialized into subtypes. If the entity type and its subtype are E and E_1, respectively, then we write, as usually,

E_1 ISA E.

The containment relation ($\subseteq$) holds between the associated entity type extensions E^*_1 and E^*. Therefore, the containment $\subseteq$ of entity sets is an inherent integrity constraint for the ISA relation.

Second, we can derive new entity types from the old ones. Then, the type specification of an entity subtype E_1 may be done by an explicit integrity constraint on the original entity type E.

In both cases there is a possibility to specify additional dimension attributes for new entity sets. For example, only video equipment (as a subclass of PRODUCT) has the attribute VideoSys.

5.1 ISA-hierarchies of tables

In the framework of dimension tables we manipulate tables and not entity types. Under the assumption of one-to-one correspondence between entity types and table schemes, we can use the same notation.

Definition 5 (**ISA_T Constraint**): Let $D(\Omega)$ be a dimension table schema and $D_1(\Omega_1)$ be a table schema with $\Omega \subset \Omega_1$. We will now define *ISA_T constraint* on D and D_1. For any dimension table D^* the statement D_1 ISA_T D qualifies such tables D_1^* that the following condition holds:

- for any row from $u \in D_1^*$ there is a row $v \in D^*$, such that $u[A] = v[A]$,

where [ ] denotes the usual relation operation projection.

Obviously, the ISA_T relation is reflexive and transitive. A meaningful relation ISA_T does not contain cycles. We will suppose that ISA_T relation represents a table hierarchy with a table D serving as its root. We will discuss the simplified situation in which D is a dimension root[7]. To denote an ISA hierarchy with the root D, we replace the index T (Table) by D and write ISA_D. According to the usual terminology of E-R modelling, we speak of *subtables* and *supertables* in ISA_D.

An interesting point arises in connection with the subtable construction. Unlike to ISA-hierarchies of entity types, we have the possibility to restrict rows of the table D via restricting values of other dimension attributes in the dimension hierarchy with the root D. A product dimension table supposed only for videos (VIDEO) could be defined in a user-friendly notation as follows:

VIDEO $ISA_{PRODUCT}$ PRODUCT (1)
with PRODUCT **restricted on** Group = 'Video'

The logical condition in (1) is a simple comparison (*atom*) of the Group value that occurs in the table GROUP belonging to the dimension hierarchy PRODUCT.

[7] In practice, ISA hierarchies built from other members of dimension hierarchies are certainly possible.

Obviously, $VIDEO^* \subseteq PRODUCT^*$ holds in each time moment. Moreover, for each row $u \in VIDEO^*$ $f_{PRODUCT,GROUP}(u) = v$ with $v \in GROUP^*$ and *v*.Group = 'Video'. Remind that $f_{PRODUCT,GROUP}$ is the associate composed roll-up function. This functional semantics is more appropriate for DW querying than the relational one. Obviously, we could write in the relational algebra

VIDEO ≡ (PRODUCT * CLASS * (GROUP(Group = 'Video'))[ArtID, Description, Class]

or, equivalently, with operation semijoin as

VIDEO ≡ PRODUCT <* CLASS <* (GROUP(Group = 'Video'))

But this approach reminds (perhaps not necessarily) a relational viewing DW.

Now, we would like to apply the approach to the relation ISA_D representing dimension tables that include some new attributes in their definition. For example, we can suppose for the table VIDEO that the attribute Brand is inherited from its supertable PRODUCT. Moreover, we could define for videos an additional attribute VidSys that has a sense only for products being videos. Extending the description (1) in this way, we obtain

VIDEO $ISA_{PRODUCT}$ PRODUCT (2)
with PRODUCT **restricted on** Group = 'Video'
attributes VidSys(Char);

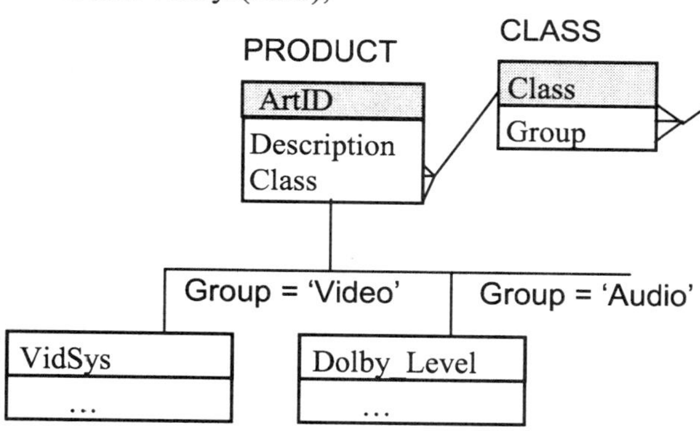

Figure 5: A dimension schema with ISA-hierarchy

A graphical form of (2) extended with the derived AUDIO table is depicted in Figure 5 (from Pokorny, 1999b). In accordance to the semantics of the ISA_T constraint, we can state

AUDIO $ISA_{PRODUCT}$ PRODUCT

Contrary to Figure 5 derived tables can be named explicitly. It depends on the purposes of using table hierarchies. Suppose a simple query language in a "query-by-example" style. Figure 6 shows a query over DW with a star schema with explicit hierarchies. Its SQL equivalent is:

```
SELECT S.SalesOrgID, S.ArtID, SUM(S.Profit)
FROM SALES S, TIME T, OFFICE O, AUDIO A
WHERE S.Month = T.Month AND S.ArtID = A. ArtID
        AND S.SalesOrgID= O.SalesOrgID
        AND T.Year  = 1998 AND O.District = 'Lublin'
        AND A.DolbyLevel = 'B3'
GROUP BY S.SalesOrgID, S.ArtID
```

It is straightforward to extend the notion of a constellation schema with explicit hierarchies by the set of **ISA** containing hierarchies ISA_D. Since each element of ISA_D is an integrity constraint, we obtain easily the set of associated admissible multidimensional databases. (Named) schemes of „subtables" given by each hierarchy ISA_D will become additional elements of the set ***D***.

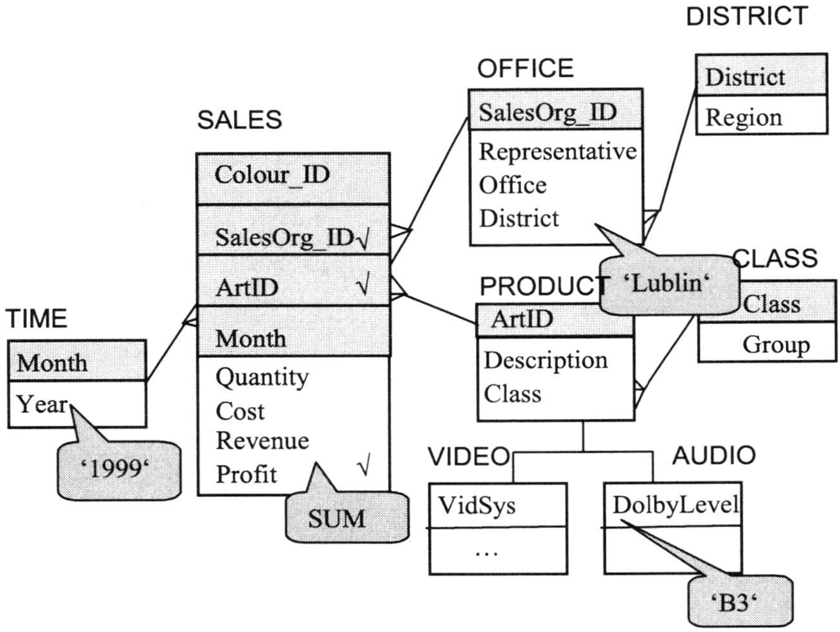

Figure 6: A query over the star schema

5.2 Constructing derived tables

It is straightforward to extend the language of restrictions from atoms to more general Boolean expressions. Any dimension attributes occurring in schemes from $\boldsymbol{D}_H$ could participate in the clause **with-restricted-on.** However, a care is necessary to ensure a correctness of such an expression. Due to the possibility of alternate and converging dimension hierarchies, the paths of hierarchy members determined by the attributes that occur in the restricting expression must be unique.

We formalize the problem. For the sake of simplicity, we suppose that the attribute names occurring in a $\boldsymbol{D}_H$ are mutually different. Further, we suppose the Boolean expressions considered are restricted on conjunctions of atoms. By definition, we add to atoms expressions like A:TRUE, where A is an attribute name. We will conceive A:TRUE as predicate that returns TRUE for all values of *dom*(A).

Consider a dimension hierarchy H and a Boolean expression E ranging on attributes of the table schemes from $\boldsymbol{D}_H$. First we propose a simple characterization of paths in H associated with E. Then we introduce the notion of well-formed Boolean expression and a number of statements allowing us to express the correctness of a table derivation in more exact way.

5.2.1 Definite paths

Let attr(E) be the set of attributes occurring in E. There is a set of tables $\{D_{i1},...,D_{it}\} \subseteq \boldsymbol{D}_H$, such that each attribute from attr(E) occurs in Ω_{ij} for an appropriate j and vice versa, i.e. each D_{ij} is restricted by at least one atom from E. We denote the set M_E and call its members *milestones*. By definition we include into M_E also the root of H.

Each Boolean expression E determines a set of rooted paths in H. In fact, there is at least one rooted path $<D_{i1},...,D_{it}>$ for each attribute $A \in$ attr(E) with $D_{i1} = D_1$ and $A \in \Omega_{it}$. Obviously, a given rooted path can be a prefix of other rooted paths. It depends on the attributes in attr(E). We will consider only the paths that are not prefixes any other paths. We denote the set of these rooted paths by path(E). According to this definition, each path from path(E) contains at least two milestones, its start node and end node.

Example 1: Consider the dimension hierarchy H depicted in Figure 7. We suppose that each $D_i(\Omega_i)$ contains the attribute A_i in Ω_i. All attributes have a common domain, e.g. integer. Let $E_1 \equiv A_3 < 5 \wedge A_7 = 4$. Then $M_{E1} = \{D_1, D_3, D_7\}$ and path(E_1) = $<D_1, D_2, D_3, D_6, D_7>$. Now, let $E_2 \equiv A_2 > 5 \wedge A_7 = 3$. Then $M_{E2} = \{D_1, D_2, D_7\}$ and path(E_2) = $\{<D_1, D_2, D_3, D_6, D_7>, <D_1, D_2, D_4,$

D_5, D_6, D_7>}. Thus, E_2 is not well-defined. On the other hand, a number of rooted paths may not make problems. For example, $E_3 \equiv A_3 > 1 \wedge A_5 = 9$ provides path(E_3) = {<D_1, D_2, D_3>, <D_1, D_2, D_4, D_5>} and the restricting is meaningful. The set of milestones $M_{E3} = \{D_1, D_3, D_5\}$.

◊

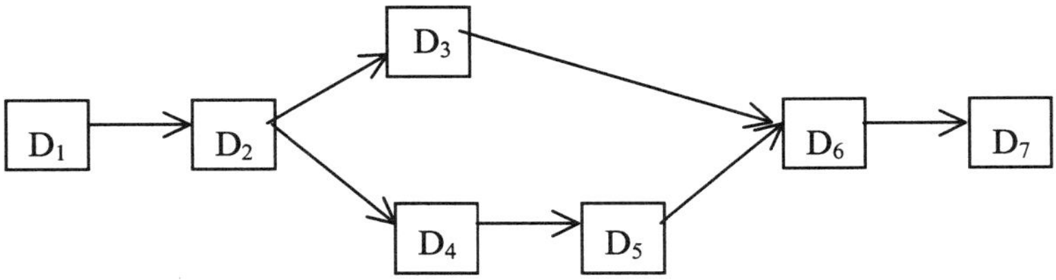

Figure 7: A dimension hierarchy

Thus, we need to ensure that path(E) does not contain two rooted paths with the same end node. In the opposite case, there are two roll-up functions whose values range the same table, but for a row $u \in D_1^*$ they return generally two different values.

In relational theory, the desirability of acyclic database schemes is often emphasized. The notion is linked to acyclic condition on a hypergraph structure of relational schemes. Viewing attributes of D_i in $\boldsymbol{D}_H$ as nodes and Ω_i as hyperedges, we obtain a hypergraph H. Its acyclicity corresponds to situations when the hierarchy H is not converging. This fact has an important consequence for an implementation. Authors of (Beeri et al., 1983) proved that acyclicity is equivalent to the claim that H has a join tree. A join tree yields a good way to join together all relation necessary to obtain a derived relation or, in query processing, an answer.

Example 2: Consider the expression E_3 from Example 1. Table schemes D_1, D_2, D_3, D_4, D_5 compose a hypergraph. The associated join tree could result in the following order of joins:

$((((D_1 * D_2) * D_3(A_3 > 1)) * D_4) * D_5(A_5 = 9))$

Consider now the hierarchy in figure 8 based on (Markowitz and Shoshani, 1991) and the expression $E_4 \equiv$ City_name = 'Poznan'. Calculating ((STUDENT * UNIVERSITY) * CITY(City_Name = 'Poznan'))[$\Omega_{STUDENT}$] we obtain tuples representing students having his/her university in Poznan. On the other hand, the relation

((STUDENT * CITY(City_Name = 'Poznan')) *UNIVERSITY) [$\Omega_{STUDENT}$]

contains tuples representing students living in Poznan. Hence, the semantics would be correct under the additional assumption that each student considered has to attend only a university located in the city where he/she lives.

◊

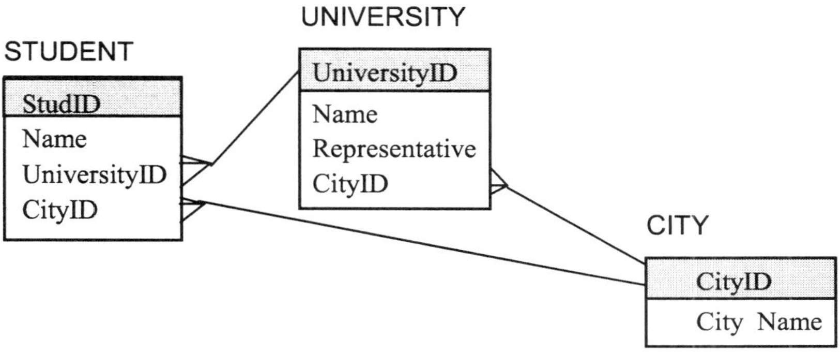

Figure 8: An example of converging dimension hierarchy

We introduce some preliminary notions that are useful in viewing the problem more formally.

Definition 6 (Definiteness of Paths): We say that a couple of nodes (D, D') of the graph H is *definite* if there is a unique path from D to D' in H. Consider a path P from path(E). According to the ordering of nodes determined by the sequence P, we can order all its milestones. Let $<D_{i1},...,D_{it}>$ be the subsequence of P composed of these milestones. Then the path P is called *definite* w.r.t. E if either

(D1) $(D_{ij}, D_{i(j+1)}) \in H$, or

(D2) $(D_{ij}, D_{i(j+1)}) \notin H$ and $(D_{ij}, D_{i(j+1)})$ is definite

for each $j \in <1, t\text{-}1>$. In the opposite case, the path is *indefinite* w.r.t. E.

Unfortunately, the definiteness of paths in path(E) is not sufficient for a correct evaluation of E. Consider, e.g., the expression

$E_5 \equiv A_2 > 5 \wedge A_7 = 3 \wedge A_3 > 1 \wedge A_5 = 9.$

Then path(E_5) = path(E_2). The only difference is that in the case of E_2 the paths are indefinite w.r.t. E_2 and definite w.r.t. E_5 in the case of E_5. We have to exclude the existence of two definite meeting paths.

5.2.2 Well-formed Boolean Expressions

We will construct now a reduced set of paths for E, say path$_{red}$(E), which contains only definite paths. The path$_{red}$(E) arises from path(E) by eliminating all its indefinite paths. Similarly to previous notation, we denote the associate set of milestones M_{ERed}.

Definition 7 (Well-formed Boolean Expression): Let H be a dimension hierarchy and E be a Boolean expression defining a subtable of the root of H. Then we say that E is *well-formed* iff it obeys the following constraints:

(WF1) any two paths for $\text{path}_{red}(E)$ are not meeting,

(WF2) $M_E = M_{ERed}$.

The dimension tables contained used in paths in $\text{path}_{red}(E)$ form a set $\boldsymbol{D}_E$. The following lemma is quite useful for deeper understanding Definition 7.

Lemma 1: Let E be a well-formed Boolean expression. Let P_1 and P_2 be two paths form $\text{path}_{red}(E)$. Then the only common nodes of P_1 and P_2 form a common prefix of P_1 and P_2.

Proof: Assume that there is a common node D of P_1 and P_2, which is not in the common prefix of P_1 and P_2. Let D be the last such node both in P_1 and P_2. Then there are two subcases:

- D is end node of both of P_1 and P_2,
- there is a path P beginning from D in H that is a suffix of P with at least two nodes.

The former is in a contradiction with (WF1). For the latter, let P_1' and P_2' be prefixes of P_1 and P_2, respectively, with end node D. Let P be the suffix of P_1 determined by D. Then $<P_1', P>$ and $<P_2', P>$ are two different definite meeting paths from path(E). This again contradicts (WF1).

Corollary 1: Let E be a well-formed Boolean expression. Then $\text{path}_{red}(E)$ forms a tree in H.

It is easy to see, that well-formed Boolean expressions ensure uniquely the paths in H that are necessary for obtaining the correct semantics of associated roll-up functions. Viewing dimension tables as relations, we immediately obtain the following result.

Corollary 2: Let E be a well-formed Boolean expression. Then $\boldsymbol{D}_E$ has a join tree.

Note that the condition (D1) in the definition 5 prefers a certain choice among conflict paths.

Example 3: Consider the situation depicted in Figure 9 and the same assumptions as in Example 1. Let $E_6 \equiv A_2 < 5 \wedge A_6 = 4 \wedge A_7 > 1$. Then $M_{E5} = \{D_1, D_2, D_6, D_7\}$ and $\text{path}(E_6) = \{<D_1, D_2, D_6, D_7>, <D_1, D_2, D_4, D_5, D_6, D_7>\}$. Obviously, the latter element of the set is indefinite w.r.t. E_6. Applying our definitions, we result in $\text{path}_{red}(E_6) = \{<D_1, D_2, D_6, D_7>\}$.

◊

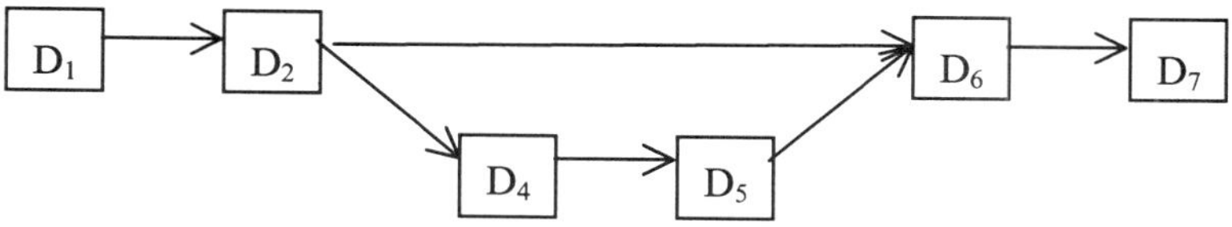

Figure 9. A dimension hierarchy

Example 3 shows that by the definition of definiteness an edge between two conflicting nodes is preferred. In other words, the path {<D_1, D_2, D_6, D_7> has a priority. This approach tries to correct the conflict intuitively in a natural way. Another possibility about how to reach definiteness arises, when we explicitly choose the path in *H*. This may be achieved when we use atoms *A*:TRUE in *E*. In example 3, we could obtain another definite path by refinement of E_6. When we add the atom A_5:TRUE, then the path <D_1, D_2, D_4, D_5, D_6, D_7> becomes definite w.r.t. $E_6 \wedge A_5$:TRUE. Refinements like this one are conservative in the sense of the selectivity of the original expressions, i.e. $E_6 \Leftrightarrow E_6 \wedge A_5$:TRUE. In addition we have a regular possibility of how to refine *E* by a non-trivial atom. The expression $E_6 \wedge A_5 > 7$ is such an example.

6. CONCLUSIONS

The paper concerns a DW modelling with dimension and fact tables and explicitly specified hierarchies. We have shown that the DW modelling offers new challenges, particularly in a new understanding of the notion of a DW schema, both on the conceptual and dimensional levels. The possibility of defining ISA hierarchies on dimensional objects has been discussed including an associated formalism. Well-formed Boolean expressions can naturally help derive new useful dimension subtables. An interesting problem arises of how to decide that a Boolean expression is well-formed. In practice, simple graph-oriented algorithms solve it. Similar problems can be met in studying correctness of view or query specifications in this class of DWs.

Many other questions arise in the study of dimension hierarchies. For example, we could ask, if it is possible to use in the Boolean expression *E,* a connection "through" the fact table. For example, the video products made before 1990 (the value of the TIME dimension member YEAR) can have some other distinguishing properties compared to videos made after 1990. To allow these possibilities means to go beyond the usual conception of dimensions. Dimensions would become dependent in this case.

Future work is supposed to focus on query capabilities over constellation schemes with explicit hierarchies and ISA-hierarchies. Well-formed Boolean expressions seem to be also suitable for this purpose.

REFERENCES

Agrawal R, Gupta A, Sarawagi S. Modeling Multidimensional Databases, Research Report, IBM Almaden Research Centre, San Jose, California, 1995, Also in: Proceeding of ICDE '97.

Beeri C, Fagin R, Maier D, Yannakakis M. On the Desirability of Acyclic Schemes. JACM, 30, 3, 1983, pp. 479-513.

Buytendijk FA. Multidimensional Data Analysis for OLAP. April 1996.

Cabibbo L, Torlone R. A logical Approach to Multidimensional Databases. Proc. of 6th Int. Conf. on Extended Database Technology, Valencia, 1998.

Gyssens M, Lakshmanan VS, Subramanian IN. Tables As a Paradigm for Querying and Restructuring. Proc. ACM Symp. on Principles of Database Systems, Montreal, 1996.

Golfarelli M, Maio D, Rizzi, S. Conceptual Design of Data Warehouses from E/R Schemes. Proc. of the Hawaii Int. Conference on System Sciences, 1998, Kona, Hawaii, 1998.

Golfarelli M, Rizzi, S. A Methodological Framework for Data Warehouse Design. Proc. of the ACM First Int. Workshop on Data Warehousing and OLAP (DOLAP 98), Washington D.C., USA, 1998.

Jagadish HV, Lakshmanan LVS, Srivastava D. What can Hierarchies do for Data Warehouses?. Proc. o the 25th VLDB Conf., Edinburgh, Scotland, 1999, pp. 530-541.

Kimball R. *The Data Warehouse Toolkit: Practical Techniques for Building Dimensional Data Warehouses*. John Wiley, 1996.

Kimball R. A Dimensional Manifesto. DBMS, August 1997.

Lehner W. Modeling Large Scale OLAP Scenarios, 6th International Conference on Extending Database Technology (EDBT'98), Valencia, Spain, 23-27, March, 1998.

Li Ch. Wang XS. A Data model for Supporting On-Line Analytical Processing. Proc. of Conf. On Integration and Knowledge Management, November, 1996, pp.81-88.

McGuff F. Data Modeling for Data Warehouses. http://members.aol.com/fmcguff/dwmodel/index.htm, 1996.

Markowitz VM, Shoshani A. Representing Extended Entity-Relationship Structures in Relational Databases: A Modular Approach. ACM Transactions on Database Systems.

Pokorny J. Conceptual modelling in OLAP. Proc. of the ECIS ' 98 Conf., Aix-en-Provence, 1998, pp. 273-288.

Pokorny, J. "Data Warehouses: a Modelling Perspective." *In Evolution and Challenges in System Development* (Eds. W.G.Wojtkowski, S. Wrycza, J. Zupancic), Kluwer Academic/Plenum Press Publ., 1999a.

Pokorny J. To the Stars through Dimensions and Facts. Proc. of the 3rd International Conference on Business Information Systems (BIS'99), Springer Verlag, London, 1999b, pp.135-147.

Pedersen TB, Jensen ChS. Multidimensional Data Modeling for Complex Data. Proc. of the 15th Int. Conf. on Data Engineering, 23-26 March 1999, Sydney, Australia, IEEE Computer Society Press, 1999.

Raden N. Modelling the Data Warehouse. Archer Decision Sciences, Inc., 1995.

Raden N. Star schema 101. http://www.netmar.com/nraden/str101_q.htm.

Chapter 14

ENHANCING THE KDD PROCESS IN THE RELATIONAL DATABASE MINING FRAMEWORK BY QUANTITATIVE EVALUATION OF ASSOCIATION RULES

Giuseppe Psaila
Università degli Studi di Bergamo - Facoltà di Ingegneria
Viale Marconi 5
I-24044 DALMINE (BG) - Italy
psaila@unibg.it

Abstract The user performing a KDD process based on the extraction of association rules may wish to reuse the association rule set, to perform new and/or different analysis tasks. We introduce the `EVALUATE RULE` operator, which performs quantitative evaluations of association rule sets over the data in the Relational Database Mining Framework; we show that the operator significantly enhances the KDD process.

1. INTRODUCTION

The extraction of association rules is one of the most popular data mining technique (Chen et al., 1996). An impressive amount of research work has been done on this topic (Agrawal et al., 1993; Savasere et al., 1995; Bayardo, 1998), which is still object of significant efforts. The main results of these research efforts are represented by general purpose tools which analyze large amounts of data and produce association rule sets; among them, significant are the works devoted to the definition of data mining frameworks. In a data mining framework, different data mining tools can be composed to perform complex data analysis tasks and assist the Knowledge Discovery Process (KDD Process, Fayyad et al., 1996); in the context of relational databases, the most frequent repositories for raw data to analyze, an important role is played by the *Relational Database Mining Framework* (Meo et al., 1996; Meo et al., 1998a; Lanzi and Psaila, 1999), in which SQL-like data mining operators take relational tables as input and produce their results (such as rule sets) as relational tables.

The user, which mines the data by extracting association rules, exploits the resulting rule sets by interpreting them; in sophisticated data mining frameworks, the KDD process can be supported by suitable tools that helps the user in comparing two rule sets. However, such kinds of analysis are qualitative, while in many cases the user wishes quantitative information.

In this paper, we introduce an operator (named `EVALUATE RULE`) that performs quantitative evaluations, over the data source, of (previously extracted) association rule sets. The goal of the proposed quantitative evaluation methods is to study, at a fine granularity level, the phenomena put in evidence by the extracted association rules, even dynamically on changing data. For example, in the classical case of basket data analysis, the relevance of each association rule might be quantitatively evaluated in terms of total amount of expense for each customer.

The operator is designed to be part of the Relational Database Mining Framework: it is based on a SQL-like syntax, takes relational tables as input and produces relational tables as output; consequently, it is interoperable with the other operators defined in the framework, included the classical SQL data manipulation operators. We will show that this feature is extremely important in perspective: in fact, it opens the way to new and complex data analysis types, enhancing the deployment of significantly complex KDD processes. New and powerful abstractions can be considered, such as meta-association rules, which model/represent/synthesize the results of the quantitative evaluation of previously extracted association rule sets.

The paper is organized as follows. Section 1.1 briefly summarizes the notion of association rule. Section 2. briefly describes the Relational Database Mining Framework, in particular illustrating the `MINE RULE` operator with the features relevant for the paper. Section 3. introduces the `EVALUATE RULE` operator, by extensively discussing its features and the quantitative evaluations it provides. Section 4. shows the effect of the `EVALUATE RULE` operator on the knowledge discovery tasks, illustrating the importance of the operator and the concept of *meta-association rules*. Finally, Section 5. draws the conclusions.

1.1 ASSOCIATION RULES

An association rule has the form

$$B \Rightarrow H$$

where both B and H are sets of values; B is called the *antecedent* or *body* of the rule, while H is called the *consequence* or *head* of the rule. A rule has associated two parameters, called *support* and *confidence* of the rule; the former denotes the frequency with which the rule is found in the data, while the latter indicates the conditional probability that the rule is found in the data having found the body. In order to obtain only the most significant rules, only rules with support and confidence greater than or equal to two minimum thresholds for support and confidence, respectively, are selected.

For example, if we consider the classical case of a data set collecting information about commercial transactions, a sample association rule

$$boots, jacket \Rightarrow shirt, s = 7\%, c = 25\%$$

may mean that the items *boots*, *jacket* and *shirt* are bought together by customers in the 7% of cases, while the conditional probability that when a customers buys *boots* and *jacket* also buys *shirt* is 25%.

Hence, association rules put in evidence frequent regularities which characterize the analyzed data. However, while association rules provide a representation form for regularities, they do not provide semantics: in fact, the same rule can be interpreted in different ways. A first element to consider is the domain which values appearing in rules belong to; for instance, rules that associate product items are different from rules that associate product categories, since they come from two distinct domains.

Furthermore, it is important to understand which is the element w.r.t. which rules express regularities. For example, a rule that associates product items may be intended at least in two distinct ways: *the rule associates product items purchased by the same customer, irrespective of the purchase transaction*, or *the rule associates product items frequently purchased in a single transaction*. Then, when extracting association rules, it is rather important to understand what kind of regularities we are looking for; in other words, it is necessary to define the semantic features that characterize the association rule problem. These considerations motivated the design of tools, such as specific query languages (see Meo et al., 1996; Imielinski et al., 1996; Han et al., 1996), to specify data mining problems based on association rule mining. Then, with the availability of several data mining tools, the problem of defining unified data mining frameworks arises naturally.

2. THE RELATIONAL DATABASE MINING FRAMEWORK

The notion of mining framework is already known from the literature and from several commercial and research products.

The need for a data mining framework arises for two reasons. First of all, the KDD process proceeds through several steps; then, the user needs to maintain intermediate results obtained during the process, and expect functionalities to analyze and compare them. Second, users desire to operate with flexible and reasonably easy to use tools, integrated each other in a common environment.

Historically, this problem has been approached in different ways.

Interface-based frameworks give a uniform interface to *collections* of algorithms for data mining, machine learning, statistics and visualization. Two important representers are *Sipina-W* and *Darwin* (see Kdd-nuggets). *Sipina-W* is a tool package that includes many machine learning and knowledge engineering algorithms. *Darwin* is a suite of mining tools developed by *Thinking Machines* that includes algorithms for classification, search (genetic algorithms), neural networks, 2D visualization and database access.

In *Flow-based* frameworks an application is described by means of a dataflow model, where nodes corresponds either to data or to algorithms and tools. An example is *Clementine*, a commercial tool that has a dataflow based GUI for building complex applications from basic modules corresponding to specific algorithms for discretization, classification and rule induction.

Finally, *library-based* frameworks integrate many different functionalities as libraries of algorithms written in a unique programming language. This is the case of MLC++ (machine learning library in C++), that has been used to build the Silicon Graphics' MineSet^{TM} (Kohavi et al., 1996), a tool for exploratory data analysis primarily centered on classification tasks. Built onto MLC++, it provides a GUI with powerful tools for visualizing the extracted knowledge, and can retrieve data from several commercial databases including Oracle, Sybase and Informix.

The aim of the *Relational Database Mining Framework*, whose development started with Meo et al., 1996 (a similar approach to the extraction of association rules has been done by Imielinski et al., 1996 and Han et al., 1996) is the definition of a mining framework fully integrated with relational databases, where operators are based on a unified and customizable semantic model. The key idea of integrating data mining tools and relational databases is motivated by the following reasons:

- all semantic options featuring the data mining task are put in evidence, in order to abstract the specification from the algorithmic implementation;
- the operators are based on a SQL syntax, where each clause expresses a precise semantic option in a declarative way;
- the output of the operators is stored again in relational tables inside the DBMS, in order to be used by successive phases of the KDD process.

Due to these features, the framework results perfectly integrated with relational environments, and achieves the goal of interoperability. In fact, the syntactic style (SQL-like) of operators makes a SQL programmer quickly able to build KDD applications; furthermore, the fact that the operators use and generate tables, allows the specification of complex KDD applications which are a free mix of traditional SQL statements and new mining statements.

Finally, this approach gives rise to another advantage: once the new operators are implemented, the same formalism can be used both to model the user problem and to actually execute the application.

At this moment, four operators constitute the relational database mining framework. The first one is the `MINE RULE` operator, which covers the problem of mining association rules (discussed in Section 2.1), the `MINE CLASSIFICATION` operator (Lanzi and Psaila, 1999), which covers classification problems, the `MINE INTERVAL` operator (Lanzi and Psaila, 1999), which covers the problem of discretizing numerical attributes (it offers several discretization techniques), and the `EVALUATE RULE` operator, fully introduced in Section 3..

2.1 THE MINE RULE OPERATOR

In the relational database mining framework, the `MINE RULE` operator (introduced in Meo et al., 1996) allows the specification of expressions to mine association rules from a relational table. This section introduces the features of the operator relevant for this paper; the other features of the operator are extensively discussed in Meo et al., 1998a. For the examples, we make use of a running example, i.e. the `Transactions` table depicted in Figure 14.1, containing data about purchases in a store. The schema of the table is

`(tid, customer, transaction, item, qty, price, amount)`

where attribute `transaction` (`tr.` in the figures) is the transaction identifier, `customer` (`cust.` in the figures) is the customer identifier, `item` is the purchased item, `qty` is the number of purchased pieces, `price` is the price of the item in the transaction (the price of an item can change in time), `amount` is the overall amount paid for the item (`qty` by `price`); finally, `tid` is a unique tuple identifier.

Consider the following two mining expressions, named `Simple` and `Filtered`. The former corresponds to the basic model for association rules; the latter exploits an important feature of the `MINE RULE` operator.

```
MINE RULE Simple AS
SELECT DISTINCT 1..n item AS BODY,
 1..n item AS HEAD,
 SUPPORT, CONFIDENCE

FROM Transactions
GROUP BY customer
EXTRACTING RULES WITH
 SUPPORT: 0.2,
 CONFIDENCE: 0.3
```

```
MINE RULE Filtered AS
SELECT DISTINCT 1..n item AS BODY,
 1..n item AS HEAD,
 SUPPORT, CONFIDENCE
 WHERE BODY.price < HEAD.price
FROM Transactions
GROUP BY customer
EXTRACTING RULES WITH
 SUPPORT: 0.2,
 CONFIDENCE: 0.3
```

The two expressions must be interpreted as follows.

Groups. The source table `Transactions` (`FROM` clause), is logically partitioned into groups (`GROUP BY` clause) such that all tuples in a group have the same value of attribute `customer`; this means that rules express regularities w.r.t. customers. The total number of groups in the source data is computed in this step; we denote it as G (used to compute rule support). To illustrate, Figure 14.2 shows the table `Transactions` grouped by `customer`.

Rules. From each group, all possible associations of an unlimited set of `items` for the body (clause `1..n item AS BODY`), with an unlimited set of `items` for the head (clause `1..n item AS HEAD`), are considered.

The number of groups that contain a rule r is denoted as G_r and the number of groups that contain the body of r is denoted as G_b.

Support and confidence. The *support* of a rule is its frequency among groups $s = G_r/G$; the *confidence* is the conditional probability that the rule is found in a group which contains the body $c = G_r/G_b$. Support and confidence are then a measure of the relevance of a rule. If they are lower than their respective minimum thresholds (`0.2` for support and `0.3` for confidence, in our sample expressions), the rule is discarded. Minimum thresholds for support and confidence are specified by the `EXTRACTING RULES` clause.

The right hand side expression, called `Filtered` has an additional optional clause (`WHERE BODY.price < HEAD.price`) called *mining condition*, that expresses a tuple predicate.

Mining Condition. Consider a group and a rule r. We can say that r is contained in the group if all the tuples in the group considered for body and head satisfy the predicate. Hence, this predicate is evaluated during the actual rule extraction phase. In our example, the mining condition selects only items for the body if all items in the head have been sold with higher price, and selects items for the head only if all items in the body have been sold with lower price.

Samples of the resulting rule sets, stored in the SQL-3 relational tables `Simple` and `Filtered`, are the following.

RULE_ID	BODY	HEAD	SUPP.	CONF.
1	{ A }	{ B }	0.75	0.75
2	{ A B }	{ C D }	0.75	1
		...		

`Simple`

RULE_ID	BODY	HEAD	SUPP.	CONF.
1	{ A }	{ B }	0.25	0.25
2	{ A B }	{ C D }	0.5	0.66
		...		

`Filtered`

Observe the effect of the mining condition on rules reported in table `Filtered`: the support is lower than in table `Simple`. For rule 1, this is due to the fact that the mining condition does not hold for any tuple in groups c_2 and c_3; for rule 2 the mining condition does not hold for group c_3.

tid	cust.	tr.	item	qty	price	amount
1	c_1	1	A	1	25	25
2	c_1	1	B	1	12	12
3	c_1	1	C	1	30	30
4	c_1	1	D	1	20	20
5	c_1	3	E	2	40	80
6	c_1	3	A	1	10	10
7	c_2	2	C	3	30	90
8	c_2	2	D	3	20	60
9	c_2	2	E	2	40	80
10	c_2	6	B	3	12	36
11	c_2	6	A	3	13	39
12	c_3	4	A	1	25	25
13	c_3	4	B	1	12	12
14	c_3	4	C	1	23	23
15	c_3	4	D	1	30	30
16	c_3	4	F	2	8	16
17	c_4	5	F	1	12	12
18	c_4	5	A	2	10	20

Figure 14.1 The table `Transactions` grouped by attribute `transaction`.

tid	cust.	tr.	item	qty	price	amount
1	c_1	1	A	1	25	25
2	c_1	1	B	1	12	12
3	c_1	1	C	1	30	30
4	c_1	1	D	1	20	20
5	c_1	3	E	2	40	80
6	c_1	3	A	1	10	10
7	c_2	2	C	3	30	90
8	c_2	2	D	3	20	60
9	c_2	2	E	2	40	80
10	c_2	6	B	3	12	36
11	c_2	6	A	3	13	39
12	c_3	4	A	1	25	25
13	c_3	4	B	1	12	12
14	c_3	4	C	1	23	23
15	c_3	4	D	1	30	30
16	c_3	4	F	2	8	16
17	c_4	5	F	1	12	12
18	c_4	5	A	2	10	20

Figure 14.2 The table `Transactions` grouped by attribute `customer`.

3. THE EVALUATE RULE OPERATOR

We now introduce the `EVALUATE RULE` operator. This operator has been designed to provide the relational database mining framework with the capa-

RULE_ID	BODY	HEAD
1	{A}	{CD}
2	{A}	{CDE}
3	{AB}	{CDE}
4	{A}	{F}
5	{ABF}	{C}
6	{B}	{A}

(a) `RuleSet`

RULE_ID	BODY	HEAD	ref-value
1	{A}	{CD}	111
2	{A}	{CDE}	154
3	{AB}	{CDE}	138
4	{A}	{F}	42
5	{ABF}	{C}	87
6	{B}	{A}	57

(b) `RuleSet2`

Figure 14.3 a) Selected rule set of interest. b) Selected rule set of interest with reference value.

customer	RULE_ID
c_1	1
c_1	2
c_1	3
c_1	6
c_2	1
c_2	2
c_2	3
c_2	6
c_3	1
c_3	4
c_3	5
c_3	6
c_4	4

(a) `Basic`

customer	RULE_ID
c_1	1
c_1	6
c_2	6
c_3	1
c_3	4
c_3	5
c_3	6
c_4	4

(b) `BasicT`

customer	RULE_ID	total
c_1	1	85
c_1	2	165
c_1	3	177
c_1	6	47
c_2	1	189
c_2	2	269
c_2	3	305
c_2	6	75
c_3	1	118
c_3	4	41
c_3	5	76
c_3	6	37
c_4	4	32

(c) `Amounts`

Figure 14.4 a) The table generated by the evaluation expression `Basic`. b) The table generated by the evaluation expression `BasicT`. c) The table generated by the evaluation expression `Amounts`.

bility of performing quantitative evaluations of association rules, previously extracted by the `MINE RULE` operator.

In the following, we discuss both the features of the operator and the different types of quantitative evaluations we considered for association rules.

3.1 PREMISE

Before starting the introduction of the operator, consider a user that executed a data mining expression based on the `MINE RULE` operator, and obtained a rule set, where each rule has associated the support and confidence values.

At this point, the user typically tries to interpret the rule set, in order to find interesting rules. Rules might be considered interesting for two reasons: a rule may be interesting because it is unexpected, then provides new knowledge to the user; a rule may be considered interesting because confirms hypothesis made by the user, hence it confirms previous knowledge.

Based on such considerations, the user selects those rules he/she considers interesting and/or useful to be evaluated from a quantitative point of view. As we will see later, support and confidence are not relevant for a quantitative evaluation of rules, then the selected rule set can appear as the rule set reported in Figure 14.3.a. In effect, support and confidence gives a measure of the relevance of an association rule w.r.t. the entire data set; by means of them it is possible to study (see Agrawal and Psaila, 1995, Agrawal et al., 1995) the dynamic evolution in time of rules. Instead, in this paper we consider the problem of measuring the relevance of a rule at a finer granularity level.

3.2 BASIC EVALUATION

Let us consider the `Transactions` table of Figure 14.1 and the rule set of Figure 14.3, stored in a table called `RuleSet`.

The simplest evaluation for the rule set the user might wish to perform is the following:

for which customers rules reported in the rule set holds ?

In other words, given a customer, we want to know which rules in the rule set holds for the customer. However, there are two possible ways to interpret this statement.

1. A rule holds if the customer bought the items associated by the rule, irrespective of the particular purchase transaction.
2. A rule holds if the customer bought the items associated by the rule all together in a single purchase transaction.

It is clear that the rule set must be evaluated in two different ways, depending on the interpretation. Here, we show how to specify both the evaluation strategies by means of the `EVALUATE RULE` operator.

First interpretation. The `EVALUATE RULE` specification for the first interpretation is the following.

```
EVALUATE RULE Basic AS
SELECT DISTINCT customer, RULE_ID
USING RULES RuleSet
ASSOCIATING item AS BODY, item AS HEAD
FROM Transactions
GROUP BY customer
```

The operator reads from the table `RuleSet` the rule set to be evaluated (clause `USING RULES`). It is specified that he operator evaluates the rule set on the table `Transactions`, containing the data to be analyzed (clause `FROM`), where each rule is defined as an association of values of the attribute `item` coming from the `Transactions` table (clause `ASSOCIATING`). Rules describe regularities w.r.t. customers in the `Transactions` table (clause `GROUP BY`); this means that each rule is evaluated w.r.t. single customers. Finally, the operator produces a table, called `Basic`, which has two attributes (clause `SELECT DISTINCT`): the first attribute denotes the customer, the second denotes the rule identifier; a tuple is inserted into this table if the rule holds for the customer.

The application of the expression to the instance of the sample table `Transactions` reported in Figure 14.2 and to the rule set of Figure 14.3.a produces the instance of the `Basic` table reported in Figure 14.4. Observe that table `Transactions` is shown grouped by customer, in order to put in evidence the fact that rules are checked for groups of tuples corresponding to purchase of a single customer-

Second Interpretation. The `EVALUATE RULE` specification for the second interpretation is the following.

```
EVALUATE RULE BasicT AS
SELECT DISTINCT customer, RULE_ID
USING RULES RuleSet
ASSOCIATING item AS BODY, item AS HEAD
FROM Transactions
GROUP BY customer
DIVIDE BY transaction
```

The operator reads from the table `RuleSet` the rule set to be evaluated (clause `USING RULES`). The rule set is evaluated on the table `Transactions`, containing the data to be analyzed (clause `FROM`), where each rule is an association of values of the attribute `item` coming from the `Transactions` table (clause `ASSOCIATING`). Rules describe regularities w.r.t. customers in the `Transactions` table (clause `GROUP BY`); this means that each rule is evaluated w.r.t. single customers.

In particular, rules must hold only for single transactions (clause `DIVIDE BY`). This means that a rule holds for a customer if there is at least a purchase transaction that contains all the items associated by the rule. Finally, the operator produces a table, called `BasicT`, which has two attributes (clause `SELECT DISTINCT`): the first attribute denotes the customer, the second denotes the rule identifier; a rule identifier is inserted into this table if there is at least a purchase transaction performed by the customer in which the rule holds.

The application of this specification to the instance of the sample table `Transactions` reported in Figure 14.1 and to the rule set of Figure 14.3.a produces the instance of the `Basic` table reported in Figure 14.4. Observe

customer	RULE_ID	total	min-price	max-price	ntuples
c_1	1	85	10	30	4
c_2	1	189	13	30	3
c_2	6	75	12	13	2
c_3	1	118	25	30	3
c_3	5	76	8	25	4

Multi

Figure 14.5 The table generated by the evaluation expression `Multi`.

that the `Transactions` table is shown grouped by customer, in order to put in evidence that rules must hold for single transactions.

3.3 INTRODUCING QUANTITATIVE MEASURES

The next step in evaluating association rules is the introduction of a quantitative measure. For instance, consider the attribute `amount` in the `Transactions` table, obtained multiplying the price by the purchased quantity. Then, the user might like to know *for which customers rules reported in the rule set holds, and which is the relevance of each rule, in terms of amount of the purchased products* ?

In other words, given a customer, we want to know which rules in the rule set holds for the customer. Furthermore, if a rule holds for a customer, we also want to know the total amount spent by the customer to buy products denoted by the rule.

The idea is the following: the total amount is obtained by summing attribute *amount* of all the tuples from which items associated by the rule come from.

This can be specified by the following expression.

```
EVALUATE RULE Amounts AS
SELECT DISTINCT customer, RULE_ID, SUM(amount) as total
USING RULES RuleSet
ASSOCIATING item AS BODY, item AS HEAD
FROM Transactions
GROUP BY customer
```

Observe that this expression is derived from the expression formulated for the simplest rule evaluation (that produces table `Basic`), by adding `SUM(Amount) as total` to the `SELECT` clause. The aggregate function operates on an attribute (in this case `amount`), whose values come from the tuples that make the rule to hold for the customer. Furthermore, since the attribute generated by the aggregate function will be in the schema of the output table, the alias `AS` is necessary for the generated attribute.

For example, the sample instance of table `Amounts` shown in Figure 14.4 is obtained by applying the expression to the table `Transactions` shown in Figure 14.2.

Observe that any of the usual aggregation functions provided by SQL can be used, i.e. `MIN`, `MAX` and `AVG`; in particular the function `COUNT(*)` counts the number of tuples that participate to the association rule.

The presence of an aggregate function does not exclude the contemporary presence of other aggregate functions: for example, we might be interested in performing four different quantitative evaluations on the `Transactions` table at the same time, such as the sum of the overall paid amount, the minimum and maximum price of the purchased products involved in the association and the total number of tuples involved in the association, as reported in the expression below.

```
EVALUATE RULE Multi AS
SELECT DISTINCT customer, RULE_ID, SUM(amount) AS total,
       MIN(price) AS min-price, MAX(price) AS max-price,
       COUNT(*) AS ntuples
USING RULES RuleSet
ASSOCIATING item AS BODY, item AS HEAD
FROM Transactions
GROUP BY customer
EXTRACTING RULES WITH total between 50 and 200,
                      max-price < 40
```

This expression also allows the user to filter the rules that will appear in the output table, by expressing conditions on the aggregate functions. Such conditions are expressed in the `EXTRACTING RULES` clause, which allows a list of comparison predicates.

Observe that this feature is not strictly necessary, since such filters can be easily performed by a conventional `SELECT` statement applied on the output table. However, adding this feature to the operator avoids the creation of excessively large output tables, this way improving the efficiency of the KDD process.

To conclude, notice that predicates in the `EXTRACTING RULES WITH` clause can be directly expressed on aggregate functions, instead of derived attributes (e.g. `total` and `max-price`). For example, the last line of the previous expression can be changed into the following.

```
EXTRACTING RULES WITH SUM(amount) between 50 and 200,
                      MAX(price) < 40
```

customer	RULE_ID	total	ntuples
c_1	1	75	3
c_1	6	37	2
c_2	6	75	2
c_3	1	118	3
c_3	4	41	2
c_3	5	76	4
c_3	6	37	2
c_4	4	32	2

(a) AmountsT

customer	RULE_ID	FREQUENCY
c_1	1	0.5
c_1	6	0.5
c_2	6	0.5
c_3	1	1
c_3	4	1
c_3	5	1
c_3	6	1
c_4	4	1

(b) RuleFrequency

Figure 14.6 a) The table generated by the evaluation expression AmountsT. b) The table generated by the evaluation expression RuleFrequency.

3.3.1 Sub-Groups and Rule Frequency.

Let us consider again the clause named DIVIDE BY. When specified, it forces the operator to further partition groups (specified by the GROUP BY clause) into sub-groups, such that all the tuples in a sub-group have the same value for the attributes appearing in the DIVIDE BY clause (*sub-group attributes*). Such sub-groups are used to evaluate rules: *an association rule holds for the group if there is at least one sub-group for which the rule holds* (i.e. there is a set of tuples in the sub-group that can be associated as indicated by the association rule). Hence, if the DIVIDE BY clause is not specified, in each group there is only the trivial sub-group, which is the group itself.

But what happens if aggregate functions are specified in the EVALUATE RULE expression together with the DIVIDE BY clause ? Consider the following expression

```
EVALUATE RULE AmountsT AS
SELECT DISTINCT customer, RULE_ID, SUM(amount) AS total,
                COUNT(*) AS ntuples
USING RULES RuleSet
ASSOCIATING item AS BODY, item AS HEAD
FROM Transactions
GROUP BY customer
DIVIDE BY transaction
```

derived from the expression Amounts previously discussed by adding the clause DIVIDE BY transaction. With such expression, the user asks to evaluate, for each customer, the overall amount paid by the customer for all the purchases described by an association rule, considering only purchases made together in the same transaction.

Applying the expression to the table `Transactions` reported in Figure 14.1, we obtain the table `AmountsT` reported in Figure 14.6. A comparison with the table `Amounts` reported in Figure 14.4 puts clearly in evidence that not only the number of rules is smaller, but also the values assumed by the `total` attribute are generally smaller than or equal to the corresponding rules in the former table.

In practice, the effects of the `DIVIDE BY` clause are the following. Consider a group.

- Since a group is partitioned into sub-groups, the first effect is that not all the rules that holds in the entire group holds in at least one of the sub-groups, because a pair of tuple that satisfies a rule in the entire group may appear in two distinct sub-groups, no longer satisfying the rule.
- If a rule holds for several sub-groups, the set of tuples that satisfy the rule in the group is now obtained uniting the set of tuples that satisfy the rule in each sub-group. The resulting set is necessarily smaller than or equal to the set of tuples that satisfy the rule in the entire group. Consequently, the aggregate functions operate on a different set of tuples, and the resulting values are different.

Rule Frequency. Consider now the following question: *for each customer, which is the frequency of each rule w.r.t. transactions ?* In other words, given a customer and an association rule, which is the number of transactions for which the rule holds on the total number of purchase transactions performed by the customer ?

Notice that the second formulation of this question is clearly based on the notion of sub-group, defined by the `DIVIDE BY` clause. Then, it is straightforward to define the *frequency* of an association rule in a group as *the number of sub-groups* in which the rule is found on the *total number of sub-groups in the group*.

The following `EVALUATE RULE` expression answers to the question.

```
EVALUATE RULE RuleFrequency AS
SELECT DISTINCT customer, RULE_ID, FREQUENCY
USING RULES RuleSet
ASSOCIATING item AS BODY, item AS HEAD
FROM Transactions
GROUP BY customer
DIVIDE BY transaction
```

The `FREQUENCY` keyword, allowed in the `SELECT` clause, generates an attribute in the output table reporting the frequency of the rule identified by

RULE_ID for the considered customer. Applying the expression to table Transactions, we obtain the instance of table RuleFrequency reported in Figure 14.6; observe the fact that some rules have frequency of 0.5, while other of 1.

Notice that, in absence of the DIVIDE BY clause, the frequency of a rule holding in a group is always 1.

The frequency can be considered as a form of aggregate function. For this reason, the FREQUENCY keyword can be used in conjunction with other aggregate functions, or to select, with the EXTRACTING RULES clause, interesting rules; this is shown in the following expression, that evaluates the frequency of rules, the total amount paid by the customer, and selects those rules having frequency less than 70%.

```
EVALUATE RULE RuleFrequencyAndAmount AS
SELECT DISTINCT customer, RULE_ID, FREQUENCY,
                SUM(amount) as amount
USING RULES RuleSet
ASSOCIATING item AS BODY, item AS HEAD
FROM Transactions
GROUP BY customer
DIVIDE BY transaction
EXTRACTING RULES WITH FREQUENCY < 0.7
```

3.4 INDEXES

Typically, the behaviour of customers may change in time, depending on several factors. The manager of a store may be interested in studying the fidelity of customers, especially to discover a reduction of fidelity and its causes.

An *index* is a simple and easy to understand tool for this purpose: given a rule r, a customer c, a quantitative measure $m(c)$ and a reference value $\overline{m}$ for the same quantitative measure, an index $i(c)$ relates the measure $m(c)$ with the reference value:

$$i(c) = \frac{m(c)}{\overline{m}}$$

If the index is much greater than 1, this means that the rule is relevant for the customer; if the index is much less than 1, this means that the rule is not relevant for the customer.

As far as the reference value is concerned, we can consider two cases.

- The reference value $\overline{m}$ depends only on the rule r, but is independent of the customer. Such a value is then general and determined a priori by the user.

customer	RULE_ID	index1
c_1	1	0.67
c_1	6	0.65
c_2	6	1.32
c_3	1	1.06
c_3	4	0.98
c_3	5	0.87
c_3	6	0.65
c_4	4	0.76

Indexes1

Figure 14.7 The table generated by the evaluation expression `Indexes1`.

customer	RULE_ID	total
c_1	1	70
c_1	6	60
c_2	6	65
c_3	1	91
c_3	4	20
c_3	5	31
c_3	6	35
c_4	4	40

(a) `Former`

customer	RULE_ID	index2
c_1	1	1.07
c_1	6	0.61
c_2	6	1.15
c_3	1	1.3
c_3	4	2.05
c_3	5	2.45
c_3	6	1.06
c_4	4	0.8

(b) `indexes2`

Figure 14.8 a) The table `Former` with the reference values for single customers. b) The table generated by the evaluation expression `Indexes2`.

- The reference value $\overline{m}$ depends on both the rule r and the user c ($\overline{m} = \overline{m}(c)$). This allows an analysis focused on the specific features of each single customer. Observe that the reference value can be computed by a previous application of the `EVALUATE RULE` operator.

The `EVALUATE RULE` operator provides constructs to evaluate indexes, as we now show.

Consider the rule set `RuleSet2` shown in Figure 14.3.b. This is the same rule set shown in Figure 14.3.a extended with the quantitative measure `ref-value`, which describes the reference value for the amount spent by a customer to purchase the items denoted by each rule. We can imagine that these values has been computed by performing a sort of pre-analysis.

If the user wishes to relate, for each customer and for each rule, the amount spent by the customer for that rule to the reference value, he/she can write the following expression.

```
EVALUATE RULE Indexes1 AS
```

```
SELECT DISTINCT customer, RULE_ID,
       INDEX(SUM(amount), RuleSet2.ref-value) AS index1
USING RULES RuleSet2
ASSOCIATING item AS BODY, item AS HEAD
FROM Transactions
GROUP BY customer
DIVIDE BY transaction
```

This expression is derived from expression `BasicT` (see Section 3.2) by extending the `SELECT` clause with the expression `INDEX(SUM(amount), RuleSet2.ref-value) AS index1`. The expression computes the quantitative measure `SUM(amount)` in the same way as described in Section 3.3, but instead of using this resulting value to generate the attribute `index1`, it divides it by the reference value of the rule, denoted as `RuleSet2.ref-value` and taken from the tuple of table `RuleSet2` describing the rule denoted by `RULE_ID`.

To understand, consider Figure 14.7, which reports the resulting table `Indexxes1` obtained applying the expression to the instance of table `Transactions` reported in Figure 14.1. Observe that the value of rule 6 is significantly under the reference value for customer c_1 and c_3 (the index has value 0.65), while the value is significantly over the reference value for customer c_2 (the index has value 1.32).

With such a result, the user might select customers with low values for specific rules and try to promote the products associated by those rules by means of, e.g., a special sale. After the promoting action, the user might apply again the same expression and compare the new index with the former index, to evaluate the effectiveness of the promoting actions.

The use of general reference values may be not enough to perform an in-depth analysis, focused on the specific behaviour of each single customer. Thus, it may be necessary to consider, for each rule, a reference value specific for each customer, value typically obtained by a former application of the `EVALUATE RULE` operator.

For instance, consider the `Former` table reported in Figure 14.8. This table might be the result of a former application of the operator.

The following expression evaluates an index, in order to compare the current value assumed by the quantitative measure with the former one.

```
EVALUATE RULE Indexes2 AS
SELECT DISTINCT customer, RULE_ID,
                INDEX(SUM(amount), Former.total) AS index2
USING RULES RuleSet2 AS A
ASSOCIATING item AS BODY, item AS HEAD
  EVALUATED IN Former(customer, RULE_ID, total)
  GROUP IS customer
```

customer	RULE_ID
c_1	1
c_1	2
c_1	3
c_1	6
c_2	1
c_2	2
c_2	3
c_2	6
c_3	6
c_4	4

(a) BasicM

customer	RULE_ID	amount
c_1	1	60
c_1	2	140
c_1	3	152
c_1	6	37
c_2	1	60
c_2	2	140
c_2	3	176
c_2	6	75
c_3	6	37
c_4	4	32

(b) AmountsM

Figure 14.9 a) The table generated by the evaluation expression `BasicM`. b) The table generated by the evaluation expression `AmountsM`.

```
FROM Transactions
GROUP BY customer
DIVIDE BY transaction
```

The resulting table, named `Indexes2`, is reported in Figure 14.8. Observe that some rules result with a high value for `index2` (around 2), meaning that their relevance increased for the customer, while other rules result with a low value (around 0.6), meaning that their relevance significantly decreased for the customer.

Hence, while the use of a general reference value allows the user to know how a rule is relevant w.r.t. the expected relevance for a generic customer, the use of a reference value specific for each single customer allows the user to study the evolution for each single customer.

Observe that the definition of index discussed at the beginning of this section may suggest that the `INDEX` function can be substituted by a simple division in the `SELECT` clause. We decided not to follow this solution because it requires an explicit join between the source and the reference tables in the `FROM` clause. In contrast, we want to hide, at the syntactic level, such a join, although this is conceptually necessary.

The computation of indexes is orthogonal w.r.t. other features of the `EVALUATE RULE` operator, then all the clauses previously discussed are still valid.

3.5 THE MINING CONDITION

One of the distinguishing features of the `MINE RULE` operator is the *mining condition* (see Section 2.1). Such condition, applied when rules are actually mined from the raw data, causes the extraction of a rule from a group only if the tuples from which the associated values come from respect the condition.

Consequently, if an association rule set has been obtained by a MINE RULE expression containing the mining condition, the quantitative evaluation should be performed by applying the mining condition as well. Consider the following expression:

```
EVALUATE RULE BasicM AS
SELECT DISTINCT customer, RULE_ID
USING RULES RuleSet
ASSOCIATING item AS BODY, item AS HEAD
WHERE BODY.price < HEAD.price
FROM Transactions
GROUP BY customer
```

obtained from the Basic expression by adding the WHERE clause after the ASSOCIATING clause, which denotes the mining condition BODY.price < HEAD.price. Such condition means that a rule holds in a group only if items appearing in the body are extracted from tuples whose value of attribute price is less than the value of attribute price in tuples from which items appearing in the head are extracted.

If we compare the instance of table BasicM reported in Figure 14.9 with the instance of table Basic reported in Figure 14.4, we notice that only rule number 6 holds for customer c_3, since tuples number 12 and 14 do not meet the mining condition: in fact, the price of item *A* is not less than the price of item *C*; consequently, all rules having item *A* in the body and item *C* in the head do not hold in the group.

Observe that the mining condition is orthogonal to the other features of the EVALUATE RULE operator.

The mining condition has effect on the evaluation of aggregate functions too. Consider the following expression, derived from expression Amounts by adding the same mining condition.

```
EVALUATE RULE AmountsM AS
SELECT DISTINCT customer, RULE_ID, SUM(amount) AS amount
USING RULES RuleSet
ASSOCIATING item AS BODY, item AS HEAD
WHERE BODY.price < HEAD.price
FROM Transactions
GROUP BY customer
```

let us compare the instance of table AmountsM reported in Figure 14.9, generated by the expression, with the instance of table Amounts reported in Figure 14.4. Consider rules valid for customer c_1. The value of attribute total

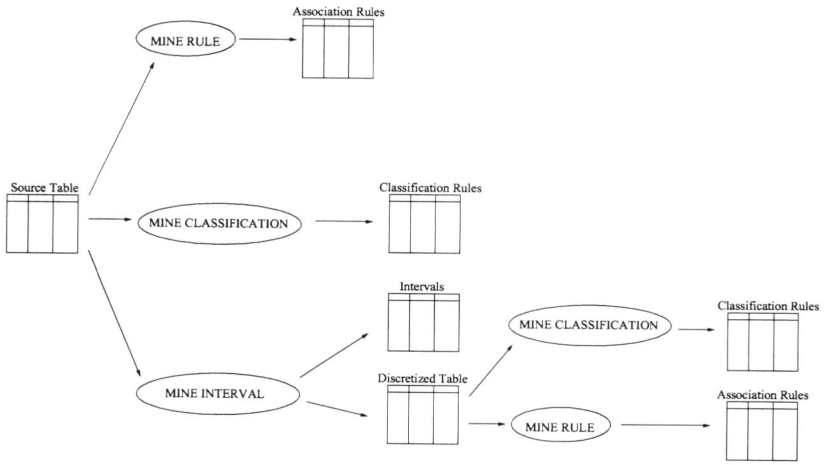

Figure 14.10 The KDD Process without the `EVALUATE RULE` Operator.

assumed by a rule in table `AmountsM` is smaller than the corresponding value in table `Amounts`: this is due to the fact that tuples number 1 and 4 do not meet the condition, thus tuple 1 does not participate to the computation of the aggregate function. However, rules 1, 2 and 3 still holds for customer `q`, due to the presence of tuple number 6 that meets the mining condition; hence, only this tuple participate to the evaluation of the aggregate function.

4. ENHANCING THE KNOWLEDGE DISCOVERY PROCESS

In the previous section we introduced the `EVALUATE RULE` operator. As the reader noticed, this operator is not a basic data mining tool, but is applied to the results of a previous data mining task, i.e. a rule set generated by the `MINE RULE` operator.

In effect the rationale behind the `EVALUATE RULE` operator is the following: the user that performed a data mining task based on the extraction of association rules, and selected a set of rules considered interesting, without this operator is not able to directly reuse them.

The scenario without the `EVALUATE RULE` operator can be represented by Figure 14.10. In our framework, three data mining operators are available.

- The `MINE RULE` operator can be applied to the source table to extract the most relevant association rules; association rules are stored into a table by the operator. This task can be performed several times, until the user finds the most significant rule set.

- The MINE CLASSIFICATION operator can be applied to the source table to produce classification rules that describe the data. An attribute of the source table is defined as *class attribute*, i.e. the attribute used in the classification process to identify the class which a record belongs to; the classifier builds the model for each class, determining the ranges of values of the non-class attributes that characterize a class. The MINE CLASSIFICATION operator generates a set of classification rules, which is also stored into a relational table.

- The MINE INTERVAL operator can be applied to the source table to discretize a numerical and continuous attribute; its output can be both the set of intervals and the discretized table (obtained from the source table by substituting the numerical attribute with the discretized version).

  Once an attribute has been discretized, it may be possible to apply the MINE RULE operator on such an attribute, in order to obtain associations of the discretized values; in effect, it is substantially useless to extract association rules from a numerical and continuous attribute, because its values are so sparse that the relevance (support) of a rule is in general very low and not significant. In contrast, the discretization step augments the frequency of values, making significant the extraction of association rules.

  Analogously, the discretized attribute can be considered as a *class attribute*, and the discretized table can be the input for the MINE CLASSIFICATION operator.

Observe that only on the results of the discretization step it is possible to apply the MINE RULE or the MINE CLASSIFICATION operators; this is not surprising, since the discretization step is normally a pre-processing step. In contrast, observe that the results of the MINE RULE and MINE CLASSIFICATION operators cannot be input of a subsequent analysis step.

4.1 THE EVALUATE RULE OPERATOR IN THE KDD PROCESS

Consider now the EVALUATE RULE operator. The operator requires the presence of a reference rule set to operate, i.e. a set of rules chosen by the user, without (but not necessarily) support and confidence values. The first step for the user, after the application of the MINE RULE operator, is the definition of the reference rule set (upper part of Figure 14.11).

- With the help of some visualization tools, the user can analyze the generated rule set and select those rules considered interesting. This step is denoted in the figure by means of the circle Selection. Observe that in

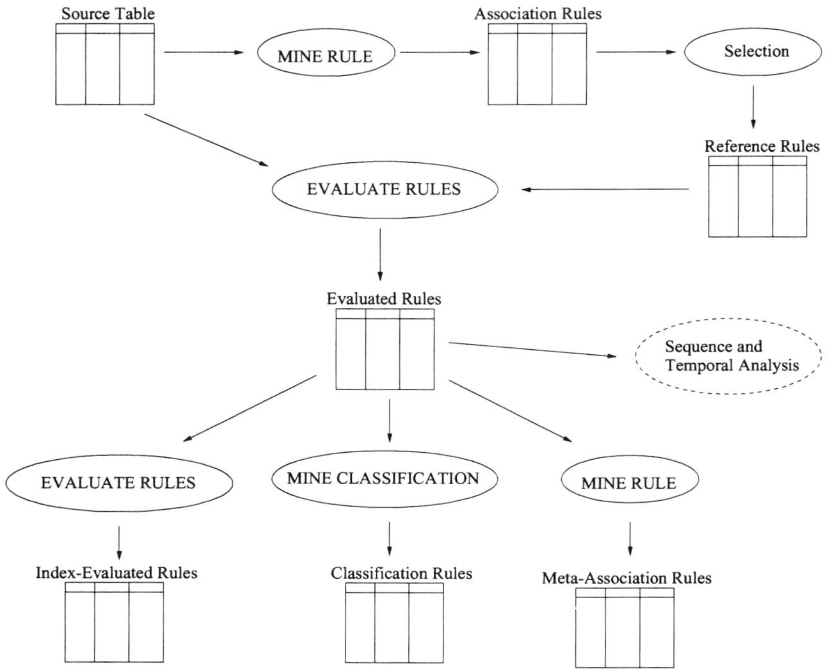

Figure 14.11 Enhanced KDD Process.

the relational environment no special tool is required to select interesting rules: a simple SQL `SELECT` statement is enough.

- The `EVALUATE RULE` operator can be now applied; it uses the reference rule set to analyze the source table, producing the so-called *evaluated rules*; for instance, if we consider the case of the `Transactions` table, rules in the reference rule set are evaluated w.r.t. customers.

The evaluated rule set can be the input for a variety of Knowledge discovery activities.

Evaluate Indexes. The first activity is a second application of the `EVALUATE RULE` operator, to evaluate rules by means of indexes. In effect, if the first application of the operator evaluated rules with a quantitative measure, this measure can be used as the basis for index computation.

Observe that this activity can be performed later in time w.r.t. the generation of the evaluated rule set, for instance when new data are appended to the source table; we can also consider that only the increment is used to evaluate indexes. This way, it is possible to analyze the evolution in time of customer behaviour.

Meta-Association Rules. The second activity is the application of the MINE RULE operator to the table containing the evaluated rules. We obtain a sort of *meta association rules*, i.e. rules which associate rule identifiers instead of items. For example, consider the table BasicT reported in Figure 14.4, obtained by the expression BasicT; applying the MINE RULE operator as follows

```
MINE RULE Meta AS
SELECT DISTINCT 1..n RULE_ID AS BODY, 1..n RULE_ID AS HEAD,
       SUPPORT, CONFIDENCE
FROM BasicT
GROUP BY customer
EXTRACTING RULES WITH SUPPORT 0.4, CONFIDENCE 0.5
```

we obtain the rule $\{6\} \Rightarrow \{1\}$, with support 0.5 and confidence 0.66. Such meta-rule means that for the 50% of customers, when the rule $6 : \{B\} \Rightarrow \{A\}$ holds, also the rule $1 : \{A\} \Rightarrow \{CD\}$ holds. Not only, the very high confidence (0.66) means that this association is really strong.

Based on this result, the user might decide to promote product B, in order to obtain a chain effect on the sells of products C and D.

Classification. The evaluated rule set might be used for a classification task, with the purpose of studying the characteristics of users for which a given rule holds.

Suppose we have a table describing customers (with properties such as age, job type, study degree, sex, etc.); let us join this table with the evaluated rule set, in order to associate customer characteristics to each rule. The rule identifier can play the role of class attribute; Hence, the resulting classification model describes the most common features of customers for which a given rule holds, in terms of age, job type, sex, etc..

Nevertheless, we might choose a different class attribute. If, for instance, we choose the job type as class attribute, the resulting classification model describes the most common features of people doing a given job type in terms of age, sex, most common satisfied rules (possibly with most common ranges for quantitative measures), etc.. Consequently, the user might decide to promote different products depending on the different job type of customers.

Sequence and Temporal Analysis. The evaluated rules can also be used for sequence and temporal analysis. For example, suppose the Transactions table is augmented with an attribute indicating the month (attribute month) in which each transaction was performed. By specifying attributes customer and month as grouping attributes, we force the EVALUATE RULE operator to evaluate rules for each customer, month by month. On the resulting evaluated rule set, we might perform sequence analysis and/or temporal analysis, e.g. to understand the most common temporal fluctuations of customer behaviour in different periods of time, or to discover cases of reduced customer fidelity. In this latter case, further analysis might be done to understand why customer fidelity decreases, for instance by means of further classification tasks or mining of meta-association rules on the data of customers whose fidelity is decreasing[1].

Temporal analysis can be also performed when new data are appended to the source table. In effect, we might apply the `EVALUATE RULE` operator only to the increment data, comparing the results with previous evaluated rule sets, or building an historical repository of the evaluated rules, on which to perform temporal analysis.

At the moment, no operator for sequence and temporal analysis has been developed for the relational database mining framework; however, we plan for the near future to address this topic.

5. CONCLUSIONS AND FUTURE WORK

In this paper, we introduced the `EVALUATE RULE` operator. The operator has been devised to address the problem of evaluating association rule sets obtained by former extraction of association rules, and filtered by the user in order to retain association rules considered interesting. Several classes of quantitative evaluations are provided by the operator, in particular aggregations and indexes, that allow the analyst to perform an in-depth analysis of selected rules w.r.t. the data.

The paper shows that the results of the operator can be used to continue the knowledge discovery process, by applying different mining techniques to the results provided by the `EVALUATE RULE` operator, possibly combined with the row data; the mining techniques considered in this paper are association rule mining, classification and discretization, but any other mining technique can be considered, such as sequence and/or temporal analysis.

In particular, the paper illustrates an interesting abstraction, i.e. the concept of *meta-association rules*, rules that associate rule identifiers instead of raw data items. This concept comes out naturally, with the availability of the `EVALUATE RULE` operator.

The operator is part of the *Relational Database Mining Framework*, a collection of tools devised in such a way they are fully integrated with the relational database environment. These tools take relational tables as input and stores their results (data and/or patterns) into relational tables too. Furthermore, they are based on a SQL-like syntax, and are based on semantic models that put in evidence all the semantic features of the addressed topic. In the end, the strong integration with the relational environment ensures the interoperability between data mining tools and the classical statements provided by SQL.

Ongoing and Future work. We are currently implementing the engine for the `EVALUATE RULE` operator, in order to actually integrate it in our framework.

The architecture of the engine is such that it exploits the presence of a relational DBMS to preprocess data and evaluate SQL predicates specified in the `EVALUATE RULE` expressions. Hence, the core of the engine is a specialized algorithm designed to operate in one single pass over the data (suitably preprocessed by the DBMS). The user must be totally unaware of this architecture, and must submit simply the expression to the engine. For this work, we are exploiting the experience obtained with the work Meo et al., 1998b.

In the near future, we plan to address the problem of performing sequence and/or temporal analysis in the context of the Relational Database Mining Framework, by defining and implementing a specific operator.

A second, but not less important, topic we plan to address is the definition of a user interface designed to assist the user in the management of complex knowledge discovery processes. We think that this user interface should be based on a really open architecture, in order to easily integrate not only mining tools, but also visualization tools and process management tools, i.e. tools that overview the execution of complex knowledge discovery processes.

Notes

1. Observe that the suggested analysis tasks involving customer personal data should be conducted in a blind way w.r.t. customer identity. In effect, it is not important why a single customer changes behaviour, but why 50 or 100 customers change their behaviour at the same time.

References

Agrawal, R., Imielinski, T., and Swami, A. (1993). Mining association rules between sets of items in large databases. In *Proc.ACM SIGMOD Conference on Management of Data*, pages 207–216, Washington, D.C. British Columbia.

Agrawal, R. and Psaila, G. (1995). Active data mining. In *KDD-95*, Montreal.

Agrawal, R., Psaila, G., Wimmers, E. L., and Zait, M. (1995). Querying shapes of histories. In *Proceedings of the 21st VLDB Conference*, Zurich, Switzerland.

Bayardo, R. (1998). Efficiently mining long patterns from databases. In *Proceedings of the ACM-SIGMOD International Conference on the Management of Data*, Seattle, Washington, USA.

Chen, M., Han, J., and Yu, P. S. (1996). Data mining: An overview from a database perspective. *IEEE Transactions on Knowledge and Data Engineering*, 8(6):866–883.

Fayyad, U. M., Piatetsky-Shapiro, G., Smyth, P., and Uthurusamy, R. (1996). *Advances in Knowledge Discovery in Databases*. AAAI/MIT Press.

Han, J., Fu, Y., Wang, W., Koperski, K., and Zaiane, O. (1996). DMQL: A data mining query language for relational databases. *In Proceedings of SIGMOD-96 Workshop on Research Issues on Data Mining and knowledge Discovery.*

Imielinski, T., Virmani, A., and Abdoulghani, A. (1996). Datamine: Application programming interface and query language for database mining. *KDD-96*, pages 256–260.

Kdd-nuggets. Knowledge discovery mine: Data mining and knowledge discovery resources. *http://www.kdnuggets.com/siftware.html.*

Kohavi, R., Sommerfield, D., and Dougherty, J. (1996). Data mining using MLC++, a machine learning library in c++. In *Proceedings of the IEEE Conference on Tools with AI*, Toulouse, France.

Lanzi, P. and Psaila, G. (1999). A relational database mining framework with classification and discretization. In *In Proceedings of SEBD-99*, Como, Italy.

Meo, R., Psaila, G., and Ceri, S. (1996). A new SQL-like operator for mining association rules. In *Proceedings of the 22st VLDB Conference*, Bombay, India.

Meo, R., Psaila, G., and Ceri, S. (1998a). An extension to SQL for mining association rules. *Journal of Data Mining and Knowledge Discovery*, 2(2).

Meo, R., Psaila, G., and Ceri, S. (1998b). A tightly coupled architecture for data mining. In *IEEE Intl. Conference on Data Engineering*, Orlando, Florida.

Savasere, A., Omiecinski, E., and Navathe, S. (1995). An efficient algorithm for mining association rules in large databases. In *Proceedings of the 21st VLDB Conference*, Zurich, Swizerland.

Chapter 15

SPEEDING UP HYPOTHESIS DEVELOPMENT

Jörg A. Schlösser, Peter C. Lockemann, Matthias Gimbel
Universität Karlsruhe, Fakultät für Informatik, PO Box 6980, D-76128 Karlsruhe, Germany

Keywords: KDD-process, materialization, query shipping, query optimization, reuse of results, management of process histories

Abstract: Knowledge discovery in databases (KDD) is a long-lasting, highly interactive and iterative process, in which the human data analyst searches for the right knowledge by repeatedly querying the database, using so-called derivation streams. Each stream consists of several data exploration steps to select, filter, transform, etc. the input data for the final analysis step (e.g., a data mining algorithm). After executing a stream the data analyst redevelops or adjusts his hypothesis by interpreting the results. This should give him new insights as to how to proceed, or how to backtrack and explore alternatives to earlier derivations. The central premises of this chapter are that current KDD systems do too little in the way of supporting the hypothesis development, that the development - or exploration - phase is closely intertwined with data mining, and that the interactive and spontaneous nature of hypothesis development in the presence of large databases requires much better performance than what is common today. The central idea is to exploit the KDD process history to overlay the general optimized query processing capabilities of an underlying relational database system (RDBMS) with a more KDD-process-oriented optimization strategy, which takes the frequent backtracking in a KDD process into account. Our approach is three-fold: First, we propose an information model for documenting the entire derivation history. On its basis we develop subsumption mechanisms for process and result matching, and introduce suitable access and retrieval facilities. Second, based on this model, we develop a strategy and technique for automatically reusing earlier results for the execution of subsequent streams whenever possible in order to avoid expensive recomputations. Since reuse requires prior materialization of intermediate results in persistent store, we introduce a strategy for automatic decisions on materialization and de-materialization. Finally, we translate data preparation steps into corresponding database queries that are transferred to the RDBMS for further optimization and execution.

1. INTRODUCTION

Knowledge Discovery in Databases (KDD) has sufficiently matured as a technology to become a widespread tool in the hands of commercial applications for extracting interesting and meaningful information, by analyzing huge and rapidly growing volumes of data. By discovering interrelationships between seemingly disparate data one hopes to gain insights, and thus knowledge, from the wealth of data collected more or less indiscriminately over long periods of time. To the naive observer the metaphor of data mining seems to suggest that all one has to do is dig into the data and come up with novel insights. And in fact, much of the research on KDD seems to support the naive view by focusing on sophisticated data mining algorithms providing the core capability for the automatic generalization of specific data to high-level information (e.g., decision trees, rules).

The metaphor implies a more sophisticated view, though. Mining is never without a specific purpose in mind: One has to know what to look for, whether it is gold, coal or iron ore. Each differs in the way where seams can be found and how they are composed, and hence, how they are to be extracted. Consequently, extraction has to be preceded by a lengthy process of exploration and preparation. To carry the metaphor over to KDD: Before one can apply data mining algorithms one must determine what to look for. The explorative phase is usually referred to as hypothesis development. Its objective is to determine the relevant data subsets, the applicable algorithms and the parameter settings.

In this chapter we go one step further by claiming that there is not even a clear separation into an explorative phase followed by a mining phase. Rather, real-world KDD is a highly user-interactive, iterative and long-lasting *process* in which a human data analyst searches for the right knowledge by repeatedly querying the data base (Figure 1). Hence, we follow other authors by emphasizing the key role played by the human data analyst in KDD (Selfridge et al., 1996). Each iteration in the process consists of several data preparation (preprocessing) steps to select, filter, transform, etc. the input data, and a final analysis method (e.g., data mining algorithm). We refer to such a collection of steps as a *derivation stream*. After executing a stream the data analyst interprets the result, hopefully gaining new insights as to how to proceed and investigate further avenues, or how to backtrack and explore alternatives to earlier derivations.

This iterative view of hypothesis development is of practical importance because many commercial KDD systems (e.g. CLEMENTINE, Intelligent Miner, Mine Set etc.) offer a large variety of extraction, sampling, statistical and discovery methods among which the user may choose for analyzing data. Hence, in principle the data analyst may start with only a very vague idea of what view of the raw data, and hence what input form, is relevant to success. Likewise, by no means will it be clear to him which method will deliver meaningful results. In general, he can be expected to rely on past experiences.

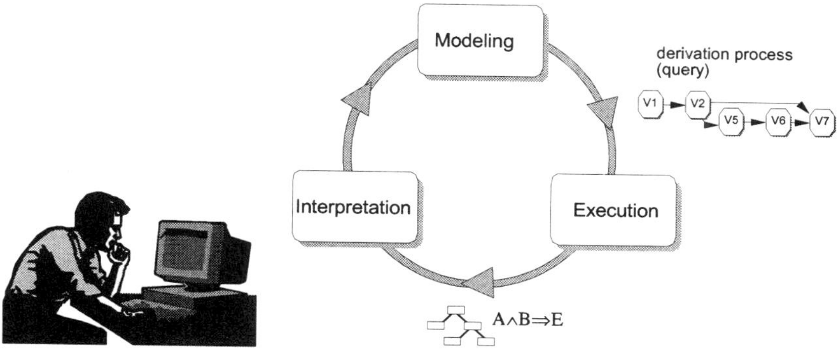

Figure 1. KDD Design Process

Of course, iteration is time consuming. If we wish to obtain meaningful results in a short time in order to react to outside events in a meaningful way, it is essential to speed up the exploration, and thus the hypothesis development. This chapter suggests two techniques to approach this goal. One is based on the very nature of iteration together with the premise of useful past experience, and gives rise to two sub-techniques:

- Documentation of earlier KDD processes or earlier steps of the current KDD process ("process history") in a repository together with the capability for consulting the history.
- Materialization of the results[1] of earlier streams, i.e. out of the process history, in order to avoid expensive recomputations, and automatic inclusion of materializations in new iterations.

The second technique is based on the assumption that the raw data is typically maintained by a relational database system (RDBMS). In most cases it would be unfeasible or at least would require a substantial amount of time to export the whole data to the KDD system and transform it suitably. Instead it should remain in the database system if possible, in order to make good use of today's commercial RDBMS capability to handle large volumes

[1] In the following we use *materialization* as a short term for "materialized intermediate result".

of data and to answer SQL queries efficiently. Even further, RDBMS should handle the materializations as well. In other words, the KDD system should "out-source" many of its explorative data inspections to the RDMBS server in the form of SQL queries. Such a strategy, called *query-shipping*, focuses on reducing the amount of data to load into the client (KDD system) by increasing the number and complexity of queries sent to the RDMBS server.

The remainder of the chapter is organized as follows. Since materialization is at the heart of the speed-up techniques, and materialization relies in turn on a suitable documentation and representation of the process history, we start by introducing a conceptual model for capturing all relevant aspects of the history. This model will be referred to in the sequel as the *information model.* Section 2 introduces the information model. Section 3 establishes a framework for the various speed-up techniques - the execution architecture of our KDD system, CITRUS. In Sections 4 and 5 we describe the methods for the automatic integration of new streams and their (intermediate) results into the IM. Then we give in Section 6 a short description of how the information model (IM) and the relational model are connected, i.e., of how IM-operations are mapped to SQL for query shipping. In Section 7 and 8 the materialization techniques are discussed: the optimization of SQL queries by using materialized intermediate results, and the automatic materialization of intermediate results. In Section 9 we discuss the viability of our approach by means of CITRUS. In Section 10 we show how our techniques can be expanded to the management of mining results. Section 11 considers related approaches. We conclude with an outlook on further work and with a claim that our approach is generally applicable and useful for any integrated, comprehensive KDD system.

2. INFORMATION MODEL

The information model must be capable of documenting the entire KDD process history. Essentially, a history is a collection of retrieval queries which produce intermediate results, and which are connected via these results or the original raw data as their input arguments. In other words, the information model expresses traces of queries. Since the information model is a static structure, its elements must reflect both the "natural" properties of the data and the operations that produced them.

The main constructs are as follows:

1. **Unitary concepts**: The chief concept is the *objectset.* An objectset is a collection of similarly structured *data objects* and captures input data or intermediate results of streams. A data object consists of an object-identifier and descriptive *attributes*. As opposed to the relational model

the IM allows *complex* attributes, i.e., attributes that reference objects in other objectsets, as well as *multi-valued* attributes. Objectsets do not represent final analysis results like rules, graphs, or decision trees. For these the IM provides the concept of *knowledge segments*. Finally, *operator-cards* act as containers for holding (parameter-) information about an operation.

2. **Operators and queries**: The information model offers a set of generic operators which - similar to the relational model - are set-oriented and can easily be combined into more or less complex queries. Each operator takes an objectset together with a subset of proper attributes as input. We refer to such a pair (objectset, set of attributes) as a *focus* of the information base. Operators for the preprocessing phase manipulate their input foci, and are defined along the abstraction principle, i.e., each operator reduces one aspect of information (and thus is orthogonal to other operators). They can formally be classified according to objectset cardinality (which is reduced by the two operators select and group), number of attributes (reduction by project), attribute domains (value computations by derive, value classification by generalize), set size of multi-valued attributes (subsetting by restrict, compactification by aggregate). Data-mining algorithms are represented by a single generic operator (discover) which takes a focus and produces a knowledge segment from it. The detailed definitions of the operators can be found in (Breitner & Lockemann, 1997).
3. **Semantic relationships**: History is defined by earlier streams (or (IM-)queries). The underlying assumption is that the operations within the queries can be reflected in the IM schema in the form of semantic relationships (Breitner, 1998). Given the instantiation (unit) of some unitary concept as the sink of a semantic relationship, this relationship identifies its origin, i.e., both the source unit and the operation that was applied to it. To identify the operation, the corresponding operator-card is attached to the relationship. The operation itself is used to classify the relationship (relationship semantics): The sub- and grp-relationships result from select- and group-operations and connect objectsets, the drv-, gen- and restr-relationships are due to the derive-, generalize- and restrict-operations and connect attributes, disc is a relationship between objectsets and knowledge segments.

   Except for the disc-relationship all semantic relationships can form lattices, if operators of the same kind are applied more than once. For instance, generalizing or restricting attributes with successive generalize- or restrict-operations will lead to several new attributes that are connected to each other via gen- or restr-relationships.

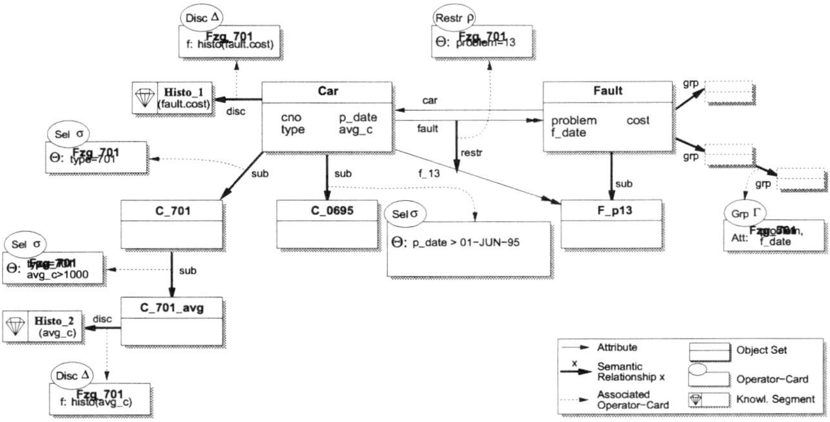

Figure 2. Exemplary Information Directory

Figure 2 shows an exemplary information directory. This simplistic image of a real world application scenario consists of cars with the attributes type, date of production (p_date), fault, and avg_c for the average costs for all faults of a car. To keep the schema legible, primitive attributes are listed with the objectsets, complex attributes are depicted with a light (double-headed if multi-valued) arrow. In the example, a fault is characterized by the cause of the fault (problem), the date the fault occurred (f_date), and the costs connected to it.

The bold arrows document semantic relationships. Attached with the broken arrows are their operator-cards. For instance, C_701 is a subset of Car and was derived by selecting only cars of type 701. Similarly, the attribute f_rad was generated as a restriction of the attribute fault to those faults with radiator problems (problem=13). Boxes with a diamond represent knowledge segments as the outcome of a discover-operation. For instance, the element labeled Histo_2 represents the distribution of the attribute avg_c for the objectset C_701_avg.

3. THE EXECUTION ARCHITECTURE OF CITRUS

The iterative process fusing exploration and mining requires a common framework. Before going into the details of our speed-up techniques we give a brief outline of our framework. Our work was part of the development of the general-purpose KDD system CITRUS (Wirth et al., 1997). As a starting point for CITRUS the existing commercial knowledge discovery tool CLEMENTINE was chosen. Developed by Integral Solutions Ltd. (ISL), it provides an environment that integrates multiple analysis algorithms with methods for data preparation, visualization and reporting. All facilities are presented and used through an intuitive graphical user interface. Based on a methodology called "visual programming" the analyst models streams by placing icons, each representing a single preprocessing step, analysis method, etc., on a drawing pane and connecting them to define the data flow. Afterwards, to execute a stream the analyst simply selects the appropriate entry on the menu of the final icon, and the result is presented to the analyst using appropriate visualizations of CLEMENTINE.

The major weakness of CLEMENTINE at the time was that the tool was based on a main-memory runtime system, i.e. all the data processed had to be loaded into main memory and all the processing took place there. This puts severe limits on the amount of data that can be processed and defies the very idea of KDD. Hence, we took it on us to extend CLEMENTINE by persistent storage. To take advantage of the many benefits that database management systems (DBMS) offer – particularly set-oriented associative access and high performance - we decided on the use of powerful relational database servers. The objectives given in Section 1 were a direct outcome of this decision.

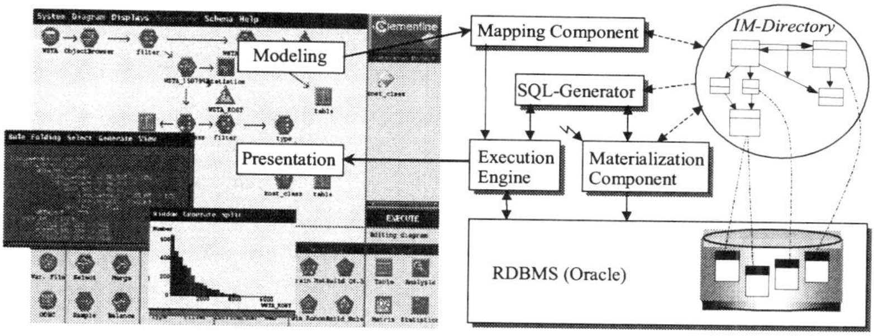

Figure 3. Execution Architecture of CITRUS

Extending CLEMENTINE by several components, CITRUS integrates the information model and the strategy for an efficient stream execution. Figure 3 shows the resulting architecture of CITRUS with its main components for the stream execution on the right, and its graphical user front-end on the left. In particular, the history is maintained in the form of an IM schema that represents the raw data, executed streams with incurred intermediate results (i.e., preprocessed data sets), and the final results (i.e., graphs, rule-sets, statistical measures, etc.). It is augmented by information on the materializations and serves as directory to the relational database. In the sequel we refer to this central repository of information as the *information directory*.

The user front-end provides the means for both, modeling the streams (IM-queries) and presenting the results. For the execution a query is handed over to the *mapping component*. The latter inspects the information directory successively for each query to determine whether and how it may be related to results of former queries. As a result the entire query or part of it may be matched by (in a precise sense to be defined) "equivalent" queries. The unmatched parts of the query are incorporated into the directory and linked to the matched elements, i.e. former queries. This component contains a retrieval component, which allows a user to query the information directory itself. It supports his interpretation of specifically named results, by reconstructing the streams (and, hence, queries in some normalized form) that gave rise to them.

Subsequently, the query is transformed to include references to corresponding elements of the information directory and then passed on to the *execution component*. The execution component performs the actual execution of the query. An important aspect is to determine whether the references correspond to materializations. The first check is on whether the final result of the query is available in materialized form. If so, this simplest case of execution consists of a single 'load-result' instruction. Otherwise, the component determines which part of the overall query can be mapped to SQL, and calls the *SQL-generator* to find an optimized SQL query for such a part, where the optimum is defined in terms of the available materializations. The resulting SQL query is then shipped to the underlying RDBMS (which will employ its own optimization strategy). The answer is fed back to the execution component to process the remaining part of the entire stream (e.g., the data mining algorithm).

The automatic materialization of useful intermediate results is the responsibility of the *materialization component*. Periodically initiated, it scans the information directory in order to select intermediate results that should be materialized or dematerialized, and transmits the corresponding SQL statements to the RDBMS. To estimate the benefit of materializations and to create the "create table ..." statements, the materialization component again uses the SQL-generator to construct optimized SQL code.

For a more detailed description of the architecture see (Schlösser, 1999).

4. SEARCHING THE INFORMATION DIRECTORY

Queries are submitted in the form of (derivation) streams that are visualized as directed acyclic graphs whose nodes represent basic operators (Figure 4). The mapping component, by searching the information directory for traces of equivalent or similar queries, pursues two objectives. First, it incorporates the query (in fact, the novel part of it) into the directory (directory evolution). Second, it passes the query together with auxiliary information collected during the mapping phase to the execution engine which determines the source data (raw, or derived and materialized).

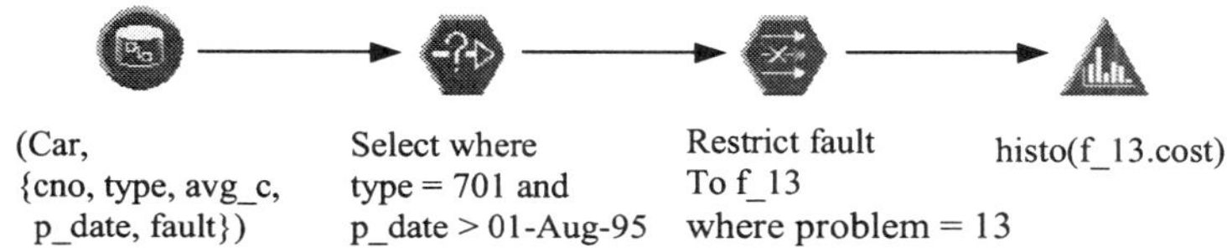

Figure 4. Query Example

The search follows a pattern-match strategy that is guided by the operators of the query. Suppose that during the search we reached in the directory a certain objectset together with a set of attributes (we refer to the objectset as the current *focus* of the query). Let *op* be the next operator in the query. Then *op* determines the kind of semantic relationship that is to be navigated from the focus. If there is a corresponding relationship (a traversal *candidate*), it can in fact only be navigated if its operator card satisfies the parameters of *op*. As a result of the navigation the focus shifts to a new unit.

As a matter of fact shifting the focus is somewhat more complicated. Because the semantic relationships of a given kind may form a lattice, the search from a given objectset may have to examine an entire hierarchical structure. Just take unit Car in Figure 2. It may well be that the focus should follow the operator disc of C_701_avg. The match may also be incomplete. In this case we examine whether one operator-card is more general than the other, i.e., subsumes it. For instance the expression type=701 is more general than (subsumes) (type=701$\wedge$ p_date>01-Jun-95). In case the query is more specific, we choose among the more general candidates within the hierarchy the most detailed - a choice that may be ambiguous. If the query is less specific than any of the operator cards in the directory, one may have to combine several of them. Due to all these complications, we refer to the search as *classification* rather than navigation. The detailed classification algorithm is given in (Breitner, 1998).

The overall search is a cycle of classifications, where each cycle picks the next operator from the query, examines candidate directory elements, and shifts the focus. The critical decision, then, is to select the initial focus. A further complication arises when an operation was already applied in the past, though not in precisely the same fashion but as part of some other operation. Hence, the search follows a fairly complicated algorithm:

- Determine the relationship that corresponds to the type of the considered operator *op*, e.g., the sub-relationship for the select-operator. Determine the root of the lattice formed by this relationship, where the lattice includes the current focus.
- Generate an operator-card for *op* and normalize the expression. Normalization eliminates differences in the structural representations so that comparisons are simplified.
- Classify the result of *op* by traversing the lattice and matching the operator-card against the operator-cards attached to the relationships.

The output of the classification is a pair consisting of the final directory element (if one already exists in the directory) together with the set of "most specific" elements on the path to the specified element from which it could be derived.

If no final directory element is found, a corresponding element is inserted into the information directory in a following evolution cycle, together with appropriate relationships from its "most specific" elements. Therefore, the overall mapping is a process of subsequent classification and evolution cycles, until the whole query has been mapped.

To give an example for the schema mapping, take the information directory of Figure 3, and the query of Figure 4 consisting of a selection followed by a restrict-operation to select for each car the subset of its associated faults, and a discover-operation for computing a distribution. The initial input focus of the query is defined by (Car, {cno, type, p_date, avg_c, fault}), i.e., the objectset Car together with all attributes.

Suppose the selection has been encountered. Then the classification proceeds as follows:

- Choose the sub-relationship. The root of its lattice is objectset Car.
- The normalized formula for the operator-card is the same as in the original query, namely (type=701$\wedge$ p_date>01-Jun-95).
- The result of the classification is (nil, {C_701, C_0695}), indicating that no exactly matching unit was found, but there are most specific objectsets {C_701, C_0695} which subsume the result of the selection.

5. DOCUMENTATION OF THE PROCESS HISTORY

In order to be able to reconstruct earlier queries and reuse their results if possible, a description of the result of the current query must be inserted into the directory (*directory evolution*). The query is specified as a sequence of operations, and insertion is such that the sequence - if executed as a trace - would have the result as its output. As noted in before, the mapping component attempts to match as much of a query as possible to the directory (*directory subsumption*). Clearly, an evolution of the information directory is necessary only if no matching directory element was found during classification. In this case the unmatched parts are incorporated into the directory in the form of new units together with connecting semantic relationships. Insertion must be at a directory location such that the relationship to earlier results is properly reflected. As a result, each executed query leaves a "trace" in the information directory, i.e., documents the history of the process.

What is desirable is to add the new information to the information directory in an automatic fashion. Consequently, the evolution is directly integrated into the classification process, by accompanying each classification cycle with an evolution step whenever necessary. We associate with each operator a procedure evolve_schema which is responsible for augmenting the information directory in an operator-specific way. It takes as arguments the result from the classification algorithm as well as the operator-card of the operator, where the result contains the matching element if existing, or at least the directory locations in the form of the most specific concepts which subsume the result of the operator. It is the output of the evolution step - a pair (objectset, set of attributes) - which is passed on to the next classification cycle. In the special case of a discover-operator, the output of evolve_schema simply consists of a knowledge segment.

We illustrate directory evolution by continuing our example from Section 4. Because no matching objectset was found, a following evolution step leads to the insertion of a new objectset, say C_701_0895, which is directly connected via sub-relationships to C_701 and C_0695. Afterwards, the focus (C_701_0895, {cno, type, p_date, avg_c, fault}) serves as the input for the classification of the restrict-operator. This classification successfully delivers (f_13, {fault}) because when following the restr-relationship from fault one encounters an exact match with the already existing unit f_13. Therefore, no further schema evolution is needed, and the starting point to classify the final discover-operator is the focus (C_701_0895, {cno, type, p_date, avg_c, fault}). Finally, the classification of the discover-operator fails since no matching knowledge segments (i.e. knowledge segments based on the same input with the same operator parameters) can be found, so that a new knowledge segment Histo_3 is inserted. Figure 5 shows how the directory in Figure 2 evolved for the query from above.

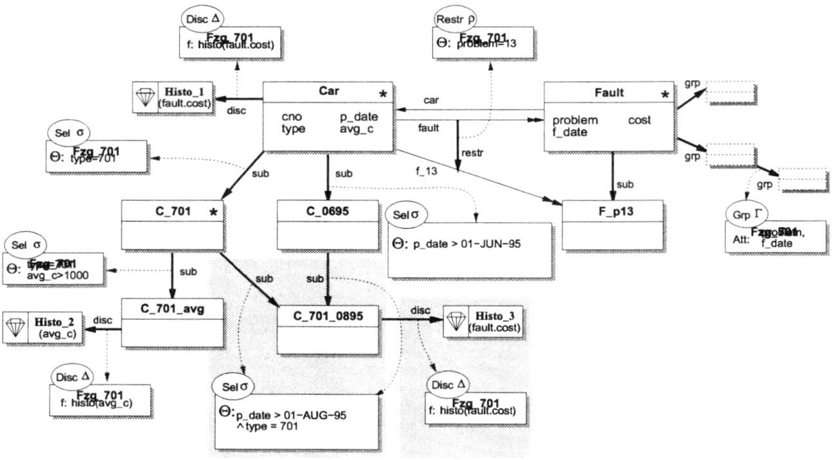

Figure 5. Information Directory after Query Mapping

We make two final observations. Usually there are alternative queries to express the same result. In order to avoid redundancies in the directory, and to detect equivalence of query and trace, a *normalization* procedure is applied during the classification. Second, as mentioned before, a critical decision during classification is the selection of the initial focus. This may of course be done manually by the user, but due to the iterative nature of the exploration the mapping component may instead act automatically by using the output of the directory evolution algorithm of the predecessor query.

6. LINKING THE INFORMATION MODEL WITH THE RELATIONAL MODEL

As mentioned earlier, our KDD framework "out-sources" data management to a relational database system (RDBMS). This has two consequences. One, the raw data is typically maintained by a relational database system, and it should stay there. Second, materialized intermediate results should be shipped to the RDBMS. All processing on the database data will then have to take place in the RDBMS. As a further consequence, our approach uses the IM only on a conceptual level. The analyst models a stream as a sequence of IM-operations, but the "IM stream" is subsequently translated to a relational query whose data preparation steps are forwarded to the RDBMS server in form of SQL queries. Such a strategy, called *query-shipping*, focuses on reducing the amount of data to load into the client (KDD system) by increasing the number and complexity of queries sent to the RDBMS server.

Two problems ensue:

- To start a KDD process on the IM level we need an IM view of the raw relational database. Hence, the information directory must be initialized, by translating the given RM schema to an initial IM directory.
- Before intermediate results can be stored as relational tables, the IM directory structure of the result must be translated to an RM schema.

6.1 RM to IM

The translation of a given RM schema is done automatically by interpreting each table as objectset, where tuples correspond to objects one-to-one. An attribute of a table leads to a primitive, single-valued attribute of the objectset, whereas a foreign key relationship is translated into two inverse, correlated complex attributes.

6.2 IM to RM

For the structural translation from IM to RM, we define a function *rel_ext*(O,***A***) which computes for a given focus (O,***A***) the corresponding relational extension. The function is highly complex due to the "impedance mismatch" between the relational model and the information model. In order to store an objectset extension as a database table, object identifiers and complex attributes have to be mapped onto combinations of primitive attributes, and multi-valued attributes must be flattened. If the multi-valued attributes are unrelated (as e.g. the extras and the repair dates of a car), in the relational model this is called multi-valued dependency and is displayed via the cartesian product of the respective attribute values. If, however, different multi-valued attributes have been derived via the same complex attribute (e.g. the repair dates and the problems causing them are derived via the same complex attribute FAULT), there are functional dependencies that must be handled in order to display the correct relational extension. To overcome this difficulty, we introduced so-called *reference-paths* that consist of a minimal subset of identifiers of those objectsets found along the derivation paths of multi-valued attributes.

Given these relational extensions, one can now develop for each preprocessing operator of the IM applied to a focus an SQL query applied to the corresponding relation. The translation rules can be determined by a constructive proof procedure (Schlösser, 1999). By successively applying the translation rules for each operation, one can express each IM query as an SQL query that computes the relational extension of a result focus from the relations that correspond to the input focus. This allows the system to stay entirely within the relational system without the need for an expensive detour through the IM. For example, for the restrict operation in Figure 4 the corresponding SQL query could look like:

```
SELECT   R_base.*, R_sub.f_13
FROM rel_ext(C_701_0895, {cno, type, avg_c, p_date, fault}) R_base
     (SELECT DISTINCT fno as f_13
      FROM   rel_ext(Fault, {fno, problem})
      WHERE  problem = 13) R_sub
WHERE    R_base.fault (+)= R_sub.f_13;
```

The last where-clause denotes a left-outer-join of the relations R_base and R_sub. An outer join is used here to preserve the object-oriented semantics of the IM with its distinction between object identities (affected by the selection operator) and attribute values (affected by the restrict operator). In our example, the query yields all cars that satisfy the selection condition, not only those with heater problems (problem = 13).

7. GENERATION OF SQL QUERIES

We now address the issue of query shipping. Even if no materializations have occurrred, an IM query must be translated to an SQL query, by tracing back the focus of the query to the raw data as represented in the directory. There may be alternative ways to do so which gives rise to an IM-induced optimization problem. Once a particular path has been determined, it will be translated to an SQL query for the RDBMS where it will undergo an RDBMS specific query optimization. In fact, the two optimizations are not mutually independent. The problem becomes even more severe if we have to account for materializations. If there are several materializations which could be used alternatively, only those leading to the most efficient stream execution should be selected.

The basic idea in all these cases is to associate an SQL template with each IM operator. An IM query is then translated by combining the SQL templates corresponding to the IM operators in the query and finally applying the resulting SQL query to the base tables corresponding to the raw or materialized objectsets.

7.1 The Optimization Problem

If materialized intermediate results are to be used, for one IM query result there may exist several ways to construct the corresponding relational extension. To find the most efficient SQL query is the task of the SQL-Generator in Figure 3. In the best case, the relational extension of the focus corresponds exactly to a materialization, i.e., a database table T. Then the SQL query consists of a simple "select * from T;" statement. Otherwise the SQL-Generator searches for other useful materializations in order to generate alternative SQL queries. For example, suppose Table 1 lists the relational extensions that have been materialized for the objectsets Car and Car_701 of the information directory of Figure 5. (Note that one has to consider in addition the "implicit" materializations of the raw data.)

Relational Extension	Materialization (Table)
Rel_ext(Car, {cno, type, p_date, fault})	R1_Car
Rel_ext(Car, {cno, fault, f_13})	R2_Car
Rel_ext(C_701, {cno, p_date, avg_c})	R1_C_701
Rel_ext(C_701,{cno, avg_c, f_13})	R2_C_701

Table 1: Materialized relational extensions

In order to get the relational extension of the focus (C_701, {cno, p_date, f_13}) the relational tables R1_C_701 and R2_C_701 combined, or R1_C_701 and R2_Car combined could be used. In both cases the resulting SQL queries consist of joining the two tables, followed by a projection to select the relevant attributes. Furthermore, if the IM operation to select the cars of type 701 out of objectset Car is translated into SQL then the two tables R1_Car and R2_Car could be used as a basis for a third SQL query.

The formal approach is based onto the following definition: A focus (O,**A**) is *covered* iff

1. at least one materialization exists for the objectset O, and
2. for any A ∈ **A**: at least one materialization exists for (a superset of) O which contains the attribute A.

Suppose $\{T_1,...,T_n\}$ is a set of materializations which satisfies the above conditions for a covered focus (O,**A**). Then the relational extension rel_ext(O,**A**) can be obtained by simply joining $T_1, ...,T_n$ and selecting the desired attribute set A with a projection afterwards. In the example above, {R1_C_701, R2_Car} is such a covering set of materializations for the covered focus (C_701, {cno, p_date, f_13}).

From this definition, we can derive two degrees of freedom for our optimization process:

- For a specified result focus there may exist several covered input foci that can be used to construct it.
- For one input focus there may exist several relational tables that can be used to construct the corresponding relational extension.

To reduce the overall complexity of the problem to generate all alternative SQL queries, we follow this distinction and apply a two-level approach. An "upper" level identifies, for a given IM query, the potential covered input foci and the query plans that make use of them, and selects the "best" plan. In order to determine the respective relational tables, it uses a "lower" level that constructs for a given covered focus its computation from the available materializations.

7.2 Higher Level Optimization Process

The higher level algorithm and, hence, the whole optimization process starts with a single initial plan that consists of the output focus of the considered data preparation query as the sole unresolved input focus. The algorithm then follows a recursive state-space-search. It expands query plans to new ones and evaluates them against a cost model. The model estimates the costs for the generated SQL query based on the costs of accessing the used materializations, the IM operators executed, and the necessary Joins to put the results together, if multiple materializations have to be combined to choose the optimal plan. A *query plan (or state)* represents the (partially) generated SQL query to obtain the searched relational extension as well as the unresolved input foci for which appropriate SQL sub-queries are still to be found. A query plan is expanded to a new one by removing an unresolved input focus and replacing its occurrences in the partial SQL query with corresponding sub-queries. If the unresolved focus is not covered, the expansion is done by backtracking along a semantic relationship in the information directory to find a focus element, and on the way reconstructing the corresponding IM operation and translating it into SQL according to the translation rules. The input foci of the newly generated sub-query are included in the set of unresolved input foci of the new query plan. If there are alternative semantic relationships for the focus element, e.g, in the directory of Figure 5 the objectset C_701_0895 is connected with C_701 as well as with C_0695, several alternative query plans will be generated.

If the unresolved focus is covered it is passed on to the lower level which selects an optimal subquery based on existing materializations. The returned subqueries are embedded into the so far incomplete query plan, perhaps giving rise to several alternative plans. The plans are evaluated against the cost model, and a SQL query, if the most efficient so far, is stored as a result of the optimization process. The process is continued with other possible input foci.

7.3 Lower Level Optimization Process

The higher level passes a covered input focus to the lower level of the SQL-Generator in order to find a SQL subquery that constructs the relational extension of the focus on the basis of existing materializations. Since none may exactly match the focus, the level may have to construct a subquery in the form of a sequence of natural join operations that combine the materializations, and a final project operation to select the relevant attributes. However, there may even be several different sets of materializations that cover the focus. The fewer materializations are used, and the smaller these materializations are, the less costly is the sequence of join operations and, hence, the more efficient is the resulting SQL subquery. Therefore, the optimization problem of the lower layer consists of finding a minimal set of materializations such that the relational extension of the given focus can be obtained. Figure 6 illustrates the optimization problem for the examplary materializations of Table 1 and a covered focus.

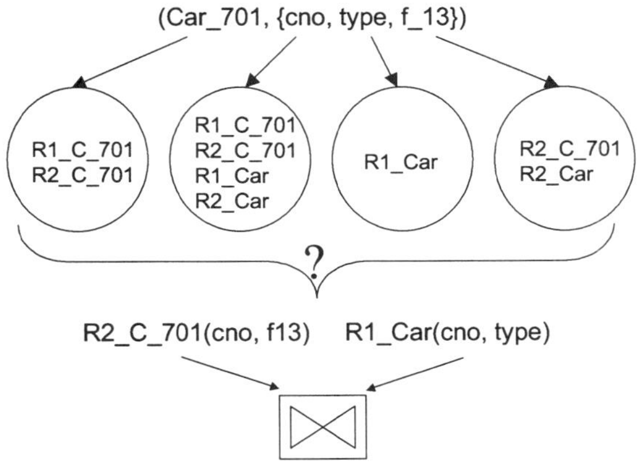

Figure 6. Optimization Problem of the lower layer

Basically, the optimization problem is a variant of the set-covering problem (Cormen et al., 1990), which is known to be NP-hard. For this problem, a greedy heuristic is proposed, because it has been proven to find a good solution with acceptable effort. At the beginning, a materialization for the objectset of the focus is selected, which comprises as many attributes of the focus as possible. Ties are broken for the benefit of materializations with smaller sizes. E.g., for the objectset C_701 in figure 6 the materialization R2_C_701 is preferred, because it covers the searched attributes cno and type, whereas R1_C_701 covers only cno. After selecting a materialization for the objectset – and maybe for some of the attributes – of the focus, further materializations comprising the residual attributes are chosen in the following, by subsequently selecting the materialization which again covers as many at that time residual attributes as possible. Ties are in turn broken by considering the sizes of alternatives. Note that, as opposed to the selection of a materialization for the focus objectset at the beginning, the additional materializations for the attributes could come from a superset of the focus objectset.

8. AUTOMATIC MATERIALIZATION OF INTERMEDIATE RESULTS

Clearly, because it is practically impossible to materialize each intermediate result (the available persistent store is limited and in general a huge number of intermediate results are computed during a KDD process), only selected intermediate results with a potential high benefit for future streams can be materialized. Consequently, materialization must be accompanied by a strategy that determines which results to materialize and, on the other hand, which to dematerialize in order to free space for new ones.

The key issue, then, is to determine which materializations are of potential benefit. Because one can hardly expect the human analyst to manage the materializations manually, what is needed is a strategy for automatic decisions on (de-)materialization of intermediate results. In Figure 3, enforcing this strategy is the responsibility of a separate system component, the materialization component. It is activated periodically, and consults with the information directory on the intermediate results incurred during the previous interval. These determine a set of potential foci, each consisting of an objectset and set of attributes. Therefore, the problem is to select the subset of potential foci which holds the highest promise for the future and thus should be materialized.

The issue is similar to classical buffer management where replacement strategies are based on a prediction model that extrapolates from the past. Compared to the crude models of buffer management we have more information available to us in the form of a large number of entire process histories. For each objectset and attribute in the information directory a reference list is maintained which registers the points in time when the objectset or attribute was part of a result focus. Based on this list, for an objectset or attribute X a reference measure *refmsr*(X) is computed which comprises the number as well as the age of previous references within a given period of time. The future process profile is then predicted as a set of foci *fut_focs* := $\{(O,\mathbf{A}) \mid refmsr(O) > 0 \wedge \forall A \in \mathbf{A}: refmsr(A) > 0.5\ refmsr(O)\}$, with the interpretation that every objectset accessed in the past will be an element of a future resulting focus together with the attributes which were accessed at least half the times when accessing the objectset. The frequency of occurrences for a future focus $(O,\mathbf{A}) \in$ *fut_focs* is computed by extrapolating *refmsr*(O).

Given *fut_focs* and a space constraint, the decision which foci should be materialized or dematerialized is a NP-hard optimization problem. Hence, we apply a heuristic in order to restrict the number of considered alternatives. It works roughly as follows: First, a pre-selection of candidate foci to consider is performed. Clearly, each predicted focus of *fut_focs* is such a candidate. Furthermore, the already materialized foci are candidates, because contrary to other foci they obviate any new materialization effort. Finally, each focus (O,**A**) is considered as a candidate, if O is a common superset of two focus objecsets out of *fut_foc* and **A** is the union of the appending attribute sets. The final selection of the foci to materialize, retain, or de-materialize, respectively, is done in a second step by estimating a benefit/cost-relationship and choosing the candidates in decreasing order (Schlösser, 1999).

9. EXPERIMENTAL RESULTS

The main application of CITRUS was the analysis of a large database of quality control data of a large automobile manufacturer. To evaluate the usefulness of our approach, we used an excerpt from this database, and an information directory that reflected the (derived) objectsets and attributes of a history of KDD processes that had earlier been performed on the excerpt. Besides the initial objectsets for the raw data, the directory included 20 derived objectsets arranged in a hierarchy of sub-relationships with five levels. Moreover, for each objectset there were approximately 40 derived attributes in the directory, each involving at least one join in the SQL query that corresponded to the attribute derivation.

Based on the information directory several access profiles were generated, each consisting of a sequence of 100 foci. Every profile was generated randomly by following the semantic relationships in the information directory. In order to simulate the properties of the explorative phase in an access profile, the probabilities for different actions (e.g., "backtracking", "access to current focus", etc.) were adjusted in accordance with the previous action.

The performance measurements were taken by processing the access profiles in the CITRUS prototype, which consists of the CLEMENTINE system extended by our techniques, and Oracle 7.3 as the underlying database server. A second machine was used for the server in order not to interfere with the operative database. Four execution modes, each with varying parameter settings, were compared:

- Data-shipping mode (DS). This is the original CLEMENTINE execution mode: For each access the needed raw data tables are loaded in entirety into the prototype, and all data preparation operations are then performed internally by CLEMENTINE built-in operations.
- Query-shipping without materialization (QS). This mode corresponds to an optimization based on the raw data only (see initial remarks in Section 7).
- Query-shipping together with materialization (QSmat). This includes all three steps, materialization, optimization, and execution. Different sizes of available storage were chosen, e.g., 20% (QSmat20) or 50% (QSmat50) of the database size.
- Net query-shipping together with materialization (QSmatnet). The measurements exclude the first step of materialization. The modification is motivated by the observation that in principle the materialization component could work in parallel to the actual query processing (or, e.g., in times of low system load). Again, different sizes of available storage were chosen, e.g., QSmat20net and QSmat50net.

Figure 7 shows the execution times for four different access profiles under the various execution modes. The results demonstrate that it is worthwhile to use both query shipping and materialization for the exploration phase of a KDD process. With mere query-shipping (QS) a performance speed-up of about 2 could be achieved compared to the original execution strategy DS. Together with materialization further efficiency gains could be attained up to a factor of 10 if the conditions for QSmatnet hold. Note, in our experiments the size of the available storage has mainly an impact on the effort for automatic materialization, but barely on the efficiency of the queries. This might be an indication that data preparation queries might be already well supported if at least a moderate-size storage for the materializations is available.

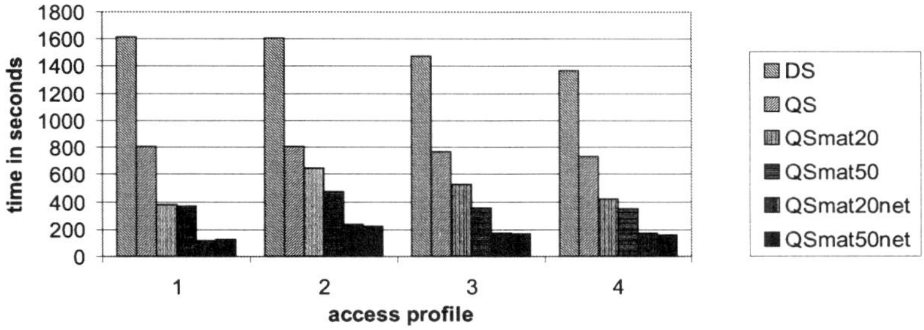

Figure 7. Execution Times for Access Profiles

10. UTILIZING PAST EXPERIENCE

The directory is an information base in its own right, which can be inspected by the analyst in order to recall and access experiences (consisting of both, queries and results) gained from past analyses. By necessity, such inspectional queries are often of a probing nature and, hence, not overly precise. To give a few examples:

- What knowledge is available concerning a certain attribute of the objectset currently examined?
- In case there are no exactly matching results, is there any knowledge which was generated for "similar" attributes or "similar" objectsets?
- Which queries have been executed which are comparable to the current query?

In "classical" database query processing only information is retrieved that precisely satisfies the given description. Approximations (which is what we expect if we think in terms of similarities) can only be recovered if one sufficiently generalizes the description, but then one will usually face a huge amount of data from which one has manually to separate the relevant information. Consequently, by introducing an appropriate measure of "similarity" and integrating it into the KDD process cycle we hope to gain the better of two worlds, high selectivity and approximation.

We define similarity as a computable relationship between units of the same kind. Units of interest are objectsets, attributes, or knowledge segments. For objectsets and attributes we link the measure of similarity to their distances in the information directory. Somewhat simplified, the distance between two units can be determined as the minimal length of an abstraction path between those units, where an abstraction path consists of semantic relationships. To account for different strengths of the various types of semantic relationships, each type is assigned a certain weight. While finding the "right" or at least an "appropriate" weight may depend on the application scenario and certainly requires further research, we have found in experiments that a very simple scheme (sub, restr = 1, grp, gen = 2, drv = 3) gives quite acceptable results for objectsets and attributes.

A different approach must be taken for knowledge segments because the different data-mining algorithms are all entered via the same discover-operator and, consequently, are represented by the same type of relationship (disc-relationship) so that, e.g., a simple distribution can not be distinguished from a far more sophisticated decision tree. We observe, however, that the "data-mining domain" is static, i.e. data-mining algorithms are not added at run time. Therefore, a distance metric - in form of a fixed table or tree as in (Motro, 1988; Breitner et. al., 1995) - can quite easily be provided by the system developer. For instance, the distance between statistical algorithms as histogram and distributions is less than between a distribution and a rule-set, the distance between a decision-tree and a hierarchical cluster-graph might be less than between a decision-tree and a set of association rules.

11. RELATED WORK

Although meanwhile a broad consensus seems to exist that KDD is a highly user-interactive, iterative, and long-lasting process with frequent backtracking, most work in the KDD field still focuses on new or enhanced automatic data mining algorithms while neglecting the necessary data preparation.

There are a few exceptions. The IMACS system (Brachmann, 1993) embodies the knowledge base system Classic which shares with our work the idea of using an object-oriented front-end to model data exploration queries. Similar to the IM, the obtained results are automatically documented in the Classic schema. IMACS pursues solely a data shipping strategy, though. Moreover, the burden of declaring the transformation rules for converting raw data into Classic objects on loading them into IMACS is left with the user, and no query optimization concepts are provided. IDEA (Selfridge et al., 1996) also offers data exploration queries together with a query-shipping strategy, but uses only the three operators to query (Q), segment (S) and aggregate (A) relational data, which - although appropriate for telephone marketing databases - are too restrictive for most applications. IDEA includes a history mechanism reflecting results and their derivation descriptions in a central information directory. A third system that provides data exploration functionality is Lockheed's RECON system (Simoudis et al., 1994). It uses a deductive information model to translate data exploration queries to SQL queries which are shipped to an underlying RDBMS for execution.

CITRUS is a system solution that draws on a number of modern techniques. One is subsumption as a central mechanism to keep redundancies off the directory and to identify materialization candidates for query optimization. Our approach appears to be novel. An earlier system that provides a schema and a subsumption mechanism for object-oriented views has been proposed with MultiView (Rundensteiner, 1992). In general the approach appears very similar to our mechanisms, but operates in a simpler context than the large-scale materializations and specialized operators needed for KDD.

Whereas query shipping seems to be a widely used technology even in the KDD context, as the previous system examples show, neither of these systems employ materialization and the ensuing query optimization strategies. On the other hand, these issues - automatic materialization of intermediate results and reusing them for query optimizing (called *query folding*) - are hot items in the area of data warehousing and OLAP. However, all this work considers a more limited context - after all, data warehousing and OLAP draw their efficiency from the fact that data analyses follow a pre-planned scenario rather than the spontaneous exploration of KDD. E.g. Harinarayan et al. and Gupta (Harinarayan et al., 1996; Gupta, 1997) introduce algorithms selecting materializations out of given aggregation hierarchies. Qian (Qian, 1996) developed a method to find for PSJ-queries[2] each partial or complete mapping on materialized PSJ-views, and Srivasta et al. (Srivastava et al., 1996) propose an approach to reformulate single-block SQL queries. WATCHMAN (Scheuermann, 1996) limits itself to a strategy that reuses cached results in a non-partial way.

Our materialization strategy resembles more what is called predicate-based, or semantic, caching. Related approaches again seem to take a narrower view. For example, (Keller, 1996) and (Dar, 1996) only support relational selection predicates over one base relation. Chen et al. (Chen et al. 94) support multiple relations and employ a simple view schema to guide the optimizer in searching for materializations. But again, the operator algebra is restricted to PSJ-Queries. In addition, the approaches described above aren't able to use multiple overlapping materializations.

[2] Project-Select-Join-Queries

12. CONCLUDING REMARKS

In contrast to most KDD developments which to date have been driven by a technology push rather than by a user pull, the development of CITRUS was strongly driven by the demands of real KDD applications. In particular, CITRUS attempts to overcome two shortcomings of present KDD systems: The lack of support for the critical phases of hypothesis development, and a weakness in dealing with large, peripherally stored data volumes and, consequently, the lack of an appropriate information management.

CITRUS is a system solution. One would expect that its strength is in integrating more or less well-known, modern techniques. However, as shown, we were forced to develop numerous novel techniques for subsumption, query optimization, query shipping and materialization. The primary basis of our work is to view KDD as a highly user-interactive, long-lasting and explorative process with frequent backtracking. Therefore, the central idea is to overlay the general optimized query processing capabilities of an underlying relational database system (RDBMS) with a more KDD-process-oriented optimization strategy, which takes the frequent backtracking in a KDD process into account. For this, we present an approach which automatically materializes intermediate results and reuses them in the sequel to avoid expensive recomputations whenever possible. Together with the query-shipping strategy for execution this achieves considerable speedup for preprocessing huge databases. Moreover, because the approach is based on the information model, a semantic data model particularly suited for the KDD process, efficiency is combined with further support, like the automatic documentation of the process history, flexible retrieval possibilities and an intuitive modeling of streams.

Our ultimate objective was to speed up hypothesis development. A maximum gain of 10 may seem extraordinary. It is modest, though, if human interaction in the presence of large databases is to be supported. Hence, as the next step we investigate the use of parallelism to further speed up the KDD-process. We plan to gain further in performance by directly executing the IM operators and using pipelining instead of static data parallelism to account for the ad-hoc nature of KDD Queries.

REFERENCES

Brachman, R.J., Selfridge, P.G., Terveen, L.G., Altmann, B., Borgida, A., Halper, Kirk, T., Layar, A., McGuiness, D.L. & Resnick, L.A. (1993). Integrated support for data archaeology. *Proc. 1993 AAAI Workshop on Knowledge Discovery in Databases*, AAAI Press, Tech. Rep. WS-93-02, pp. 197-212.

Breitner, C. Freyberg, A., & Schmidt, A. (1995). Towards a flexible and Integrated Environment for Knowledge Discovery. *Workshop on Knowledge Discovery and Temporal Reasoning in Deductive and object-oriented databases KDOOD,* Singapore, pp. 28-35

Breitner, C. & Lockemann, P.C. (1997). Information modeling and management for efficient KDD processes. *Beiträge zum 10. Fachgruppentreffen Maschinelles Lernen.* University of Karlsruhe, Faculty of Computer Science, Faculty of Economics, Karlsruhe, Germany, pp. 7-13.

Breitner, C. (1998). An information model for derivation processes and their results in the knowledge discovery process. Ph.D. thesis. Infix Verlag, Sankt Augustin. (In German).

Cormen, T.H., Leiserson, C.E., & Rivest,, R.L. (1990). Introduction to algorithms. MIT Press.

Chen, C.M., Roussopoulos, N. (1994). The Implementation and performance evaluation of the ADMS Query Optimizer. Integrating Query Result Caching and Matching. *Proc. 4th Intl. Conference on Extending Database Technology,* LNCS Vol. 779, Springer Verlag, pp 323-336.

Dar, S., Franklin, M.J., Jonsson, B. T., Srivastava, D., Tan, M. (1996). Semantic Data Caching and Replacement. *Proc. 22nd Intl. Conf. on Very Large Databases (VLDB),* Morgan Kaufmann, pp. 330-341.

Gupta, H. (1997). Selection of views to materialize in a data warehouse, *Proc. Intl. Conf. on Database Theory (ICDT),* LNCS Vol. 1186, Springer Verlag, pp. 98-112.

Harinarayan, V., Rajaraman, A. & Ullman, J.D. (1996). Implementing data cubes efficiently, *Proc. ACM SIGMOD Intl. Conf. on Management of Data,* ACM Press, pp. 205-216.

Keller, A. M., Basu, J. (1996): A predicate-based caching scheme for client-server database architectures. VLDB Journal, 5(1):1996, pp. 35-47.

Motro, A. (1988). VAGUE: A user interface to relational databases that permits vague queries. *Transactions on Office information systems,* 6(3):1988, ACM Press, pp187-214.

Qian, X. (1996). Query folding, *Proc. Intl. Conf. on Data Engineering (ICDE),* IEEE Computer Society, pp. 48-55.

Rundensteiner, E. (1992). MultiView, a Methodology for Supporting Multiple Views in Object-Oriented Databases. *Proc. 18th Intl. Conf. on Very Large Databases (VLDB),* Morgan Kaufmann, pp. 187-198.

Scheuermann, P., Shim, J., Vingralek, R. (1996): WATCHMAN: A Data Warehouse Intelligent Cache Manager. *Proc. 22nd Intl. Conf. on Very Large Databases (VLDB),* Morgan Kaufmann, pp. 51-62.

Schlösser, J. (1999). Efficient query processing in the knowledge discovery process. Ph.D. thesis. Shaker Verlag, Aachen. To appear. (In German)

Selfridge, P.G., Srivastava, D., & Wilson, L.O. (1996). IDEA: Interactive data exploration and analysis, *Proc. ACM SIGMOD Intl. Conf. on Management of Data,* ACM Press, pp. 24-34.

Simoudis, E., Livezey, B., & Kerber, R. (1994). Integrating inductive and deductive reasoning for database mining, *Papers from the AAAI-94 Workshop on Knowledge Discovery in Databases,* AAAI Press, Tech. Rep. WS-94-03, pp. 37-48.

Srivastava, D., Dar, S., & Jagadish, V. (1996). Answering queries with aggregation using views, *Proc. 22nd Intl. Conf. on Very Large Databases (VLDB),* Morgan Kaufmann, pp. 318-329.

Wirth, R., Shearer, C., Grimmer, U., Reinartz, T., Schlösser, J., Breitner, C., Engels, R., Lindner, G. Towards Process-oriented tool support for KDD. Proc. *1st European Symposium on Principles of Data Mining and Knowledge Discovery (PKDD'97),* LNCS Vol. 1263, Springer Verlag, pp. 243-253.

Chapter 16

SEQUENCE MINING IN DYNAMIC AND INTERACTIVE ENVIRONMENTS

Srinivasan Parthasarathy
Computer Science Department, University of Rochester, Rochester, NY 14627
srini@cs.rochester.edu

Mohammed J. Zaki
Computer Science Department, Rensselaer Polytechnic Institute, Troy, NY 12180
zaki@cs.rpi.edu

Mitsunori Ogihara
Computer Science Department, University of Rochester, Rochester, NY 14627
ogihara@cs.rochester.edu

Sandhya Dwarkadas
Computer Science Department, University of Rochester, Rochester, NY 14627
sandya@cs.rochester.edu

Keywords: Frequent Sequences, Sequential Patterns, Incremental and Interactive Algorithms, Data Mining, Knowledge Discovery

Abstract: The discovery of frequent sequences in temporal databases is an important data mining problem. Most current work assumes that the database is static, and a database update requires rediscovering all the patterns by scanning the entire old and new database. In this paper, we propose novel techniques for maintaining sequences in the presence of a) database updates, and b) user interaction (e.g. modifying mining parameters). This is a very challenging task, since such updates can invalidate existing sequences or introduce new ones. In both the above scenarios, we avoid re-executing the algorithm on the entire dataset, thereby reducing execution time. Experimental results confirm that our approach results in execution time improvements of up to several orders of magnitude in practice.

1. INTRODUCTION

Dynamism and interactivity are essential features of all human endeavors, be they in a scientific or business enterprise. The collection of information and data in various fields serves as an exemplar, where every moment we are faced with new content (dynamism) and are required to manipulate it (interactivity). For example, consider a large retail store like Walmart, which has a data-warehouse more than a terabyte in size. In addition, Walmart collects approximately 20 million customer transactions every day. It is simply infeasible to mine the entire database (the original terabyte data-warehouse, and the new transactions) each time an update occurs. As another example consider Web Mining. Let's assume we have mined interesting browsing patterns at a popular portal site like Yahoo! that receives millions of hits every day. Once again it is not practical to re-mine the site logs each time an update occurs.

Given the inherently dynamic nature of data collection, it is somewhat surprising that incremental techniques have received little to no attention within knowledge discovery and data mining. It is worth noting that without incrementality, interactivity also remains a distant goal. True interactivity is not possible if once is forced to re-mine the entire database from scratch each time. This paper seeks to address the problem of mining frequent sequences in dynamic and interactive environments. For example, incremental updates of the most frequent sequence of items purchased by customers, or real-time mining of browsing patterns (i.e., sequences of web-pages) on the Internet.

Sequence mining is an important data mining task, where one attempts to discover frequent sequences over time, of attribute sets in large databases. This problem was originally motivated by applications in the retail industry (e.g. the Walmart example from above), including attached mailing, add-on sales and customer satisfaction. Besides the retail and Internet examples, it applies to many other scientific and business domains. For instance, in the health care industry it can be used for predicting the onset of disease from a sequence of symptoms, and in the financial industry it can be used for predicting investment risk based on a sequence of stock market events.

Discovering all frequent sequences in a very large database can be very compute and I/O intensive because the search space size is essentially exponential in the length of the longest transaction sequence in it. This high computational cost may be acceptable when the database is static since the discovery is done only once, and several approaches to this problem have been presented in the literature. However, many domains such as electronic commerce, stock analysis, collaborative surgery, etc., impose soft real-time constraints on the mining process. In such domains, where the databases are updated on a regular basis and user interactions modify the search parameters, running the discovery program all over again is infeasible. Hence, there is a need for algorithms that maintain valid mined information across i) database updates, and ii) user interactions (modifying/constraining the search space).

In this paper, we present a method for incremental and interactive sequence mining. Our goal is to minimize the I/O and computation requirements for handling incremental updates. Our algorithm accomplishes this goal by maintaining information about "maximally frequent" and "minimally infrequent" sequences. When incremental data arrives, the incremental part is scanned once to incorporate the new information. The new data is combined with the "maximal" and "minimal" information in order to determine the portions of the original database that need to be re-scanned. This process is aided by the use of a vertical database layout — where attributes are associated with the list of transactions in which they occur. The result is an improvement in execution time by up to several orders of magnitude in practice, both for handling increments to the database, as well as for handling interactive queries.

The rest of the paper is organized as follows. In Section 2. we formulate the sequence discovery problem. In Section 3. we describe the SPADE algorithm upon which we build our incremental approach. Section 4. describes our incremental sequence mining algorithm. In Section 5. we describe how we support online querying. Section 6. presents the experimental evaluation. In Section 7. and Section 8. we discuss related work and conclusions, respectively.

2. PROBLEM FORMULATION

In this section, we define the incremental sequence mining problem that this paper is concerned with. We begin by defining the notation we use. Let the *items*, denoted $\mathcal{I}$, be the set of all possible attributes. We assume a fixed enumeration of all members in $\mathcal{I}$ and identify the items with their indices in the enumeration. An *itemset* is a set of items. An itemset is denoted by the enumeration of its elements in increasing order. For an itemset i, its *size*, denoted by $|i|$, is the number of elements in it. An itemset of size k is called a *k-itemset*.

A *sequence* is an ordered list (ordered in time) of non-empty itemsets. A sequence of itemsets $\alpha_1, \ldots, \alpha_n$ is denoted by $(\alpha_1 \rightarrow \cdots \rightarrow \alpha_n)$. The *length* of a sequence is the sum of the sizes of each of its itemsets. For each integer k, a sequence of length k is called a *k-sequence*. A sequence α is a *subsequence* of a sequence β, denoted by $\alpha \preceq \beta$, if α can be constructed from β by striking out some (or none) of the items in β, and then by eliminating all the occurrences of $\emptyset \rightarrow$ and $\rightarrow \emptyset$ one at a time. For example, $B \rightarrow AC$ is a subsequence of $AB \rightarrow E \rightarrow ACD$. We say that α is a *proper subsequence* of β, denoted $\alpha \prec \beta$, if $\alpha \neq \beta$ and $\alpha \preceq \beta$. For $k \geq 3$, the *generating subsequences* of a length k sequence are the two length $k-1$ subsequences of α obtained by dropping exactly one of its first or second items. By definition, the generating sequences share a common suffix of length $k-2$. For example, the two generating subsequences of $AB \rightarrow CD \rightarrow E$ are $A \rightarrow CD \rightarrow E$ and $B \rightarrow CD \rightarrow E$, and they share the common suffix $CD \rightarrow E$. A sequence is *maximal* in a collection $\mathcal{C}$ of sequences if the sequence is not a subsequence of any other sequence in $\mathcal{C}$.

Our database is a collection of *customers*, each with a sequence of *transactions*, each of which is an itemset. For a database D and a sequence α, the *support* or *frequency* of α in D, denoted by $support_D(\alpha)$, is the number of customers in D whose sequences contain α as a subsequence. The *minimum-support*, denoted by $min\_support$, is a user-specified threshold that is used to define "frequent sequences": a sequence is frequent in D if its support in D is at least $min\_support$. A rule $A \Rightarrow B$ involving sequence A and sequence B is said to have *confidence* c if c% of the customers that contain A also contain B. Suppose that new data δ, called the *incremental database*, is added to an *original database* D, then the *updated database* is denoted by $D + \delta$. For each $k \geq 1$, $\mathcal{F}_k$ denotes the collection of all frequent sequences of length k in the updated database. Also FS denotes the set of all frequent sequences in the updated database. The *negative border* (NB) is the collection of all sequences that are not frequent but both of whose generating subsequences are frequent. By the *old sequences,* we mean the set of all frequent sequences in the original database and by the *new sequences* we mean the set of all frequent sequences in the join of the original and the increment.

For example, consider the customer database shown in Figure 16.1. The database has three items (A, B, C), and four customers. The figure also shows the Increment Sequence Lattice (ISL) with all the frequent sequences (the frequency is also shown with each node) and the negative border, when a minimum support of 75%, or 3 customers, is used. For each frequent sequence, the figure shows its two generating subsequences in bold lines. Figure 16.2 shows how the frequent set and the negative border change when we mine over the combined original and incremental database (highlighted in dark grey). For example, C is not frequent in the original database D, but C (along with some of its super-sequences) becomes frequent after the update δ. The update also causes some elements to move from NB to the new FS.

Incremental Sequence Discovery Problem. Given an original database D of sequences, and a new increment to the database δ, find all frequent sequences in the database $D + \delta$, with minimum possible recomputation and I/O.

Some comments are in order to see the generality of our problem formulation: 1) We discover sequences of *subsets* of items, and not just single item sequences.

DATABASE

CID	TID	Items
1	10	A B
	20	B
	30	A B
2	20	A C
	30	A B C
	50	B
3	10	A
	30	B
	40	A
4	30	A B
	40	A
	50	B

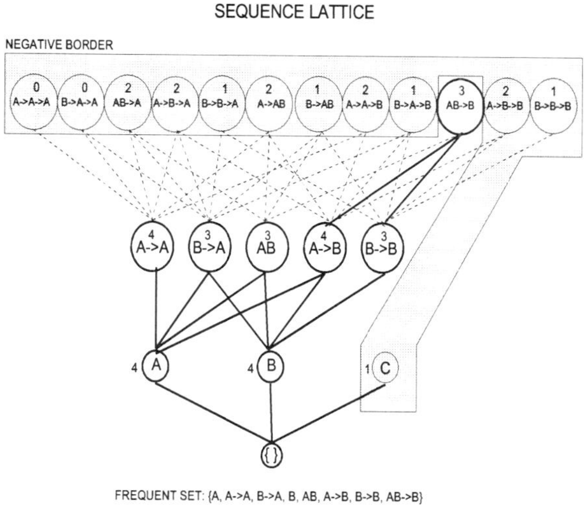

Figure 16.1 Original Database

DATABASE

CID	TID	Items
1	10	A B
	20	B
	30	A B
	100	A C
2	20	A C
	30	A B C
	50	B
3	10	A
	30	B
	40	A
	110	C
	120	B
4	30	A B
	40	A
	50	B
	140	C

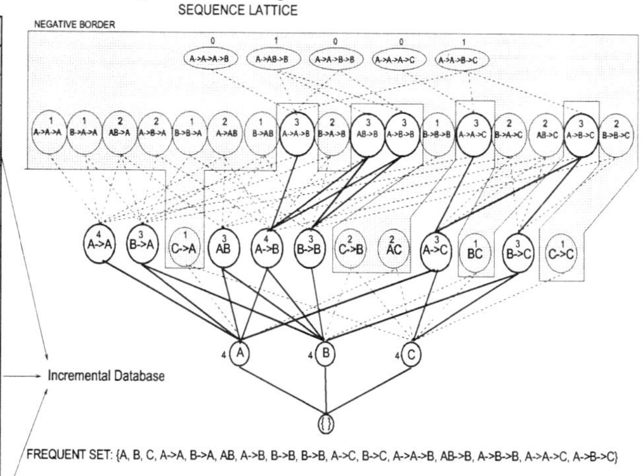

Figure 16.2 Original plus Incremental Database and Lattice

For example, the itemset CD in $(CD \rightarrow E)$. 2) We discover sequences with arbitrary *gaps* among events, and not just the consecutive subsequences. For example, the sequence $(A \rightarrow A)$ is a subsequence of customer 1 (see Figure 16.1), even though there is an intervening transaction. The sequence symbol $\rightarrow$ simply denotes a *happens-after* relationship. 3) Our formulation is general enough to encompass almost any categorical sequential domain. For example, if the input-sequences are DNA strings, then an event consists of a single item (one of A, C, G, T). If input-sequences represent text documents, then each word (along with any other attributes of that word, e.g., noun, position, etc.) would comprise an event. Even continuous domains can be represented after a suitable discretization step.

3. THE SPADE ALGORITHM

In this section we describe SPADE (Zaki, 1998), an algorithm for fast discovery of frequent sequences, which forms the basis for our incremental algorithm.

Sequence Lattice. SPADE uses the observation that the subsequence relation $\preceq$ defines a partial order on the set of sequences, i.e., if β is a frequent sequence, then all subsequences $\alpha \preceq \beta$ are also frequent. The algorithm systematically searches the sequence lattice spanned by the subsequence relation, from the most general (single items) to the most specific frequent sequences (maximal sequences) in a depth-first manner. For instance, in Figure 16.1, the bold lines correspond to the lattice for the example dataset.

Support Counting. Most of the current sequence mining algorithms (Srikant and Agrawal, 1996) assume a *horizontal* database layout such as the one shown in Figure 16.1. In the horizontal format, the database consists of a set of customers (*cid's*). Each customer has a set of transactions (*tid's*), along with the items contained in the transaction. In contrast, we use a *vertical* database layout, where we associate with each item X in the sequence lattice its *idlist*, denoted $\mathcal{L}(X)$, which is a list of all customer (*cid*) and transaction identifier (*tid*) pairs containing the item. For example, the idlist for the item C in the original database (Figure 16.1) would consist of the tuples $\{\langle 2, 20\rangle, \langle 2, 30\rangle\}$.

Given the per item idlists, we can iteratively determine the support of any k-sequence by performing a temporal join on the idlists of its two generating sequences (i.e., its $(k-1)$ length subsequences that share a common suffix sequences). A simple check on the support (i.e., the number of distinct cids) of the resulting idlist tells us whether the new sequence is frequent or not. Figure 16.3 shows this process pictorially. It shows the initial vertical database with the idlist for each item. The intermediate idlist for $A \rightarrow B$ is obtained by a temporal join on the lists of A and B. Since the symbol $\rightarrow$ represents a temporal relationship, we find all occurrences of A before a B in a customer's transaction sequence, and store the corresponding time-stamps or tids, to obtain $\mathcal{L}(A \rightarrow B)$. We obtain the idlist for $AB \rightarrow B$ by intersecting the idlist of its two generating sequences, $A \rightarrow B$ and $B \rightarrow B$, but this time we are looking for *equality join*, i.e., instances where A and B co-occur before a B. Since we

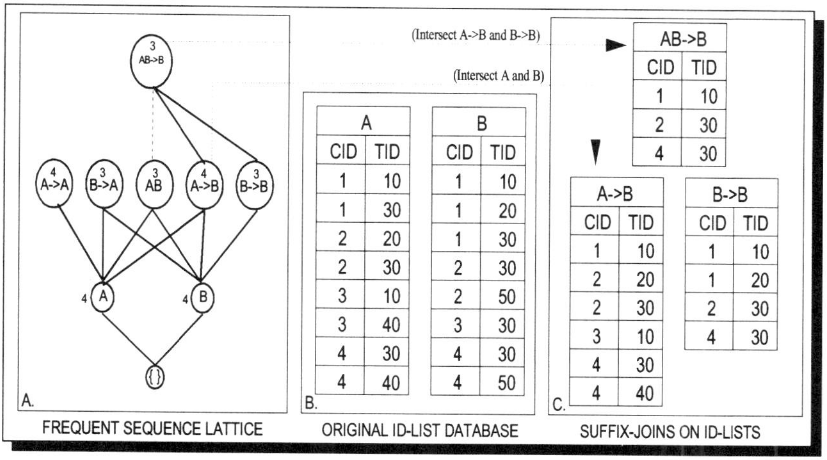

Figure 16.3 A. Frequent Sequence Lattice; B. Initial Idlist Database; C. idlist Intersections

always join two sequences that share a common suffix, it suffices to keep track of only the tid of the first item, as the tids of the suffix remain fixed. Please see (Zaki, 1998) for exact details on how the temporal and equality joins are implemented.

If we had enough main-memory, we could enumerate all the frequent sequences by traversing the lattice, and performing intersections to obtain sequence supports. In practice, however, we only have a limited amount of main-memory, and all the intermediate idlists will not fit in memory. SPADE breaks up this large search space into small, manageable chunks that can be processed *independently* in memory. This is accomplished via *suffix-based equivalence classes* (henceforth denoted as a class). We say that two k length sequences are in the same class if they share a common $k-1$ length suffix. The key observation is that each class is a sub-lattice of the original sequence lattice and can be processed independently. Each suffix class is independent in the sense that it has complete information for generating all frequent sequences that share the same suffix. For example, if a class $[X]$ has the elements $Y \to X$, and $Z \to X$ as the only sequences, the only possible frequent sequences at the next step can be $Y \to Z \to X$, $Z \to Y \to X$, and $(YZ) \to X$. It should be obvious that no other item Q can lead to a frequent sequence with the suffix X, unless (QX) or $Q \to X$ is also in $[X]$.

SPADE recursively decomposes the sequences at each new level into even smaller independent classes. For instance, at level one it uses suffix classes of length one (X,Y), at level two it uses suffix classes of length two (X $\to$ Y, XY) and so on. We refer to level one suffix classes as *parent* classes. These suffix classes are processed one-by-one. Figure 16.4 shows the pseudo-code

BEGIN Enumerate-Frequent-Seq($[S]$):
  for all elements $A_i \in [S]$ **do**
    $[A_i] = \emptyset$;
    for all elements $A_j \in [S]$ **do**
      $R = A_j \cup A_i$; /*sequences R formed by generating
        subsequences A_j and A_i with A_i as a suffix*/
      $idlist(R) = idlist(A_j) \cap idlist(A_i)$;
      if $support(idlist(R)) \geq min\_sup$ **then**
        $[A_i] = [A_i] \cup \{R\}$;
  for all $[A_i] \neq \emptyset$ **do** *Enumerate-Frequent-Seq*($[A_i]$);
END Enumerate-Frequent-Seq($[S]$):

Figure 16.4 Enumerating Frequent Sequences

(simplified for exposition, see (Zaki, 1998) for exact details) for the main procedure of the SPADE algorithm. The input to the procedure is a class, along with the idlist for each of its elements. Frequent sequences are generated by intersecting (Zaki, 1998) the idlists of all distinct pairs of sequences in each class and checking the support of the resulting idlist against *min_sup*. The sequences found to be frequent at the current level form classes for the next level. This level-wise process is recursively repeated until all frequent sequences have been enumerated. In terms of memory management, it is easy to see that we need memory to store intermediate idlists for at most two consecutive levels. Once all the frequent sequences for the next level have been generated, the sequences at the current level can be deleted. For more details on SPADE, see (Zaki, 1998).

4. INCREMENTAL MINING ALGORITHM

Our purpose is to minimize re-computation or re-scanning of the original database when mining sequences in the presence of increments to the database (the increments are assumed to be appended to the database, i.e., later in time).

In order to accomplish this, we use an efficient memory management scheme that indexes into the database efficiently, and create an Increment Sequence Lattice (ISL), exploiting its properties to prune the search space for potential new sequences. The ISL consists of all elements in the negative border and the frequent set, and is initially constructed using SPADE. In the ISL, the children of each nonempty sequence are its generating subsequences. Each node of the ISL contains the support for the given sequence.

Theory of Incremental Sequences. Let C', T' and I' be the set of all cid's, tid's and items, respectively, that appear in the incremental part δ. Define D' to be the set of all records (in $D \cup \delta$) with cid in C' and $D'' = D' \setminus \delta$. For the sake of simplicity assume that there is no new customer added to the database. This implies that infrequent sequences can become frequent but not the other way around. We use the following properties of the lattice to efficiently perform incremental sequence mining.

By set inclusion-exclusion, we can update the support of a sequence in FS or NB based on its support in D' and D''.

$$\begin{aligned} & support_{D+\delta}(X) \\ = \; & support_{D}(X) + support_{D'}(X) - support_{D''}(X). \end{aligned} \tag{16.1}$$

This allows us to compute the support at any node in the lattice quickly, by limiting re-access to the original database to D'.

Proposition 1 *For every sequence X, if $support_{D+\delta}(X) > support_{D}(X)$, then the last item of X belongs to I'.*

This allows us to limit the nodes in the ISL that are re-examined to those with descendants in I'.

We call a sequence Y a *generating descendant* of X if there exists a list $[Z_1, Z_2, \ldots, Z_m]$ of sequences such that $Z_1 = Y$, $Z_m = X$, and for every i, $1 \le i \le m-1$, Z_i is a generating subsequence of Z_{i+1}. We show that that if a sequence has become a member of $FS \cup NB$ in the updated database, but it was not a member before the update, then one of its generating descendants was in NB and now is in FS.

Proposition 2 *Let X be a sequence of length at least 2. If X is in $FS_{D+\delta} \cup NB_{D+\delta}$ but not in $FS_D \cup NB_D$, then X has a generating descendant in $NB_D \cap FS_{D+\delta}$.*

Proof The proof is by induction on k, the length of X. Let X_1 and X_2 be the two generating subsequences of X. Note that if both X_1 and X_2 belong to FS_D then X is in $FS_D \cup NB_D$, which contradicts our assumption. Therefore, either X_1 or X_2 is out of FS_D. For the base case, $k = 2$, since X_1 and X_2 are of length 1, by definition both belong to $FS_D \cup NB_D$, and by the above, at least one must be in NB_D. For X to be in $FS_{D+\delta} \cup NB_{D+\delta}$, X_1 and X_2 must be in $FS_{D+\delta}$ by definition. Thus the claim holds, since either X_1 or X_2 must be in $NB_D \cap FS_{D+\delta}$, and they are generating descendants of X. For the induction step, suppose $k > 2$ and that the claim holds for all $k' < k$. Suppose X_1 and X_2 are both in $FS_D \cup NB_D$. Then, either X_1 or $X_2 \in NB_D$. We know $X \in FS_{D+\delta} \cup NB_{D+\delta}$, so X_1 and X_2 belong to $FS_{D+\delta}$. Since X_1 and X_2 are generating subsequences of X, the claim holds for X. Finally, we have to consider the case where either X_1 or X_2 is not in $FS_D \cup NB_D$. We know that as $X \in FS_{D+\delta} \cup NB_{D+\delta}$, both X_1 and X_2 belong to $FS_{D+\delta} \cup NB_{D+\delta}$. Now suppose that $X_1 \notin FS_D \cup NB_D$. We know that X is in $FS_{D+\delta} \cup NB_{D+\delta}$, X_1 is in $FS_{D+\delta} \cup NB_{D+\delta}$. Therefore from the induction step (since X_1 has length less than k) the claim holds for X_1. Let Y be a generating descendant satisfying the claim for X_1. Since X_1 is a generating subsequence of X, Y is also a generating descendant of X. Thus the claim holds for k. The same argument can be applied to the case when $X_2 \notin FS_D \cup NB_D$. ∎

Proposition 2 limits the additional sequences (not found in the original ISL) that need to be examined to update the ISL.

Memory Management. SPADE simply requires per item idlists. For incremental mining, in order to limit accesses to customers and items in the increment, we use a two level disk-file indexing scheme. However, since the number of customers is unbounded, we use a hashing mechanism described below.

The vertical database is partitioned into a number of blocks such that each individual block fits in memory. Each block contains the vertical representation of all transactions involving a set of customers. Within each block there exists an item dereferencing array, pointing to the first entry for each item. Given a customer, and an item, we first identify the block containing the customer's transactions using a first level cid-index (hash function). The second item-index then locates the item within the given block. After this we perform a linear search for the exact customer identifier. Using this two level indexing scheme we can quickly jump to only that portion of the database which will be affected by the update, without having to touch the entire database. Note that using a vertical data format we were able to efficiently retrieve all affected item's cids, without having to touch the entire database. This is not possible in the horizontal format, since a given item can appear in any transaction, which is found by scanning the entire data.

Incremental Sequence Mining (ISM) Algorithm. Our incremental algorithm maintains the incremental sequence lattice, ISL, which consists of all the frequent sequences and all sequences in the negative border in the original database. The support of each member is kept in the lattice, too. There are two properties of increments we are concerned with: whether new customers are added and whether new transactions are added. We first check whether a new customer is added. If so, the minimum support in terms of the number of transactions is raised. We examine the entire ISL from the 1-sequences towards longer and longer sequences to compute where each sequence belongs. More precisely, for each sequence X that has been reclassified from frequent to infrequent, if its two generating sequences are still frequent we make X as a negative border element; otherwise, X is eliminated from the lattice. Then we default to the algorithm described below (see Figure 16.5).

```
PHASE 1:
compute D'(i), D''(i) for all items i
for all items i in I'
    Q.enqueue(S);
while (Q is not empty)
  p = Q.dequeue(); Compute_Support(p);
  if (support(p) ≥ min_sup )
    k = length(p);
    if (p is in the negative border)
      NB-to-FS[k].enqueue(p);
    else if (D'(p) ≠ ∅)
      for all k + 1-sequences S in ISL that are
          generating ascendents of p
        Q.enqueue(S);

PHASE 2:
for each item i in NB-to-FS[1]
  construct suffix class [i];
  NB-to-FS[2].enqueue([i]);
for (k = 2 to ...)
  for each class C in NB-to-FS[k]
    Enumerate-Frequent-Seq(C);

Compute_Support(p):
A = generating_subsequence1(p);
B = generating_subsequence2(p);
support_D'(p) = intersect(D'(A), D'(B));
support_D''(p) = intersect(D''(A), D''(B));
support(p) = support(p) + support_D'(p)
  −support_D''(p);
```

Figure 16.5 The ISM Algorithm

The algorithm consists of two phases. Phase 1 is for updating the supports of elements in *NB* and *FS* and Phase 2 is for adding to *NB* and *FS* beyond what was done in Phase 1. To describe the algorithm, for a sequence p we represent by $D'(p)$ and $D''(p)$ the vertical id-list of p in D' and that in D'', respectively.

Phase 1 begins by generating the single item components of ISL: For each single item sequences p, we compute $D'(p)$ and $D''(p)$ and put p into a queue Q, which is empty at the beginning of computation. Then we repeat the following until Q is empty: We dequeue one element p from Q. We update the support of p using the subroutine Compute_Support, which computes the support based on Equation 16.1. Once the support is updated, if the sequence p (of length k) is in the frequent set (line 10), all length $k+1$ sequences that are already in ISL and that are generating ascendents of p are queued into Q. If the sequence, p, is in the negative border (line 8) and its support suggests it is frequent, then this element is placed in *NB-to-FS*$[k]$.

At the end of Phase 1, we have exact and up-to-date supports for all elements in the ISL. We further have a list of elements that were in the negative border but have become frequent as a result of the database increment (in *NB-to-FS*). In the example in Figures 16.1 and 16.2, the following elements had supports updated: $A \to A \to A, B \to A \to A, A \to A \to B, B \to A \to B, A \to B \to B$, and C. Of these, the following moved from the negative border to the frequent set: $A \to A \to B, A \to B \to B$, and C.

We next describe Phase 2 (see Figure 16.5). As to Phase 1, at the end of Phase 1 the *NB-to-FS* is a list (or an array) of hash tables containing elements that have moved from NB to FS. By Proposition 2 these are the only suffix-based classes we need to examine. For all 1-sequences that have moved we intersect it with all possible other frequent 1-sequences. We add all such frequent 2-sequences into the queue *NB-to-FS*[2] for further processing. In our running example in Figures 16.1 and 16.2, $A \to C$ and $B \to C$ are added to the *NB-to-FS*[2] table. At the same time all other evaluated two-sequences involving C that were not frequent are placed in $NB_{D+\delta}$. Thus, $C \to A, C \to B, AC, BC$ and $C \to C$ are placed in $NB_{D+\delta}$. The next step in Phase 2 is to, starting with the hash table containing length two sequences, pick an element that has not been processed and create the list of frequent sets, along with associated id-lists from $D \cup \delta$, in its equivalence class. The next step is to pass the resulting equivalence class to *Enumerate-Frequent-Set*, which adds any new frequent sequences or new negative border elements and associated elements to the ISL. We repeat this until all the *NB-to-FS* tables are empty. As an example, let us consider the equivalence class associated with $A \to C$. From Figures 16.1 and 16.2 we see that the only other frequent sequence of its suffix class is $B \to C$. As both the above sequences are frequent, they are placed in $FS_{D+\delta}$. Recursively enumerating the frequent itemsets results in the sequences $A \to A \to C$ and $A \to B \to C$ being added to $FS_{D+\delta}$. Similarly, the sequences $AB \to C, B \to A \to C, B \to B \to C, A \to A \to A \to C$, and $A \to A \to B \to C$ are added to $NB_{D+\delta}$.

5. INTERACTIVE SEQUENCE MINING

The idea in interactive sequence mining is that an end user be allowed to query the database for association rules at differing values of support and confidence.

The goal is to allow such interaction without excessive I/O or computation. Interactive usage of the system normally involves a lot of manual tuning of parameters and re-submission of queries that may be very demanding on the memory subsystem of the server. In most current algorithms, multiple passes have to be made over the database for each ⟨*support, confidence*⟩ pair. This leads to unacceptable response times for online queries. Our approach to the problem of supporting such queries efficiently is to create pre-processed summaries that can quickly respond to such online queries.

A typical set of queries that such a system could support include:

1. **Simple Queries:** identify the rules for support x%, confidence y%.

2. **Refined queries:** where the support value is modified ($x + y$ or $x - y$) involves the same procedure.

3. **Quantified Queries:** identify the k most important rules in terms of support, confidence pairs or find out for what support/confidence values can we generate exactly k rules.

4. **Including Queries:** find rules including itemsets $i_1, \ldots, i_n$.

5. **Excluding Queries:** find rules excluding itemsets $i_1, \ldots, i_n$.

6. **Hierarchical Queries:** treat items $i_1\,(coke), \ldots, i_n$ (pepsi), as one item (cola) and return the new rules.

Our approach to the problem of supporting such queries efficiently is to adapt the Increment Sequence Lattice. The preprocessing step of the algorithm involves computing such a lattice for a small enough support S_{min}, such that all future queries will involve a support S larger than S_{min}. In order to handle certain queries (**Including, Excluding** etc.), we modify the lattice to allow links from a k-length sequence to all its k subsequences of length $k - 1$ (rather than just its generating subsequences). Given such a lattice, we can produce answers to all but one (**Hierarchical queries**) of the queries described in the previous section at interactive speeds without going back to the original database. This is easy to see as all of the queries will basically involve a form of pruning over the lattice. A lattice, as opposed to a flat file containing the relevant sequences, is an important data structure as it permits rapid pruning of relevant sequences. Exactly how we do this is discussed in more detail in (Parthasarathy et al., 1999).

Hierarchical queries require the algorithm to treat a set of related items as one super-item. For example we may want to treat chips, cookies, peanuts, etc. all together as a single item called "snacks". We would like to know what are the frequent sequences involving this super-item. To generate the resulting sequences, we have to modify the SPADE algorithm. We reconstruct the id-list for the new item $(i_1, \ldots, i_n)$ via a special union operator, and we remove from consideration the individual items $i_1, \ldots, i_n$. Then, we rerun the equivalence class algorithm for this new item and return the set of frequent sequences.

6. EXPERIMENTAL EVALUATION

All the experiments were on a single processor of a DECStation 4100 using a maximum of 256 MB of physical memory. The DECStation 4100 contains 4 600MHz Alpha 21164 processors. No other user processes were running at the time. We used different synthetic databases with size ranging from 20MB to 55MB, which were generated using the procedure described in (Srikant and Agrawal, 1996). Although the size of our benchmark databases fit in memory, our goal is to work with out-of-core databases. Hence, we assume that the database resides on disk.

The datasets are generated using the following process. First N_I itemsets of average size I are generated by choosing from N items. Then N_S sequences of average length S are created by assigning itemsets from N_I to each sequence. Next, a customer of average T transactions is created, and sequences in N_S are assigned to different customer elements, respecting the average transaction size of T. The generation stops when C customers have been generated. Table 16.1 shows the databases used and their properties. The total number of transactions is denoted as $|\mathcal{D}|$, average transaction size per customer as T, and the total number of customers C. The parameters we used were $N = 1000$, $N_I = 25000$, $I = 1.25$, $N_S = 5000$, $S = 4$. Please see (Srikant and Agrawal, 1996) for further details on the dataset generation process.

Database	C	T	$\lvert\mathcal{D}\rvert$	Total Size
C100.T10	100000	10	1000,000	20 MB
C100.T12	100000	12	1200,000	25 MB
C100.T15	100000	15	1500,000	30 MB
C150.T10	150000	10	1500,000	31 MB
C200.T10	200000	10	2000,000	42 MB
C250.T10	250000	10	2500,000	55 MB

Table 16.1 Database properties

To evaluate the incremental algorithm, we modified the database generation mechanism to construct two datasets — one corresponding to the original database, and one corresponding to the increment database. The input to the generator also included an increment percentage roughly corresponding to the number of customers in the increment and the percentage of transactions for each such customer that belongs in the increment database. Assuming the database being looked at is C100.T10, if we set the increment percentage to 5% and the percentage of transactions to 20%, then we could expect 5000 customers (5% of 100,000) to belong to C', each of which would contain on average two transactions (20% of 10) in the increment database. The actual number of customers in the increment is determined by drawing from a uniform distribution (increment percentage as parameter). Similarly, for each customer in the increment the number of transactions belonging to the increment is also drawn from a uniform distribution (transaction percentage as parameter).

Database	Simple	Refined	Priority	Including	Excluding	SPADE
C100K.T10	0.06	0.011	1.11	negligible	0.07	75
C100K.T12	0.06	0.014	1.08	negligible	0.06	82
C100K.T15	0.08	0.026	1.90	negligible	0.08	90
C150K.T10	0.085	0.022	2.48	negligible	0.09	94
C200K.T10	0.08	0.022	1.5	negligible	0.08	102
C250K.T10	0.044	0.02	1.28	negligible	0.16	150

Table 16.2 Interactive Performance: Time in Seconds

Incremental Performance. For the first experiment (see Figure 16.6), we varied the increment percentage for 4 databases while fixing the transaction percentage to 20%. We ran the SPADE algorithm on the entire database (original and increment) combined, and evaluated the cost of running just the incremental algorithm (after constructing the ISL from the original database) for increment database values of five, three and one percent. For each database, we also evaluated the breakdown of the cost of the incremental algorithm phases. The results show that the speedups obtained by using the incremental algorithm in comparison to re-running the SPADE algorithm over the entire database range from a factor of 7 to over two orders of magnitude. As expected, on moving from a larger increment value to a smaller one, the improvements increase, since there are fewer new sequences from a smaller increment.

The breakdown figures reveal that the phase one time is pretty negligible, requiring under 1 second for all the datasets for all increment values. It also shows that the phase two times, while an order of magnitude larger than the phase one times, are still much faster than re-executing the entire algorithm. Further, while increasing database size does increase the overall running time of phase 2, it does not increase at the same rate as re-executing the entire algorithm for these datasets.

The second experiment we conducted was to vary the support sizes for a given increment size (1%), and for two databases. The results for this experiment are documented in Figure 16.7. For both databases, as the support size is increased, the execution time of phase 1 and phase 2 rapidly approaches 0. This is not

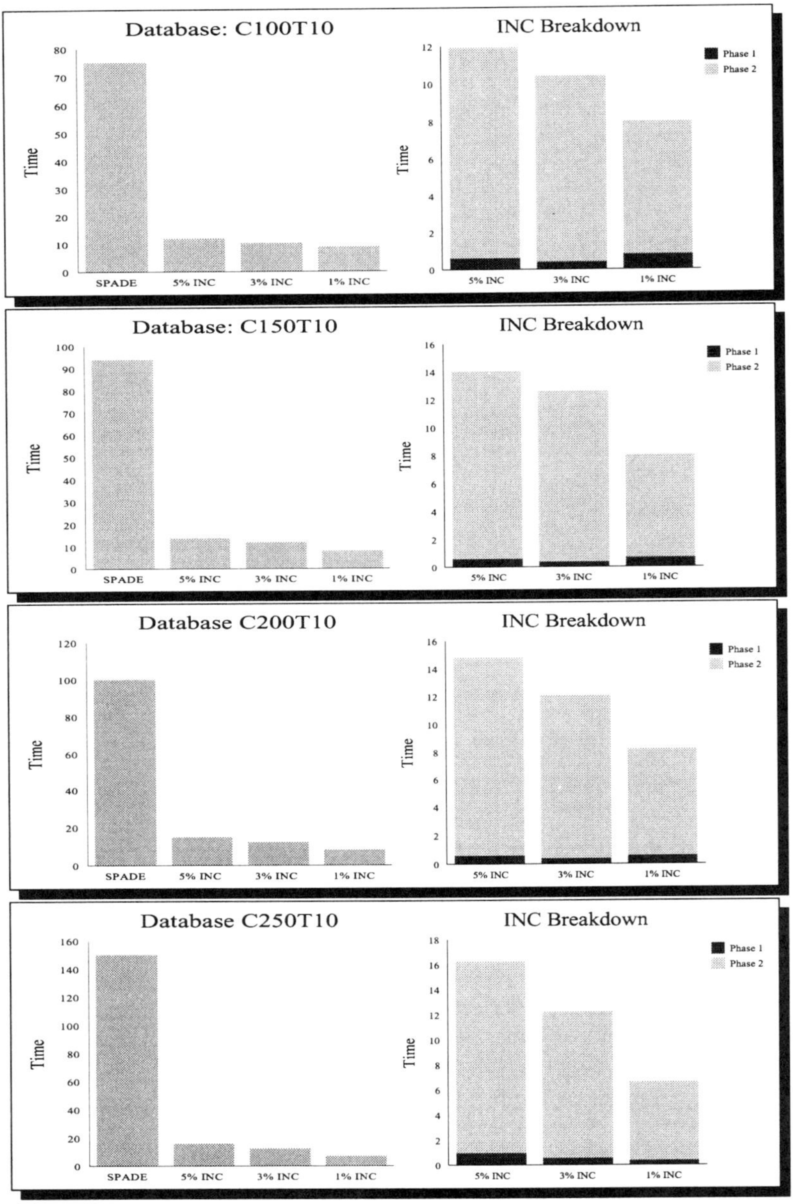

Figure 16.6 Incremental Algorithm Performance Comparison (Time in Seconds)

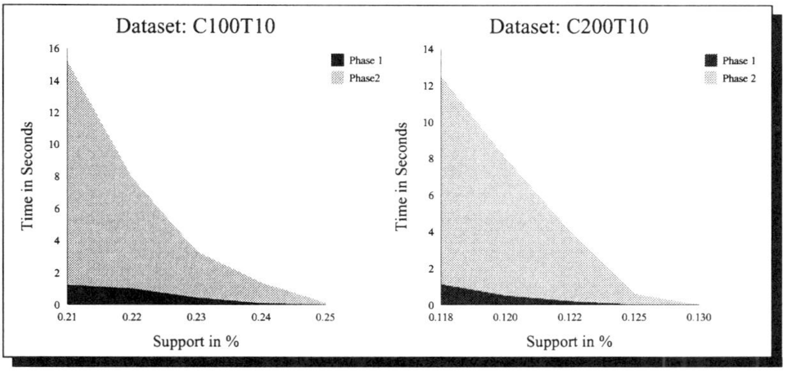

Figure 16.7 Effect of Varying Support: C100.T10 and C200.T10

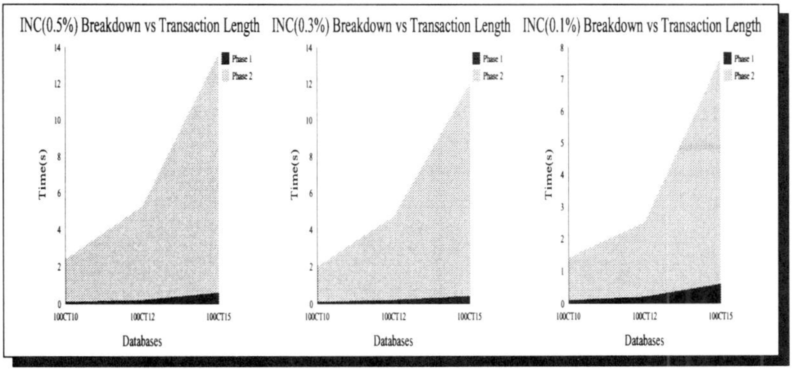

Figure 16.8 Effect of Varying Transaction Length

surprising when you consider that at higher supports, the number of elements in the ISL are fewer (affecting phase 1) and the number of new sequences are much smaller (affecting phase 2).

The third experiment we conducted was to keep the support, the number of customers, and the transaction percentage constant (0.24%, 100,000, and 20% respectively), and vary the number of transactions per customer (10, 12, and 15). Figure 16.8 depicts the breakdown of the two phases of the *ISM* algorithm for varying increment values. We see that moving from 10 to 15 transactions per customer, the execution time of both phases progressively increases for all database increment sizes. This is because the number of sequences in the ISL are more (affecting phase1) and the number of new sequences are also more (affecting phase2).

Interactive Performance. In this section, we evaluate the performance of the interactive queries described in Section 5.. All the interactive query experiments were performed on a SUN UltraSparc, 167MHz processor with 256 MB of memory. We envisage off-loading the interactive querying feature onto client machines as opposed to executing on the server, and shipping the results to the data mining client. Thus we wanted to compare executing interactive queries on a slower machine. Another reason for evaluating the queries on a slower machine is that the relative speeds of the various interactive queries is better seen on a slower machine (on the DECs all queries executed in negligible time).

Since hierarchical queries simply entail a modified execution of phase 2, we do not evaluate it again. We evaluated simple querying on supports ranging from 0.1%-0.25%, refined querying (support refined to 0.5% for all the datasets), priority querying (querying for the 50 sequences with highest support), including queries (including a random item) and excluding queries (excluding a random item). Results are presented in Table 16.2 along with the cost of rerunning the SPADE algorithm on the DEC machine. We see that the querying time for refined, priority, including and excluding queries are very low and capable of achieving interactive speeds. The priority query takes more time, since it has to sort the sequences according to support value, and this sorting dominates the computation time. Comparing with rerunning SPADE (on a much faster DEC machine) we see that the interactive querying is several orders of magnitude faster, in spite of executing it on a much slower machine.

7. RELATED WORK

Sequence Mining. The concept of sequence mining as defined in this paper was first described in (Srikant and Agrawal, 1996). Recently, SPADE (Zaki, 1998) was shown to outperform the algorithm presented in (Srikant and Agrawal, 1996) by a factor of two in the general case, and by a factor of ten with a preprocessing step. The problem of finding *frequent episodes* in a single long sequence of events was presented in (Mannila et al., 1997). The problem of discovering patterns in multiple event sequences was studied in (Oates et al., 1997); they search the rule space directly instead of searching the sequence space and then forming the rules. Sequence mining has been successfully used in a number of practical applications (Hatonen et al., 1996; Lesh et al., 2000; Zaki et al., 1998); our incremental and interactive algorithm can be used to enhance these applications.

Incremental Sequence Mining. There has been almost no work addressing the incremental mining of sequences. One related proposal in (Wang, 1997) uses a dynamic suffix tree based approach to incremental mining in a single long sequence. However, we are dealing with sequences across different customers, i.e., multiple sequences of sets of items as opposed to a single long sequence of items. The other closest work is in incremental association mining (Cheung et al., 1996; Feldman et al., 1997; Thomas et al., 1997). However, there are important differences that make incremental sequence mining a more difficult problem. While association rules discover only intra-transaction patterns (itemsets), we now also have to discover inter-transaction patterns (sequences). The set of all frequent sequences is an unbounded superset of the set of frequent itemsets (bounded). Hence, sequence search is much more complex and challenging than the itemset search, thereby further necessitating fast algorithms.

Interactive Sequence Mining. A mine-and-examine paradigm for interactive exploration of associations and sequence episodes was presented in (Klemettinen et al., 1994). Similar paradigms have been proposed exclusively for associations (Aggarwal and Yu, 1998). Our interactive approach tackles a different problem (sequences across different customers) and supports a wider range of interactive querying features.

8. CONCLUSIONS

In this paper, we propose novel techniques that maintain data structures for mining sequences in the presence of a) database updates, and b) user interaction. Results obtained show speedups from several factors to two orders of magnitude for incremental mining when compared with re-executing a state-of-the-art sequence mining algorithm. Results for interactive approaches are even better. At the cost of maintaining a summary data structure, the interactive approach performs several orders of magnitude faster than any current sequence mining algorithm. One of the limitations of the incremental approach proposed in this paper is the size of the negative border, and the resulting memory utilization. We are currently investigating methods to alleviate this problem, either by refining the algorithm or by performing out-of-core computation.

Acknowledgments

This work was supported in part by NSF grants CDA–9401142, CCR–9702466, CCR–9705594, CCR–9701911, CCR–9725021, INT-9726724, and a DARPA grant F30602-98-2-0133; and an external research grant from Digital Equipment Corporation.

References

Aggarwal, C. and Yu, P. (1998). Online generation of association rules. In *14th Intl. Conf. on Data Engineering*.

Cheung, D., Han, J., Ng, V., and Wong, C. (1996). Maintenance of discovered association rules in large databases: an incremental updating technique. In *12th IEEE Intl. Conf. on Data Engineering*.

Feldman, R., Aumann, Y., Amir, A., and Mannila, H. (1997). Efficient algorithms for discovering frequent sets in incremental databases. In *2rd ACM SIGMOD Workshop on Research Issues in Data Mining and Knowledge Discovery*.

Hatonen, K., Klemettinen, M., Mannila, H., Ronkainen, P., and Toivonen, H. (1996). Knowledge discovery from telecommunication network alarm databases. In *12th Intl. Conf. Data Engineering*.

Klemettinen, M., Mannila, H., Ronkainen, P., Toivonen, H., and Verkamo, A. I. (1994). Finding interesting rules from large sets of discovered association rules. In *3rd Intl. Conf. Information and Knowledge Management*, pages 401–407.

Lesh, N., Zaki, M. J., and Ogihara, M. (2000). Scalable feature mining for sequential data. *IEEE Intelligent Systems and their Applications*, 15(2):48-56. Special issue on Data Mining.

Mannila, H., Toivonen, H., and Verkamo, I. (1997). Discovery of frequent episodes in event sequences. *Data Mining and Knowledge Discovery: An International Journal*, 1(3):259–289.

Oates, T., Schmill, M. D., Jensen, D., and Cohen, P. R. (1997). A family of algorithms for finding temporal structure in data. In *6th Intl. Workshop on AI and Statistics*.

Parthasarathy, S., Zaki, M. J., Ogihara, M., and Dwarkadas, S. (1999). Incremental and interactive sequence mining. In *8th Intl. Conf. Information and Knowledge Management*. Expanded version available as Technical Report 715, U. of Rochester, June 1999.

Srikant, R. and Agrawal, R. (1996). Mining sequential patterns: Generalizations and performance improvements. In *5th Intl. Conf. Extending Database Technology*.

Thomas, S., Bodgala, S., Alsabti, K., and Ranka, S. (1997). An efficient algorithm for incremental updation of association rules in large databases. In *3rd Intl. Conf. Knowledge Discovery and Data Mining*.

Wang, K. (1997). Discovering patterns from large and dynamic sequential data. *J. Intelligent Information Systems*, 9(1).

Zaki, M. J. (1998). Efficient enumeration of frequent sequences. In *7th Intl. Conf. on Information and Knowledge Management*.

Zaki, M. J., Lesh, N., and Ogihara, M. (1998). PLANMINE: Sequence mining for plan failures. In *4th Intl. Conf. Knowledge Discovery and Data Mining*.

Chapter 17

INVESTIGATION OF ARTIFICIAL NEURAL NETWORKS FOR CLASSIFYING LEVELS OF FINANCIAL DISTRESS OF FIRMS: THE CASE OF AN UNBALANCED TRAINING SAMPLE

Jozef Zurada
Department of Computer Information Systems
College of Business and Public Administration
University of Louisville
Louisville, KY 40292, USA
email:jmzura01@athena.louisville.edu

Benjamin P. Foster
School of Accountancy
College of Business and Public Administration
University of Louisville
Louisville, KY 40292, USA

Terry J. Ward
Department of Accounting
College of Business
Middle Tennessee State University
Murfreesboro, TN 37132, USA

Keywords: artificial neural networks, cascaded neural networks, financial distress and bankruptcy prediction, classification, data mining, knowledge discovery

Abstract: Accurate prediction of financial distress of firms is crucial to bank lending officers, financial analysts, and stockholders as all of them have a vested interest in monitoring the firms' financial performance. Most of the previous studies concerning predicting financial distress were performed for a dichotomous state such as nonbankrupt versus bankrupt or no going concern opinion versus going concern opinion. Many studies used well-balanced samples. Much less than one-half of firms become distressed and firms generally progress through different levels of financial distress before bankruptcy. Therefore, this study investigates the usefulness of artificial neural networks in classifying several levels of distress for unbalanced but somewhat realistic training samples. The chapter also compares the classification ability of neural networks and logistic regression through extensive computer simulation of several experiments. Results from these experiments indicate that analysis with two cascaded neural networks produce the best classification results. One network separates healthy from distressed firms only, the other network classifies those firms identified as distressed into one of three distressed states.

1. INTRODUCTION

An important task for auditors and financial statement users such as bank lending officers, financial analysts, investors, is to forecast reliably the financial health of firms. For decades, traditional statistical techniques such as regression analysis, logit models, or discriminant analysis assisted in this task. More recently, much research has focused on the use of the new data mining paradigms such as artificial neural networks for predicting the future financial health of companies.

Because firms progress through different levels of financial distress before they go bankrupt, and predicting these levels is crucial to financial analysts, we revisit the same, unbalanced, but somewhat realistic data sample that we once processed. The training and test samples contain firms that experienced the following four levels/states of distress: healthy (state 0), dividend cuts (state 1), loan defaults and accommodations (state 2), and bankruptcy (state 3). In this chapter, we perform a more thorough investigation of neural networks' ability to properly classify firms into different levels of financial distress when the training sample is not balanced for each state. Our goal is to improve the classification rate of the distressed states 1-3 that contain relatively few firms in the training and testing samples. We examine thoroughly whether any of the following techniques and experiments improves the classification rates of the networks for these states.

First, we apply principal component analysis to try to reduce, without losing information, the number of input variables used for training and to remove correlation between them. Second, we more effectively balance a training sample by repeating the same observations for the states with few observations. Third, we allocate a certain number of the observations from the training set to a validation set to try to improve the networks' generalization. Finally, we explore whether two cascaded neural networks classify financial distress more accurately than the network with four output neurons representing the healthy and three different distressed states used by Zurada *et al.* (1997, 1998-1999). One neural network is designed to distinguish observations between a healthy (state 0) and a distressed state only (states 1-3 are collapsed to 1). The second neural network is designed to classify firms identified as distressed by the first network into one of the three distressed states.

Our objective is to perform and report on several experiments that test the effectiveness of neural networks in properly classifying firms compared to an incumbent technique. The study should interest an audience of business information specialists and researchers dealing with data mining techniques for knowledge discovery (KDD) in business as well as financial analysts, auditors, and senior management. The chapter is organized as follows. Section 2 provides further motivation and reviews previous literature. Section 3 covers logistic regression and neural network fundamentals, and briefly discusses the principal component analysis. Section 4 describes research methodology, sample data, the variables used, and the performed experiments. Section 5 presents and discusses the results. Section 6 provides conclusions and some directions for future work. Finally, a sample of the useful MATLAB commands is described in appendix.

2. MOTIVATION AND LITERATURE REVIEW

Many previous studies concerning financial distress were performed on well-balanced data samples for dichotomous states (for example, auditors' going concern opinion versus unmodified opinion and healthy versus bankrupt). Back *et al.* (1996) designed several neural network models to classify the financial distress of Finnish companies. They trained and tested a neural network using 76 randomly selected small- and medium-sized manufacturing firms equally divided into a training set and a test set. Each set contained 19 failed and 19 nonfailed matched pairs. They compared the classification capability of neural networks using four different models for bankruptcy prediction. Two of the models were based on accrual data, and two others were based on funds-flow data. They obtained highly accurate classification rates with the accrual data (95% and 90%) and funds-flows data (87% and 84%).

Other studies compared the classification accuracy of neural networks and more traditional statistical techniques with dichotomous response variables and balanced data sets. Coats and Fant (1991-1992) defined financial distress by the type of auditors' opinion received. They used five variables (eg., working capital/total assets) to distinguish between the groups of 47 healthy and 47 distressed firms in separate training and holdout samples. They reported that for the holdout sample, the neural network correctly classified 96% of healthy firms and 91% of distressed firms compared to 89% of healthy firms and 72% of distressed firms correctly classified by multiple discriminant analysis. Fletcher and Goss (1993) used three independent variables: current ratio, quick ratio, and income ratio. Their training sample contained 18 failed and 18 non-failed firms. They found that a neural network more accurately predicted bankruptcy than a logistic regression model. Lenard *et al.* (1995) also found neural networks superior to a logistic regression model in predicting auditors' going concern opinions. Koh and Tan (1999) developed a neural network that better predicted healthy versus bankrupt firms than a probit model or the auditors' going concern opinion.

Some studies have addressed the issue of balanced sample sets not being representative of the actual population of healthy and distressed firms. Coats and Fant (1993) performed a follow-up analysis to their 1991-1992 study using the same independent variables, but samples of 94 healthy to 47 distressed firms. The neural network still classified the firms better than multiple discriminant analysis. Wilson and Sharda (1994) began with a balanced sample of 65 bankrupt and 64 healthy firms. They examined whether an unbalanced data set would affect the results by repeating observations from the healthy group to create data sets that were 20% bankrupt and 80% healthy, and 10% bankrupt and 90% healthy. Neural networks were generally better at classifying the firms than discriminant analysis in each data set.

Other studies with unbalanced samples include Salchenberger *et al.* (1992). They began examining a balanced sample of 100 failed and 100 surviving thrift institutions, but also examined a set of 100 failed and 329 surviving thrifts. They found neural networks superior to logistic regression models for classifying both data sets. Barney *et al.* (1999) also found neural networks superior to logistic regression analysis in distinguishing between farmers defaulting on Farmers Home Administration loans. They used data sets including information from approximately three farmers who made timely payments for each one who did not.

Agarwal *et al.* (1997) reported the neural network classification accuracy for a four-state level state response variable. They used training and holdout samples very similar to those used in our current study and Zurada *et al.* (1997, 1998-1999). However, they only examined one set of ten variables as input to a neural network, logistic regression model, and multiple discriminant analysis. They reported classification results for original and balanced training samples, and used measures of classification accuracy based on the distance and direction of classification errors. They concluded that neural networks classified the best overall.

Results are not unanimous in supporting the superiority of neural networks over other methods. Altman *et al.* (1994) claimed no difference between the prediction ability of neural networks and multiple discriminant analysis. They also were skeptical of neural network results because they found illogical weightings on variables and over-fitting in the neural network. Greenstein and Welsh (2000) could not say neural networks were superior to logistic regression models when their sample included a more realistic (unbalanced) proportion of firms that might become distressed.

In our previous research (Zurada *et al.*, 1997, 1998-1999) we compared the ability of neural networks and logistic regression models to distinguish between an unbalanced holdout sample of firms. Our samples included firms that were: (1) healthy (state - 0) or were experiencing one of three different levels of distress (dividend cuts - state 1, loan defaults and accommodations - state 2, and bankruptcy - state 3), and (2) firms that were healthy (state 0) or bankrupt (states 1-3 were collapsed to state 1). Results from initial computer simulations indicated that the complexity of the financial distress response variable appeared to affect classification rates. When a distress variable was more complex (contained four states) and the training sample was unbalanced, the overall classification accuracy of neural networks was better than logistic regression models. The neural network performed significantly better in 9 out of 12 cases, primarily because of excellent classification of healthy firms (state 0) which highly dominated the training sample. Although it appeared that logistic regression analysis gave slightly more accurate predictions than the neural network for the other distressed states 1 through 3, both techniques performed rather poorly in classifying these states. We also found no significant difference in the overall classification rates between the neural network and logistic regression models for the two-state (healthy vs. bankrupt) distress variable. Tables 2-4 (columns two and three) present a sample of the classification results from our previous studies (Ward and Foster, 1996; Zurada *et al.*, 1997, 1998-1999).

The above mentioned studies typically used multi-layer feed-forward neural networks that were trained in a supervised manner. Therefore, the study performed by a Finnish scientist, Kiviluoto (1998), requires a special attention. This individual used the self-organizing map for analysis of financial statements, focusing on bankruptcy prediction. He analyzed the phenomenon of going bankrupt in the qualitative and the quantitative manner. In the qualitative stage of processing, Kiviluoto employed the Kohonen self-organizing network to assign the healthy and bankrupt companies to two separate clusters. In the quantitative analysis, he used three classifiers that utilized the self-organizing map (SOM) and compared them to linear discriminant analysis and learning vector quantization. Using the Neyman-Pearson criterion for classification, Kiviluoto found that the SOM with radial basis function network classifier performed slightly better than any other classifiers used in that study.

To summarize, most previous studies analyzed data for a two-state distress variable (healthy vs. distressed) with balanced samples of healthy and distressed companies for both training and testing. Before a company goes bankrupt (or even obtains an auditor's going concern opinion), it may experience different levels of financial distress. Therefore, Zurada *et al.* (1997, 1998-1999) examined four levels of financial health or distress and compared the classification accuracy of neural network and logit regression models. They found that the overall classification accuracy of the neural network was better than logit regression, but both methods performed rather poorly in classifying the three distressed states. None of the literature, except ours and Agarwal *et al.* (1997), reported the classification accuracy of neural networks for multi-state response variables for uneven but somewhat realistic training and testing samples. Therefore, this study extends our previous research using the same data samples, by investigating more thoroughly the classification ability of neural networks for a multi-level distress variable. Our focus in all conducted experiments is to increase the classification rate for the three distressed states that have few observations in the training and testing samples. This may also increase the overall classification accuracy of the network.

3. LOGIT REGRESSION, NEURAL NETWORK, AND PRINCIPAL COMPONENT ANALYSIS FUNDAMENTALS

This section discusses the logit regression technique used by Ward and Foster (1996) and the fundamentals of neural networks and principal component analysis. As mentioned previously, logit regression is an incumbent statistical technique that has traditionally been used for the tasks of prediction and forecasting, and can be useful in doing so for businesses. Neural networks are relatively new artificial intelligence data mining tools for KDD, and the principal component analysis is a well-established statistical technique which allows one to reduce the dimension of input data and extract features.

3.1. The Logit Regression Model

One purpose of logit regression analysis is to obtain a regression equation that can be used to predict into which of two or more groups an observation should be placed. Ward and Foster (1996) constructed their financial distress prediction models using proportional odds ordinal logistic regression (OLR). (Interested readers should review Agresti (1984) for a discussion of various OLR models.) Using transformed cumulative logits, this procedure fits a parallel lines regression model.

For example, the equation may have p predictor variables and a response variable with the ordered values 0, 1, 2, and 3. Given a vector $\mathbf{X} = (X_1, X_2, \dots, X_p)$ of independent variables, we can define CP_i as the cumulative probability that a firm is in state i or lower. We can estimate the cumulative logit (CL_i) as:

$$CL_i = \ln[CP_i / (1 - CP_i)] = a_i + \sum_{i=1}^{p} b_i X_i \qquad (1)$$

for each state $i = 0$ to 2.

and then:

$$CP_i = P(FINDIS < i \mid X) = \frac{e^{CL_i}}{1 + e^{CL_i}} \qquad (2)$$

where i = 0 to 2, CP_i = the cumulative probabilistic predictor, *FINDIS* = levels 0 to 3 of financial distress, a_i represent intercept parameters, and the b coefficients show the effect of the first through pth explanatory variable on a firm's probability of ending up in state i or lower.

Because the response variable has ordered values of 0 to 3, the following formulas provide the conditional probability that the kth observation belongs to response i:

$$P(FINDIS = 0 \mid X_k) = CP_0 \qquad (3)$$

$$P(FINDIS = 1 \mid X_k) = CP_1 - CP_0 \qquad (4)$$

$$P(FINDIS = 2 \mid X_k) = CP_2 - CP_1 \qquad (5)$$

$$P(FINDIS = 3 \mid X_k) = 1 - CP_2 \qquad (6)$$

where X_k is the kth observation's known vector of predictor variables.

In OLR, an ordinal relationship between the dependent and independent variables is assumed. OLR produces one parameter estimate and one test statistic for each independent variable, like ordinary least squares regression. However, OLR does not make an assumption concerning the intervals between the levels of the dependent variable. Thus, the intercepts differ between the states of distress. For more detailed explanation the reader is referred to (Agresti, 1984; Afifi and Clark, 1990; Manly, 1994; Christensen, 1997).

3.2. Neural Networks

Neural networks are mathematical models that are inspired by the architecture of the human brain. They are nonlinear systems built of highly interconnected neurons that process information. The most attractive characteristics of these networks are their ability to adapt, generalize, and learn from training patterns. Jain *et al.* (1996) mention many other desirable features of neural networks. They require no *a priori* system model and provide fault tolerance and robustness that are not available from computer programs derived from precise algorithms. When neural systems are implemented in hardware, they possess additional useful characteristics such as massive parallelism, and distributed representation and computation. On the negative side, a neural network behaves like a "black box" whose outcomes cannot be explained adequately, making it difficult to associate the network's weights with simple if-then rules.

Artificial neural systems are no longer the subject of computer science alone. They have become highly interdisciplinary and have attracted the attention of researchers from other disciplines, including business. Typically neural network models are characterized by their three properties: (1) the computational property, (2) the architecture of the network, and (3) the learning property. We discuss these three properties in the next three subsections. Other subsections provide more detail on supervised training for feed-forward algorithms, describe ways to attempt to prevent overfitting, and specify the neural network methods used in this study.

3.2.1. The Computational Property

A typical neuron contains a summation node and an activation function (Figure 1). A neuron accepts an R-element vector $\mathbf{p}$ on input, often called a training pattern. Each element of $\mathbf{p}$ is connected with the summation node by a weight matrix $\mathbf{W}$. The summation node produces the value of $n = \mathbf{Wp} + b$ that is used as the argument in the activation function. The formulas in (7) provide examples of continuous sigmoid and hyperbolic tangent sigmoid (tansig) activation functions, respectively.

$$a = f(n) = \frac{2}{1+e^{-\lambda n}} - 1 \quad \text{or} \quad a = f(n) = \frac{e^{\lambda n} - e^{-\lambda n}}{e^{\lambda n} + e^{-\lambda n}}, \tag{7}$$

where λ is the steepness of the function (Hagan *et al.*, 1996). Neurons form layers and are highly interconnected within each layer.

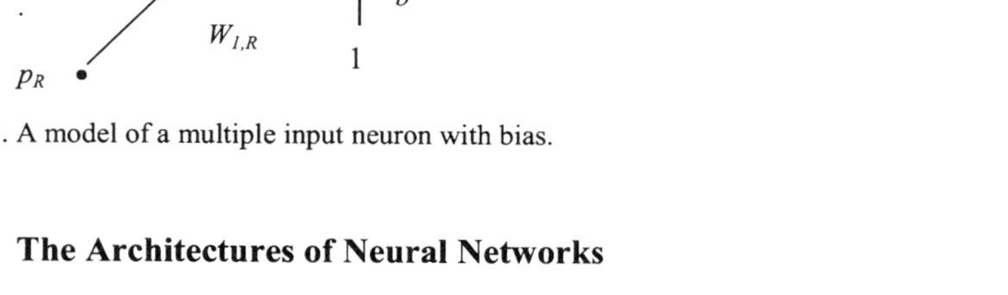

Figure 1. A model of a multiple input neuron with bias.

3.2.2. The Architectures of Neural Networks

Over the years several types of neural network architectures have been developed. The most common type of networks is a two-layer feed-forward neural network with error back-propagation, which is typically used for prediction and classification tasks[1]. We use this network in this and the previous studies. The network has two layers, a hidden layer and an output layer[2]. The neurons at the hidden layer receive the signals (values of input vectors) and propagate them concurrently to the output layer. In case of a multi-layer network that has more than one hidden layer, the neurons at the first hidden layer receive the signals and propagate them concurrently through the remaining hidden layers to the output layer. Often networks with a single hidden layer are favored because they are simple, train faster, and can effectively approximate very complex non-linear functions in the same manner as networks with more hidden layers.

3.2.3. The Learning/Training Property

Neural networks' learning is a process in which a set of input vectors **p** is presented sequentially and repeatedly to the input of the network in order to adjust its weights in such a way that similar inputs give the same output. Neural networks learn in three basic modes, the supervised mode, the unsupervised mode, and the reinforcement mode. In supervised learning, the training set consists of (1) the training patterns/examples, vectors **p**, that appear on input to the neural network (one at a time or all of them in batch mode), and (2) the corresponding desired responses, represented by vectors **t**, provided by a teacher. The differences between the desired response, vectors **t**, and the network's actual response, vectors **a**, for each single training pattern modify the weights of the network in all layers. The training continues until the *mse* performance function (8), the mean sum of squares of the network errors, for the entire training set containing Q training vectors is reduced to a sufficiently small value close to zero.

$$mse = \frac{1}{Q}\sum_{i=1}^{Q}(\mathbf{t}_i - \mathbf{a}_i)^2 \quad (8)$$

---

[1] Among other network architectures, the Kohonen feature maps, the Hopfield network, the radial basis function network, and the probabilistic neural network are worth noticing. For example, the Kohonen network is commonly utilized for clustering or finding similarities in input data (see the work of Kiviluoto (1998) concerning bankruptcy prediction mentioned in section 2 of this chapter), and the Hopfield network is used for optimization.

[2] Following the approach used in some literature (Zurada, 1992; Hagan *et al.*, 1996), we do not consider an input layer as a layer. If one considers an input layer as a layer, the network would have three layers.

In unsupervised learning, only the input vectors (training patterns) are available, and a teacher is not present. The network is able to find similarities in input data and classify them into clusters. In reinforcement learning, a teacher is present, but gives less specific help. In all types of learning, the knowledge (what the network learned) is encoded in weights of the network.

3.2.4. Supervised Training Algorithms for Feed-forward Networks

Standard back-propagation is a gradient descent algorithm used for training feed-forward networks. There are many variations of the back-propagation algorithm. The simplest back-propagation algorithm updates the weights and biases in the steepest descent direction - the negative of the gradient of the performance function (8). One iteration of this algorithm can be written

$$\mathbf{x}_{k+1} = \mathbf{x}_k + \alpha_k \mathbf{g}_k \tag{9}$$

where $\mathbf{x}_k$ is a vector of current weights and biases, $\mathbf{g}_k$ is the current gradient, and α_k is the learning rate. There are two different ways in which gradient descent algorithms can be implemented: incremental and batch mode. The incremental mode method computes the gradient and adjusts the weights after each input is applied to the network, whereas in the batch mode method all of the inputs are applied to the network before the weights are updated. Although the performance function in the back-propagation algorithm decreases most rapidly along the negative of the gradient, it does not necessarily produce the fastest convergence.

Conjugate gradient algorithms produce generally faster convergence than steepest descent directions. Most of these algorithms perform a line search at each iteration along conjugate directions. This line search is computationally expensive, because it requires that the network response for all training inputs to be computed several times for each search. Moller (1993) designed the scaled conjugate gradient algorithm that avoids the time consuming line search. The basic idea of this algorithm is to combine the model-trust region approach used in the Levenberg-Marquardt algorithm (Hagan and Menhaj, 1994) with the conjugate gradient approach.

Newton's method is one of the alternatives to the scaled conjugate gradient method for fast optimization. The basic step of Newton's method is

$$\mathbf{x}_{k+1} = \mathbf{x}_k - \mathbf{A}_k^{-1} \mathbf{g}_k, \tag{10}$$

where $\mathbf{x}_k$ is a vector of current weights and biases, $\mathbf{g}_k$ is the current gradient, and $\mathbf{A}_k$ is the Hessian matrix (second derivatives) of the performance index at the current value of weights and biases. Although Newton's method usually converges faster than the scaled conjugate gradient method, it is complex and expensive to compute the Hessian matrix of second derivatives. The quasi-Newton (or secant) method is based on Newton's method, but it does not require calculation of second derivatives. It updates, as a function of the gradient, an approximate Hessian matrix at each iteration of the algorithm (Gill *et al.*, 1981; Battiti, 1992).

3.2.5. Overcoming Overfitting During Training

One problem that occurs during network training is overfitting. Overfitting happens when the network memorizes the training examples, but does not learn to generalize to new situations. In other words, the error on the training set is driven to a very small value, but when new data is presented to the network, the error is large. One method for improving generalization is to reduce the size of the hidden layer in a network. The problem is that it is difficult to know beforehand how large a network should be for a specific application.

There are two other methods for improving network generalization: regularization and early stopping (see Neural Network Toolbox for Use with MATLAB, 1998, pp. 5-38). Regularization involves modifying the *mse* performance function (8) by adding a term that consists of the mean of the sum of squares of the network weights and biases:

$$msereg = \gamma mse + (1-\gamma)msw, \tag{11}$$

where γ is the performance ratio, and $msw = \frac{1}{n}\sum_{j=1}^{n} w_j^2$.

Using this performance function should cause the network to have smaller weights and biases, and consequently the network response should be smoother and less likely to overfit. The problem with regularization is that it is difficult to determine the optimum value for γ.

Therefore, early stopping may be a preferable method for improving generalization. This technique divides the available data into three subsets: the training subset, the validation subset, and the test subset. The training subset is used for computing the gradient and updating the network weights and biases. The error on the validation subset monitors the training process. When the validation error increases a specified number of times, the training stops, and the weights and biases at the minimum of the validation error are returned. The test subset error is not used during training, but it is used to compare different models.

3.2.6. Neural Network Methods Used in this Study

To conduct analysis for all computer experiments presented in the chapter, we apply two-layer feed-forward networks with error back-propagation. We use the early stopping technique with the scaled conjugate gradient algorithm or the quasi-Newton method (10) to train the neural networks in batch mode. We use version 3.0.1 of the MATLAB Neural Network Toolbox (discussed in the Appendix).

3.3. The Principal Component Analysis

The principal component analysis (PCA) is a well-established statistical method for feature extraction and data compression (Duda and Hart, 1973; Diamentras and Kung, 1996). The analysis has three effects. First, it orthogonalizes the components of the input vectors (so that they are uncorrelated with each other). Second, it orders the resulting orthogonal (principal) components so that those with the largest variation come first. Third, it eliminates those components that contribute the least to the variation in the data set.

The PCA determines an optimal linear transformation

$$\mathbf{y} = \mathbf{W}\mathbf{x} \tag{12}$$

of a real-valued, *n-dimensional,* zero-mean random input data pattern $\mathbf{x}$ ($E[\mathbf{x}]=0$), into another pattern *m-dimensional* ($m \leq n$) transformed feature vector $\mathbf{y}$. The $m \times n$ fixed linear transformation matrix $\mathbf{W}$ is designed optimally (from the point of view of maximum information retention) by exploring statistical correlations among elements of the original patterns. PCA then finds a possibly reduced compact data representation retaining maximum nonredundant and uncorrelated intrinsic information of the original data. Exploration of the original data set $\mathbf{x}$ is based on computing and analyzing a data covariance matrix, its eigenvalues and corresponding eigenvectors arranged in the descending order. The elements of the *m-dimensional* transformed feature vector $\mathbf{y}$ will be uncorrelated and organized in the descending order according to decreasing information contents. For a more formal approach, see Bishop (1995) and Cios *et al.* (1998).

4. RESEARCH METHODOLOGY

4.1. Sample Data and Time Period Investigated

The Ward and Foster (1996) sample provided the data for analyses conducted for this study and our earlier studies (Zurada *et al.*, 1997, 1998-1999). They searched the *Wall Street Journal Index* and *Compact Disk Disclosure* to identify companies that became bankrupt or defaulted on loan interest or principal payments or received a favorable debt accommodation in 1988 or 1989. They also performed a search with *Compustat* tapes to identify companies that cut their dividend by at least 40% after paying a dividend for each of the three prior years. Then, Ward and Foster (1996) randomly matched healthy companies to distressed companies from the same industry. Ward and Foster (1996) examined companies' annual reports and 10-Ks and eliminated firms: (1) for which they could not verify the distress event (for distressed firms) or lack of a distress event (for the healthy firms), (2) that did not have complete data on *Compustat* tapes, (3) that did not have audited financial statements prepared in accordance with U.S. GAAP, and (4) whose management was under investigation for fraudulent financial reporting.

The 1988 firms and a holdout sample of the 1989 firms are used for training and testing, respectively. An unbalanced, but somewhat realistic training sample contained 204 firms of which 150 were healthy, 16 experienced dividend cuts, 21 experienced loan default, and 17 filed for bankruptcy, was used for training. A holdout sample of 141 firms, of which 103 were healthy, 12 experienced dividend cuts, 14 experienced a loan default, and 12 filed for bankruptcy, was used for testing. Unlike many samples used in previous studies, in this sample distressed companies were not as numerous as the healthy ones. These uneven samples contained several levels of distress and included both small and large firms. The firms came from several different industries such as manufacturing, retailing, and restaurant, but excluded firms from the financial services and utility industries.

To compare results to Ward and Foster (1996) and Zurada *et al.* (1997, 1998-1999), we examined data for each of the three years before the distress event. For the 1988 companies, we developed neural network models from each year's data for 1987, 1986, and 1985. We then applied the results from these analyses to the 1989 holdout sample's data 1988, 1987, and 1986. Thus, for a multi-state response variable, we compared the relative ability of logit models and neural networks to predict financial distress one, two, and three years prior to the distress event. For a detailed description of the sample and sampling techniques employed, the reader is referred to Ward and Foster (1996).

4.2. Variables

For this study, we use the same response variable as Ward and Foster (1996) and Zurada *et al.* (1997): a four-state ordinally-scaled response variable with companies coded as: 0 = healthy, 1 = dividend cut, 2 = loan default or favorable debt accommodation, or 3 = bankruptcy. To compare neural network and logit regression model results, we also examine the same nine independent variables that Ward and Foster (1996) and Zurada *et al.* (1997, 1998-1999) used in their studies. The variables are traditional accounting ratios or traditional ratios adjusted for accounting allocations. Eight of these variables were:

(1) SALESCA = sales/current assets,
(2) CALC = current assets/current liabilities,
(3) OETL = owners' equity/total liabilities,
(4) CATA = current assets/total assets,
(5) CASHTA = cash plus marketable securities/total assets,
(6) SIZE = log (total assets),
(7) CFFF = estimated cash flow from financing activities/total liabilities, and
(8) CFFI = estimated cash flow from investing activities/total liabilities.

Ward and Foster (1996) developed four different logit models for each of the three years prior to distress. Each model included the eight independent variables described above. Unique models were created by using one of the following as the ninth variable in the model:

(9a) NITA = net income/total assets,
(9b) DPDTADJ = depreciation and amortization and deferred tax allocations adjusted operating flow/total assets,
(9c) NQAFLOW = net-quick-assets operating flow/total assets, or
(9d) CFFO = estimated cash flow from operating activities/total assets.

The Ward and Foster (1996) study investigated the impact of accounting allocations on predictive models. Therefore, they adjusted the scaling measures of total assets, total liabilities, and owners' equity by removing the impact of depreciation and deferred taxes in the models including DPDTADJ, NQAFLOW, and CFFO. Also, because the sample period includes years before companies issued statements of cash flows, Ward and Foster estimated CFFI, CFFF, and CFFO from income statement and balance sheet information. For a more thorough description of the variables, see Ward and Foster (1996).

4.3. Description of the Experiments

We examined thoroughly whether any of the following techniques and experiments improved the classification rates of the network in detecting the distressed states (1 through 3). First, we applied principal component analysis to try to reduce, without losing information, the number of input variables used for training and to remove correlation between them. Then, we conducted experiments that involved repeating observations in the distressed states, using a validation sample, and using cascaded neural networks.

4.3.1. Principal Component Analysis (PCA)

The size of the training set must be sufficiently large to cover the ranges of inputs available for each feature/variable. Unfortunately, there is no simple rule to express a relationship between the number of features and the size of the training set. Berry and Linoff (1997) state that it is desired to have at least several (5-10) training examples for each weight in the network or several dozen training examples for each feature. For a network with n inputs variables, h hidden neurons, and o output neurons, there are $n*(h+1)+o*(h+1)$ weights in the network. For example, for a network with 9 input variables, 10 neurons in the hidden layer, and 4 neurons in the output layer (each neuron designed to detect one of the four states), there are 143 weights in the network. Consequently, one may need from 715 to 1430 training examples divided equally into four classes.

The above computations imply that given the small number of training patterns (204 cases), it is advisable to use a relatively small network and reduce the number of input variables. Therefore, we first ran the PCA to find if the components of the nine input vectors in all 12 scenarios (four models for the three years) are highly correlated (redundant), and consequently, if the dimension of the input vectors could be reduced. As mentioned, the smaller number of input variables should allow one to use a smaller network that needs less neurons in the hidden layer and training examples. Such a network is also easier to train because it will have a smaller number of local minima. It is also more likely that a training algorithm will find a true global minimum instead of a local one, which might improve the classification accuracy of a network.

We tried to conservatively retain those principal components which account for 99% of the total variation in the data set. There was no significant redundancy in the data set, since the principal component analysis did not reduce the number of the input variables (to a number less than 9). Next, we tried to eliminate those principal components which contribute less than 5% of the total variation in the data set. The number of variables was reduced to 6. The results from the initial computer simulation showed, however, that the network with 6 input variables did not classify the distressed states better than the network with 9 variables. Therefore, we decided to use the original number of 9 variables in further experiments.

4.3.2. Neural Networks Used

We used one of the most frequently used networks in financial applications, two-layer feed-forward neural networks with error back-propagation. Each network contained 10 neurons in the hidden layer and, depending on the experiment, 4, 3, or 2 neurons in the output layer. This size of the hidden layer appeared to produce the best classification results when run on the test set. With data discussed above, we trained and tested the networks on the nine input variables for the four models. To prevent saturation of the network, we transformed input variables into normalized values in the range [-1,1]. Each neuron used a tansig nonlinear activation function to produce values within the range [-1,1].

For the four-state response variable, the true teacher's responses were: [1, -1,-1,-1], [-1,1,-1,-1], [-1,-1,1,-1], and [-1,-1,-1,1]. They represent a healthy firm (state 0), a firm that experienced dividend cuts (state 1), a firm that experienced loan default (state 2), and a firm that filed for bankruptcy (state 3), respectively. For the three-state response variable, the true responses of a teacher were: [1,-1,-1], [-1,1,-1], and [-1,-1,1] to represent a firm that experienced dividend cuts (state 1), a firm that experienced a loan default (state 2), and a firm that filed for bankruptcy (state 3), respectively. Likewise, for the two-state response variable, the true responses of a teacher were: [1,-1] and [-1,1] to represent a healthy firm (state 0) and a distressed firm (states 1, 2 or 3), respectively.

For training, we used a scaled conjugate gradient or a quasi-Newton method complemented with the early stopping technique that may improve generalization. The training stopped if one of the following conditions was met: the maximum number of 2500 training cycles was reached, the performance function had been minimized to the goal of *mse*=0.01, the performance gradient fell below 10^{-7}, or validation performance increased more than 1200 times since the last time it decreased. As in the previous studies (Zurada *et al.*, 1997, 1998-1999), the decision of the network was determined by the largest of its four outputs for the four-state response variable, the larger of its three outputs for the three-state response variable, and the larger of two outputs for the two-state response variable.

As gradient descent was performed on the error surface, it was possible for the network solution to become trapped in one of the local minima. This may happen depending on the initial starting conditions. Settling in a local minimum may be harmful if it was far from the global minimum and if a low error was required. Therefore, back-propagation will not always find the optimum solution. To guarantee the most accurate solution, in each experiment we re-initialized and re-trained the network for each model several times and recorded the best results.

4.3.3. Experiment One

Berry and Linoff (1997), in their practical guide to data mining techniques, suggest that in case of uneven sample proportions, one may balance a training sample better by repeating the same observations for the uneven states. Following that suggestion, we balanced the training sample more effectively by repeating the same observations 9, 7, and 9 times for the underrepresented states 1, 2, and 3, respectively. This way we obtained a new expanded training sample comprising 150, 144, 147, and 153 patterns representing states 0, 1, 2, and 3, respectively. The test patterns included 141 firms described earlier. Figure 2 illustrates the neural network used in this experiment.

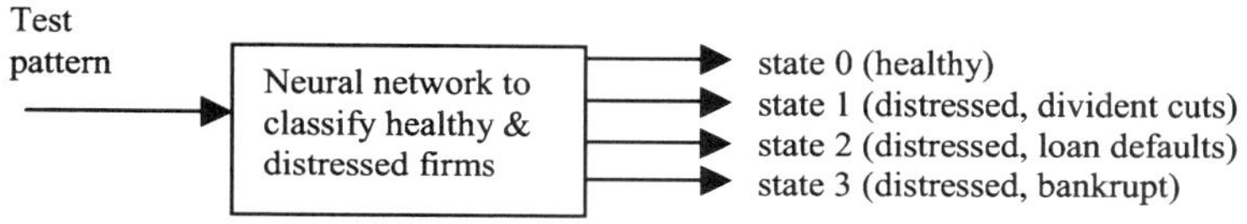

Figure 2. Architecture of a neural network used in experiments one and two.

4.3.4. Experiment Two

In this experiment, we used exactly the same network and the same training algorithms. The test set containing 141 observations remained unchanged, but we randomly extracted 20% of the observations from the training set for a validation set. As a result, the training set and the validation set comprised 120, 13, 17, 14 and 30, 3, 4, 3 observations, respectively, representing states 0, 1, 2, and 3. Then to balance the training and validation samples, we repeated each state 1, 2, and 3 in the training and validation sets 9, 7, and 9 times, respectively. This produced the expanded training and validation sets containing 120, 117, 119, 126 and 30, 27, 28, 27 observations, respectively. Table 1 presents a composition of the training, validation, and test sets. Figure 2 also illustrates the neural network used in this experiment.

Table 1. Composition of the training, validation, and test sets for three experiments.

Training & Test Sets	Number of Patterns			
	Experiment 1	Experiment 2	Experiment 3 NN1	NN2
Original:				
State 0	150	150	150	0
State 1	16	16	54	16
State 2	21	21	0	21
State 3	17	17	0	17
Expanded:				
State 0	150	150	150	0
State 1	144	144	162	48
State 2	147	147	0	63
State 3	153	153	0	51
Training:				
State 0	150	120	120	0
State 1	144	117	130	38
State 2	147	119	0	50
State 3	153	126	0	40
Validation:				
State 0	0	30	30	0
State 1	0	27	32	10
State 2	0	28	0	13
State 3	0	27	0	11
Test:				
State 0	103	103	103	0
State 1	12	12	38	12
State 2	14	14	0	14
State 3	12	12	0	12

4.3.5. Experiment Three

In this experiment, we designed two cascaded neural networks (Figure 3). The first network was used to detect healthy and distressed companies. Thus, the network had only two outputs. The second network was supposed to classify distressed companies into classes 1, 2, and 3 described above. Thus, that network had three outputs. We trained the two networks separately as follows. The first network was trained using the same training sample of 204 firms. However, for this network we collapsed distressed states 1, 2, and 3 into one category (a distressed state of 1) to produce the dichotomous variable taking values of 0 and 1 only. Consequently, we obtained 150 healthy firms and 54 distressed ones. Next, to balance the sample we repeated the same distressed states three times to obtain 162 observations that represent state 1. Thus, we obtained a training set containing 312 cases. In addition, from the training set we randomly extracted 20% of the observations, from states 0 and 1 for a validation set.

We trained the second neural network using a sample of 54 distressed firms only, of which there were 16, 21, and 17 firms representing states 1, 2, and 3, respectively. Because the number of training patterns was relatively small, we repeated the same observations in the training sample 3 times to obtain a training sample of 162 firms. Then we randomly assigned 20% of the observations representing states 1, 2, and 3 equally to a validation sample. The test set remains unchanged and contains 141 observations dominated by 103 cases representing healthy firms (state 0). Table 1 summarizes the sample numbers used in the experiments.

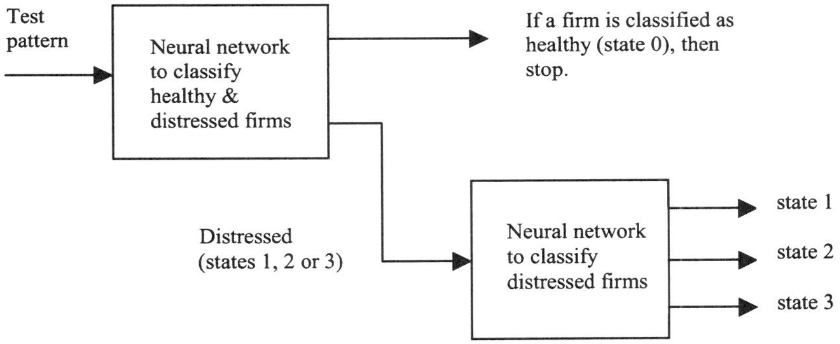

Figure 3. Architecture of two cascaded neural networks used in experiment three.

5. DISCUSSION OF THE RESULTS

Tables 2 through 4 present the results obtained from logit regression (Ward and Foster, 1996), initial simulation using neural networks (Zurada *et al.*, 1997, 1998-1999), and the three experiments. Tables 2-4 also contain results from proportional z tests used to test for significant differences between the accuracy rates (Bhattacharyya and Johnson, 1977, p. 310). We calculated z scores for differences between the overall classification accuracy rates, the classification accuracy rates for healthy firms, and classification accuracy rates for the distressed firms in total (states 1, 2, and 3, combined). We did not conduct significance tests on the individual states of distress because of the small sample size in each state.

As far as the overall classification rate was concerned, the neural network model from experiment one outperformed logistic regression 11 times out of 12 and the two methods classified firms equally well one time. Furthermore, the neural network outperformed logit regression 10 times out of 12 in correct classification of class 0. Also, comparing the classification accuracy within classes 1 through 3 for the four models for the three years (36 classes), revealed that the neural network outperformed logistic regression 27 times. The neural network used in our previous studies (Tables 2-4, col. 3) outperformed the logit regression only 15 times and the two methods classified firms equally well one time.

Although the results are not particularly impressive, balancing the training sample, even with the same training patterns, apparently improved the classification accuracy of the network. Comparing experiment one with the previous neural network revealed that improvement generally came in the ability to correctly classify distressed firms at the expense of properly classifying healthy firms. Significance tests verified that effect.

The neural network model in experiment two apparently performed better than the logit regression model, but showed little change from the experiment one neural network results. It is worth noting that the neural network model had some difficulty in classifying firms three years prior to the distress event (Table 4, col. 5). Excluding some training patterns from the already small original training set and assigning them to a validation set produced results difficult to interpret.

The cascaded neural networks in experiment three produced the best classification results. The networks produced the highest overall classification rates in all cases, significantly so in eight of the 12 cases. Moreover, the networks properly classified the distressed firms more accurately than any other method in all cases, significantly so in nine of the 12 cases. Clearly, using a combination of two cascaded neural networks in experiment three produced results superior to those achieved with the networks used in experiments one and two. Note that in experiment three we still repeated observations in the uneven states and used a validation sample.

Table 2. Classification Rates for Multi-state Response Variable by Ordinal Logistic Regression and Neural Network Models (Year - 1). Shows the percentage of firms classified correctly. (Number of firms classified correctly/Total number of firms).

Model	Year – 1				
	Regression (Ward & Foster, 1996)	NN Zurada *et al.* (1997, 1998-1999)	NN Exp. 1	NN Exp. 2	NN Exp. 3
NITA:					
All firms	63.3	74.5**	74.5	69.5	76.6* (108/141)
State 0	77.7	89.3**	88.4	80.6#	85.4 (88/103)
State 1	8.3	16.7	25.0	16.7	50.0 (6/12)
State 2	7.7	57.1	57.1	50.0	64.3 (9/14)
State 3	53.9	25.0	25.0	50.0	41.7 (5/12)
States 1-3	21.1	34.2	36.8	39.5	52.6 (20/38)
DPDTADJ:					
All firms	70.9	74.5	73.1	73.8	82.3** (116/141)$
State 0	80.6	90.3**	85.0	87.4	90.3 (93/103)
State 1	41.7	16.7	25.0	16.7	66.7 (8/12)
State 2	61.5	50.0	57.1	57.1	71.4 (10/14)
State 3	30.8	25.0	33.3	33.3	41.7 (5/12)
States 1-3	47.4	31.6#	39.5	36.8	60.5** (23/38)
NQAFLOW:					
All firms	69.5	75.2	69.5	70.9	82.3** (116/141)$
State 0	79.6	93.2**	81.3###	85.4	90.3 (93/103)
State 1	66.7	16.7	33.3	41.7	66.7 (8/12)
State 2	46.2	42.9	50.0	42.9	50.0 (7/14)
State 3	15.4	16.7	25.0	8.3	66.7 (8/12)
States 1-3	42.1	26.3#	36.8	31.6	60.5*** (23/38)$
CFFO:					
All firms	66.0	75.2**	73.7	71.6	80.9** (114/141)
State 0	80.6	94.2***	88.4#	85.4	91.3* (94/103)
State 1	33.3	16.7	25.0	33.3	58.3 (7/12)
State 2	23.1	35.7	50.0	42.9	50.0 (7/14)
State 3	23.1	16.7	25.0	25.0	50.0 (6/12)
States 1-3	26.3	23.7	34.2	34.2	52.6* (20/38)$

Results of 2-tailed proportional z-tests performed on the overall classification rates (All firms), classification rates for the healthy firms (State 0), and classification into the proper distress state for all distressed firms (States 1-3). The small number of observations in each distress state precluded meaningful significance tests for each individual distressed state.

* Significantly better than previous column (* at .10, ** at .05, *** at .01).

\# Significantly worse than previous column (# at .10, ## at .05, ### at .01).

$ Significantly better than best other technique ($ at .10, $$ at .05, $$$ at .01).

Table 3. Classification Rates for Multi-state Response Variable by Ordinal Logistic Regression and Neural Network Models (Year - 2). Shows the percentage of firms classified correctly. (Number of firms classified correctly/Total number of firms).

Model	Year – 2				
	Regression (Ward & Foster, 1996)	NN Zurada *et al.* (1997, 1998-1999)	NN Exp. 1	NN Exp. 2	NN Exp. 3
NITA:					
All firms	57.5	68.8**	68.8	69.5	80.1** (113/141)$$
State 0	70.9	86.4***	79.6	78.6	86.4* (89/103)
State 1	0.0	16.7	33.3	41.7	83.3 (10/12)
State 2	38.5	21.4	42.9	42.9	42.9 (6/14)
State 3	23.1	25.0	41.7	50.0	66.7 (8/12)
States 1-3	18.4	21.1	39.5**	44.7	63.2*** (25/38)$$$
DPDTADJ:					
All firms	65.5	69.5	74.5	68.1	83.7***
State 0	74.8	85.4**	89.2	76.7###	(118/141)$$
State 1	33.3	0.0	16.7	58.3	90.3*** (93/103)
State 2	53.9	28.6	28.6	28.6	83.3 (10/12)
State 3	23.1	50.0	58.3	50.0	57.1 (8/14)
States 1-3	39.5	26.3	34.2	44.7**	58.3 (7/12)
					65.8*** (24/38)$$$
NQAFLOW:					
All firms	61.7	71.6**	66.7	70.9	82.3** (116/141)$$
State 0	72.8	85.4**	75.7###	79.6	89.3** (92/103)
State 1	0.0	33.3	25.0	41.7	75.0 (9/12)
State 2	84.6	21.4	57.1	42.9	35.7 (5/14)
State 3	7.8	50.0	41.7	58.3	83.3 (10/12)
States 1-3	34.2	34.2	42.1	44.7	63.2*** (24/38)$$$
CFFO:					
All firms	60.3	70.2**	66.0	66.7	80.1***
State 0	72.6	87.3***	72.8###	75.7	(113/141)$$
State 1	25.0	8.3	58.3	16.7	87.4** (90/103)
State 2	30.8	28.6	35.7	50.0	58.3 (7/12)
State 3	23.1	33.3	50.0	58.3	71.4 (10/14)
States 1-3	26.3	23.7	47.4**	42.1	50.0 (6/12)
					60.5 (23/38)$$

Results of 2-tailed proportional z-tests.
* Significantly better than previous column (* at .10, ** at .05, *** at .01).
# Significantly worse than previous column (# at .10, ## at .05, ### at .01).
$ Significantly better than best other technique ($ at .10, $$ at .05, $$$ at .01).

Table 4. Classification Rates for Multi-state Response Variable by Ordinal Logistic Regression and Neural Network Models (Year - 3). Shows the percentage of firms classified correctly. (Number of firms classified correctly/Total number of firms).

Model	Year – 3				
	Regression (Ward & Foster, 1996)	NN Zurada *et al.* (1997, 1998-1999)	NN Exp. 1	NN Exp. 2	NN Exp. 3
NITA:					
All firms	53.2	62.4*	58.9	51.1#	75.9*** (107/141)$$$
State 0	66.0	78.6**	69.9#	55.3##	81.6*** (84/103)
State 1	0.0	0.0	8.3	33.3	50.0 (6/12)
State 2	46.2	50.0	28.6	35.7	50.0 (7/14)
State 3	7.7	0.0	50.0	50.0	83.3 (10/12)
States 1-3	18.4	18.4	30.0	39.5	60.5** (23/38)$$
DPDTADJ:					
All firms	56.7	65.3*	58.6	63.1	75.9*** (107/141)$$
State 0	68.0	83.5***	63.1###	76.7**	81.6 (84/103)
State 1	8.3	0.0	41.7	0.0	50.0 (6/12)
State 2	46.2	42.9	50.0	71.4	57.1 (8/14)
State 3	15.4	0.0	41.7	0.0	75.0 (9/12)
States 1-3	23.7	15.8	44.7***	26.3##	60.5***(23/38)$
NQAFLOW:					
All firms	51.1	66.7***	58.2	49.6	69.5*** (98/141)
State 0	64.1	84.5***	68.9###	52.4###	71.8*** (74/103)@@
State 1	0.0	8.3	25.0	0.0	41.7 (5/12)
State 2	38.5	28.6	42.9	42.9	71.4 (10/14)
State 3	7.7	16.7	16.7	83.3	75.0 (9/12)
States 1-3	15.8	18.4	44.7***	42.1	63.2** (24/38)$$
CFFO:					
All firms	53.9	66.7**	57.5	50.4#	72.3*** (102/141)
State 0	68.0	83.5***	65.1###	51.5##	77.7*** (80/103)
State 1	8.3	8.3	41.7	16.7	33.3 (4/12)
State 2	30.8	42.9	42.9	57.1	64.3 (9/14)
State 3	7.7	8.3	25.0	66.7	75.0 (9/12)
States 1-3	15.8	21.1	36.8*	47.4	57.9 (22/38)

Results of 2-tailed proportional z-tests.
* Significantly better than previous column (* at .10, ** at .05, *** at .01).
# Significantly worse than previous column (# at .10, ## at .05, ### at .01).
$ Significantly better than best other technique ($ at .10, $$ at .05, $$$ at .01).
@ Significantly worse than best other technique (@@ at .05).

Improvement may have resulted from making the number of the original training patterns representing states 1-3 more even to the patterns representing the healthy firms in the first cascaded network, and eliminating domination by the patterns representing the healthy firms in the second network. The gradient on a multidimensional error surface was influenced proportionally by the training cases representing states 1-3 in the first network, and was not affected by the cases representing state 0 at all for the second network because they are not present in the training sample. In our previous studies, the healthy firms that dominated the training sample overwhelmingly affected this gradient.

6. CONCLUSIONS AND FUTURE RESEARCH DIRECTIONS

Very few studies have addressed the predictive accuracy of logit regression models and neural networks for a multi-state response variable and uneven but realistic training samples. In this study, we performed several experiments and examined the predictive ability of neural networks to distinguish between different levels of financial distress for unbalanced training samples. It appears that two cascaded neural networks, used in the third experiment, yield the best results. A big advantage of the cascaded neural networks is that the improvement in overall accuracy comes from more accurately identifying the distressed firms. Compared to logit regression and other neural network models, this approach produces relatively high classification accuracy for all scenarios tested. The two data mining tools for KDD could also complement each other by using them in parallel to produce a more reliable classification.

An extension of this study would be to examine how much of the improvement in the cascaded neural network over logit regression resulted from the procedures performed in experiments one and two. Would the cascaded neural network classify as accurately as in this study when the training sample was not balanced by repeating observations of the distressed firms and without using a validation sample?

Small and uneven training and test samples may cause some concern in this study, especially in the second stage of the cascaded neural networks. Possibly, no analysis could predict more accurately the multi-level distress variable based on the given independent variables and training cases. To accurately predict each class of input, training samples should represent each class of input well to come up with a sound neural network model. Therefore, to make our findings more generalizable, we recommend performing a similar classification rate analysis on larger training and test samples. Examining different independent variables could also increase generalizability.

Future studies could also perform sensitivity analyses to determine the significance of input variables for experiment three. Likewise, calculating two other useful evaluation criteria such as sensitivity and specificity defined by Cios *et al.* (1998) could be enlightening. It would also be advisable to calculate the classification ratios using different cut-off points and incorporating the cost of the Type I and Type II misclassification errors into comparisons.

In addition, a reasonable step would be to use radial basis function networks (RBFNs) and probabilistic neural networks (PNNs) instead of feed-forward networks with back-propagation. These may prove to be excellent architectures that may further improve classification accuracy. Three possible advantages to RBFN and PNN support this suggestion. First, unlike all supervised learning algorithms in feed-forward neural networks with error back-propagation, RBFNs, for example, are able to find a global minimum. Second, the architectures of the RBFNs and PNNs are simple to set up and do not require guessing the appropriate number of neurons in the hidden layer as with back-propagation. Third, training time for RBFNs and PNNs is short compared with back-propagation. Finally, one may try to employ another data mining technique such as decision trees to improve the classification accuracy and interpretation of analyses' results.

APPENDIX - NEURAL NETWORK TOOLBOX

As mentioned previously, to perform all the presented experiments we used the MATLAB Neural Network Toolbox. Therefore, we present a brief overview of some commands that were used.

The Neural Network Toolbox for use with MATLAB is a very comprehensive and powerful set of functions and commands that allow one to create different neural network architectures, train them using a variety of efficient algorithms, and finally test their performance. In addition to many useful statistical functions such as the principal component analysis, the toolbox contains several functions that allow preprocessing and post-processing of data. We briefly present a sample of the MATLAB commands used in computer simulations presented in this chapter.

The function *newff*

net = *newff* (*pr*, [10,4], {*'tansig'*, *'tansig'*}, *'trainscg'*);

creates a multi-layer feed-forward back-propagation neural network object and also initializes the weights and biases of the network making it ready for training. Most typically, the function requires four input parameters and returns the network object *net*. The first input *pr* is an *R*x2 matrix of minimum and maximum values for each of the *R* elements of the input vectors. The second input [10,4] is an array containing the sizes of each layer. There will be 10 neurons in the first (hidden) layer and 4 neurons in the second (output) layer. The third input *{'tansig', tansig'}* is a cell array containing the names of the transfer functions that each layer uses. The hidden and the output layer use a hyperbolic tangent sigmoid transfer function for all neurons. The last input parameter *'trainscg'* contains the name of the training function used by the network. The abbreviation stands for the scaled conjugate gradient. The quasi-Newton training algorithm uses a literal *'trainbfg'*. We briefly described the features of both training methods in section 3.2.4 of this chapter. The function *newff* automatically calls the function *init* to initialize the network with the default parameters when the network is created.

The function *train*

[*net*, *tr*] = *train* (*net*, *ptr*, *ttr*, [], [], *validation*, *t*);

trains the network in batch mode according to the training algorithm specified in the earlier command *newff*. The function returns a new neural network object *net* and a structure *tr* that represents the training, validation, and test performance over each epoch. The first input parameter is an object *net* of the initialized network created by the function *newff*. The second parameter *ptr* is an R×Q matrix of input (column) vectors, where *R* is the size of the training vector (the number of training variables) in each training pattern and *Q* is the number of all training patterns. The third parameter *ttr* is *V*×*Q* matrix of the network's targets, where *V* is the number of targets. The fourth and the fifth parameters coded by the square brackets [], [] represent input delay conditions and are not used. The sixth parameter *validation* and the seventh parameter *t* are structures representing validation vectors and test vectors, respectively. Although in the example above the function has 7 input parameters, most typically the first three are used to train a network without validation vectors or an early stopping technique. One may use the validation vectors to stop training early if further training on the primary vectors will hurt generalization to the validation vectors. One can also measure test vector performance to verify how well the network generalizes beyond primary and validation vectors.

Once a network is trained, a function *sim* may be used to simulate the network and check its performance. The function *sim* with two input and one output parameter is as follows:

[*a*] = *sim* (*net*, *p*);

sim takes the network input vectors *p* that have not been introduced during training, the network object *net*, and returns the network output vectors *a*.

The function *prepca* transforms the network input training set by applying a principal component analysis so that the elements of the input vector set will be uncorrrelated. In addition, the size of the input vectors may be reduced by retaining only those components that contribute more than a specified fraction (*min_frac*) of the total variation in the data set. The syntax for the function is as follows

[*ptrans*, *transmat*] = *prepca* (*p*, *min_frac*);

where *p* is an $R\times Q$ matrix of centered input (column) vectors and *min_frac* is a minimum fraction variance component to keep. It is assumed that the input data set *p* has already been normalized using a function *prestd* so that it has a zero mean and the standard deviation of 1. The output parameter *ptrans* contains the transformed input vectors, and *transmat* is the principal component transformation matrix. After the network has been trained, this matrix should be used to transform any future inputs which are applied to the network. It effectively becomes a part of the network, just like the network weights and biases.

REFERENCES

Afifi, A.A, and Clark, V., 1990, *Computer-Aided Multivariate Analysis*, Van Nostrand Reinhold Co., New York.

Agarwal A., Davis, J., and Ward, T.J., 1997, Ordinal Four-State Financial Condition Classification Model Using Neural Networks, Working paper.

Agresti, A. 1984, *Analysis of Ordinal Categorical Data*. John Wiley and Sons, Inc.: New York.

Altman, E.I., Marco, G., and Varetto, F., 1994, Corporate Distress Diagnosis: Comparisons Using Linear Discriminant Analysis and Neural Networks (the Italian Experience), *Journal of Banking and Finance*, Vol. 18, No. 3, pp. 505-529.

Back, B., Laitinen, T., and Sere, K., 1996, Neural Networks and Bankruptcy Prediction: Fund Flows, Accrual Ratios, and Accounting Data, *Advances in Accounting*, Vol. 14, pp. 23-37.

Barney, D.K., Graves, O.F., and Johnson, J.D., 1999, The Farmers Home Administration and Farm Debt Failure Prediction, *Journal of Accounting and Public Policy*, Vol. 18, pp. 99-139.

Battiti, R., 1992, First and second order methods for learning: Between steepest descent and Newton's method, *Neural Computation*, Vol. 4, No. 2, pp. 141-166.

Berry, M.J., and Linoff, G.S., 1997, *Data Mining Techniques for Marketing, Sales, and Customer Support*, John Wiley & Sons, Inc., New York.

Bhattacharyya, G. K. and R. A. Johnson, 1977, *Statistical Concepts and Methods*, John Wiley & Sons, New York.

Bishop, C.M., 1995, *Neural networks for Pattern Recognition*, Oxford Press.

Christensen, R., 1997, *Log-Linear Models and Logistic Regression*, Springer, New York.

Cios, K., Pedrycz, W., and Swiniarski, R., 1998, *Data Mining Methods for Knowledge Discovery*, Kluwer Academic Publishers, Boston.
Coats, P.K., and Fant, F.L., 1991, A Neural Network Approach to Forecasting Financial Distress, *Journal of Business Forecasting*, Vol. 10, No. 4, pp. 9-12.
Coats, P.K., and Fant, F.L., 1993, Recognizing Financial Distress Patterns Using a Neural Network Tool, *Financial Management*, Vol. 22, September, 142-150.
Diamentras, K.I., and Kung, S.Y., 1996, *Principal Component Neural Networks. Theory and Applications*, Wiley.
Duda, R.O., and Hart, P.E., 1973, *Pattern Recognition and Scene Analysis*, Wiley.
Fletcher, D., and Goss, E., 1993, Forecasting with Neural Networks: An Application Using Bankruptcy Data, *Information & Management*, Vol. 24, No. 3, 159-167.
Gill, P.E., Murray, W., and Wright, M.H., 1981, *Practical Optimization*, Academic Press, New York.
Greenstein, M.M., and Welsh, M.J., 2000, Bankruptcy Prediction Using *Ex Ante* Neural Network and Realistically Proportioned Testing Sets, *Artificial Intelligence in Accounting and Auditing*, Vol. 6 (forthcoming).
Hagan, M.T., Demuth, H.B., and Beale, M., 1996, *Neural Network Design*, PWS Publishing Company.
Hagan, M.T., and Menhaj, M., 1994, Training Feedforward neural Networks with the Marquardt Algorithm, IEEE Transactions on Neural Networks, Vol. 5, No. 6, pp. 989-993.
Jain, A.K., Mao, J., and Mohiuddin, K.M., 1996, Artificial Neural Networks: A Tutorial, *Computer*, Vol. 29, No. 3, 31-44.
Kiviluoto, K., 1998, Predicting Bankruptcies with the Self-Organizing Map, *Neurocomputing*, vol. 21, no. 1-3, 191-201
Koh, H.C., and Tan, S.S., 1999, A Neural Network Approach to the Prediction of Going Concern Status, *Accounting and Business Research*, Vol. 29, No. 3, pp. 211-216.
Lenard, M.J., Alam, P., and Madey, G.R., 1995, The Application of Neural Networks and a Qualitative Response Model to the Auditor's Going Concern Uncertainty Decision, *Decision Sciences*, Vol. 26, No. 2, pp. 209-227.
Manly, B.F.,1994, *Multivariate Statistical Methods: A Primer*, Chapman & Hall, London.
Moller, M.F., 1993, A Scaled Conjugate Gradient Algorithm for Fast Supervised Learning, *Neural Networks*, Vol. 6, pp. 523-533.
Neural Network Toolbox for Use with MATLAB, User's Guide, Version 3, 1998, The MathWorks, Inc.
Salchenberger, L.M., Cinar, E.M., and Lash, N.A., 1992, Neural Networks: A New Tool for Predicting Thrift Failures, *Decision Sciences*, Vol. 23, No. 4, pp. 899-916.
Tam, K.Y., and Kiang, M.Y., 1992, Managerial Applications of Neural Networks: The Case of Bank Failure Predictions, *Management Science*, Vol. 38. No. 7, pp. 926-947.
Ward T.J., and Foster, B.P., 1996, An Empirical Analysis of Thomas's Financial Accounting Allocation Fallacy Theory in a Financial Distress Context, *Accounting and Business Research*, Vol. 26, No. 2, pp. 137-152.
Wilson, R.L., and Sharda, R., 1994, Bankruptcy Prediction Using Neural Networks, *Decision Support Systems*, Vol. 11, pp. 545-557.
Zurada, J., Foster, B.P., Ward, T.J, and Barker, R.M., 1997, A Comparison of the Ability of Neural Networks and Logit Regression Models to Predict Levels of Financial Distress, *Systems Development Methods for the 21st Century*, (G. Wojtkowski, W. Wojtkowski, S. Wrycza, and J. Zupancic , eds.), Plenum Press, New York, pp. 291-295.
Zurada, J., Foster, B.P., Ward, T.J., and Barker, R.M., 1998-1999, Neural Networks Versus Logit Regression Models for Predicting Financial Distress Response Variables, *Journal of Applied Business Research*, Vol. 15, No. 1, pp. 21-29.
Zurada, J.M., 1992, *Introduction to Artificial Neural Systems*, West Publishing Company, St. Paul, Minnesota.

Index